1000 x
EUROPEAN
ARCHITECTURE

The Deutsche Nationalbibliothek lists this publication in the Deutsche National-
bibliografie; detailed bibliographical data are available on the internet at
http://dnb.d-nb.de.

ISBN 978-3-03768-087-2
© 2012 by Braun Publishing AG
www.braun-publishing.ch

1st edition 2012

Editor: Chris van Uffelen
Editorial staff: Julia Chromow, Nicole Felhösi, Christine Maier, Anne Osherson,
Lisa Rogers, Manuela Roth, Sarah Schkölziger, Georgia van Uffelen
Translation: Lisa Rogers
Art direction: Michaela Prinz

IMPRINT

1000 x
EUROPEAN ARCHITECTURE

BRAUN

CONTENT

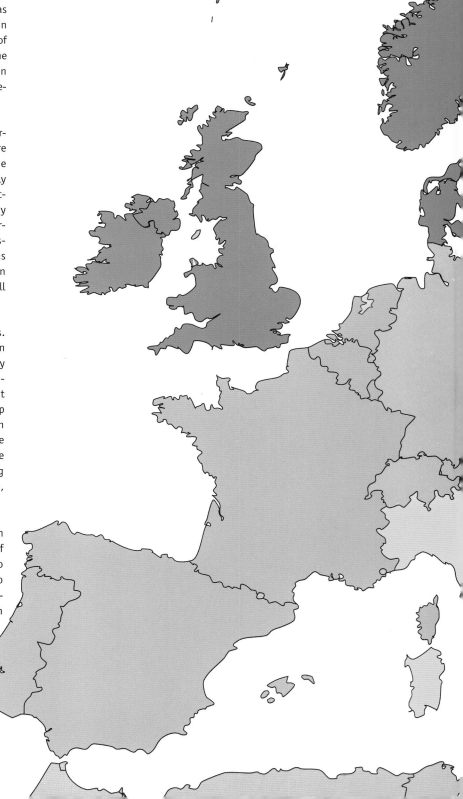

1000xEuropean Architecture is one thousand European buildings from the last five years: it is neither a small selection, which is a typical limitation of architectural monographs, nor a "census", which would not only be impossible but also undesirable as it would present too many "buildings" and not enough "architecture". The one thousand buildings in *1000xEuropean Architecture* are far more an example of carefully selected architecture, a cross section of "collective" European architecture, which simultaneously considers individual achievement. Taken from within the timeframe of the last five years, the buildings included have emerged from widely divergent economical backgrounds: a large section of the projects included was built in the building boom before the financial crisis, or at least planned during this time. A second group was faced with great financial difficulties, either in the early execution phase or in the late planning stages. A third group was built in a time of full awareness of the financial crisis, a situation that is still continuing in many countries. The final group involves projects that were either built at a time where confidence in economic recovery was beginning to return or, because of a short building timeframe, were completed with the knowledge that they had overcome the crisis.

The diversity of *1000xEuropean Architecture* also allows for the inclusion of architecture offices from outside of Europe who have built important work here and even offers space for countries rarely given consideration. At the same time, unusual building categories were also considered, which otherwise rarely find their way into architectural publications. It is precisely these building categories that clearly show the national differences across Europe: one country has a disproportionately high number of hotels; another has numerous kindergartens; and this despite the fact that this result is not what you would necessarily expect from these countries. A third country – very surprisingly – has a high proportion of luxury villas; the exact locations of which must remain confidential. Even when no attention is paid to the topography, the reader will notice that the country has changed after viewing just a few projects.

Even more recognizable is the difference between each of the five regions. Eastern Europe in particular has changed significantly since the first edition of *1000xEuropean Architecture*. Five years ago, Eastern Europe was defined by a wealth of Post-modern architecture, but it has now managed to forge a connection to the rest of Europe. This region offers the last "white areas", but also the greatest growth potential. The "white areas" of the European map are gradually being filled, not only enhancing examples of great European architecture but also strengthening the province: five years ago, there were fewer clearly defined urban centers of architecture and the dominance of these is now much weaker. Although they still dominate in terms of sheer building numbers, this advantage is no longer based on the prestige of the projects, which are located both in the countryside and in medium-sized towns.

The thousand projects featured here are sure to be thought-provoking; both in comparison to the first edition of *1000xEuropean Architecture* and in terms of this book. These comparisons are not listed here, as this fun should be left to the reader. *1000xEuropean Architecture* should offer the reader the chance to draw their own conclusions, to discover connections and to recognize not-so-old acquaintances as well as to see the brand new gems and jewels of European architecture.

PREFACE

NORTHERN EUROPE

NORTHERN EUROPE

01

02

03

Utzon Center

The Utzon Center is situated in the harbor front along the park sequence, which is characteristic for this area of Aalborg. It is a concept of individual buildings, creating a unique place around a courtyard on a platform, with the surrounding sculptural and varied roofscapes. The auditorium, the boat hall and the library are designed with dramatic and very tall sculptural roofs. The orientation of the three significant roofs and the views through the building respond to the varied nature of the site, from the windy harbor front to the blooming park next to the city Center of Aalborg.

01 Auditorium, exterior view | 02 Library, interior view | 03 Roof of library | 04 Section of boat hall and library | 05 Side view

04

05

01

Iceberg Dwellings

The Aarhus harbor development provides an enormous opportunity for Denmark's second largest city to develop in a socially sustainable way by renovating its old, out-of-use container terminal. A third of the apartments will be set aside as affordable rental housing, aimed at integrating a diverse social profile into the new development. The project's main obstacle is that the desired size is in conflict with the specified height restrictions and the intentions of providing ocean views and good daylight conditions. The Iceberg negotiates this problem, forming 'peaks' and 'canyons'; eliciting the project's iconic strength while ensuring that all flats will be supplied with a generous amount of natural lighting and waterfront views.

01 View from dock | 02 Interior | 03 View from the harbor | 04 Floor plans

02

03

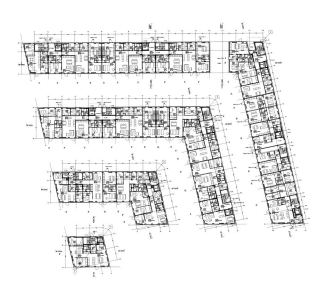

04

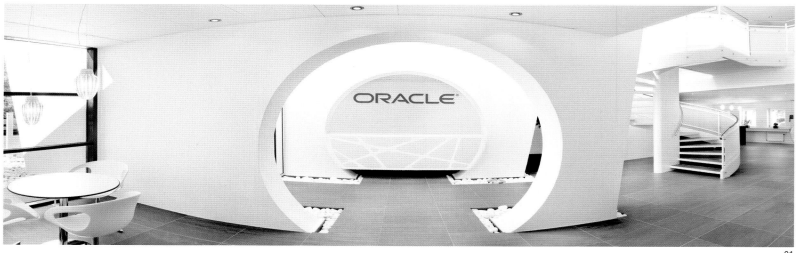

01

02

O-Zone, Oracle Headquarters

The architecture and the interior design are based on a vision of offering inspiring and functional surroundings for the employees and on Scandinavian minimalism mixed with organic shapes. Oracle's employees were involved in the design of O-Zone from an early stage. The office space is divided into four areas suited for different types of work – the Call Zone, Dialog Zone, Project Zone, and Quiet Zone. Employees don't have permanent desks, but instead have a private locker and are welcome everywhere in the house. Based on the American high school model, this emphasizes the campus feel of the building. The day starts off in the locker area fetching one's carrier, before deciding on today's workspace.

01 Reception and lobby | 02 Call Zone | 03 Library Zone | 04 Ground floor plan | 05 Main entrance

03

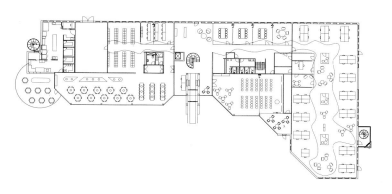

04

05

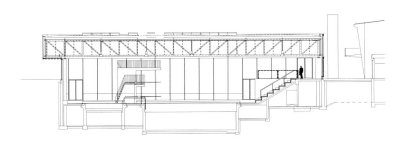

01

02

03

Bellahøj Swim Stadium

The Bellahøj Swim Stadium is a beautiful building situated in an overlooked but spectacular position in Copenhagen. It has created a focus point and a public space in an area hitherto regarded as only a gigantic crossroad. It incorporates a modern Olympic regulation competition facility, with a park and a water playground for children. At night the roof can be lit from inside with energy saving LED lights. It embodies a combination of architectural quality, landscaping, urban design and social responsibility.

01 Sections | 02 Swimming pool | 03 Exterior view | 04 View from north | 05 Square outside stadium | 06 View from outdoor water playground

04

05

06

01

The New Royal Playhouse

Located on the harbor front in Copenhagen, the new Royal Playhouse fits into its urban environment, embraces the harbor, and opens to theater-goers as well as passersby. The building consists of several compositional elements: the foyer, a broad 'sidewalk' floating over the water, the auditorium and scene tower, and the service area, located on the roof level. The composition completes the surrounding urban structure and serves the purpose of creating the optimal conditions for the meeting of the public and the theatrical spectacle.

01 General view | 02 Plan | 03 General view of foyer | 04 Service area | 05 North façade at night

02

03

04

05

01

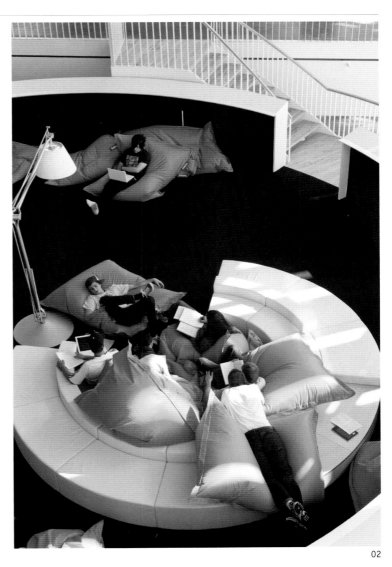

02

03

04

Ørestad College

Ørestad College is the first college in Denmark based on the new visions of content, subject matter, organization and learning systems in the reform of the educational system of the Danish 'high-school' for students aged 16–19. Communication, interaction and synergy have been key issues. The project displays a visionary interpretation of openness and flexibility regarding team sizes, varying from the individual to groups, to classes and assemblies, and reflects international tendencies aiming at achieving a more dynamic and life-like studying environment and introducing IT as a main tool. The intention is also to support the students' abilities to learn on their own, both through teamwork and individual assignments.

01 Exterior at night | 02 Furniture | 03 Interior view | 04 Staircase | 05 Floor plan

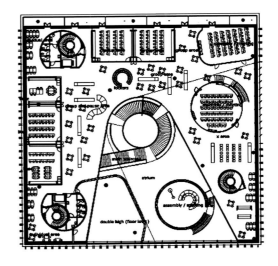

05

01

Crystal Sports and Culture Center

This new building will be used for a variety of daily sport and cultural activities such as concerts and theater performances. The dynamic landscape that unfolds inside lets these activities take place on different levels, while remaining in visual contact with each other. The most pronounced feature is a large translucent membrane that stretches between the sports arena and the culture center. The irregular, trailing form of the space results from the continuum created with the four walls of the neighboring buildings; the regulations guiding the structure and the program requirements. Steel and timber covered with opalescent polycarbonate panels with a low U-value were used as building materials. The translucent cover creates excellent lighting conditions and, together with the green flooring, hints at an open-air experience. The translucent outer skin dissolves the volume of the building, and at night, makes the structure appear as a glowing crystal.

01 Exterior view at night | 02 Sections | 03 Façade | 04 View over the roof | 05 Interior view towards courtyards

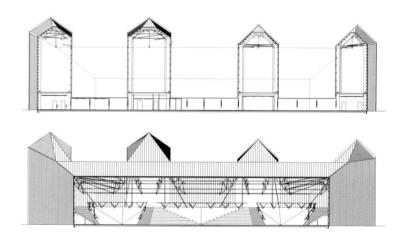

02

03

04

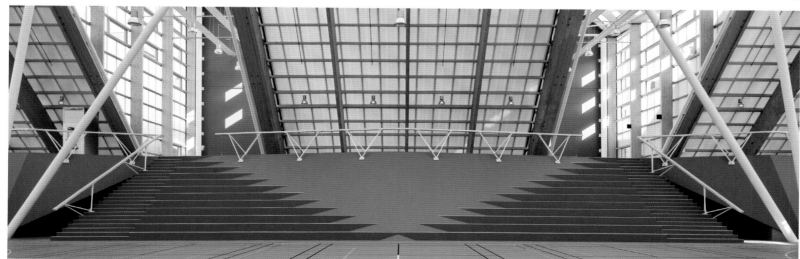

05

01

02

03

04

05

Mountain Dwellings

This complex consists of two-thirds parking space and one-third living space with the parking area as the base upon which terraced housing is placed - like a concrete hillside covered by a thin layer of housing, cascading from the eleventh floor to the street edge, merging the two functions into a symbiotic relationship. The north and west façades are covered by perforated aluminum plates, which let in air and light. In some places the ceiling reaches up to 16 meters, which gives the impression of a cathedral-like space. All apartments have irrigated roof gardens facing the sun, amazing views and parking on the tenth floor.

01 North façade detail with view inside | 02 Parking area | 03 Sloping elevator and ramps | 04 View from southwest | 05 View of the roof gardens | 06 West elevation

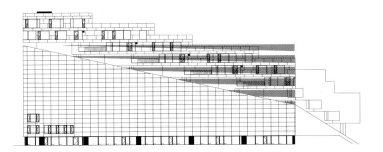

06

01

02

Saxo Bank

The new head office of the Saxo Bank in Copenhagen is designed by 3XN, and the architecture takes Saxo Bank's profile as its point of departure. The main lines of the structure explore the balance between dynamic expression and trustworthy solidity. The colors of the sea and the sky in the green glass and white façade elements interchange in the cut-up structure with many shapes reminiscent of the letter X in the name of the bank. Inside, the open plan design centers around a softly shaped top-lit atrium with a winding main staircase enhancing the sense of team spirit.

01 Side view | 02 Atrium with spiral staircase | 03 Third floor plan | 04 Exterior view with entrance | 05 Staircase from below

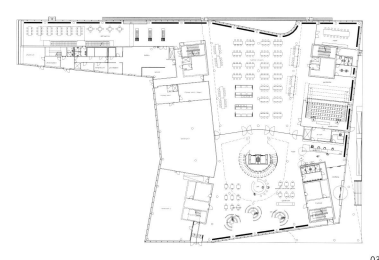

03

04

05

01

02

03

04

World Health Organization

This building tries to bring together man and architecture, humanism and minimalism, in a kind of 'huminalism'. Functions, surfaces and volumes were split up into individual elements and then recombined in a composition without transitions, e.g. between the façades and roofs. The landscape and building volumes are perceived as coherent commensurate elements as well. A floating entrance bridge protrudes from the building, while inside the building, the bridge sequence is a long concrete slab that is cut off and folded to produce stairs and landings. Around the atrium, the workplaces are located in open office landscapes, and a new office system, "Flexus", was specially designed as an extension of the building's 'huminalistic' architecture.

01 "Flexus" workspaces | 02 Longitudinal section | 03 Bird's-eye view of entrance | 04 Stairway | 05 Bridge and balcony at night | 06 Front view at night

05

06

01

02

8 House

"8 House" is located in Southern Ørestad on the edge of the Copenhagen Canal. It is a big house, offering all types of homes, for people in all stages of life: the young and the old, nuclear families and singles, families that grow and families that become smaller. The bow-shaped building creates two distinct spaces, separated by the center of the bow, which hosts the communal facilities. Instead of dividing the different functions of the building into separate blocks, they have been spread out horizontally. The apartments are placed at the top, while the commercial program unfolds at the base of the building. The apartments benefit from the view and fresh air, while the offices merge with life on the street.

01 View from canal at night | 02 View from above | 03 Basement floor plan | 04 Façade | 05 View from canal | 06 Rear view | 07 Interior view

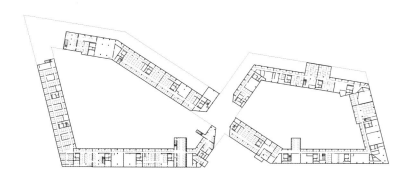

03

04

06

05

07

01

02

03

04

The New National Archive

The new Danish National Archives building is located on DSB's old freight rail site at Ka-
lvebod Brygge. The complex is incorporated into the master plan as a significant urban
and park element, which stretches from Bernstorffsgade to Dybbølsbro. The National
Archives consists primarily of two massive, enclosed high-bay warehouses placed in tandem and coupled to the former freight terminal via a low intermediate building. A 'garden street' runs along the full length of the roof of the building, serving as a new public
and recreational space in the urban area. The very rigorous geometry of the archive
building is set in motion by a graphic relief on the façades, which is reminiscent of rune
characters and represents the historical collections within.

01 Corridor in office building | 02 Exterior view | 03 Interior view of archives | 04 Bird's-
eye view | 05 Section

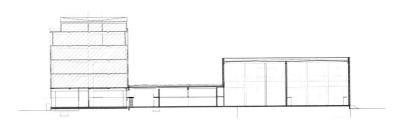

05

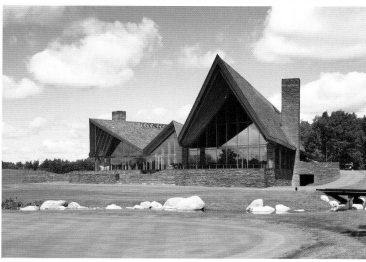

01

02

Scandinavian Golf Club

Located in the beautiful, hilly landscape of the former training area of Farum military barracks, the Scandinavian Golf Club comprises an exclusive nature park and golf course with two courses, each of 18 holes. The architectural vision was to bridge the gap between the traditional American golf club and the functional architecture of Scandinavia. The golf club is a traditional wing house but is built from rustic materials with large cantilevers and oblique angles. The roof floats above the plateau as a sculptural element integrated into the hilly landscape.

01 Exterior view | 02 View of lawn | 03 Woodwork detail | 04 Staircase | 05 Dining area | 06 Interior view | 07 Design sketch

03

04

05

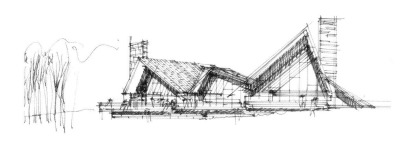

06

07

01

Clubhouse for the Royal Danish Yachting Club

The mellow form of this clubhouse is a reference to the curves of a boat and the soft character of water. It addresses the waterfront, with fully exposed façades in glass from floor to ceiling. Materials are limited to a selection of hardwood, steel, glass, and concrete. To ensure and support the desire for a homogeneous form, the building is clad in black roofing felt without indicating seam joints – framed by a white painted steel profile as a reference to the white hull of a a large ship. The form is internally paneled with wood as a direct reference to a ship's wooden decks and internal fittings.

01 Harbor site and terrace at night | 02 Floor plan | 03 Passage to the terrace | 04 Dining area

02

03

04

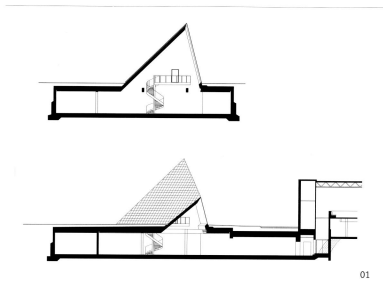

01

02

Carl-Henning Pedersen & Else Alfelt Museum

This museum is built up around a large collection of works by the Danish artist couple Carl-Henning Pedersen and Else Alfelt, who were both active in the CoBrA movement. The museum is characterized by the unity of art and architecture in the sculptural form. The façade is clad with ceramic tiles decorated with Carl-Henning Pedersen's colorful mythical beasts. The shape is entirely geometric, with a circular main building and a square extension underground. A small extension is also planned, which will create a link to the nearby Herning Art Museum. The geometry interacts with the other buildings in the cultural and educational center, most of which were designed by C.F. Møller Architects.

01 Section | 02 Aerial view | 03 Ground floor interior | 04 Main entrance ramp |
05 View from park | 06 Exhibition area

03

04

05

06

01

02

03

04

Vitus Bering Innovation Park

Having teaching and business start-up office facilities side by side is the philosophy behind the extension of the existing 1970s University College Vitus Bering Denmark. The building's dynamic and innovative character is expressed by its spiral shape – on the façades, the movement is present in the glazing strips that stretch towards the sky, while internally it is expressed via the green staircase, which runs as a spiral between the floors of the common internal atrium up to the common meeting facilities and roof terrace. It is one of the first office complexes in Denmark to be classified as low-energy class 1 – two times lower than the minimum required by the Danish building regulations.

01 View downwards through atrium | 02 Atrium full view | 03 Stair detail | 04 Exterior view | 05 Floor plan top floor and roof terrace

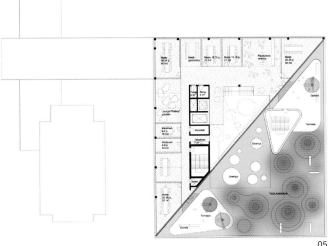

05

01

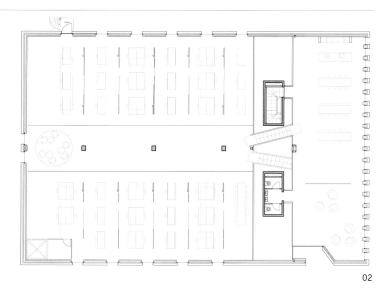

02

03

COMM2

This IT company's concern for long term investment in well-being and job satisfaction was of high importance from the early stages of the project, along with the company's virtues – high quality, efficiency, innovation and concern for details. The structural concrete beams and the heavy masonry pillars of the former industrial building were incorporated in the new design. Big white surfaces vertically divided by glazing from ground to roof create a homogeneous and simplistic backdrop for refined details in steel, glass, and high gloss surfaces. A suspended bridge makes the arrival to the headquarters a special experience, and divides the inner calmness of the house from the surrounding industrial area.

01 Arrival with suspended bridge | 02 Floor plan upper levels | 03 Reception and lobby | 04 Lobby lounge and meeting rooms | 05 Extreme openness | 06 Black cores in the atrium

04

05

06

01

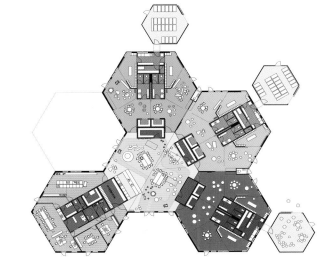

02

Paletten

Like a flower whose seeds are surrounded by petals, the common room of this daycare center is a central area accessed from the surrounding group rooms. In this way, all functions are closely connected to the common room and to each other, which is extremely practical whilst also manifesting the symbolic importance of community in the spirit and design of the project. Each room is shaped as a hexagon and therefore connected to all others and part of a unified whole. Each room is also a different color, allowing the children to address concepts of uniqueness and identity. The materials used for the façades and roof supports further emphasize the key concept of diversity alongside recognition.

01 Playground with sandbox | 02 Playground with extended garden | 03 Hexagonal floor plans | 04 Classroom | 05 Aerial view | 06 Activity room

03

04

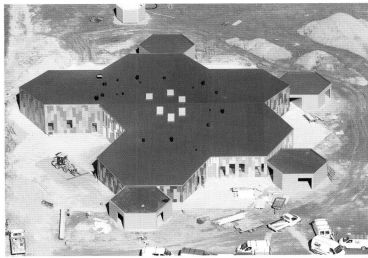

05

06

01

02

03

04

05

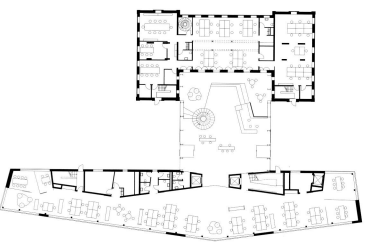

06

Max Bank

Max Bank head office consists of a new building that is integrated with Kanalgården – a former workhouse from 1882. The old building is connected with a new wing-formed structure that downscales the building and underlines the reflections of the façade. This results in a lean, vertical expression towards the city of Naestved. Max Bank has a simple, raw and industrial expression, reflecting the harbor as a former industrial working place. The primary materials are concrete and steel, put together in a modern architectural language. The translucent glass façade reflects the water and the sky, changing the expression of the head office throughout the year.

01 Lobby | 02 Interior view | 03 Exterior view | 04 View from river | 05 General view | 06 Floor plan

01

02

FDF Activity Center

This project was designed for the FDF, one of the largest Christian organizations for children and youth in Denmark. By simple means, the qualities of the site are used constructively in a clear concept, fulfilling FDF's challenging request for extensive flexibility. An ideal and challenging framework has been established to accompany the activity center's multiple activities and the flexible applicability of the facilities allows their optimum utilization, inside and outside. The activity center readily encourages use – by parents and children, young and old, on all sides, outdoors and indoors, up and down, around the clock, summer and winter.

01 Front view | 02 Side view | 03 Interior view common space | 04 Ground floor plan

03

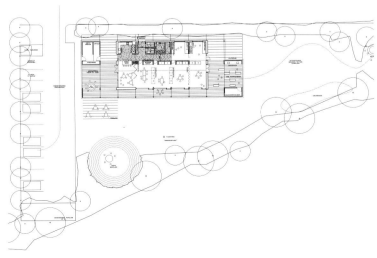

04

01

02

03

Skybox House

This project is situated near the northern coast of Sealand, Denmark. The plot is the result of the partitioning of a larger plot belonging to an old, thatched house. The two buildings at each end of the plot are inhabited by two generations, and the layout of the site plan was careful to provide both with separate and shared spaces. The main architectural focus concentrated on adding space and light to the relatively small area. The plan separates the bedrooms from the living space and introduces an open hallway. In working with the section, the ceiling height was minimized to give contrast to the "skyboxes" that add spatiality and air.

01 Kitchen | 02 Exterior view | 03 Living room | 04 Design sketch | 05 Side view

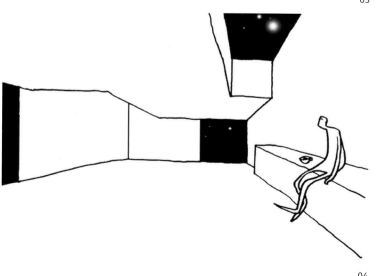

04

05

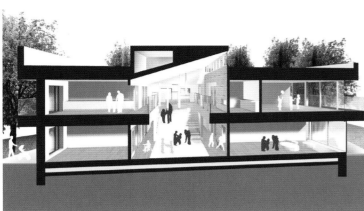

01

02

Dragen Children's House

The integrated kindergarten sets new standards with a sustainable and pedagogically conceived design using largely "Nordic Swan" eco-labelled components. The simple and clear architecture has two levels, linked by staircases and ramps designed to stimulate and challenge the children's sensory and motor skills. Dragen has small niches distributed throughout, offering space to play, read or just withdraw. In addition, there are purpose-built areas, giving the children special opportunities: a small theater, atelier, motor skills room, and pedagogical kitchens, indoors and out. Another feature are small 'loopholes' in the walls, allowing the children to play across the room divisions.

01 3D section | 02 Interior of main space | 03 Wall with multiple windows at children's heights | 04 Playground with sandbox

03

04

01

02

03

Vestas

Vestas wind turbine factory lies alongside the motorway and has been extended in several stages since its inauguration, most recently in 2002 with warehouse and administration facilities. The project included both external areas and interiors of the buildings. The architecture consequently finds expression on scales both large and small as a powerful unifying concept, providing the complex with a clear identity. The factory has been expanded in sync with the growing international success of Vestas. The complex shows that it is possible, despite changing demands, to maintain an overall architectural expression in a dynamic design process.

01 Research and development center | 02 Logistics center | 03 North view | 04 Site plan | 05 Common areas | 06 Stairway

04

05

06

01

02

03

04

Performance House Folk High School

Performance House, situated at the heart of the Paper Mill's revitalized industrial area, is a modern interpretation of a performing art institution. The old heating plant has been transformed into a winter garden, with an instruction room and a performance area, while an adjacent plaza links the historic building with its modern counterpart. The architectural style and choice of materials are simple and bold, expressing the area's industrial heritage. The demarcation between interior and exterior and between the individual elements in the academy organism are continually redrawn, making it possible for passersby to hear music or catch a glimpse of theatrical performances.

01 Façade of new building | 02 Interior | 03 New building at night | 04 Foyer |
05 Ground floor plan old boiler building

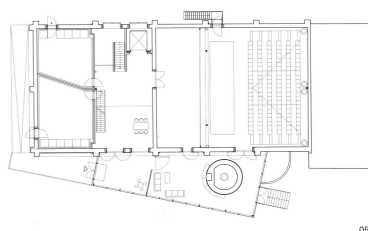

05

01

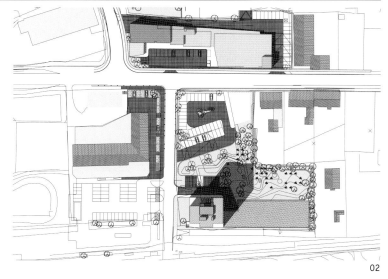

02

Siloetten / The Sil(o)houette

These new apartments are a mix of single story flats and maisonettes, so that the lower levels enjoy a full view and no two flats are the same. The silo contains staircases and lifts and serves as the base of a common roof terrace. Around the tower, the apartments are built up on a steel structure in eye-catching forms, which protrude out into the light and the landscape. This unusual structure of protrusions and displacements provides all of the apartments with generous outdoor spaces. The nature of the silo's 'rural high-rise' is unique and – since it is a conversion – no other building in the area can be built to the same height, guaranteeing its status as a free-standing landmark.

01 Side view | 02 Site plan | 03 Living area | 04 Exterior view | 05 Two-story apartment

03

04

05

01

Taastrup Theater

This project involved the extension and renovation of Taastrup Theater and has improved the general appeal and functionality of the building by introducing a second façade around the rough concrete structure. The new façade is conceived as a translucent curtain of acrylic prisms, elegantly embracing the existing building and creating a new open foyer. A whole new spatial dimension is added to the building, newly connecting the formerly enclosed interior with the outside.

01 Façade at night | 02 Entrance | 03 Foyer | 04 Ground floor plan | 05 Interior view

02

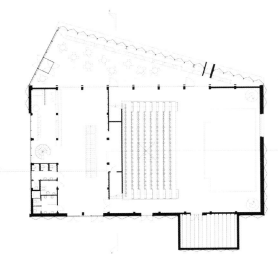

03

04

05

01

02

Fuglsang Art Museum

This new museum is a low-rise structure, which sits within a loose assembly of rural buildings. Similar to the red barn and the forge in the surrounding countryside, the museum extends into the fields with an axial but offset relation to the most significant of the buildings, the Manor House and its formal surroundings. A connection between the two buildings is further established by the profile of the museum with its arrangement of three diagonal roof lights. The façades of the museum are constructed from brick. In order to complement the barn on the west side of the court, they are painted white, with roof lights of grey brick to match the color of the roofs of the surrounding buildings.

01 Southeast corner | 02 Southwest corner with entrance | 03 Site plan | 04 View of the central gallery | 05 Daylight from the roof lights

03

04

05

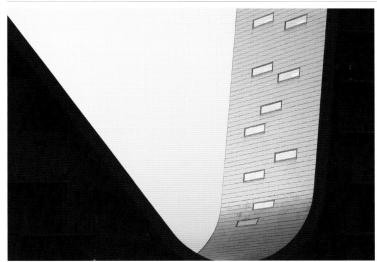

01

02

03

The Wave

The new landmark of Vejle is a distinctive, nine-story residential building with a magnificent location by the bay Skyttehusbugten and Vejle Fjord. With its five characteristic
wave crests, The Wave in Vejle stands out as a sculptural icon both respecting and challenging its location. Architecturally, the building relates to its fantastic location by Vejle
Fjord. During the day, the building will be characterized by the soft movements of the
waves reflected in the water surface of the fjord. At night, the characteristic profile of
The Wave will appear as an undulating mountain landscape of light and color. The building comprises 100 flats - many of which have two stories.

01 Wave detail | 02 Design sketch | 03 Balconies | 04 Façade | 05 Exterior view

04

05

01

02

03

04

Advice House

This building has an open and flexible office layout, in which various tenants share the same large space, of dramatic perspectives and angles. The building is shaped around two angled office wings, separated by an equally angled atrium, resulting in a plan resembling a hexagon with one corner pushed inwards. The two wings are connected by walkways across the atrium and the open and transparent interior is naturally ventilated. The building's unusual geometry offers passersby a dramatic and changing appearance, enhanced by the special color-changing cladding and textures of the façades.

01 Façade | 02 View from canteen | 03 View from motorway | 04 Stairwell | 05 Typical floor plan

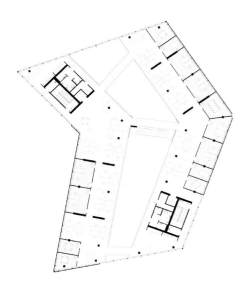

05

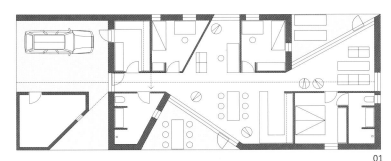

01

02

Sinus House

The pleated façades of Sinus House combine the wish of having large glass surfaces and view with the desire for privacy. This unusual 164 square meter country home is a great mix of pastoral settings and modern architecture. Designed with a black roof and façade to contrast the stark white incisions in its exterior walls, the structure charms with its interiors, where comfort blends perfectly with contemporary. With expansive floor-to-ceiling windows, enhanced open spaces, and an amazing kitchen with a black and white island, the Sinus House draws attention.

01 Floor plan | 02 Kitchen and dining area | 03 Living room with sliding doors | 04 Pleated façades

03

04

01

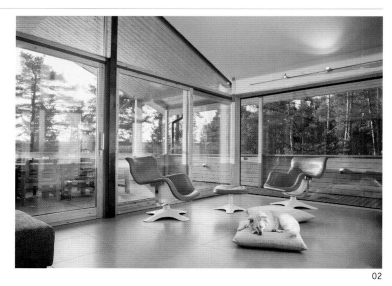

02

03

Kekkapää House

The simple form topped with a pitched roof integrates the building into the wider context. The western slope of the woodland site is divided into two areas of differing character; the back part with pines and the rocky ground, covered with moss and the dry peat forest to the front. This division is retained because the front yard is filled with activity; it contains the main entrance, the children's playground, the terrace and a workshop. On the opposite side of the main building, with a more fragile nature, is a solitary path leading to the sauna. The main building comprises three zones: living, working, and a glass-roofed conservatory linking the two.

01 Entrance bridge | 02 Winter terrace | 03 Dining and living area | 04 Conservatory | 05 Section | 06 Upper terrace

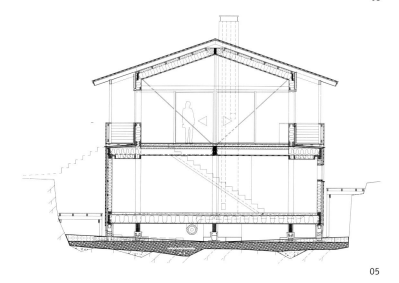

05

04

06

01

02

03

Kindergarten Espoo

This construction was confined to the sloping south side of the plot, where there are favorable climatic and construction conditions. The building has the shape of an organic, living entity that feeds the imagination. In the sheltered embrace of the building, the yard opens up towards the favorable southerly orientation. The interiors vary in height and utilize the attic space below the shallow roof planes. An essential part of the architecture is the seemingly arbitrary placement of the windows and the artificial landscape of slopes formed by the roof, where 'light lanterns' stand as miniature buildings, as well as enlivening the interior.

01 Playground | 02 Façade | 03 Hallway | 04 Playroom | 05 Site plan | 06 Entrance

04

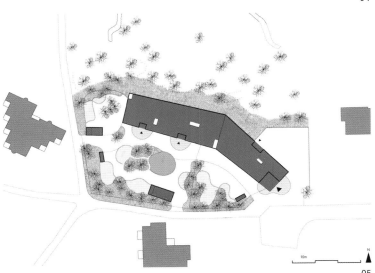
05

06

01

02

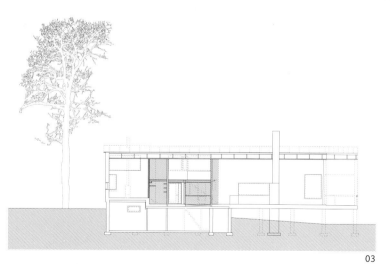

03

04

Humlegård House

This building is in the village of Fiskars, a few kilometers away from the center of the old ironworks. It stands on a small knoll at the edge of an overgrown glade, and is orientated in a north-south direction. The garden boundary is defined to the west by a shed and a garage, on the south by a field with an old winding village road, and is sheltered by a high cliff on the north. A log sauna has been built to the east of the house where Fiskars Lake can be seen through the forest. The house consists of three parts: two kitchen/living rooms linked by a balcony, a bathroom and a walk-in wardrobe below. The high window openings catch the first rays of the sun, which are reflected into the interior by the ceiling.

01 Living area | 02 Bedroom in open loft volume | 03 Section | 04 Exterior at night | 05 Timber west façade with blinds open

05

01

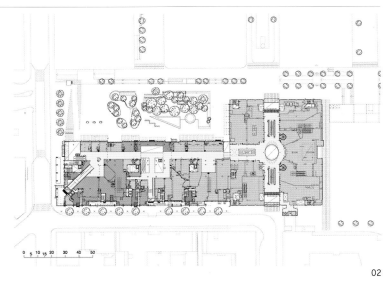

02

Kamppi Commercial Center

The cityscape of the new Kamppi district is characterized by functional design. Facing Mannerheimintie Street, the commercial spaces complement the service range of the city center and improve its competitiveness compared with other commercial hubs nearby. The interior space represents the 21st century, where the choice of materials is ruled by lifespan philosophy: they are aesthetic, functional, technically durable, and economical, now and in the future. A functional context takes on the main role through the wide removable glass walls and lighting that utilizes the latest technology.

01 Department store and Narinkka Square | 02 Floor plan | 03 Aerial view from east | 04 Atrium | 05 Tennispalatsi Square

03

04

05

01

02

03

04

05

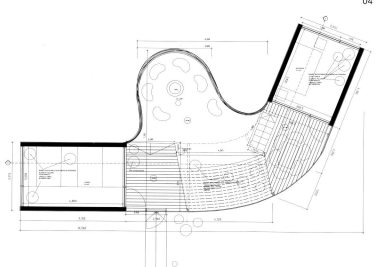

06

Wisa Wooden Design Hotel

The inspiration for this project came from the architect eating toffee caramels, where the outer edge breaks away to reveal a soft interior. The application of this idea to the design for a wooden architecture competition was natural. The site specified for the construction was located at the northern edge of Valkosaari, Helsinki. Birch wood was used to create a simple interior, while exterior surfaces were treated with water based wood treatment, providing the gray color. In addition to the actual designing and structural execution, the location of the site on an islet at the mercy of the weather, required particularly precise organization in terms of logistics and time scheduling.

01 Detail wooden trellis | 02 Exterior view | 03 Sculptural wooden trellis between two box-like ends | 04 Interior view | 05 Side view | 06 Floor plan

01

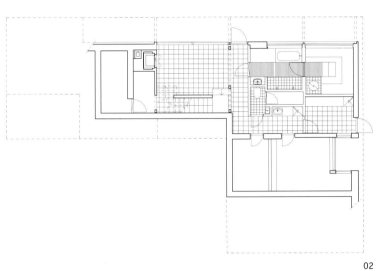

02

03

Villa Nuotta

The top of this steeply sloping rock gives an open view of the wide lake. The wild yet beautiful terrain and views provided the guidelines for building. In order to protect the undergrowth, which is very sensitive to wear and tear, the human footprint was limited as much as possible. The house is built of wood and planned for use as a holiday home all year round, and encloses a sheltered entrance yard. The exterior and interior spaces overlap, offering a variety of views and elevations. Visitors do not see the lake view until they are inside the house, when the view opens along the full width of the house.

01 Living room | 02 Basement floor plan | 03 View from balcony | 04 Interior view |
05 Front view

04

05

01

02

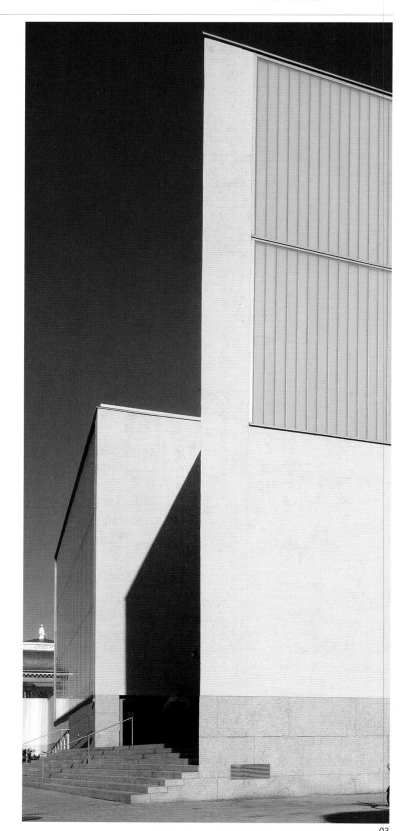

03

City Library in Turku

The new city library in Turku is located at the historical center of the city. The building is the latest addition to a block with several historical buildings. The new main entrance opens onto the corner of two main streets. Public spaces are situated mainly on two floors surrounding the inner courtyard. The main room is reached through a stairway, which opens to a monumental space. For the interior, mostly European oak is used in the wall covering and furniture; the façades are mainly plastered. Natural stone is used extensively on the façades, the stairway and the grounds surrounding the building. Glass was also given a seminal role both in the outer architecture and the interior world. Transparency befits this type of building; a public library building should evoke the idea of openness.

01 Wooden furniture in the library | 02 Exterior view from the inner courtyard | 03 Entrance area | 04 Ground floor plan

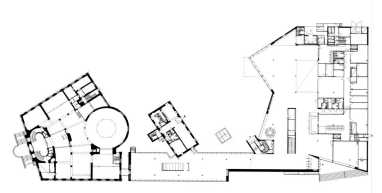

04

01

02

03

04

Hof Culture Building

The Hof Culture Building was designed to become a vortex of cultural life in the city of Akureyri and the surrounding area. This can clearly be seen from the circular shape of the building and the public street that runs right through it. HOF is rooted in the Icelandic nature by its exterior, which is covered with slabs of Icelandic Studlaberg granite, the narrow windows mirroring glacier cracks and ravines and the interior, which resembles a chasm between cliffs. Smaller openings give access to the cultural functions of the building: the concert hall seating 600, the mixed-use hall and the sculpture yard. The chasm and its cafes with spectacular views of the fjord can be visited also when Hof is closed to the public.

01 Façade | 02 Lobby | 03 Concert hall | 04 View from harbor | 05 Ground floor plan

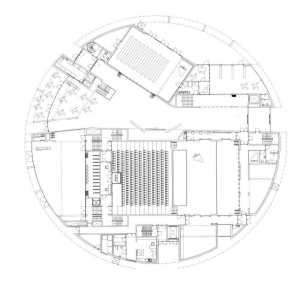

05

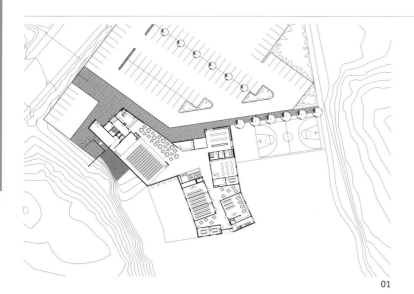

01

02

Borgarfjordur College

Located on a spectacular site, this building establishes a dialogue with the immediate environment, ringed by both rocky landscapes and vegetation. The building is formed by rectangular concrete blocks, which contain the main functional areas of the school. These are carefully placed on the site, creating open spaces between them and complementing the surroundings. The materials are elegant yet durable; the buildings are clad in brass, which will weather to a golden brown color, referrencing the color of the rocks on site. The roofs are covered with gravel made from the same rocks.

01 Ground floor plan in site plan | 02 View from inside towards fjord | 03 Exterior view | 04 Main view

03

04

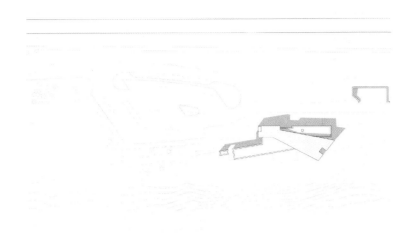

01

02

03

Snaefellsstofa Visitor Center

This building is divided into three parts so that it can be utilized in different ways, depending on the season. The eternal creative force of the glacier inspires the building's form; how it breaks its way through terrains, or retreats and carves new, ever changing natural wonders into the landscape. These creations provide the inspiration for the spaces and forms found in the building. The materials used are largely local in origin, such as local larch, turf roof and landscaping walls of local rock. In addition, horizontal and gently tilted tertier lava layers are reflected in the building with pronounced angles and the deep valley is reflected in its appearance.

01 Site plan | 02 Turf roof | 03 Walking path | 04 Exterior view

04

01

02

03

Hof

This country residence is in a remote and very special location, less than 100 kilometers from the Arctic Circle. It rises from the tufted site as a series of sheer cedar and concrete walls with the displaced grass of the field reinstated on the roof. Raw or painted concrete was used for all innermost walls. Ceilings, doors, and carpentry consist predominantly of oiled oak with steel detail. The house is highly insulated and thermally stable due to massive concrete walls, stone floors, and balanced fenestration. Water heated by geothermal energy is used for floor heating, radiators and all domestic uses. Electricity consumption is minimized by the design and sourced from hydroelectric and geothermal sources.

01 Parlor | 02 Main bathroom with marble tiles | 03 Open fireplace in the living room | 04 Sections | 05 Front view

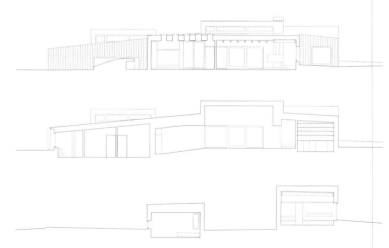

04

05

01

02

03

E-Tube

This extension was envisaged as a light membrane suspended between the existing enclosed space and the exterior. While providing a sheltered communication space between previously unconnected classrooms, it simultaneously adjoins the outdoor space to the school structure. The rhythm of transparent glass and translucent polycarbonate, which forms the envelope, allows continuous natural light into the classrooms and plays with the views: framing the Atlantic coast beyond, while blurring the immediate neighborhood. Unfinished timber and rudimentary detailing of the structure, exposed in the interior, are the third dimension of what externally appears to be a weightless screen – the mirror and the extension of the vast surrounding landscape.

01 Southwest view | 02 Interior view | 03 Extension at dusk | 04 Elevations and floor plan

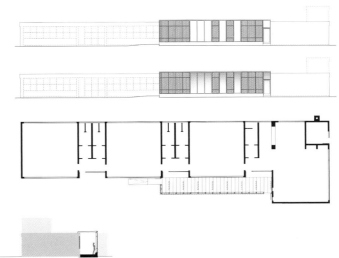

04

01

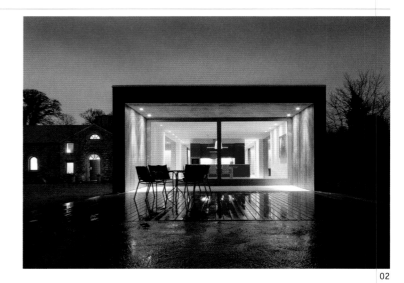

02

03

04

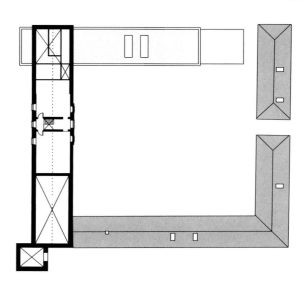

06

05

Farmhouse at Ballymahon

The introduction of this new wing to a group of 18th century farm buildings was an attempt to complete the courtyard, whilst allowing visual transparency between the courtyard and the woodlands beyond. Large expanses of frameless glazing allow the user to engage with both the courtyard and the surrounding landscape. Externally, the oiled cedar cladding connects the new wing to the woodland, whilst offering a new warmth to the inner courtyard, dominated until now by slate, brick, and stone. Raised off the ground, the wing seems to float, contrasting with the existing rooted buildings. A protruding section to the rear of the farmhouse houses the master bedroom and forms an eye to the surrounding woodland.

01 View of new building extension | 02 Deck at night | 03 Exterior view, old meets new | 04 Bedroom with open views to landscape | 05 Floor plan | 06 Living room

01

02

03

Visual

The Visual, Center for Contemporary Art & George Bernard Shaw Theater, provides Ireland with a significant new exhibition space to showcase contemporary visual arts and a theater of national and international importance. Located in the picturesque setting of the grounds of St. Patrick's College, it features expansive gallery space for touring international contemporary exhibitions. The entrance, located on the south elevation, opens into a foyer of cast concrete and dark timber, which leads up a short flight of stairs to the galleries, or left to the George Bernard Shaw Theater, located in the southwest corner of the building. It contrasts with the serene neutrality of the gallery spaces and is defined by a deep red feature wall in the foyer bar and red seating in the auditorium.

01 Entrance area at night | 02 East view | 03 Northeast corner | 04 Sketch of interior | 05 Link gallery | 06 Theater bar | 07 Link gallery

04

05

06

07

01

02

03

04

Pre-Cast House

This project is defined in conceptual terms as three discrete forms: garage, house, and swimming pool, their respective heights determined by their function. Each form is detailed in the same manner and is constructed of polished pre-cast concrete. The surface tension across the façades is maintained by the flush detailing of the windows and the glass balustrades. At the first floor (entry) level, the plan is open, with the primary living spaces overlapping with the entrance. The continuous stone floor is offset with rich walnut cladding. The open nature of this space creates a panoramic connection to the landscape and seascape beyond. The depth of the plan is illuminated with three roof lights.

01 Exterior view from garden | 02 General view | 03 Living room terrace looking towards the Irish Sea | 04 Study room | 05 Sketch

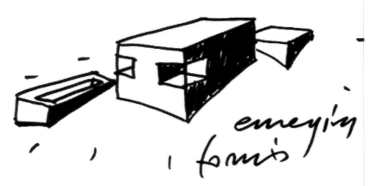

05

01

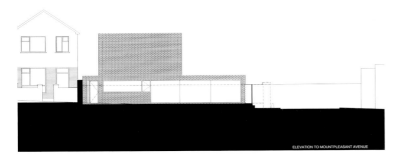

02

Single-Family House

This house is located in a protected area close to Dublin's city center, on a small but prominent infill corner site. Two stories of the house remain largely in character with the nearby terrace of houses and form a low book-end building to Richmond Place. They also offer a strong contextual response to both the prevailing architectural context and the unusual site configuration, which is the principal generator of the building form. The ambition was to build on the entire site, maximizing the footprint of the building and visually extending the living area into the external courtyards formed on each side. Externally the house is faced entirely in a stock brick, directly referencing the gable ends of neighboring period houses.

01 Exterior view | 02 Elevations | 03 Detail of external courtyard

03

01

02

Elm Park

This project offers the possibility of a new type of urban environment in Dublin, one which is firmly lodged in its natural environment, while fine-tuned to energy conservation and generation and the functional potential of its components. It is a large, functionally diverse ensemble of elements integrated into a continuous energy-balanced piece of urban landscape. It is a place where buildings are oriented so as to minimize their energy demand and maximize their use of natural light. Landscape facilitates movement, creates connections between activities and people, provides a place of density and concentration, for people to live, work, and engage in leisure.

01 Structural elements | 02 Day clinic and hotel | 03 Offices and conference center | 04 Site plan | 05 Canopy construction

03

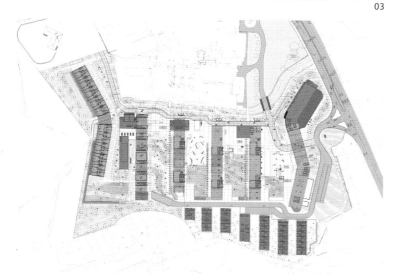

04

05

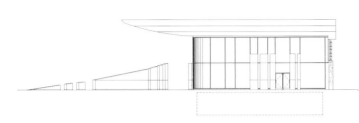

01

02

Glasnevin Trust Museum

The Glasnevin Trust identified the need for a new building, which would present in visual form the history of the cemetery and the achievements of the one and a half million people who are buried there. This building evolved into the new museum. There was only one site available within the cemetery, located beside the main entrance and parallel to Finglas Road, all other areas in the cemetery contained burial areas or places of special interest. The plan and roof of the building curves outwards and upwards pointing towards the tower, while the graves are sheltered from the museum by a curving freestanding stonewall formed of polished stone elements of varying modular sizes.

01 West elevation | 02 Interior view | 03 Main staircase | 04 Main entrance | 05 View of historic graves | 06 Museum with former Cemetery Superintendent's Lodge

03

04

05

06

01

02

Aviva Stadium

Developed on the site of the world's oldest international rugby ground at Lansdowne Road, the 50,000 seat Aviva Stadium is Ireland's home for Rugby and Soccer. The building's organic form, mass, materials and aspect were derived as a response to its site and surroundings. The undulating form is expressed in a skin of transparent polycarbonate shingles, which reflect the sky and light conditions, resulting in a constantly changing building façade. The shingles allow light to be drawn into the interiors, an element which enhances the drama created by the elegant structure and allows for the development of exciting and intimate spaces suitable for sporting events, as well as the many other non-match day uses.

01 Aerial view | 02 Inside stadium | 03 Entrance lobby | 04 Site plan

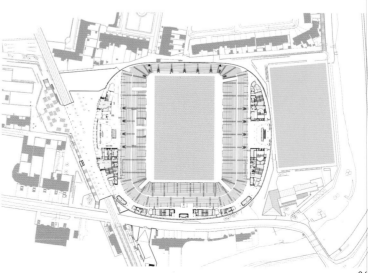

03

04

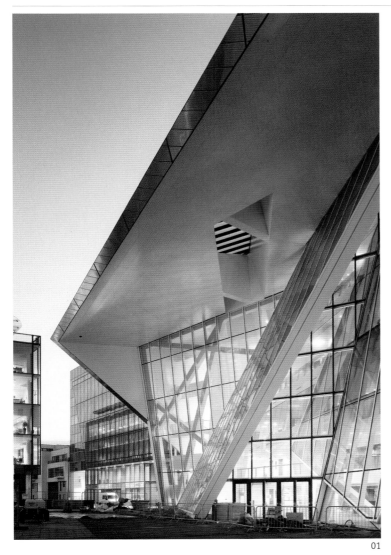

01

02

03

04

Grand Canal Square Theater

The concept of the Grand Canal Square Theater and Commercial Development is to build a powerful cultural presence expressed by dynamic volumes sculpted to project a fluid and transparent public dialogue with the cultural, commercial and residential surroundings. The design also seeks to communicate the various inner forces intrinsic to the theater and office buildings. This composition creates a dynamic urban gathering place and icon, mirroring the joy and drama emblematic of Dublin itself. The theater becomes the main façade of a large public piazza that has a five star hotel and residences on one side and an office building on the other. From its rooftop terrace, the theater offers spectacular views out over Dublin harbor.

01 Façade detail | 02 Interior view | 03 General view | 04 Foyer | 05 Section

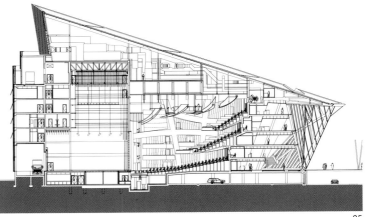

05

01

02

03

04

05

Westmeath County Council Headquarters

Westmeath County Council headquarters is a low-energy civil services office building located at the heart of an important archaeological site. The open and transparent building was carefully woven into the historic context, creating an ensemble of new and old
buildings around this public site. On the inside, the new building is a sculpture of light,
created primarily with glass, timber and concrete, while on the outside it represents an
open and transparent expression of local government. The building is principally organized in two axes and two buildings; a north-south axis which contains the library and
cafe, and an office block that curves east to west. The entirely naturally ventilated building has a double façade combined with an atrium, which ventilates the office building.

01 Main entrance | 02 South façade | 03 Library | 04 Urban composition | 05 Site
plan | 06 Reading room

06

01

02

03

Atrium Cabin on Vardehaugen

This project is a coastal cabin 35 meters above sea level with a panoramic view in virtually all directions. The building is inspired by the traditional Norwegian farmyard, in which flexible half-climatic outside spaces and a clear social organization are the leading principles. The planning of the cabin was executed during a year of regular trips to Vardehaugen to get the most complete impression of the varying climatic conditions affecting the property. To provide maximum protection for the cabin, the black roof folds in and becomes wall surfaces towards the most exposed directions.

01 Exterior | 02 Deck | 03 General view | 04 Front entrance | 05 Interior | 06 Living area

04

05

06

01

03

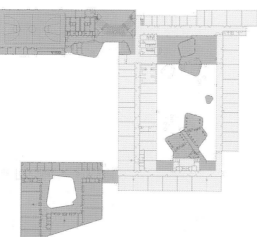

02

Oslo International School

The existing 1960s structure was worn down, but had obvious architectonic qualities which the architects aimed to preserve, including organization on one level enabling easy orientation, good natural lighting and close contact to the outdoors. A pavilion separate from the rest of the school houses the smallest children in ten classooms. The room sizes are flexible and can be altered according to the number of children on each level. Daylight from the atrium floods the common areas. The organically shaped walls are clad with specially milled wooden paneling in convex and concave shapes, treated with clear tar, and the façade is covered with fiber cement boards in ten different colors.

01 Main entrance | 02 Floor plan | 03 Hallway | 04 General view | 05 Outdoor area

04

05

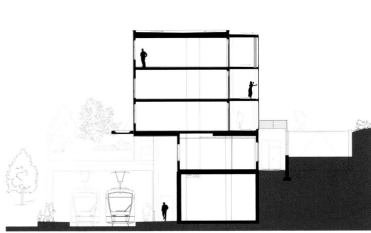

01

02

Fantoft Student Flats

The Fantoft area is a part of the municipality of Bergen. 3RW Architects' work with the student accommodation area at Fantoft started in 2006. Today, the 'Student City' at Fantoft, consists of five large residential blocks, built in typical 1960s and 70s style. With 1,344 units all together, including Bergen's highest building, the area makes quite an impact at a local scale. The development plan displays a condensation proposal where new buildings are to be established in areas unsuitable for outdoor and recreational activity. It also stresses the importance of adding an urban quality by providing an emphasized central area in connection to a new shopping street and the city tram stop.

01 Section | 02 View of new square | 03 Street painting | 04 Night view | 05 Public square | 06 Housing block

03

04

05

06

01

02

03

Tautra Maria Convent

This project is a new monastery for 18 nuns, complete with a small chapel and all facilities needed for sustainable living. The original plan was reduced by around 30 percent by eliminating almost all corridors in the project. This was made possible by analyzing the way the monastery works. Usually, when all the nuns are assembled, they gather in one of the four main rooms, which can therefore also act as 'corridors' and circulation areas. Most of the rooms are unique and have very different requirements. This created a need for architectural flexibility, as well as adequate daylight for each of the rooms located within the horizontal layout. For this reason, the project consists of a system of spaces connected to each other at the corners using courts.

01 Façade creates patterns of light and shadow | 02 Glass façade | 03 Chapel, interior | 04 Roof construction | 05 General view | 06 Detail façade

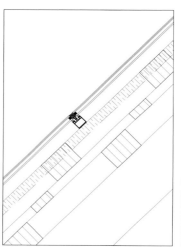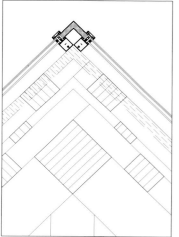

04

05

06

01

Service Buildings Flydalsjuvet

The site is located on the ridge of the steep mountain chain that rises from the Geiranger fjord. The timbered modules were collected from a local site and have been refurbished by traditional craftsmen. The house was part of an old farm and had fallen into disrepair. This is a general problem in Norway: traditional farmhouses become ruinous symbols of a culture in the process of change from farming to tourism. Instead of reusing these buildings for new purposes, the building industry is facilitating tourism by using a traditional building system, but within an architectural framework that typically seems to refer to something between national romanticism and a post-modern Viking castle. In this project, the old timber modules are mounted on a five-centimeter-thick glass base, which allows light to enter under the massive wooden walls. Thus, an old local building tradition is preserved for the future, floating on a modern glass structure.

01 Buildings with scenery | 02 Rear view | 03 Interior | 04 Construction detail | 05 Detail wood – glass

02

03

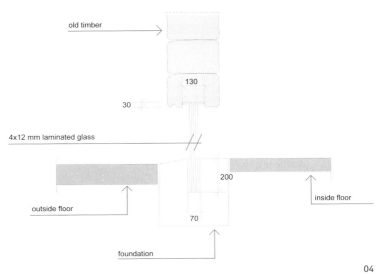

old timber

130

30

4x12 mm laminated glass

200

outside floor

inside floor

70

foundation

04

05

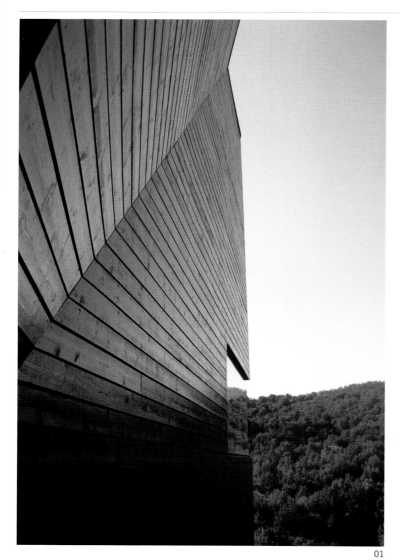

01

02

03

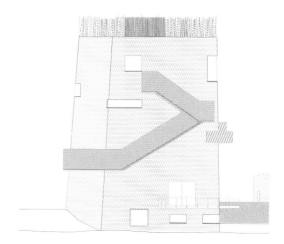

04

Hamsun Center

This center is dedicated to the writer Knut Hamsun. It is located above the Arctic Circle, near the village of Presteid in Hamarøy and the farm where the writer grew up. The center contains exhibition areas, a library and a reading room, a café and an auditorium equipped with film projection equipment. The concept for the museum is 'building as a body,' creating a battleground of invisible forces. Many features of the building are inspired by the vernacular style, such as the characteristic stained black wood exterior skin of the great wooden stave Norse churches. The long grass on the roof garden is also a modern interpretation of the style of the traditional Norwegian sod roofs.

01 View into the landscape | 02 Roof detail with long bamboo | 03 Building in context |
04 Section | 05 Staircase

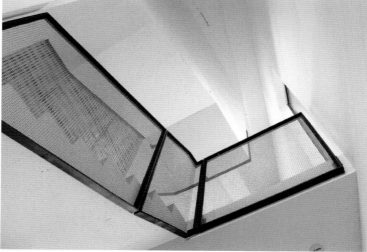

05

01

02

Service Building Hereiane

This small building is situated near Jondal, along national road 550. The rest area has a fantastic view over the Hardanger Fjord and sea access via a rocky landscape filled with moorland herb. The building consists of two main elements: a monolithic slate-construction and a yellow base. The shape and materials are based on local crafting traditions. The yellow concrete flows under the whole building. The strong yellow and iconic shapes are designed to catch the attention of the passing drivers. The contrast between the glossy concrete and the dry stone underlines the building's tactile quality and encourage visitors to stop and appreciate it.

01 View from parking lot | 02 General view | 03 Façade and concrete seating | 04 Interior detail | 05 Window and façade detail | 06 Elevations, section and floor plan | 07 Slate wall and glass door

03

04

05

06

07

01

02

03

04

Villa G

Villa G lies like a white landmark in the soft landscape of Hjellestad, near Bergen. The house is large and modern but not dominating. It has a futuristic form but is built with traditional Nordic materials and architectural elements, and has a good base in Norwegian building methods. The house has an over-built outside space, the second floor covers the entrance below allowing the house to work together with the rough climate on the west coast of Norway. The stair is one solid piece of one-centimeter thick steel, galvanized with white sand corn making it slip resistant. The kitchen bench is eight meters long and has plenty of drawers for kitchen equipment. None of the electrical outlets are visible and all technology is controlled by a main control panel in the kitchen.

01 Night view | 02 Bedroom and bathroom | 03 Projecting angles of building envelope | 04 Kitchen and dining area | 05 Floor plan

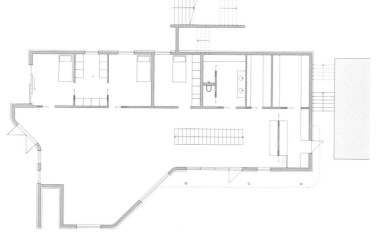

05

01

Farm House Gamleveien

This building replaces an old derelict barn comprised of a courtyard, together with the existing main building. It now accommodates a small apartment, sauna/fitness room and a double garage with storage space. The three, pitched roofs represent a new interpretation of the old saddle roof and provide extra, useful space on the upper level. The two gable-pitches face the magnificent view towards the west horizon. The middle east-oriented pitch opens up towards a steep hillside nearby and gives additional daylight to the rooms on ground level. A flybridge connects the upper level for easy access to storage space on the upper level, heat pump and highly insulated construction contribute to energy efficiency.

01 Exterior view | 02 Side view | 03 Storage space | 04 Interior view | 05 Dining room | 06 View from upper floor | 07 Elevations

02

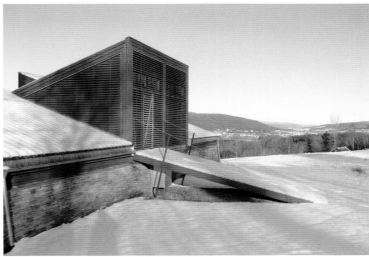

03

04

05

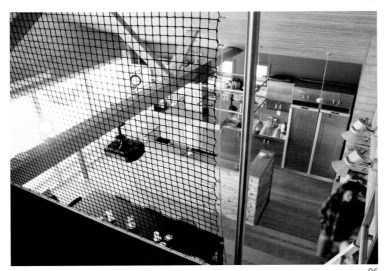

06

07

01

02

Preikestolen Mountain Lodge

The client is Stavanger Turistforening, an association that facilitates hiking in the mountains through small cabins open to all. They needed a new building to serve the rapidly increasing amount of tourists hiking to Pulpit Rock. It was clear that the old cabin, built in 1947, with bunk beds and a shared shower in the hallway did not meet modern standards. The client's wish was to create a modest accommodation building with upgraded bathroom facilities. The building features a restaurant with room for 100 guests, a small conference room, universal access, and is built with environmentally friendly materials.

01 Side view | 02 Exterior | 03 Bedroom and bathroom | 04 Dining area | 05 Living area | 06 Bedroom

03

04

05

06

01

Buholmen Cottage

02

This cottage replaces an old shed. It is twofold, with one residential zone and one bed-room area, and a wind-protected patio between the two. A new outhouse and pier were also part of the project. The situation forms an open wing plan, which opens towards the south. The south wing contains the private zone with compact sleeping cabins. The east wing consists of one large open living room/kitchen area, divided by a split-level, em-phasizing the view towards Jomfruland. The dynamic form, with its wedge-shaped plan and tilted roofs, embraces the view to the bay in front of the cottage. The pine façade is treated with iron-sulfate which, together with the sedum-moss roof, captures the colors of the environment.

01 View from water | 02 Cottage and annex | 03 Waterfront | 04 Ground floor plan | 05 Deck

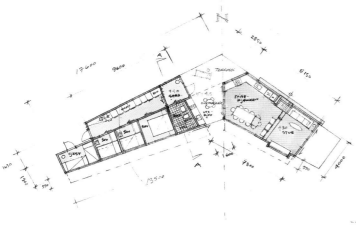

03

04

05

01

02

04

Parisholmen Cottage

This planned summer cottage spans across a gap between the rocks. The design presents a sequence of levels, leading up to the viewpoint overlooking the fjord and open sea in the east. The green roofscape emphasizes the shape of the terrain and creates a dynamic interior which corresponds to the different levels. In conjunction with the sides of the rocks, the positioning of the building forms a natural atrium, providing room for private space and a swimming pool. The façade is clad with untreated hardwood pine and the sedum-moss roof covering blends in with the surroundings.

01 Waterfront | 02 Exterior view | 03 Interior view | 04 Artistic impression

03

01

03

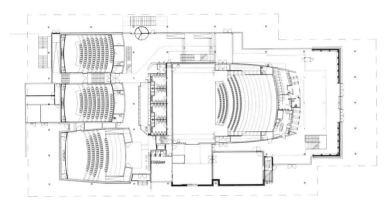

02

Cultural Center The Wave

The dominating form of this cultural center is comprised of a wood-clad main hall and a stage area with 550 seats. This main element breaks through a thin metal-clad roof surface, accentuating its lightweight nature. Tall glass walls with delicate frameworks girdle the hall and public spaces, allowing an expansive view of the fjord, river and city. In the rising landscape to the west, three cinemas have been fitted into the partly underground area. These are made of poured concrete, with an art gallery positioned above them, opening out towards the city. The design is characterized by industrial simplicity.

01 Main entrance | 02 Ground floor plan | 03 Interior view | 04 Night view | 05 Waterfront

04

05

01

02

Trollwall Restaurant and Service

The architecture of this new visitor's center is a result of the site's close connection to the impressive mountain wall, one of Norway's many nature attractions. The building has a simple but flexible plan, with a characteristic roof that draws inspiration from the majestic landscape. The glass façade of the structure reflects the dramatic landscape and allows daylight to flood into the interior. The wooden sections of the exterior also help to blend the structure with its surroundings, creating a building that complements, rather than contrasts, the natural environment. The building's simple design gives the structure its character and identity making the service center an eye-catcher and an architectural attraction in the region.

01 General view | 02 Detail interior | 03 Façade detail | 04 Ground floor plan | 05 Rooftop structure

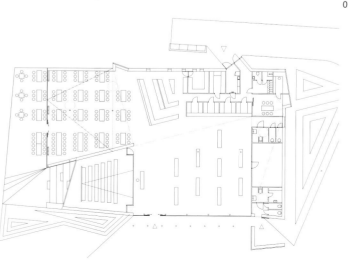

03

04

05

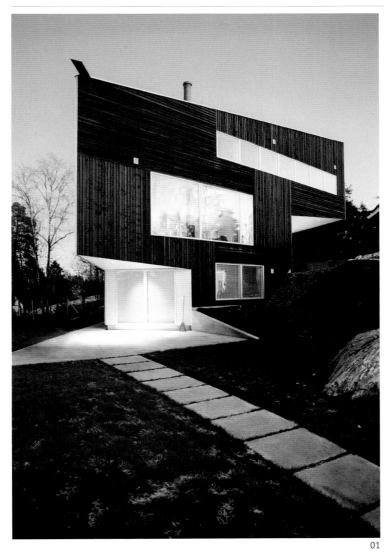

01

02

03

04

Triangle House

This house is situated with a view towards the sea from between the branches of the surrounding pine forest. The vertical lines of the building emphasize the shape and the height of the roofline. While the window openings frame the views of the exteriors, the interior is more fluid, with overlapping sequences of space and light shaping the layout. The exterior cladding of wooden panels follows the shape of the window openings. The interior is clad with OSB-boards and the floors are cast in concrete, partly covered with sisal mats. The bathrooms are paneled with brushed aluminum panes and mirrors, while a collection of books cover the walls and soften the acoustics.

01 West view at night | 02 Dining room | 03 North façade | 04 Living room | 05 Floor plan

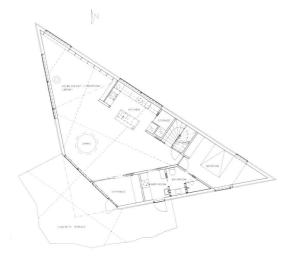

05

01

02

03

04

Gunnar's House

This house was built based on a traditional six-inch timber frame construction, cantilevering beyond the forest floor, over a covering of lichen and moss. High pine trees frame the building volume, comprised of two floors and a basement. The timber frame structure defines the zones in the house and the plan is organized within a three-by-three meter grid. The exterior appears fairly closed from the east and north, but the other façades allow light in, creating a bright interior with windows on all outer walls and ceilings. The semi-covered outdoor spaces on the gable walls evoke retracted balconies in more traditional storehouses.

01 View from forest | 02 Staircase | 03 Kitchen and dining area | 04 Side view | 05 Ground floor and gallery floor plan

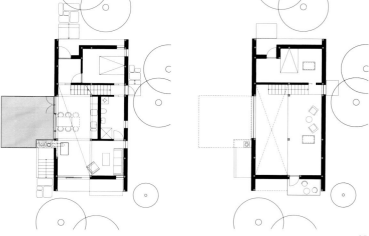

05

01

Opera House

The Opera House is the first element in the planned transformation of this area of the city. The marble-clad roofscape forms a large public space in the landscape of the city and fjord. The public face of the Opera House looks west and north, while the building's profile is also visible at a distance from the fjord to the south. The building connects city and fjord, urbanity and landscape. To the east, the view of the Opera House as a 'factory' is articulated and varied. One can see the activities within the building: ballet rehearsal rooms at the upper levels; workshops at street level. The connection to a lively new district will add greater meaning to this feature. Snøhetta's architecture is narrative. It is the materials that form the defining elements of the spaces and it is the meeting of materials that articulates the architecture through varied detail and precision.

01 View from plaza | 02 Façade detail | 03 First floor plan | 04 Exterior view | 05 View from Oslofjord | 06 Detail of marble 'carpet'

02

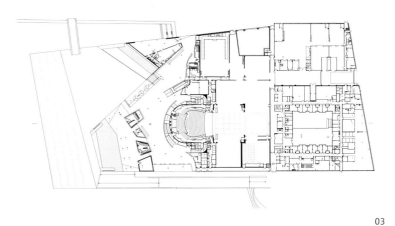

03

04

05

06

01

02

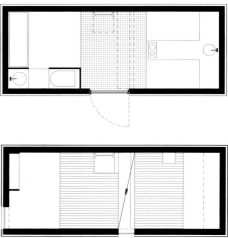

03

04

Boxhome

In the north, all residential buildings have high energy demands and must follow certain regulations due to the extreme climate. Smaller homes are therefore economically and environmentally advantageous. Boxhome is a 19-square-meter dwelling with four rooms covering the basic living functions: kitchen with dining, bathroom, living room, and bedroom. The project focuses on the quality of space, material and natural light, and tries to reduce unnecessary floor area. As a consequence, the price is one third of that of any apartment of the same size in the area. It is a small, peaceful home, a kind of urban cave that offers withdrawal from the intensity of the surrounding city.

01 Façade detail | 02 Interior | 03 Floor plans | 04 Resting area | 05 Front façade

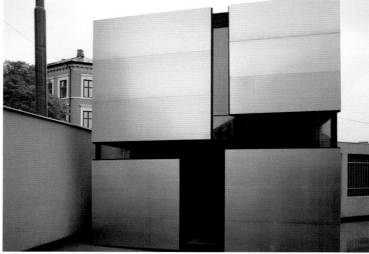

05

01

02

03

New Holmenkollen Ski Jump

This design aims at unifying the various elements present in a ski jump into one single expression, shape and action. Rather than having a series of dispersed pavilions on site, the architects have managed to combine them into one organism. The judges booths, the commentators, the trainers, the royal family, the VIPs, the wind screens, the circulations, the lobby, the entrance to the arena and the arena itself, the lounge for the skiers, the shop of souvenirs, the access to the existing museum, the viewing public square at the very top. Everything, is contained in the shape of the jump in a symbiosis of programs and experiences, giving the jump a harmonic contextual relationship to the surrounding landscape.

01 General view | 02 Stainless steel façade | 03 View from stands | 04 Site plan

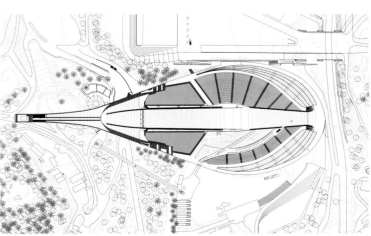

04

01

02

03

04

House Kollstrøm/Østberg

This house is pulled back from the road, establishing a southwest facing garden. A carport with a narrow garden shed shelters the garden from the road. The garden is separated from the entrance path by an 18-meter-long carp pond. The house consists of two elements, a concrete base and a folding timber envelope. The aim is to give character to the living spaces, which are the less defined parts of the program, by cultivating the configuration of spaces for program elements of definite and predictable proportions. This dualism constitutes the basic hierarchy of the house. The timber envelope unfolds in three displaced sections, the resultant openings permitting light and views.

01 View from garden | 02 Waterspout and entrance to basement | 03 Façade facing forest | 04 Kitchen and living room | 05 Section

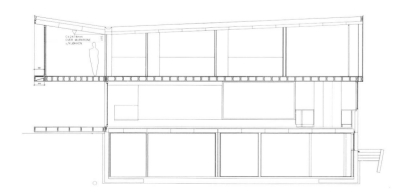

05

01

02

03

Kindergarten Fagerborg

RRA has designed a new kindergarten for Fagerborg Congregation in central Oslo. The kindergarten offers two units for children between one and three years of age and two units for children between three and six years of age. The gross area of the building is around 1,000 square meters. There were many cultural heritage guidelines to be considered in the project site. As a requirement from the local authority, the kindergarten is to have a contemporary expression. With its location in the middle of a small city park, the kindergarten has an outdoor area that is protected like an enclosed garden. The planning solution enables the four kindergarten units to function both independently and together as required.

01 Exterior view | 02 View at night | 03 Interior view | 04 Section and ground floor plan | 05 Contemporary building design

04

05

01

02

Summer House Inside Out

This house is beautifully situated on the top of a hill overlooking the ocean and the horizon, placed in the midst of an uncultivated landscape on a small peninsula. The design of the house allows a close interaction with the surrounding nature and the beautiful scenery. It provides a feeling of being outdoors when inside. The small scale of the house, together with the use of wooden materials that will gradually develop a gray patina allows the project to interact and fit in with the existing shape and natural colors of the surrounding landscape. At the same time, the design contrasts with the traditional building practice of the area.

01 Exterior view from below | 02 Deck | 03 Floor plan | 04 Bedroom | 05 Exterior view

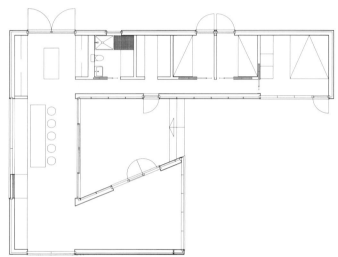

03

04

05

01

02

03

04

Vestfold Crematorium

Vestfold Crematorium seeks to meet both the functional and emotional needs related to cremation services. This involves creating dignified spaces for relatives grieving the deceased, as well as for the staff. The building's location, along a forest boundary, forms an outdoor space sheltered from noise coming from the highway to the north. There are large windows facing the forest in both the relatives and staff areas. The rooms for cremation are designed with the same degree of dignity and quality as the public spaces. Simple lines of movement are important in facilitating the daily work in the crematorium.

01 Interior ceremony space | 02 Staff office | 03 Interior view | 04 Exterior view at night | 05 Floor plan

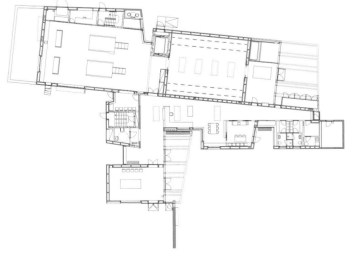

05

01

04

02

03

05

Solberg Tower and Park

Sarpsborg is a green, flat and calm area of South Norway and a traditional stopover for travellers on the route to and from Sweden. A low-walled ramp spirals around the rest area, defining the area's limits, while spring-flowering fruit trees adorn the courtyard. Within it, Saunders Architecture designed seven small pavilions, working with graphic designer Camilla Holcroft. The flatness of the landscape meant that the beauty of the surrounding nature could only be enjoyed from a certain height, so the creation of a tower quickly became a main part of the brief. Named Solberg, the tower's aerial views towards the nearby coastline and the Oslo fjord are truly dramatic.

01 Wooden platforms and tower | 02 Boardwalk | 03 Information booth | 04 General view | 05 Outdoor recreational area | 06 Ground floor plan

06

01

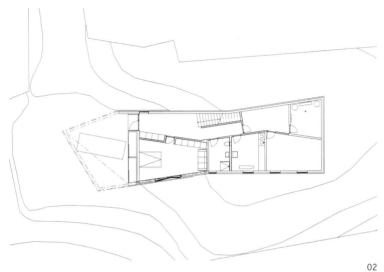

02

03

White House

Situated in a rather dense suburban setting, this house dynamically combines sheltered areas for privacy and open ones with interesting views. The central space of the house catches the morning light among the pines in the east, and the western sun on the horizon of the Oslo fjord. The house's interior and exterior are both clad with painted wooden panels. Walls and ceilings on the first floor are finished in oak, while floor and walls of the ground floor consist of exposed concrete casted on site.

01 Living room | 02 Ground floor plan | 03 Dining area | 04 View from east | 05 General view

04

05

01

02

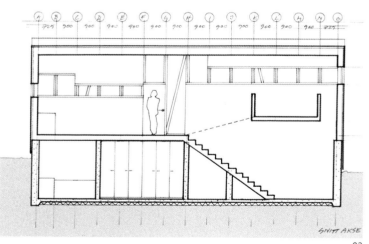

03

04

Farm House

This is a small house for two historians and their children, overlooking lake Mjøsa at an abandoned farm which they have inherited. The 100-year-old cladding of the old barn was recycled for both the exterior cladding and terraces of the new house. Some of the old planks are cut with widths that vary from the bottom to the top. These diagonals are used to adjust the horizontality of the cladding towards the sloping lines of the ground and the angle of the roof. The spatial complexity, exposed construction, and material simplicity of the barn have also inspired and informed the new architecture in a wider sense.

01 Ramp to upper floor | 02 Kitchen | 03 Section | 04 Exterior | 05 Rear entry

05

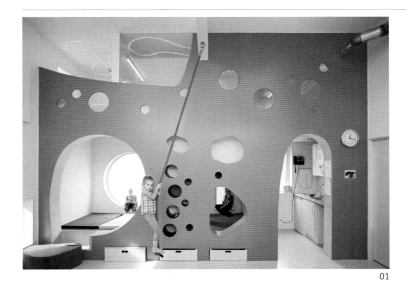

01

Somereng and Fjellvegen Kindergarten

This kindergarten is organized in a number of linear zones – from a series of roofed out-door terraces and an 'indoor street' with water-play areas and a winter garden feel, to intimate reading nooks and mezzanines. These zones enable a soft transition from the exterior to the interior spaces – from the exposed wide landscape to the private and quieter zones. The rooms themselves offer a variety of functions: simple moves can transform the size and feel of each space. Adjustable walls contain a variety of play elements: pull-out furniture, climbing walls and puppet shows. The concept is an exploration of a child's imaginative world with themes of transition, conversion and surprise.

01 Play area | 02 Playing and crawling walls | 03 Theater and performance area | 04 Exterior view | 05 Sketch | 06 Puppet theater section

02

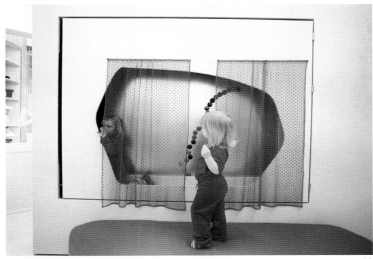

03

04

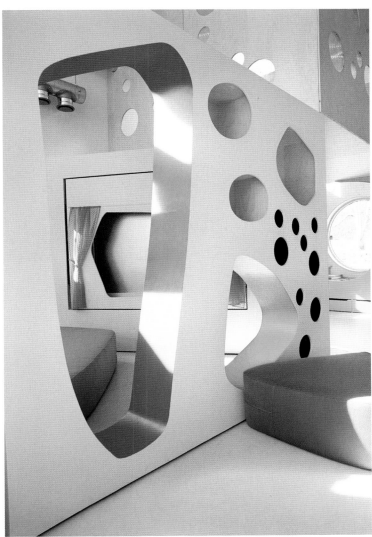

05

06

01

02

Strandkanten Urban Development

Strandkanten is a new housing area south of Tromsø's center, on a reclaimed area of the Tromsø strait. The area is crucial to the city's development strategy, as its concentrated growth will strengthen the downtown activities and reduce the need for transportation. The entire area is planned to include 900 dwellings on a site of 88 areas. The development plan focuses on ensuring the quality of the outdoor areas, while maintaining a high population density. The contents and quality of the outdoor areas will be a deciding factor for the development.

01 View from the sea, building F | 02 Blocks E and F | 03 Building F in arctic winter night | 04 Outdoor area with greenhouses | 05 Site plan, area III

03

04

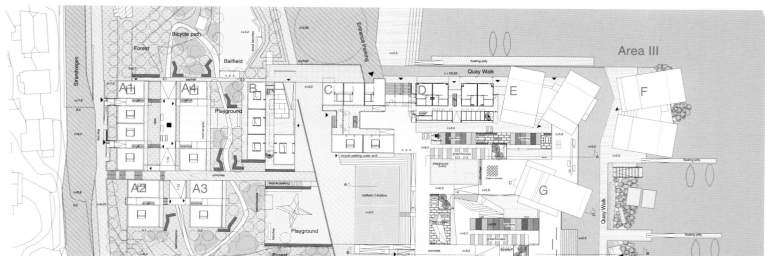

05

01

02

03

04

Branntomta / Borkeplassen

These buildings were conceived as modern interpretations of merchant homes featuring a mix of businesses and residential spaces. Their open urban planning and strict style, along with the narrow alleys that divide them, contribute to the renewal of the center's variety of buildings. The central square is surrounded by shops, outdoor cafes and restaurants, constituting a meeting place for the new buildings. The outdoor areas between the flats also enhance the standard of living. Some of the apartments have larger private outdoor areas, while others have French balconies or screened-in, half-private areas directly linked to the apartment. There is also a common outdoor area: the bridge gallery towards Borkeplassen. This solution satisfies the minimum requirement of ten square meters of outdoor space per apartment.

01 West façade | 02 Façade detail | 03 Exterior view | 04 South façade | 05 Floor plan

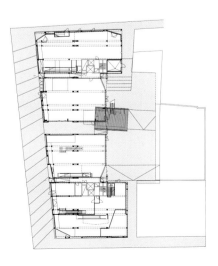

05

01

02

03

04

05

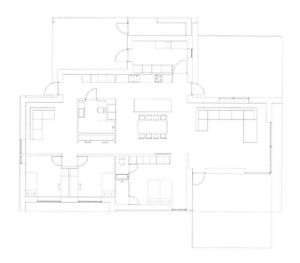

06

Line House

Line House utilizes a unique building system which is a refinement of a 'standard' SIP (Structural Insulated Panels). It is 100 percent damp proof, extremely airtight and well insulated, making this house the first to be certified according to the Swedish government's strict regulations on passive housing. Combined with highly efficient windows and foundations, the house does not require any active heating, even when the temperature drops to -20 degrees celsius. The house is divided into a children's and an adult zone, which are connected through a common office-cum-passage. The roof is raised above the social areas adding and defining a feeling of space. The master bedroom is linked with the living area by its floor to roof door. The raised roof then continues on the outside of the house, creating coverage over the terrace.

01 Kitchen and dining area | 02 Living room | 03 Side view | 04 Corner view | 05 Terrace | 06 Floor plan

01

02

03

04

Umeå School of Architecture

Umeå School of Architecture enjoys a unique location by the Umeå River. With its interior landscape of open floor levels and sculpturally shaped stairs, the building has a strong artistic expression. As a growth center for future architecture, the main function of the building is to provide a framework for inspiration and innovation. From the outside, the building has a cubic expression with its larch façades and square windows placed in a vibrant, rhythmic sequence on all sides. The interior space of the building is designed as a dynamic sequence of stairs and split, open floor levels where abstract white boxes hang freely from the ceiling filtering the light coming in through the high skylights.

01 Façade detail | 02 Staircase | 03 Exterior view | 04 Interior view | 05 Sketch

05

01

02

03

04

Mirage

The Mirage dance hall is situated 200 meters from the beach in a small pine wood grove at the southern-most tip of Sweden. The project was the result of an international competition to replace an existing, much-loved dance hall that had been destroyed in a fire. Set in a nature reserve, the new building occupied the site and footprint of its predecessor. Sympathetic to its surroundings, the building's façades comprise of dark walls that recede into the forest and a pattern of mirrored panels that reflect the surroundings, echoing the façade pattern of the old dance hall. The abstracted forest pattern used on the interior walls further acts to connect the building with its surroundings, blurring the boundaries between indoor and out.

01 Entrance at night | 02 Façade detail | 03 Night view | 04 Restaurant | 05 Section and floor plans

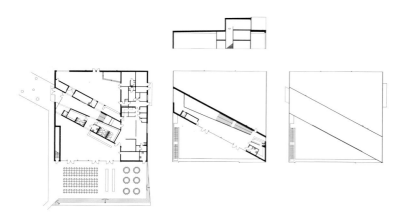

05

01

New Discfilter Facility, Rya Wastewater Treatment Plant

KUB arkitekter was brought into this process in 2006. The task determined that a good working environment should be created by using the construction consultant's structure as a starting point. At KUB it was also felt that the important function of the building needed a strong physical manifestation and that the closeness to the forest Rya skog needed to be taken into special consideration. The result is a simple building with a sophisticated shape. Two long glass façades are united into an oval shape by a sweeping roof. Towards the woods it rests on a concrete foundation, but seen from a distance the building seemingly floats just above the basin surfaces.

01 General view at night | 02 South corner | 03 Interior north hall | 04 Water sculpture | 05 Floor plan

02

03

04

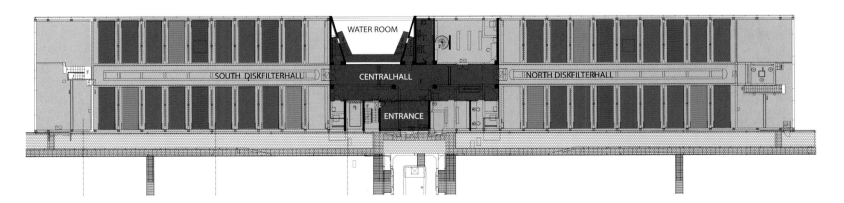

05

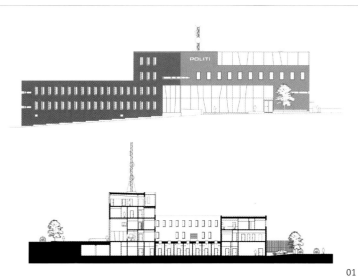

01

02

Hedmark Police District Headquarters

The 6,500-square meter Hamar police station is the headquarters of Hedmark Police District. The project forms and occupies a city block in a new urban development with close proximity to the city center, strategically located next to a main artery into the center of Hamar. The public entrance to the police station faces this main street from a new square. The building is executed as a monolithic, dark volume towards the surrounding streets. The atrium in the middle appears as if it has been carved out of the main body of the building, providing natural light into the surrounding offices. The architecture aims to signal the function and role of the police in today's society – transparency, safety, neutrality, discipline and order.

01 Elevation and section | 02 View from atrium | 03 East view | 04 Front façade

03

04

01

02

Kalmar Museum of Art

The conceptual idea of this museum is a series of open platforms for art. It is a black four-level cube, clad with large-scale wooden panels and large glazed openings. The main spaces are the white box, with one side that can open towards the park, and the top floor gallery that is lit by shed head light shafts, doubling its ceiling height. There is also a public art library, a children's atelier and workshops. The floors are stacked on top of each other, reaching up into the trees, with different spatial experiences while offering views of the environment.

01 Old restaurant in front of the museum | 02 Façade facing the water | 03 Ground floor plan, museum and restaurant | 04 Top floor gallery | 05 Exhibition room, white box | 06 Main staircase

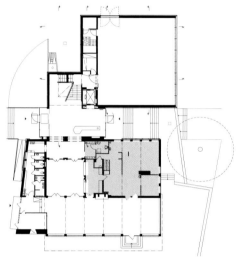

03

04

05

06

01

02

03

04

Kivik Art Center – Refugium

A pale concrete structure is embedded in the lushness of a slope. Secretive, it does not immediately reveal itself to its visitor. The entire form is gathered around a nave made out of wood; a passage and an inner space are spun between wood and concrete. The boundary between what is inside and what is outside is blurred. The idea is to inflict as little damage as possible on the site, conceptually as well as visually. The foundation is laid in the back, which allows the structure to rise above the ground and leave a large part of the site untouched. The materials, wood and concrete, are allowed to age in the hope that over time, the experience of both space and place will become further enhanced.

01 Exterior view concrete block | 02 Entrance staircase | 03 Entrance | 04 Side view of concrete and wood | 05 Floor plan

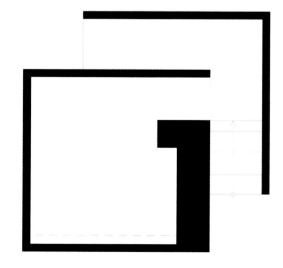

05

01

02

03

04

Townhouse

This narrow site is sandwiched between very old buildings. It is barely five meters wide, with a surface area of 75 square meters and faces the street. The architects wanted to create a sharp contrast to express clarity, but more importantly to highlight the beauty of the surroundings. They aimed to create an interior that gave the feeling of being outdoors. Because of this, the architects made a single space, softly partitioned by thin steel slabs, spanning the entire width of the house and dividing its functions. This creates an array of different spatial experiences in the small space. The continuous interior space opens up to the street, to the middle of the block and to the sky above.

01 Street view at dusk | 02 Bathroom and interior terrace over living room | 03 Front view | 04 Interior view | 05 Section

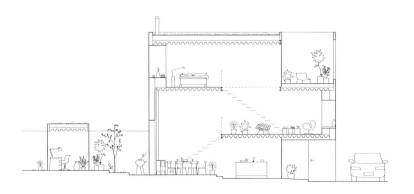

05

01

02

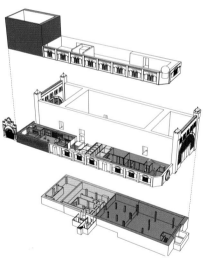

03

04

Modern Museum

This new art museum, housed within a former electricity plant, represents a rare opportunity to create a new focal point within the city, changing the urban balance and developing the surrounding neighborhood. In order to comply with the highest international standards for displaying art exhibitions, it soon became clear that a building within a building had to be built, a contemporary addition within the existing shell. This radical reconstruction provided a challenge as well as an opportunity. The extension provides a new entrance with a perforated, orange façade that connects to the existing brick architecture and introduces a contemporary element to the neighborhood.

01 Exhibition room | 02 Machine hall | 03 Exploded view drawing | 04 Exterior view | 05 Café

05

01

02

03

04

The Glass Bubble

The Glass Bubble is a sculpture, organism and a paradise all rolled into one. In the darkness of the winter the bubble is a big, brightly lit volume. Its location close to the sea is stormy, extremely barren and exposed. The only thing that separates the inside from the outside is a partition wall made of thin glass. The function of the glass is similar to that of a membrane. The inside becomes a bubble filled with warmth and life. Inside, the climate is controlled, keeping the temperature at a warm and pleasant level. A sensual, luxuriant and flowering garden with murmuring water, flowers, colors, fruits, verdure and floral splendor is created inside the bubble. Exotic species like citrus, camellia and magnolia grow in the raised flowerbeds.

01 View towards the sea | 02 Interior view | 03 Exterior view | 04 Natural meeting place |
05 Site plan

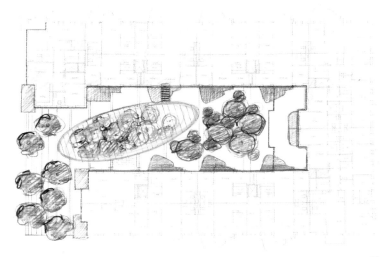

05

01

02

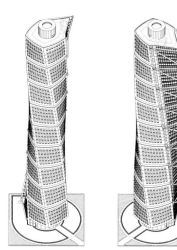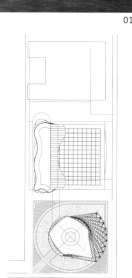

03

04

Turning Torso

Western Harbor is rapidly becoming a mixed-use residential district. Given the opportunity to enhance and enlarge a public area that is defined by the intersection of two main roads Calatrava conceived of this project as a freestanding sculptural element. The design is based on one of his sculptures, Turning Torso, in which he abstracted the human form in movement as a stack of cubes elegantly positioned around a core. The spiraling form is composed of nine box units, shaped like cubes with triangular tips. The main load-bearing structure is a circular reinforced concrete core, the center of which corresponds exactly to the rotation center of the floors. Inside the core are the elevator and the staircase, which is a secondary structural element.

01 View from south | 02 View from east | 03 Plans | 04 View from west

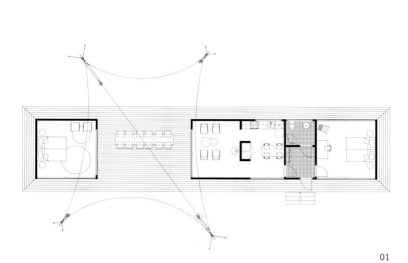

01

02

Momo

This modular-based interpretation of a traditional weekend cottage combines the architectural concept of a house in a box with the flexibility of a prefab module that is only 4.5 x 2.25 meters. The house comprises eight modules divided into two sections. Volumes made of solid wood containing different living functions are held together by a relaxation area covered with a tensile fabric roof structure. The smaller section contains an area for guests, while the larger section houses the living area, kitchen, bathroom and bedrooms. Natural insulation in the walls keeps the house warm in the winter and cool in the summer. On the roof, water storing succulents and grass provide further insulation.

01 Floor plan | 02 Living room with fireplace | 03 Bedroom with panoramic view |
04 General view

03

04

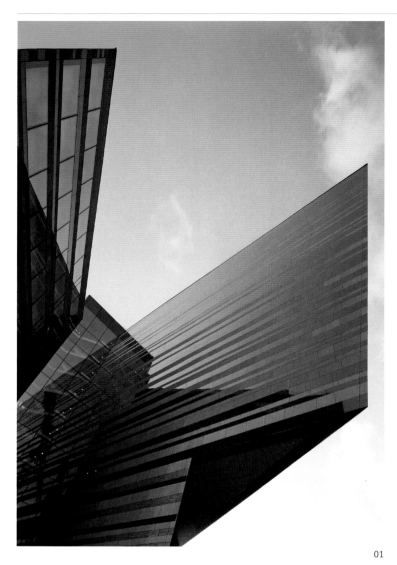

01

02

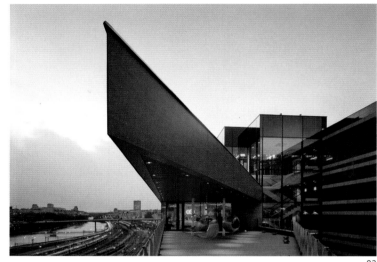

03

04

05

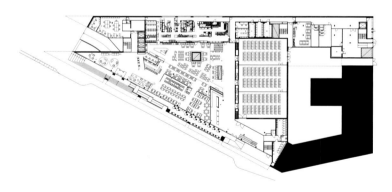

06

Clarion Hotel Sign

The architects divided the façade into five large, outwardly inclined oriels separated by five pillars and extending the full height of the building. The size echoes the scale of the city center with its beautiful stone buildings. Each oriel has its own rhythm, defined by breast walls of different heights. The hotel presents two sharp points to the south. Irrational, dynamic and concealing the true scale of the hotel, they cut the air space. This is the first thing many people encounter when they arrive on foot from the central station.

01 South façade detail | 02 Exterior view from east | 03 Roof terrace | 04 Exterior view from west | 05 Floor plan entrance level | 06 Reception area

01

02

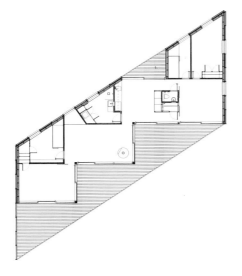

03

Archipelago Home

Conceived as a lightweight construction in wood and glass, this summer house is built in the outer Stockholm archipelago. The horizontal character of the black stained exterior relates to the verticals of tall pines and the mirrored views of the Baltic Sea. The geometry of the plan is generated by the specifics of the site, the house being fitted into the flat surface between two mountain rocks and turning simultaneously towards the sun in the south and towards the sea in the west. With the small rooms placed in the back, the social areas of the house stand out as an open platform crisscrossed by sliding glass. The zig-zag layout also creates a series of outside places sheltered from the strong winds.

01 Front façade | 02 Angled deck | 03 Bedroom with panoramic view | 04 Floor plan | 05 Living room with fire orb | 06 Bedroom

04

06

05

01

02

03

AH#062

The contrast between the closed, toned-down and open façades is this structure's key characteristic. Inside, the building is dominated by the openness created by the huge expanses of windows. The social area has an open plan kitchen and living room, protected from the entrance by the centrally located staircase. On the first floor, there is a day room, two bathrooms, and four bedrooms, along with two built-in wardrobes. The foundation is a cast concrete slab and the walls are manufactured in blocks in the factory and put together on site. The external wood panels, made from Swedish spruce, is fitted on site in order to avoid block joints in the façade. AH#062 is available in three sizes.

01 Kitchen | 02 Bedroom with open view to surroundings | 03 Dining and living room | 04 Floor plans | 05 Exterior rear view | 06 Bathroom

04

05

06

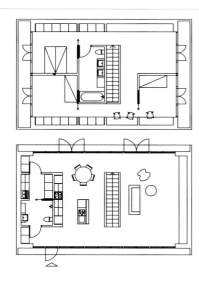

01

02

AH#001

The basic form of AH#001 is almost generic – a two-story home with the roof angles and proportions of a traditional Swedish barn. Except for the basic form, however, there is nothing traditional about this design. It features open floor plans without normal window openings and walls made entirely of glass moved inwards to create protected and shadowed zones. When the sight lines of the longer ground floor walls and the first floor gable ends are laid on top of each other, an abstract symbol ('plus' sign) is formed. Everything apart from the concrete foundation, the exterior paneling and roof covering is manufactured in a factory before being transported and erected on site.

01 Floor plans | 02 View inside from terrace | 03 View to living room from entrance | 04 Terrace

03

04

01

02

03

Hill Hut

Visiondivision was commissioned to design an extension to a villa in a picturesque lake setting in southern Stockholm. The owner of the old house had met his new wife in Thailand and the couple wanted to move and settle down in Sweden along with her two children. The beautiful nature surrounding the plot and the fact that two children would occupy the house became the key elements of the design. Instead of designing a house with expensive materials and detailing, the architects deliberately chose affordable windows and façade materials. This allowed a bigger budget for a more playful architecture such as an outdoor cinema, private caves and an undulated landscape going through the living room.

01 View from lake | 02 Outdoor cinema | 03 Cave | 04 Axonometric projection

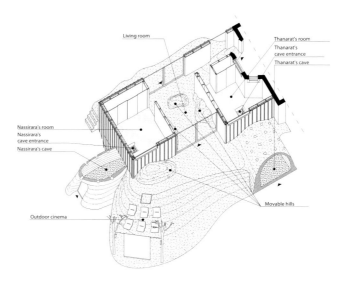

04

01

02

03

04

Pionen, White Mountain

This project is situated in a former 1,200 square meter anti-atomic shelter. An amazing location, 30 meters under the granite rocks of the Vita Berg Park in Stockholm. The starting point of the project was to consider the rock as a living organism. The humans try to acclimatize themselves to this foreign world and bring the 'best' elements from earth: light, plants, water and technology. The architects created strong contrasts between rooms where the rock dominates and where the human being is a stranger against rooms where the human being took over totally. The client had a strong vision from the first brief and the result is only possible because of their persistence. The main room is not a traditional space limited by surfaces but defined by the emptiness inside a mass.

01 Meeting room | 02 Granite cave | 03 Office | 04 Hall | 05 Underground floor plan

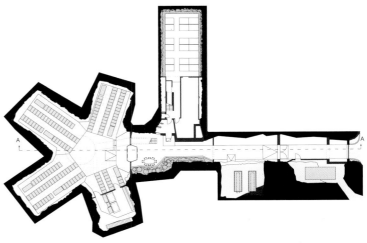

05

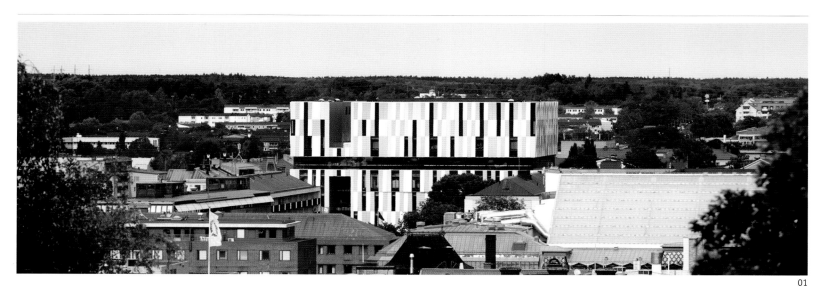

01

02

Uppsala Concert and Conference Hall

With its metallic façades, the Uppsala Concert and Conference Hall looks like a large split crystal. The vertical cleft in the building allows access from two sides – the old historical town and the modern, lively Vaksala Torg square. The horizontal cleft presents a view of the characteristic skyline of Uppsala, dominated by the palace, cathedral and library. The Concert and Conference Hall contains about 14,600 square meters, covering a total of eight levels including the basement. The concert hall houses exhibition areas and three halls, the largest of which has 1,150 seats and is planned for symphonic music.

01 General view | 02 Site plan | 03 Southwest façade and entrance 'cleft' | 04 Main concert hall | 05 Northeast façade detail

03

04

05

01

02

03

04

Refugium of a Forester

The Grimeton Nature Reserve is a dramatic environment that rises over the flat arable lands along the seaboard. Here the forest opens up and creates a place where the encounter between the modern forestry and the old forest are made visible. The Refugium is situated on the top of the hill, low-voiced and functional, with a dark introverted façade where only the entrance box breaks the otherwise austere façade. The varying wood façade folds in under the volume and follows the jutting and suppressed parts, externally as well as internally. The window details are made out of teak, while the fireplace and the exposed surfaces are of concrete. A foundation high above the ground indicates the wish to leave the ground untouched.

01 Lake façade | 02 Entrance box detail | 03 Façade opened towards lake | 04 Interior living space | 05 Floor plan

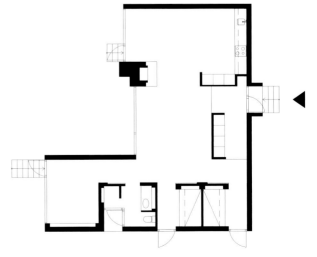

05

01

02

Sommarnöjen – Summer Cottages

This project idea derives from a Swedish regulation stating that you are allowed to build a 15-square meter house without a permit. The client wanted a house that could be pre-produced, in a few different designs that would appeal to different clients and different sites. The architect's have designed three types of houses: one inspired by the traditional red painted Swedish house with a Japanese touch, one square, like a small pavilion. The third can be overgrown by plants and hidden in the lush Swedish nature. The clients decide the program for the house. It can be a sauna, a summer cottage, a guesthouse, an atelier or a home office.

01 House C | 02 Floor plan of House C | 03 House B | 04 House A

03

04

01

02

Barnsley Digital Media Centre

Barnsley Digital Media Centre contains individual office units of various sizes. The building's form is a single large atrium surrounded by office units, articulated as three interconnected towers. Stone is the predominant material used for civic buildings in Barnsley and this building continues and explores this tradition. The building is grounded at the base by gabion stone in cages, reflecting the rough stone of an existing retaining wall. A lightweight stone composite panel is used at upper levels. This system allows the stone to be hung sufficiently far from the structure to enable insulation within the cavity, thus preserving the building's thermal mass. Colored crumpled mesh shutters on the south façade provide some shading and contrast with the solidity of the stone.

01 Building in context | 02 South view | 03 View from east at dusk | 04 Second floor plan | 05 Main entrance

03

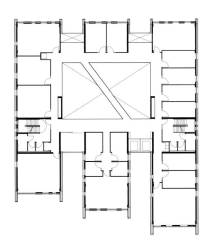

04

05

01

02

03

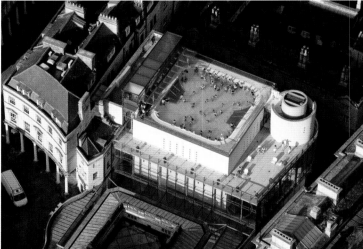

04

Thermae Bath Spa

Thermae Bath Spa marks the revitalization of the city's spa quarter. The spa complex comprises one new building – the New Royal Bath – and the sensitive restoration and adaption of another five Grade I and II listed buildings. Requirements for the new spa facility and listed building parameters have inevitably led to a very closely integrated design with a direct and intimate interplay between new and old. The difference in levels between existing buildings has been carefully resolved with the use of split level planning and the clear articulation of the connecting spaces as transparent bridge links which open up vistas along, across and through the complex.

01 Interior view | 02 Entrance | 03 Rooftop pool | 04 Bird's-eye view | 05 Floor plan

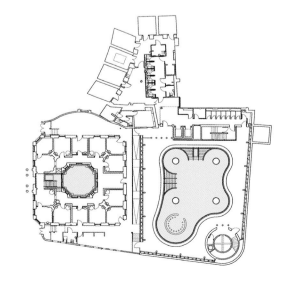

05

01

BaleHaus@Bath

BaleHaus@Bath is a highly sustainable domestic property that offers an entirely renewable way to construct homes. Made from natural materials that are beautiful, affordable and sustainable, it provides practical ways of reducing CO_2 emissions without compromising on comfort. BaleHaus@Bath utilizes ModCell's revolutionary prefabricated straw bale construction system. ModCell uses replenishable and locally sourced materials (timber, straw, hemp, lime) to create walls that breathe and have a less than zero carbon footprint. The precision engineered frames use sustainable FSC and PEFC wood, are fabricated close to the site in a 'Flying Factory' and then in-filled with locally sourced straw.

01 Exterior view from garden | 02 Staircase | 03 Elevation

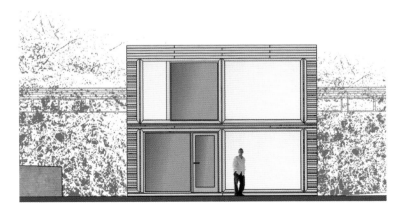

02
03

01

02

03

04

05

Headlands House

This house demonstrates how traditional brick construction can be used in tandem with other local crafts and materials to provide beautiful contemporary solutions that are ecologically, socially and economically sustainable. The unusual organic form of the building has evolved from a unique response to external orientation, site constraints, privacy and views across the valley as well as from an understanding of how the client and his family live and move internally around their home. Its plan is based on the tradition of the hearth being the social and communal focus of the home. The organic building form can be seen as an evolutionary response to these local issues and constraints.

01 Interior view | 02 View from southeast | 03 View from southwest | 04 Living room | 05 View from patio | 06 Ground floor plan

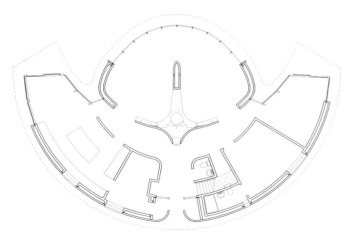

06

01

02

03

04

Gateway

Gateway is the centerpiece of the ongoing redevelopment of Buckinghamshire New University's campus in High Wycombe. Located on a constrained and sensitive urban site, the new landmark building accommodates a learning resource center, a multi-purpose sports and events hall, a gym, music and video recording studios, and a drama space. The vision was to create a sustainable and contemporary building that provides facilities for the entire student body and that contrasts with the existing campus architecture to establish a new and distinctive identity for the university. The exciting mix of uses reinforces the public nature of the campus. Providing 24/7 access, it creates a memorable and appropriate 'gateway' building for BNU and High Wycombe, consequently raising the expectations and experiences of students, staff and public alike.

01 Exterior view | 02 Study area | 03 Library | 04 Central atrium | 05 First floor plan

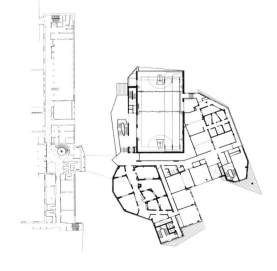

05

01

02

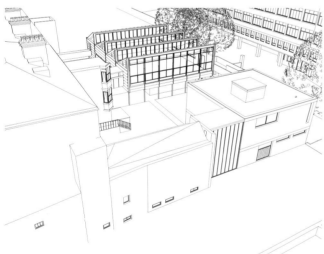

03

04

University of Cambridge Studio Building

The new studio building forms part of a refurbishment and expansion of the Department of Architecture, responding to a brief uniting teaching and research functions. The new studio building sits to the rear of the terrace adjacent to Colin St John Wilson's seminal 1950's extension. Space for the new building was limited: planning constraints meant that existing listed trees needed to be preserved and sufficient space given to the rear of the listed Georgian terrace to preserve its integrity. The placement of the building creates a central cloistered garden space between the new building and the existing extension. The form of the building is determined by its function, and a desire to build a naturally cooled timber-frame building that embodies the department's commitment to sustainable design.

01 Exterior view | 02 Aerial view | 03 Perspective | 04 Façade | 05 Window detail

05

01

02

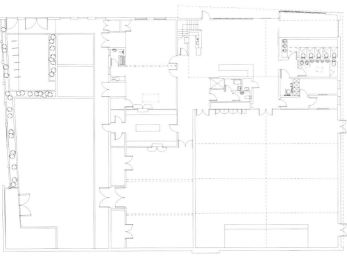

03

Salvation Army Chelmsford

Breaking the mold of the traditional brick citadel, both in terms of plan and materiality, the RIBA award-winning Salvation Army Citadel Corps in Chelmsford is constructed
entirely of timber and clad with an undulating zinc roof, providing 900 square meters of
new accommodation for the mission. The building uses a cross-laminated timber panel
system, akin to jumbo plywood, which offers all the advantages of reinforced concrete
construction without the environmental cost. The building plan offers flexibility for the
two sides of the mission, providing an assembly hall for worship as well as recreational
facilities for its wide range of community outreach activities.

01 Contemporary steeple | 02 Zinc-clad façade | 03 Ground floor plan | 04 Interior view
with reception

04

01

02

Civic Heart

This designing project involves a market square and develops the idea of a 'red carpet'. The floorscape contains color-changing integrated lights that slowly pulse a blue rhythm referencing the culvert below. The archway shape is inspired by the viaduct form at the end of the market square. 10,000 handmade textured bricks were used for the project so that all surfaces have sensuality even in dull light. Seb Boyesen realized this project with ingenuity and extreme sensitivity. The 'red carpet' is defined by granite seats with original poems by the artist's father, John Fairfax, lightly etched into the surface. The top of the arch has 480 polycarbonate tubes that slowly change color during the evening. The locals dubbed this feature, the "Mohican of the North".

01 Tubes on archway | 02 Archway by night | 03 Colored illumination: polycarbonate tubes on archway and lights in the floorscape | 04 Model of rib construction | 05 Archway with 'red carpet' and granite seats | 06 Granite seats | 07 Floorscape detail

03

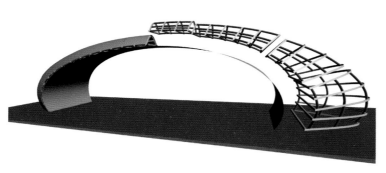

04

05

06

07

01

02

Corby Cube

Corby Cube is the striking, glazed focal point of a major regeneration program to revitalize the former industrial town. Envisaged as a town hall for the 21st century, the civic hub and arts center combines council administration and cultural activities within a five-story building at the heart of a central new town square. The facilities, which include a library, theater, cafe, council chamber, one-stop shop and civic offices are arranged around an internal 'promenade architecturale' and composed into a coherent cube form. The building illustrates a new paradigm for civic architecture enabling access for all, promoting leading edge design, achieving BREEAM excellence and bringing together wider arts and civic activities into one inclusive community building.

01 East façade | 02 Exterior view | 03 Interior view | 04 Ground floor plan

03

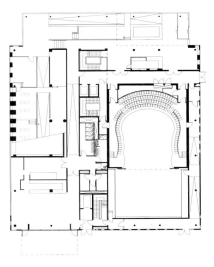

04

01

Junction Arts & Civic Center

Junction is a small arts center that incorporates a 170-seat auditorium and performance workshop, together with Goole Town Council's offices and council chamber. The ground floor of the center is organized as an enfilade of spaces: auditorium, foyer, café and performance workshop. The first floor accommodates the chamber and offices, the excess volume affording double-height spaces below. The building replaces a 1980s extension to the Victorian Goole Market Hall, reusing a steel portal frame that is reformed with a brim. Subtle distortions in perspective accentuate the curious nature of the original frame. It links the historic high street with the Wesley Square retail development, mixing art and politics with commerce.

01 Exterior view | 02 Auditorium | 03 Interior view | 04 Section

02

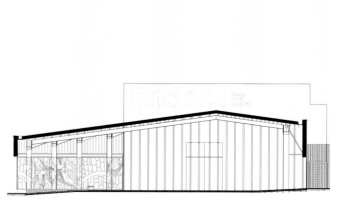

03

04

01

The Pod

The Pod was designed to provide recreational 'intermediate' accommodation and offers a comfortable shelter that serves a similar function to a tent but is more secure against the elements. It is designed to have a low carbon footprint, high durability and aesthetics that integrate well with most natural environments. In late 2007 permission was granted to Martyn and Sara Merckel to create a campsite 'village' of ten Pods in Eskdale in the English Lake District National Park. The Pods were craned into a wooded area with poor access and a high water table. This flagship project opened in March 2008 and The Pod is now established throughout the United Kingdom and parts of Europe.

01 Front façades | 02 Floor plan | 03 General view of site

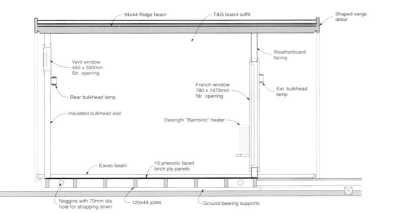

94x44 Ridge beam   T&G board soffit   Shaped verge detail

Vent window 450 x 330mm Str. opening

Weatherboard facing

French window 780 x 1475mm Str. opening

Ext. bulkhead lamp

Rear bulkhead lamp

Insulated bulkhead wall

Delonghi "Bambino" heater

Eaves beam   15 phenolic faced birch ply panels

Noggins with 70mm dia. hole for strapping down   120x44 joists   Ground bearing supports

02

03

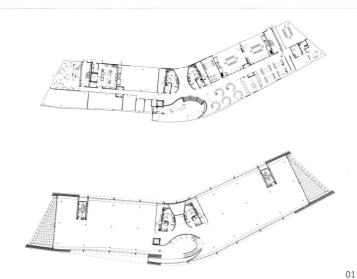

01

02

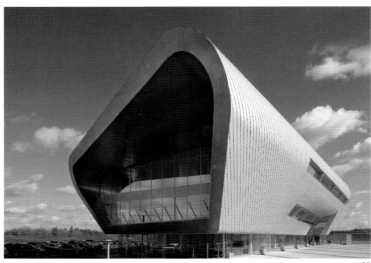

03

Tag Farnborough Airport

The 5,000-square-meter terminal building houses offices and operations rooms. It extends over three floors, linked by one central atrium area with panoramic views over the airfield. The asymmetric construction uses floor plates of varying sizes that give the building a dynamic profile. The wing-shaped exterior is clad in mill-finished aluminum shingles similar to the textured finish of the control tower, and set in a sculptured landscape. A key design feature is direct access between aircraft and car transport, consistent with TAG's strategy to create the most modern airport dedicated to business aviation in Europe.

01 Plans | 02 Foyer | 03 View from west | 04 View from south

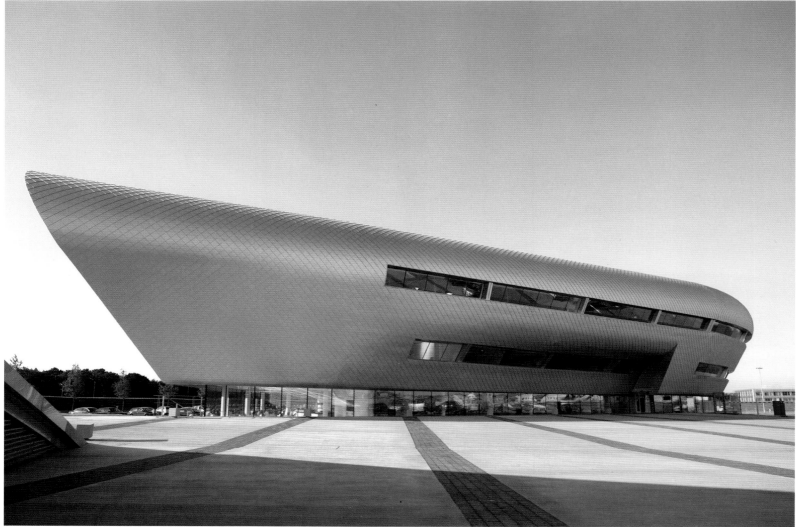

04

01

Hazelwood School

The aim was to develop a school building without the institutional feel. Its form winds among the trees, creating a series of small gardens suitable to the small classes and maximizes the potential for external teaching environments. Internally, the curved form of the building reduces the scale of the main circulation area, removing the institutional feel conveyed by a long corridor. The design team developed a palette of highly textured natural materials, which are stimulating to touch and smell. Naturally weathering timber boarding, reclaimed slate tiles, and zinc give variety and contrast on the outside.

01 'Interactive' façade made from different materials | 02 Outdoor teaching spaces | 03 Corridor | 04 Sections | 05 Classroom

02

03

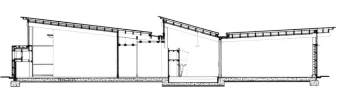

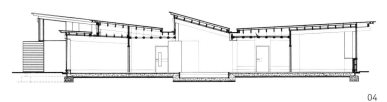

04

05

01

02

03

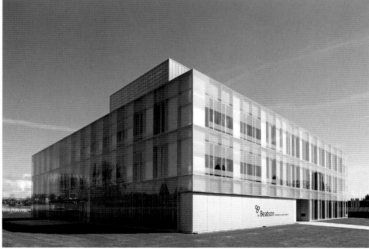

04

Beatson Institute for Cancer Research

This major research laboratory building accommodates a directorate, seminar rooms, lecture theater, social areas and laboratories with support spaces for a staff of 250. It is located on the premises of the walled-in garden grounds of the University of Glasgow's existing Garscube Estate research campus. The new building takes the form of a horizontally layered crystalline glazed cube. The ground floor, containing lecture, meeting and café areas, opens up to the enclosed garden. Above, a series of highly serviced laboratories encircle a central communal area. A solar screen grid was 'drawn' onto the glazed walls of the exterior. This cutting-edge, glazed skin building is seen as a world leader in part due to its excellent open debate, forum and research environment.

01 Façade detail | 02 Interior view | 03 General view | 04 Crystalline cube | 05 Site plan

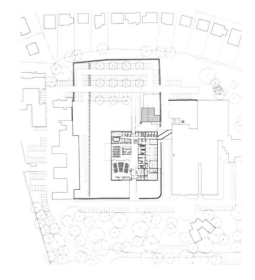

05

01

02

03

04

Round Tower

The Round Tower is a Grade II listed folly, previously reduced to ruin by a fire and years of neglect. Located on the crest of a hill, the exposed site is visually integral to the setting of this listed structure. The design maintains an open relationship with the surrounding agricultural landscape by developing a substantial yet discreet underground open plan extension to the tower. Sunlight enters the subterranean living spaces through a central sunken courtyard and a lateral 'landscape scoop' that conceals the new swimming pool and associated sun terraces from public view. The tower maintains a dominant presence, providing the entrance to the four bedroom family house and means of vertical circulation leading to a roof terrace to enjoy panoramic views of the surrounding landscape.

01 Interior view | 02 Interior skylight | 03 Tower and pool at night | 04 Sunken courtyard | 05 Cross section

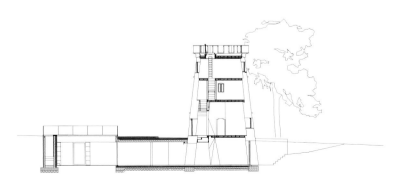

05

01

02

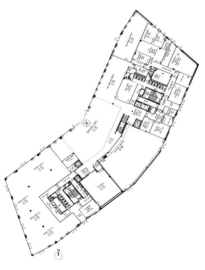

03

Ravensbourne

The main design strategy for Ravensbourne, a university sector college leading in digital media and design, was to produce a structure, which encourages collaboration between the different disciplines and practitioners. To achieve this, the building has been structured around a system of two interconnected atria. The atria are systematically attached to the external façade allowing them to be used as ventilation devices as well as to visually connect the core of the public spaces inside the building to the perception of the urban surroundings. In order to have optimum environmental performance, low maintenance and high flexibility, the massing has been kept as compact as possible with a very low ratio of façade to area.

01 Entrance | 02 Façade | 03 Ground floor plan | 04 Interior view

04

01

02

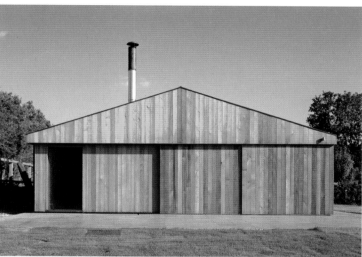

03

04

05

Basing Farm

Basing Farm provides a sustainable and environmentally sensitive model for the conversion of a redundant industrial chicken shed to a high quality modern family house. The agricultural quality of the original structure appropriate to this rural setting is maintained. The converted shed is a timber framed building, highly insulated and cedar clad. Sliding shutters prevent light pollution ensuring the building has the appearance of a complete timber volume with no specific openings and identical in character to the former agricultural structure. All heating is provided by geothermal heat source. The selected natural materials will weather and age to ensure the integration of this converted shed into the landscape of the site.

01 Glazed entrance | 02 Façade open | 03 Façade closed | 04 Exterior view | 05 Interior view | 06 Floor plan

06

01

Black Rubber Beach House

Dungeness Beach in Kent is a classic example of Non Plan. The houses that populate the beach have developed through improvisation and being thrown together at random. This scheme develops this tradition in a way that responds to the drama and harshness of the landscape. The original 1930s fisherman's hut, a product of many changes and extensions since it was built, has been stripped back to its timber frame, restructured, extended to the south and east to capture the extraordinary views, and clad both internally and externally in Wisa-Spruce plywood. Externally both walls and roof are clad in black rubber, a more sophisticated version of the layers of felt and tar found on many local buildings.

01 South façade | 02 View from east | 03 Interior view | 04 3D view | 05 Draught lobby

02

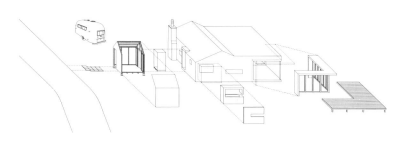

03

04

05

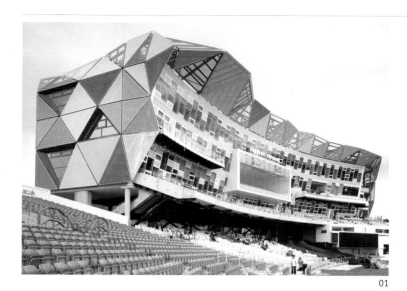

01

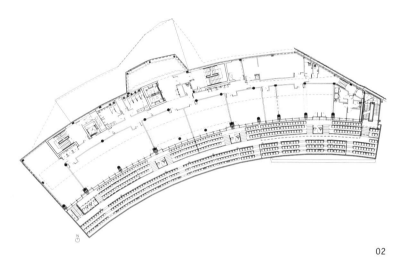

02

03

Carnegie Pavilion

The shared vision of Leeds Metropolitan University in partnership with Yorkshire County Cricket Club (YCCC) was to replace the existing, substandard Wintershed and Media Center with the new dual-use "Carnegie Pavilion". The upper ground level is split in half by the shared reception and entrance foyer. The three-dimensional rain screen façade is formed out of perforated aluminum panels, supported on a triangular sub-frame. The triangular cladding is itself punctuated by an irregular pattern of triangular windows, tinted with purple and yellow tones. The upper ground and lower ground are enclosed with curtain walling to maximize the openness and transparency at entrance level.

01 View from arena | 02 Floor plan | 03 Interior view | 04 View from street | 05 General view

04

05

01

02

03

04

05

David Wilson Library

The requirements of the university were very clear in its brief. The library should be an excellent environment for people as well as for books, putting the needs of students and researchers at the very heart of the project. The relaxation of the strict environmental criteria of the storage of books in lieu of natural ventilation is an example. There is a tendency for people to assume that libraries are just storehouses rather than workplaces. This emphasis on the users of the building suggested the key aspects of the design should give it a surprise factor, a lot of natural light, a layout which was easy to navigate, local control of services, energy efficiency, and a high quality of materials and finish. All of these aims have been successfully achieved.

01 Feature lighting in new atrium | 02 Main entrance and podium | 03 Rear atrium formed at connection with listed building | 04 Mono crystalline PV array within glazed brise soleil on south façade | 05 First floor plan

01

02

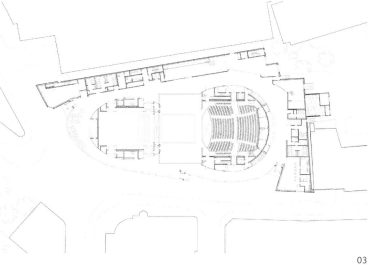

03

04

Curve

Curve is an innovative, democratic building which respects Leicester's history, while helping to redefine its future. The cutting-edge design turns the typical theater configuration 'inside out' by exposing all components of the theater to the public and integrating all aspects of performance into the life of the city. For the very first time, audiences and passersby will be engaged in the actual process of theater-making, behind the scenes. Conceived as islands within a public foyer, a central stage sits at street level between two colored volumes and a system of metal shutters enables the creative team to place the audience in a variety of configurations, creating possibilities for either conventional or technically more ambitious theater production and design.

01 Glazed façade at night | 02 Interior view | 03 Ground floor plan | 04 Theater | 05 Curve

05

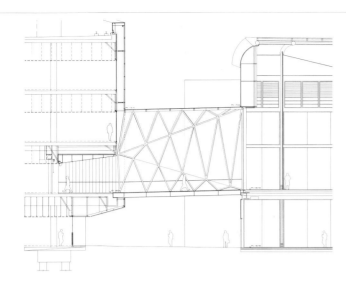

01

John Lewis Department Store and Cineplex

The design of the John Lewis Department Store provides retail flexibility, while maintaining the urban experience of shopping. The cladding is designed as a double-glazed façade with a pattern that makes it look like a net curtain. This creates transparency between the store interior and outside, allowing the exterior views and light to penetrate inside. To cater for the twelve cinema screens it encloses, the Leicester Cineplex's curtain is designed as an opaque stainless steel rain screen, with a mirror finish, and pleated at different scales to diffuse the large volume into smaller reflective surfaces.

01 Section of pedestrian link to neighboring mall | 02 Pedestrian link to parking lot | 03 Exterior view | 04 Façade detail | 05 Double-glazed façade

02

03

04

05

01

02

Art & Design Academy

Merging the John Moores University's art and design faculties, the building's serpentine form bends and curves to reflect the shape of the site, aligning primarily with the base of the Metropolitan Catholic Cathedral. The sculptural form is emphasised by the splayed walls of the studios which provide shade from direct sunlight while maximizing natural light from the north. Spanning three stories, this entrance draws students, staff, and visitors into the central atrium, the social heart of the building. The 11,000 square meters of floor space is distributed over six floors. The lower and ground floors provide shared facilities, including the Tate café, seminar rooms, a 350-seat multi-purpose space, galleries and exhibition spaces.

01 Exterior view | 02 Gallery | 03 Façade | 04 Elevation with cathedral in background

03

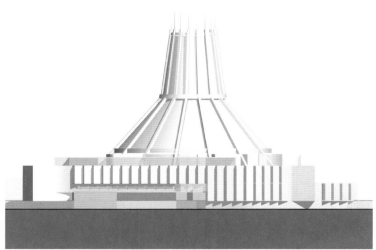

04

01

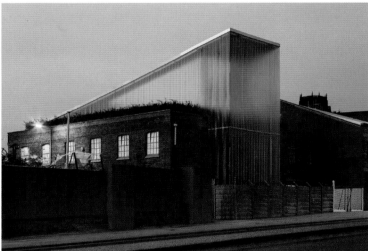

02

03

Kunsthuelle LPL

Kunsthuelle LPL was a temporary installation for a major new contemporary art venue in Liverpool. The rooftop structure was designed as a playful and experimental space for lectures, performances and events. It appeared to merge into the old factory, incorporating an existing staircase and the rooftop, and extending out over the public façade of the building. It divided the rooftop into two terraced spaces, lined with green hedges. A permeable membrane allowed visitors to walk from one zone to another, passing through PVC curtains that flexed and warped. The Kunsthuelle responded to the shifting environment, with changes in light and wind playing across the curtains, creating a dynamic and lively character. Karsten Huneck and Bernd Truempler were responable for the design.

01 View from street | 02 Exterior view | 03 Interior view | 04 Section

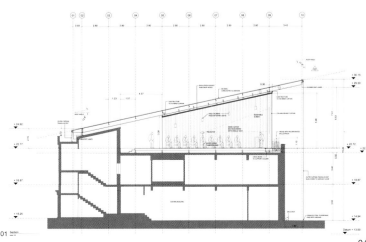

04

01

02

03

04

05

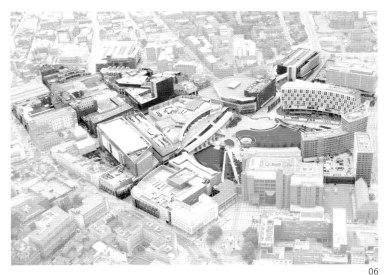

06

Liverpool One Masterplan

Liverpool One Masterplan repairs and reconnects the city center. It creates a framework for architecture, landscape and lighting design of the highest quality. The masterplan takes great care in connecting into the existing fabric of the city, from the intimate spaces of the Bluecoat Triangle to the civic scale of Chavasse Park. Vistas of Liverpool's famous landmarks root the development in the city and provide a real sense of place. The commitment to creating individual buildings in the city has been fulfilled by the selection of appropriate architects for each site within the masterplan. Liverpool One has breathed life into the heart of the city.

01 Bridge between buildings | 02 Façade | 03 View towards the city | 04 Entrance steps | 05 Arcade | 06 Site plan

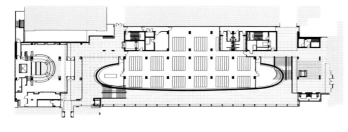

01

02

Darwin Center

The extension of the Natural History Museum takes the form of a huge concrete cocoon, surrounded by a glass atrium. The architecture reflects the museum's dual role as a tourist attraction and a scientific research center. The cocoon forms the inner protective element, while its shape and size give an understanding of the collection's volume. The exposed thermal mass of the continuous sprayed and reinforced concrete shell provides a stable internal environment and minimizes energy loading. Public access to the scientific core of the center takes the form of a visitor route up and through the cocoon, overlooking the science and collection areas.

01 Ground floor plan | 02 Exhibition space | 03 Atrium with cocoon | 04 Old and new together | 05 View into laboratories

03

04

05

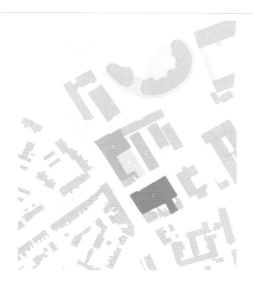

01

02

Sackler Building

The new Sackler Building provides new, purpose-made accommodation for all the painting students at the Royal College of Art to work together under one roof for the first
time in over ten years. The Sackler Building is the first phase of the RCA's plan for a
major new campus in Battersea, also designed by Haworth Tompkins. The second phase
started on site in January 2010. The Sackler Building was always conceived as a conversion; the old building – a single-story factory – has been transformed into a series of
new day lit spaces under a dramatic new roof form, by inserting a new independent steel
structure within the existing brick enclosure. This has significantly increased the height
of the building, providing several double-height studios along with a mezzanine level,
which houses a number of smaller top-lit studios, whilst retaining a predominantly open
plan environment.

01 Site plan | 02 Profiled studio roof | 03 Entrance | 04 Studio | 05 Naturally lit studios |
06 General view

03

04

05

06

01

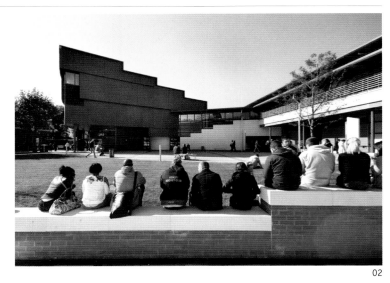

02

03

04

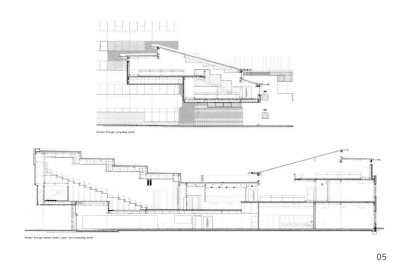

05

Computer and Conference Center

This building consists of a 400-seat lecture theater, foyer and a university entrance, general teaching rooms, and a 400-screen computer library. The lecture theater on the first floor, which acts as an architectural pivot between the entrance road and the new College Green, is clad in fiber-cement and features two unique corner windows. The entrance foyer is located underneath it. A fire-escape doubles as a direct passage to a vomitorium entrance to the theater above (also useful for late-comers). However, the main entrances are the entrance to the teaching accommodations in the rear and an angled staircase with a direct view of the computer library on the first floor. Externally, a vaulted passage links the first College Green courtyard to the emerging second courtyard.

01 Interior view | 02 View towards lecture theater | 03 Exterior view | 04 View across new College Green | 05 Sections | 06 Computer center

06

01

02

UEL Cass School of Education

This building is organized around a simple idea – everything should be visible on entry and there should be no corridors. A top-lit atrium offers three floors of teaching accommodation on the north side, balanced by four floors of offices to the south. Since the floor to ceiling heights differ on either side, this results in a journey between two stairs on either side from floor to floor to the top. Both offices and teaching rooms are glazed in front so that all the building's activities are clearly visible. There are two 'special' features. First, a plywood-clad tower, which cantilevers out into the main space overhanging the entrance desk on the ground floor contains one-to-one interview rooms and an open meeting space at its top. And second, a small music performing room has been placed adjacent to the entrance and implemented as an external object.

01 Exterior view | 02 Interior view | 03 Atrium | 04 Second floor plan

03

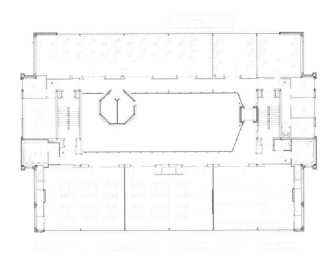

04

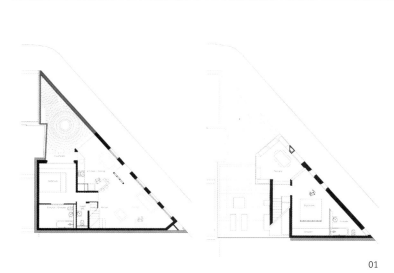

01

Palmwood House

This is a prototype building for problematic urban sites – a small vacant lot severely constrained by height restrictions and poor planning history. The building works with a gradation of spaces, views and daylight to achieve an extensive living experience despite its restricted volume. The site has a tight, triangular shape, at the end of a terraced row in the riverside district of Battersea. The development encompasses the equivalent of three terraced houses cut across their diagonal. The construction combines low energy and sustainable materials with advanced building technologies that minimize energy consumption. These included high-tech insulants, high performance insulated glazing, reclaimed brickwork, recycled flooring and sustainable woods – including the first use in Europe of palmwood, an ecologically-sound plantation hardwood.

01 Floor plans | 02 Balcony and courtyard | 03 Exterior view

02

03

01

Guy's Approaches

In the course of restructuring the entrance area of Guy's Hospital, the boiler house was improved. This building is situated in front of the entrance and contains vital machinery. Heatherwick Studio designed the "Boiler Suit" – a tiling system to wrap around the boiler house that provides an adequate shelter for the machinery within, ensures building ventilation and brings the façade to life in a very special way. The tiles used in the façade are human scale, standing 2.4 meters by 2.4 meters. They are gently curved and breathable, formed from stainless steel braid woven through frames. In sunlight this surface becomes animated, reflecting surrounding colors. At night, lighting concealed within the façade provides a dramatic luminous surface, while improving pedestrian safety.

01 "Boiler Suit" by night | 02 Detail woven tiles | 03 Section

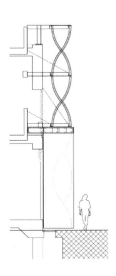

02

03

01

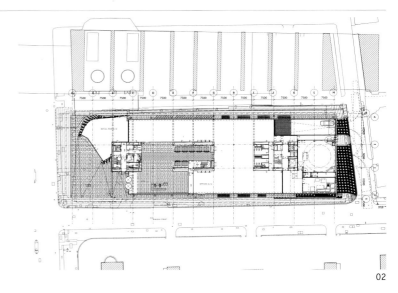

02

03

Palestra Office Building

The Palestra commercial scheme provides large, straightforward and flexible floor plates, to be used in open plan or cellular formats. The building resembles a raised box, with retail and restaurant space at ground level next to public routes. The offices are on two levels, separated by an open 'social space' level. The building's appearance belies its simple layout. The façades use the most advanced glazing technology, benefitting not only the working environment and climate control, but also the aesthetics of the building. The glazing includes a bold abstract pattern within the individual glass sheets.

01 Façade detail | 02 Ground floor plan | 03 General view | 04 View from the street

04

01

02

03

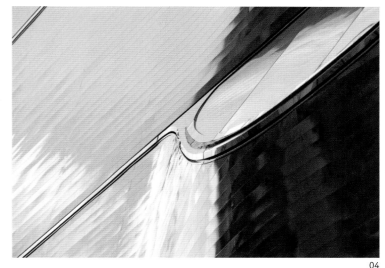

04

10 Hills Place

Lack of daylight in the narrow streets was a key issue for the design inspired by the art work of Lucio Fontana. A slashed aluminum skin with large glazed areas facing the sky uses high quality ship hull technology for an ingenious sculptural façade assembled on-site. Self cleaning glass and hidden gutters ensure the façade remains low maintenance. The fine faceting of the aluminum strips creates complex reflections of sky and street, making the building highly visible from Oxford Street. At ground level, a glass, mesh and dichromatic film sandwich is animated with fiber optics to create a visual depth of field and a dynamic moiré pattern on an otherwise blank façade.

01 View from Oxford Street | 02 Window detail | 03 Roof terrace | 04 Façade detail | 05 Elevation

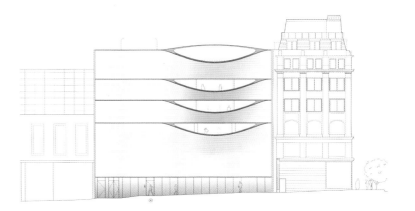

05

01

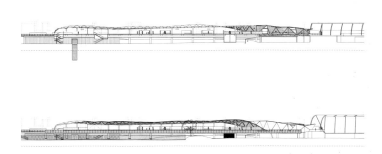

02

03

Stratford DLR

The old Stratford Docklands Light Railway station, a four meter-wide single-track platform, was diagnosed as suffering from increasingly severe congestion at peak travel hours. Since the environs did not allow for broadening or enlargement of the existing station, a new station with an improved commuter capacity had to be constructed. The new DLR station is longer than its predecessor, allowing three train cars to dock. One of its most striking design features is the irregular structure of the outer skin, which consists of aluminum panel cladding. The platform provides a clear and inviting atmosphere as well as a high degree of passenger safety.

01 Ceiling structure | 02 Longitudinal sections | 03 Light rail station | 04 Aerial view |
05 Roof structure and cladding

04

05

01

Baldry Gardens

Baldry Gardens is a new general practitioner surgery and community health center in south London. The 1,030-square-meter two-story brick building features interiors designed to create a calm and therapeutic environment. The building form is L-shaped in plan, providing two wings of cellular rooms arranged either side of a central corridor separated by a reception area and waiting room. Given the clinical setting, any conflict that might have arisen between a day lit interior and a concern for dignity is resolved by placing clinical rooms and consulting rooms on the first floor. Simple massing, monolithic polychromatic brickwork and the distribution and apparent scarcity of windows give this modest community building an enduring but benign presence in the city.

01 View from street | 02 General view | 03 Interior view | 04 Ground floor plan

02

03

04

01

02

03

04

The Blizard Building

Queen Mary University's vision of creating a world-class medical school at the cutting edge of teaching and research has been realized through a stunning new landmark building. The building includes category two and three laboratories with full support services, write-up offices, and a 400-seat lecture theater, setting a high standard for the college and for the further regeneration of the Whitechapel area. SMC Alsop and Amec's new building will facilitate better scientific research and discovery through collaboration and shared resources. It provides a common identity and functionality to the research disciplines while allowing the flexibility necessary to accommodate their changing needs over time.

01 Interior view | 02 Laboratories | 03 Exterior view | 04 Detail interior | 05 Ground floor plan

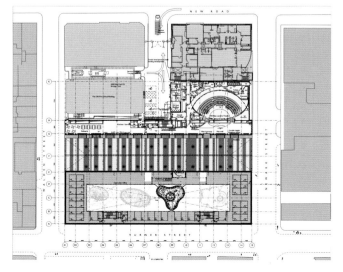

05

01

02

03

04

Gap House

Gap House is situated on a plot just over two meters wide, within a conservation area in west London. The low-carbon four-bed family home maximizes light and space and proves that sustainable architecture is achievable without compromise within the constraints of a tight and awkward urban site. Each room benefits from good daylight and feels spacious. This has been achieved by stacking the smaller bedrooms at the front of the house facing the street and organizing the rear rooms in a cascading configuration with a courtyard that brings light into the ground floor reception space. A number of green strategies, including high levels of insulation, a ground coupled heat pump and rainwater harvesting have been employed to minimize the house's carbon footprint.

01 View from street | 02 Courtyard | 03 Living room | 04 Interior view | 05 Section

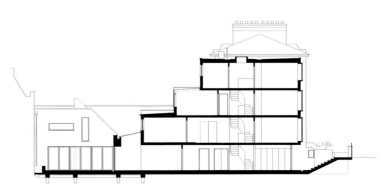

05

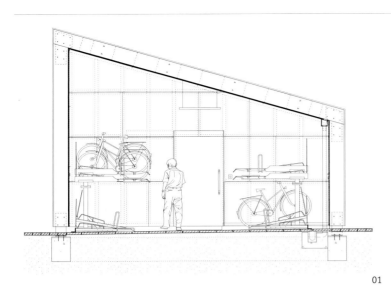

01

02

Bermondsey Square Bicycle Station

This scheme provides a new enclosure to securely store and shelter 76 bikes for the residents and office workers in the Bermondsey Square regeneration area. The square is the site of the historic Bermondsey antiques market. The enclosure is formed by 13 Douglas Fir portal frames clad on the internal face with translucent glass reinforced plastic sheeting to provide natural diffused light. The external skin is formed by a series of scattered triangular stainless steel cladding panels, arranged in forms referring to the gem-like bollards used in the external landscaping scheme. Integrated lighting raises awareness of the bicycle store and acts as a deterrent to criminal activity.

01 Cross section | 02 Façade detail | 03 Side view | 04 Main façade

03

04

01

02

03

04

05

ExCeL Phase 2

ExCeL London's brief required the extension of their existing building to provide more flat-floor exhibition space. The distinctive form of the striking, yellow spiral was settled upon by the design team as providing a strong visual orientation, which aided wayfinding across levels. Stretching away from the spiral is the Grand Boulevard, continuing on from Phase I's central spine. Once the two phases combine, this will be the longest corridor in Europe. The architectural design is intended to combat 'exhibition fatigue' by providing generous provision for natural light and ventilation, resulting in an entirely unconditioned space. Bold, energetic colors are used throughout the non-exhibition spaces to further energize visitors.

01 Exterior view | 02 Front view | 03 Aerial view | 04 Interior view | 05 Detail | 06 Hall

06

01

02

03

W London Leicester Square

Designed by award-winning architects Jestico + Whiles, the glamorous new Starwood Hotel W London in Leicester Square is now open to visitors. Developed by McAleer & Rushe, the new ten-story building houses retail, leisure and residential accommodation, including a spa, 11 penthouse apartments and a new retail-leisure experience provided by a leading global brand. The façade of the hotel has been wrapped in a second skin of frameless glazing, which is suspended from the face of the building like a floating sheer veil and etched with an undulating, abstract pattern, reminiscent of the folds in a theater curtain and evoking the cinematic legacy of the locale.

01 Façade | 02 View from street | 03 Façade detail | 04 Ground floor plan

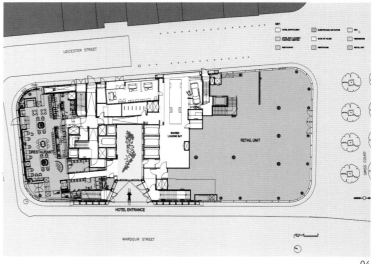

04

01

02

03

04

Faceted House 1

The project brief was to remodel and extend this three bedroom, two-story house, which was in a decrepit state and in need of considerable refurbishment and modernization. Paul McAneary Architects responded to the brief by demolishing the existing 1980s rear extension to the property that was crumbling and dilapidated. The concept driving the whole design is a 30 degree twist that allows physical and perceptive overlapping between the indoor and the outdoor spaces, between the garden and kitchen thresholds. Technology is also hidden as much as possible, to fully integrate all requirements so as the space could remain as calm, uncluttered and contemplative as possible.

01 View from roof | 02 Kitchen and dining area | 03 Terrace and garden | 04 Living area | 05 Ground floor plan

05

01

02

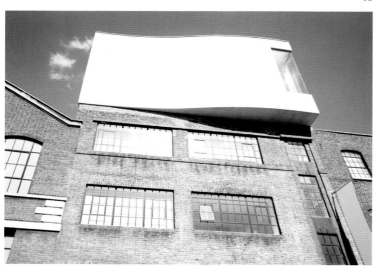

03

Victoria Miro Private Collection Space

The Victoria Miro Private Collection Space is housed in a new building, erected on the roof of a Victorian brick warehouse in Islington. The new extension is a significant urban gesture, expressing its art content through a configuration that acts as both container and sculpture. The external white rendering gives a sense of lightness and abstraction, in contrast to the earthy weight of the existing building. Inside, a dramatic staircase of 72 steps leads to the collection on the top floor. Glass windows face east and south, bathing the space in light. Art, architecture and natural light complement one another here, exhibiting a simple splendor that maintains their individual identities: thus the feeling of serenity.

01 Interior view | 02 View from street | 03 Façade detail | 04 Floor plan

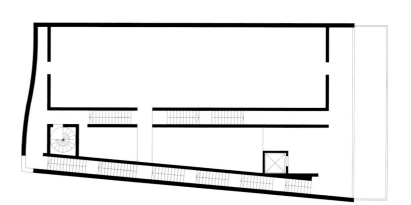

04

01

02

03

04

05

Glass House

A German art collector commissioned the Glass House in Richmond, on the outskirts of London, in 2005 as a latter-day 'folly' in her back garden. The brief proposed a tranquil space for meditation, to house a very fine 16th century Khmer Buddha. The client was looking for a design that would incorporate the ancient Hindu 'Vaastu' principles; a system of spatial organization based on the directional alignments, which derive from the elements of earth, fire, water, air and space. The Glass House is constructed with steel frame, 24 glass panels and slate floor. The building is four meters wide, eight meters long and just over three meters in height.

01 Interior view | 02 Garden | 03 Khmer buddha | 04 Night view | 05 Diagonal view | 06 Floor plan

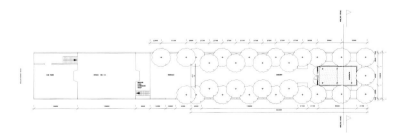

06

01

Serpentine Gallery Pavilion 2006

Each summer, the Serpentine commissions an internationally renowned architect to design a temporary pavilion for its lawn. The Serpentine Gallery Pavilion 2006 was co-designed by prize-winning architect Rem Koolhaas and structural designer Cecil Balmond. The pavilion is an eye-catching ovoid-shaped, inflatable canopy that floats above the 346-square meter gallery area. It is made from translucent material and can be raised or lowered according to the weather. The enclosure below the canopy functions both as a café and forum for public programs, accommodating up to 300 people. LCD TV screens in the façade provide information.

01 Main view of the pavilion | 02 Façade detail | 03 Interior

02

03

01

02

03

04

Eco Funnel

Conceived as a community hall and serving as temporary accommodation while the main school building is being refurbished, the Eco Funnel also acts as an example for green building techniques. It is situated in the corner of the playground and built from pre-fabricated solid wood panels by Eurban. The roof and rear walls are clad in black EPDM rubber, while the front walls are timber board and a special low window gives panoramic views of the playground for children. PV panels on the south and west roof slopes generate power; rainwater is funneled from the roof and is used to water the community garden. The Eco Funnel was short-listed in the 2008 Wood Awards and featured in Open House London.

01 Exterior view | 02 Entrance | 03 Front view | 04 Interior view | 05 Floor plan

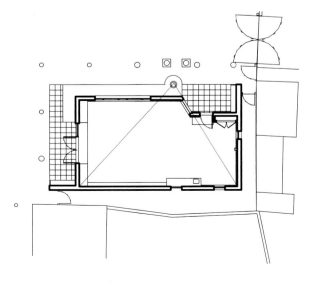

05

01

02

03

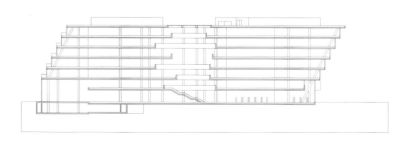

04

City of Westminster College

The new flagship campus for the City of Westminster College is designed to support new ways of teaching and learning. The college provides much greater amounts of open learning spaces than typical colleges in the United Kingdom. The building is designed to embrace interaction and diversity and allow students to learn from each other, formally and informally, through the adaptability and flexibility of the learning spaces. The building has been designed from the inside-out, responding to the needs of the diverse groups who use the college, as well as taking into account the sensitive local context. With its simple geometric forms, rotating around a terraced atrium, it appears as a clean-cut, modern building with a distinct Scandinavian heritage.

01 View towards café | 02 Atrium | 03 Main entrance | 04 View from Paddington Green | 05 Section

05

01

02

03

04

Lumen United Reformed Church

Theis + Khan Architects were commissioned by members of the Regent's Square United Reformed Church to redesign an existing 1960s church building in order to create a new church and community center open to people of all faiths. The existing church space is divided in two, with a community café at the front and church at the rear, with the shaft of light worship space in its pivotal position at the core. The center also includes a new, accessible entrance and three community rooms, as well as ancillary accommodation. A new garden was created from the existing car park at the rear. The aim for honesty and simplicity is reflected in the use of materials.

01 Exterior view | 02 Shaft of light | 03 Community room | 04 Café | 05 Axonometric sketch

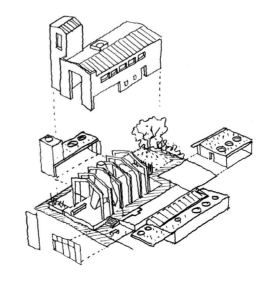

05

01

02

03

04

KX200

KX200 has transformed three existing buildings on Pentonville Road, Kings Cross into a vibrant mix of student accommodation, private and social housing as well as retail and office space. Driving the design was the desire to create different architecture for the two elements of the project. The reused concrete frames of the office towers were reclad in lightweight glazed unitized curtain walling, reinventing the corporate architecture with a variegated pattern of blue shades. Both the curtain walling and the pre-cast concrete were mass-produced off-site in the United Kingdom. Repetitive internal elements such as the student's bathrooms and kitchens were also mass-manufactured and delivered fully finished, ready to be plugged in and used.

01 View from side street | 02 Student café area | 03 Student living space | 04 Courtyard | 05 Ground floor plan

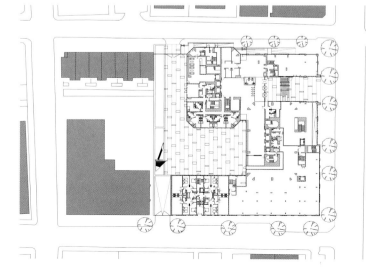

05

01

02

03

04

New Change

This building's architecture is one of vibrating materiality, contrasting light, transparencies, reflections and glass. Inflections in the façade between Bread Street and Cheapside, differentiated treatment of rounded corners, the view onto the shining steel cylinders at ground level, terraces embossed into the glass rooftop on which objects are posed to exploit the anamorphosis, all work to create new questions, new mysteries and new intrigues. The mass of the building is contradicted by the lightness of its materials and the depth of its transparency. The immense floor slabs provide great flexibility on both sides of the passage; through-floor connections are possible on several levels above the porch.

01 Retail space | 02 Street view | 03 Aerial view | 04 Interior view | 05 Site plan

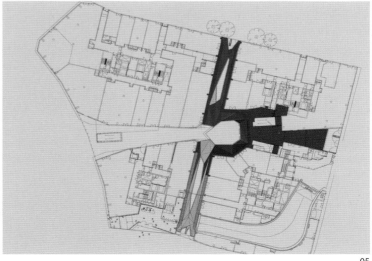

05

01

02

03

04

Skyroom

Skyroom provides an unexpected outdoor event venue with a mix of covered and open space on the rooftop of a five-story office building in central London. A central courtyard opens to the sky and a cantilevered balcony offers breathtaking views of the city. It is a bespoke structure constructed of steel with copper mesh façades, with larch flooring and topped with six ETFE cushions. The structure and materials used were chosen for their lightness and varieties of transparency and to satisfy the local authority's requirement for quality finishes that would age well and complement the conservation area. Skyroom demonstrates the opportunity to adapt London's skyline even when faced with rigorous planning controls within a conservation area.

01 Exterior view with cantilevered balcony | 02 View from street | 03 Aerial view | 04 Central courtyard | 05 Axonometric projection

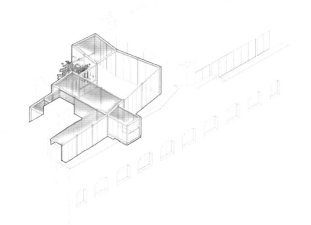

05

01

02

Chips

Quirky, bold and robust, "Chips" forms the first major development for the Archial-designed masterplan for New Islington in Manchester. Designed by Will Alsop, the building was inspired by three fat chips piled on top of one another. The building comprises three equal-height, long, thin new build masses (Chips) approximately 100 meters long by 14 meter wide stacked and staggered upon one another creating an elevated ground floor and eight levels comprising 142 one, two and three bedroom apartments. The building is clad in a composite wall, faced with a cladding covered in newspaper print with text that echoes the industrial heritage of the local area. The scheme achieved a BREEAM Eco-Homes Excellent rating.

01 Section | 02 Folding door divides the room | 03 Interior view | 04 Exterior view |
05 Side view | 06 Stacked volumes

03

04

05

06

01

Manchester Civil Justice Center

The new headquarters of the Ministry of Justice in the northwest of England, Manchester Civil Justice Center is the biggest court complex to be built in the United Kingdom since the Royal Courts of Justice. The building provides accommodation of around 34,000 square meters on 15 levels. It houses 47 courtrooms and 75 consultation rooms in addition to office and support spaces. The working courts and offices are designed as long rectilinear forms, articulated at each floor level, and projecting at each end of the building as a varied composition of solid and void.

01 East façade | 02 View from north | 03 Floor plans

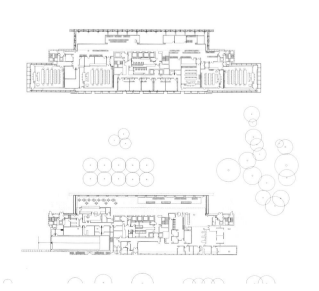

02

03

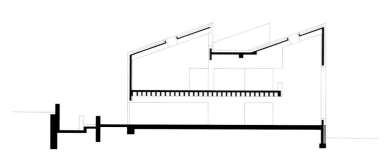

01

02

Turner Contemporary

This new gallery is located on a prominent seafront in Kent, the former site of a guest-house frequented by the English painter William Turner (1775–1851). The new two-story building is formed from six identical crystalline volumes with single-pitch roofs bringing light to the gallery spaces and revealing daily and seasonal light changes. The building is constructed with a concrete frame and acid etched glass skin. The envelope has to withstand the corrosive nature of the sea, high humidity levels, strong winds and the occasional wave topping over the entire site. Internally, the material palette is reduced to hard-wearing screed floors and dry lining to facilitate the hanging of changing exhibitions as the gallery does not have a permanent collection.

01 Section | 02 Gallery space | 03 Reception | 04 Waterfront | 05 Exterior view | 06 View of ensemble

03

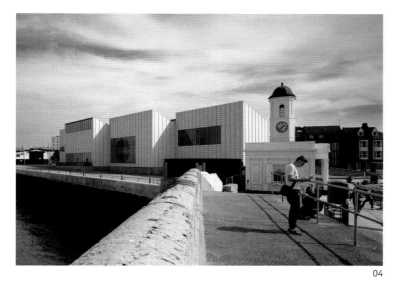

04

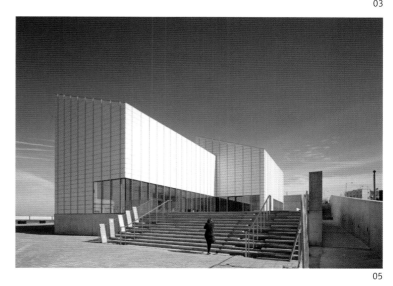

05

06

01

02

03

04

MIMA – Institute of Modern Art

The MIMA is part of an urban regeneration scheme, intended to revitalize the heart of the city. The applied materials and scales respect and relate to the existing surroundings. The new public square, an integral part of the project, was designed in co-operation with architects West 8. The foyer, the defining space within the gallery, forms a transition between gallery and public square. Its height, of more than 16 meters, reveals a central staircase, which is framed by a suspended stone curtain. Interaction between the two is stimulated by the enormous transparent façade, inviting visitors and inhabitants to embrace the gallery as the heart of the new cultural quarter of Middlesbrough.

01 Suspended stone curtain | 02 Staircase | 03 View at night | 04 Exhibition room | 05 Ground floor plan

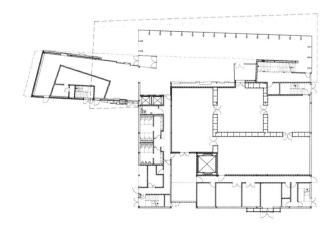

05

01

The Coach House

A timber and glass structure extending the rear elevation replaces an unsightly neo-victorianconservatory added to the house in the 1980s. On the ground level this creates a reception room and office area, which benefit from uninterrupted panoramic views of the surrounding countryside. The full height glazing is supported by a series of sections of solid oak cantilevered off the amended floor slab. At the front of the house, one of the twin garages has been removed to provide space for a white calacatta limestone kitchen, which has been relocated from the first floor. The removal of the garage door on the north façade created an opening in the entrance elevation masonry, which has been glazed to function as a picture window.

01 General view | 02 Kitchen | 03 Ground floor plan

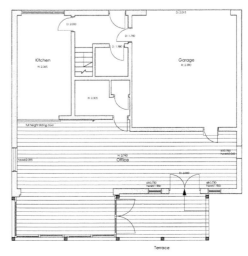

02

03

01

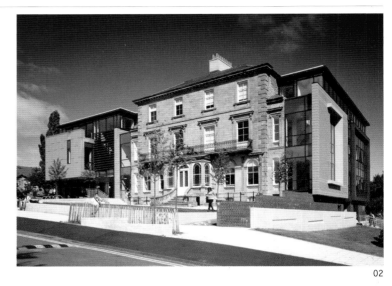

02

03

04

05

Newcastle College

RMJM has designed five major projects at Newcastle College's Rye Hill Campus. The series of new projects are seen as playing a major role in regenerating the campus and surrounding community. The award winning new buildings include the Performance Academy, which combines the Music, Performing Arts and Media; SPACE, a reconfiguration of the existing 1960s concert hall to provide a Higher Education Center with bar, café, exhibition, and conference space; the refurbishment of grade B listed Ryehill House provides student support and administration facilities; the Lifestyle Academy combines food, hospitality, beauty, travel, customer services and sport departments, with the facilities being open to the public; and lastly the Sixth Form College.

01 Façade | 02 Ryehill House | 03 Night view | 04 Interior view | 05 Perspective | 06 Visualization

06

01

02

University of Wales Newport City Campus

This city center campus highlights the important role of the university in the social and economic regeneration of the city and its region. The new building occupies a highly visual waterfront site, bringing together business, technology, art, design and media disciplines into a single collaborative environment under a single roof. Housing sound and television studios, screening theaters, lecture theaters, learning support, exhibition space, teaching studios and academic offices, the design approach is to provide a sociable and convivial environment, which fosters interdisciplinary learning, research and outreach. The shape of the building maximizes visual and physical connections with the city and the waterfront setting.

01 View from water | 02 Façade | 03 Ground floor plan | 04 Corridors | 05 Atrium | 06 View from upper floor | 07 Street view

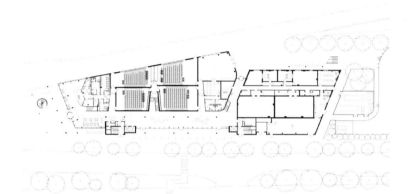

03

04

05

06

07

01

02

03

04

Freya and Robin

Freya's Cabin and Robin's Hut are two structures imagined through the writing of a love story and inspired by the stunning man-made landscape of Kielder Water and Forest. The two characters, Freya and Robin, are personifications of two spots on opposite banks of the lake. Robin's simple hut is on the north bank amongst fir trees and rocks. Freya fell in love with Robin and built him a cabin to entice him to come over to meet her on the south bank. She modeled it on her flower press, balancing it up high on the tallest straightest stems she could find. When Robin didn't arrive, Freya cried tears of gold and wrapped the cabin in them. Robin saw the golden tears glistening in the sun, rowed over and whisked Freya away on an adventure.

01 View from below | 02 View out to the water | 03 Winter view | 04 Façade detail | 05 Elevation

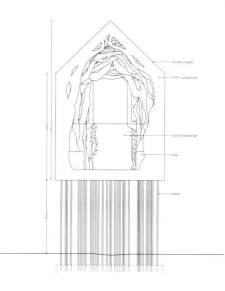

05

01

02

03

Kielder Observatory

The design of this astronomical observatory sited in a remote spot in Northumberland, close to Scotland, in an area with a very low level of light pollution, envisions a building in the form of a land pier that is able to house two telescopes and a warm-room used for research activities. Timber was chosen as the main material because of its relation to the surrounding forest and its carbon neutrality. The power strategy was developed with a local renewables specialist and encompasses a two and a half kilowatt wind turbine which utilizes the windy weather conditions of the site for operating power needs, and photovoltaic panels to power deep cell batteries.

01 Entrance area | 02 Raised foundations protect landscape | 03 View along corridor | 04 Floor plans | 05 Exterior view

04

05

01

Highfields Automotive & Engineering Training Center

A joint venture between Castle College Nottingham and car manufacturer Toyota, the new 6,600-square meter regional training center in Highfields Science Park Nottingham consists of specialist wings with expandable workshops, linked by a brightly colored central hub. Seen as an exemplar of collaboration, the facilities provide high-level training and research facilities for automotive engineering, including hybrid engine technology and biofuels. The center is the first building to complete in Highfields Science and Technology Park in Nottingham and a winner of a RIBA Award in 2009.

01 Exterior view | 02 Interior view | 03 Workshops above car park | 04 Sections

02

03

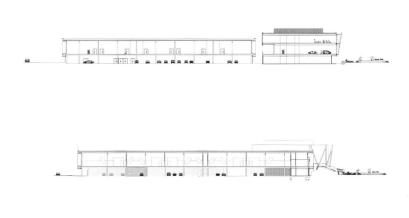

04

01

02

03

04

The North Wall Arts Center

Built on the grounds of St Edward's School, this center is shared by the school and town. It houses a flexible 300-seat theater, a rehearsal space, dance studios and an art gallery. The design unites an ancient stone boundary wall, a Grade II listed Victorian former swimming pool and a new building to form a carefully scaled streetscape to the public side and a new courtyard to the school. The scheme has been envisaged as a linear series of connected 'barns' built against the weathered stone boundary wall. Vernacular forms, contemporary detailing, and traditional but unfamiliar materials emphasize the building's role as a place for innovation and creativity within an historic environment.

01 Gallery with foyer | 02 Theater | 03 Façade detail | 04 Dance studio | 05 Ground floor plan

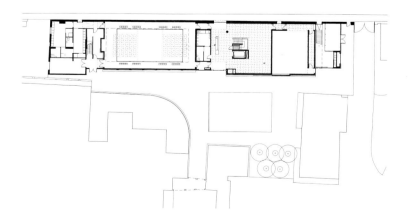

05

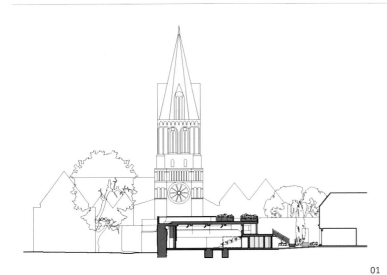

01

02

Corpus Christi College Auditorium

Rick Mather Architects designed a new flexible multi-purpose performance space for Corpus Christi College in Oxford. Corpus Christi is one of Oxford's oldest colleges founded in 1517. The building site lies in the southwest corner of the college within a bastion of the 13th century city wall. A flexible space was created to accommodate seminars, 136-person lectures, drama, music, a 40-person round-table, banquets for 80 diners and college parties. The new building replaces the existing smaller music room. A skylight above the theater gives views up to Christ Church Cathedral, and a large picture window opposite gives views back to the trees of the college gardens.

01 Section | 02 Auditorium | 03 View across courtyard | 04 Exterior view | 05 View from park | 06 Auditorium at dusk

03

04

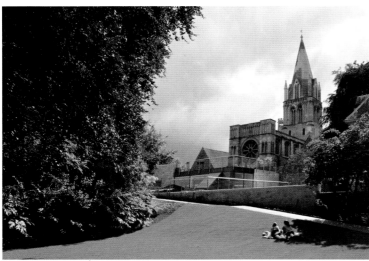

05

06

01

02

03

04

Ecospace's Project

This building acts as a sanctuary away from the main house, allowing the client to work from home in isolation without domestic distractions. Similarly, the relaxing space and guest accommodation act as a self-contained, detached space. The clients required a sustainable, fast track project with minimal disturbance to their busy lifestyles. The cedar-clad building with a birch wood interior and a sedum-planted roof was built with modern methods of construction, using prefabricated structurally insulated panel systems, resulting in a fast track construction time of just ten days to completion.

01 South view | 02 Study space | 03 Exterior view | 04 Living space | 05 Floor plans

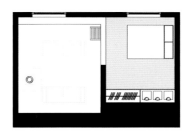

05

01

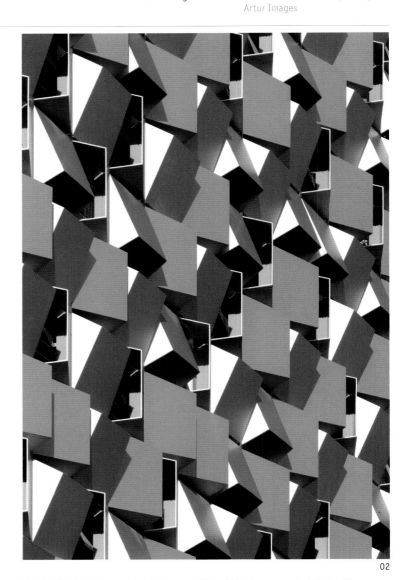

02

03

04

Charles Street Parking Lot

This multi-story parking lot provides public car parking in Sheffield city center and forms part of the regeneration of the Heart of the City project. It provides 520 parking spaces over ten floors, above retail space. The structure consists of pre-cast concrete columns, walls and floors. The external envelope is finished in natural anodised aluminum panels, painted green on the inside. Each is manufactured from a single sheet of folded aluminum, cut to an angle on two sides, and hung in four different orientations. This provides natural ventilation and hides the structure behind a homogeneous surface. The appearance of the panel system varies between day and night.

01 Main entrance | 02 Aluminum panels | 03 Parking spaces | 04 Spiral ramp | 05 Floor plan

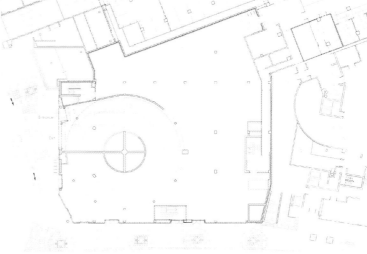

05

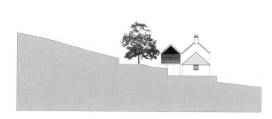

01

02

The Dairy House

The space was pragmatically redesigned for conversion into a five-bedroom house with a small pool. Lean-to sheds were removed and an extension was added. During the design process, the requirements changed from a rental property to those of a weekend house for the client. The intervention was to appear as a natural extension of the existing structure, with an 'un-designed' design to combine privacy and seclusion with openness to the wider landscape. The inspiration was both local, in the stacked timber in the yard opposite, and literary, in the 18th century "La Petite Maison – an Architectural Seduction" architectural treatise and erotic novella by Jean-Francois de Bastide.

01 Sections | 02 Living room | 03 Bathhouse | 04 View into passageway | 05 Interior

03

04

05

01

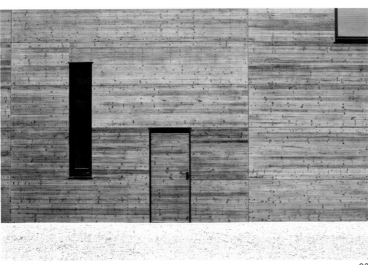

02

03

Welham Studios

This project started with a study of placement; watching objects in clay and observing how they create shapes through their interaction with the wind and rain. The project seeks to find a union between object and environment. One aspect developed into the basic forms using triangulation. This work was the basis of a project with the Swinomish Tribal people of Fidalgo Island Washington State. This project developed into a series of buildings of which Welham Studios is the prototype. The building is constructed with structurally insulated panels; the insulation material thermoform three-ply cladding was used. The roof is an EPDM membrane with an inbuilt roof barrier.

01 General view | 02 Façade detail | 03 Exterior view | 04 Elevations | 05 Exterior view in winter

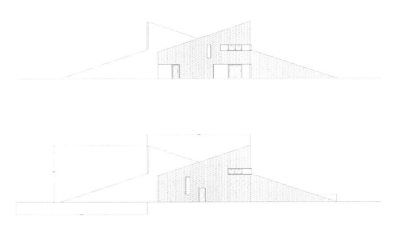

04

05

01

02

Balancing Barn

This house engages the landscape and reinterprets the simple volumes of Vermont rural architecture. Three clearings in the forest punctuate the long gravel driveway and provide views of meadow, pond and house. In the final clearing, the house is broken into three volumes arrayed around a large rock outcropping with open spaces that frame vistas of the Green Mountains. Each volume has a distinct programmatic function: a shed volume serves as a workshop and storage outbuilding, and two connected volumes form the main living quarters of the house. The house provides a weekend gathering place for three generations of family from around the region.

01 Worm's-eye view | 02 Exterior covered in reflective metal sheeting | 03 General view | 04 Floor plan | 05 Bird's-eye view | 06 Bedroom | 07 Living room

03

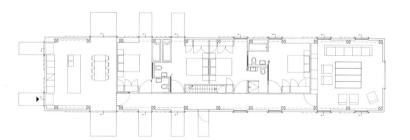

04

05

06

07

01

Read-Nest

Measuring only ten square meters, Read-Nest is a small structure designed to sit in the landscape like an architectural folly. Being flexible in situation and use, it can be located wherever the owner desires and used for study, relaxation or both. The exterior is clad in vertically striated natural oiled wood slats that are designed to interact well with the immediate environment. Inside, Read-Nest is fitted with a wall of shelves, as well as a bed that can be folded into the wall. There are views to the outside from the skylight above the bed and from the worktable through a large window, which can be folded horizontally to create an outdoor cover. The interior is clad in waxed birch plywood.

01 Exterior view | 02 Interior with fitted bookshelf and foldable bed | 03 Floor plans and elevations

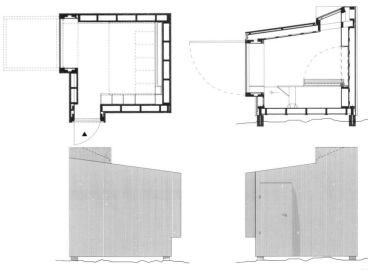

02

03

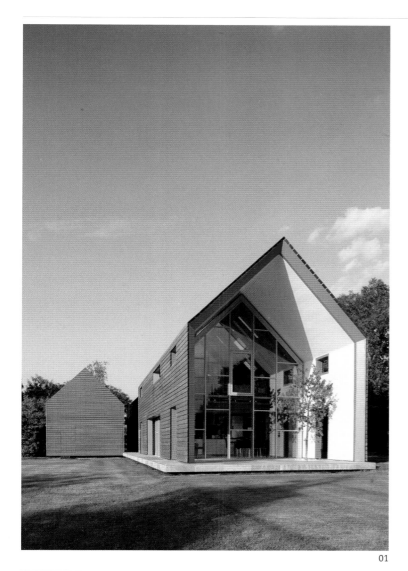

01

02

03

04

Sliding House

The brief was a self-build house offering a rural retreat. The result is a structure with conventional building forms and unconventional detailing. A 28-meter linear building of apparent simplicity is sliced into three programs: house, garage, and annex, each defined with a distinct finish of red rubber membrane and glass, red and black stained larch respectively. These separated forms can be transformed by the fourth and largest element in the group, the 20-ton mobile roof and wall enclosure which traverses the site. This autonomous and insulating structure passes over the annex, house and glasshouse, creating elements of enclosure, open-air living and framing of views according to position.

01 Front façade | 02 Open-air bathtub | 03 Glass house | 04 Dining room | 05 Sketch

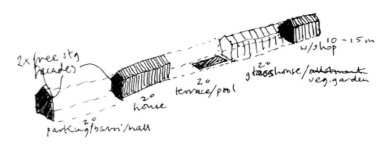

05

01

02

03

04

Bavent House

Responding sensitively to its rural surrounding, Bavent House is a striking new four-bedroom family house situated in the Suffolk countryside. Inspired by the architecture of the locale, which includes agricultural barns and the humble beach hut, the design employs robust economical materials – an engineered timber frame, black zinc and Iroko timber cladding – that will weather with time and harmonize with its setting. The house is arranged in a U-shaped plan with rooms around a southfacing courtyard. At the center of the plan is a double-height space forming the hub of the house, from here the building is divided into two wings, with living areas and bedrooms either side.

01 Ground floor with double-height space | 02 Upper floor | 03 Front view | 04 Rear view | 05 Ground floor plan

05

01

02

03

04

Dovecote Studio

The Dovecote Studio forms part of the internationally renowned music campus at Snape Maltings, on the Suffolk coast. A large roof window provides consistent light for artists, while a small mezzanine platform with a writing desk incorporates a fully opening, glazed corner window that gives long views over the marshes towards the sea. Decaying existing windows were left alone and vegetation growing over the dovecote was protected to allow it to continue a natural process of ageing and decay. The Corten structure itself is fabricated from full size 1,200 by 2,400 milimeter sheets with regular staggered welded joints, into which door and window openings are cut in locations dictated by internal layout.

01 View from north | 02 Exterior view | 03 View out to marshes | 04 Design sketch | 05 Entrance

05

01

02

03

The Hepworth Wakefield

The Hepworth Wakefield is a purpose-built art gallery, located in the historic waterfront area south of Wakefield city center. The monolithic appearance and composition is accentuated by the use of pigmented insitu concrete. The program is split horizontally between the ground floor and the first floor. The ground floor contains the reception, shop, cafeteria, auditorium, and learning studios, as well as offices and back-of-house areas. The main source of daylight in each gallery is a light slot running the full width of the ceiling at the highest end of each space. The varying angles of each ceiling have been calculated to admit and diffuse light in the best possible way, complementing the artificial lighting system.

01 North view | 02 Side view | 03 Interior view | 04 First floor plan

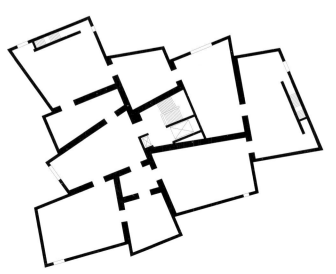

04

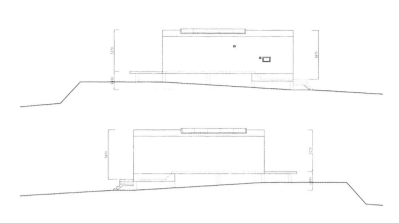

01

02

03

Beach House

This beach chalet, with a floor area of 36 square meters, is built on galvanized steel stilts to protect it from flooding. The outside of the chalet is clad with cedar shingles and the inside with sawn softwood. Since the land slopes away from the beach, steps were constructed inside and outside to create a level interior surface. The added height at the rear of the building meant that there was space for a mezzanine level, which serves as a sleeping area, with space for two double mattresses. The oblong-shaped window above it provides beautiful views over the countryside, which is one of the focal points of the design. Behind the kitchen are the children's bunk beds and the bedroom.

01 Sections | 02 General view | 03 Exterior clad with ceddar shingles | 04 Kitchen | 05 Living area

04

05

01

The Stonehenge Project

The new Stonehenge center will provide amenities, interpretative exhibitions and educational facilities. The structure is designed to sit lightly in the landscape. Its modern construction utilizes a steel structure and lightweight framed walls, requiring minimal substructure and enabling reversibility. A thin, undulating canopy floats above, evoking the gentle swell of the landscape, and is supported by slender columns. Two enclosed pods sit beneath the canopy; a glass pod housing the café, retail and education spaces; and a solid timber-clad pod containing the interpretative exhibition space, information point and toilets. The floating canopy defines and shelters, whilst views and movement encourage an outdoor landscape experience.

01 Visitor center | 02 Sketch | 03 Undulating roof canopy above landscape

02

03

01

02

03

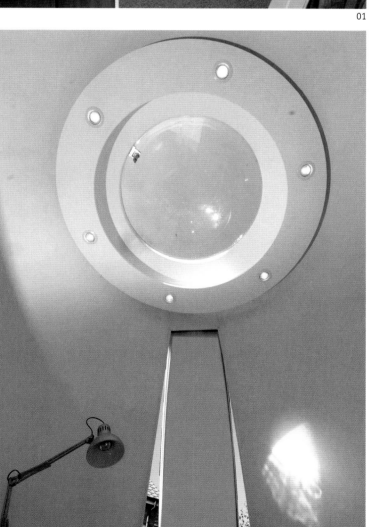

04

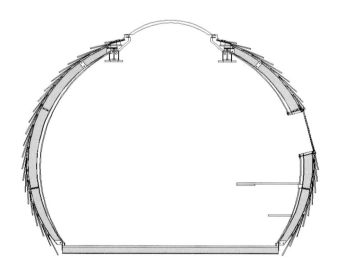

05

Archipod Garden Office

This self-contained garden office, playroom, or treehouse is built from timber from FSC sources and clad in Western Red Cedar. Archipod's aim was to create a garden office building specifically designed to complement a garden landscape as well as being ergonomic, efficient and unusual. They chose wood as the world's most replenishable construction material and insulated the pod to a standard exceeding that of current building regulations. The interior has a plastered finish with no visible internal jointing strips. A double-skin polycarbonate roof dome maximizes natural light and ventilation. The structure can be delivered complete with power and lighting, or assembled on site from components.

01 View into office | 02 Exterior view | 03 Façade detail | 04 Window detail | 05 Section

01

02

03

04

The Lift

The Lift, a new parliament, is a proposal for a new type of meeting and performance space. Its brief was developed by AOC with Lift and 200 East London residents through a six-month program of workshops culminating in a sharing event in a 1:1 mock up at Stratford Circus. Part theater, part village hall, part social condenser, the Lift's distinct shape and evolved quilt pattern create an instant icon wherever it is located. A large external window provides a billboard, hanging space, natural ventilation and allows the interior to enjoy both blackout and daylight. An adaptable box of tricks, its internal deployable roomscape and curtains actively encourages users to adapt the space or create the spaces they need, when they want it.

01 Festival Square, Southbank Centre, London | 02 Stratford Park, London | 03 Outdoor cinema | 04 Space for performance – deployables raised | 05 Floor plan

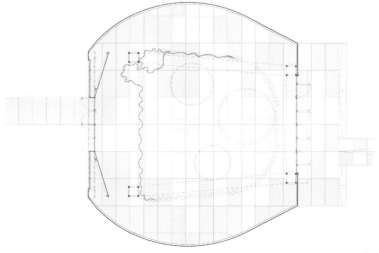

05

01

Blob VB3

The design originally proposed by dmvA for a house extension was repeatedly rejected by local building regulations. DmvA responded by designing a mobile unit, a blob, which skirted around the strict building codes with its strongly artistic features. A timber frame was constructed, covered with a stretch material and plastered with polyester, which was sanded repeatedly to create the smooth egg shape. Inside, the space was built up with niches and the gap between the outer and inner shells filled with PUR insulation. The egg houses all necessary functions: bathroom, kitchen, lighting, a bed and several storage niches. The nose can be opened automatically and functions as a porch.

01 View inside | 02 Night view | 03 Front view | 04 Elevations

02

03

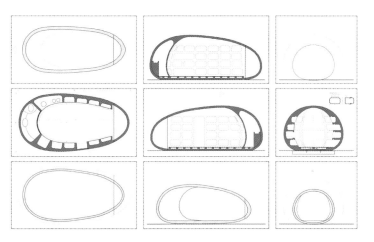

04

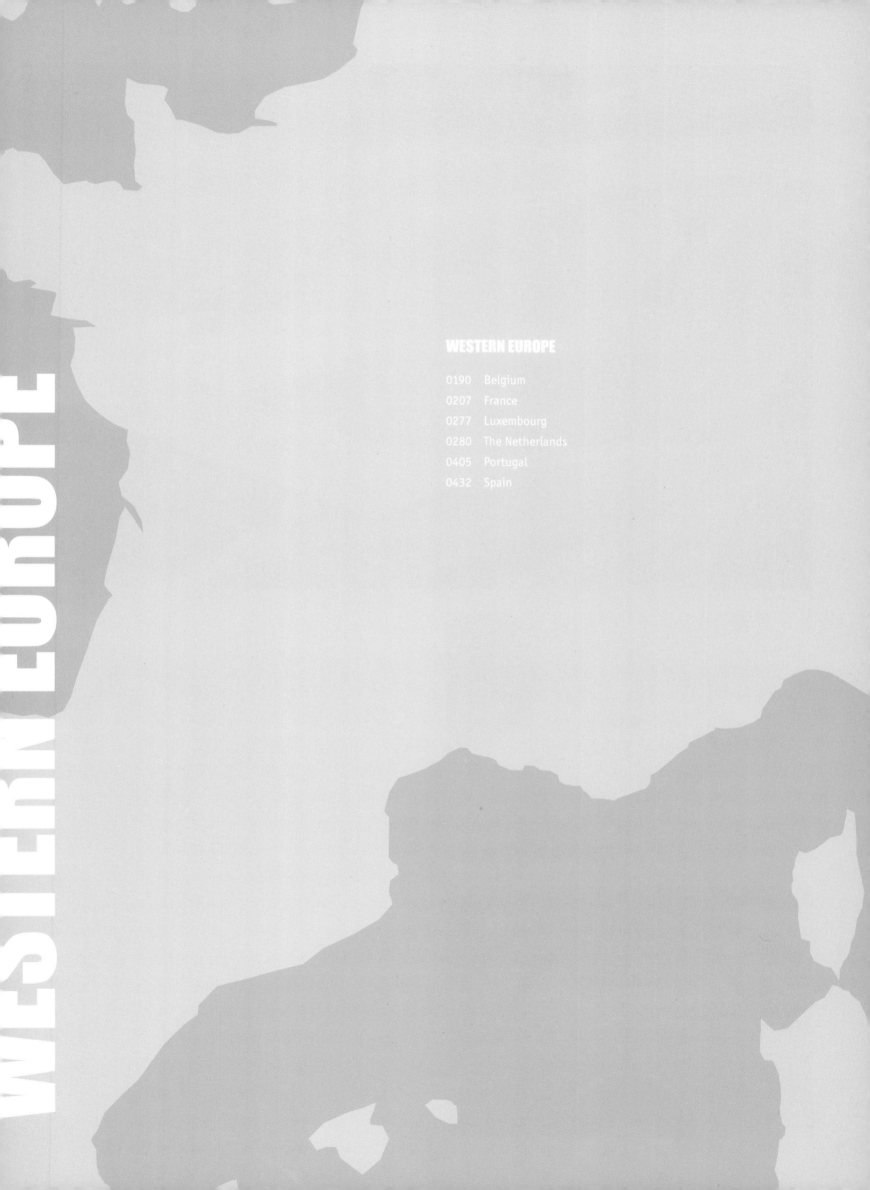

WESTERN EUROPE

WESTERN EUROPE

01

02

03

Q8 Service Station

The architecture of this service station building was intended to fit optimally in the topography of the surrounding site and also to adhere to a sustainable program. The structure has been designed to capitalize on available sunlight and other climatic parameters specific to the site. With the twofold aim of catering to user comfort and respecting the environment, the design choices were geared towards natural and/or recyclable materials such as a timber substructure and a partially green roof. Similarly, the technical choices fell on high environmental quality systems such as solar protection, low heat loss glazing, underfloor heating, light management, water cycle, as well as solar and photovoltaic panels.

01 Bird's-eye view of site | 02 Glass façade detail | 03 Timber structure | 04 First floor with mezzanine

04

01

02

03

04

Smallest House of Antwerp

The task consisted of finding a concept for a rest space of two and a half meters in width. Four wooden floors between two existing walls, hanging in a steel skeleton, divide this house into a work area on the ground floor, first floor dining room, second floor living room, third floor bedroom, and a view on the roof. The façade is all glass, which not only lets in needed light, but adds a modern touch. This transparency coupled with the black window frames gives the impression of a living painting, hinting at its former function in this neighborhood – a bordello.

01 First and second floor | 02 Bedroom | 03 Bathtub on the roof | 04 Living room | 05 Section

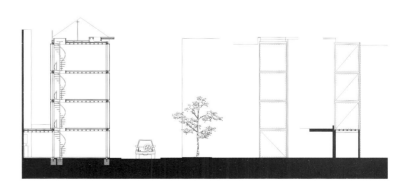

05

01

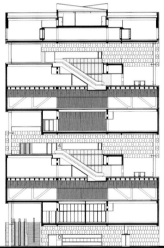

02

03

MAS | Museum aan de Stroom

The "Museum aan de Stroom" stands between the old docks in the center of the Eilandje. Ten gigantic natural stone trunks are piled up as a physical demonstration of the heaviness of history, full of historical objects that are the legacy of our ancestors. Each story of the tower has been rotated a quarter turn, creating a gigantic spiral staircase. This spiral space, in which a façade of corrugated glass is inserted, forms a public city gallery. The top of the tower accommodates a restaurant, a party room and a panoramic terrace. Façades, floors, walls and ceilings of the tower are entirely covered with large panels of hand-cut red Indian sandstone, evoking the image of a monumental stone sculpture.

01 View from east | 02 Section | 03 View from dock | 04 Fourth floor plan

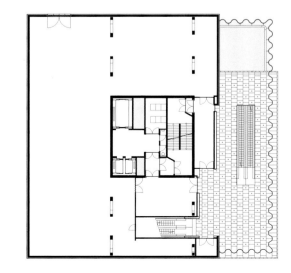

04

01

02

Antwerp Law Courts

This 40,000-square meter law court complex, located in the heart of Antwerp, was the winner of a RIBA European Award in 2007. The structure is shaped almost like an octopus and includes courts, offices, archives and meeting rooms. The distinctive spiky roof resembles a series of church steeples or ship sails. Each of the courtroom roofs are formed by four interconnecting, timber hyperbolic paraboloids. An elevated courtroom deck, made from bonded together concrete pre-cast units, supports these. As well as blending in well with the existing landscape, and having a positive visual impact, this award winning law court is a symbolic gateway to the city, and a lively hub for the surrounding area.

01 Lobby stairs | 02 Exterior view | 03 Entrance | 04 Entrance interior | 05 Exterior view at night | 06 Courtroom

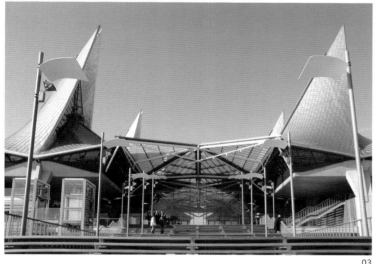

03

04

05

06

01

02

03

04

05

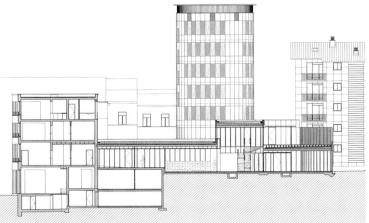

06

Childcare Center and Welfare Office C.P.A.S.

This complex belongs to the city of Brussels and includes social units, such as child care and social services. The building is a small cylindrical tower with six levels. The outer diameter is kept as small as possible, so that the building does not appear so strikingly visually. The tower houses, offices and medical rooms and the interior walls are clad with treated or untreated wood, the windows and door frames are made of stainless plissel. The top floor is a conference room with panoramic views, a covered terrace with roof garden and a playground. A veil of metal is attached, acting as wind protection and safety net.

01 Staircase | 02 Corridor | 03 View of entrance | 04 Interior view | 05 Side view | 06 Section

01

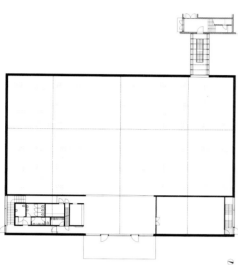
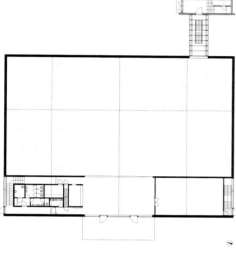

02

03

Sports Hall KA Hiel

The KA Hielschool site acts as a green space within the urban context. The campus area features great differences in height as well as much diversity in buildings and pavilions. According to the campus philosophy, the new sports hall has been introduced as an autonomous object. The building shows a harmonious transition between the main building and the small-scale nursery school. A natural incision in the sloping terrain provides the entrance to the sports hall. The concrete volume features colored sports field lines that can be used as tennis, soccer or climbing wall. The structure of the roof consists of a wooden frame, suspended from upside-down beams, giving the building a sculptural character.

01 Interior court | 02 First floor plan | 03 Tunnel to school | 04 Wall detail | 05 Exterior view

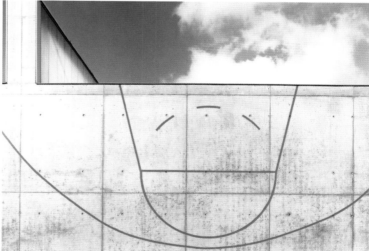

04

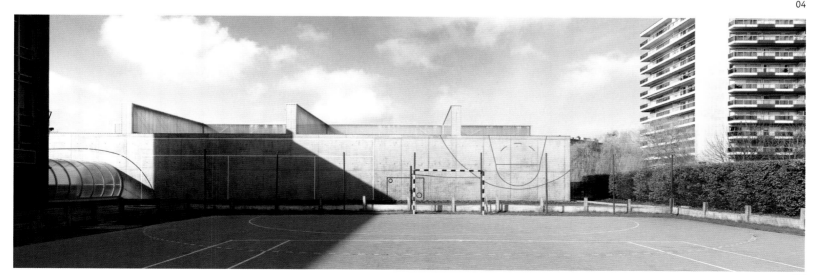

05

01

02

03

04

Square Brussels Meeting Center

This architectural proposition offers a newfound visibility to the former congress center by means of a poetic emblem embodied in the glass cube that forms the entry to Square. Its tree-like structure and an aesthetic based on transparency and light shares a dialogue with R. Pechère's historic garden. The cube contains suspended stairs and catwalks that connect the different access levels to the 52,000-square-meter complex. Square offers 27 meeting rooms with 3,538 seats, an exhibition hall, a restaurant and a brasserie with 420 seats. It therefore constitutes an attractive technological jewel at the heart of the city and consumes the transformation of an important historic site by respect for its history and ambition for its future.

01 Main entrance with exterior auditorium | 02 Interior looking upwards | 03 View from garden | 04 View over René Pechère's historic garden | 05 Section

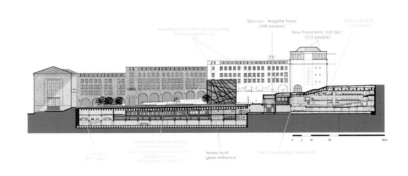

05

01

02

The Cube

The Cube – dining with a view – is a pavilion designed by Park Associati (Filippo Pagliani, Michele Rossi) to house an itinerant restaurant commissioned by Electrolux. Designed to be placed in unexpected and dramatic European locations, it has been launched in Brussels where it will sit atop of the Parc du Cinquantenaire. The Cube has been conceived as a module that can be put up and taken down relatively easily, one that suits all climatic conditions, even the most extreme, while always expressing the maximum in living comfort. The construction has the lightness and versatility of an exhibition stand, yet with the design complexity of a building. It uses materials that are highly innovative in terms of technology, sustainability and energy saving as well as enabling constant re-use.

01 Exterior at night | 02 Side view | 03 Atop the Parc du Cinquantenaire | 04 Terrace | 05 Conceptual drawing | 06 Interior view | 07 Dining room detail

03

04

05

06

07

01

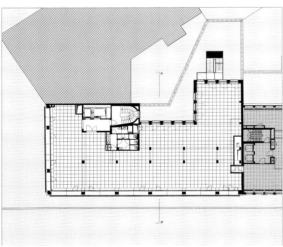

04

02

03

05

06

Office Building for Immobiliere SEM

The original building dates from the 1960s and was completely renovated and thus adapted to suit the new use. The building structure was exposed to permit a panoramic view of the Royal Park and parts of southern Brussels. The new façade is made of wood and glass and adjustable slats of bamboo and glass offer protection from sun and wind. The balconies are accessible from the inside. A continuous glass roof protects the balconies on the first five floors from rain. On the ground floor, the curtain of slats is broken and the façade is clad in stainless steel.

01 Interior view | 02 View from the street | 03 Balcony detail | 04 Typical floor plan | 05 Perspective | 06 View from windows

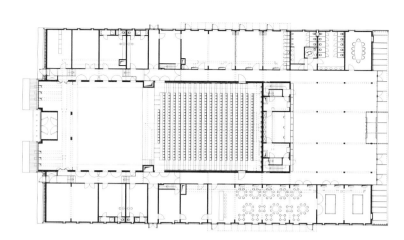

01

02

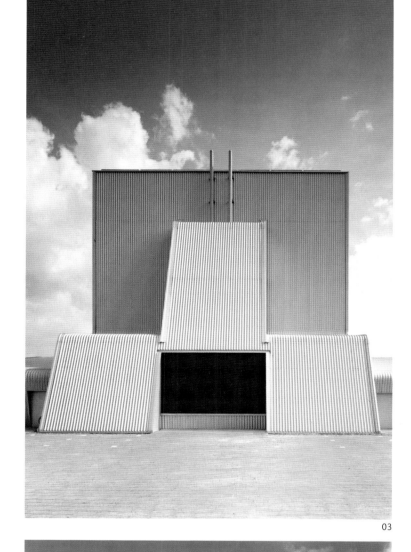

03

Cultural Center and Services

This multi-purpose building is located in a park on the outskirts of the city. The space has been created to host various concerts and events. The stage and the auditorium, with retractable seats, are located in the central nave of the building. Two wings flank the nave and house the cafeteria, multipurpose rooms, green room, dressing rooms, storage and technical facilities. Some administrative offices are located between the hall and foyer. The building consists of concrete blocks and reinforced concrete slabs and has a corrugated outer skin of galvanized steel. The high walls are there for the stability of the structure and must also fulfill the function of sound insulation.

01 Ground floor plan | 02 Auditorium | 03 Main view from parking area | 04 Side view | 05 Exterior view

04

05

01

02

03

04

Sint-Janspoort Shopping Center and Housing

This new shopping center at Sint-Janspoort covers a whole block in the center of Kortrijk. The project is in two parts: a shopping center with a floor area of 34,000 square meters, spread across four floors, and a detached ten-story block of flats. With its interiorized street pattern and monumental atrium, this shopping center forms a diagonal link between Steenpoort and Veemarkt. The existing Sioen Street has been incorporated into the route of the inner area. The surrounding streets are visible from several places in the interior 'market place'. The tower closes off one end of the Romeinselaan. The volume of the block, which contains offices and homes as well as shops, matches the scale of the surrounding buildings.

01 Street view | 02 Exterior view | 03 Balconies | 04 Interior of shopping center | 05 Ground floor plan

05

01

02

03

Euro Space Center

The Euro Space Center is responsible for providing information concerning space exploration activities and telecommunications. The project houses diverse enterprises active in these sectors, located in modules consisting of low-rise wooden constructions. A large structure, like a raised horticultural greenhouse, provides a common roof for the ensemble. The glass façade along the highway is lengthened by a 120-meter-long gallery that covers the existing building. The three-dimensional structure is the ideal support for large banners, signaling the nature of the activities of this center. The southern slopes of the roof and façade elements are equipped with photovoltaic panels.

01 General view | 02 Façade detail | 03 Inner courtyard under photovoltaic roof | 04 Sketch

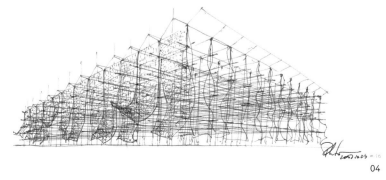

04

01

02

03

Médiacité

The Médiacité project ties together all the disparate elements of the site to create a new axis through the city of Liège. The 350-meter-long mall weaves through the fabric of the refurbished market center at one end, through the new two-story building on the old steelworks site and connects to the new Belgian national television center at the other. The mall is modeled on the internal 'street' of the traditional galleria and arcade, where the architecture unifies rhythm and proportion. The lattice of steel ribs overhead, mirrored in the floor pattern, sculpts the volume of the mall beneath, drawing a sinuous pathway through each of the zones, revealing diverse vistas and forming a variety of different spatial experiences.

01 View across Meuse river | 02 Exterior view | 03 Sawtooth interior | 04 3D model |
05 Terrace

04

05

01

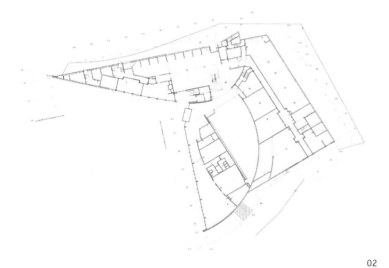

02

Art Museum in Louvain-la-Neuve

This new art museum is sited between the main square of the town of Louvain-la-Neuve, Belgium and an existing lake and park. The concept was to create a building that preserves the park setting and extends it to the town square, while also acting as an element marking the entrance to the town center. The museum consists of two massing elements: an exhibition tower, housing the museum's permanent collection, and a park-covered base, offering space for public functions and temporary exhibits. The roof of this base provides pedestrian connections within an elevated park. The exhibition tower slopes out of the landscape, forming a vertical element, which marks the vehicular and pedestrian entrances to the town square.

01 View from lake | 02 Ground floor plan | 03 North façade | 04 View of terrace | 05 Lobby

03

04

05

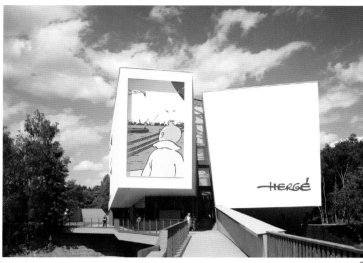

01

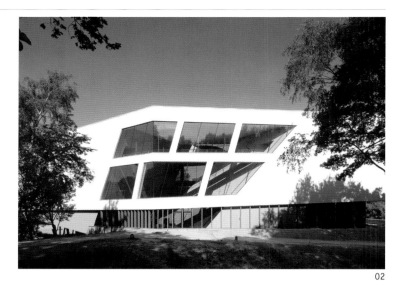

02

Hergé Museum

The Hergé Museum is built on a straight-edged concrete slab with a car park underneath. The architects took the decision to disengage the new museum building from the town, moving it towards the nearby woods. This results in an interior bathed in light, against the darker backdrop of the forest. The visitor is confronted with four landscape objects, corresponding to Hergé's drawing style. The museum's architecture was inspired by the collection in that it must pay tribute to Hergé, but also by a desire to respond to the surroundings. The generous glazing permits views of the woods while also allowing natural light in, to illuminate the exhibits and the elegant interior.

01 View of entrance | 02 Exterior view | 03 Interior view | 04 Second floor plan | 05 Walkway | 06 Exterior view at night

03

04

05

06

01

02

03

04

Château d'eau

On a small site in the middle of the flat Belgium landscape rises this 30-meter water tower, built between 1938 and 1941 for and by the village of Steenokkerzeel. The tower was in service until the beginning of the 1990s and was used by the Nazis in World War II as a watchtower. The preservation of existing concrete elements such as the main water conduit, concrete ceilings, concrete stairs and the 250,000-liter concrete water basin, was essential in maintaining the building's strong identity. Every visible concrete element inside was painted a dark gray in order to differentiate the old from the new. This choice also works to give the interior a contrasting bright and dark appearance.

01 View from kitchen | 02 Bathroom | 03 Exterior view at night | 04 Kitchen | 05 Elevation and section

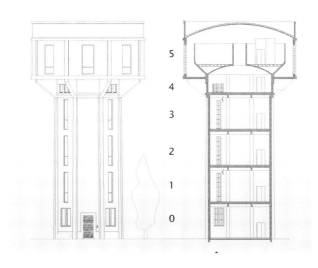

05

01

02

Picanol Site Reconversion

When the city of Ypres acquired the former Picanol factory, it cleared the path for an important new urban development: the re-evaluation of the canal area and its integration with the city center. The city council made a strategic decision to assign public services a location in this new district together with private functions. The project maintains the most important factory buildings and groups the library and the art and music academy on the industrial site, giving the new single family homes and apartment buildings a strategic location on the site and rethinking the design of the public space. The project functions as generator for a broader development that will be addressed in later design stages.

01 Overview | 02 Exterior view | 03 Façade | 04 Library

03

04

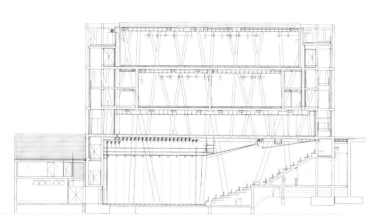

01

National Choreography Center

This project aimed to challenge mathematics. The structural solutions celebrate effort and work, skin and bones, weak against strong. Due to the restrictions of the location, the project is limited to skin on bones. In the architectural quarrels (neo-modernism vs. degenerated postmodernism vs. high-tech colonialist) it is an emergency gesture that could be confused with utopia, the act of reconstituting a gesture. The need for open floors, completely free of constraints, required the shift of the structural load to the façades. Expansive floors were chosen to avoid walls or interior pillars.

01 Section | 02 'Skin and bone' exterior structure | 03 Interior view level 7 | 04 Exterior view | 05 Staircases | 06 Façade at night

04

05

02

03

06

01

02

Grand Théatre de Provence

The proposed project will transform the theater complex and its facilities into an ensemble arrangement that allows visitors to walk on the roofs of the various volumes, thus creating a series of urban public sites at various levels, theatrically inhabitable and diversified. The principle of inhabitability is underlined by the unity of the stone covering material and by the variegated textured finish of the coverings, a clear reference to the layers of a large geological mass. The structure is crowned by the trees on the highest terrace, thus further emphasizing its inhabitability. The volume of the theater is oriented around the ideal axis that connects the location with the historic city; this axis dialectically communicates with the historic center via two rectilinear ramps that allow movement between the planes of the volumetric whole and are in turn connected to the atrium of the theater by the circular entrance plaza from the city.

01 Total view | 02 Rendering of theater | 03 Stage and concert hall | 04 Foyer | 05 Front view of the ramps

03

04

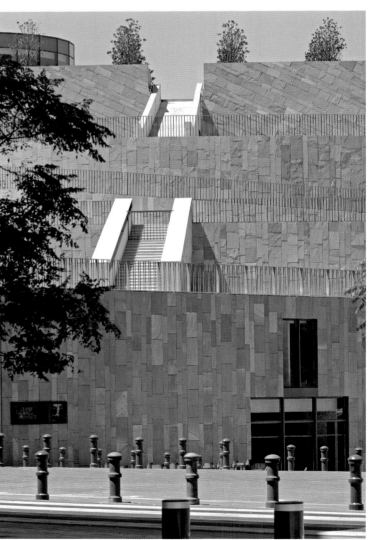

05

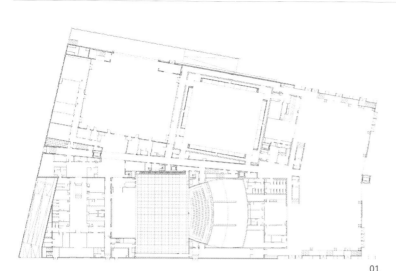

01

02

03

Le Quai

This theater is a major project for both the town and the region. Developed around the trend of 'creation, training, and urban animation', the theater's architecture enhances urban character and strengthens the link between town, performance areas and dance school. Le Quai theater is a location where live shows are created and three rhythms, each with specific requirements, co-evolve: the rhythm of performance needs preserved and autonomous venues; the rhythm of the audience is aided by venues that are integrated with the urban space; and finally, the rhythm of the dancing school, which requires specific educational spaces. The town and the theater were linked using a peristyle open onto the town, framing magnificent views on the King René Castle.

01 Ground floor plan | 02 Main auditorium | 03 Inner façade of the forum | 04 Façade |
05 Exterior view from La Maine river

04

05

01

Sarthe et Loir Health Center

With only 300 beds on three different levels, this hospital has human dimensions. Overlooking a valley, it features a technologically sophisticated architecture that strongly contrasts with the rural setting. High vertical windows structure the façade of printed glass. The horizontal succession of the various functions leads to increased transparency, facilitates communications within the building, and is compatible with a future extension. Color plays an important role in the green courtyards, where different kinds of materials structure the space and underscore the importance of art within the hospital.

01 Patio and façade | 02 Façade detail | 03 Pink patio | 04 Pink corridor | 05 Ground floor plan | 06 Reception in hall

02

03

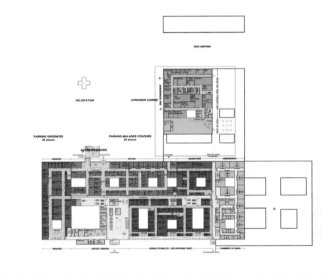

04

05

06

01

02

03

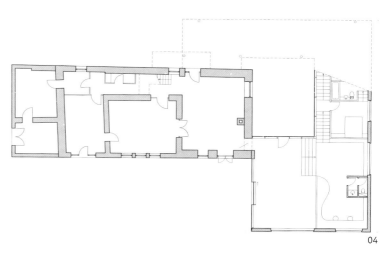

05

04

Spiral House

This typical Burgundy farmhouse is situated on a large site and required an extension that would approximately double the size of the house. The family required a large extension, on both the upper and lower floors of the house. Powerhouse Company designed the extension as a spiral, creating a succession of rooms that connect the more public living room on the ground floor to the more private bedrooms on first floor of the house. The spiral contains a living room extension, a study, two guest rooms with bathroom, a playroom and a child's bedroom. The spiral creates an intimate patio, a sloping roof garden, extending the house, but also extending the family's way of life; creating a continuous 'loop' for living.

01 Entrance | 02 View from garden | 03 Spiral shape creates an intimate patio area | 04 Ground floor plan | 05 View from patio | 06 Side view

06

01

02

The Lighthouse Sports and Events Arena

The new sports arena of Belfort is located on the site of Fort Hatry, a 19th century defense structure. The design of the new building creates a strong contrast to the existing stonewalls. Similar to the fluidity and the dynamics of sports activities, the façade of the sports arena creates a flexible and generous movement through the landscape. The envelope of the building, made of glass, picks up the subtle coloring of the natural light, the sky and the landscape. At night the building is transformed into a bright beacon, fully representing the events taking place inside.

01 Main hall | 02 Ground floor plan | 03 View from southeast | 04 View from northeast | 05 Circulation hallway

03

04

05

01

02

03

04

05

Children's Toy Library

The Bonneuil-sur-Marne children's toy library is a public building as well as a play space for children. It is located in an area where 1960s social housing has had a strong physical and social impact. The architects wanted to create a strong urban symbol able to stand out from its environment, whose shell would protect its core. The architects designed a building that appears timeless, an urban symbol standing out from its environment. The monolithic elevations are closely linked to the surrounding urban context. The result is a bunker-like volume that seems always to have been there.

01 Glazed edge of the building | 02 Exterior view | 03 Inner courtyard | 04 View to inner courtyard | 05 Main play area | 06 3D model

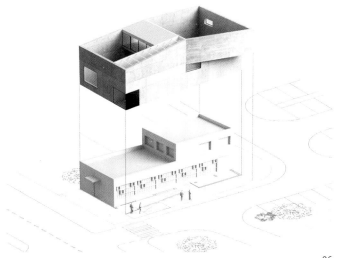

06

01

02

03

04

Seeko'o Hotel

A regular pattern of evenly proportioned openings covers the two façades of the hotel. These windows and French windows ensure a remarkable visual continuity in the extension of the 18th century's façade of the waterfront. The project emphasizes the lack of decoration and the pure, clean lines of its design. The choice of a smooth, abstract outer skin made up of large, immaculately white plates of Corian® creates the strong identity of the project. The final level of the hotel, an attic, is set recessed from the façades. The rooms there benefit from an unspoiled view of the surroundings.

01 Urban context | 02 Bathroom | 03 View from northeast | 04 Hotel room | 05 Front, east, rear elevation, cross section

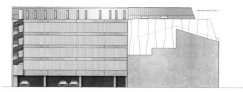

05

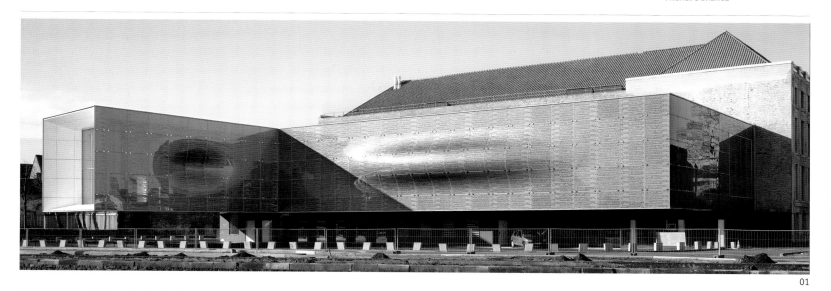

01

Calais International Center for Lace and Fashion

In this project, technology steps aside in favor of imagination and age-old tradition. The new façade of the "City of Lace and Fashion" arouses curiosity. From the canal, it masks the old mill. Like moving images of changing periods, the nearby canal and roads are reflected in anamorphoses on the two façades, one concave, the other convex. Their fine silkscreen patterns, in metallic enamel, reproduce the perforations of the Jacquard weave cards once used on British weavers looms. With the passing of time, these high-tech cards have become artifacts themselves.

01 New glass façade | 02 Master plan | 03 Interior façade | 04 Interior view | 05 Façade detail

02

04

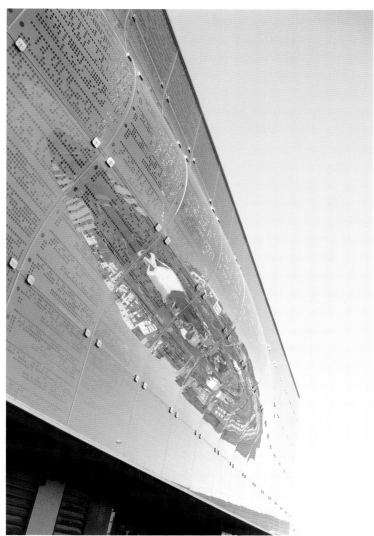

05

01

Albert Camus Multimedia Library

This white Madagascan marble building overlooks a garden carved out of rock, which expands the space and creates perspectives, lengthens distances and eliminates boundaries. Inside, the multimedia library takes up the entire hall. Visitors can see the whole collection at once. A large window overlooks the road and nearby trees. There are also three 'alcoves' – the records room, the music and reading room and an area dedicated to storytelling. These different areas are organized around a long, narrow patio. The flooring is made up of crushed Madagascan marble reflecting soft and welcoming light.

01 Section and elevation | 02 Long patio | 03 North façade detail | 04 Forecourt of southern entrance | 05 Interior view

02

03

04

05

01

02

03

04

Fiteco

The public accounting group Fiteco wished to bring its head office and its local branch together in one area, situated in the suburb of Laval. The French architecture office Colboc Franzen & Associés decided to go further and to design a single building. This resulted in lower construction costs, reduced environment impact and optimal internal organization. All communal facilities are situated on the first floor. The local branch settled down on the second floor and the head office on the third floor. The heart of the building is composed of an atrium, two cores of services, staircase, elevators, restrooms and photocopy room.

01 Corner detail | 02 Atrium | 03 Night view | 04 Exterior view | 05 Section

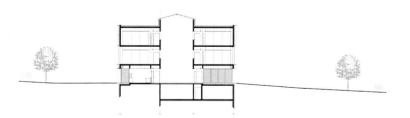

05

01

02

Carré d'Etoiles

Carré d'Etoiles is a window to the sky, an invitation to rediscover nights of stargazing through a pioneering accommodation concept. With its daring cubic structure, this reversible and nomadic tiny house offers a highly original way to sleep in the open, while remaining in a cocoon-style interior. Conceived to meet a demand for 'get away from it all' tourism, it can be used as a holiday home, shelter, guest room, or private studio. Minimalist and environmentally friendly, it is ready to use and features a double-loft bed, a shower, separated toilets, a kitchen corner with amenities, and a lounge with sofa bed, flat screen television, and electric heating. All this in nine square meters.

01 Exterior view | 02 Exterior view at night | 03 Bird's-eye view | 04 Interior view to second floor | 05 View inside | 06 Living room | 07 Elevations

03

04

05

06

07

02

Louis Armand Secondary School

Behind the perforated aluminum-clad façade, a 1,000-square meter atrium with a height of three stories can be found. Each floor has its own color. The colors meet again in the atrium and form a work of art in the style of Mondrian. The architects have managed to establish a connection between the old and new building to enable a stable educational work.

01 Façade | 02 Exterior view | 03 Atrium | 04 Site plan | 05 Atrium | 06 Classroom

01

03

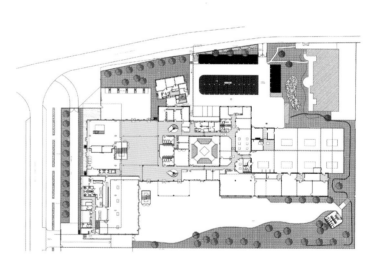

04

05

06

01

Epinay Nursery School

This nursery is located on the edge of a 1970s estate characterized by tall, massive, and rectangular features. With its bright colors and modern look, this nursery is at odds with the surrounding buildings, but entirely in tune with the imaginative world of childhood. The project consists of five entities, all linked to childhood, but each one distinct and requiring its own configuration and access. These small units lie at right angles to the main access road and alternate with strips of vegetation. Each unit has a panelled roof whose slope differs according to the activities underneath. The difference in height and the resulting available internal space are linked to the room's importance.

01 Play area | 02 Classroom | 03 Passage linking different units | 04 Floor plan | 05 Aerial view | 06 View to courtyard

02

03

04

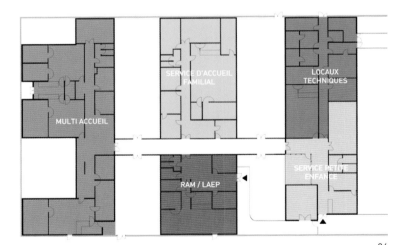

05

06

01

Würth Museum

02

This museum is a new two-story rectangular building made of smooth, raw concrete. The entrance to the 70-meter-long rectangular structure is located on the central line of the building. The laterally positioned exhibition halls are illuminated by two rows of sky lights. An auditorium with 224 seats is situated in the 'blind' center. The raw concrete and the simple white plaster contrast with the art objects. Two light boxes on the flat roof allow daylight to penetrate the rooms. The amount of this light can be adjusted depending on the weather situation. Shutters and artificial lighting can create cold and warm hues.

01 Exterior view during twilight | 02 Main entrance | 03 Exhibition space | 04 Ground floor plan

03

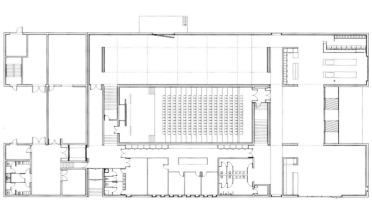

04

01

02

03

Champollion Museum

This museum occupies three buildings in the heritage area of the old town. The screen façade on Place Champollion gives the museum its own identity — it is a metaphor of writing and deciphering of animated alphabets. It represents a 'polyglot typographic moucharabieh', expressing poetic modernity inspired by living vibrating light. The old stone façade ensures continuity of the urban fabric. The screen façade is set back from the alignment and designed as a composition of glass and copper. Between these two façades, loggias are open to the public, and higher up there is a soleilo, a feature borrowed from the vernacular architecture of the region. The depth of the façade forms a public space of transition between the square and the museum.

01 Exhibition with the Mediterranean room | 02 Façade | 03 Detail between the two façades | 04 Elevations | 05 Façade detail

04

05

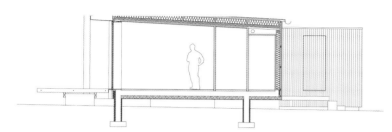

01

02

SLM Residence

The site is a large meadow near an ancient hamlet and its chapel. The simple volume of the chestnut-sided house, its long façade oriented towards the sun, seems to float above the grass. This house, like most traditional farmhouses in Brittany, is oriented south-southeast, with the southerly façade open to the meadow and the sun. Two substantial 'bookends', punctuated by strong horizontal window openings, frame a long wooden terrace that naturally extends the living room and bedroom spaces. The north façade on the opposite side is very different; it is closed and protected against the elements. The attention to orientation and thermal qualities results in a very energy-efficient building, heated by a single wood stove. In this project, wood is used both as wall structure and siding.

01 Cross section | 02 View from southeast | 03 South terrace | 04 Living room

03

04

01

02

03

04

Firminy Church and Museum

In April 2002, the Communauté d'Agglomération Saint-Etienne decided to continue construction of the Eglise Saint-Pierre de Firminy-Vert, an unfinished project of the Le Corbusier site at Firminy. The only one of its kind in Europe and the architect's second most important work after Chandigarh in India, Le Corbusier designed the architectural ensemble between 1954 and 1965 but died before it could be built. José Oubrerie, who had assisted Le Corbusier in drawing up the plans and begun the construction, was also in charge of its completion, marking the crowning achievement of a great human adventure.

01 View of the "bouchon" (cap) | 02 Interior view | 03 South façade | 04 West façade "canon à lumière" (light canon) | 05 Main church floor plan

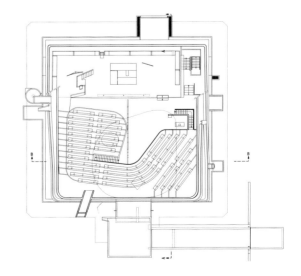

05

01

02

03

Maison en Bois

This weekend house integrates the latest criteria regarding comfort, cost-saving and environmental friendliness. The users can come here to appreciate quiet leisure-time together with their friends. The architecture suggests a mountain lodge as well as a ship cabin. The light structure offers various community rooms and combines functions freely: a bath tub with a view near the oven, an elongated kitchen with direct access to the terrace and a dormitory with hanging bunks. The monochrome natural materials contrast with the colors of the surrounding meadow. Every room affords selected views on the landscape, thus interconnecting the interior and the exterior.

01 Bathroom wall | 02 Interior | 03 Second floor | 04 Exterior | 05 Bathroom under stairs

04

05

01

02

03

04

Ocher Mines Bruoux

This building under a wooden trellis unites all the common features of entrance facilities, like a ticket desk, shop, sanitary units and a refreshment stall. Its orientation responds to the geographical situation and protects it from the dominant western wind. The outer walls, with an openwork wood façade, do not just echo the vertical rhythm of the trees, but also work as a filter for the rising sun. A wall in natural and ocher-colored concrete is positioned against a hill. It constitutes the technical area, including patios that diffuse natural light and a vegetal roof. The wall and the hill are the backbone of the thermoactive system connected to the technical area.

01 Aerial view | 02 Wooden structure | 03 Perspective | 04 Exterior at night | 05 Plans

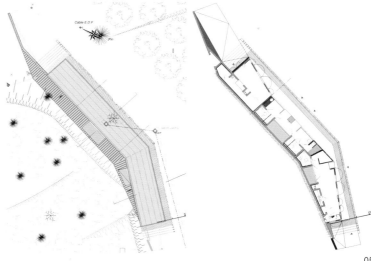

05

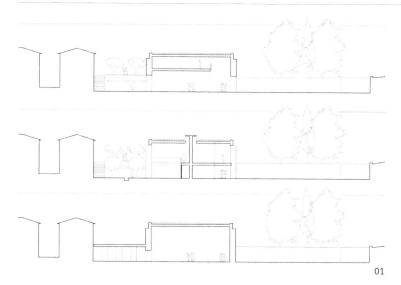

01

02

Solan Monastery Wine Storage

Solid limestone from the Provence is the main building material used for the wine warehouse. It is ideally suited for wine storage and, being mined with a relatively low energy expenditure and with no application of chemicals, it is one of the most ecologically sound materials overall. Stone buildings are raised quickly, produce little waste at the site and their building material can be used again and again. The stone format of the two-story building, which was built by monks, is standardized, and the architecture concentrates on the essentials. Douglas fir roof beams reverberate the play of light and shade on the walls.

01 Sections | 02 Wine storage | 03 Exterior view | 04 Exterior detail | 05 New and old stone façade

03

04

05

01

02

T1 Tower, GDF Suez Headquarters

The T1 Tower was conceived as a giant 200-meter-high glazed surface, curved to the south and cut by a gradual arc on its north face. This new shape, the appearance of which changes depending on the viewer's vantage point, assures its insertion within its complex urban context. Following the sun's path, this giant glazed surface, silk-screened to limit thermal loads, rises in the east to culminate in the south and descend in the west. The tower's geometry provides vast panoramic floor plates at each level. Its design associates quality working conditions and functional efficiency.

01 View from La Defense | 02 Ground floor plan | 03 T1 Tower at night | 04 View from street

03

04

01

EQWater

This project is inscribed in a program of urban requalification for the entry of Issy Les Moulineaux. The building is part of an eclectic existing urban fabric, comprised of three volumes and articulating a transition of scale between the town and Sequana tower. It responds to the tower by means of a game of opposites and proportions in its design: the horizontal is opposed to the vertical, taut lines and the curves of the interior of the hall are in opposition to the elliptical plan and orthogonal distribution of its interior. The façade finds it's expression in the opaque and glazed elements and this, in response to orientation and potential solar gain, creates a unique cladding of the two exterior volumes.

01 Exterior | 02 Typical floor plan | 03 Façade detail | 04 Building at night

02

03

04

01

Microsoft European Headquarters / EOS

02

This 46,000-square meter office development houses the headquarters of Microsoft Europe and the French branch of the European Development Center for Internet research. The solution met the dynamic architectural and strict environmental needs without compromising issues like security and natural daylight. A rectangular prism establishes an urban edge, anchors the development and serves as a buffer from the adjacent railway activity. Three sculpted volumes stand forward reaching out towards the river, appearing as freestanding objects in the composition. The building was awarded the highest possible environmental rating in France and the Eco-Building Forum's Grand Prix award.

01 Exterior from riverside | 02 Three sculpted volumes | 03 View from the street | 04 Façade at night | 05 Master plan | 06 Ground floor plan

03

04

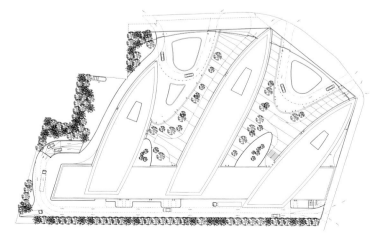

05

06

01

02

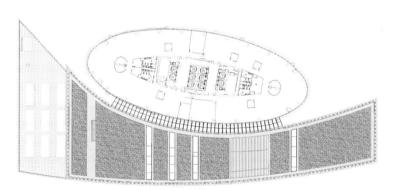

03

04

Tour Bouygues Télécom / Séquana

This 25-story tower has an elliptical form that gives the building multiple fronts. Its softly shaped edges imply a democratic space and a certain sensuality in its relationship to the green landscape that surrounds the building. The elliptical prism is eroded as it reaches the sky, following the angles of the envelope; this results in two angled planes that reveal the curved plan in elevation. The receding floor plates provide additional space that introduce executive floors with smaller footprints and angled glass surfaces that act as greenhouses. The building was awarded the Grand Prix award by the Eco-Building Forum a top international prize for achievements in sustainable design.

01 Exterior | 02 25-story, elliptical tower and extension at night | 03 Typical floor plan | 04 Interior with staircase

01

02

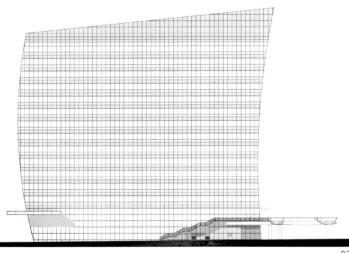

03

04

Exaltis Tower

Exaltis Tower is a new, 15-floor, 23,000-square-meter office building with three levels of underground parking in La Défense. Conceived as a tower of glistening glass, Exaltis defines the axis of the Avenue Gambetta. In form, the building is a rectangular prism that is modified and sculpted by the introduction of two curves along its short façades. These curving surfaces transform the rigid rectangles into fluid forms. The two curves radiate from different points somewhere below the ground and splay as they rise towards the sky. The two end walls present contrasting forms, one convex and the other concave. The result is a building with dynamic quality, implying horizontal movement along the axis of the avenue.

01 Exterior view | 02 Reception | 03 North elevation | 04 View from plaza | 05 Elevators

05

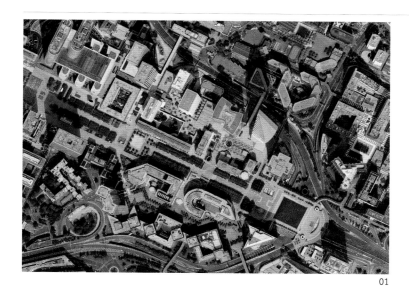

01

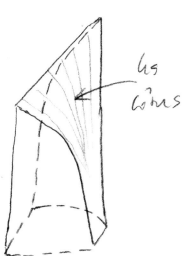

02

Generali Tower

In the district of La Défense, next to the GAN and AXA towers, this proposal for the Generali Tower constitutes a major urban opportunity. The dynamic landmark can easily be spotted from the center of Paris, and offers multiples sight perceptions: oblique lines, curves and a spire reinvent the Paris skyline. The ground floor and the lower levels offer space for a kindergarten, the building hall, restaurants and conference rooms, all of which are conceived as pavilions. Associated with Neuilly - La Défense's housing block, they compose a legible and lively square. The office tower asserts the distinctive scales of the site: the street level, the skyline.

01 Aerial view | 02 Sketch | 03 Exterior view | 04 General view

03

04

01

02

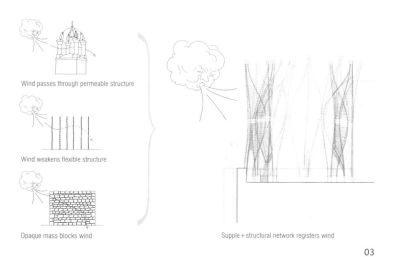

Wind passes through permeable structure

Wind weakens flexible structure

Opaque mass blocks wind

Supple + structural network registers wind

03

Windshape

Windshape was an ephemeral structure commissioned by the Savannah College of Art and Design as a venue and gathering space near their Provence campus. Built by nArchitects and a team of SCAD students, it became the small town's main public meeting space, and hosted concerts, exhibitions, and ceremonies throughout the summer of 2006. The two eight-meter high pavilions dynamically changed with the Provencal wind. Fifty kilometers of white polypropylene string was threaded through the lattice to create swaying enclosures. The string was woven into dense regions and surfaces and pinched to define doorways, windows and spaces for seating. The string responds to the wind in several ways by varying tension to create anything from rhythmic oscillations to fast ripples across its surfaces.

01 Interior view | 02 Detail | 03 Structure diagram | 04 Worm's-eye view | 05 Aerial view

04

05

01

02

03

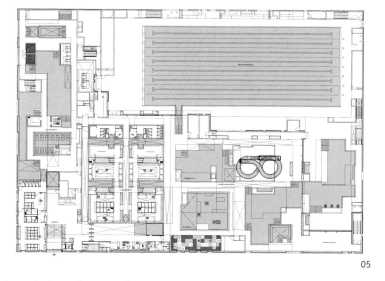

05

04

Les Bains des Docks

This aqua center built along the quay in Le Havre harbor is shaped as a massive metal carapace that reacts to the change of light. Random openings on the façades provide views of the rich interior waterworld. The entrance is located on Quai de la Réunion, opposite the future Seaworld Center. It consists of several spaces in a row that function as initiation filters for visitors on their way from outside to inside. The architects conceived both the entrance hall and various spaces within the aqua center as massive blocks with a surprising and varied geometry that articulates the different water basins.

01 Children and family area | 02 General view of the swimming pool | 03 Mirrored architecture | 04 Indoor leisure area | 05 Plan

The Docks Dombasles

This architects' mixed-use office and housing building is part of an initiative to preserve and reuse the industrial heritage of the southern quarters of Le Havre. Through its scale, rhythm, shape and materials, the project forms an integral part of a re-envisioned harbor landscape. A 19th century brick warehouse, or alvéole, was conserved and incorporated into the project to house the office space required in the program. The warehouse's silhouette and scale subsequently inspired the module that was repeated for the housing portion of the project. The use of modules allowed for a prefabricated construction system.

01 Floor plans | 02 View from park | 03 Terrace | 04 View from river basin

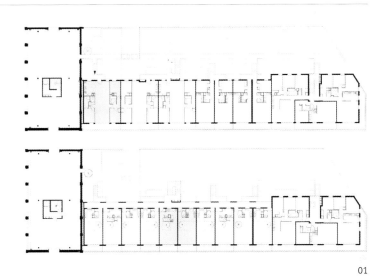

01

02

03

04

01

02

03

Groupe Scolaire Les Géraniums à Lyon

This project involved the restructuring and expansion of a 1960s school building, with the aim of providing a comfortable, functional and modern environment. Existing buildings have been wrapped in a new outer skin; the development of this new thermal layer improves the appearance of the structure as well as reducing energy use and increasing the functionality of the entire building. The building has also been extended at both ends, to the north and to the south, this works to enhance the quality of the space and its flexibility. The wood slats and glass of the façade allow an abundance of light into the school, giving it a light and airy interior.

01 Varied façade structure | 02 Hall | 03 Exterior view | 04 Section | 05 West façade

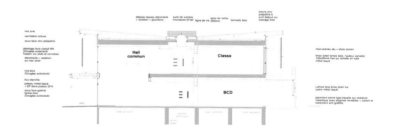

04

05

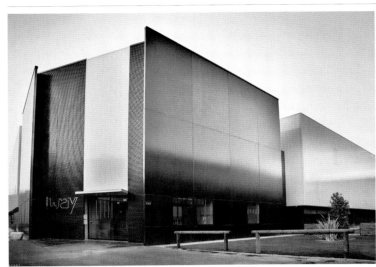

01

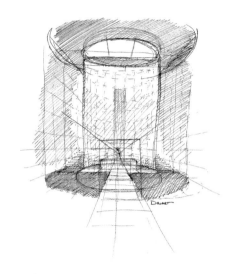

02

03

I-Way

Inaugurated in July 2008 in Lyon, 'I-Way' is an international first. This exclusive building is entirely dedicated to automobile simulations. Simulator technology offers six degrees of freedom inspired by the aeronautics industry, providing the public with access to eighteen machines. Organized around three simulation zones – Formula 1, Endurance, Rally/Touring – the complex also includes a fitness room, alcohol-free bar, bar/restaurant lounge with terraces, two conference rooms, meetings rooms and offices. Light sources, whether visible or hidden, are designed to make every space appear radically different.

01 Façade | 02 Design sketch | 03 Main staircase | 04 Interior view | 05 Lounge and restaurant

04

05

01

The Orange Cube

The ambition of the urban planning project for the old harbor zone, developed by VNF in partnership with Caisse des Dépôts and Sem Lyon Confluence, was to reinvest the docks of Lyon on the riverside and its industrial patrimony, bringing together architecture and a cultural and commercial program. The project is designed as a simple orthogonal cube into which a giant hole is carved, responding to necessities of light, air movement and views. This hole creates a void, piercing the building horizontally from the riverside inwards and upwards through the roof terrace. The cube's light façade, with seemingly random openings, is completed by another façade, pierced with pixilated patterns that accompany the movement of the river.

01 View from street | 02 View from river | 03 Interior view | 04 Floor plan

02

03

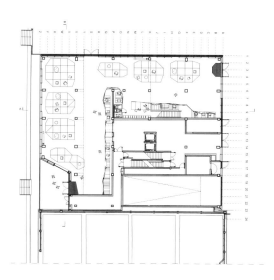

04

01

Le Monolithe

The development of this new inner city quarter, close to the central station of Lyon, can be described as a classical urban plan, with open split blocks occupied by apartments and leading to a sea of similar buildings. By 'gluing' the suggested five blocks together, a possible recognizable element can be introduced: one big block. This figure is divided into five sections. Each part is designed by a different architect and has a differentiated program, infrastructure and façade; from the wooden entrance in the north, a strict concrete interior and a modest dark section, finishing with an aluminum southern section that accompanies the entrance from the basin.

01 Front view | 02 View with bridge | 03 Public plaza | 04 Floor plan

02

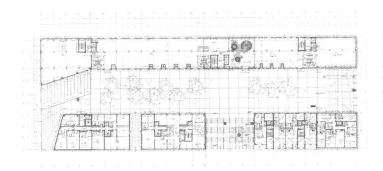

03

04

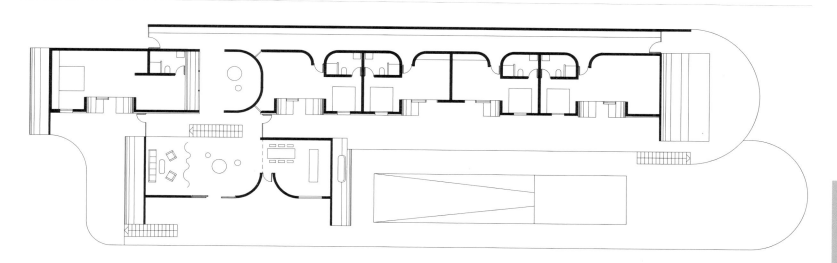

01

La Vague

Located on a southern slope, overlooking the sea at the Esterel Massif, La Vague is gently embedded into the mountains of the Cote d'Azur and takes the form of the waves of the Mediterranean. Layered natural stonewalls and exposed concrete are in line with the typical materials of the region. The floor levels are connected to the flowing landscape by stairs. Over time, the surrounding mimosa forest will grow over the curved roof space. Wide cantilevered roofs offer protection from the hot midday sun. The huge house can be divided into two main levels of up to five units for families, singles or even entire seminar groups. The building is heated and cooled with geothermal energy and the use of the swimming pool as a hot water storage tank.

01 Ground floor plan | 02 Rear side | 03 Overall view

02

03

01

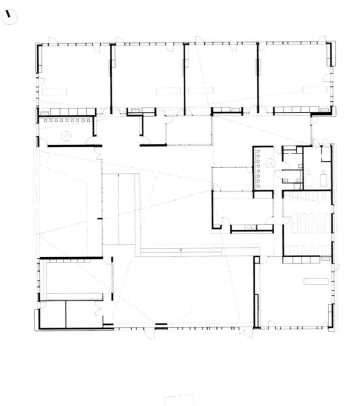

02

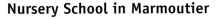

03

Nursery School in Marmoutier

The geometrical simplicity of the building and the widespread use of natural materials reveal this kindergarten's respectful relationship with its environment. Fences are made of dried heather and the grounds are covered in fine sand, while a basin in the middle of the school collects rainwater. All five classrooms benefit from two orientations which allow natural light and ventilation to flow into the rooms. A cell measures the exact quantity of light necessary, thereby eliminating superfluous energy consumption. Aside from the environmental aspects, the spaces themselves are the key concept of the project: they are varied, playful and scaled to the children who use them.

01 Detail of interior roof planes | 02 Classroom | 03 Floor plan and section | 04 Exterior view from garden | 05 Building incorporated into the landscape

04

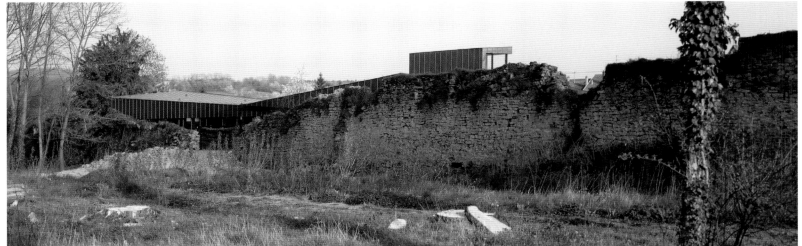

05

01

02

03

05

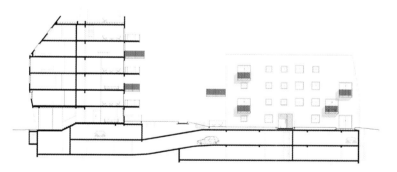

04

06

Housings in Massy

These 70 dwellings are located away from busy routes in the heart of this new district of the city of Massy Palaiseau. The architects did not wish to design a dense, homogeneous city construction, but wanted to create a framework as part of a landscape, situated in the heart of an island. The volumes built are the maximum size allowed by city regulations. The buildings are designed to free up land space and extend the adjoining garden space. The complex is further split into three volumes; these take the appearance of the rocks, placed in a garden.

01 Two volumes | 02 Balconies | 03 Street view | 04 Section and elevation | 05 Facetted façade | 06 Flat façade with balconies

01

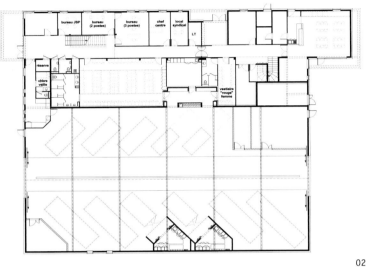

02

03

Meyzieu Fire Station

This building is compact and functional, with the outer areas situated around the core. A large parking area provides ample space for emergency vehicles. The main building houses all service functions, accommodation areas and locker rooms. The architecture is functional but also modern, providing a much-needed alternative to the area's fragmented and heterogeneous architecture. The areas to the north of the site include office space and meeting rooms as well as areas for training and sports. This section has a large circulation area and good views of the surroundings. The fire hall allows direct and fast access for emergency vehicles.

01 East façade | 02 Ground floor plan | 03 West façade detail | 04 West view | 05 South façade

04

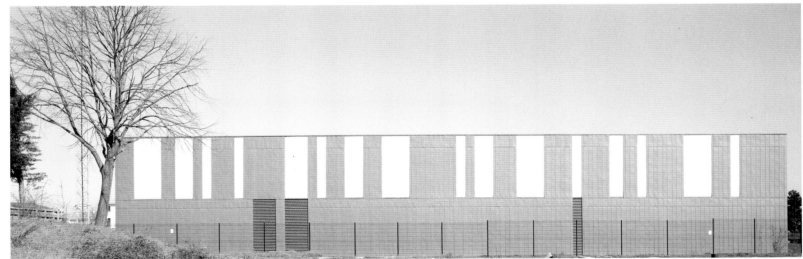

05

01

02

03

04

Atelier Bugatti

In 2005 the production plant of the 1001-HP Bugatti Veyron was opened south of Molsheim in a landscape park with the Château St. Jean (1857) at its center. The flanking outbuildings (from 1788 and 1853) are used for vehicle transfer to the customer, as restoration workshops and as apartments for guests. The whole group of edifices is expanded by the new production building, an oval studio building and three test modules, where the final construction phase of the Bugatti vehicles takes place. The assembly places are located in the middle of the oval with the motor preassembly located in the front end. The building is positioned on a continuous base, which presents the building as if it were floating.

01 Main view | 02 Workshop interior | 03 Motor preassembly | 04 Entrance | 05 Site plan

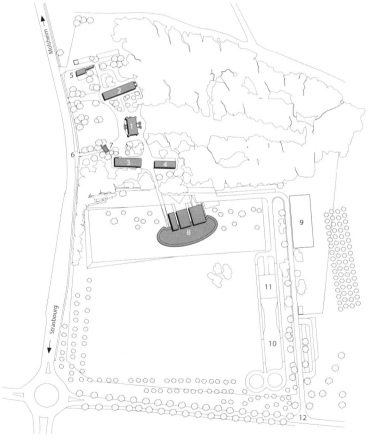

Key:

1 Château	5 Concierge	9 Logistic hall
2 North depot	6 Entrance to Château	10 Test track
3 South depot	7 Entrance gate	11 Helicopter landing pad
4 Orangery	8 Atelier	12 Entrance to atelier

05

01

02

03

Flake House

The Flake House is a nomadic dwelling based on the concept of 'folie'; a wooden structure is broken into two halves, thus establishing a radical spatial boundary and an unusual entry sequence. Combining low- with high-tech features and contrasting the traditional external log cladding with a smooth, stripped down interior, the architects designed a balanced structure that would enhance any possible environmental context. The shape recalls a broken branch with an unconventional scale and this forms the key concept. The house was created in 2006 for the "Petites machines à habiter" competition held by the CAUE 72.

01 External log cladding | 02 General view | 03 Wooden interior | 04 Elevations

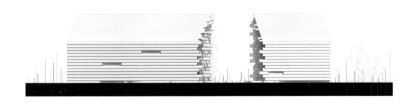

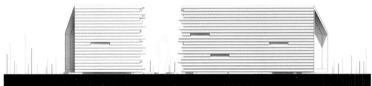

04

01

03

02

Vitam'Parc – Sports, Leisure & Shopping Center

Vitam'Parc is a sports and wellness complex formed by a water park, a spa, a hotel, a restaurant and a shopping area. It is located in the country at the foot of the Salève. This location presented a challenge in terms of the design as a project of this size has to be integrated as harmoniously as possible into the surroundings. The design aimed to recreate the pre-existing topography, made of folds and valleys. Moreover, some of the buildings organically blend into the landscape and thanks to their green roofs appear to be an extension of the surrounding greenery. The materials used, such as wood and ETFE, reinforce this sensation, creating a membrane whose transparency and lightness gives the impression that it is floating above the landscape.

01 Relaxation area | 02 Floor plan | 03 Indoor swimming pool | 04 Outdoor swimming pool | 05 Exterior view

04

05

01

02

36 Apartments + Medical Center

This project is both the physical and political heart of the AUC's redevelopment project for the Courtillières quarter. The aim was to return much needed public facilities to this troubled, urban area. The building represents a commitment to urban rebirth. Defined by the duality of its program, the building provides an important dialogue between public and private, where the housing is enriched by the presence of the medical center and vice versa. Their coexistence is put into evidence by the game of peek-a-boo created by the courtyard at the heart of the building, giving chance views into the inhabitants' daily life and social interaction.

01 Towering volumes | 02 Façade detail | 03 Courtyard | 04 Balcony detail | 05 Section

03

04

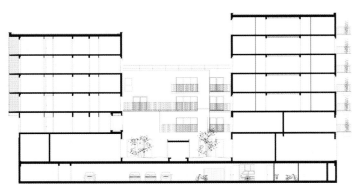

05

01

02

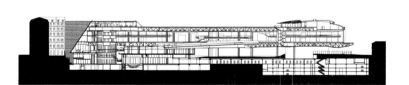

03

04

The Quai Branly Museum

This museum collects various exhibits stemming from non-European cultures which were previously dispersed among the city's various museums. The building is located in a generous garden, and the ground story remains open, allowing the garden sections to fuse underneath the museum. The 18,000-square-meter garden takes up diverse vegetation as its theme. A 12-meter-high, 200-meter-long glass wall shields the park from the busy Quai Branly. The 800 square meters of the exterior and 150 square meters of the interior of the green wall along the west perimeter along Quai Branly bring together 15,000 examples of plants from Japan, China, the Americas, and Central Europe.

01 Vegetal wall By Partick Blanc | 02 Exterior view | 03 Sections | 04 Glass palisade

01

02

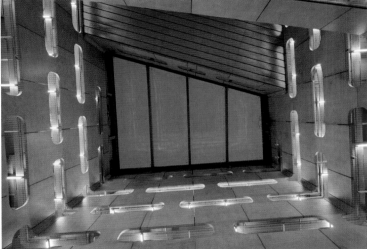

03

04

05

Jussieu University Atrium

The building on the Jussieu University campus completes the grid plan designed by Edouard Albert in the 1960s. As opposed to the original single patio, Périphériques planned two. One of which has bridges raised on piers, creating shortcuts in the circulation route and forming a 'vertical space' that concentrates all movement within the building. The heaviness and hardness of this space contrasts with the light-weight metal cladding of the outer skin, giving the façades complex and variable depth. It consists of panels perforated by circular holes that filter daylight and reflections.

01 View from gallery | 02 General view | 03 View to the roof | 04 Lit façade and entrance | 05 Façade detail | 06 Section

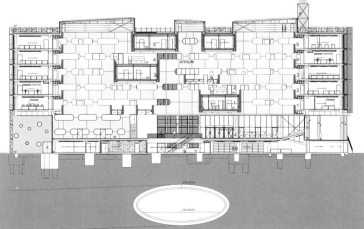

06

01

02

Halle aux Farines

Heavy restructuring was needed to install university facilities in this reinforced concrete market built in 1950. The volumetry of the building was preserved because the envelope structure provides its main strongpoint and architectural interest. The building has therefore been totally preserved, with its towering ceilings, vaulted reinforced concrete shell, and skeleton façades filled with huge prefabricated concrete panels. Only the central bay was entirely emptied to make way for the lecture halls, with no intermediary load-bearing point. These almost back-to-back spaces, which sit inside the existing envelope like a 'ship in a bottle', compose a linear form that is independent of the two side bays and determines an open space beneath the vaulted ceiling in which computer cabins have been installed for the students.

01 View from street | 02 Entrance | 03 Façade at night | 04 Sections and floor plan | 05 Staircase | 06 Lecture hall | 07 Interior view

03

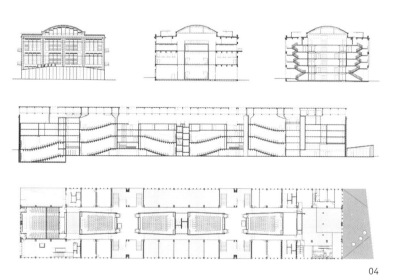

04

05

06

07

02

01

03

04

05

Les Petits Lardons Nursery

An unusual architecture amid one of Paris's first ZAC development areas, the "Les Petits Lardons" nursery extension scheme is based on a maximalist will, spatial generosity taken to the limit. The final volume is merely the outcome of the available space. The building imposes itself in its playful modernity, on the scale of the small child. The structural lattices and opacities are handled by a mathematical reading between the interior and the exterior. Inside, a simple contemporary 'movable architecture' structures the different sections. It is organized in the most sensitive way between ergonomic and programmatic considerations.

01 Building in landscape | 02 View to interior from garden | 03 Detail of side façade | 04 Activity room | 05 Interior view with reflection | 06 Elevation

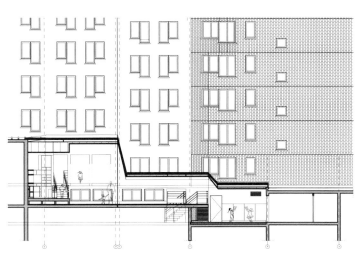
06

01

118 Elysées

AW² was commissioned with the complete refurbishment of an existing office building on the Avenue des Champs Elysées in Paris. The existing façades were completely refurbished, along with all the interiors. The courtyard was modified by introducing a vertical garden, which, in the contrived allowed space, changes both the look and feel of the whole building. This is the strongest feature of the design, which will contribute to a renewed quality of the workspace for all users. The entrance hall was also totally redesigned by introducing a white Corian wall decorated with a backlit plant pattern, which recalls the vertical garden of the central courtyard. All office levels were entirely refurbished, allowing the workspaces to reflect a contemporary and luxurious environment.

01 Courtyard with vertical garden | 02 Office | 03 Reception of the offices | 04 Section

02

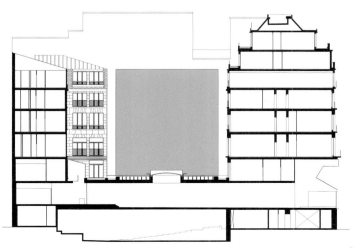

03

04

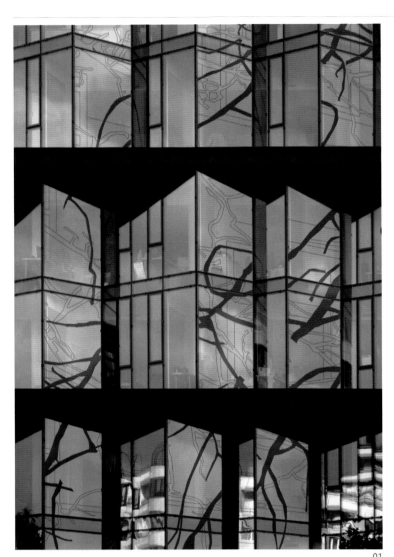

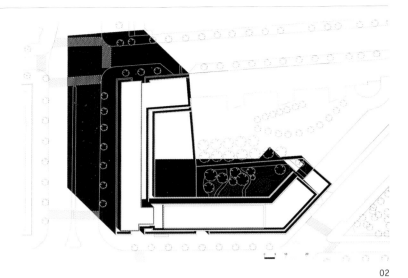

01

02

Cinetic Office Building

A strategic link in the restructuring of Paris's Porte des Lilas, the Cinetic office building respects the area's symmetry and assumes the role of a gateway between Paris and the contiguous suburbs. The project presents different strongly identified façades matching the styles of the nearby buildings, in particular the northwest façade which is distinguished by its innovative, irregular, folded patterns. The folds facing north on the suburban side are made of clear glass, while those facing west on the Paris side are made of silk-screened glass, serving as the medium for a work by artist Elisabeth Ballet, representing a close-up of a chestnut tree and its branches.

01 Silk-screened glass detail by Elisabeth Ballet | 02 Plan | 03 General view

03

01

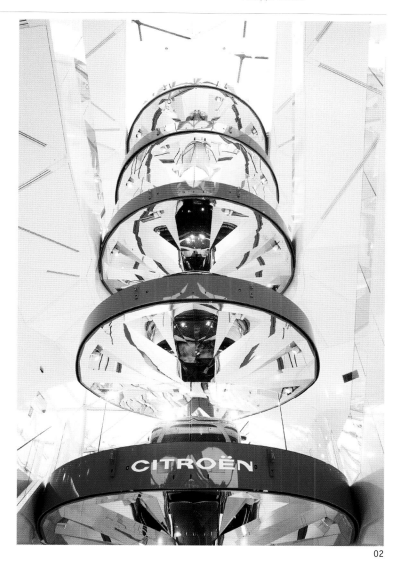

02

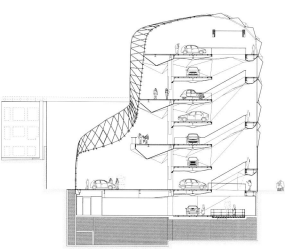

03

04

C42_Citroën Flagship Communication Center

This project is a gigantic upright display around which visitors move in a spiral movement via stairs and landings. At the top, the sculpture offers superb views up and down the avenue, over the city, and across the nearby gardens and river. The cars are displayed on revolving circular platforms under a faceted mirrored ceiling that fragments and multiplies their lines and details. The skin is of faceted glass and plays on the distinctive shape of the Citroën logo – the chevron. At street level on the Champs-Elysées, the façade begins as a simple flat curtain wall. The glass front unfolds like a gigantic origami.

01 View from the Champs-Elysées | 02 Upright display | 03 Cross section | 04 Reception desk | 05 Top of the building

05

01

02

03

04

05

Eden

This project comprises 100 new apartments and ateliers for artists, some new community rooms and a small, renovated restaurant. The density of the program is situated in the center of the site, along the original alleys, where maisonettes and buildings with vegetal façades face each other. The new ensemble can be seen as a contextual patchwork made of red shingles, timber pillars, zinc, whitewash and exposed concrete. Every house has its own façade, its own cladding to differentiate it from the others. The whole ensemble is held together by a ribbon of red shingles that wraps around it. The stairs lead to two apartments on each level, each apartment has a window on both sides and a balcony oriented due south.

01 Stairs to apartments | 02 Houses differentiate in height | 03 Every house has an individual façade | 04 Elevation | 05 Corridors of greenery

01

I'm lost in Paris

This project involves the design of a private laboratory. 1,200 hydroponic ferns are used in the design, together with 300 glass beakers. These are designed to harvest the bacteria Rhizobium, which increase the percentage of Nitrogen without the use of chemicals or manure. The beakers add to the uniqueness of the design and bring extra light to the area by refraction. Large windows and a glazed door in the rear of the building offer views onto the closed courtyard. The green wall of the courtyard and additional greenery are watered with collected rainwater, fed with a mechanical drop by drop system.

01 Greenery detail | 02 Exterior view | 03 View from inside | 04 Diagram

02

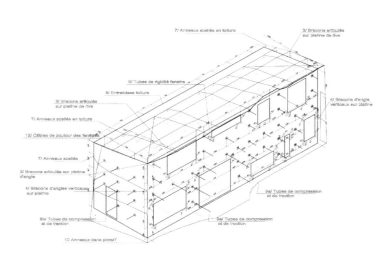

03

04

01

Children's Recreation Center

This new children's recreation center in Pierrelaye is an extermely ecologically-friendly project. The construction includes an new public space and a play area for children, which offers learning materials about form and color. At the center of the bulding is an open space, allowing lots of room for movement as well as being functioinally flexible. The exterior has a bright and cheerful appearance, suitably fitting its function. Ecological aspects of the project include double-flow ventilation, the use of solvent-free paint and incorporated research into the study and protection of glass façades.

01 Façade | 02 Exterior view | 03 Hall | 04 Site plan | 05 Group room

02

03

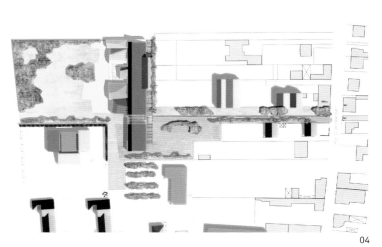

04

05

01

02

03

04

Library in Proville

The new mediatheque of Proville opens onto the village and becomes a place of exchange and culture, a public library and a surprising and enthusiastic place inviting everyone to the pleasure of reading. The idea was to create a contemporary building dealing with the environment and the existing elements. The mediatheque has a metallic frame clad in wood that will turn gray as it ages. Large aluminum windows let in lots of natural light, allowing the users of the library to communicate with the town. The roof, overlooking the church tower and the trees, can be used as a terrace for reading outdoors.

01 Exterior view | 02 Roof of the library | 03 Office space | 04 View inside from roof | 05 Ground floor plan | 06 Interior

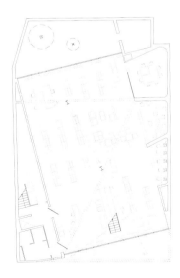

05

06

01

02

03

Provins Police Station

Located on a triangular parcel next to the entrance of the city, the Police Station of Provins is part of the creation of a new civic center. The outside of the base consists of a concrete wall covered with local white stone and a greenery-covered roof, which gives the building a softer appearance. The more confidential quarters are wrapped in thick concrete, pierced here and there with window openings, allowing an abundance of light to flood in. The front is glazed, dressed with copper slats angled slightly downwards, making it an extension of the roofing surface. Its treatment, in contrast with the thick mineral sheeting of the other three façades, emphasizes the frontal aspects of the police station.

01 Front façade | 02 Exterior view | 03 Hall | 04 Ground, first and second floor plans | 05 Façade

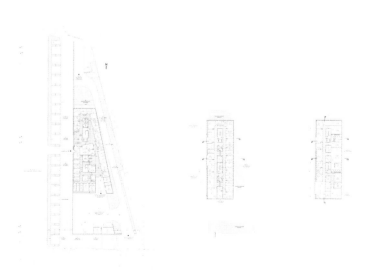

04

05

01

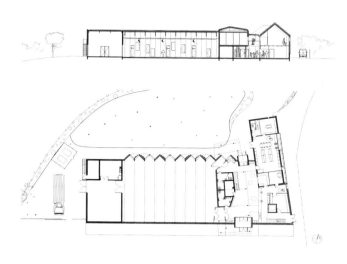

02

03

The Pays de Rennes Ecomuseum

Within its strong natural context, this project's wooden façade reflects the nature of the ecomuseum inside. The extension of the existing building includes the new entrance hall and the temporary exhibition, built in timber framework and timber cladding. On the southern side, the timber framework extends down an ecological concrete wall base, tinted with natural pigments. Above this, the timber cladding is made of natural wood shingles arranged in graphic patterns. Pillars are made of raw tree trunks, though most of the site's trees have been conserved.

01 Entrance hall | 02 Cross section and ground floor plan | 03 Entrance hall with reception desk | 04 Entrance | 05 View from north | 06 Side view

04

05

06

01

02

03

Pathé Gaumont

This project is situated in Rennes, close to the new train station and to Champs Libres, another project inaugurated by Christian de Portzamparc in 2006. The multiplex, with 13 theater rooms, is part of the general organization of the esplanade Charles de Gaulle (urban master plan by Nicolas Michelin). The project is structured by a transversal grand hall, which leads to two floor levels. The hall was designed to give shape to one of the front façades on this esplanade. Its architecture consists of large horizontal planes and slanting lines which reflect daylight. At night, the gradients of the artificial lights create a dialogue with Champs-Libres, further emphasized by the similar materials and volumes of the newly constructed building. The concrete was developed in a special way with architectonic moulds designed by Christian de Portzamparc and the sculptor Martin Wallace.

01 Aerial view | 02 Perspective | 03 Side façade | 04 Entrance | 05 Section and floor plan | 06 Front view

04

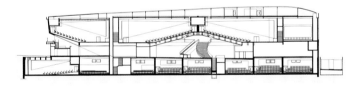

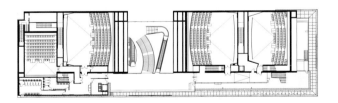

05

06

01

02

03

04

05

Rouen Convention Center

Located in the ancient commercial harbor, this project focuses on the extension of an old storage hangar between the railroad tracks and the Seine River, providing space for an auditorium and exhibition spaces. In the middle of the building, a large mashrabiya captures and diffracts light. At night, the lattice becomes a lantern emerging from the floor beneath the hangar's frame. The auditorium sits partially beneath the old hangar, a concrete structure independent of the existing building frame. The surprise lies at the end of the room, where the back wall of the stage opens, and the harbor is invited to join the conversation – to a greater or lesser degree, depending on the rotation of the vertical blinds.

01 Mashrabiya staircase | 02 Auditorium | 03 Mashrabiya staircase detail | 04 Darkened auditorium | 05 Exterior view | 06 Section

06

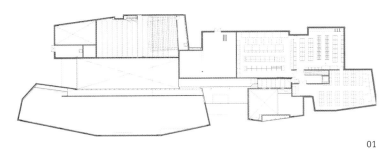

01

The Grande Lande Ecomuseum

The main highlight of the "Pavilion des Landes de Gascogne" building project is the development of a contemporary architecture which references the local context. Despite an impressive surface area and an amorphous architectural form, it is integrated without colliding with its environment. It is in sync with the linearity of the tracks, the volume of the neighboring detached houses and the façades of the traditional sheds. According to the different angles of view, it can be seen as a unique building with supple and broad forms, or as a whole made of several buildings whose masses echo the buildings of the railway station and of the town of Sabres.

01 First floor plan | 02 Exterior view from west | 03 View from south | 04 View of temporary gallery | 05 Large glazed section in temporary gallery

02

03

04

05

01

02

La Cité des Affaires

This site offers a vital liaison point between the center of Saint-Etienne and the new Chateaucreux neighborhood, to which it forms a major entranceway. The project is like a large 'Aztec serpent' rising on the lot. Its body has three identical outer faces, and an underside that is different: a skin of silvery transparent scales and a bright yellow 'throat', shiny and opaque. This dual treatment of surfaces obeys a simple logic shared throughout, which aims at expressing clarity in folds. Depending on these movements, the yellow underside is either a floating canopy or an interior vertical wall, accompanying internal pedestrian movements with its rich luminous presence.

01 Façade | 02 Night view | 03 Perspective | 04 Longitudinal section | 05 Interior view | 06 Entrance

03

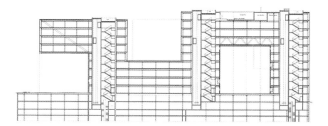

04

05

06

01

Zénith Music Venue

The Zénith is a state-of-the-art music and cultural facility for Saint-Etienne which places the former industrial city on the cultural map, forming the heart of an exciting project aimed to revitalize the area to the northeast of the city center. On the outside, it is characterized by a large, cantilevered roof which utilizes the valley winds to assist natural ventilation and cooling. A broad ramp provides access to the glazed foyer which spans across a busy road and houses the artists' and backstage facilities. The plazas in front of the building and the foyer are shaded by a deep overhang of the roof canopy. Inside, the venue offers flexible performance space and auditoriums which can be configured for capacities that range from 1,100 to 7,200.

01 Front view | 02 Canopy | 03 Roof | 04 Auditorium | 05 Floor plan

03

02

04

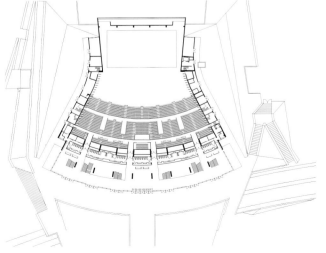

05

01

Gymnasium Pierre Mendès France

This project is part of an ambitious development that has various functions, including residential elements, a nursery school and various landscaping elements. The building is compact and makes optimal use of the limited space. It is wrapped with a modern façade that establishes a direct relationship between the building and its environment through the positioning of window openings and entrances, which are positioned to collect as much light as possible. The main hall shares a visual connection to the other areas and offers ample space to serve its purpose as sports hall. It also includes technical elements such as lighting and heating panels and basketball facilities.

01 General view | 02 Façade detail | 03 Interior of sports hall | 04 Ground floor plan | 05 Corridor

02

03

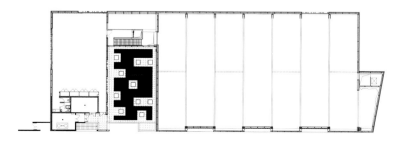

04

05

01

Alvéole 14

The submarine base of Saint-Nazaire is a raw and impressive structure, transformed with minimal interference. Two of its former cells were turned into cultural elements: LiFE and VIP. The hall for the international center for emerging art forms (LiFE) is a minimalistically equipped 'Monospace', situated in a former submarine basin and opened up towards the harbour. VIP, a venue for contemporary music, occupies one of the volumes inside the bunker. On the roof, a geodesic dome from the Berlin Tempelhof Airport serves as a 'think tank' for art and music projects. A newly defined street with an enigmatic atmosphere traverses the entire base. It creates interaction between the various already existing spaces and the newly created ones.

01 General view | 02 Interior view | 03 Site plan

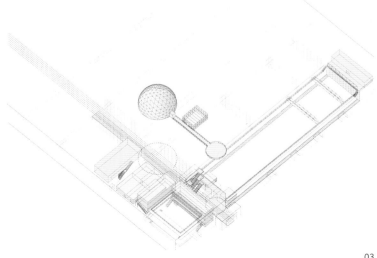

02

03

01

02

Zénith Music Venue

This building is an autonomous sculpture. The design gains dynamism from the layering and rotating of the ellipsoid metal façade structure. This is underlined by the translucent textile membrane which covers the steel-frame and creates magnificent light effects. Projections on the outer skin create playful effects and convert the façade into a billboard communicating upcoming events to passersby. The building's daytime appearance has a monolithic calmness that mutates at dark. The inner experience is transmitted to the outside through the transparent skin – the building becomes a 'light sculpture'.

01 General view at night | 02 Foyer | 03 Auditorium | 04 Floor plan up to level two | 05 Façade detail

05

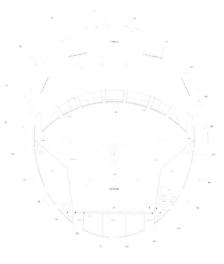

04

03

01

02

André Malraux Library

The river landscape demands to be understood horizontally. Everything in the setting complies with the logic of the river – the linearity of the quays, the stretch of the jetty, the alignment of the trees. Even the buildings themselves are lined up from one end of the jetty to the other, perfectly regular in their continuity parallel to the quays, vertically punctuated at their ends, like prows, by their silos. On this long tongue of land surrounded by water, it is less the buildings that define the space than the relation between them; the succession of masses and voids, the play of horizontals and verticals, the axes, as well as their strict alignment with the quays.

01 General view | 02 Interior view | 03 Section | 04 Reading room | 05 Layering

03

04

05

01

02

03

04

New General Building of the Council of Europe

This new office building stands as a monolithic building which is visible from the canal and the city. The glazed façade presents a softer appearance towards the city, while a totally different façade faces the countryside. The primary concern was the occupants' comfort and intelligent individual control of interior space. The project utilizes the benefits offered by sun and wind orientation, the presence of water and greenery, underground conditions and the temperate continental climate to increase comfort and reduce running costs. The office building features meeting rooms, a crèche and a landscaped garden.

01 Exterior view | 02 Atrium | 03 Entrance at night | 04 Conference rooms | 05 Scheme of solar chimneys

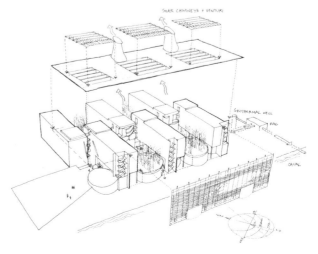

05

01

02

GO-House

Organized in three levels over a below-ground parking garage, this building has outline glass 'profilit' façades that offer thermal isolation as well as intimacy. This translucent envelope is slanted and the levels are shifted in relation to each other. The windows in the walls behind the profilit panels often do not follow their outline, being organized to best accommodate the rooms and views from the house. A zinc roof continues the glass wedge metaphor. The house can be accessed from the street by a ramp; near the main door, a large stair leads to the first floor, four and a half meters above.

01 View from street | 02 Bathroom | 03 First floor plan | 04 Construction

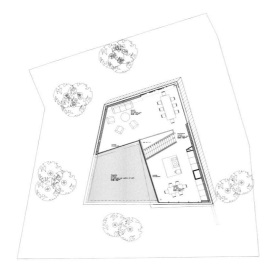

03

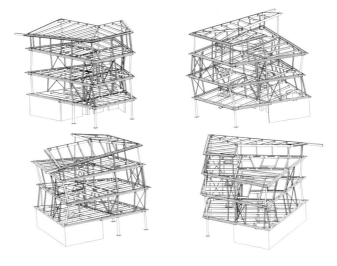

04

01

02

03

04

Valbonne 2.0

This small house divides the functional area across two open levels. The living and bath-room are situated on the lower level and direct access to the outside and the main house is possible from the living space. The sleeping areas and a roof terrace are situated on the upper floor and a table is incorporated into the wall, offering a space for reading or writing, with a view into the garden. The house is more open towards the southeast; large glazed surfaces and oak-framed sliding windows create a direct relationship to the garden. The different façades and roof openings provide a variety of different lighting and formulate individual zones in the space.

01 Façade | 02 Staircase detail | 03 Exterior view | 04 Interior view | 05 Floor plans and sections

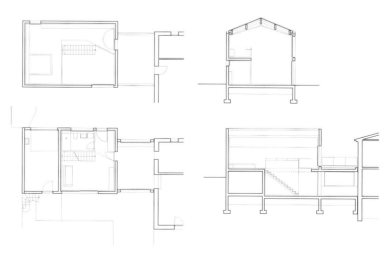

05

01

02

03

04

7 Houses

Situated less than two kilometers from Paris, this building complex is located at the end of a cul-de-sac. To ensure the privacy of each unit, the houses are juxtaposed, not on top of one another and not overlapping. The organization of the volumes ensures long diagonal views between residents, in contrast to the frontal relationships that one might have feared in such a situation. Invisible from the bottom or from directly opposite, huge light boxes illuminate the double-height of the first floor living spaces from directly above. The austerity of the exteriors gives no hint of the generous natural lighting of the houses or of the habitability of the rooftop.

01 Terrace | 02 Exterior view | 03 Façade | 04 Interior view | 05 Section

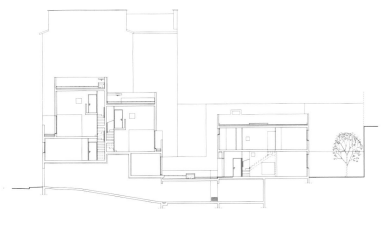

05

01

02

2+2 Houses

This project is settled at the back of a nice private wooded plot. The construction branches into the landscape. The project could be modified in the future, by joining the four apartments to form either one unit or two. The entrance walkway leads to the central patio, a common space that gives access to the four units that comprise the 2+2 Houses. The ends of each wing are twisted, following the natural restrictions of the surroundings. The space is flexible, liberated from any technical constraints to make any future change in the use of the house easier. The architects have used a metallic frame, which adapts to the site and respects the differences of height or dips and hollows in the ground.

01 Night view | 02 Patio at night | 03 Wings | 04 Ground foor plan | 05 Detail house | 06 Patio | 07 Detail living room

03

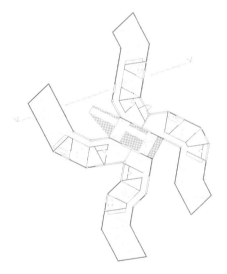

N

04

05

06

07

01

03

02

LAM

LAM is the Lille Métropole Museum of Modern, Contemporary and Outsider Art. Rather than install the new section at a distance, the architects chose to wrap the extension around a corner of the 'old' building. The project, for the Communauté Urbaine de Lille, aims to reconstitute the museum as a continuous ensemble, by adding new galleries to house a collection of Art Brut works in a travelling movement that extrapolates existing spaces. The architecture of the extension wraps around the northern and eastern ends of the angular brick building in a double splay of long, fluid and organic volumes. On one side, the new wing extends in narrow folds to contain a restaurant opening onto a central patio, while on the other, it extends in larger folds, each of which houses one of the five Art Brut galleries.

01 Exterior | 02 Night view | 03 Model (1/200) | 04 Interior of the extension | 05 View of patio

04

05

01

02

CIPA Haaptmann's Schlass Berbourg

This integrated residential and residential care home for senior citizens (CIPA) in Berbourg will be developed with a residential area of 72 rooms and further infrastructure. The extension consists of three, two-story pavilions grouped around a common courtyard and another section, connecting the old and the new buildings. At each level the pavilions offer space for 12 rooms, rooms for nursing staff and a communal area with cooking facilities for the residents. Inside each of the pavilions lies a landscaped atrium which is accessible from the common room on the ground floor. The rooms are located on the external façades facing east, south and west and have views across the valley.

01 Residential area | 02 Corridor | 03 Elevations | 04 Corridor along courtyard | 05 Courtyard | 06 West view | 07 South view

03

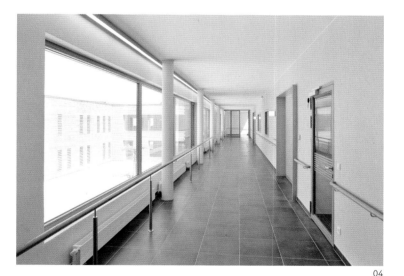

04

05

06

07

01

02

03

Children's Day Nursery and Pre-School Hamm

The two-story nursery and pre-school was constructed of timber frames as a low energy building. The upper floor contains plant rooms, in which the children can harvest plants from a variety of continents including coffee, bananas and pineapples. A covered recreation hall is open over both floors and has an energy regulating effect: the special planting has a positive impact on air quality and micro climate. An information board in the hall displays the current supply of energy produced by the photovoltaic elements on the roof. The constant visibility of the energy values aims to raise the awareness of the children to the issue of renewable energy.

01 Foyer | 02 Detail façade | 03 Interior planting | 04 Floor plan | 05 Exterior view | 06 Front façade

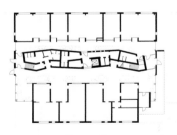

04

05

06

01

02

03

04

05

C.N.I. Syrdall Schwemm Recreational Baths

This swimming pool includes different worlds of experiences. In addition to a large swimmer's area, outdoor pool, deck areas, slides and children's area, visitors can relax in the sauna, spa and restaurant. As a visible sign, a compact, dynamic structural shape floats above the large glazed swimming hall. The golden façade relates to the property's description "On the Sand" and becomes a bright eye-catcher. The sculpted nature of the exterior flows through the building and continues into the pool area. The swimming pool offers an optimal combination of a user-oriented architecture with high quality and atmospheric choice of materials, as well as an energy optimization.

01 Glazed façade | 02 Exterior view | 03 Interior view | 04 Dynamic structure floats above glazed swimming hall | 05 Swimming pool | 06 Ground floor plan

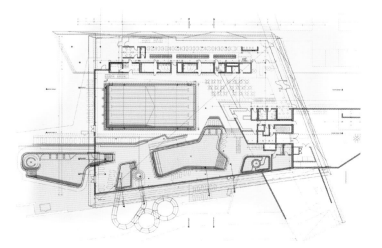

06

01

Fire Station Alkmaar

This building is characterized by a complex structure, partly resulting from the necessary proximity of the fireman's rooms to the depot, in a volume that must conform to stringent town planning conditions. A design was chosen that runs from its abutment with council offices up towards the railway tracks. It rises to a height of about 20 meters and accentuates the entrance to the city center. There is parking on the roof, invisible from the ground floor. The visible, strong slanting line on the front and back of the building forms the access ramp to the parking area. LIAG and the municipality Alkmaar joined forces to devise a plan for a sustainable and energy efficient building.

01 General view | 02 Ramp to rooftop parking | 03 Façade | 04 Site plan and section

02

03

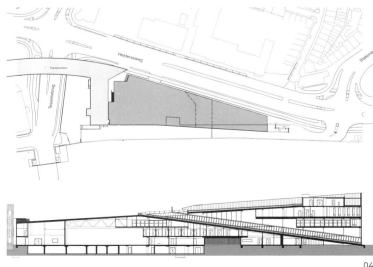

04

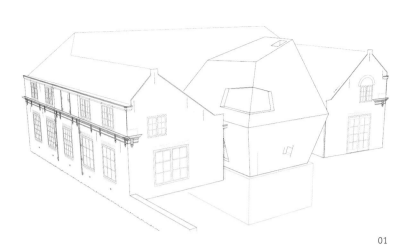

01

Van Alckmaer voor Wonen Office

The housing organization "Van Alckmaer voor Wonen" occupies a new office in the center of Alkmaar in the former "Stadtstimmerwerf", which dates back to 1600. In 2003 the office and the organization were transformed, so Klous + Brandjes Architecten used the analysis of the organization and the building history as the basic principle for the design of the office. This resulted in the removal of obscure annexes and the restoration of the U-shaped head structure. The organization needed a larger floor area than the old building could provide, so a new development was required. This resulted in a diamond-shaped volume that responds to and contrasts with the environment while imperceptibly connecting the old with the new.

01 Draft sketch | 02 View from Oude Gracht | 03 Interior view

02

03

01

02

Schuurman Headquarters

The headquarters of the Schuurman Group, an electro-technical firm, is situated in a prime location alongside the A9 highway. To profit from the qualities of the location, the building is designed as a sculptural freestanding object; conceptually the volume has uplifted corners with huge glass sheets, to accentuate the special functions of the program. The strong lines of the exterior give the building a distinctive expression and allow the landscape to flow through the building. On the top floor a patio-garden brings light deep into the building, providing a visual and physical link between the offices and the warehouse-area. The newest sustainable measures have been incorporated, forming a green environment.

01 Front façade | 02 Patio | 03 Interior view | 04 Second floor plan | 05 Staircase

03

05

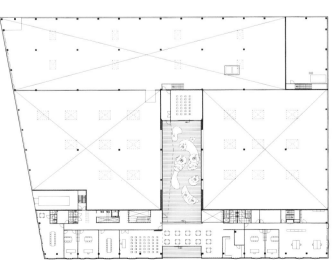

04

01

02

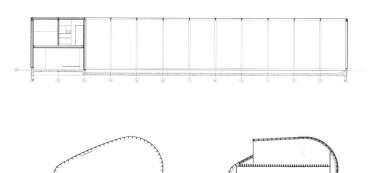

03

04

Sheep Stable

The city of Almere has a sheep population of about 80 that keep Almere's 'bears-breech' weeds under control. The stable has an asymmetrical homogeneous layout. The sheep's part of the building is relatively low; with the high part situated above the pathway and the hay storage section. This shape creates a natural airflow; as the air enters through slits at the foot of the long sides of the building. The construction and cladding are made of wood, the curved girders of steel, and the vertical inner walls are clad in beech plywood. On the second floor there is a room for the shepherd and a small office.

01 Façade detail, shepherd's rooms | 02 Interior view beech plywood | 03 Sections | 04 General view with entrance | 05 Front view

05

01

02

03

De Citadel

Located at the heart of the new town of Almere, the dual-purpose block, designed by Christian de Portzamparc, fits into Rem Koolhaas's multi-layered urban plan. The block is fragmented by the crossing of two pedestrian high streets built onto a structural plate, which accommodates the public car network and parking below ground. Above the high streets, colorful houses are distributed around a large convex meadow, preserving the intimacy of the inhabitants.

01 Pedestrian area | 02 Exterior view | 03 Façades | 04 Colorful houses | 05 View from roof | 06 Aerial view | 07 Crossing over the streets

04

05

06

07

01

02

03

The New Library

This new public library is situated in Almere's new city center. The block accommodates several different functions: apartments, retail and offices. But, the principal function is the library unfolding in a succession of spaces, which together form a route of around 400 meters in length. Glass walls throughout allow contact to be maintained with the outside world, while the light wells and garden provide contact between the different parts of the building. The building has a figure-of-eight ground plan and the combination of several loops gives the library its clarity and flexibility. In the elaboration of the façades and interior, the building was treated as a monolith and emphasis was put on the spatial experience.

01 Main entrance | 02 Exterior view | 03 Night view | 04 Reading garden | 05 Interior view | 06 Main hall

04

05

06

01

02

03

04

Kaboutergarage

Block 11, a garage with 413 parking spaces, is part of the expansion of the city center of Almere-Buiten. The plan is characterized by a lot of green, a clear urban structure, and many experiments on innovative materialization and new constructions. The unique façade of the garage contains natural elements, like integrated plant containers with specific prlants related to the orientation of the façade. By using a thermoforming technique – commonly utilized in the automotive industry – the perforated façade panels show characteristic images of the province of Flevoland, like birds, windmills, garden gnomes and birdhouses. The perforation supplies natural ventilation in the parking garage and creates an open atmosphere, especially at night.

01 Plant container | 02 Exterior view | 03 Façade detail | 04 Night view | 05 Ground floor plan

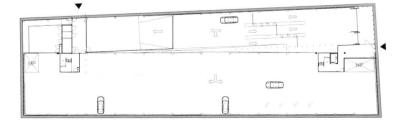

05

01

02

03

Villa Overgooi

This five-in-one villa was designed under commission by Villa van Vijven residents' collective, a group of five private clients. These five dwellings have been created with the outward appearance of one villa. Each individual dwelling is designed in such a way that it has the same qualities as a freestanding house, namely an outside view in all directions. Moreover, the villa is elevated, allowing each dwelling a view of the Gooimeer from the second floor viewing rooms. In each dwelling, the first floor has been turned a quarter-turn, this gives it a view of the street but also to provides access to the elevated garden on the southwest side. Underneath the building is a collective plaza, which all the front doors open on to.

01 View from street | 02 Terraces connecting first floor with elevated garden | 03 Interior view | 04 Elevation and section

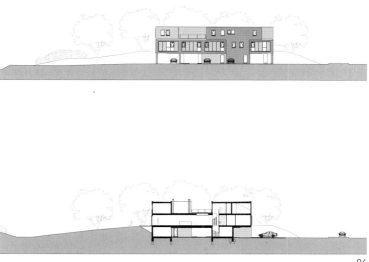

04

01

02

Esprit Head Office Benelux

The Esprit Head Office Benelux is a sustainable mixed-use building, consisting of three layers of showroom spaces and offices. The landscape is lifted and extended into the building, creating a welcoming and transparent entrance and restaurant area. An oblique-shaped volume forms the superstructure, with windows carved in lopsided shapes. Aluminum plating forms a filigree, free formed pattern in relief. Large boulders carry the volume and anchor the building in the landscape. The interior is dominated by a large monumental staircase connecting the three floors, leading to the patio on the top floor. Voids and skylights bring transparency and openness to the building, reflecting the philosophy of the company.

01 Main entrance | 02 Evening view | 03 Interior view | 04 Second floor plan | 05 Main staircase

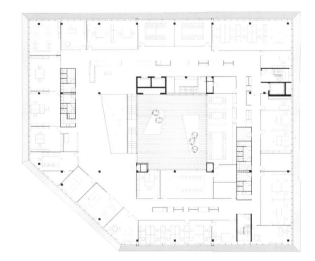

03

04

05

01

02

03

04

Amsterdam Public Library

The new city library will be the centerpiece of the Oosterdokseiland, a redeveloped area in Amsterdam. The total built area is 28,500 square meters and is located in an urban envelope with a volume of about 40 meters in height, 40 meters in width and 120 meters in length. The library was designed as an interior meeting place and an easily discernable landmark in the Amsterdam townscape. Form, function and technique are inextricably linked. The materialization of the exterior in natural stone continues in the the interior. The library is one of the three European ECO Buildings and received various awards, among them the WAN Award Public Building of the Year in 2009.

01 Atrium | 02 Reception area | 03 Southern façade | 04 Workstations | 05 Design sketch

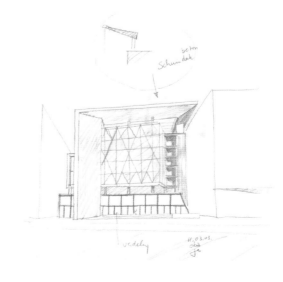

05

01

02

03

Bijlmer Park Theater

This cultural building consists of an ellipsoid, with the upper two floors slightly displaced in relation to the ground floor. This creates a covered entrance area located in a logical position within the routing of the plan's urban development. The building's shape necessitated the search for a financially viable way of reproducing this rounded shape in the façade, partially of glass. The solution was found by pairing wooden slats and vertical aluminum strips against the steel-and-glass sections of the façade. As a result, the intersection points of the segmented façade are invisible, and the building exhibits a rounded, dynamic and somewhat abstract appearance which changes continuously as you walk around it.

01 Façade | 02 Exterior at night | 03 Interior view on first floor| 04 View into auditorium | 05 Foyer | 06 Axonometric projection of floors

04

05

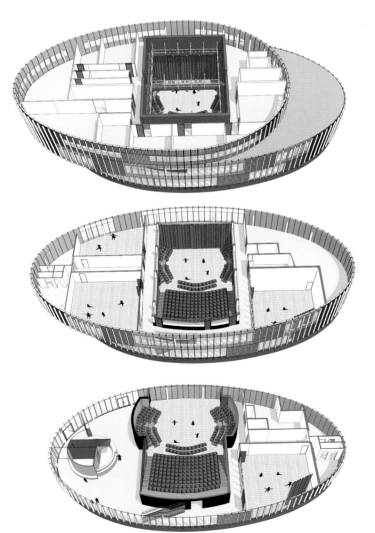

06

01

02

Library of Special Collection

This complex includes the University Museum and the special collections belonging to the university library. The crux of the plan is an 'interior street', which gives the complex a new main structure. This feature endows the cluttered rear of the buildings on the side of the Binnengasthuis grounds with an ambience worthy of a traditional court. The solar court doubles as a glass case for displaying the obliquely placed back section of the building – a physical reminder of the site's medieval land division. The narrow old gateway, the Gasthuishofpoort, has become the new, architecturally spruced up entrance with a tall, narrow light court topped off with a glass roof.

01 Exterior view | 02 Courtyard façade | 03 Rosenthaliana Library | 04 Site plan | 05 17th century brick arch

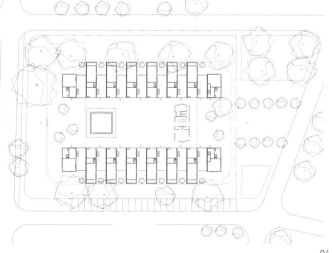

03

04

05

01

02

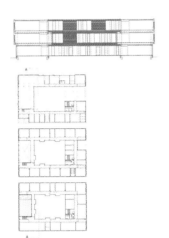

03

04

Secondary School No. 4

In 2008 HVDN architects designed the Secondary School No. 4 building in Amsterrdam. This modular building is located in the Houthavens. Because of a number of innovations, the building is not only moveable, it also has technical and aesthetic qualities and a level of finishing that are similar to permanent traditional construction. The 4,100-square-meter school building was completed in six month and is characterized by expressive colors and a smart routing.

01 Schoolyard | 02 Exterior view | 03 Section and floor plans | 04 Hall with view to yard | 05 Interior view | 06 Schoolyard

06

05

01

Booster Station South

Booster Station is a public utility building covering a pumping-engine for sluicing out sewage. The building is a reference to a streamlined engine. The aerodynamic skin is an envelope for the building's technical elements, and the building reveals its ducts to emphasize the relation between form and function. The constant stream of passengers perceives the Booster Station as a futuristic sculpture. With its cladding of stainless steel panels it reflects the movements, shapes and colors of its environment. At night the illuminated seams in the steel skin make the building look like a mesh-model.

01 General view | 02 Aerodynamic skin | 03 Façade as a mesh | 04 Metaphorical link to a streamlined engine | 05 Plan | 06 Exterior view at night

02

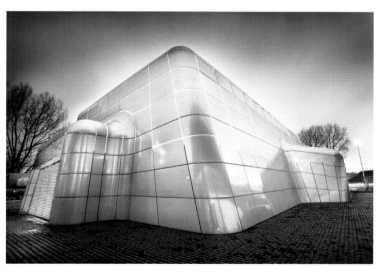

03

04

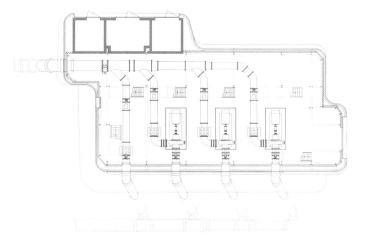

05

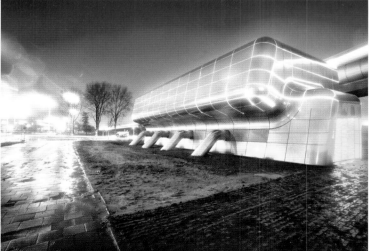

06

01

02

03

04

Open Café-Restaurant

Open café-restaurant is a pure, transparent, glass volume that fits precisely onto the existing bridge. It is composed of a floor, a roof and a glazed façade formed entirely bofpivotal windows, all of which can be opened. The pivotal windows add a subtle refinement to the principle of the purist, modernist box, introducing the quality of elegant, undulating movement. Two detached green volumes inside contain the kitchen, cloakroom, toilets and bar. A pleated wooden ribbon meanders along the inside of the glazed façade, constituting benches, a bar with seating, and railing. A staircase and a lift attached to the no longer functional brick pillar on the quayside provide access to an outdoor serving area on top of it.

01 General view | 02 Platform | 03 Detail windows | 04 View from river | 05 Ground floor plan

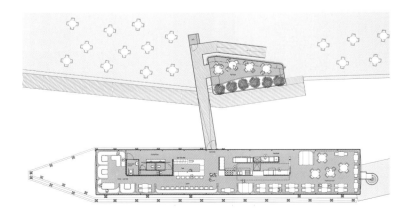

05

01

02

03

IJburg House

The 140-square-meter house is located on a small plot in IJburg; a recently developed suburb in the city of Amsterdam, and is designed as a vertical garden in a densely ur-banized area. Closed private spaces contrast with open collective spaces, creating a sense of depth and mass. Three bedrooms, a small bathroom and a 'multipurpose hall' are situated on the ground floor, while the first floor remains completely open, flooded with daylight. The façade contains special brick detailing inspired by techniques from the famous Amsterdam School style from the 1920s. Hedra, kiwis, grapes and apples will overgrow the house and create a 'natural curtain' around it, uniting nature and culture in a unique way.

01 View from the street | 02 Front view | 03 Green façade | 04 Living room | 05 Interior detail

04

05

01

02

03

The Blue House

Steigereiland, near Amsterdam, is the location for Pieter Weijnen's experimental wooden home. The house, painted a vibrant blue, refers to traditional houses of nearby Durgerdam, where spaciousness is the keyword in the design. The ground floor consists of a roomy live-in kitchen, and upon entering the house, a lounge hanging from the ceiling like a floating island is present. The shape has been interpreted as a boat or basket, giving the space below a homely atmosphere. To ensure stability, old docking poles were used as diagonal braces behind the front wall. The glass façade facing south allows plenty of daylight and heat to penetrate indoors, while air-conditioning is based on an ancient Arabian system.

01 Exterior view | 02 Dining area and underbelly of living room | 03 Floor plans | 04 View to hanging living room

04

01

DJ's Garden

In a former sewage treatment plant that was converted into a residential building with seven apartments in 1999 by De Architectengroep, a penthouse has recently been extended by an extraordinary roof terrace – including a pavilion – called DJ's Garden. By utilizing the entire roof area, the living space has been doubled. The pavilion has the character of a fully-fledged room with garden view and can be used in many different ways, from its vantage point in the middle of a 'green roof' with plants, mosses, sedums and a pond. Thereby the necessity of the gravel roof of DJ's Garden has been turned into a delightful roof garden with a flexible and sheltered outdoor area.

01 Bird's-eye view | 02 View from the pond | 03 Top floor

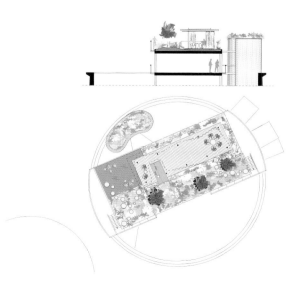

02

03

01

02

03

04

Multifunk Residential, Office, Kindergarten

Multifunk is a flexible building that can easily change its functions. It can be gradually transformed from a residential building into an office building and vice versa. Since the complex consists of a fixed structure that can be freely filled in, the flexibility of the concept not only leaves room to mix or alternate functions, but it can also meet the different needs for space that these functions require. The building stands on Steigereiland which forms the main entrance to a new city quarter with mixed-use area for housing and offices. It mediates between these contrasting areas. The recycled material corresponds to the second life that the Multifunk building can and will have by definition. KLP, the unique material by Lankhorst Recycling, gives the complex both an exclusive and an informal feel. The plastic is environmentally friendly, durable, maintenance-free, splinter-free easy to apply and doesn't contain any harmful substances.

01 Façade detail | 02 Detail plastic cladding | 03 General view | 04 Northeast façade | 05 Concept sketches

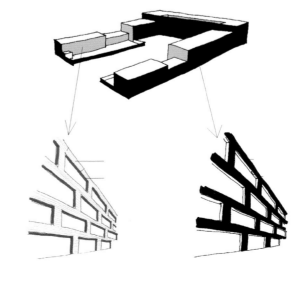

05

01

02

03

04

05

06

Atradius Headquarters

With its dynamic sculptural design, the new insurance bank headquarters is a conspicuous eye-catcher. An innovative office concept that is immediately observable from the outside was developed especially for this building to encourage communication and human contact. 'Space to meet one another' was the theme on which the spatial organization of the requirement plan was based. Areas in which employees of different departments can meet one another in an informal atmosphere were created by arranging 11 voids across the building in the shape of green atria. These atria, which differ in shape and height, are intended to serve as municipal parks, connected by stairs, or tree-lined squares.

01 Staircase | 02 Central atrium | 03 Restaurant | 04 South view | 05 Competition sketch | 06 View from courtyard

01

02

Kraanspoor

The lightweight office building was built on top of a concrete crane dock in Amsterdam's old harbor. The new construction, with 270 meters of length, offers a phenomenal expansive view of the river IJ and the old city center of Amsterdam. Fully respecting its foundation, the building is lifted by slender steel columns three meters above the dock. To help minimize the weight, a light-weight steel structure in combination with a thin floor system was chosen for the new development, reducing the total building weight nearly by half. Ecological claims are fulfilled by a double-glazed climate glass façade across a concrete core used for the infrastructure and floor, as well as hydrothermal heating and cooling.

01 View of stairwell | 02 City view from inside | 03 Elevations and sections | 04 Stairwell with dock | 05 View from waterside | 06 Stairwell and entrance

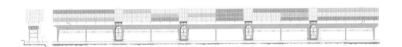

03

04

05

06

01

Oost-Watergraafsmeer District Office

These district offices are located in a building with a stepped gable on the south side that mediates between the different heights of the complex. The new façades are made partly of brick and partly of stone. Four original façades of buildings from the gasworks have been retained on the south side. Two of the original plant buildings have been restored to accommodate the art library. The community school is located in a new building with an entirely different syntax of long, horizontal bands of windows and an arched entrance. The transition between public and private spaces in the complex is seamless. The building encloses two long, semi-public areas, one of which is covered.

01 Interior of Center for Fine Arts | 02 Ground floor plan | 03 General view

02

03

01

02

MTV Networks Benelux

In 2007 the carpentry workshop on the former NDSM shipyard was transformed into the bustling headquarters of MTV Networks Benelux. The 1927 monument was to be fused with today's high-tech world. Inside the stripped hall, a detached concrete frame consisting of four layers is fitted with a new thermal wall, about one meter behind the existing masonry and single glass walls. One half of the new building contains the recording studio with the directors' offices on top, between the roof structure and skylights. The other half contains the various business units, on four floors around the entrance hall with a large void. The cantilevered glass restaurant gives the building a new front to the river IJ.

01 New thermal skin behind original façade | 02 Northwest façade with cantilevered restaurant | 03 Seating | 04 Central hall | 05 General view | 06 Original roof construction | 07 Ground floor plan

03

04

05

06

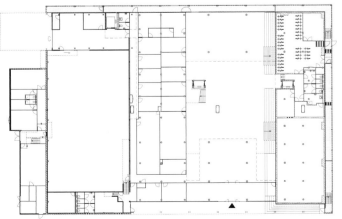

07

01

02

Parking Garage P23

The construction of Parking Garage P23 offers around 400 parking spaces and is a part of the restructuring of Amsterdam Zuidoost, where particular attention was given to the Amsterdamse Poort shopping center. The fundamental idea was to provide a sustainable, socially responsible and safe design. The high staircases allow light to enter the building but also act as 'night lights', illuminating the area around the garage. Perforated plates on the approach to the ramps create a lively light display, and this view is affected by the headlights of inbound and outbound cars.

01 Exterior view of entrance | 02 Ground floor entrance to parking level | 03 Ramp | 04 Section and floor plan of parking level

03

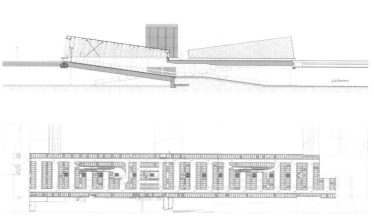

04

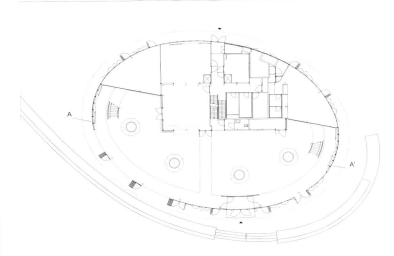

01

02

03

Jinso Pavilion

The original building consisted of an elongated, two-story box measuring 20 by eight meters. The concept eventually evolved into a transparent glass oval, more than 12 meters high and measuring 43 meters length and 30 in width. The façade consists of cold-bent insulation glass, which was bent on-site and placed by means of suckers. On the ground floor, the façade can be opened over more than three quarters of its length by means of a facetted folding wall in which every separate part has a different radius. The roof is more than two and a half meters high and comprises eight large pneumatic cushions mounted on a refined detailed steel construction of facetted deltabeams.

01 Ground floor plan | 02 Interior view | 03 Façade | 04 Exterior view

04

01

De Bomentuin

The Slotermeerhof is one of multiple locations within the Western Garden Cities of Amsterdam that is being renewed as part of a large-scale urban operation. The project is situated on the site of a former apartment complex belonging to a residential home for the elderly. The new ensemble consists of two apartment buildings and two rows of family houses. The whole complex is three stories high. Each floor is reflected by prefabricated concrete strips in the brickwork and by the horizontal lines of the balustrades. The ground floor apartments and terraces are slightly raised from the garden level in order to optimize the view of the green surroundings. The choice of brickwork combined with wood, concrete and the soft colors of the frames, allow the project to fit naturally into the neighborhood.

01 Block A at night | 02 Street view Block A | 03 Front view Block C | 04 Site plan

02

03

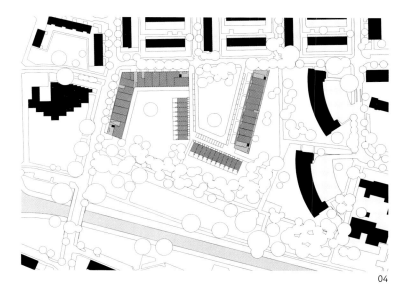

04

01

02

03

House on Steigereiland

In 2006 the clients were informed that they have been allotted a plot on the Steigereiland on island IJburg. This design by Emiel Lamers Architectures complies with building regulations but also develops the size of the building envelope to the absolute maximum. The two-story house is 15 by six meters. A small playroom is situated downstairs, next to the entrance hall and is connected to the three-meter-high living area and open kitchen by a window. Four bedrooms and a spacious bathroom are located on the upper floor. A frosted window, positioned on the side of the house, provides plenty of light for the landing. The house was built within a short timeframe, with a pre-cast concrete building system.

01 Overview | 02 Rear façade | 03 Living room | 04 Ground and first floor plan

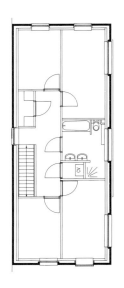

04

02

01

03

04

Blok K / Verdana

Blok K is part of a master plan for 550 dwellings by Frits van Dongen of de Architecten Cie. It is part of 16 blocks that are referred to as 'hidden delights'. The ten units within the building are organized according to a 'back to back' system and are accessed from a corridor in the middle of the block; all have direct access on street level. Water and gas meters are located towards the interior hallways and stairs, tucked away into the darker areas, allowing the façades to benefit from the light and view of the park. In order to optimize the urban envelop, all dwellings are deformed, but the blocks keeps it's initial total volume. By shifting the access alley all units are both stretched and compressed, either in height or length, but each still has the given volume of about 630 cubic meters.

01 Bird's-eye view | 02 Entrance | 03 Roof | 04 Exterior view | 05 Section

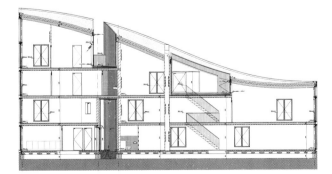

05

01

02

Het Funen

Het Funen is a former industrial yard, bordering on a sports ground, at the interface of the inner city and the Oostelijk Havengebied. Taking into account the ambitious nature of the substantial program, a complete new architectural concept was developed for this site: living and working in inner-city densities combined with sufficient green space. The inner area consists of a park-like landscape with a great diversity of smaller building typologies – each with its own identity and program – these are concealed there as 'Hidden Delights'. To ensure the diversity and to emphasize the exceptional quality of the area, the 'Delights' were designed by various architects.

01 General view | 02 Exterior view | 03 Façade | 04 Section | 05 Interior view

03

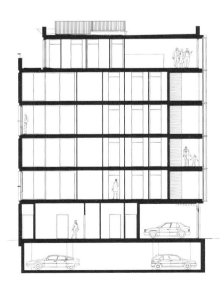

04

05

01

02

03

04

OZW VU University of Amsterdam

The OZW healthcare and welfare training institute is a new landmark for the architectural landscape of the VU University. It embodies an innovative training concept that combines intermediate and higher level vocational training programs and university programs. The window spacing emphasizes the verticality and main lines of the exterior and immediately draws attention to the transparency and vitality of the interior: a playful combination of training centers around atria. The private offices are at the far ends of the building. The public base is transparent and the volume of the lecture hall catches the eye. The training institute is a playful landscape to roam in, see and meet people.

01 Exterior view and playing field | 02 Interior view | 03 Atrium | 04 Auditorium | 05 Section

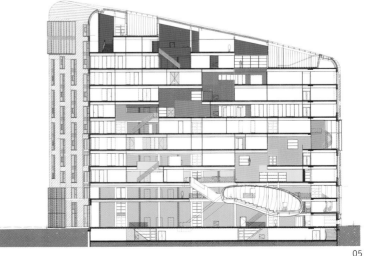

05

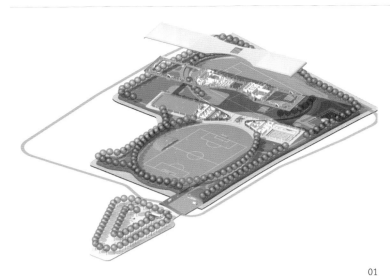

01

02

Ronald McDonald Center

The Ronald McDonald Center is a sports center for disabled children. The terrain and buildings serve grandstand and sports functions at the same time. The center of the complex is the clubhouse, which is wedged between the two oval arenas. The clubhouse offers views of all outdoor and indoor activities. The clubhouse, trees and grandstand stairs around the arenas provide a sense of an ever-present audience. The center has many innovations such as pools with movable floors, drowning detection system, lockers with fingerprint recognition and the world's first sports floor with LED lines. The entire project was made possible by sponsoring.

01 Axonometry | 02 Pool | 03 Sports hall | 04 Exterior view | 05 Front façade

03

04

05

01

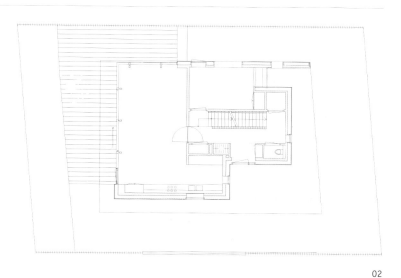

02

03

Villa Rieteiland Oost

This villa is located on the artificial island of 'RieteilandOost' in Ijburg, an extension of Amsterdam. All houses on this island are detached. The house is oriented towards the surrounding vegetation, giving it a strong sense of privacy and openness. The residence consists of three floors. The façade has the maximum height permitted and acts as the back of the house, turning it to the courtyard. From this large façade the building mass slants downwards to the side where the residence has an open character with large glass windows and the creation of loggias and roof terraces. Fitting the complete sloping roof with anthracite solar panels enhances the abstraction of the villa.

01 Exterior view | 02 Ground floor plan | 03 Living room and kitchen | 04 Exterior view at dusk

04

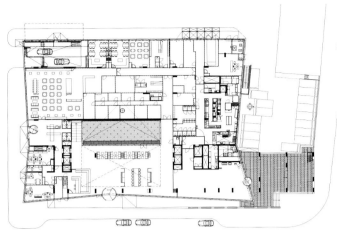

01

02

Casa 400

The unique feature of the Casa 400 concept is the combination of student housing and its use as a commercial hotel. Students live in the 370 hotel rooms from October to May. From June through September, these same rooms are rented as hotel rooms in the three-star category. The development of 150 permanent hotel rooms is one of the new additions to the existing casa concept, aside from a brasserie that is also designed for passersby, a spacious conference level with 12 meeting rooms in different sizes and the necessary conference facilities to accompany them, as well as a large area for students where they can cook and eat in groups. Casa 400 has been awarded the Green Key eco-label.

01 Ground floor plan | 02 West façade | 03 Indoor garden | 04 Exterior view

03

04

01

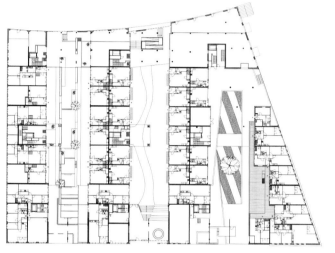

02

03

La Grande Cour

MVSA designed the spatial master plan for La Grande Cour. The dwellings are organized around three courtyards. Large openings ensure that most dwellings have views through the courtyards and make it possible to deliver a pleasant living environment despite the high density of 300 dwellings per hectare. For the same reason, the tall buildings were designed as 'periscopes' that cantilever above the perimeter buildings to focus on the panoramic views. Three different architectural firms, MVSA, Heren 5 and De Architekten Cie, designed the architecture of the block. Each area includes a courtyard and it is here that the individual architectural styles are most in evident.

01 Courtyard | 02 Ground floor plan | 03 Courtyard and periscope | 04 View from south |
05 View from southeast

04

05

01

02

03

Floating Catering Building

Waterstudio designed the Floating Catering Building for a company that takes care of the catering for the canal boats in Amsterdam. The building is situated in the single canal in Amsterdam. The roof, end walls and ground level form a continuous line framing the working area and office and accentuating the entrance and elevator by bending down in the middle. The kitchens are situated partly underneath the water level. The elevator brings the food to the ground floor level. By using materials like aluminum, glass and metal shutters the building has been given an industrial look. The big glass façades show the lime green interior that brings the color into the building. At night this gives a nice green glow over the water.

01 Waterfront view | 02 Bird's-eye view | 03 View from shore | 04 Floor plans

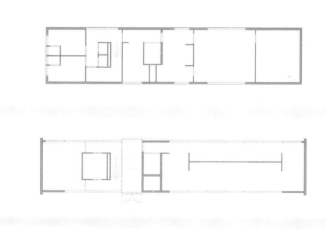

04

01

02

03

04

Watervilla de Omval

This tautly designed houseboat floats in the Amstel river of Amsterdam. The design is contemporary without losing the characteristic appearance of the typical houseboat. The clients wanted a boat with an open floor plan where they could enjoy the water and the outdoor space to the max. The distinguished curved line of the façade derives from this desire and is also due to the restriction that the boat couldn't be more than three meters above the waterline. A sun terrace could only be realized by lowering the roof of the watervilla. The white plastered walls and ceilings follow the curve of the façade, creating a seamless transition from the exterior to the interior.

01 Night view | 02 Central staircase | 03 View of Amstel river | 04 Waterfront façade | 05 Façades and sections

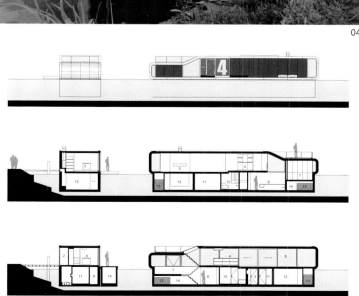

05

01

Walterboscomplex

This project involves the expansion of the Inland Revenue Department. It was immediately evident that the spectacular view across the forest could make working in these high-rise blocks attractive. This feature became the main theme within the design and resulted in the flowing, asymmetrical form that prevents the panorama being obstructed by the existing office buildings. The space around the core is free to be laid out according to the users' preference and can be arranged as an open-plan office or as separate rooms. The façades are constructed of glass and stretch from floor to ceiling. For sun shading, and also to give the buildings more expression, special awnings with synthetic slats were developed.

01 Exterior view | 02 View outside | 03 Third floor plan

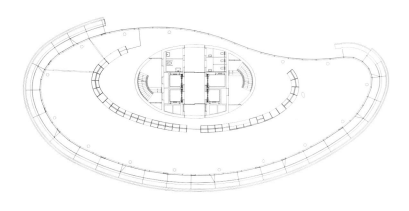

02

03

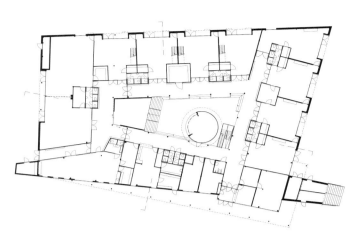

01

De Uitkijck

This center for education and childcare houses a primary school and two organizations for baby- and childcare. The building is planned around an open central space used by all parties and containing a yellow, cone-shaped volume with the libary and a small theater. Organized by age, the building houses the younger children on the ground floor and the older children on the first floor with its French balcony. A sloping roof gradually rises from one to two and a half stories, creating more space in some sub-level floors and a dry main entrance. Both inside and outside, wide stairs lead from the ground floor to the first floor. These stairs are also used as galleries during events.

01 Floor plan | 02 Side view | 03 Lobby | 04 Front façade

02

03

04

01

02

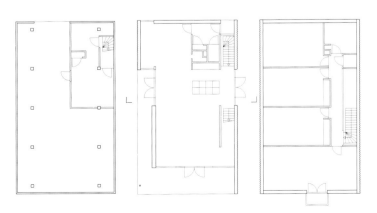

Dijk House

This unique barn house design has made a modern statement in its small town of just 1,500 homes. Overlooking water and surrounded by a magnificent landscape, this contemporary design comes in the form of an old-fashioned barn with a newfangled twist. Wrapped in clear 'skin', this house features a roof and façade of anthracite-colored corrugated sheets, strategically placed so as to allow entry of natural light and the surrounding views. Inside, this barn house features a 'soft' look with walls clad in light woods, and a spacious layout. The home's basement level is slightly above ground, creating a podium and placing the main level one meter above the ground, lending it a unique floating feeling.

01 Front façade facing garden | 02 View from waterside | 03 Interior view | 04 Floor plans

03

04

01

02

03

04

Het Turfschip

The redevelopment of the Turfschip area included the construction of a mega movie theater, a fitness center, offices and an underground parking garage. The area is conveniently located near the historic city center within easy reach of its commercial, cultural and recreational activities. The cinema foyer, with its glass drum-like façade, can be used as a giant projection screen. Seven theaters are housed in the building, serviced by one central control room. Both offices and apartments are located in the 12-story zinc clad building on the east side. The lower elongated building on the west side houses luxury apartments. The apartments and a low-rise housing block wrap around the cinema. The central axis leading towards the main entrance is accentuated by the pavement, which resembles a giant carpet.

01 Façade | 02 Inside rounded façade | 03 Front view | 04 Interior view | 05 Third floor plan

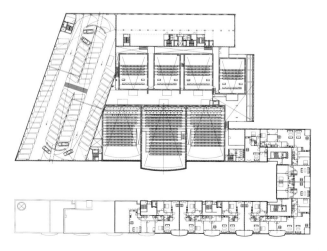

05

01

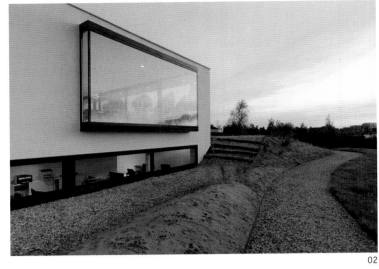

02

House S

House S is located on the edge of the Asterdplas in Breda's Haagse Beemden district. The living area is raised above the surrounding land, optimizing the view of the natural environment. Further solidifying the home's connection to nature, large floor-to-ceiling windows frame the view, while giving the house a light and transparent character. Since the residents work from home, employees and customers are regular visitors to the house. Private and business rooms are separated in an ingenious manner, whereby they touch but never cross. The working space is partly situated below ground and fitted with a horizontal window, allowing excellent views and generating a bright, naturally lit lower level.

01 View from beach | 02 View to cantilevered window | 03 Exterior view | 04 Sections | 05 Living room | 06 Sundeck

03

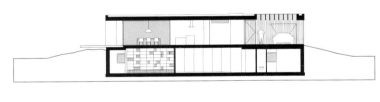

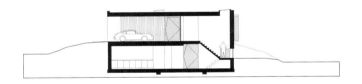

04

05

06

01

02

House KVD

The residents expressed a desire to experience the green environment of the Teteringen woods in the most intense way possible and this ambition formed the main concept of the building. The house blends in with the trees, giving new and surprising perspectives on the forest from every angle. A partly raised square volume embraces an open court-yard containing the entrance. Framework on the outside of the building filters direct sunlight and creates a 'cut out' view of the forest, while intensifying the sculptural char-acteristics of the volume. The façade is formed of vertically fitted, black stained wooden sections. The ground floor houses living rooms, with bedrooms on the first floor.

01 Exterior view from garden | 02 Side view | 03 Exterior view | 04 Bedroom | 05 Floor plan |
06 Living room with double-height ceiling

03

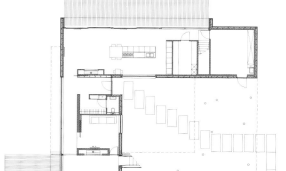

04

05

06

01

Fuiks Eten en Drinken

MIII architecten have designed a restaurant on the site of the former Vuyk shipyard in Capelle aan den IJssel. This distinctive building is an overdue reminder of Vuyk's long and remarkable tradition of master craftsmanship. The wooden structure, marine lining and carpentry as well as the sloped, angular surfaces lends this building its dynamism and nautical feel. The key concept here was to envelope a building encased in a wooden coat. The smooth wooden cladding alludes to the master carpentry of the past. The open front coping has several advantages above a closed one; for example, wind can freely flow along the front end of the building, and by doing so, naturally dehydrates these parts while also ventilating the rear. For the wooden cladding, MIII chose scraped laths of Oregon pine.

01 Rear view | 02 Exterior view | 03 Roof detail | 04 Floor plan

02

03

04

01

02

Datacenter

Beneath racing Dutch clouds, green glass sparkles in the grey concrete of the new data center on the campus of Delft University of Technology. Functionality, security and the need for a short construction period determined the basic form and materialization of this design. By examining and using the potential of prefab concrete, this functional, robust box was provided with an elegant exterior. The concrete was used to wrap the building in a sturdy, unruly skin. To realize the graphic slanted lines, special elements were developed in collaboration with a concrete manufacturer, finished in a number of ways but using the same mold.

01 Northwest façade | 02 Exterior view | 03 Façade detail | 04 Ground floor plan

03

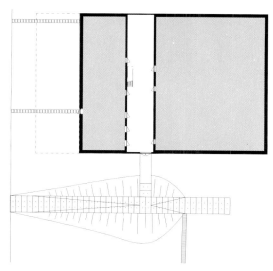

04

01

Daycare Center Felsoord

This project concerns the extension and renovation of an existing daycare center for the mentally disabled, situated in a natural wetland area near Delft. The limitations of the patients make the sensory and tactile quality of the building a key issue in the design process. The extension is situated to the rear of the building. Its organic shape and thatched cladding makes the building dissolve into the surrounding woodland. The existing façades are clad with silk-screened glass combined with a grid of pinewood lamellas. In the entrance hall, both the thatched façade and the pinewood façade are continued into the interior, ending in the form of a huge sky-light hovering over the reception desk.

01 General view | 02 Ground floor plan | 03 Roof detail | 04 Interior view | 05 Entrance

02

03

04

05

Delft Media Center

The renewal of the Media Center is characterized by color and light as well as the contrast between contemporary and traditional materials, which results in various atmospheres. This, in turn, creates an inextricable unity, fitting in with historical architecture in Delft. Traditional orange-colored brick and dark boarding have been used, and together with hardstone details, they create a classic urban look. In each department, color and organizing elements produce distinction and identification. At the entrance, a ten-meter-high glass construction is placed as an extreme 'welcoming gesture'. A light well created using a void and a striking glass roof covering the breadth of the building has been added. Light is given great depth and led into the very heart of the building, letting its interior be understood with just one glance.

01 First floor plan | 02 Comic book room | 03 View from main staircase | 04 Entrance area at night

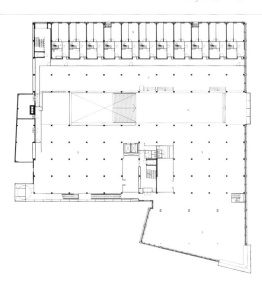

01

02

03

04

01

02

03

Bloemershof: School, Firestation and Gym

This urban ensemble consists of three buildings, each with a different function, coming together in one mixed-use unit and comprising of a vocational school, sports hall and fire station. The ensemble is designed as an enclosed courtyard in an H-shape. The middle zone is a green and transparent public space, designed as enclosed inner courtyards and allowing views of the surrounding area. Starting with a formal garden, the green courtyards form a link with the green landscape of the Veluwe. The buildings consist of a transparent base with concrete columns, and a structure elaborated with wooden slats. Conceptually, the ensemble is designed as a 'stone forest'. The interiors are light, transparent and extremely functional.

01 Main hall | 02 Elevations | 03 Interior view of sports hall | 04 Exterior view school |
05 Façade supports designed as a stone forest

04

05

01

02

ROC Graafschap College

Graafschap College, a regional school with 700 pupils, is situated on the outskirts of the center of Doetinchem. The rolling green landscape extends over Graafschap College, with large gaps in the grassy hills, allowing for a good view and plenty of light. The grassy mound houses function as the theory classrooms and the main hall. These areas can be divided up flexibly. The college presents itself with the high building facing the Energieweg, where the restaurant, sports accommodation and other facilities are located. The restaurant, kitchen, bakery and hairdressing salon combine with the main entrance to give character to the street on this side.

01 Entrance | 02 Rear view | 03 Central corridor | 04 Ground floor plan | 05 Entrance area | 06 Atrium

03

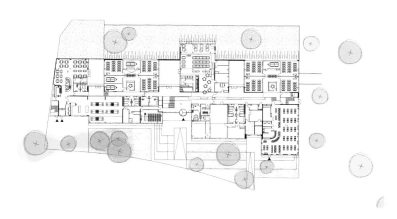

04

05

06

01

02

03

Outside-in turned Townhouse

Within the existing walls of a former dwelling, a contemporary alternative to the courtyard house has been designed. The courtyard is the heart of the house and simultaneously also the resting point upon which the surrounding circulation is focused. The complete house is redefined by the inversion of outside and inside. The bedrooms and the
library are situated in the most protected places behind the solid façade. Natural light
does not enter the house from the façade, but from the center courtyard. In this way an
apartment is created that is protected but still open. By the stepping into the bay window it is possible to experience a more direct contact with the town.

01 Living room | 02 Patio | 03 Exterior view | 04 Plan | 05 Red room with skylight

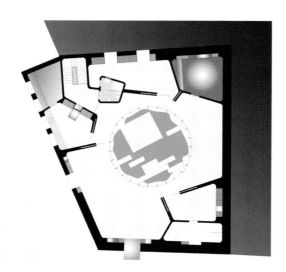

04   05

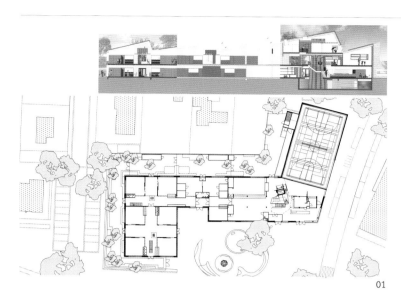

01

02

03

MFA De Zonneboom

This design for a multi-functional facility was central in the plan for a new community center in Doetinchem. It consists of two primary schools, a small café, a multi-use room, a large gymnasium and space for social service institutions. All functions have been centralized under a conspicuously shaped roof that refers to the typical Oosseldse roofs of the area. This roof divides the building up into smaller parts so that its scale is in tune with the rustic character of the surroundings. In case of major events, the café, the activity room, the playroom and the multi-functional room can be interconnected, forming one large space with the hall. The classrooms are situated around learning domains.

01 Section and site plan | 02 Corridor with learning attic | 03 View towards classrooms |
04 Gymnasium | 05 Staircase detail | 06 Front view

04

05

06

01

03

02

Da Vinci College, Learning Park

The Da Vinci College is part of the Dordrecht Learning Park. The various materials, including Corten steel, brickwork, stucco, zinc, aluminum, and glass, show pride of craftsmanship. A fresh colored skin of glass panels drapes around three vertical cones containing meeting rooms and a conference center. The transparent façades on the ground floor offer a view of the student service center, practice rooms and training facilities. The architects emphasized the diverse characteristics of the training houses by giving each a unique design, its own entrance, and different use of space and materials.

01 Restaurant | 02 First floor plan | 03 Exterior view restaurant | 04 View from courtyard | 05 View from street

04

05

01

02

03

04

Renovation WY Building

The new entrance, part of a complete renovation of the WY building, is designed as a slender and transparent volume in contrast to the heavy office building itself. The WY building dates from 1968 and has been one of the scene-setting laboratory buildings on the High Tech Campus in Eindhoven. It has recently undergone a complete renovation. The out-of-date laboratories have been transformed into light, transparent offices and test spaces, and a new entry hall volume was added. The use of steel and glass in the entry hall construction refers to the high-tech character of the campus, whereas the walls, built of natural stone, refer to the architecture of the 1960s, which used to be omnipresent here. The renovation of the building reveals an interesting three-way dialogue between rough stone, refined steel and glass.

01 Exterior view | 02 Entrance | 03 Front view | 04 Entrance area | 05 Entrance section and ground floor plan

05

01

HTCE Parking Lot

The concrete-coated landscape of this former-industrial area has been transformed. The campus serves as a social space, while the cars disappear, out of sight, into the parking lot. The parking lot, in the center of the High Tech Campus Eindhoven, offers 1,200 parking spaces and room for 550 bikes. The construction itself is striking and marks the entrance onto the campus. The 160-meter façade rises above the main body of the building, increasing the height of the construction in relation to its width. The façade is made out of aluminum sections and hanging glass panels of different colors and transparencies. The aquamarine color of the façade is decorated with fish, their rolling pattern representing the coming and going of cars.

01 Exterior view | 02 Exterior view from park | 03 Regular floor plan | 04 Upper level

02

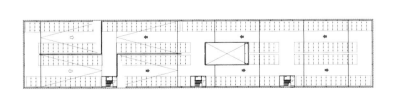

03

04

01

HTCE Five Parking Lots

This High Tech Campus in Eindhoven marks the development of the area from industrial to social, to a meeting place within the landscape. The five 'green' parking lots can accommodate 650 cars and 600 bikes and make no concessions in terms of functionality and economics. The architects made use of a large technical repertoire, employing cutting-edge technology. The walls are constructed of gabions, which allow the light and air to circulate inside the building and encourage climbing plants to grow on the outside, thus softening the appearance and allowing technology to be united with nature. The natural landscape is being encouraged to reclaim the space, leaving no place for asphalt and metal.

01 Exterior view | 02 Façade detail | 03 Floor plan

02

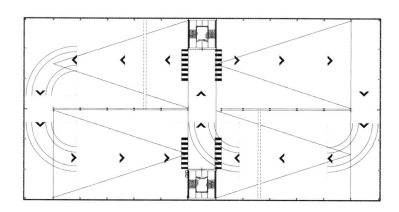

03

01

The Hangar

This project involves the addition of two volumes to the characteristic airplane hangar. A large part of the hangar has been kept empty, allowing space for a covered square that also functions as the entrance to the complex. A central corridor connects the square to a playground that opens towards an ecological green zone. The corridor is enclosed on one side by a colorful, transparent volume that houses a community center with library. On the other side lies a volume, situated partially in the ground, with a playground on the roof. It houses a sports center and a gathering space. The buildings are connected by means of an underground volume.

01 Covered square at night | 02 Community center | 03 Playground | 04 Central corridor | 05 Sports hall interior | 06 Ground floor plan

02

03

04

05

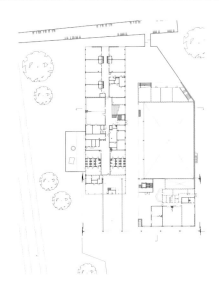

06

01

02

03

04

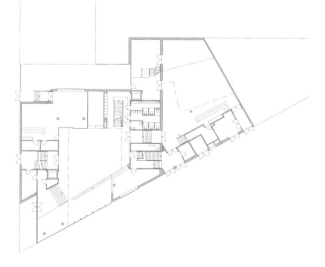

05

Dynamo

This youth center presents itself as a striking volume with two different façades. One façade is characterized by a large urban window, measuring 12 meters in height. This window provides a vibrant connection between the Catharina Square and the atrium inside the "Dynamo" building. The adjacent façade shows a more introvert character, relating to the existing historic buildings next to it. The entrance to the building, positioned on the point where both façades converge, leads visitors straight to the atrium to which all public facilities are connected. The level of this internal square is slightly raised above city level, giving the space a measure of privacy without overruling transparency.

01 Exterior view | 02 Evening view urban window | 03 Atrium | 04 Open staircase | 05 Entrance to atrium level | 06 Ground floor plan

06

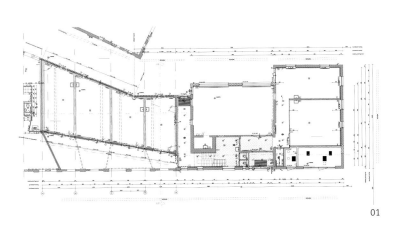

01

02

03

Roombeek Culture Cluster

Enschede's textile history is present in the 'woven' form of the tower. The saw-tooth roof stems from the visible profile of the old factory wall and transforms into a pedestrian bridge, connecting the tower to the warehouse on the opposite side of 'culture street'. The building and the warehouse are also connected underground. All areas, including the residences, can be accessed from the street. The floor area of the houses is limited, resulting in tall and narrow façades. The entrance hall is similarly squeezed so that each function receives access to the 'culture street'.

01 Floor plan | 02 Exterior view of pedestrian link | 03 Interior view of pedestrian link | 04 New museum tower with 'woven' façade

04

01

02

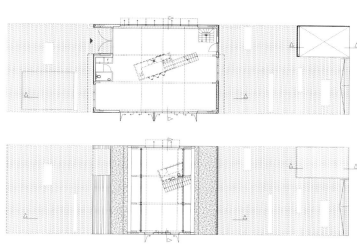

03

04

Housing for the Groote Scheere

This black wooden house has strict contours. The roof opens up to the landscape and becomes a private outdoor space. The wooden terrace lies just above the landscape, making a demarcation of the private space superfluous. The façade is made up of a series of
shutters which play an essential role in the appearance of the dwelling. Large vertical
shutters on the side allow light to enter. When opened in summer, they also function as
sun blinds. The horizontal shutters on the opposite side are smaller and narrower. They
are reminiscent of slits in the façade of a farmhouse. Instead of overlapping shingles,
the panels are slightly opened for the particular moment where light can protrude into
the living space.

01 Main façade with vertical shutters | 02 Sloped roof | 03 Main façade with closed
shutters | 04 Floor plans

01

02

03

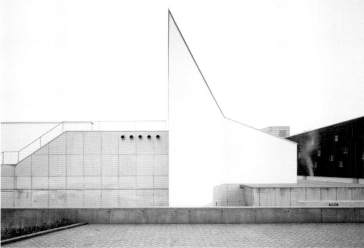

04

Nedap Groenlo

Ruud Bartijn was commissioned in the early 1990s to create new offices for Nedap that would reflect the changing outlook of the company's management. The existing production facility received a facelift and new spaces, terraces, sky bridges, and a forecourt were created. Freestanding columns in the forecourt represent rudimentary traces of the earlier factory. Thus, the company has grown into an entire office park in which the different market groups can operate from their own premises. Sunscreens, which are spaced away from the eaves, appear to connect the different buildings; separate yet attached, characterizing Nedap's new home in Groenlo.

01 Exterior view | 02 Interior view | 03 Courtyard | 04 Exterior view of backyard | 05 Ground floor plan

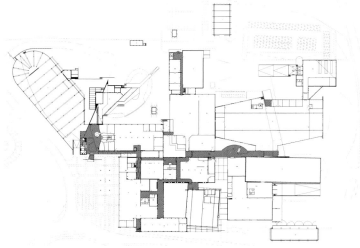

05

01

02

The New Martini Hospital

The design for the New Martini Hospital placed the new building next to one already halfway through its 40-year lifespan, which will also eventually be replaced by a new building. Furthermore, the function of the building can become totally interchangeable in the design phase and when the building is in use. A nursing department can be converted into an outpatient clinic or offices, for example. Extensions can also be randomly attached to the façade to gain extra floor space, allowing the accommodation of bigger departments. The only fixed elements are the service shafts, which will always remain at the center of the block.

01 Exterior view at night | 02 Glazed façade | 03 Hallway | 04 Ground floor plan | 05 Interior detail | 06 Workspace | 07 Multi-story interior

03

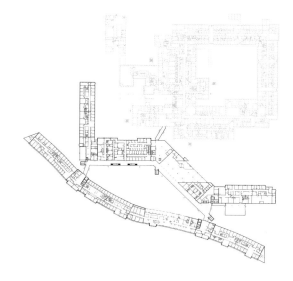

04

05

06

07

01

02

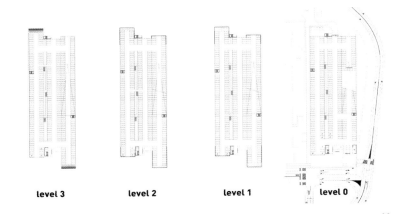

level 3   **level 2**   **level 1**   **level 0**

03

04

05

Martini Hospital Parking

The parking garage for the Martini Hospital has space for up to 1,200 vehicles. The form of the garage has been divided into three longitudinal forms, each with its own parking lane. The outer two forms are connected by the middle parking lane. The design of the outer façade expresses the route that vehicles take within the garage, which suggests the idea of a parking machine. The dynamic character of the façade has been emphasized by rounding one end of each form. These rounded ends have been diagonally mirrored, creating a stimulating view and emphasizing the shifting nature of the outer two forms.

01 Side view of parking structure | 02 Façade detail | 03 Floor plans | 04 Exterior view | 05 View from first floor

01

Education Executive Agency and Regional Tax Office

This Public Private Partnership project involves the building of a new office for the Education Executive Agency and Regional Tax Office. Sustainability and innovation are important items and are therefore integrated in the design. The façade has been designed in such a way that sun blinds, wind regulation, entry of daylight, ventilation and construction have been integrated. The aerodynamic shape of the building plays along with the northwest wind. Terraces, rounded angles and the design of the façade 'vins' result in a minimal disruption of the microclimate in the nearby forest. In the long term the building can be reused for housing. The project was led by the consortium DUO2 (Strukton, Ballast Nedam and John Laing).

01 Worm's-eye view | 02 Office tower | 03 Office tower detail

02

03

01

Medical Faculty, University of Groningen

The grounds of this Medical Faculty are squeezed in between a 19th century building and high-rise from the 1960s. The building houses lecture rooms, laboratories, a main lecture hall for 450 students, a large foyer, a canteen and an underground parking for 1,300 bicycles. The building is characterized by its gleaming golden 'shawl' – a double-curved aluminum skin enveloping the entire building, built with the help of a shipbuilder. All of the double-curved surfaces, which are also visible from the inside were made as prefabricated parts. All that remains open is the face of the university, visible from a distance and wrapped in the golden shawl. This façade, the only one of which is not of a piece with the roof, faces the inner city.

01 Exterior | 02 Golden shawl | 03 Façade detail | 04 Interior | 05 Section

02

03

04

05

01

02

Prisma

This 16-story building is part of a large-scale renovation of post war residential areas across the Netherlands. Prisma offers 52 apartments. The desired apartment types are stacked one above the other, with the smaller ones at the top. The balconies are then smoothly draped around the building, contributing to its characteristic shape. As a consequence of the geometry of the tapered structure, the outdoor spaces vary in width and depth. The balconies in principle are all sized equally, while at the same time they are all unique and individual. The ground level houses additional facilities, such as a nursery and a medical facility.

01 Exterior view | 02 Façade setup | 03 Additional facility | 04 Façade

03

04

01

04

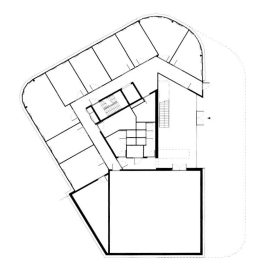

06

02

03

05

Duisenberg Pavilion

On the campus of Groningen University, pvanb architecten built an extension to the Duisenberg Building, which houses the Faculty of Economics & Business and Spatial Science. In order to fit the program into a lucid and compact volume, it was organized in a pentagon around a central void. The void brings light into the building and clarifies the spatial layout. The top floor contains the Netharbary, below this are two floors of offices and a lecture hall. The plain façades have been given depth by the application of a second skin consisting of white, yellow and red aluminum coffers, profiles and variously perforated expanded metal sheeting. This produces a moiré effect over the entire façade surface.

01 Central staircase | 02 Front façade | 03 Main entrance | 04 Library | 05 Night view | 06 Ground floor plan

01

Research Laboratory

UNStudio has designed a deceptively simple envelope constructed from flat, vertical aluminum slats, which, in places, are twisted outwards in bowed forms. Tall vertical undulations are generated presenting an open or a closed aspect depending on the angle at which they are viewed. On the lower level the color yellow is used, gradually changing to green towards the top of the building. Consequently the laboratory minimizes or even prohibits both the incursion of daylight and views into the building and yet still responds to its surroundings, offering some visual stimulus and presenting a semblance of transparency.

01 Exterior view | 02 Stairs | 03 Facade detail | 04 Ground floor plan

02

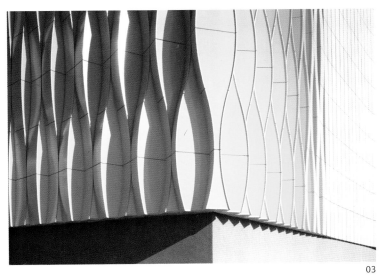

03

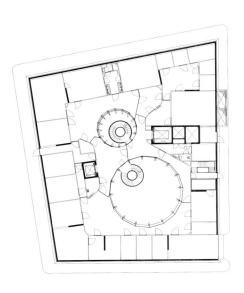

04

01

02

03

Haarlem City Theater

The cultural landmark in this historic city center dates back to World War II is a listed monument. The existing theater no longer met contemporary theaters' technical production facility, and building accessibility requirements. The new design included renovation, careful restoration and extension of the existing theater. The most striking intervention on the monument is the replacement of the original flight tower by a new, expanded structure. The visual impact of this extension is minimized through the cascading layering of the façade, letting it dissolve into the air. Brickwork, ornamented porcelain and partially screen-printed glass are integrated into the existing eclectic Art Deco façade.

01 Exterior view | 02 Entrance | 03 Auditorium | 04 Ground floor plan | 05 Hallway | 06 Bar

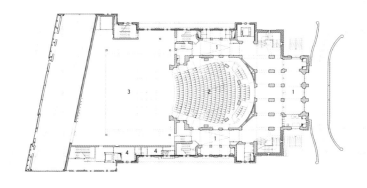

04

05

06

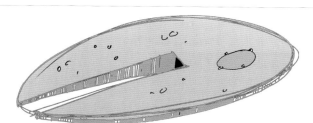

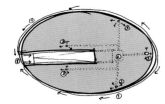

01

Hageveld Estate

In 2002 a plan was made to transform the Hageveld Estate into private housing and expand the space for the school's sporting activities. The landscape design enhances the green character of the estate and restores the heavily damaged planting on the west side of the estate with trees. A large pond was designed on top of a new underground parking lot, creating space for the increasing number of visitors, without destroying the peaceful landscape. The entrance slope to the parking lot slits through the water and glass panels ensure daylight entering the underground space. At night-time the light from the underground parking lot shines upwards through the panels results in a very special effect. In addition, the liveliness of the water is increased by special fountains that are switched on at night.

01 Sketches of pond and parking lot entrance | 02 Entrance ramp | 03 Access to underground car park

02

03

01

02

03

04

05

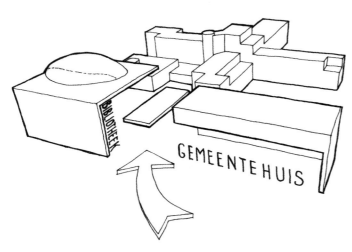

06

Town Hall Extension, New Library

The center of Heerhugowaard is changing dramatically. The reason is a new city plaza next to the Town Hall. A new wing of the Town Hall, with information and social services for the public, opens up the building to the outside world and invites it to come inside. The existing brick buildings are joined by a municipal department, clad in bluestone, and a library with a wooden exterior. The nine-meter-high entrance hall provides spatial coherence. A walkway around the adjacent courtyard connects the existing cube of the meeting hall with the new free-form spaces containing service counters, the library with cafés, the art lending library, and the wedding room. A cupola topped with a mezzanine offers a splendid view of this new heart of Heerhugowaard.

01 Entrance | 02 View of library and townhall | 03 Entrance area | 04 Interior | 05 Reception desk | 06 Concept sketch

01

Columbus Dalton School

The multifunctional center is situated between trees in a large park. The school consists of 14 classrooms, a daycare center and a gymnasium. By placing the auditorium and the playroom in the central space of the building, they become 'the heart' of the organization. The 'heart' connects three different levels and provides visual and spatial connections between the classrooms, the daycare center and the gymnasium. To moderate daylight in the school, PV cells have been applied in the glass, thus creating an interesting interplay between light and shadow.

01 Exterior view | 02 General view | 03 Interior view | 04 Site plan

02

03

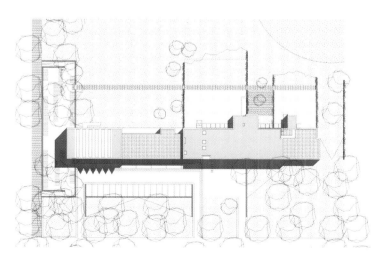

04

01

02

Bronckhorst Town Hall

This town hall building is exceptionally sustainable and extremely energy efficient integrated into the landscape of the Achterhoek in the Netherlands. Five small local authorities in the Achterhoek merged and became a single local municipality with the name Bronckhorst. Two office wings project slightly outwards and have been placed next to each other. Openings have been introduced in both inner sides at the middle of the wings: a high one for the council chamber, a low one for the public counters. The shutters around the building are an eloquent example of intelligent exploitation of the principles of passive building. They are intended to keep an excess of solar warmth outside to prevent the building from overheating during the daytime.

01 General view | 02 Shutters, decorated by the artist Jaap Drupsteen | 03 Interior of façades | 04 Shutters exploit principles of passive energy saving | 05 City council room | 06 Ground floor plan | 07 View from upper level

03

04

05

06

07

01

02

03

04

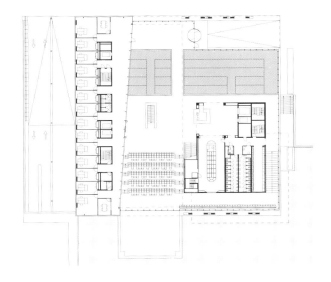

05

Netherlands Institute for Sound and Vision

This building is horizontally divided into two sections above and below ground. The portion below ground contains the archives vault, with fixed climatic conditions but without daylight. Bridging the gap between the two sections are the public spaces, client reception and services. A large light well opens to the south allowing the afternoon sun to penetrate to the core of the building and reflected light to skim over the inner façade wall of the offices. Light enters through the skylights, while colored and tempered light enters through the glazed façade.

01 Central hall | 02 Lit façade and entrance | 03 Permanent exhibition "The Experience" | 04 View to archives from central hall | 05 Ground floor plan

01

02

New Fire Station

This fire station is situated on the edge of Houten, in allotments along the De Kruisboog road. Wood and transparent materials inspired by greenhouse architecture were translated into the building in a contemporary manner. The building is robust, despite the fragile nature of the cladding material. It features a timber supporting structure with double walls of transparent plastic sheets and black recycled plastic. The design is one of a simple beauty; it not only looks attractive, but is also extremely sustainable and durable. The choice for a materialization in wood and recycled plastic, with sober and clean detailing, resulted in significant savings in material usage and expenses.

01 Fire truck | 02 Interior view | 03 Exterior view | 04 Firefighters' area | 05 Ground floor plan

03

04

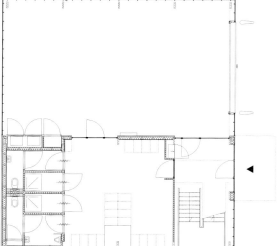

05

01

02

03

04

05

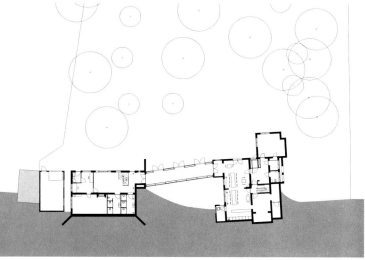

National Glass Museum in Leerdam

The four pedestrian bridges draw everything together in an elegant manner. Visitors can idle through extensive rooms; only one lift is needed and an enormous amount of space is gained. The bridges serve as exhibition space, where all the museum's objects are on display. In the historical villas not much work was needed. Repairs were carried out where necessary, with some later additions removed. The bridges were constructed from several layers of polycarbonate panels and covered by a translucent skin of gray, powder-coated, aluminum mesh. During the day they contrast sharply with the refined old villas, whereas at night they glow in reflection of the 9,000 glass objects inside them.

01 Night view | 02 Day view | 03 View from garden | 04 Side view | 05 Interior | 06 Ground floor plan

06

01

Leeuwarden Multifunctional Center

Two elementary schools, a community center for young and old, a crèche and a sports hall are combined in a compact and dynamic building. The building functions as a 'guiding light' for the whole neighborhood: literally through its transparent façade and more figuratively through the functions it accommodates. The different user groups are organized within the building in such a way that they can use it autonomously, each with their own entrance, so preserving their identity. It is also possible to link or exchange the spaces for the various user groups. The building is heated and cooled with the use of concrete core activation in combination with a heat pump.

01 Exterior view at night | 02 Elevations | 03 Schoolyard | 04 Wooden staircase

02

03

04

01

02

03

04

Leeuwarden Zuiderburen

Zuiderburen is located to the south of Leeuwarden, on the other side of the Van Harinx canal. The plan will realize around 1,900 houses as tasked by the Vinex plan. The residential program is subdivided into three neighborhoods. Other program elements include planting new woods and digging a number of large water areas. The existing twin village of Hempens-Teerns forms the pivot-point in a landscape composition that is carefully rooted in its environment and is directed towards the vast Frisian landscape.

01 Site plan | 02 Aerial view of pier houses | 03 View from water | 04 Water houses | 05 Pier house | 06 Panorama of new forest

05

06

01

02

03

04

Essent Heating Plant

Energy company Essent asked Bonnema Architects to come up with a design for a standardized, but modulated heating plant. It was necessary to create a design that would not disrupt the identity and company logo of the standardized design. The building had to be a shell to the internal heat source. The design for Essent looks like an armadillo; an animal that protects itself with bravery and a modulated body armor, the ultimate internal heat source. The armadillo nestles in the Zuidlanden, on the edge of a new extension of Leeuwarden.

01 Exterior view | 02 Façade detail | 03 Exterior view | 04 Night view | 05 Site plan

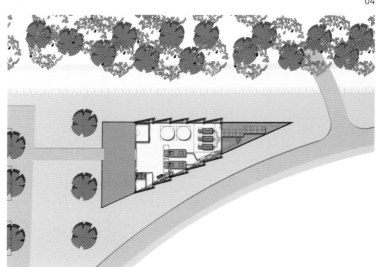

05

01

02

Lorentz School

This primary school for 900 pupils contains not only a multimedia library, but also a playroom with after-school group and a gymnasium. The heart of the school, located in the center and easily accessible from all directions, is the auditorium. This multifunctional space can be transformed into a ballroom with foyer, gallery and theater for monthly performances. Many ways can be used to approach the school, but most of them meet again in the center. Sliding doors to the classrooms and huge windows bring light to the inner corridors and create an open learning atmosphere.

01 View of library and media center | 02 Schoolyard | 03 Exterior view | 04 Staircase | 05 Floor plan

03

04

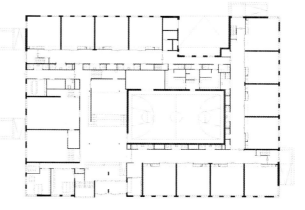

05

01

02

03

05

04

V21K07

In order to profit from direct sunlight and the panoramic views over the city, the functions of the house were organized in an unusual way. The living area on the top overlooks the historical center of Leiden. Bedrooms are in the middle and a multipurpose room for playing, working, reading or collective activities is located on the ground floor. Private life meets public life on the entrance porch outside the building. The black wooden façade refers directly to the historical black houses in the region. In order to minimize costs, details were reduced to a bare minimum and only one window format was used. The building meets all low-energy standards.

01 Interior view | 02 Terrace with swing | 03 Roof terrace | 04 Exterior view | 05 Cross section

01

Agora Theater

This building is part of the master plan for Lelystad by Adriaan Geuze, aiming to revitalize the town center. Both interior and exterior walls are designed to reflect the prismatic
experience of the theater. In the Agora Theater, drama and performance extend to create an urban experience. The interior is colorful; a handrail designed as a pink ribbon
extends down the main staircase, winds itself all around the center of the open foyer
space on the first floor, and then extends up the wall towards the roof, changing color
from violet, crimson and cherry to almost white. The main theater is all in red.

01 View from southwest | 02 Foyer | 03 Main hall | 04 Ground floor plan

02

03

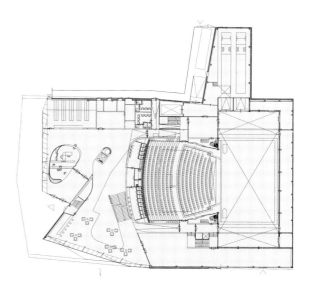

04

01

02

03

Floriade 2012 and Venlo Greenpark

The Floriade must provide an answer to the demand for sustainable construction. Living and landscape will be combined seamlessly, the gray industrial zone will change color. The tension of the area lies in the overlap of the various layers. Archaeology and new buildings of the business park as well as the landscape lines, contours and spaces create a mutual entwining for a new diversified overall picture and stimulate the experience of this diversity. The passive characteristics of the building, in terms of external energy profit, avoid overheating and limit energy loss, in combination with the maximum exploitation of the surroundings, the soil and the solar energy, have been integrated in the design.

01 Main view | 02 Atrium | 03 Interior view | 04 Site plan

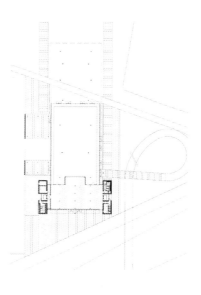

04

01

02

03

04

H House

H House was designed for a couple with a strong interest in the arts. It is situated in a hilly suburban area of Maastricht near the Netherlands-Belgium border. The clients formerly occupied a home directly adjacent to the site before appointing WielArets Architects to design what would become their new home, the H House. Individually an actor and a dancer and now both landscape architects, the owners are able to keep their landscaping skills honed in the formal garden behind the house, which they occasionally open to the public.

01 Kitchen | 02 Staircase | 03 Exterior view | 04 Garden view in winter | 05 Ground floor plan

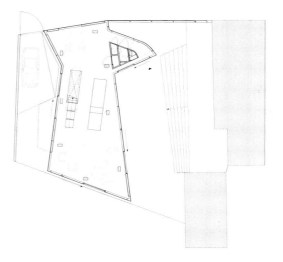

05

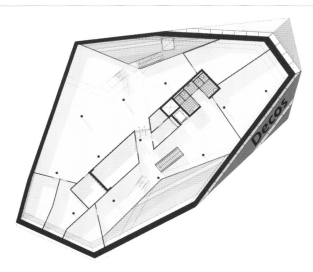

01

02

03

Decos

After winning the competition based on a contextual concept, a structure was designed that has become a representation of the company's technologies. The enthusiasm of the client is illustrated by his ambition to associate with the adjacent ESTEC-campus. "Decos" makes software so organizations can convert paper processes into digital. This offered the opportunity to fundamentally reconsider the office and the way people work. The building's cladding, a smooth seamless ice-blue skin cut by continuous window strips, contributes to the effect of alienation and wonder. The main feature is the experience of the skin recurring in the interior by partially detaching the floors from the skin and creating views across all levels.

01 Floor plan | 02 Interior view | 03 Exterior view at night | 04 Staircase | 05 Exterior view

04

05

01

Betty Blue

In Roermond Retail Park, visitors enjoy a new experience, a world in which shop and customer communicate with each other. The building is ambiguous it is in relation to its shape and color; it is sometimes straight and other times round, from the one side purple and from the other side blue. The lighting is dynamic, communicating a sense of energy and modernity. In the shelter of this enormous lifted and stretched drop of water, an inner square with almost exotic conditions has been shaped, as if it has taken on a life of its own, in which façade openings, billboards, lampposts, wastebaskets, bicycle sheds and road markings have gone through a joint and balanced growth.

01 Exterior view | 02 View from parking lot | 03 Interior view | 04 Site plan

02

03

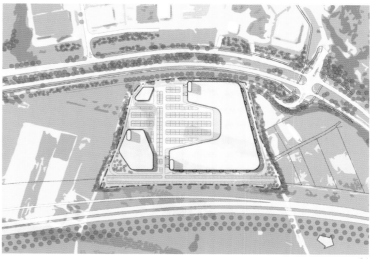

04

01

Pavilion on Roosendaal

In 2001 the city of Roosendaal decided to ban cars from the New Market in the center of town by building a huge two-story underground parking. In order to create a new public square, the city of Roosendaal asked the urban design office Quadrat to make a proposition. Rene van Zuuk were then later asked to design an additional pavilion. Because of the market activities, which occupy the entire square twice a week, the terraces of the pavilion needed to be placed above the ground floor. Originally the terraces could only be reached by going through the pavilion. Rene van Zuuk decided to make the terraces accessible from the outside of the building as well so it is possible to walk from the square up onto the sloped roof to the terraces.

01 Main view | 02 Staircase to terraces | 03 View from street | 04 Floor plan

02

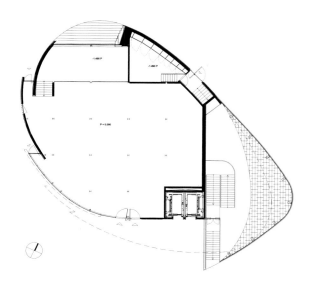

03

04

01

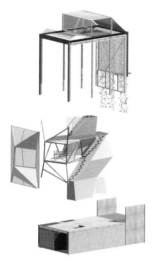

02

Body House

This private house is part of a residential redevelopment of a harbor pier in Rotterdam. A living room with cooking an dining space was to be the heart of the house. The heart has developed into a body that connects, organizes, and structurally holds the urban stack of three small projects. Below is the fixed, internalized, dark, heavy, robust, concrete socle. On top is the roof terrace with a free, open, light, flexible, nylon tent. In between is the big living space with the body that attached itself in the big façade opening and deformed itself towards the panoramic view onto the river.

01 Living room with stairs | 02 Exploded drawing | 03 Lit façade openings | 04 General view from street

03

04

01

Caballero Fabriek

The former tobacco factory has been transformed into a lively working environment with offices for companies from the culture, IT and media sectors. The leading theme of the design is cross-fertilization. The interior seeks to stimulate interaction amongst the tenants and between tenants and visitors. The industrial building remained intact, while new functions stand out by their different designs. A new broad corridor including a meeting area, functions as the backbone of the building; with common areas for tenants as well as visitors all located on this corridor. Because of its lively character, the Caballero Fabriek is able to attract a wide audience, giving a strong new impulse to its surroundings.

01 General view | 02 Communal terrace | 03 Entrance and lunch café | 04 Ground floor plan | 05 Door between corridors | 06 Conference 'box' and corridor

02

03

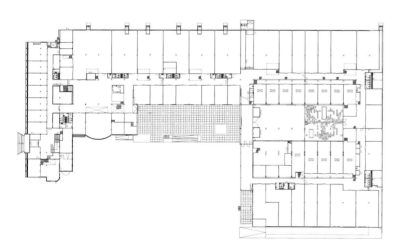

04

05

06

01

02

03

04

deBrug/deKade Unilever Rotterdam

The lowest floor of the new building is 25 meters above the quay, spanning the old factory complex. The main entrance is located between the classic 19th century building and the deKade office. The elevator and staircase to the floors are in the inner court. The offices offer a breathtaking view of the city center. Atriums and patios allow light to enter the building. The vacant spaces are strategically located to ensure adequate illumination in the central zone. Transparency is visible on the outer façade and contributes to give the entire building a communicative character. deBrug therefore adequately responds to the need for a dynamic office organization in which consultations can be held in an informal atmosphere.

01 Atrium | 02 Interior view | 03 Front façade of deBrug and deKade | 04 Street view from the Nassaukade | 05 Sections

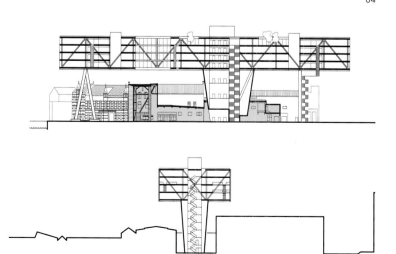

05

01

Brainpark III Office

The investor together with the tenant, a law firm, decided to establish a sustainable building on the office premises at Brainpark III. It is one of six office villas of four floors each at the edge of Brainpark III that constitute the transition between the high rise buildings of the area and the Fascinatio residential area. The buildings show the typical modernist style of office buildings, yet the variations in the understated details express a villa-style individualism. Large windows dominate the façade. Their offset arrangement and the positioning of some windows at an angle promote transparency throughout the building. The all-round façade has been provided with a few modifying accents near the entrance to the terrace and occasional jutties.

01 General view | 02 Sections | 03 Reception | 04 Interior view

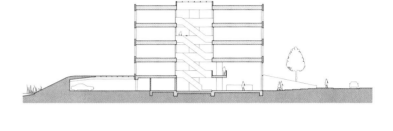
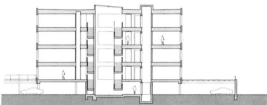

02

03

04

01

02

Private House

This 620-square meter villa was built within a rural context that is currently being developed into a high quality residential area with a green and open character. With the large glass walls and slender pillars the building refers to modernist architecture, while masonry, wood and especially thatching keep up the rustic, local tradition. The organic ground plan and the sculptured roof soften the large volume of the three-story building. The long crown of the roof gives a horizontal accentuation. Parts of the volume are embedded in the modeled terrain. Interior and landscape design are by Erick van Egeraat as well, making the project a real Gesamtkunstwerk.

01 Exterior view | 02 View of entrance | 03 Interior view | 04 Basement plan

03

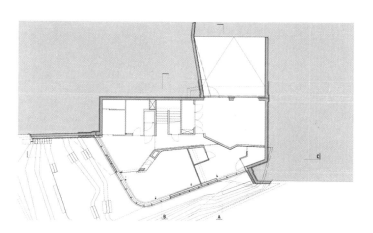

04

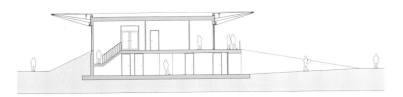

01

02

Sports Pavilion Zestienhoven

Within the open space between the airport and newly developed houses in the park, the aim of this design was to create a transparent and 'lightweight' pavilion. The building is divided into two levels. The clubhouses and the boardrooms are situated on the top floor of the building. This level is directly connected to the pitches by grass-covered slopes. These slopes cover the ground floor with its dressing rooms and storage areas, and provide a natural grandstand for spectators. The final piece of the building is the translucent cantilevered roof. This roof filters direct sunlight and shines out like a lantern in the evening thanks to the integration of LED powered lighting.

01 Cross section | 02 Stairs on natural grandstand | 03 View of interior and terrace | 04 Night view

03

04

01

02

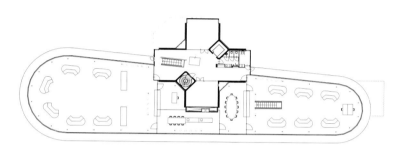

03

04

Rotterdam Traffic Control Center

The original shore radar stations, over 30 in total, were designed in the 1980s by Broek-bakema. The existing space of the Rotterdam Traffic Control Center was unsuitable for the new function, both in terms of size and the required flexibility. However, the pro-gram demanded that the design of the tower be maintained. One of the requirements was that the traffic controllers have an unobstructed view from the extension in virtually every direction. Two slim horizontal 'discs' form the roof and floor of the extension, with a slanting glass façade sandwiched in between them. The floating appearance is achieved by the extremely slender support structure, four pairs of V-shaped columns, which are drawn back from the façade.

01 Exterior view | 02 View from water | 03 Floor plan | 04 Interior view | 05 View from shore | 06 Aerial view | 07 View from harbor

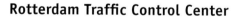

05

06

07

01

02

Periscope Houses

The final concept for the Periscope Houses evolved out of an exclusive competition, which demanded a design for 12 large water residences. The houses were to be expressive and appealing and should mark the Waterwijk in Rotterdam/Nesselande. Within each cluster, three houses are brought together to form a solid, three-story center. Soft shining volumes slice through this cube. Like periscopes, the houses look in different directions, thereby ensuring the privacy of the individual balconies. The materials applied are durable and low maintenance. Apart from the choice in materials and the flexible floor plans sustainability is further sought in extra isolation and energy saving mechanisms.

01 View from water | 02 View from northeast | 03 Terrace detail | 04 Floor plan | 05 Façade detail

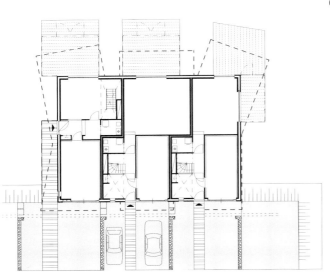

03

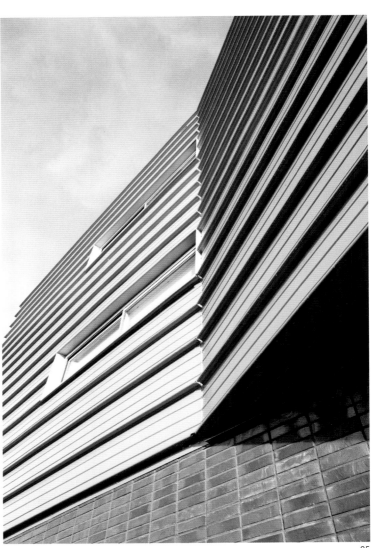

05

04

01

02

03

04

Kraton 230 / Schiecentrale phase 4A

The Kraton 230 building is part of the redevelopment of the former Schiecentrale and houses the new headquarters of regional radio and television station RTV Rijnmond, as well as several other firms. It completes the heart of the audio-visual sector in Rotterdam along with Schiecentrale, the 25kV building, Stroom hotel and restaurant and the new building of phase 4B. The sturdy character of Kraton 230 is a direct reference to the large size of the Schiecentrale, a former electricity generating station, and to the imposing ships that used to dock on the quay nearby. The façade of the building is made of rusty brown cast-iron panels that are decorated with maritime and audio-visual motifs designed by Studio Job.

01 Entrance | 02 Façade detail| 03 General view | 04 Interior view | 05 Ground floor plan

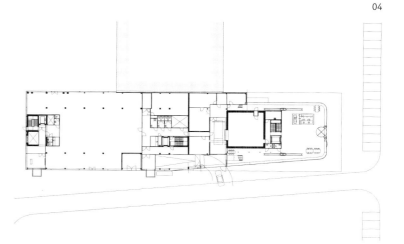

05

01

Villa Rotterdam

This detached house in Rotterdam has been extended several times in recent decades. Ooze architects translated the owner's desire to recycle the 'soul' of the house by transforming it in an unusual way. The firm began with a commission to design a kitchen that then evolved into a complete renovation. Inside, the building manifests itself through a formal language based on prefabricated, solid wood triangles that have a direct reference to the old roof. Through the creation of a void, the architects transformed the dark and cramped existing stairwell into a bright and social space. The exterior references traditional Dutch farms through the use of sedum green roofs and black stained Accoya planks.

01 General view | 02 Entrance | 03 Glazed façade | 04 View from meadow | 05 Interior view | 06 Dynamic façade creates light and shadow effect | 07 3D model

02

03

04

05

06

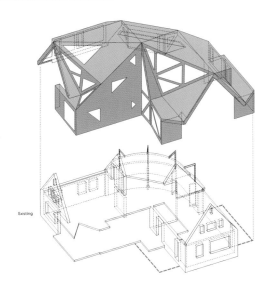

07

01

02

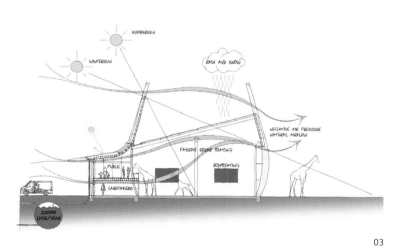

03

04

Sustainable Giraffe House

This residence is a sustainable shelter for giraffes. It provides protection against the natural elements, but also uses them to create a comfortable environment and a distinctive architecture. Oriented towards the prevailing wind and sun, the shelter has a healthy indoor climate with natural ventilation and natural light. The transparent roof allows the sun to enter, providing natural warmth. The height of the façade is also designed to make the most of solar potential and shade. The oval shape and the bulging façade provide excellent freedom of movement for its residents. Due to the holistic design approach it is a sustainable, healthy and animal friendly environment, where humans can experience these magnificent creatures in a unique way.

01 Façade detail | 02 Interior view | 03 Principle of sustainability | 04 Exterior view | 05 3D model

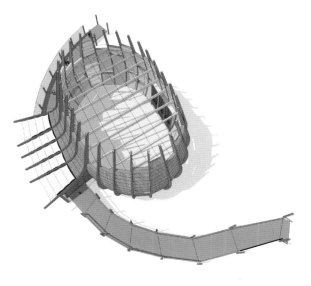

05

01

Le Medi

The concept for this urban block provided the starting point for Le Medi, in accordance with the master plan for Punt-Schippersbuurt. A dynamic world is created within the walled perimeter of the block, through a series of rooms of different shapes and sizes. A fountain lies under two lines of trees and two small courtyards can be accessed from this square. The properties can be accessed from two sides; there is a formal entrance on the street side and an informal one on the side of either the garage or the garden. The ornamentation and the use of traditional elements taken from Arabian, North African or Andalusian building traditions are given a modern twist.

01 Main entrance | 02 Residential house | 03 Ground, first and second floor plans and section

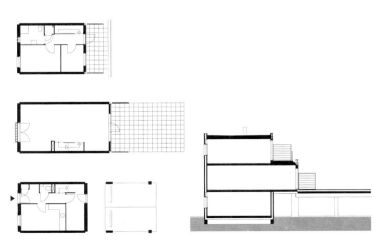

02   03

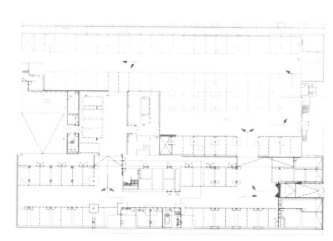

01

02

INHolland University

In order to accommodate the rapid growth of INHolland University in Rotterdam, 15,000-square meters hosting study areas, classrooms, commercial functions and offices were added to the original building from 2001. The extension was delivered in 2008 and consists of three interconnected parts. A lower, three-level building is situated parallel to and connecting with the original building. It supports one end of a nine-level bridge building that spans 35 meters over the courtyard and underlying Metro line and rests on a student apartment building at the other end. Finally a higher volume, partially cantilevered from the bridge building, offers panoramic views towards the harbor. The façades of each building volume differ, while their architectural language relates to the original INHolland University building to form a coherent ensemble.

01 Floor plan | 02 View of waterfront | 03 Dining area | 04 Exterior view

03

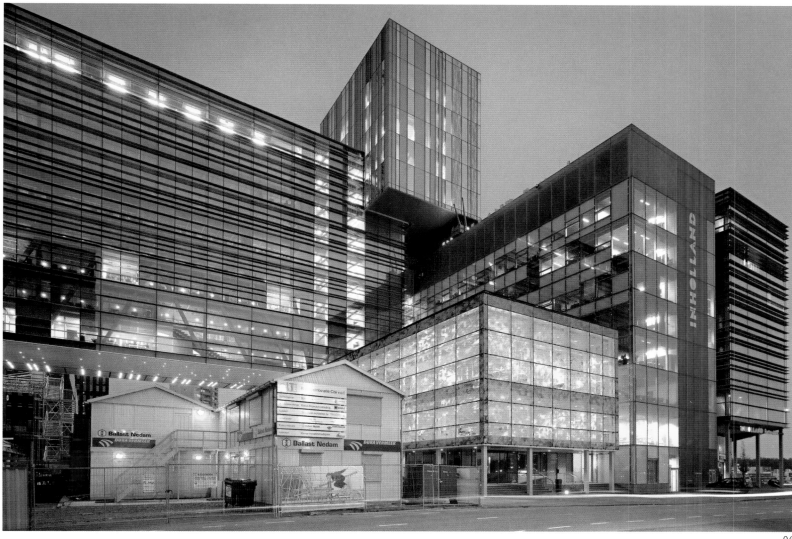

04

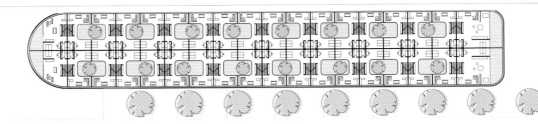

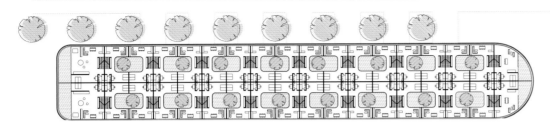

01

Arche XXI

These two buildings follow the system of a back-to-back townhouse. They have been designed to provide living space for several generations living in close proximity or to be rented out to holidaymakers on a short-term basis. Each unit shares a courtyard with its neighbor, which ensures the internal illumination of the houses while serving as a private garden. Parking, engineering and storage space are all located on the ground floor, while the upper levels offer three-story units. As a semi-detached house, two generations can live together. If required, the division of the space can be varied. Parts of the ground floor are designated as shops and insurance institutions. The size of the buildings is limited to just provide the essentials, in an attractive location on an artificial dune.

01 Floor plan | 02 Bird's-eye view | 03 View from sea

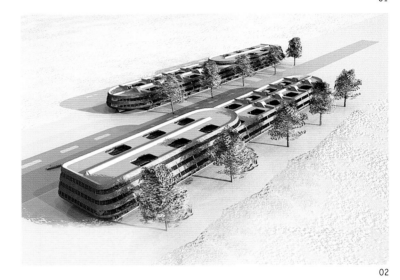

02

03

01

02

Van Der Zwan & Zn. Office

The fishing company Van der Zwan established itself on a peninsula across the harbor entrance of Scheveningen. The 360-degree orientation demanded by the location, the light glass box placed on a concrete base with sturdy concrete V-columns, the balcony on the south façade, and the stalwart image desired by the company all came together in the image of a navigating bridge. The west side is by far the most spectacular, with its view of the open sea and the sunset at the end of a work day. High quality materials were chosen for durability and sustainability in the extreme sea side conditions. The building accommodates offices, conference facilities, bar and warehouse, plus fish inspection rooms and logistics.

01 Main entrance hall with lighting sculpture by Scabetti | 02 Exterior view from seaside | 03 View from balcony | 04 Exterior view of double skin façade | 05 Second floor plan | 06 Board room

03

04

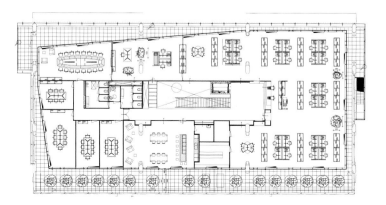

05

06

01

02

03

04

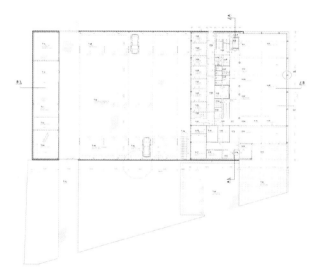

05

Police Station

This police station is the new district office for the municipalities of Schijndel, Sint Oedenrode and Sint Michielsgestel. The client chose a single three-storied structure, with a fully gated car park for police vehicles. The building opens up near the entrance, creating a gradual transition from public to private area. The dark brick building opens at the front, giving a sense of an immediate entrance. The natural lighting of this outer hallway is the result of an opening in the roof and the roof terrace on the second floor. Behind the public area are the police offices. This area of the building receives a lot of sunlight thanks to the transparent roof of the central stairwell. The building is entirely constructed of evenly finished black brick with deeply recessed dark joints.

01 Exterior view | 02 View from park | 03 Patio detail | 04 Exterior view at night | 05 Ground floor plan | 06 Horizontal detail of light strip

06

01

02

Lightcatcher

This pavilion contains a concrete basement with toplights and a first floor fully constructed from timber. Its size is almost equal to that of an additional house, which can be used as a guesthouse, orangery or as a workshop space. Functioning as a 'lightcatcher', the pavilion also offers a grand view of the historical town center and the banks of the Eemriver. This project attempts to prove that contemporary architecture can peacefully co-exist with a historical site as long as it can measure up to its surroundings in terms of quality and craftsmanship.

01 Front façade | 02 View towards historic town | 03 View towards Eem river | 04 Animated section | 05 Ground floor and basement plans | 06 Basement | 07 Ground floor

03

04

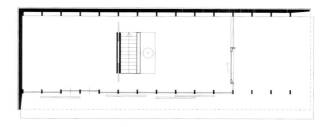

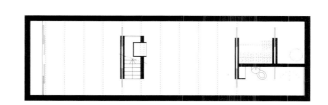

05

06

07

01

Fire Station Teteringen

A public garden in the village center is the unusual location for this new fire station. The core task of the design was to make a plain and functional building, focused on the logistics of turn-out at ground level. The building doubles as a clubhouse after stressful call-outs and as a meeting place/educational facility. A feature of this fire station is its transparency; offering views outwards as well as making the activities of the fire service visible. Wood is not the obvious choice for a fire station. However, this finish allows the building to blend into its green surroundings, and is more reminiscent of a pavilion than the usual range of industrial materials selected for this function.

01 Entrance | 02 Rear view | 03 Elevations | 04 Side view

02

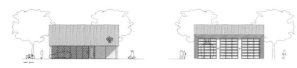

03

04

01

02

03

04

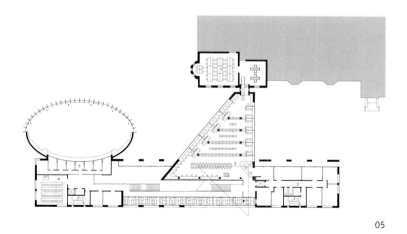

06

05

Library and Conference Center, Peace Palace

This building provides space for the international law library, academy events and for court proceedings. The design exterior is marked by the connection and penetration of geometric forms: A narrow, four-story cube on the south façade of the Peace Palace houses the function rooms and offices and provides access to the different areas. Its brick façade corresponds in color and materiality with the Peace Palace. The triangular library reading room 'floats' as a connecting element between the new building and the palace. Another smaller reading room juts out as a wedge at the second long façade. The transverse axis of the parks points precisely to the elliptical conference hall of the new building.

01 Detail of reading room | 02 Reading room | 03 View of ensemble | 04 Interior view of reading room | 05 First floor plan | 06 Conference center

01

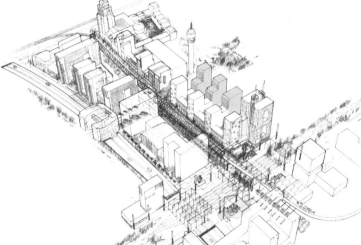

02

Prinsenhof

These three high-rise residential blocks, with 207 apartments featuring from two to five rooms, are part of a multifunctional complex, which also includes offices, shops, a hotel, a car park, and three public gardens. The residential building consists of a five-story plinth on top of which the elegant blocks rise to 72 meters. To stress the great urban significance of the plan, it reaches up over the offices. The structure – a core with free-standing oval columns – guarantees high flexibility for the floor plans. The blocks are a 'Rubik's cube' of 63 different housing types which often have several floors and a view from several sides of the building, to obtain as much sunlight as possible.

01 General view | 02 Urban development plan | 03 Interior view | 04 View to the sky

03

04

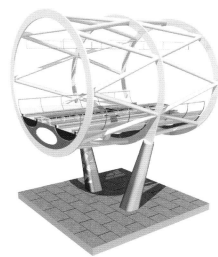

01

02

03

Beatrixkwartier Station

The RandstadRail project involved the creation of a new light rail network for the area between the Hague and Rotterdam. The 400-meter-long viaduct by Zwarts & Jansma comprises a ringed skeleton of mild steel bands with a circumference of about ten meters, interconnected by hollow, diagonally arranged bars to form an open tube structure. The considerable structural height of the tube allows it to easily cover the large spans. The structure is supported by V-shaped columns and provides room for two rail tracks, allowing two trains to pass within the tube. Thanks to the massive spans of 40 and 50 metres there are relatively few columns at street level. There is also hardly any visual obstruction at eye level, so that pedestrian and traffic safety are not compromised.

01 Axonometric projection | 02 View along tracks | 03 View of station | 04 Tubular structure resting on V-shaped columns

04

01

02

03

04

05

06

Council of State

The building complex of the Council of State has been renovated and expanded. The first phase concerned a new office building and the refurbishment of the 19th century houses. To transform the labyrinthine complex into a logical entity with workable office space Merkx + Girod devised an ingenious solution: a void and a logistic highway that overcomes all existing differences in level, connects all offices and provides also extra daylight to all floors. Only the original rooms on the street side were retained. Each floor has its own individual finish in material. The addition of roof gardens and the restored public garden integrates the complex into the fabric of the city. Phase two will be completed in 2011.

01 Facility area in aluminum | 02 Facility area in oak | 03 Void | 04 Connection between existing mansions and new expansion | 05 Renovated mansions | 06 New expansion | 07 Floor plans

07

01

ROC Mondriaan Laak II

This new school building is situated on a narrow plot, perched between the busy railway lines at the Hague HS Station and Waldorp Street. The position, close to the public transport node is an excellent strategic choice. The building forms a powerful and colorful completion to the square and, when seen from the train, it acts as a showpiece for ROC Mondriaan Laak II. The building has a grid-shaped concrete façade and the individual squares are all brightly painted. An arcade follows the pedestrian route from the station to the dwellings and the shopping mall. Large glass areas along the arcade provide a view into the school: transparency and a display window for vocational training are combined here with increased social safety.

01 Exterior view | 02 View from station | 03 Façade detail | 04 Section

02

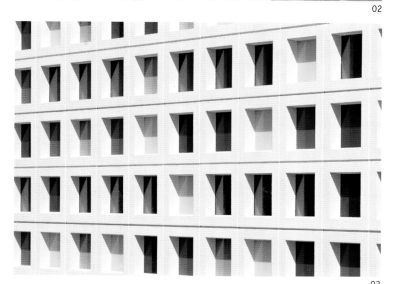

03

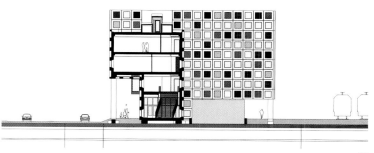

04

01

02

Renovation Ministry of Finance

The renovation of the Ministry of Finance is the first building project that the Dutch government has tendered as a public-private partnership, encompassing design, building, finance, maintenance and operations. The building, dating from 1975, is a prominent example of Dutch Brutalist style, but was also bulky, inward looking and impersonal. Now, the building provides office space for 1,750 employees as well as meeting rooms, a library, a restaurant and parking and sport facilities underground. By covering the garden with a glass roof, the architects created an atrium as the heart of the building, as well as a welcoming central entrance area and a more open, transparent character.

01 Entrance and semi-public square | 02 Atrium | 03 Entrance to the Platanenhof | 04 Ground floor plan | 05 Main entrance hall

03

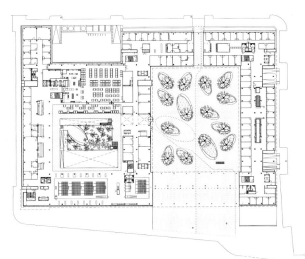

04

05

01

02

03

04

05

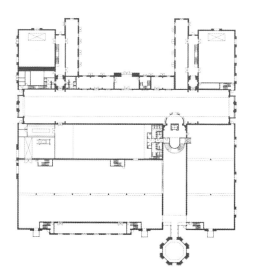
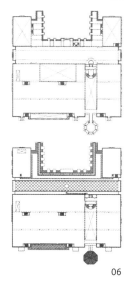

06

Louwman Museum

The Louwman Museum, home to a preeminent collection of vintage automobiles, is located in a park in an historic section of the Hague adjacent to the Queen's palace. The 102-square meter program includes secure exhibition galleries, an auditorium, a reception hall, a conference center, food service and workshops for automobile conservation and repair. The barrel-vaulted great hall creates an east-west spine, separating the double-height volume of the exhibition area from the U-shaped public spaces that define the entry court. With its distinctive brickwork and steeply sloped peaked roofs and dormers, this section breaks down the scale of the overall building, making the museum contextually appropriate.

01 Octagonal pavilion | 02 Front façade | 03 Rear façade | 04 Spyker Hall | 05 Vintage automobiles | 06 Ground, first and second floor plans

01

02

Tilburg Audax Textile Museum

The Textile Museum in Tilburg has been renovated and extended. The entrance has been designed as an abstract glass volume. Its unique steel supporting framework has been left completely visible, creating a contrast with the historical qualities of the 19th century original construction. Inside, a second, smaller volume gives the illusion of defying the law of gravity. A new, entirely closed archives building is placed above an existing exhibition building and has been allocated an exterior of water proof PVC material that gives the construction a taut, abstract and geometric look.

01 Old building | 02 Archives building | 03 Top level | 04 Museum store | 05 Front view |
06 Side view | 07 Sections and elevations

03

04

05

06

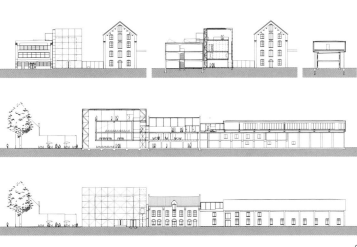

07

01

02

Top Sports Hall T-kwadraat and Ireen Wüst Ice-Skating Rink

At the beginning of the competition to design this project, the architects wanted to create a design that was more than just a sports hall. The diverse public program drove them to create a site-specific sports palace; a recognizable center around which the new Stappegoor area can thrive. From the outside, the building appears to be an abstract monolith with randomly placed oval windows. On approach, finer details and patterns can be seen on the façade until the interior is unveiled behind the glass plinth. The interior is organized around the main sports hall. The gorge, a giant naturally lit space, visually as well as physically connects all spaces and activities. The sports hall is thus defined as a contemporary social arena.

01 Rear façade detail | 02 Interior view | 03 Staircase and gallery | 04 Interior view with vibrant colors | 05 Exterior view | 06 Second floor plan

03

04

05

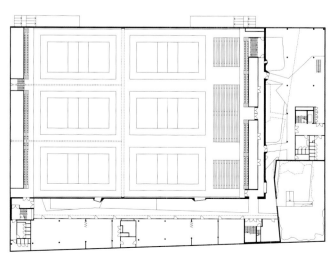

06

01

02

03

04

Bierings House

From a basic form, defined by the municipal urban plan, sculptural 'eyes' emerge with direct views to the varied countryside. The form and orientation of the building avoid visual contact with the adjacent houses: on the ground floor, the angled ceiling of the kitchen accentuates the intensive contact with the garden. On the first floor, the differently shaped openings in the roof and façade offer, like 'fingers of light', varied daylight experiences.

01 Floor-to-ceiling book shelf | 02 Interior detail | 03 Terrace | 04 Dining room | 05 Ground floor plan

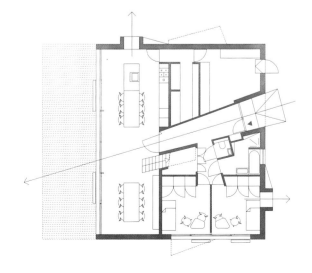

05

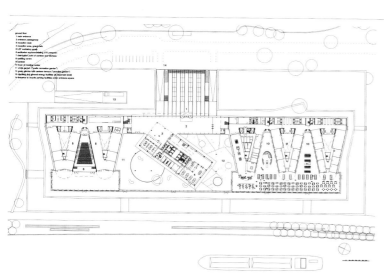

01

02

03

Westraven

The existing high-rise construction has been completely renovated and reorganized, and an elongated four-story building has been realized around the foot of the tower, both for the offices of the Ministry of Public Works. Façades, made entirely of glass and voids in the floors, dominate the spatial structure of the high-rise block. Atriums, conservatories and inner gardens in the low-rise part stimulate spatial awareness, and also help visitors to orient themselves. Many of the working areas have been designed as flexible work stations, making it possible to work at various places in the building. Much attention has been devoted to implementing a perfect equilibrium between low energy consumption and an optimum working climate.

01 Ground floor plan | 02 Textile second skin of high-rise | 03 General view | 04 Conservatory at low-rise | 05 Worm's-eye view of atrium roof

04

05

01

02

03

04

De Cope Utrecht Parking and Offices

This project combines public parking and office spaces in one building. The design consists of two abstract units, connected by a crossway. The parking garage functions separately from the office spaces on the three top floors, which are currently occupied by a business center. As the façade is built around both the parking decks and the office-floors, there is no way to visually distinguish between the different functions. The façade consists of inwardly curved panels with a golden, metallic look. The gradual changes in the perforations and the protruding panels create the impression of a woven structure. Form, color, and detail provide the building with a different look depending on weather and light.

01 Northwest façade | 02 Main entrance to offices | 03 Transparent bridge between building volumes | 04 Lobby | 05 Office and parking level floor plan and elevation

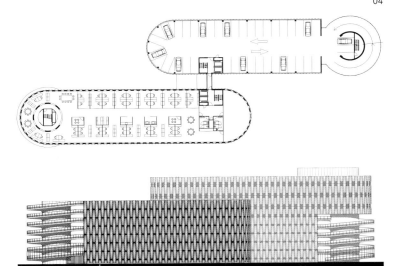

05

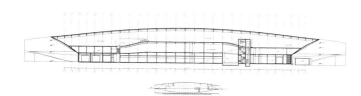

01

02

Hessing Cockpit in Acoustic Barrier

The Acoustic Barrier is a one and a half kilometers long and 13 meter high structure that protects new apartment buildings from the noise of the A2 highway, which counts 14 lanes since its reconstruction. The Hessing Cockpit houses the showroom, annex and garage of the Hessing company, national dealer of luxury cars. The concept for both the Acoustic Barrier and the Cockpit building, which is immersed in the elongated volume, was design adapted to the speed of passing cars [120 kilometer per hour].

01 Longitudinal section of cockpit | 02 Showroom | 03 Acoustic barrier seen from highway |
04 General view at night

03

04

01

Music Center XXI

"Music Center XXI" is a large scale project that had to be realized in a small scale, built up area. The design follows the conditions of the context: it is a small village that transforms into a large volume, fitting into the morphology of its surroundings. The building is a conglomerate of open and closed volumes. The music studios and the rehearsal room have been positioned separately, resulting in two closed volumes. The service functions depend on daylight, such as the entrance, stairs, foyer and office, because of this they are situated in the intermediate space formed by the two volumes. Monochrome colors turn the conglomerate of various spaces into a single building.

01 Corner view | 02 Façade view | 03 Rehearsal hall | 04 First floor plan

02

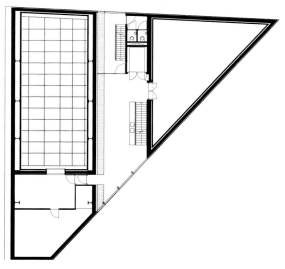

03

04

01

Villa 1

Set in the woodlands of Holland, Villa 1 is optimally oriented towards the views of the terrain and sun. Half of the building is pushed below ground to meet local zoning regulations. This creates a clear dichotomy in the spatial experience of the house; a 'glass box' ground floor where all mass is concentrated with furniture elements and a 'medieval' basement, where the spaces are carved out of the mass. Its Y-shaped floor plan results in a landscape of different spatial perceptions, creating a landscape of spatial intimacies that goes beyond the mere pragmatic diagram of functionality.

01 Northwest view | 02 Ground and basement floor plans | 03 Southeast façade | 04 Library | 05 View from terrace towards kitchen and central hall

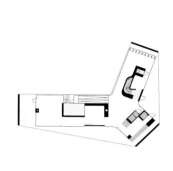
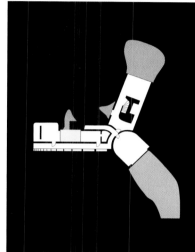

02

03

04

05

01

Schuitvaartgracht

These 64 apartments combine an urban lifestyle with a small scale living environment. The apartments are accommodated in two round, six-story buildings with an underground parking garage. They are situated in a small, wooded park on Schuitvaartgracht. At the junction with the outside space, the façade is recessed by a meter and a quarter, while the floor extends outwards by the same distance, creating wide terraces. On the upper levels, the floors on the south side are set back a number of times, resulting in elevations of double-height. The fifth floor is still further recessed and is bordered by a terrace, producing an enormous diversity of apartments, in terms both of area and organization.

01 View from water | 02 General view | 03 Floor plan

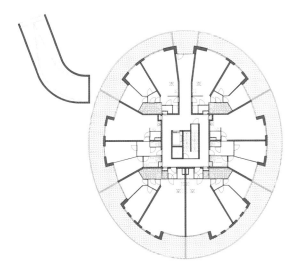

02

03

01

Tea House on Bunker

This project aimed to redesign a historical and derelict building through renovation and expansion. The 1936 bunker remains intact except for a portion of the concrete roof where the new structure is connected. The new umbrella-like addition can be removed and does not permanently influence the historic structure. The space is designed with steel structures within its two main walls that act as floor-to-ceiling beams. The beams are balanced off-center on two columns positioned directly in front of the existing bunker. Stability is achieved by using the massive concrete shell of the bunker as a counterweight.

01 Panoramic window | 02 Side view | 03 Rear view | 04 Section

02

03

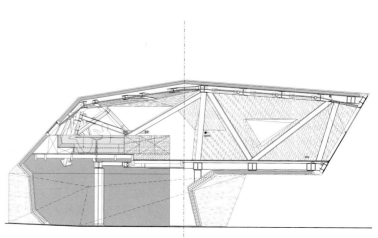

04

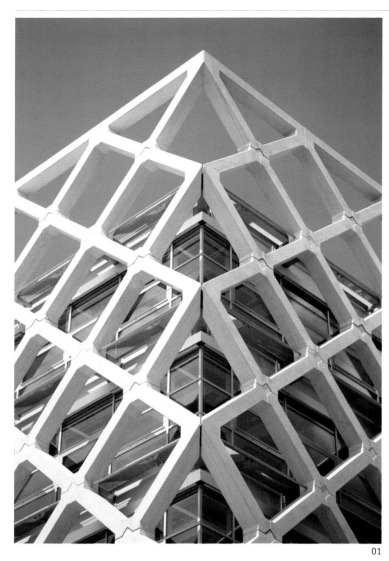

01

02

03

04

Atlas Building

Viewed from the outside, the Atlas Research Center looks like an abstract, cubic sculpture in the landscape. Placing the main supporting structure outside the building created the sculptural expression. X-shaped prefab concrete elements, each one-story-high, constitute a transparent network set 70 centimeters from the glass and aluminum curtain wall. This concrete network supports both the floors of the various stories and the glass wall. The offices, laboratories and other functions are arranged across seven floors surrounding a spatial core: a single large void extending from the first floor right up to the glass roof. Slender steel ramps intersect the void, creating flowing connections between the individual floors.

01 Façade detail | 02 Atrium | 03 Exterior view | 04 Entrance bridge | 05 Section

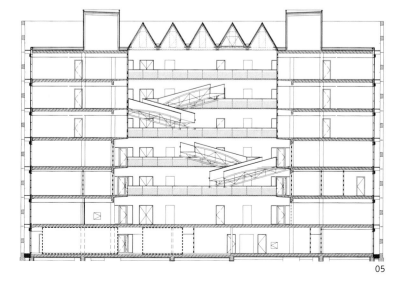

05

01

City Hall Zaanstad

The new city hall Zaanstad is linked to the new bridge over the railway and the highway. The short side, where the main entrance and the public functions are housed, runs along the plaza on this bridge. The long side of the city hall, where the offices are located, is elevated between the railway and the provincial highway, above the bus station. The city hall was designed as a chain of several large Zaandam houses, in which the features of the local architecture have been applied in a new way. Zaandam houses are famous for their typical façade architecture: the wooden façades are very flat and painted in all sorts of green hues. The new city hall also features façade architecture in green and white.

01 View from street | 02 Impression | 03 West façade | 04 Section and ground floor plan

02

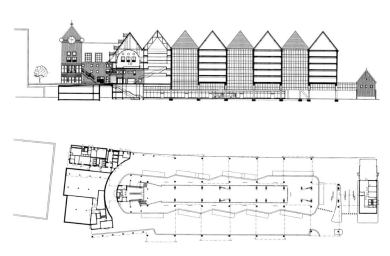

03

04

01

WWF Headquarters

Rau transformed a former 1950s agricultural laboratory into the first CO_2-neutral and self-sustaining office in the Netherlands. By breaking through the rigidity of the existing structure and adding an organic blob at the center, the rejuvenated building has been given a friendly and inviting appearance. Being one of the world's foremost environmental organizations, the World Wildlife Fund expected its identity to be translated into the design of the new headquarters. With its outstanding energy performance, natural ventilation, healthy indoor environment and the use of child-labor free, environmentally friendly materials the building meets high standards of sustainability.

01 Exterior as organic blob | 02 Ground floor plan | 03 Back side | 04 Staircase system

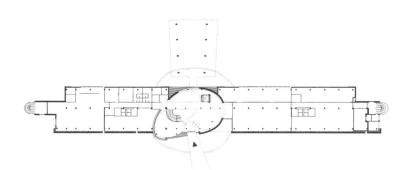

02

03

04

01

02

Spazio

The expansion of the center to the west of Zoetermeer was necessitated by the strong growth of the new city. Spazio will revive the intersection point of both centers with a mixture of shopping, leisure, residential and office space. A promenade with two bordering shopping floors cuts through the building volume. Resting on both sections above the promenade, a prominent "UFO" is found. This emblematic volume houses a fitness center. The towers, with residential units and a row of offices, stand above the shopping floors.

01 General view | 02 "UFO" | 03 Promenade | 04 "UFO" and residential units

03

04

01

02

03

04

Cultural and Educational Center de Binding

Next to the Langedijk town hall, the Cultural and Educational Center de Binding offers accommodation to asecondary school, a library, a music school, an artist's studio, a toy lending center and a youth work center. In addition, the complex hosts numerous cultural and educational activities, such as lectures, exhibitionsand theater performances. The layout of the building reflects the historical town structure of the villages of Langedijk. It consists of three parts: the islands, the route and the elements. Each part has its own materials and architecture. The 'islands' are functionally flexible as well as allowing for future changes. A lot of natural daylight and open views makes the building easy to navigate.

01 Balcony | 02 Connecting passage | 03 Entrance | 04 Library | 05 Ground floor plan

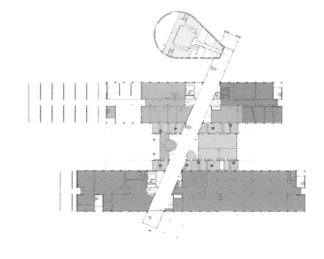

05

01

02

Social and Cultural Center

This Social and Cultural Center is organized in two volumes that are vertically connected to each other by a gallery. The volume rests on a big thick slab of concrete. Underneath this, the ground floor is organized into a set of volumes separated by courtyards, accesses and circulations. The first floor fits in a white volume situated on the highest part of the topography and suspended over the ground floor, the interior is mainly white, with bright, modern lighting that effectively illuminates the interior space. The outside area will be preserved as a green public space for outdoor activities.

01 View from south | 02 View from park | 03 Main corridor on first floor | 04 View from east | 05 Playground | 06 Atelier | 07 Ground floor plan

03

04

05

06

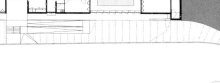

07

01

02

03

House in Vale Bem

The middle axis of this house appears to divide the space into common and private areas. It is also this axis that demarcates the entrance with a strong vertical image. On one side, a long and low volume defines the private area, where the bedrooms are located, to the other side is a strong volume with high ceilings and a strong exterior expression. This part includes common areas, such as living room, dining room and kitchen. These are all spatially related to the garden and swimming pool. The design meets the client's wishes and creates a homely space, which continues a dialogue with nature as well as maintaining privacy where necessary. The wooden façade allows natural light into the house.

01 East façade and patio | 02 South façade | 03 Swimming pool | 04 Living room and staircase | 05 Interior view towards kitchen | 06 Ground floor plan

04

05

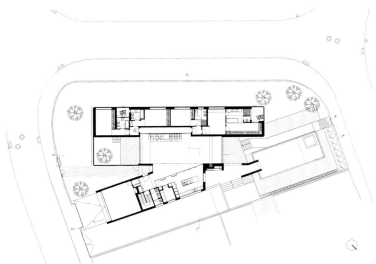

06

01

02

03

04

Ganesh Club

The concept for this club was to create a massive object that gives the impression that it simply grew out of the Portuguese mountains. The emerging black volume suffered rhythmic subtractions, linking its form to the surrounding terrain. The interior was designed to resemble a cult area focused on entertainment. The DJ stage became the altar and two secondary wings were created for his followers. Inside, white aleatory stripes subtract matter from the thick volume. Light and laser beams can be displayed without contempt. The building's layout allows several activities, such as concerts and foam parties. It can even become a showroom for cars exhibitions.

01 Night view | 02 Main entrance | 03 Façade at night | 04 Day view | 05 Exterior at night | 06 Interior view | 07 Floor plan

05

06

07

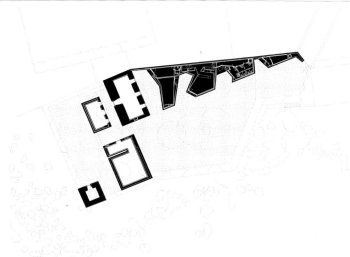

01

02

Santa Marta Lighthouse Museum

In this 17th century site, the various intentions, materials and technologies of each era resulted in a succession of additions, adaptations and subtractions. The project thus has a significant legacy with shapes, spaces and constructive systems rooted in historical processes. These are present in the morphology and state of the building and express a clear vision of the future in the first phase of the competition program. The aim is to replace the original order and, by including time, memory, and function, to create a new use based on the old functions.

01 Site plan | 02 General view | 03 Courtyard | 04 Passage | 05 Courtyard and lighthouse

03

04

05

01

02

03

04

Paula Rêgo Museum

After surveying the trees, especially their tops, the architects developed a set of buildings with different heights that represent a built 'positive' juxtaposed to the 'negative'
tree top structures. This 'Yang' and 'Yin' interaction between building and nature was
also elemental in deciding the exterior material: a red concrete which is complementary in color to the green wood. In the meantime, the surrounding plant structure was
reduced for protective reasons. The architects additionally established a hierarchy by introducing two big pyramids — skylights — in the entrance axis, which house the library
and the café. It was considered important that every exhibition room always have an
opening to the exterior garden.

01 Exhibition hall | 02 Shop | 03 Courtyard | 04 General view | 05 Sketch

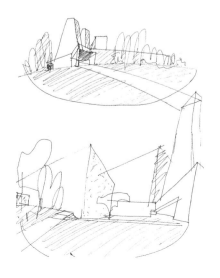

05

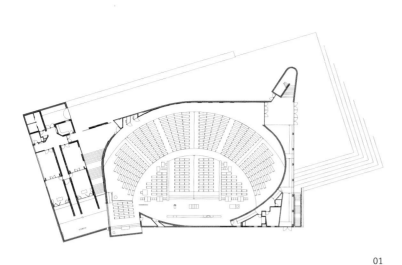

01

02

03

Boa Nova Church

This site was one of the city's last slums, called 'End of the World'. The local community needed a new identity. The conceptual elements were two empty spaces: the courtyard and the nave. The courtyard offers an extroverted space, connecting the city to a valley with distant seashore views. The nave provides an introspective space which, by following the creative paths suggested by the work of Bernini and Piranesi, became infinite and irrepresentable. Today, the 'End of the World' is known as 'Our Lady of Good News'. The church stands as an anthropomorphic object, marking the suburban surroundings with an iconic tower.

01 Floor plan | 02 Auditorium | 03 Church nave | 04 Exterior view | 05 Courtyard

04

05

01

02

Cork House

The client convinced the design team to build the Cork House at a minimum cost. The shaped body is securely wrapped in cork panels with a few radical ruptures that create a friendly distance from the neighborhood. The cork skin on the outside provides extensive insulation for the building. To minimize electricity consumption, the functional rooms were placed at the north side of the building, while the living spaces face south, to allow extensive daylight penetration. Inside, the spaces have a simple geometry with no partition walls.

01 Side view | 02 Entrance area | 03 Façade | 04 Interior view | 05 Section | 06 Façade detail

03

04

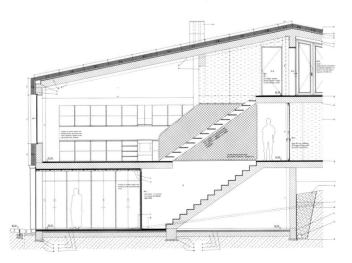

05

06

01

02

03

Paço de Pombeiro

This project involves a manor house located on a farm with ten hectares of land, 90 percent of which are used as vineyards. The main building was built in the 16th century, together with several little constructions, which are either very damaged or ruins. In a landscape with strong rural features, the new building is inspired by what already exists. All spaces spread out from the main house, which is also the owner's permanent home, and from the ruins where new spaces have been integrated. The individual and exterior gritted access paths introduce visitors to the rural character of the landscape.

01 Aerial view | 02 Exterior view | 03 Entrance | 04 Ground floor plan

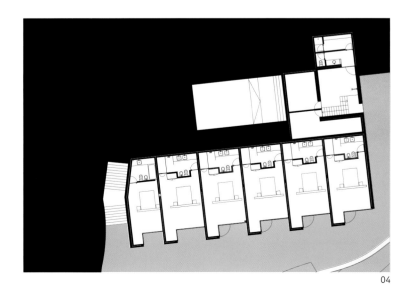

04

01

02

03

04

05

Casa no Gerês

This project involved the reconstruction and augmentation of a ruin into a weekend retreat. The chosen plot had extraordinary characteristics, situated near to the Cavado River and its tributary. The clients desired that the exceptional view should become an integral element of the house; for the architects, the interior should be large and spacious. The weightless intervention enhanced by the overhanging part that shoots off the riverbank maximizes the transparent appearance from the river, reducing land occupancy and avoiding all existing trees.

01 View towards ruin | 02 View from river | 03 View from living room to nature | 04 Dining room | 05 Living room | 06 Ground floor plan

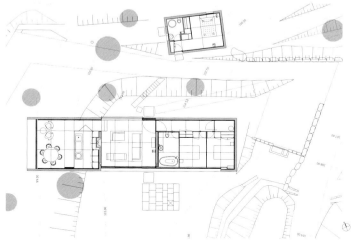

06

01

Shopping Alegro

The Alegro shopping mall was a direct result of the changing retail market in Portugal, the quality demands made by consumers and tough competition from new retail centers in the greater Lisbon area. The existing retail facility consisted of a Jumbo (Auchan) hypermarket with related convenience shops and an electrical household goods store. The refurbishment and extension of the existing facility was a complex process as the hypermarket had to remain fully functional throughout the building process. The hypermarket underwent a comprehensive renovation and new access stairs and escalators were installed between the parking lot and the new retail areas.

01 General view | 02 Façade detail | 03 Northeast façade detail | 04 Design sketch | 05 Glass totem

02

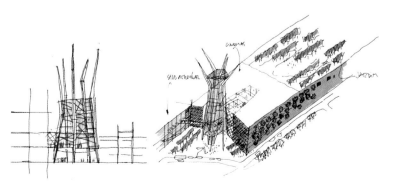

03

04

05

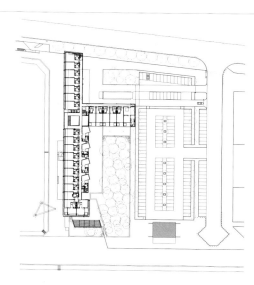

01

02

03

Altis Belém Hotel

Altis Belém Hotel is situated in Belém, on the waterfront to the east of the Bom Sucesso Dock and opposite the Belém Cultural Center. It is a five star hotel with 50 rooms and a number of facilities intended to support water sports. It is designed not to constitute a visual obstacle along the axis between the Belém Tower and the Monument to the Discoveries. The hotel is also composed of a rectangular platform, which incorporates the restaurant and creates a 'pocket' designed to increase privacy. A narrow structure, which sits between the hotel and the restaurant, possesses a strong identity of its own that is related to the look of the nearby Popular Art Museum. The interior design was by FSSMGN Architects.

01 Floor plan | 02 Restaurant | 03 Reception area | 04 Façade detail | 05 Exterior view | 06 Main entrance

04

05

06

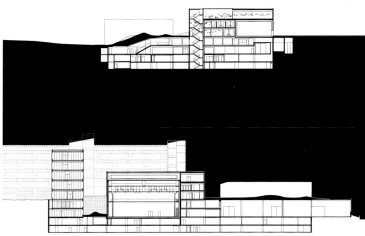

01

02

03

Headquarters and Studios R.T.P./R.D.P

The volatility of media and the image of speed are expressed through mutation, move-ment, and dynamism. The toughness and neutrality of the concrete volumes (studios) oppose the dynamics of the partially printed glass façades (administrative services) and the ductility of metal (technical services), underlining the abstract character of the project. Functionally it results in a flexible structure that provides physical proximity between the existing building and its expansion, assuring the interaction between these parts through two underground passages, while giving each autonomy.

01 Sections | 02 Interior view | 03 Exterior view | 04 Bird's-eye view

04

01

Mora River Aquarium

Echoing the rural barns of the Évora district in the Alentejo region of Portugal, this building was conceived as a single and monolithic pitched roof shed of white pre-cast concrete trusses with single spans of 33 meters. Inside, this remote hut shelters a complex water sanctuary moving through diverse fresh water habitats with more than 500 specimens. This project has been developed in collaboration with Boston architectural and marine biology firm cosestudi, a studio with which Promontório has teamed up for various international aquarium projects.

01 Façade with pitched roof | 02 Section | 03 Walkway over exterior pond | 04 Bird's-eye view | 05 Trusses

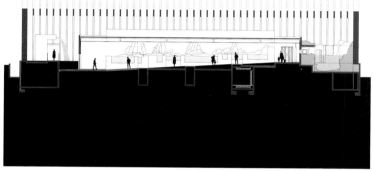

02

03

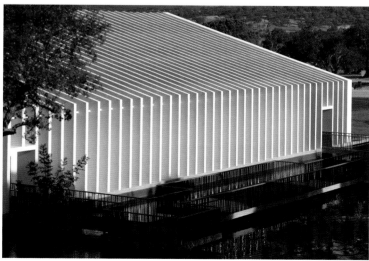

04

05

01

02

03

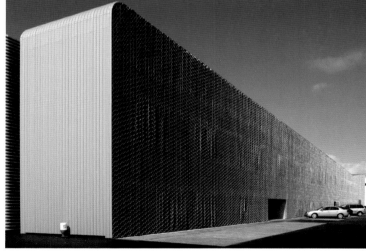

04

Inapal Metal Industrial Plant

This complex is composed of two volumes. One consists of two wings and a cantilever for storage, production and delivery. The other contains the maintenance and staff quarters, spread across two floors. The design deals with material homogenization and continuity, and embraces a strategy of structural modulation and constructive rationalization. The building design focuses on its 'skin'. A single material – trapezoidal metal cladding – is used and applied in various ways: revetments sheets are used to create closed spaces, and sliced metal sheeting is fixed in a honeycomb pattern for shade, illumination, or ventilation.

01 Space between the staff and industrial areas | 02 Distribution corridor | 03 Industrial wing and cantilever | 04 View from southeast | 05 Sections

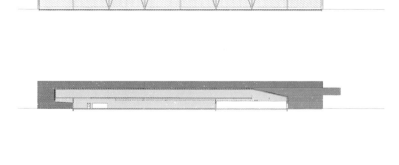

05

01

02

03

04

05

Santo António's Church and St. Bartolomeu Social Center

Seen from the outside, the building looks like an elementary structure made of white surfaces. The main space is defined by the continuity from the street, to the quartz stone, through the portico, to the courtyard with two ramps on each side, the community center side wings and finally to the church itself. Another patio creates a stage setting for the church room. The church's assembly room is almost square. The altar is also a square table. The simplicity of the design creates a sense of freedom, with the people and the events as the main characters.

01 Entrance portico | 02 View from the street towards the church | 03 Courtyard with ramps | 04 Courtyard | 05 View towards the quartz stone | 06 Ground floor plan

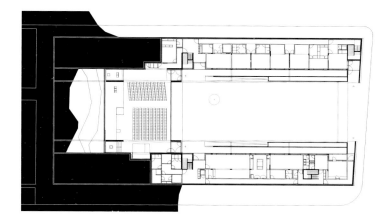

06

01

Dolce Vita

This shopping center is an elliptical, vertical atrium space that rises from below the ground to break through the roof of the building. Each of the elliptical walkways that project into the space of the atrium is a bolted cantilevered, steel and glass structure. Underneath these translucent glass walkways are upward-facing lights (responsible for giving the translucent glass floors a mystical shimmer) and downward-facing lights (providing adequate illumination for the floor below). At the top of this elliptical space is a 'folded butterfly' ceiling of perforated metal panels that provides a gossamer effect and allows views beyond to the trusses that support the ceiling.

01 Aerial view | 02 'Folded butterfly' ceiling | 03 Master plan | 04 Atrium | 05 Main façade | 06 Assemblage of glass and lighting systems

02

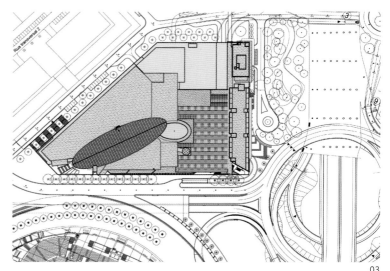

03

04

06

05

01

Fez House

This house was built by Alvaro Leite Siza Vieira and took 12 years to complete; from assembling the site, designing the house and then building it. The house is sculptural in nature, with a strongly defined horizontal axis. Multiple entrances and exits are located in the angular niches and sculptural elements of the house work to blur the boundaries between interior and exterior. Wood, concrete and white granite, together with the stark white interior, give the house a museum-like feel. Inside, an unusual stairway leads visitors down to the indoor swimming pool.

01 View from garden | 02 Corner view | 03 Interior view | 04 Sections | 05 Garden

02

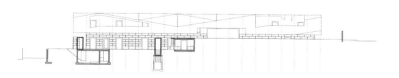

03

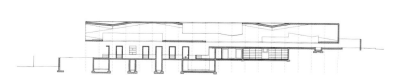

04

05

01

02

03

04

Temporary Bar

This bar was the winning entry of an academic competition, organized by the Faculty of Architecture in Oporto. Fast construction and a low budget had to be taken into consideration in the design of this temporary structure, which had to be built in just one week with voluntary help from students. The project is a modular building made out of different depth storage boxes. These stand as a visual reference, capable of dramatically changing its appearance: by day a white abstract and closed volume, by night a box of changing light following the DJ set. The vibrancy of the small, brightly lit structure reflects its purpose as an entertainment venue, as well as setting it apart from the surrounding architecture.

01 Temporary bar | 02 Night view | 03 Exterior view | 04 Façade detail | 05 Floor plan and elevation

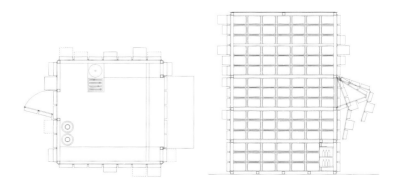

05

01

Arena Dragão Caixa

The construction of Arena Dragão Caixa is particularly important in urban terms because it complements the urban area and fills an open slot in the ring of buildings surrounding the stadium. The restrictions imposed by the location and shape of the site was instrumental in the project design. The site consists of one building and two outdoor spaces, one to the north and one to the south. The space to the south acts as a public square, the one to the north provides access for loading and unloading. The boxy shape of the building's front gives it a contemporary appearance; this is emphasized by the modern interior lighting and color scheme.

01 Front view | 02 Interior view | 03 Indoor court | 04 Ground floor plan in situation

02

03

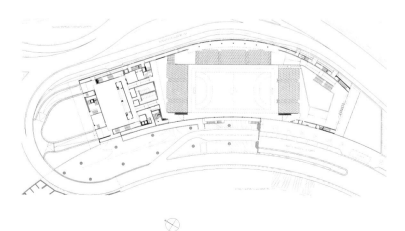

04

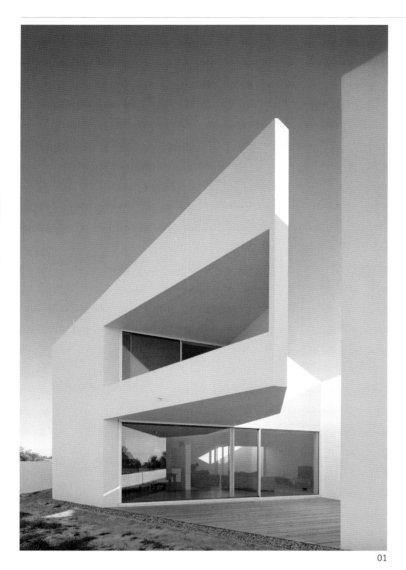

01

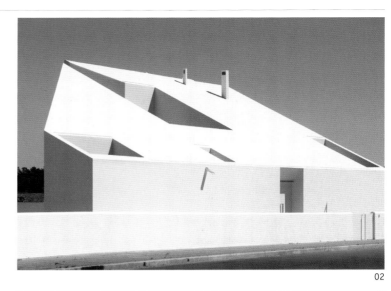

02

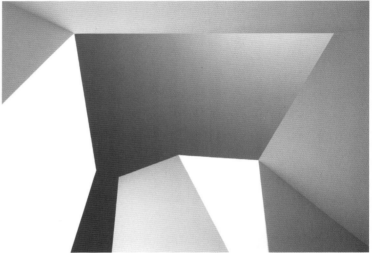

03

04

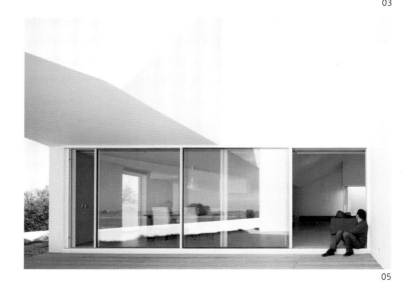

05

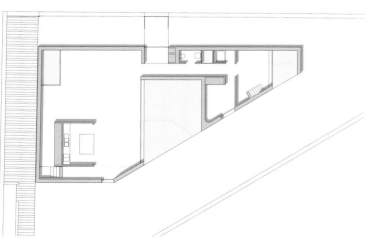

06

House in Possanco

The owners required a small vacation house that would allow a casual and relaxed enjoyment of their weekend. The first challenge confronting the architects was the triangular shape of the small lot which, when applying the legal distance measures, barely allowed any formal alternatives. The most interesting views stand to the north and not to the south of the site, where the windows should be placed in their quest for light. To the south are the street, traffic and passersby. The decision was taken to install almost all windows facing north, allowing them to frame the views of the amazing landscape. The architects explored the expressiveness of the white block and its abstract personality. The totality of the volume is white, while the patios resemble bluish excavations, delicately enhancing the strong character of the house.

01 Exterior view | 02 Street view | 03 Skylight | 04 Interior view | 05 Patio | 06 Floor plan

01

02

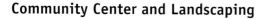

03

04

Community Center and Landscaping

This community center and landscaping project was part of the intention to redevelop and reuse this urban area, as well as endowing it with necessary public facilities. The proposal aims to recycle the existing urban structure through the creation of a natural platform and to implant the building in the north limit, defining an urban front for the square and allowing room for an exterior leisure space in the interior of the block. It also involved the redesign of the passages between different squares and organized the program, guaranteeing its autonomy and its link with the public services.

01 Façade | 02 Main corridor | 03 View from south | 04 View from west | 05 Sections

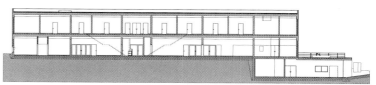

05

01

02

03

04

Santa Ana's Chapel

The location of this chapel is at the intersection of five streets, and at the bottom corner of an ascending topography. It is developed on one level, varying only its height towards the altar at the head of the chapel. The shape of the church and the plot that it is located on allow space for Mass to be celebrated outside. The unique architecture and the way it is fitted to the slope create a unique worshipping experience of light and transparency. The perforated skin of the façade allows light into the white interior, brightening the space and giving it a more open appearance.

01 View towards altar | 02 View from street | 03 Façade | 04 Bird's-eye view | 05 Night view | 06 Floor plan

05

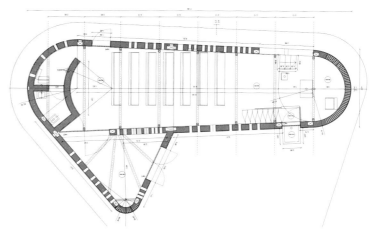

06

01

02

Refuge Pavilion

This project anticipates the rearrangement of an already existing construction annexed to a small house, consisting of a refuge pavilion of 50 square meters with energy-efficient concepts. The pavilion layout departs from a nucleus of sanitary and shower fittings, placed between the yard and the covered area, while trying to strengthen the direction of the entrance through its compression, to release all the remaining space in a single multifunctional compartment. The inner space is marked by structural porches and carpentry façades, which, when shut, totally enclose this inner space, and when opened, allow an 180-degree view of the surrounding landscape.

01 East façade | 02 Exterior view | 03 Living area | 04 Sections

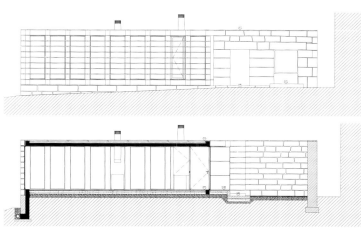

03

04

01

02

Modernization of Sebastião da Gama School

This project is based on improving the school and its relationship with the city of Setúbal. This process includes both exterior and interior areas. The project orders, rearranges and locates not only the program and circulations but also the design of the outside area. The starting point for the project is the setting – both symbolically and functionally – of an exterior central space, creating a square perceptible as the center of the school. For this system to become intelligible and effective, the creation of the new building, which contains the library, multi-use room, café and outdoor playing field, between the old ones was important. The project aims to bring a logical conclusion to the site.

01 Exterior view | 02 Classroom | 03 Exploded view | 04 Façade detail

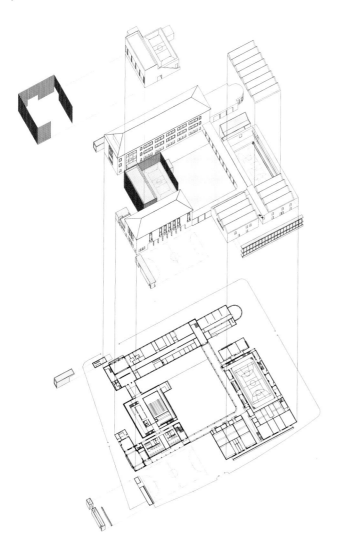

03

04

01

02

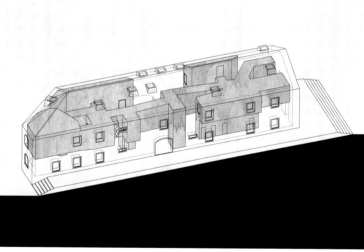

03

Environmental Monitoring and Interpretation Offices

This project is a conversion of a formerly rundown infrastructure. The new program comprises two distinct areas: a public area for exhibitions and a private area consisting of lecture rooms and accommodation for invited artists. The design maintains the entire external perimeter construction, while its rundown interior has been totally scooped out. The new construction establishes itself as the anatomy of the existing building. The private areas are volumetrically defined within the structure and optimized for inhabitability. The social life, exhibitions and meetings take place in the interstitial space around the new structure and are characterized by the programmatic events defined by the enclosed spaces.

01 General interior view | 02 Main staircase volume | 03 Axonometry | 04 Main open space area

04

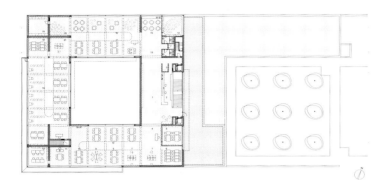

01

Viana do Castelo Library

This library sits on the L-shaped ground floor and consists of a raised square. The building has an area of 45 x 45 meters, including an inner courtyard of 20 x 20 meters. In order for the landscape to flow continuously, the large volume should not disturb the view to the river from the street and the surroundings. The architect preserves the view of the river through this elevated construction and creates framed views on the street level, with a large riverside inner garden. The ground floor hosts the entrance, offices, conference rooms and archives, while the actual library is on the first floor, additionally lit by skylights. The façade consists of exposed white concrete, while the natural stone cladding of the building's base is in harmony with the surrounding nature.

01 First floor plan | 02 View towards the city | 03 Elevated first floor framing the view towards the river | 04 Interior | 05 Library with skylights

02

03

04

05

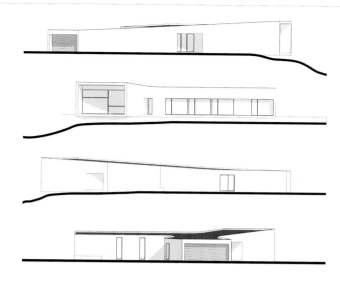

01

02

03

Casa Jorge Guedes

Located at top of a valley, Jorge Guedes's house appears as a large window that covers the landscape. The building rises to the principles of the varied volumes of the region's architecture. The architects have devised an organic whole, composed of three bodies, which extend along the ground, searching for the best orientation for each volume. A Y-shape forms an intersection point between the arms and is both the entry and distribution space, separating the public from the private areas. The bathroom, laundry and kitchen do not face the valley and are fitted with a small orange patio that allows them to benefit from direct sunlight without creating imbalances in elevation.

01 Elevations | 02 View from street | 03 View from above | 04 View towards valley |
05 View from lawn | 06 Interior view | 07 Night view

04

05

06

07

01

South Tenerife Convention Center

The Convention Center on the Adeje Coast of Tenerife coexists with a difficult environment due to the proximity of the South Tenerife motorway. The only reference points in the surrounding area are the rocky, semi-desert landscape and the sea, its imposing presence framing the building with a constant view of La Gomera Island in the background. The response to this situation arises from an appreciation of the landscape, which the architects have extended by means of geometric rocks that house the program functions. The fault lines of the rock encourage the flow of the roof, which was imagined as moving liquid that engulfs the space in every direction. The liquid splits and multiplies, producing cracks of light and ventilation that intensify the sense of lightness on the undulating surface. The main entrance to the large foyer leads visitors to the coffee shop or the auditorium.

01 Exterior view | 02 Conference hall | 03 Aerial view | 04 Floor plan, lower level

02

03

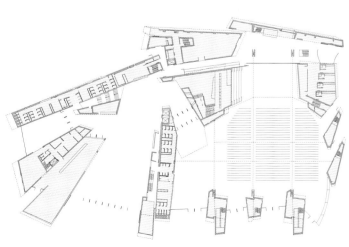

04

01

02

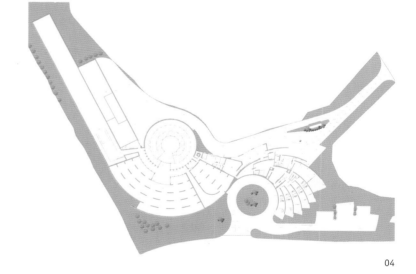

03

Bodega Antión

The intention was to mold the plot of land, which was uneven and relatively shapeless. Most of the bodega is located underground, covered by a green blanket, with no alteration to the landscape. These underground buildings gradually emerge from the land in different ways, each with their own distinctive identity. In this way, the top of the production building can just be glimpsed from the north, whilst almost the entire building stands out in the south, designed with a ventilated façade to protect it from the direct impact of the sun. Colored, exposed monolithic concrete is predominant in the complex, only altered by the stainless steel crowning the great cylinder in the winemaking room.

01 Front view | 02 Lateral view | 03 Barrel area | 04 Floor plan | 05 Sections

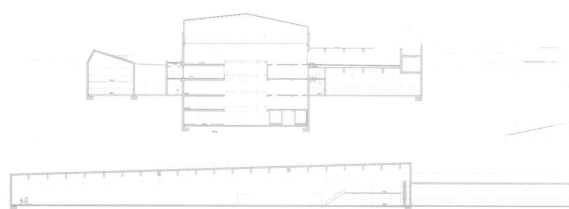

04

05

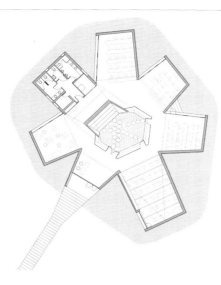

01

02

Wifi Pavilion

The idea of this project is the construction of an exportable wifi-media pavilion, located in the heart of a university campus. The building performs as a virtual interface providing public Internet access and a place for students to hang out and relax. The star-shaped pavilion is divided into five different spaces surrounding a central courtyard that guarantees maximum natural light and ventilation. The spaces are designed in order to offer a wide range of configurations, since the final use of the building was not clearly specified. The island rises one and a half meters above ground level, re-enforcing the identity and singularity of the pavilion as an 'object trouvé'.

01 Floor plan | 02 Interior view and patio | 03 Patio | 04 Interior view | 05 General view | 06 Main entrance

03

04

05

06

01

02

03

04

Holiday Home

This steeply sloping slight was made of pure rock and was previously considered virtually unattainable. The dynamic form of this holiday home results from the existing contour lines and the terrain profile. Through the flexible floor plan, the main apartment can be divided up into three separately developed units. Another small annex complements the family house. A terrace offers a 180-degree view of the surroundings. The roof of the terrace is adapted to the path of the sun and offers protection from rain and strong sunlight. Fully glazed façades permit an impressive view of the rugged mountains on one side and the Spanish town of Altea with the sea on the other side.

01 Main floor plan | 02 Exterior view | 03 General view | 04 Terrace | 05 Interior view | 06 Swimming pool with view of surrounding area

05

06

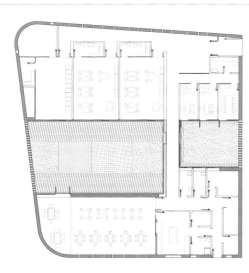

01

02

Kindergarten in Sotillo de la Adrada

A solid perimeter fence, sometimes following the outline of the plot, sometimes seeking the best route over land, separates this new center for pre-school education from the numerous new housing units surrounding the site. Inside the fence, the building is condensed into two closed spaces connected by an arm of light and glass, and two patios. The interior reveals spaces with qualities of color bestowed by the lacquered finish of the aluminum carpentry work and colored ceramic surfaces. The circulation spaces have been designed to allow the children their own visual relationship with the spaces outside. The uppermost limits of the classrooms are marked by hanging lamps.

01 Floor plan | 02 Activity room | 03 Glass façade revealing colorful interior | 04 Inner façade with skylight

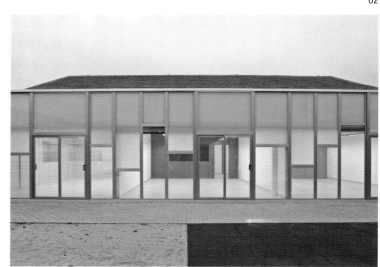

03

04

01

02

House 10.1

This house was conceived as an industrialized extendable prototype adapted to the basic program of its inhabitants, that will be able to grow as their needs or interests grow. The initial design phase focuses on the interior space, which features double-height ceilings and houses the typical living functions: kitchen, dining room and living room. On the other hand, the corners and transition spaces offer places to sleep, to work, and to store, together with the vestibule and the bathroom. On the outside, a disproportionate terrace sometimes acts as an observation platform and as an artificial fragment of the landscape marked by the house.

01 Exterior night view | 02 House within landscape | 03 Front façade | 04 Ground floor plan with deck | 05 Interior view | 06 Deck | 07 Kitchen and dining area

03

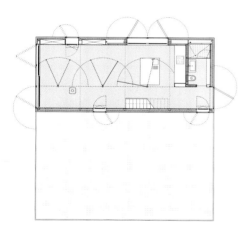

04

05

06

07

01

02

03

04

Hotel Me by Meliá

This tower stands out on the Barcelona skyline like a metal needle; a 'jewel', with red, blue and green glass distributed at random along the façade like a giant stained glass window. At night the tower turns into an urban lantern, a luminous diagonal symbol. The interior design is based on the generous views from each room, like a giant screen overlooking the city. This screen is articulated by a series of smaller screens resembling television sets that form a 'wall of images'. The result is a building clad in a protective skin of thick sheets of anodized aluminum - dense, stiff and corrosion-proof.

01 General view from the park | 02 Outdoor space | 03 Terrace on an elevated level | 04 View of a suite | 05 Pool on an elevated level

05

01

02

Gym 704

A simple prismatic volume is deformed only by the slope of the deck, which has been attached parallel to the access ramp so as to avoid casting a shadow on the track, allowing an alternate use when the school is closed. The porch becomes the theme for the composition, providing access to locker rooms and the gym, while connecting them to the level of the track sport area. The formalization of the building is achieved using constructive logic, which was part of the initial intention to build using microlaminated wood. The outer coating is made with polycarbonate panels, which contribute to energy savings on the southern façade and bring light to the north façade.

01 Exterior view | 02 Side view | 03 Perspective | 04 Section | 05 Corner | 06 Interior view

03

04

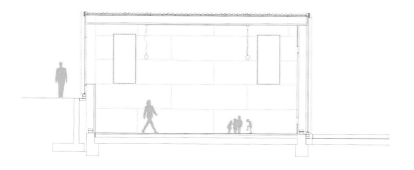

05

06

01

02

03

04

05

06

House 205

The setting of this project is a plot with steep slopes and a large amount of trees and bushes. The aim is building a house without causing any serious impact on the land. The house is built on a natural rocky platform, which is used as both the exit and the garden of the house. The only uneven area is the path ramp, which crosses the piece of land diagonally. The inner layout of the house is based on a lineal sequence of rooms of different proportions linked to the structure. There are great sliding opened areas, which provide both harmony and versatility.

01 Deck connecting with interior | 02 Rear view | 03 Exterior view | 04 Kitchen | 05 Hallway serving as children's area | 06 Sections

02

01

04

03

05

Parclogistic ILLA-B1

This brand-new building of Abertis, constituting the second phase of Barcelona's "Logistic Parc," is a 13,000-square meter office building that accommodates on its five floors the different business areas of the company: telecommunication infrastructures, airports, parking, and logistics. A central Greek-cross shape open space provides access from the lobby to the flexible working zones. The building is meant to be part of a group of three buildings with a continuous angled façade that forms an interior plaza sheltered from the highway. The interior plaza contrasts with the double glass wall, while elements of Mediterranean and Catalan architecture in red stucco are reintroduced to this patio.

01 Night view | 02 General view | 03 Offices corridor | 04 Entrance to the offices | 05 Site plan

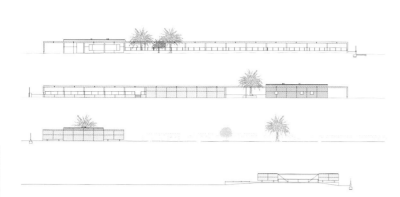

01

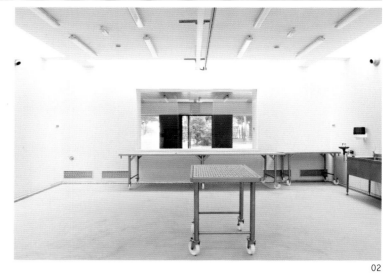

02

CRAM.

CRAM Foundation for the Rehabilitation and Conservation of Marine Animals is an organization dedicated to the protection of the environment and the species that inhabit it. A center without references, a pioneer in Europe, incorporating the three basic guidelines of the foundation: the clinic, and rescue of marine protected species which varies from reintroduction, the tasks of conservation, research and training and finally the social awareness campaigns on the state of the marine environment and its problems. The project seeks to balance the clinical program of research and public program with minimum possible means to ensure that the conditions of the activity become the key factors in defining the architectural features and volume of the whole.

01 Elevations | 02 Postmortem building interior | 03 Façade | 04 Administration building | 05 Clinic entrance

03

04

05

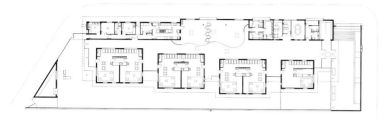

01

02

03

04

Uni Dori Municipal Nursery School

This project occupies a total built up surface area of 1,271 square meters, with four sets of classrooms for up to 107 pupils. The sets include a 76-square-meter wing on one side for babies up to a year old, plus three modules, each of 130 square meters, containing a total of six classrooms, three for children from one to two years old and three more for children from two to three years old, each one with the capacity to accommodate 20 children. The project is comprised of brightly colored wooden cubes, for each of the different groups of children, based on a partially roofed, translucent surface. The design is a kind of boulevard or street, containing and developing the full range of school activities.

01 Floor plan | 02 Classroom | 03 Classroom detail | 04 Indoor playgound | 05 Exterior view | 06 Exterior playground

05

06

01

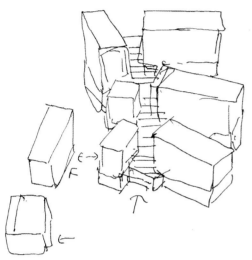

02

City of Justice

Barcelona's new law courts complex breaks down the 240,000-square meter program into nine buildings, four of which are linked by a continuous four-story-high concourse building. The site is on the border between the cities of Barcelona and l'Hospitalet on the site of a former military barracks. A group of four large judicial buildings are situated around the perimeter of a linking concourse building. The concourse building gathers people at the start and completion of their judicial visit within a central public room, which overlooks the exterior plaza. Four other independent buildings comprise a judicial services building for l'Hospitalet, a forensic sciences building, and two commercial buildings with retail facilities at ground level.

01 General view | 02 Sketch | 03 Entrance | 04 Interior view | 05 Foyer

03

04

05

01

02

03

Can Framis Museum

This museum is located in the 22nd district of Barcelona, which is now a high-rise, heavily built-up area. Can Framis aimed to play on contrasts, with a surrounding garden providing a quiet breathing space. The main interest of the two buildings to be preserved lies in the contrast of their location, based on the former agricultural plan prior to the Cerdà plan. The project involved the restoration of two factory buildings and the construction of a new building to link the different entities. The three buildings form a courtyard where the main entrance is located. Outside, the lime mortar blends with the existing stonework and merges with the exposed concrete. The façade then becomes a collage of textures.

01 Street view | 02 Rear view | 03 Interior view | 04 Floor plans | 05 Main entrance

04

05

01

02

03

Hotel W

The sail-shaped Barcelona Port Hotel, located at the new entrance to Barcelona's harbor, rises like a modern icon above the Mediterranean Sea and is a landmark for an area slated to be redeveloped with upmarket office and entertainment facilities. The reflecting façade of silvered glass blends with the color of the sky and sea. This volume is inserted into the low-slung atrium building, the lobby of which affords views of the sea and enjoys natural zenithal light. Public activities are housed beneath a platform designed in the form of two huge terraces. The sizeable volume of the conference hall with its large glass frontage overlooking the sea breaks the horizontal lines of the podium.

01 Interior view | 02 Hotel room | 03 General view | 04 Floor plan | 05 View of sea | 06 Exterior view

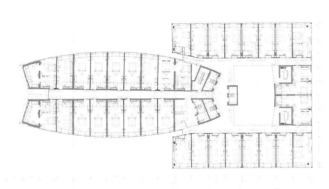

04

05

06

→ Toyo Ito & Associates with Carlos Basso and
UDA Arquitectos
→ Hotel
→ 2009
→ Barcelona
→ Spain
→ Photos: Courtesy of the architects

01

02

Suites Avenue Apartment

Toyo Ito & Associates Architects were responsible for the renovation of the front façade and the internally facing façade of this building, which fronts the main street, Paseo de Gracia in Barcelona. Carlos Basso and Toni Olaya of UDA Arquitectos participated in the building renovation. The design proposed the use of 'waves' as a representation of movement. These were made of curved steel plate and seamlessly integrated with one another. Their convexity and concavity were shifted at different areas, conveying the undulating wave movements towards the city's fabric. The surface is coated with a light tint of pearl pink, allowing the color to react to the light conditions. The landscape seen from the balcony is trimmed by the undulating waveforms, giving the hotel guests a view of uniquely reformed scenery.

01 Façade | 02 Street view | 03 View to Casa Mila by Gaudí | 04 Façade detail | 05 Floor plan

03

04

05

01

04

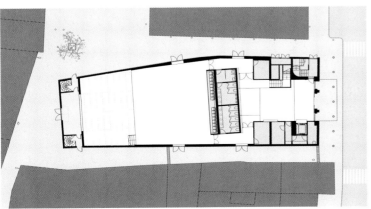

06

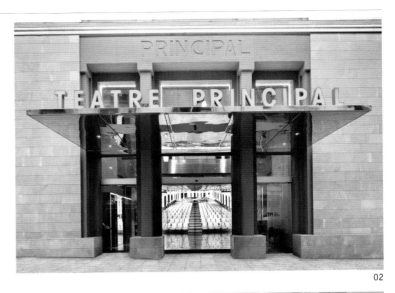

02

03

05

Renovation of the Teatre Principal

This building houses the Teatre Principal and belongs to the Badalona Town Council. Built in 1930, it was initially used as a cinema and was last renovated in 1998. It is currently used for the programing of shows of varying formats, aimed at a range of different audiences. The initial idea of the project was to create a multipurpose space for drama productions and other events and to provide the building as a whole with a spatial quality and design continuity that it had lost over the years as a result of its various changes in usage, multiple modifications and a certain lack of upkeep.

01 Front façade | 02 Entrance | 03 Main hall | 04 Interior view of second floor | 05 Theater | 06 Ground floor plan in situation

01

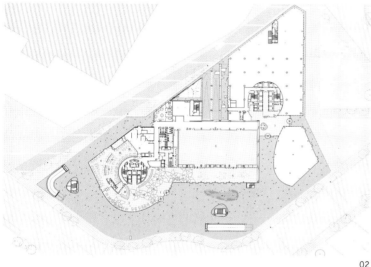

02

03

Torres Porta Fira

Within the "European Plaza", a pair of towers now stands as part of the urban regeneration project for L'Hospitalet, the neighboring city to Barcelona. The project consists of three parts: a hotel tower and an office tower, both about 110 meters tall and a lower compartment with a roof garden that connects the two towers. The hotel tower has 345 rooms, an entrance hall, restaurant, and the banquet hall, which is also used for conferences or exhibitions. On the mezzanine level, there are conference rooms, which can be divided into four spaces by sliding partitions and three small meeting rooms. The office tower has 22 office floors, two leasable shops and an entrance hall on the ground floor.

01 General view | 02 Site plan | 03 Foyer | 04 Restaurant | 05 Exterior view

04

05

01

Tellada House

Raised above the ground, this environmentally friendly house follows the slope of the land and blends effectively into its wooded environment. Large glazed openings ensure a close relationship between the interior and the external landscape. Wood, combined with aluminum frames, dominates both the interior and exterior. This house was awarded the Fundación Juan de Vega prize and was praised especially for its balance between good design (which is consistent with the intended uses) and the integration of the work in its natural environment (a small forest of oak, birch, and chestnut trees), which also contributes to the materials chosen, predominantly wood.

01 Front façade | 02 Winter terrace | 03 Work area | 04 Kitchen and dining area | 05 Large window connecting exterior and interior

02

03

04

05

01

02

03

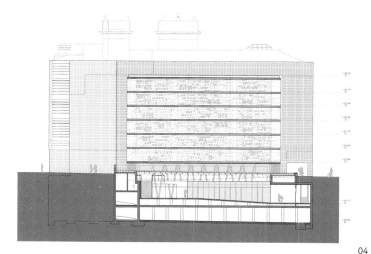

04

The Regional Library of Bizkaia

This site includes an existing building, which had to be reformed, and an open space permitting a new construction according to client requirements. The new construction includes two new buildings. The first one, covered with stone, houses the administration. The second one serves to store the books and is designed like a glass container. The texture of the books is used to establish a cultural claim and make evident the dialogue between the interior of the building and the public space in the outside. During the day, the image of the printed serigraphies, which represent the written content of the books, is dominant. At night, the artificial illumination intensifies the aura of the books stored in the shelves.

01 Exterior view at night | 02 Lecture room | 03 Interior view | 04 Section | 05 Façade detail

05

01

BTEK Technology Interpretation Center

The new BTEK Technology Interpretation Center is designed to be a reference point in the landscape. It has two, apparently freestanding, pyramidal volumes; the first is a black volume that emerges from the earth. This has a heavier composition, enclosed on three sides and a roof formed by a grid of solar panels. Two curtain wall façades and a grass roof, conceived as a continuation of the land, generate the second volume. The roofs of the below-gradient connection, also of grass, merge into the site and the surroundings. The entrance is generated through the first volume, in the fold of a corner that marks the entrance to the building.

01 Green roofs | 02 Northwest view | 03 Integration with the landscape | 04 Sections | 05 Exhibition space

02

03

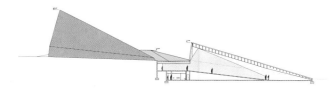
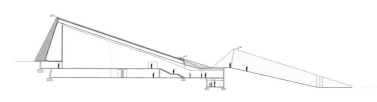

04

05

01

02

03

04

La Charca School Extension

This new building at the west end of the school complex is a prismatic box with voids in two opposite corners, creating the main entrance and the classrooms openings, covered by porches in both cases. The roof gives the image of the extension from the adjacent buildings, while the side façades are the background to the schoolyard. Next to the entrance, a lobby is directly connected to the multipurpose room, the rest of the classrooms and functional spaces. The simplicity of the interior space is enhanced by a patio that articulates the main circulations. Simplicity, according to the scale of the proposal, is evidenced by the structural system, in which the load-bearing walls are also the classrooms separations.

01 South view | 02 View from the entrance | 03 View from the schoolyard | 04 General view | 05 Conceptual plans

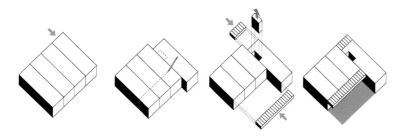

05

01

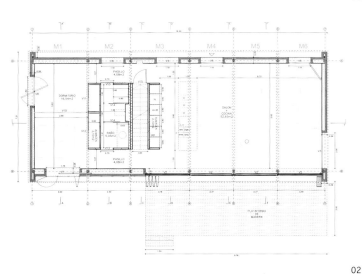

02

03

04

Prefab House

Constructed off-site using beams and galvanized steel columns for the frame, this prefab was transported by truck to the site and assembled in just three days. The design was inspired by the surrounding pitched roof farmhouses and abundant eucalyptus forests that pepper the steep hillside. The house comprises six modules: two contain the bathroom, stairs and kitchen, three provide living areas, and the last houses a bedroom with a moveable partition wall. The roof and perimeter walls are clad with Viroc, a prefabricated mixture of cement and wood shavings, which is characteristically strong, lightweight and echoes the colors of the eucalyptus forests nearby.

01 View down to living room | 02 Floor plan | 03 Detail | 04 Living room | 05 Rear façade

05

01

Between Cathedrals

Between Cathedrals seeks to create an intervention worthy of the most significant location in the historical town of Cádiz; the empty space facing the sea located between the Old and New Cathedrals. The basic premise is to cover and protect an archeological excavation. Additionally, this new plane serves as a base for a space facing the ocean, a raised public area providing clear views, unobstructed by cars passing on the ring road. A light, white platform is thus conceived, poised over the excavation as if on tiptoe, and reached by a side ramp. Over this plane, a huge canopy structure is built to offer protection from the sun and rain.

01 Waterfront | 02 Exterior view | 03 Entrance ramp | 04 Site plan

02

03

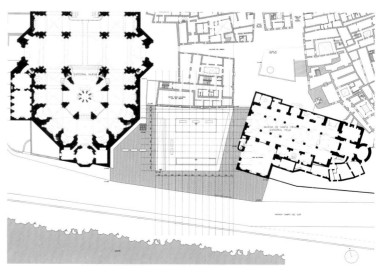

04

01

02

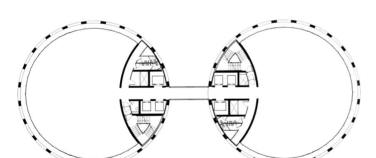

03

Hercules Towers

The Hercules Towers, two cylindrical towers of identical volume, are located in the Bay of Gibraltar on a plot of 12,000 square meters. They are joined by a crystalline prism which houses the hallways connecting the two buildings. The 100-meter towers, which allude to the legendary "Pillars of Hercules", rise like rigid structures from the body of water that surrounds them. On the façade, giant letters spell out the sentence "Non plus ultra", protecting the offices from solar radiation. The circular floors are 25 meters in diameter and the vertical core houses vertical communications facilities and services, while general facilities are placed in the basement and on the roof.

01 General view | 02 Glass connection between the two towers | 03 Typical floor plan | 04 Roof terrace

04

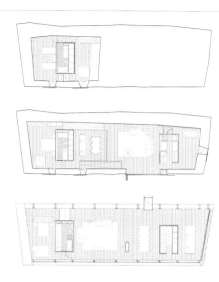

01

02

03

House in the Pyrenees

Located in a small town in the Pyrenees, Canejan, Catalonia, this dry stone house is a comfortable residence that consists of two units within one envelope, for a father and a son. It features impressive views over the valley and of the summit mountain. The design of the house not only respects the envelope, but also the historical values of the architecture. The new technologies and knowledge of age are applied to create a sustainable house, even in an extreme climate.

01 Floor plans | 02 Night view | 03 Living and dining room with double-sided fireplace | 04 View to stone terrace | 05 Kitchen with open views to surroundings

04

05

01

02

03

04

The Roman Theater Museum

The aim of this project was to incorporate the Roman Theater into the city by connecting pre-existing buildings and voids with the urban framework, thereby creating a museum-like route that leads from the lower levels of the port up to the Cerro de la Concepción. The Center for Roman Studies and the museum are located along this itinerary, culminating in the space of the Roman Theater. The 'promenade' flows through exhibition spaces lit by a system of skylights. The construction encompasses two buildings, connected by a corridor, surrounding a yard. The first one contains service rooms and provides access from the Riquelme Palace. The second building is located in General Ordoñez, connected by a terrace to the Old Cathedral.

01 Foyer | 02 Corridor | 03 Bird's-eye view | 04 Exhibition room | 05 Site plan

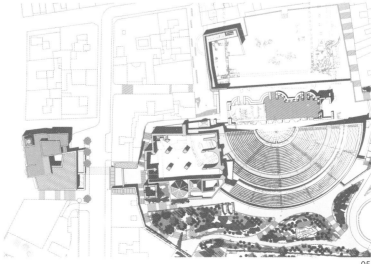

05

01

Casa del Estudiante

This project involved the rehabilitation of an existing building to create a student center and provide services and space for a range of activities carried out by the students of the Cartagena's Polytechnic University. These aims allowed for a generic design program with offices, meeting rooms, an auditorium and a large multi-purpose space with double-height ceilings. The intervention goes beyond the limits of the original construction – a modest residential building from the early 20th century protected by urban zoning regulations – to invade the adjacent public space and occupy the area underneath it in an effort to expand the available surface area.

01 General view | 02 Façade detail | 03 Interior view of second floor | 04 South elevation | 05 View from west

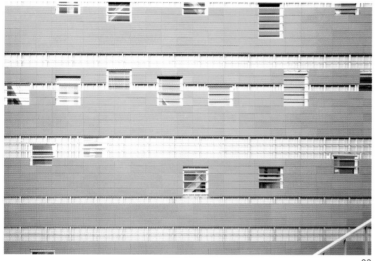

02

03

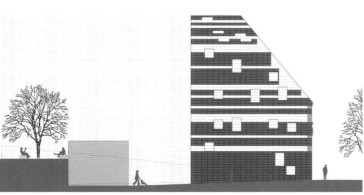

04

05

01

Bodegas Portia

Bodegas Portia is a new winery for the Faustino Group, located in the Ribera del Duero, one of Spain's foremost wine-producing regions. The building's trefoil plan expresses the three main stages of production: fermentation, ageing and maturation. After harvesting, the grapes are delivered to the winery via a road that rises on to the roof, from here they are dropped directly into the hopper. Gravity then helps to move the harvest around the building, maximizing energy efficiency and minimizing damage to the grapes. The roof canopy shades the glazed atria and exposed vats and incorporates photovoltaics. The structure is clad in Corten steel shingles, whose color complements the natural tones of the vineyards.

01 Aerial view | 02 Exterior view | 03 Stairs | 04 Interior view

02

03

04

01

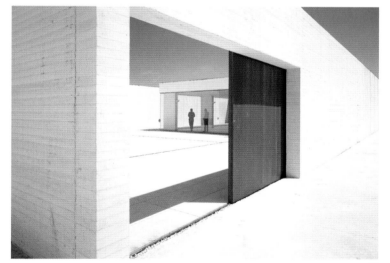

02

Madinat al Zahra Museum

The Madinat al Zahra archaeological site is considered one of the most significant early Islamic archaeological sites in the world. Excavations are still ongoing, so the museum development needed to be carefully considered. The final design is reminiscent of a cloister building; the building articulates its new uses around a sequence of full and empty spaces, covered areas and open patios. From the main vestibule, a broad patio spreads out on a square plan, blue from the reflection of the pond presiding over it. The materials respond to the prevailing criteria of the project: walls of poured concrets, interior walls of iroko wood and courtyards paved with limestone.

01 View from roof | 02 Exterior view | 03 Interior | 04 Floor plan

03

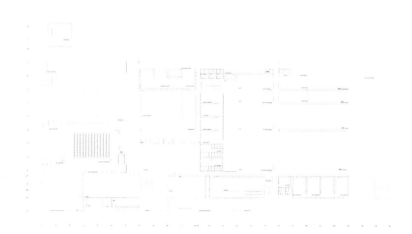

04

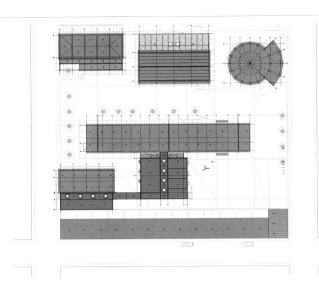

01

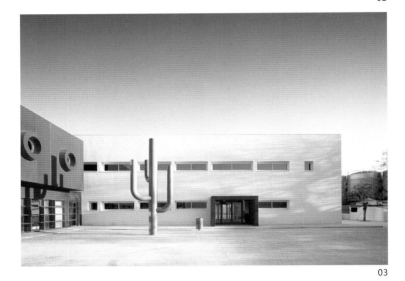

02

Hermanos Amorós Public School

The original school was divided into six pavilions of traditional architecture unconnected to each other. The approach taken by the architects was to create the seventh piece on the existing complex, which would resolve the functional requirements and behave as joint organization between elementary education pavilion and high school. As the architects embarked upon the project, it became clear that the school required more interventions than the scope of the competition initially suggested. The intervention transforms the existing relationship between buildings and creates new social spaces.

01 Floor plan | 02 Library entrance | 03 Northern façade | 04 View from the street | 05 View from the playground | 06 Roof | 07 Inside the library

03

04

05

06

07

01

02

03

Las Vinas Infant Educational Center

Located in the northern part of Cullar Vega's city center, this project was conceived around the idea of creating a permeable building, in which the exterior space and its relation to the interior play the leading roles. Two main complementary, perpendicular axes, one enclosing public activities and administration, the other, longer, the teaching activities and classrooms, structure the building. All spaces receive natural light and ventilation and are interconnected in order to achieve visual integration of all inner areas. The perimeter wall is dense, in order to align the school with its urban surroundings, yet also permeable, allowing views of the grounds from beyond the wall.

01 Front façade | 02 Playground | 03 Main entrance | 04 Sections | 05 Outdoor area

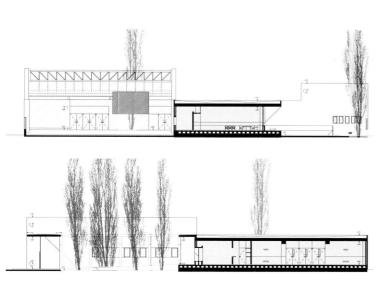

04

05

01

02

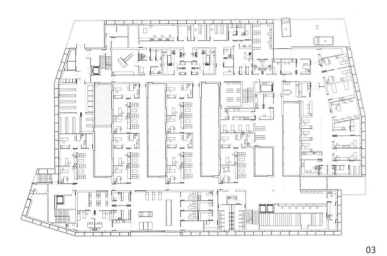

03

04

Daimiel's Health Care Center, Outpatient Specialty Center

On the outside, this project solves the problem of a public building fitted into a residential neighborhood, being covered with a metallic skin of louvers made out of micro perforated galvanized plates that helps lessen the scale of every single window. Inside, the building is open to five patios clad with a galvanized undulated sheet, with the consulting rooms on one side and corridors and waiting areas on the other side, maximizing optimal conditions of natural lighting and ventilation through the glazed enclosures. The interior is made of white materials, mosaic tiles, compact laminate panels and glass.

01 Metallic skin of louvers | 02 Front view | 03 Ground floor plan | 04 Entrance view | 05 Metallic skin detail | 06 Inner courtyard

05

06

01

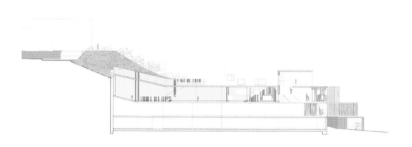

02

03

04

05

Kindergarten and Parking in Sansaburu

Opening towards the south and southeast, Sansaburu kindergarten is composed of two wings surrounding a central courtyard. Each arm of the building has two stories in which the various elements are organized. The classrooms have been arranged in order to receive the most possible natural light at the times when they are in use. Large windows at ground level allow light to flood into the interior spaces and also create a relationship between interior and exterior. The warm colors that clad the interior extend beyond the internal spaces through a random arrangement of gaps in the façade. An arrangement of lamps in the front entrance above the tramex closure draws the gaze of passersby.

01 Bird's-eye view | 02 Section | 03 Tramex building closure | 04 Scale windows in corridors | 05 Staircase

01

02

03

Marqués de Riscal Hotel

The central part of this complex is the building designed by Frank O. Gehry, housing the company headquarters and hotel complex. This ambitious project combines top architecture, local landscape and enjoyment of wine. A mix of modernity and tradition, the Marqués de Riscal Hotel is Gehry's homage to this region. The building resembles a great vine and is distinguished by its form and materials, which resemble those used in the Bilbao Guggenheim Museum. Here the titanium covers feature the colors of the hotel – pink for the wine, gold for the mesh covering bottles and silver for the bottle cap.

01 General view with hotel and garden | 02 View of roof | 03 Terrace | 04 Section

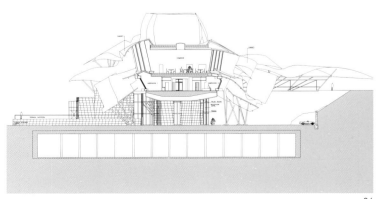

04

01

02

03

Andalusia Memorial Museum

This project complements the central headquarters of the Caja Granada Savings Bank, built in 2001 by the same architects. A podium building, measuring 60 x 120 meters, is three stories high, so that its upper floor coincides with the podium of the main Caja Granada building. Everything is arranged around a central courtyard, in an elliptical form in which circular ramps rise, connecting the three levels and creating a spatial tension. Like a gate to the city, a strong vertical piece emerges, the same height and width as the main building of the Caja Granada. To finish the entire operation, a large horizontal platform serves as a public space, running all the way to the river.

01 General view | 02 Elliptical courtyard | 03 Courtyard | 04 Site plan and silhouette | 05 Bird's-eye view | 06 Screen building

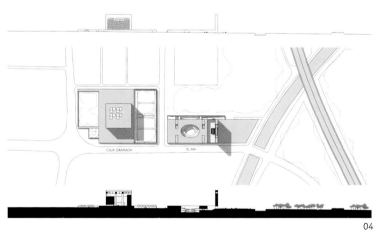

04

05

06

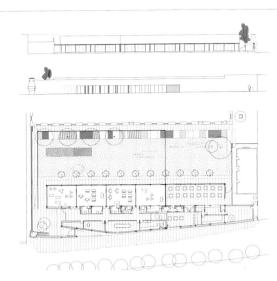

01

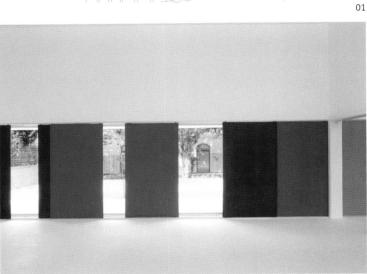

02

03

Los Mondragones

A vast military block north of Granada has been transformed into an administration complex including a daycare center and municipal dining hall. The peculiarities of the site, its topography and orientation as well as its specific use, presented a variety of challenges. The daycare center is in three modules and, on the recommendation of a team of pedagogues, is based on the concept of creating spaces that favor learning and the development of psychomotor activity. The classrooms have double-ighting and high windows that face the morning sun, while a glass wall to the west opens onto a garden full of plants. Energy consumption was optimized by the installation of thermal insulation and insulation against humidity.

01 Floor plan | 02 Activity room | 03 Hallway with sliding wall elements | 04 Exterior view from street | 05 Garden side

04

05

01

R. Lopez de Heredia Pavilion

The client approached Zaha Hadid Architects with the wish that a pavilion be created to contain an older pavilion that was discovered in the client's outhouses and had been restored. The great-grandfather had originally commissioned the old pavilion for the world fair exhibition in 1910. Made from timber and designed in a fin-de-siecle style, the old pavilion became a jewel within the new container. Various studies led to a container developed in sectional cuts. The section distorts from a rectangle around the old pavilion to a shape resembling a decanter. This was not an intentional end point, but once noticed it could not be ignored. The architects had designed a new bottle for an old wine.

01 Façade detail | 02 Interior view | 03 Exterior view | 04 3D model

02

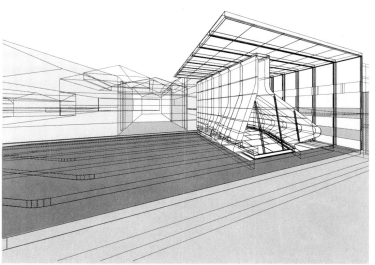

03

04

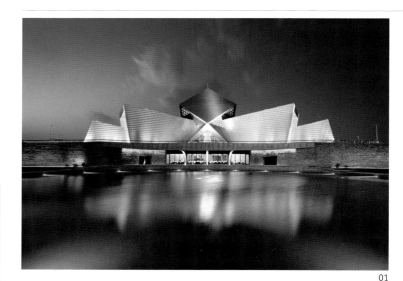

01

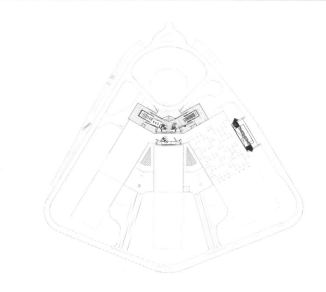

02

Bodega Irius

Most of this winery is situated below ground level and covered by a green layer without blotting the landscape. In the working part of the winery, the need for a balanced temperature means that, wherever possible, it is advisable to provide protection from outside influences. The working area contains three large areas (vinification, oak ageing and bottle ageing) with axes radiating from the center. This design leaves intermediate spaces, which can grow as the production units expand. The meeting point of the two axes generates a sense of order, which governs the small world of this winemaking business. The shape of the building is based on sharp blocks that appear to have been piled up randomly.

01 Front view | 02 Lateral view of the sharp blocks | 03 Floor plan main plant building access | 04 Tasting room | 05 Floor plan plant warehouse | 06 Restaurant | 07 Barrel area

03

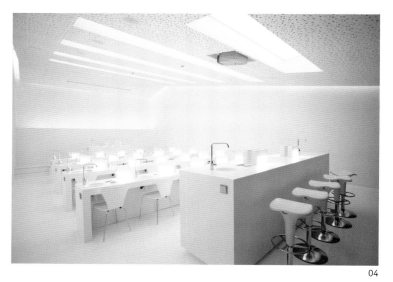

04

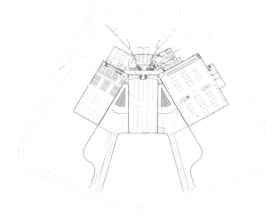

05

06

07

01

02

03

Vivienda en Bares

This house is the result of the reconstruction of stone ruins in Bares, the northern-most point of Spain. The new house is built entirely in the dimensions of the old building and many of the original stonewalls were incorporated into the design. Inside, where only a staircase remained, the structure has been completely redesigned. The house won an architectural prize awarded for the preservation of architectural and historical heritage.

01 Exterior view | 02 Interior detail | 03 Façade detail | 04 Section | 05 Wall detail on second floor

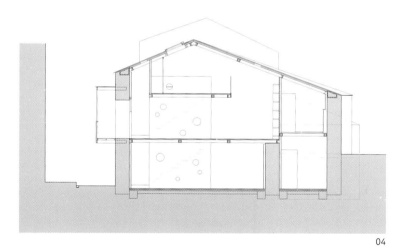

04

05

01

02

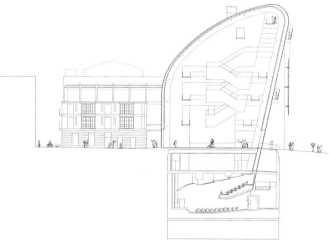

03

Caixa Galicia Art Forum

The design had to be sensitive to the distinctive architecture of the building's neighbors, resulting in a tilted parabolic shape. The form's apex peaks at the front, then falls steeply down the street façade on an inverse incline to plunge below ground. The main elevation of the art gallery is clad in glass paneling with a marble interlayer; this translucent skin gives the building luminosity and allows daylight to enter it. In darkness, it is softly illuminated. The glass panels on the main elevation also double as louvers. The curved rear façade is a composition of glass, marble and honeycomb aluminum.

01 Front view at night | 02 Double-glass cladding detail | 03 Section | 04 Rear view

04

01

02

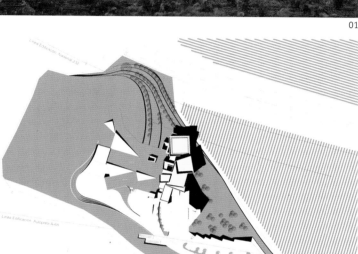

03

Bodega Darien

This design focused on blending the building with the landscape. This was achieved by building the bodega into the slope, positioning the warehouses underground and only revealing those sections which need natural light and external contact. The architects provided the bodega with an exceptional thermal and acoustic balance. The bodega rises up, reminiscent of the projecting jagged stones common to the area. The interior layout and design are rational, connecting spaces and passageways and creating dynmaic, changing atmospheres; going from the bright hall to a sequence of darker spaces.

01 Front view | 02 Rear view | 03 Site plan | 04 Balcony to barrel area | 05 Restaurant | 06 Barrel area

04

05

06

01

02

03

OS House

OS House allowed the architects to put an architectural experiment into practice. The owners presented the architects with a program of unusual complexity for this typology, one which reflected very differing needs. Firstly, the program had to serve a possible variation in the number of users of the house, from two to 30 or more, and all the possibilities inbetween. Secondly, the usual seasonal use of a second home was exacerbated by the number of users. A final factor that was introduced into this array of possibilities was the uncertain future of this program. The owners' age, the future growth of their children's families and a possible change from second to first home were the final factors in the challenging program situation.

01 General view | 02 Side view | 03 View to the sea | 04 Floor plans

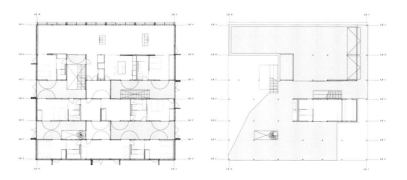

04

01

02

03

Eco-Boulevard of Vallecas

The proposal for the eco-boulevard in Vallecas, a new suburb of Madrid, can be defined as an urban recycling project with a threefold action plan: to place "air trees" as socially revitalizing elements within an existing urban environment; to densify existing trees; and to reduce and asymmetrically rearrange traffic circulation. Superficial interventions (perforations, fillings, paint, etc.) are also used to reconfigure the existing urban environment. Three pavilions, or "air trees", have been designed as open structures to multiply the range of activities that local residents can practice here. Installed in the 'non-city' as temporary prostheses, they will be used only until air-conditioned spaces are no longer needed, when the area has been thoroughly regenerated. When that happens, these devices should be dismantled, leaving spaces that resemble forest clearings. The "air tree" is a light structure, easily dismantled and self-sufficient in terms of energy: it consumes no more than it can produce by means of photovoltaic panels.

01 "Air tree" | 02 Outer skin of "air tree" | 03 Media tree | 04 Diagrams

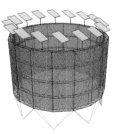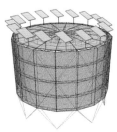

04

01

02

Telefónica District C

The new Telefónica headquarters will house all 14,000 employees of the company in one single corporate campus. All buildings are distributed around a canonical patio – the lawn of the campus – within a framework of squares set out in the corners of the premises. An environmental canopy with photovoltaic panels unites, covers and defines the perimeter of the campus. Two different hierarchies organize the spaces: one dedicated to business activities and one to employees' social and cooperative activities. Glass developed specifically for this project appears transparent from the inside and opaque from the outside.

01 General view | 02 Site plan | 03 Exterior view | 04 Interior view | 05 Façade detail

03

04

05

01

02

11th March Memorial Station

This memorial was inaugurated three years after the terrorist attacks at this very site, facing the train station building. It is an oval shaped glass cylinder that is 11 meters high and has a diameter of eight by ten and a half meters. The monument consists of two parts, the glass cylinder and an underground presentation room. Both parts are linked visually by a round window. The design creates the impression that the memorial, is a 'shimmer of hope' rising up towards the city from the depth of the train station, the 'site of sorrow'. Inside the glass cylinder, spontaneous expressions of sorrow from citizens were engraved into a transparent plastic film.

01 Memorial at night | 02 Passageway | 03 Memorial room | 04 Plan

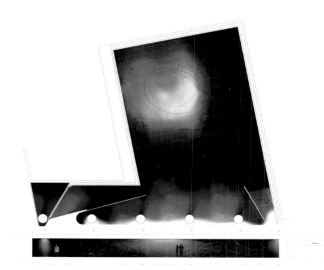

04

03

01

02

03

04

Canoeing Training Center of the Royal Spanish Federation

This boat store is an existing building. It can be considered a good example of the rural architecture from the second half of the 20th century, with its stone walls of granite masonry covered in Arabic tiles. It was restored in a way that deliberately preserved its characteristic feature. The gym and social areas are resolved in two separate volumes in order to optimize space and leave the communication elements uncovered. The walls are clad in prefabricated panels of laminated Bakelite, finished in wood. To the side of the reservoir, the boxes are opened with large windows that let visitors enjoy the landscape from the inside. In the façade panels, small windows are placed with metal shutters which allow light and ventilation of the rooms.

01 Exterior view | 02 Entrance and pier | 03 General view | 04 Interior view | 05 Ground floor plan

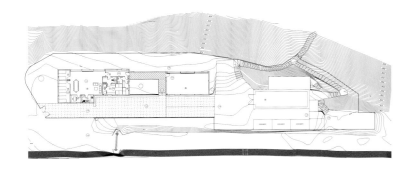

05

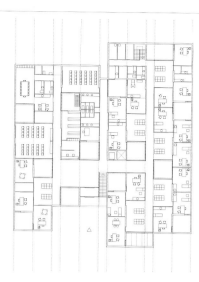

01

02

Villaverde Health Care Center

The Villaverde HCC belongs to a series of three Health Care Centers built with the same program and plan. The program is developed extensively on a single floor. The units are ordered by generating a sparse orthogonal grid, where 13 yard elements are distributed through three non-corridors. The corridor ceases to exist as a linear structure, because of the alternative arrangement of empty spaces and waiting rooms. The glazed skin of the building, without openings, reflects the surrounding space without allowing an interior-exterior visual relationship.

01 Floor plan | 02 Interior view | 03 Exterior view | 04 Façade

03

04

01

Caja Madrid Tower

This new headquarters building for Caja Madrid – the largest bank in Spain – continues investigations into the flexible workplace that can be traced through a family of recent office towers, most notably for Swiss Re and Commerzbank. Compositionally, the building can be thought of as a tall arch, the services and circulation cores framing the open office floors. At ground level, a 22-meter, glazed atrium provides the transition from the street, and accommodates a 'floating' glass-walled auditorium. The cores are strategically positioned so as to block west/east direct sunlight, a move that has the added benefit of framing spectacular views of the hills of Sierra de Guadarrama to the north and the center of Madrid to the south.

01 Street view | 02 Side view | 03 Detail

02   03

01

02

03

05

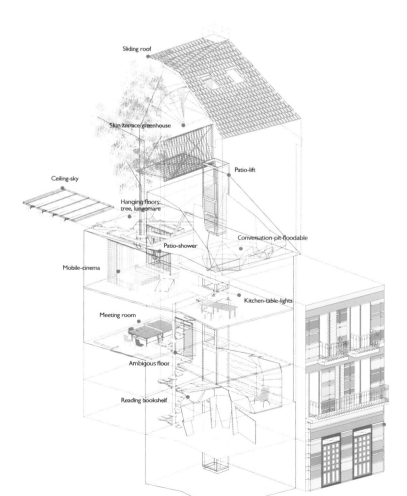

Sliding roof

Skin &terrace/greenhouse

Ceiling-sky

Patio-lift

Hanging floors:
tree, lungomare

Patio-shower

Conversation-pit-floodable

Mobile-cinema

Kitchen-table-lights

Meeting room

Ambigous floor

Reading bookshelf

04

TSM3 Unstable House

Above an 18th century ground floor, this new construction is in a state of flux. The architecture does not define limits through fixed elements; it defines potential actions or situations. Obeying municipal regulations, the façade is inspired by 19th century design. A 19th century façade may be composed following visual criteria based on gravity. A 20th century façade may be composed of an abstract skin following geometric rules. A 21st century façade will be automatically composed, as a result of the relation between inside and outside, natural light, sun exposure, ventilation, privacy, or the wish to linger in an intermediate private-public position. Form and function follow the weather.

01 Living space | 02 Façade | 03 Kitchen | 04 Axonometry | 05 Interior façade

01

02

New Youth Center in Rivas-Vaciamadrid

From the beginning, this project was conceived as the chance to make the 'underground' visible, a construction devised as a radical manifestation of Madrid's youthful spirit in general, and of Rivas' youth groups in particular. The project aspires to become an explicit 'teen' communication vehicle by appropriating their language and their voices as the ingredients of the project. In this way, the project's team embraces all Rivas' youth groups by means of an open participation process, in which the future users of the center, combined with technicians and politicians, will contribute their decisions, their concerns, their fantasies and their aesthetics to create a contemporary 'social monument'.

01 Main façade | 02 Bird's-eye view | 03 'Movement space' | 04 Media library | 05 Chill out zone | 06 Roof balcony | 07 Axonometric projection

03

04

05

06

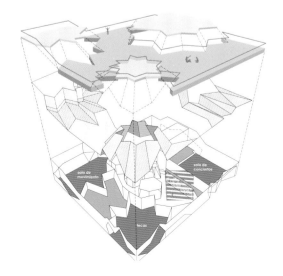

07

02

03

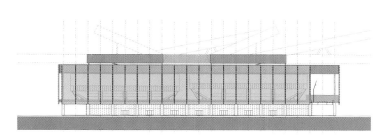

05

01

04

Olympic Tennis Center

As a candidate for staging the Olympic Games in 2016, the Spanish capital has begun a campaign to build spectacular facilities; among them, the Olympic Tennis Center. Working in an indistinct peripheral area, the main challenge was not so much to design a building as to stage manage architectureand invent scenery. The "magic box" concept encloses sports and mixed-purpose buildings, but opens up and adapts itself to the various uses, projecting a changing and lively silhouette in the cityscape. Its vibrant skin filters the sunlight, serves as a windbreak and shelters the sports hall in a lightweight shell. What has been created is an architectural landscape that flows and ripples like a garment, a venue that is alive day and night.

01 View from inside | 02 Exterior view | 03 Tennis court | 04 Exterior view with open roof | 05 Elevation

01

02

03

04

Parish Church of Santa Monica

The shape of this site determined the nature of this building by allowing the work to be created by edges and pinnacles, in an explosion of north-facing skylights. The sonorous piece shows a clear and categorical respect for the buildings subject: faith and holiness. Light is allowed to flood into the building, giving the space character. The project focuses on the search for ways in which to unite earth and sky, matter and light. The natural light gives the space something special. The limit, and boundaries become blurred, eliminating the existence of matter.

01 Rear view | 02 Side façade | 03 Sculpture in contemporary context | 04 Interior view | 05 Section

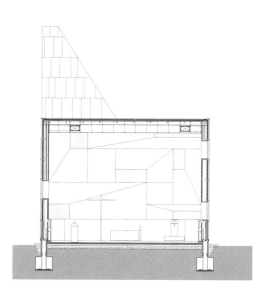

05

01

02

03

04

05

Casa Paz

This entire design is developed inside a metal, cube like structure, clad with a skin of stretched sheet metal. This rests on a reinforced concrete base – the container for the pool water and for installations and the guts of this iron artifact, where all vital fluids are concentrated. The columns are the only contact the house has with the ground. To maintain structural equilibrium and a certain gravitational logic, the house is suspended five and a half meters over the river without any support, and the same amount is projected towards the road, where it ends up being only 40 centimeters above ground at the entrance. By doing this, a balance in weight is achieved.

01 View from road | 02 View from valley | 03 Side view | 04 Overhang detail | 05 Interior view | 06 Construction process

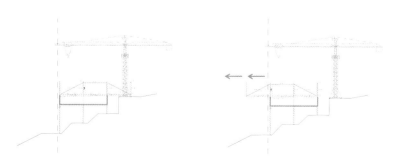

06

01

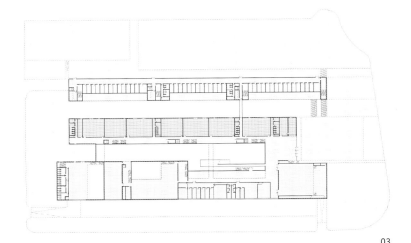

02

Faculty Building of the Economics and Social Sciences

These architects treated the planning as an urban project. The program suggested a small city in which the continuity of the public spaces remains permanent. It consists of three large rectangular blocks. This composition allows pedestrian streets to be established among them, lying parallel to the building and the campus roads of the University of Malaga. These interior streets have different roles, depending on the function of the blocks. The landscape, its topography with a north-to-south slope, and the inclined campus streets were determining factors from the beginning.

01 General view | 02 Street view | 03 First floor plan | 04 Interior view | 05 Hall | 06 View of entrance

03

04

05

06

01

02

03

Health Center

This building is organized on two levels. The first one reflects the topographical richness; the second one echoes its degree of permeability or integration into the environment. The construction of the building also followed the two-volume pattern. The volumes, although sharing the structural solution, differ in their outer shell, which gives them individual character. The volume including the surgery offices has a multilayer façade, whereas the waiting area is enclosed with double-glazing. The outer layer of wood, opaque in the surgery area, gradually becomes lattice and finally disappears.

01 Exterior detail | 02 Exterior view | 03 Glazed façade | 04 Ground floor plan | 05 Interior view | 06 View toward first floor with glazed waiting room

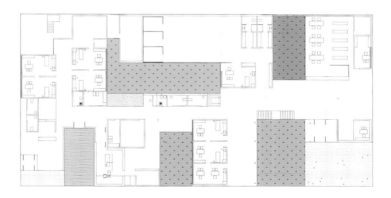

04

05

06

01

Noain City Hall

This building is made up through a superposition of membranes. The inner layer with its strict geometry is formed by a translucent double-skin separated by an air chamber. It guarantees the decrease of lighting and energy consumption. The external membrane is a metallic latticework with an organic form where vegetation will grow producing a 'cloud' that will change its density and colors throughout the year. Thus the building is perceived as a landscape that changes, displaying the course of days and seasons. In summary, it acts as an index of the everyday life and the yearly cycles of the Noain citizens.

01 Main view | 02 View from garden | 03 Front façade | 04 Section

02

03

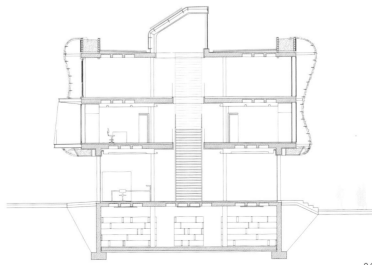

04

01

02

Casal de la Juventud de Novelda

This building is situated in Novelda, a small town near Alicante. The project involved the renovation of an old school building and its yard to give it a new, public use. The proposal suggested the reuse of the old buildings, adapting them to meet contemporary needs. The function of the building focuses on social groups, determined by their age, who don´t have a physical place for cultural activities and leisure. The plaza is raised as a hub of social activity in Novelda. This system consists of connecting paths that also define soft areas that can adapt and establish links with what is happening inside the building. The building was built by CrystalZoo, composing of José Luis Campos, Ana Cantero, Leticia Ballester.

01 Street view | 02 Façade lighting | 03 Main hall | 04 Cross section | 05 Main entrance

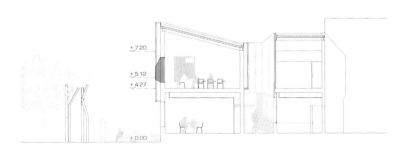

03

04

05

01

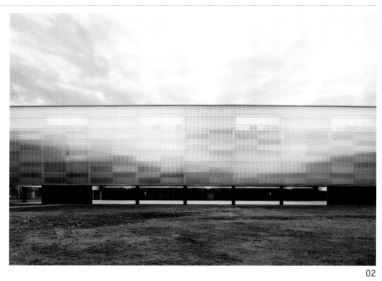

02

03

04

05

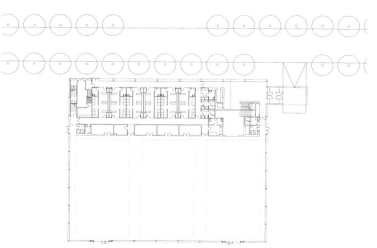

06

Sports Hall and Skating Rink

This project involved the creation of two new sports areas. The indoor skating rink is actually an extension of an existing sports pavilion. Both volumes have been designed with the most clear and convincing geometry possible. The façade of the skating rink volume is resolved by a neutral colored metal façade, micro-perforated on the upper band. The volume integrates itself naturally with the old pavilion. The new sports hall is built on the land where a thick grove of trees once grew. The green of the leaves and the shadows are reproduced in the pixel pattern of the new pavilion's façade. A second polycarbonate skin blends the colors of the façade and the real dimensions of the building.

01 Sports hall entrance | 02 South façade | 03 Skating rink façade | 04 Seating area | 05 Staircase | 06 Ground floor plan

01

02

03

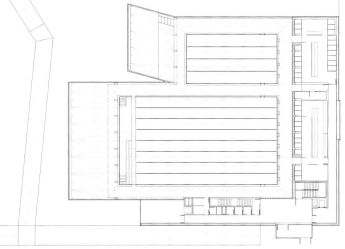

04

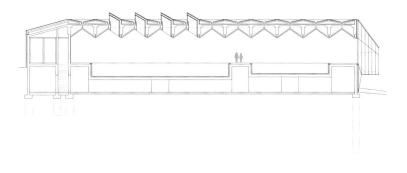

05

Swimming Pools for Vigo University

This chosen plot is located at the highest point of the university campus, a location that gives it a special value in the relationship between the city of Orense and the campus. Opting for a program oriented towards leisure, and that may thereby serve both the university community and the people of Orense, will help to heighten the value of the building as an element of urban interaction. The proposal was drawn up as a large platform overlooking the campus. The users of the installations enjoy the views over the university complex from the elevated platform that contains the swimming pools. The other central piece of the project is the roof. From the interior, its geometry aims to be a determining element in the configuration of a space.

01 Interior view | 02 Glazed exterior | 03 Projecting building from street level | 04 Ground floor plan | 05 Cross section | 06 Swimming pools contained in an elevated platform

06

01

02

03

Kameha Bay Portals

Kameha Bay Portals creates a new world within a naturally grown environment. The combined use of sophisticated materials and surfaces, architecture by tec Architecture Swiss, and design by Marcel Wanders Studios, creates a unique ambience. The exuberantly designed pool deck situated on top of the cascade of terraces affords views to the Mediterranean as well as plenty of sunshine and privacy. In a stunning design move, the building becomes part of the pool courtesy of a nearly 20-meter vertical water feature that graciously weaves into the actual pool. Lush lawns as well as beautifully laid out terrace surfaces blend the outside space seamlessly with the architecture. The floral ornamentation of the façade at times takes on a natural green hue.

01 View to pool and hotel | 02 Entrance area | 03 Terrace with waterfall | 04 Site plan

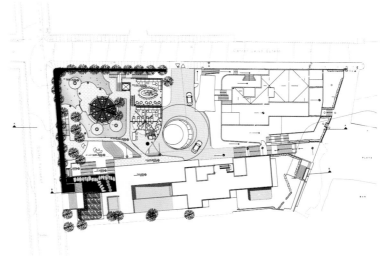

04

01

02

03

04

05

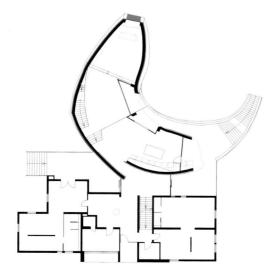

06

Casa Son Vida

Located approximately 15 minutes outside of Palma de Mallorca in an exclusive community called Son Vida, the eponymously named Casa is an example of design poetry in motion. The completion of this home marks the arrival of third millennia architecture on the island of Mallorca. The task at hand was straightforward: take a very ordinary existing Mediterranean villa constructed in the 1960s and transform it into something extraordinary. The 800-square-meter luxury villa transgresses the constraints of site and context, redefining luxury architecture as it is typified by the traditional and prolific Mediterranean and Tuscan styles otherwise found on the island.

01 Master bathroom | 02 Exterior | 03 Pool area | 04 Bathroom | 05 Living room | 06 Floor plan

01

Shelter for the Homeless

As well as satisfying residents' needs for shelter and food, the new "Shelter for the Homeless" offers an opportunity to improve the quality of life of a socially excluded group. A silent box is proposed that protects visitors from the curiosity of onlookers and adequately integrates its reduced scale into the semi-urban environment. An exterior lattice of aluminum profiles guarantees the desired privacy of the users and at the same time resolves the possible intrusion problems that may occur in such a center, as wells as configuring an homogeneous and unified exterior image, adapting the scale of the building to its environment.

01 West view | 02 Sections and floor plan | 03 Interior view | 04 North façade

02

03

04

01

Nursery School in Pamplona

This building is organized as a series of four parallel bodies in which fully built and empty areas are alternated. A body with administration services is located at the west of the site and filters the traffic noise from this side. The empty central space is illuminated through a skylight that emerges above the rest of the building and a third body houses the children's areas, including classrooms, workshops, refectories and bedrooms. Lastly, the external backyard is conceived as an extension of the classroom spaces through the opening of large windows. Diverse colors and textures (concrete, rubber and grass) create suggestive and varied playing spaces for the children.

01 Exterior view | 02 Central space | 03 Central area with double-height ceiling | 04 Floor plan and sections | 05 Play area | 06 Enclosed outdoor area

02

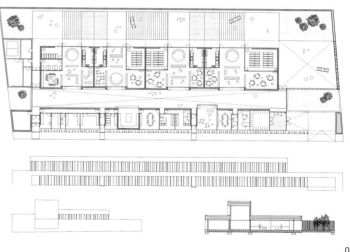

03

04

05

06

01

02

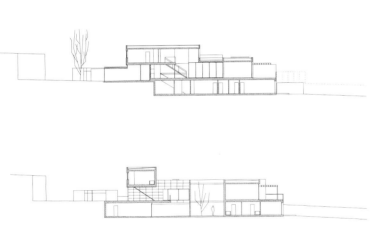

03

04

Semi-Detached House

This project is an attempt to conjugate two archetypes of modern housing architecture: the viewpoint house, open and expansive, and the patio house, enclosed and intimate. The patio in House A is a static, calm and contemplative space, while a second patio in House B has a more dynamic character, linking the pedestrian entrance with the garage and the garden. Although the site is small and located in a complex residential environment, it also offers distinct advantages such as a slope to allow natural terracing of the three floors and excellent views of the sea and local landmarks. The ventilated façades are formed of zinc and ceramic panels in white with a large format.

01 Main entrance | 02 View from second floor | 03 Sections | 04 Front façade | 05 Rooftop

05

01

02

Innova

Since the beginning of the industrial revolution, the debate around work spaces has been a constant topic in architecture. The necessity to accommodate new uses because of new activities has introduced new typologies. In this sense, it is easy to remember good examples of both buildings and cities. But administrative advances and computer technologies completely transformed the way of thinking of these spaces. This project proposes functional strips for the different areas of each floor. The entire building is a big technological black box based on the idea of neutrality, elegance and expressiveness.

01 Exterior view | 02 Glazed boxes | 03 Ground floor plan | 04 Box spaces | 05 Terrace | 06 Interior space

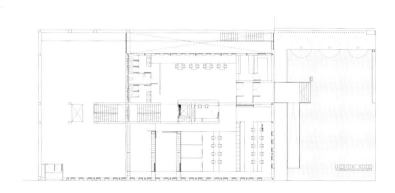

03

04

05

06

01

02

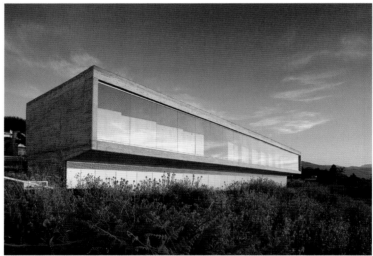

03

04

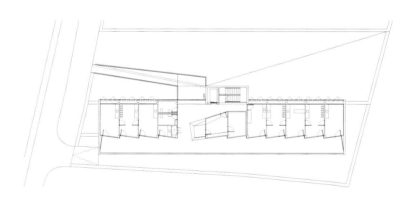

05

Ravelo Medical Clinic

This building has been designed with two levels and street-level pedestrian access. The main floor is occupied by the medical surgeries, while the lower floor houses multipurpose, administrative and staff areas. The project is characterized by a dialogue between the external, concrete frame and an internal wooden layer that transforms the empty space of the frames into a series of rooms, separating the areas for specific private use from the public ones. To the north, the panoramic window embraces the distant countryside, incorporating it into the everyday life of the clinic.

01 Surgery | 02 Access | 03 Glazed façade | 04 Reception area | 05 First floor plan | 06 Waiting area

06

01

Bodegas Real Winery

This project is an extension of a 17th century farmhouse and wine cellar in the country-side of La Mancha, which creates a center devoted to wine culture. A new star-shaped piece is placed in the ancient courtyard, connecting old buildings and new ones. Its large scale is fragmented into smaller open spaces, each of them linked to the surrounding functions. The courtyard, which is the hub of activity of the old farmhouse, is transformed by this star shaped construction but maintains its character as an exterior space. The peaks of the star open towards the landscape; in this way the complex acquires a new relationship with the surroundings.

01 Main entrance | 02 Multi-purpose room | 03 Axonometry | 04 Old meets new

02

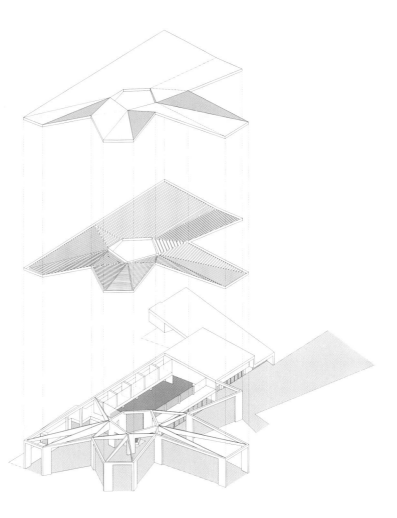

03

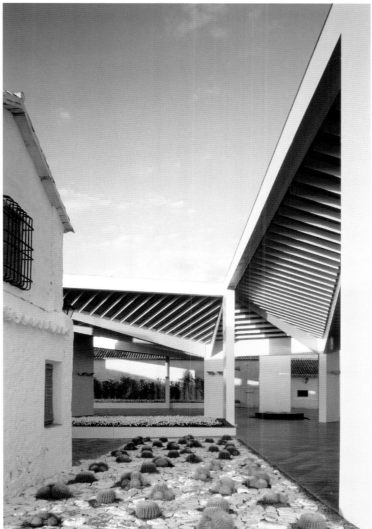

04

01

02

03

04

Casa Camino in Roses

Situated on a steeply sloping plot in Costa Brava, this house offers a stunning view across the Gulf of Roses. The large windows offer a panoramic view of the landscape, stretching from the Mediterranean Sea to the lofty heights of the Pyrenees. Just like at the cinema, the residents look out through a wide band of glass. Sky, sun and sea appear close enough to touch. The house has two floors and nestles, sickle-shaped, into the sloping site. Far projecting concrete roofs and walls frame the glass façade. The upper level cascades backwards, making room for a large, flowing roof terrace that continues on three sides of the upper level. The bay looks almost as if it has been brought into the house.

01 Exterior at dusk | 02 Exterior with swimming pool | 03 Bathroom | 04 Living room | 05 Upper floor plan

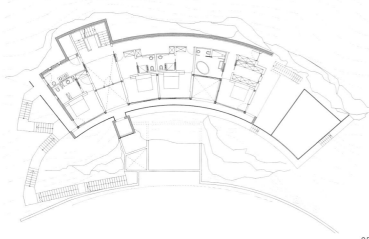

05

01

02

03

San Agustín de Guadalix Service Station

This service station is located on one of Spain's six major national highways, near the town of San Agustín de Guadalix, outside of Madrid. The project is comprised of three curvilinear canopy structures and a rectangular building, which houses, in addition to the service station's facilities, a full service restaurant. In the 1940s and 1950s the design of service stations exuded optimism and modernity; the structures employed cantilevers and projections that gave a sense of magic to the spaces below. Perhaps the difference between those service stations and this one is that this one has a more playful character, thanks to the curved shape of the canopies. It is not only a shelter, it is fluid movement, clearly reflecting the natural landscape of rolling hills in the distance.

01 End view | 02 Roof landscape | 03 Long view | 04 Elevation | 05 General view

04

05

01

Culture Center and House of Peace and Human Rights

Located in the monumental Aiete Park in San Sebastian, the complex program included the Culture Center and a House of Peace and Human Rights. The project required the restoration of the historical Palace of Aiete and the construction of a new building. The project had to provide a balance that would maintain the essential nature of the pre-existing structure. The new center is conceived as an intervention in the landscape that extends the park's romantic plot to the north side of the palace. The access to each main use is always through two 'bubbles', where double doors provide privacy and necessary acoustic control and security.

01 Exterior view old and new | 02 Night view | 03 View of library | 04 Section | 05 Second floor and staircase of palace

02

03

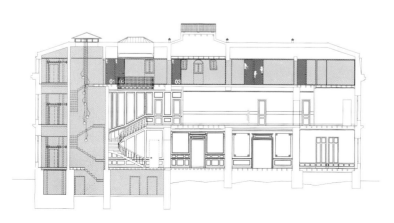

04

05

01

02

Never Never Land House

This site on the island of Ibiza is on a slope with an average gradient of 20 percent. It faces the northwest, allowing views of the setting sun, over a landscape with few buildings and continuous vegetation. The building design focused on the need to preserve the qualitative continuities of the valley's natural base in the building to the greatest possible degree. The design feeds into this idea by minimizing tree and shrub removal or pruning on the allotment, raising more than 80 percent of the building mass on piles to avoid any sort of disturbance and clustering all the waste filtering and treating equipment, as well as the water tank, into a compact reinforced concrete vessel.

01 Pool | 02 Elevated building | 03 Façade | 04 Interior view | 05 Site plan

03

04

05

01

02

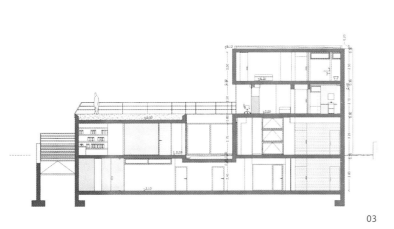

03

Casa P3

Casa P3 stands for a fold (pliegue) that structures, defines the different levels of the house and marks what is empty or full. The fold in a metallic U-shape sets the operative beginning of the project. "P" for platform, that invites us to stare at the landscape from the eco-roof. "P" for patios, three spaces where the landscape is controlled and where light is brought to the most private areas. The first entrance patio is through a suspended footbridge; the second one focuses on the exterior views from the studio; and the last one is at the center of community life - living room, dining room and kitchen. The façade is a projection of the different levels, explained by the limit of the fold.

01 General view | 02 View from street | 03 Section | 04 Side garden

04

01

Insular Athletics Stadium Tenerife

This project, in the form of a crater with fixed slopes covered by volcanic rock, reflects the island's volcanic origins. The proposal integrates a range of different uses. Its dimensions lay claim to its iconic value, while minimizing the impact on the environment. The crater provides a new public space, finished in irregular basalt stone, establishing a visual relationship to the Atlantic Ocean. Inside, different facilities, including a high performance center, a gymnasium, warming up track, press room, and a lecture theater with a capacity for 200 people, open onto the space via mobile screen walls.

01 Stands | 02 Aerial view | 03 Rear view of stands | 04 Plan | 05 Access

02

03

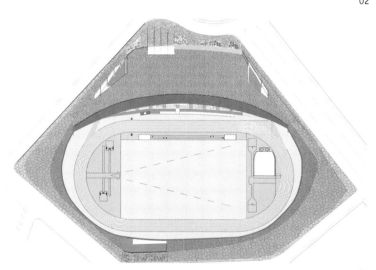

04

05

01

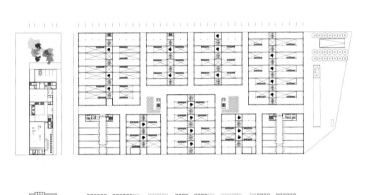

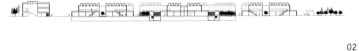

02

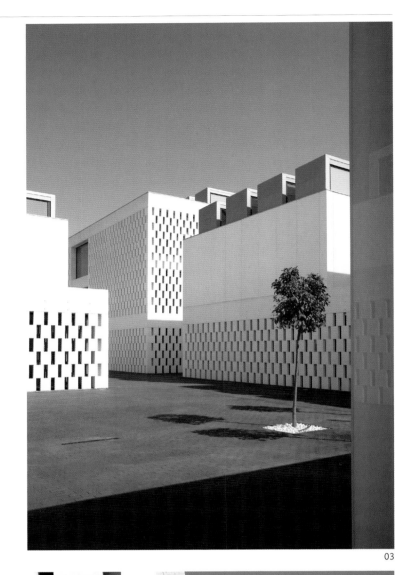

03

Sacred Art Business Park

The Sacred Art Business Park in Seville is made up of ten buildings that form a unique and compact urban fabric. The project is proposed as an architectural reinterpretation of the souk and its main objective is to preserve the intimate atmosphere in which crafts-men have traditionally worked. The point of departure is an atelier able to be expanded under different functional requirements. Lighting is solved according to functionality: areas next to the façade are illuminated by a continuous concrete lattice while light in inner spaces comes from northwest oriented skylights. The project is completed by a long steel canopy that highlights the park access and a mixed-use building with exhibi-tion areas and conference halls for artisans.

01 Main lobby | 02 Ground floor plan and section | 03 Courtyard | 04 View of interior street | 05 Workshop

04

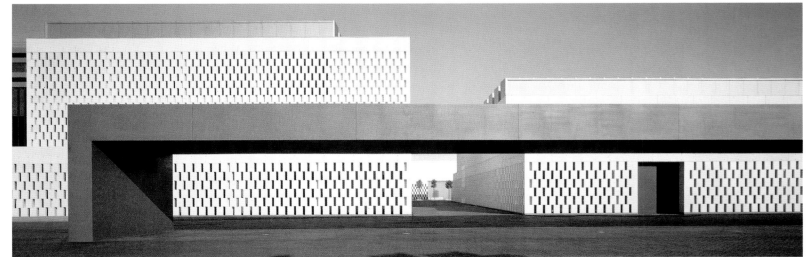

05

01

Police Station Seville

The program for this police station in Seville is organized in a star-shaped plan. As high-rise dwellings surround the building, a horizontal and extended volume that seems not to touch the ground gives it a representative image towards the city. A continuous suspended wall made of white concrete wraps the perimeter of the building. The glass beneath is sheltered from the harsh sunlight by the wrapping, which changes according to the viwer's orientation. The program is organized in the four peaks of the star with the public areas right next to the entrance, all of them provided with natural light. An artificial green slope borders the volume and a transparent fence closes the police station towards the city.

01 Bird's-eye view | 02 Façade detail | 03 Window detail | 04 Ground floor plan

02

03

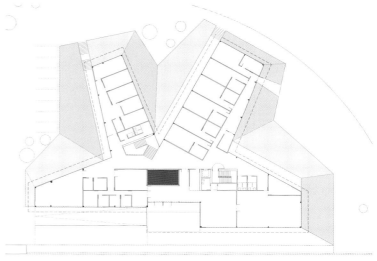

04

01

02

03

04

Ferreries Cultural Center

The old market of Ferreries, after falling into disuse for several years, has been restored and extended to become the new Ferreries Cultural Center. Sections of the main building have been preserved and through their extension a new transition space is generated in order to enable to connect the existing building and Joan Monclús Square. An important relationship is established between the market and its extension. The white interior contrasts a new, dark façade, which is finished with a grooved texture, creating a surface of accentuated shadows.

01 Interior view | 02 Wood strips to muffle acoustics | 03 Front view | 04 Night view | 05 Ground floor plan

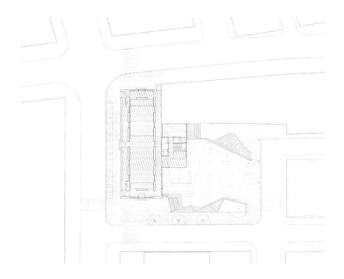

05

01

02

03

04

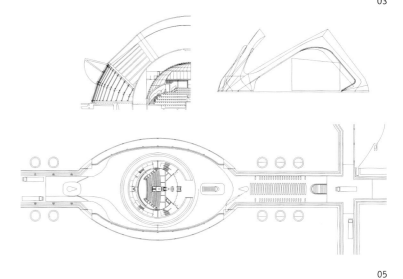

05

City of Arts and Sciences

The government of Valencia resolved to establish a museum of national importance. The 35-hectare site chosen for this initiative is located in the dry bed of the Turia river, midway between the old city and the coastal district of Nazaret. In 1991, Calatrava won the competition for the original project, then later that same year received the commission to develop the whole complex, which also included a science museum and a planetarium. The science museum, like the grand exhibition pavilions of the past, is a longitudinal building, created from the modular development of transverse sections that repeat along the length of the site. The triangular structures that brace the ends of the building also mark the entrances.

01 Príncipe Felipe Science Museum | 02 "Umbracle" | 03 Hemisphere | 04 Aerial view | 05 Plans | 06 Night view

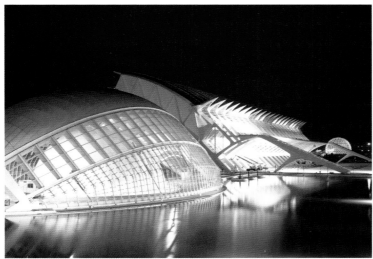

06

01

02

03

04

Galicia Architectural Association

This project aimed to maximize the building's volumetric envelope and to highlight it as an object made independent by its abstraction. In the course of its sculpting process, ephemeral marks were left. An entire free urban void was configured in unison with the building. Together, they make up part of a topography that moves from the plane to the envelope, with a full choreography of entrances and connections related to the richness of the street layout. These resolve the different levels of the place in a continuous line, linking them to the building and also to others. By organizing the vehicle traffic and creating rest areas, the project creates a uniform urban area.

01 Interior view | 02 Bird's-eye view | 03 Upper floor | 04 Entrance area | 05 Diagram

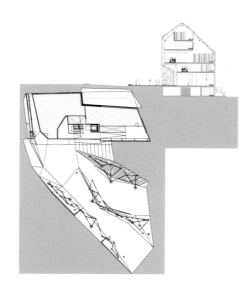

05

01

02

03

GM House

GM House is a 318-square-meter, three-story house located in Vilafranca del Penedés. The basement offers space for a garage and children's play area; kitchen and living room are located on the ground floor and bedrooms are on the first floor. The design was based around the idea of a central element that includes a lift, fireplace and storage units. This feature allows the balanced organization of dining areas and kitchen on one side and living area on the other. The house is made of natural stone a gray-colored wood, giving it a modern, elegant appearance.

01 Terrace | 02 Street view | 03 First floor plan | 04 Living area | 05 Bedroom | 06 Kitchen

04

05

06

01

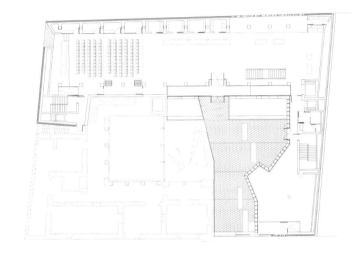

02

Álava Museum of Archeology

This building adjoins the Palace of Bendaña, currently the museum of Naipes Fournier. Access to the building is through the same courtyard that leads to the palace. Because of the slope of the terrain, the courtyard is accessed via a bridge over a garden that lets light into the lower areas, which would otherwise have no natural illumination on this side. In the permanent exhibition halls, all horizontal surfaces are dark, the wooden floors are almost black, and the continuous ceilings are black. However, the exhibition pieces are organized around white glazed prisms which draw light in from the roof during daytime.

01 Façades defining the courtyard | 02 Glazed prisms in the exhibition hall | 03 Ground floor plan | 04 Brazen façade | 05 Staircase

03

04

05

01

02

03

04

Ataria – Salburúa Nature Interpretation Centre

This project had five aspects to consider. A unique place, a natural wetland area close to the center of a big city; a suggestive program, a threshold between urbanity and nature; the smell of wood, the material which gets better with time; the opportunity to take risks and to try something totally new; and great joy in defying gravity. The architects did not want to make a wooden-looking building, but a real wood building. The building is now a reality, the environment must catch up, and the wood will surely improve with age.

01 View of cantilever from the exhibition terrace | 02 Play of light inside the building | 03 General view from west | 04 Main hall | 05 Section

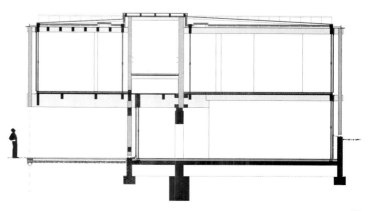

05

01

Savings Bank Headquarters

The headquarters of a local savings bank reproduces the scale of the surrounding woods. The floor plan is shaped like a chromosome with four arms. The structural concept is based on pairs of exterior metal supports, clad in stainless steel composite panels. One of the arms has been conceived as a 26-meter cantilever. In this case, the concept changes and the pairs do not have any structural function. A double-height hall located at the heart of the building has its two façades enclosed by a work of art. They have been provided with red polyurethane panels with a hand-painted biological pattern. The idea is to present the building as a living organism in motion.

01 North façade at night | 02 Ground floor plan | 03 Façade detail | 04 Workshop area | 05 Interior courtyard

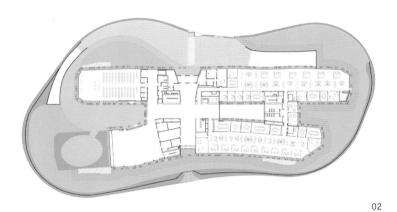

02

03

04

05

01

Offices for the Junta de Castilla y León

This project was completed in collaboration with Pablo Fernández Lorenzo, Pablo Redondo Díez, Alfonso González Gaisán and Francisco Blanco Velasco. The exterior wall is deliberately reminiscent of the architectural style of the nearby cathedral and demarcates the outline of the site. This design creates a garden space where leafy trees, flowers and foliage have been planted. The openings in the stone wall frame spectacular views of the cathedral. In this garden, a glass building has been constructed; the transparency forges a connection between the interior and exterior spaces. The design is a stone box, open to the sky that holds a crystalline box and protects it, immersed in the midst of a wonderful garden.

01 Courtyard | 02 Exterior view | 03 View towards city | 04 Site plan

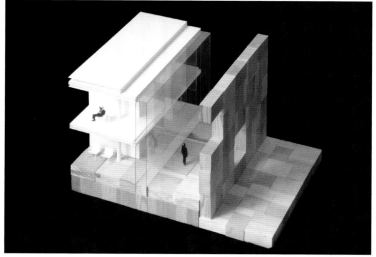

02

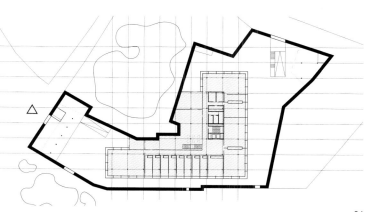

03

04

01

02

03

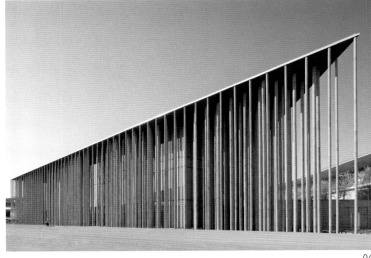

04

Spanish Pavilion for EXPO Zaragoza 2008

The desire to reproduce a forest of bamboos on a layer of water is the subconscious basis for this project. The choice of materials (terracotta and cork, amongst others) turns the pavilion into the expression of a relationship between means and end, as a basis that can and must achieve the maximum degree of meaning and representation of the host country, Spain. Aiming to provide the pavilion with a certain independence from the immediate context of the Expo has defined a project and its details by encouraging a very dry, meccano-like construction with elements that can be built and moved to and from any given place.

01 Interior view | 02 Interior "bamboo forest" | 03 Exhibition room | 04 Exterior view | 05 Section

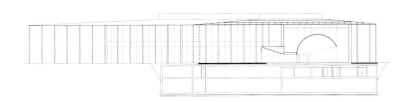

05

01

Zaragoza Bridge Pavilion

The Zaragoza Bridge Pavilion is organized around four main elements, or 'pods', that act both as structural elements and as spatial enclosures. Each 'pod' is a specific exhibition space. The 'pods' intersect and brace each other, allowing the weight of the bridge to be distributed across the four trusses instead of one main element. This reduces the size of load-bearing beams required to span the sections of the bridge that cross the Ebro River. The pedestrian viaduct, whose shape resembles a gladiola, uses the Osterberg Cell to ensure the correct laying of the foundations.

01 Triangular entrance | 02 Exterior view at night | 03 View from the river | 04 North elevation | 05 Roof and ramp | 06 Window detail

02

03

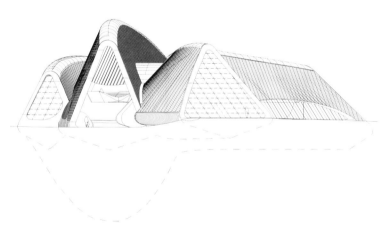

04

05

06

01

02

St. Isabel Kindergarten

The floor plan and layout of the school is conceived as two boxes of concrete, glass and wood. The austere exterior contrasts with the materialization of light in the interior, where the subtle light variations of the classrooms, the play of longitudinal visions and the rhythm of courts redirect the attention to the playground. The concrete paneling accentuates a vertical break-down and ensures that in the texture of the surrounding, one does not lose the warmth of the wood used in the paneling, which initiates a playful interaction between the materials.

01 Façade made of wood, concrete and U-glass | 02 Exterior view at night | 03 Design of walls ensures maximum amount of natural daylight | 04 Entrance area | 05 Ground floor plan | 06 Interior view | 07 Corridor

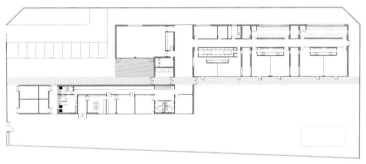

03

04

05

06

07

Kindergarten in Rosales de Canal

This project is based closely on children's perception of the constructed environment: Magén Arquitectos wanted to combine the general volumetrics with a domestic scale and the sensory relationship between children and architecture. The classroom forms the basic unit and the roofing style is repeated to cover spaces that occupy a larger surface area such as the multipurpose hall and the dining room. The general configuration of the building responds to clearly organizational criteria, with the classrooms placed around the patio, with service spaces situated between them. A combination of horizontal and vertical wooden panels and colored boards forms an apparently adventurous composition.

01 Floor plan | 02 Brown classroom | 03 Lobby | 04 Courtyard

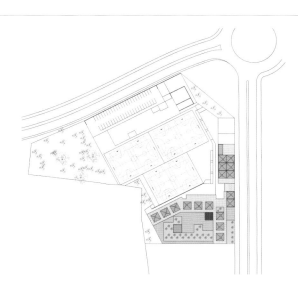

01

02

03

04

01

02

Environment Service and Public Spaces Headquarters

This proposal is the answer to a public need and an opportunity to construct an urban landscape. Because of the differences in the levels of the site, the main entrance to the building is on the upper floor. This floor houses the administrative spaces and the classroom. The main hall joins and separates both spaces, enabling them to be used independently. The roof is an essential element within the landscape design of the building. It is configured as a viewpoint at different levels, which are joined together by gentle ramps and a terraced grandstand. The contrast between the roughened, black tinted, concrete panel and the different textures of the upper level defines the formal configuration of the building.

01 Side view | 02 Front view | 03 Interior view | 04 Sections | 05 Façade detail

03

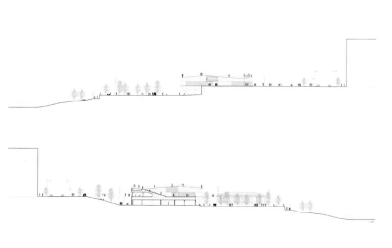

04

05

01

02

03

04

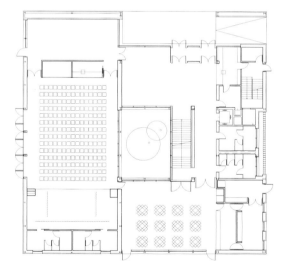

05

06

Library and Coexistence Center

This Coexistence Center and library are divided into three floors and a basement, organized with a central courtyard scheme that connects the four floors, providing natural light and relating the different users. The idea of the project is determined by the building's own program and the interaction or non-interaction of uses, generating quality spaces that are determined by the mixture of the areas greatest in volume. The main access is through a porch located at the north, the point where there is maximum openness to the plot. The lobby is proposed as a large space inside the building connecting the two side streets, causing an extension of the public space from the street into the building.

01 Inner courtyard | 02 Street view | 03 Façade | 04 Library | 05 Floor plan | 06 Courtyard entrance

CENTRAL EUROPE

01

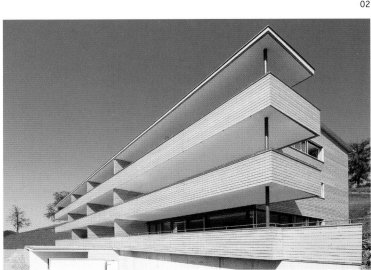

02

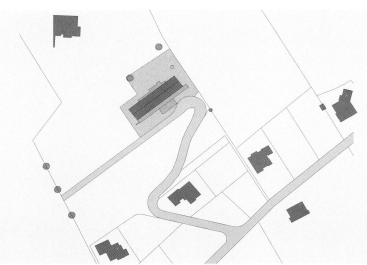

03

Residential Complex

This complex, made up of 12 residential units, is situated in a meadow, on the outskirts of Alberschwende. Due to its exposed position and the slope of the terrain, the building receives sunlight throughout the day and all year round. The building is comprised of a basement, with garage and cellar, built into the incline of the hill, as well as three residential floors that are accessible from the hillside, via an open balcony. All of the apartments are orientated towards the open balcony. Cooking, dining and living areas all have room-height windows and three meter deep balconies, facing the valley. The entire façade of the building is clad with natural white pine wood taken from the local region.

01 Southwest view | 02 Terrace | 03 Southeast view | 04 Site plan | 05 East view

04

05

01

02

03

04

Bleibergerhof Hotel, Therma and Spa

The challenge for the architects of the new Bleibergerhof Hotel, Therma and Spa was to double the capacity of the existing space and bring the existing buildings together to form a unified whole. In the central section, the building structure was maintained. Sections to the north and south were partially demolished, in order to implement a new, more efficient room layout. The small existing bedrooms in the middle sections were combined to form large suites and the structure was further extended at both ends. An inside and outside pool leads the guests out of the glazed wellness area into the mountain landscape. The main entrance with lobby, reception and hotel bar is located at street level and one level above.

01 Hotel room | 02 Bathroom | 03 Bar | 04 Fireplace room | 05 Ground floor plan | 06 Pool | 07 Sauna

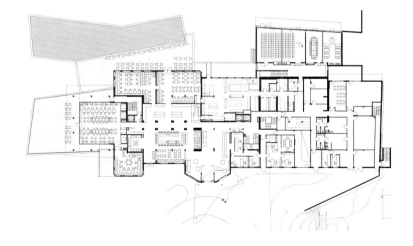

05

06

07

01

02

03

04

05

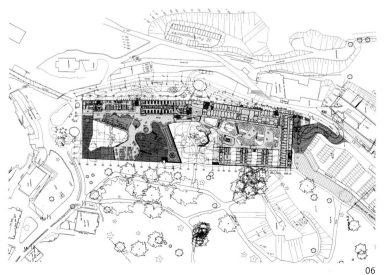

06

Life Medicine Resort Das Kurhaus Bad Gleichenberg

This project is situated in a protected park and consists of a treatment area with about 50 different rooms for medical treatments, a four star hotel with several different restaurants and cafes, and a public thermal bath for the patients and other guests. The waiting areas in the middle of the treatment rooms are shaped around courtyards allowing sun light to flood in and providing views of the trees, giving the patients the impression of waiting in the park itself. Between treatments, the patients wait in the open and transparent waiting areas where the park is always close. One of the main aims of the architecture has been to un-institutionalize the architecture, so that it bears as little resemblance to a hospital as possible. The interior was designed by an advertising office.

01 Exterior view | 02 Green roof | 03 Outdoor thermal bath | 04 View towards terrace with magnolia tree | 05 Corridor medical treatments | 06 Site plan

01

02

Falkensteiner Hotel & Spa Bad Leonfelden

The Falkensteiner Hotel in Bad Leonfelden is located in the middle of the mill district, which is characterized by soft hills and dense spruce forest. The main entrance is situated in the center of the building. A traditional stone wall builds the base of the hotel, while the bedrooms are situated above and are reminiscent of an airy, bright hayloft. The public spaces allow for easy orientation. The restaurant can be seen from the library and room height windows offer views across the landscape. A slit in the wall near the spa area allows views of the pool. All spaces and functions are designed so that the sun follows the movement of the guests throughout the day: the restaurant catches the early morning sun, then the inside pool area stays sunny until dusk.

01 Reception area | 02 Bedroom | 03 Building diagram | 04 Exterior with wooden terraces

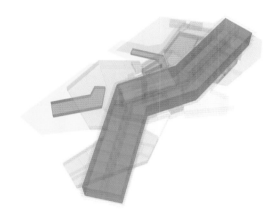

03

04

01

02

03

Grimming Thermal Spa and Aldiana Salzkammergut

This thermal spa is presented as a malleable, rolling and transparent structure; while the club hotel itself has a more cubic form. The sauna and wellness area in front creates a strong contrast to the design of the thermal bath building. Inside, gallery-style lounging areas and a restaurant are situated around the outside of the baths. Ten-meter high glazed openings integrate the Grimming Mountains into the architectural concept, where they serve as both namesake and dramatic backdrop. In addition to the large, transparent building structure, local larch wood is also used, particularly in the design of the roof.

01 Reception | 02 Thermal baths interior | 03 Thermal baths outdoor pools | 04 Ground floor plan | 05 Exterior view

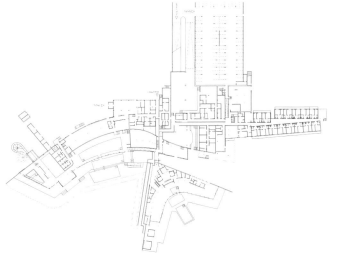

04

05

01

Festival Hall

Located on the banks of Lake Constance, Bregenz, the Festival Hall has been renovated and expanded in several stages and now serves as an efficient theater as well as an event and conference center. Architecturally of the highest quality, this building defines the lakeside site and creates a distinctive location. Two eye-catching, oversized bar-shaped building elements divide the area into three main sections: studio and workshop, the main stage and an open-air theater. The public square in front of the main entrance is half urban and half open space, offering a stunning view of the lake. The inside of the main stage is lined with acacia wood and provides a perfect theater atmosphere in a modern setting.

01 Main stage | 02 Main entrance | 03 Foyer | 04 Site plan

02

03

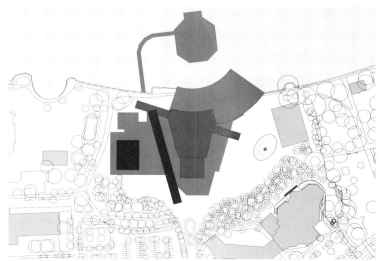

04

01

02

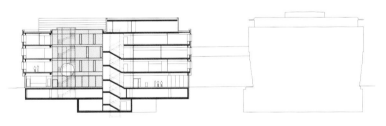

03

04

Hypo State Bank Vorarlberg

This project involved the overall refurbishment and modification of the Hypo State Bank.
This distinctive building opens on the train station side of the inner city pedestrian zone
of the provincial capital. Constructed in 1921, the unique state parliament building is
built in the Neo-Baroque style and is part of a complex that covers the entire city block.
This is functionally integrated into the bank by a glass corridor and connected by bridges
on all levels. The new façades include bright fiber-reinforced concrete slabs and glazed
surfaces, which offer protection from the sun and give the complex a sense of discrete
openness.

01 Glass corridor between old and new | 02 New façade | 03 Cross section | 04 Service
area | 05 Main view in the evening light

05

01

Family House Schwendebühel

This property is located on a sloping site above the town of Dornbirn and is oriented westwards, towards the Rhine Valley. To make the most of the views, the living areas have been positioned as high as possible; the bedrooms are located one level lower. The house rests on concrete discs, with the open level functioning as a supporting mechanism. Two large, covered and overlapping terraces are situated on the south and west sides of the house, ensuring that the architecture itself offers protection from the sun and weather. The pool is located on the terrace in front of the bedrooms and projects partially out, over the supporting wall towards the valley. This, together with the leafy terrace, fulfills one of the client's wishes.

01 Access and southeast façade | 02 Terrace with pool | 03 West view | 04 Upper floor plan | 05 Exterior at night | 06 Ground floor plan | 07 Living room

02

03

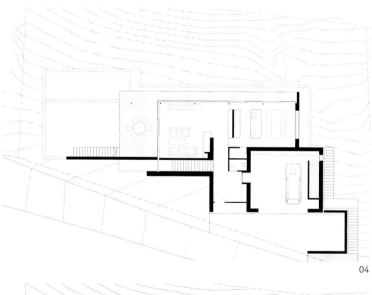

04

05

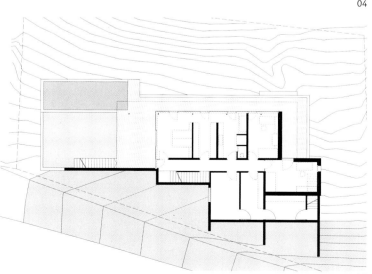

06

07

01

02

Residential Care Home Dornbirn Höchsterstraße

A striking feature of this site is the park-like vegetation. In accordance with this, the building is generous in size, freestanding and oriented to its surroundings on every side. The window openings lie flush with the façade and reach almost to the ground, this allows a view into the park even from a sitting position. The raised parapet on the community terrace is visible through small openings in the façade, which allow light to filter playfully through. The ground floor is set back slightly, and contains the most important common areas. It offers place for movement and the chance to be outdoors even in bad weather.

01 Entrance court | 02 Community terrace | 03 Section | 04 Exterior view

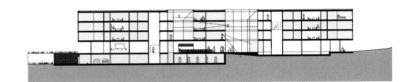

03

04

01

Raiffeisen Finance Center Eisenstadt

The design of this building conforms to the necessary building code restrictions, as well as the differing demands of the program for each story, by developing a unique exterior form, which encompasses the complete form of the bank. The continuity of the building envelope communicates employee and customer identity, and its volumetric formulation ensures it a prominent place in the city. The design consists of aluminum sandwich-panels, the color of which carries connotations of coins or the corporate identity of the bank. Slim window openings, positioned in carefully calculated areas of the façade, meet the demands of Austrian employment law, ensuring that glare from the windows is not reflected by the computer screens.

01 Exterior view | 02 Detail façade | 03 Projecting façade elements | 04 Fifth floor plan

02

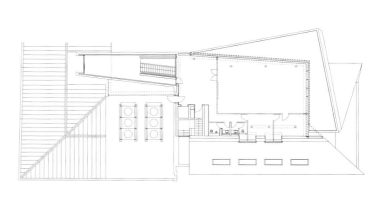

03

04

01

House of Generations Götzis

This new three-story building has different exteriors, created by three incisions. Because of this unusual structure, light is drawn deep into the building's interior. The horizontal incision creates a raised terrace in front of the care area and a projecting frame with a retractable sunshade completes the overall contours of the building. The two vertical courtyard incisions create entrances to the public facilities, which reach from the nurses' station to the kindergarten. The design of the nursing area is in accordance with the residents' wishes for light, easy orientation and variety. The building was awarded the International Architecture award, 2009, Best of Austria Award 2008/2009 and the Innovation Prize, 2008.

01 Entrance new building | 02 Front view | 03 Entrance clouding | 04 Site plan

02

03

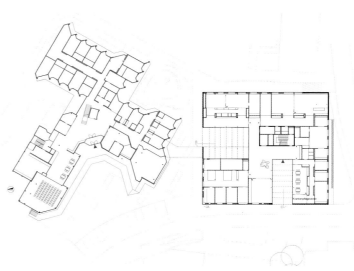

04

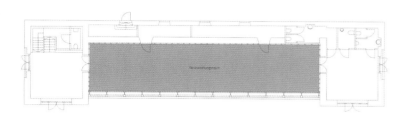

01

02

Orangerie d'Or

This classical building in the midst of the palace gardens in Graz originally served as a winter storage area for tropical plants. Based on the desired use of the main room as a representative ceremonial room for banquets, dinners and concerts, the two side wings have been designed as an entrance hall and a catering zone. The opulent ornamental design and the use of mirror effects make the edges of the room disappear, enhancing the room's atmospheric mood. The challenge was to create uniform finishes on different substructures and with varying surface requirements. The basis for surfacing consists of MDF panels for the walls and ceilings and concrete screed for the floors. The substructures are coated with a metallic paint as grounding for the application of foils with ornaments. Several coats of high-gloss clear varnish form the top and finishing layers.

01 Ground floor plan | 02 Exterior view | 03 Wall detail | 04 Hall of mirrors

03

04

01

New Chemistry TU Graz

This new chemistry institution creates space for five chemistry institutes. The aim of the project was to close the existing gap in the U-shaped New Technology building and to open the site by upgrading the existing urban area as well as creating new access routes. The entrance area is a two-story foyer space, this forges a spatial connection to a large lecture hall by means of a corridor, which then leads to the courtyard of the New Technology building. Laboratories for the students are located on both the ground and first floors – making up the public area. The research laboratories and measuring facilities of the institute are situated above these. At the top of the east and west areas are the offices corresponding to the laboratories, these are sometimes situated on different levels.

01 Main façade with entrance area | 02 Section | 03 Inner courtyard | 04 Stairs office area

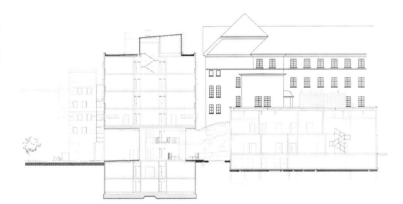

02

03

04

01

Residential House

The unique panorama and the slope to the south influenced the design of this project. Two perpendicular wings of the building are cut into the slope. The resulting courtyard offers a beautiful view of the surrounding hills. With its simplicity and clarity the roof shape considers the view of the surrounding buildings. The building height is kept low and develops from the slope, so the overall impression of the structure conveys restraint. The interior of the house is divided into single zones; the outer space has a large terrace with great views. The whole garden façade is glazed and surrounds the terrace. Large glass elements provide passive solar energy, and exterior shutters protect against overheating during the summer.

01 East view | 02 East façade | 03 South view | 04 Sketch | 05 View direction sleeping wing | 06 West view

02

03

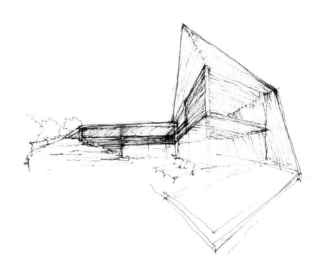

04

05

06

01

Seminar and Family House

This building consists of two parts: a two-story structure containing the office and living areas, with a gallery to the north, and a ground floor bedroom wing. Both structures stand at right angles to each other and open out, L-shaped, towards the south. This makes good use of solar energy and the beautiful views of the surrounding landscape. The building fulfils the requirements of a passive house. The wooden straws of the façade draw up from the foundation strips, which form a basement in the downwards-sloping terrain.

01 South façade | 02 Diagram of light path through the seasons | 03 Living room | 04 South-southeast façade

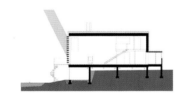

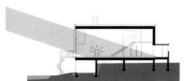

02

03

04

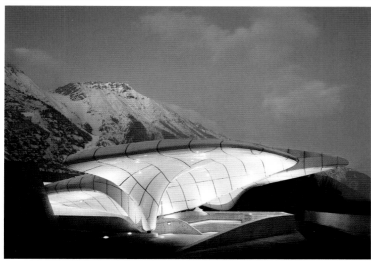

01

02

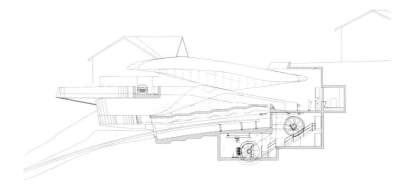

03

Nordpark Cable Railway

The one mile long railway, comprised of four new stations and a cable suspension bridge over the river Inn, travels from the center of Innsbruck to the top of the mountain in less than half an hour. The design for each station adapts to the specific site conditions at various altitudes, while maintaining the overall architectural language of fluidity. Starting underground, the railway travels through a tunnel, crosses the river Inn, starts its steep ascent, and finally arrives at Hungerburg village.

01 View of entrance | 02 Cable railway | 03 View of station and glass shaft | 04 Longitudinal section Hungerburg Station | 05 Side view by night

04

05

01

Thermal Spa and Hotel Tauern Spa Zell am See Kaprun

This four star hotel has 160 rooms with 360 beds and an exclusive hotel spa on the top floor, connected to a public sauna and water world. Combined, the seminar rooms in the Tauern Spa Hotel accommodate up to 240 people. The architectural composition rises out of the valley in front of Kaprun. It is recognizable as a complete sculpture, in combination with the surrounding mountains. The geometric spiral form, crowned by the trademark hotel spa affords an incredible view of the stunning mountain scenery from all public areas and from all bedrooms. The relationship with nature is the most important element of the design both in terms of the architecture and the interior design.

01 Exterior view hotel with panorama pool | 02 Sauna building | 03 Spa | 04 Sections

02

03

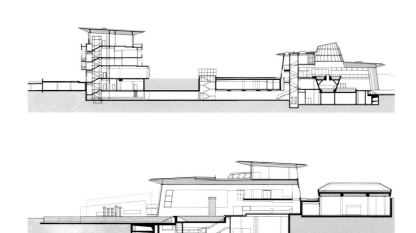

04

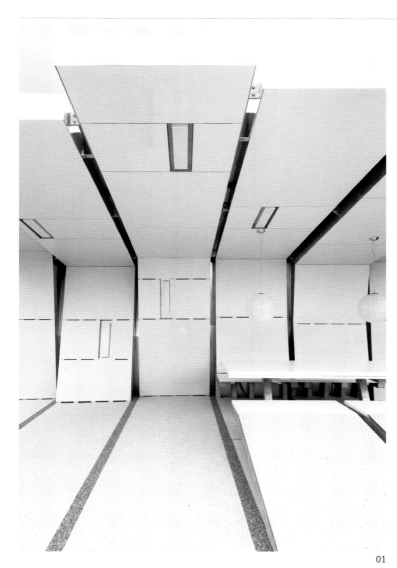

01

02

03

04

05

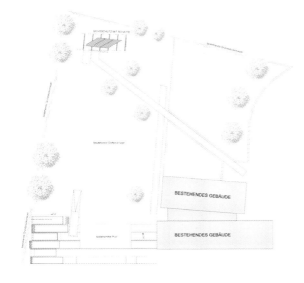

06

Hausplatz Jordan

Hausplatz Jordan comprises a structural intervention in the garden of a family home. Geometrically developed paths lead through the garden, serving different functions and requirements. They serve as accessible areas around the swimming pool, as seating areas, lounging areas, tables and roofs or work to give a feeling of protection. In the pool areas, six strips are arranged together and have different functions according to requirement. A fragmented-strip serves as a ramp and absorbs the transition to the lawn. Every single strip of the screen belongs to the paths that lead to and through the garden. The foliage and screen are composed of a steel construction and draped with 'ivory' cement plates.

01 Front view | 02 View across lawn to pool | 03 Side view | 04 Front view with pool | 05 Sheltered seating | 06 Site plan

01

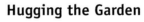

02

Hugging the Garden

This kindergarten in Klosterneuburg, near Vienna, has one main focus: to convey a sense of security, communication and freedom to the children. The two-story wooden building closely hugs the large garden and affords views of the valley. The supporting wooden frame of the glazed building offers the possibility to sit and play, allowing the children to experience nature, the weather and the changing of the seasons. The entrance, with a cloakroom and secondary zones communicates order, while the six group rooms offer space for free play and allow for a variety of functions. Open rooms for movement and exercise extend the circulation areas and create more room for playing and frolics.

01 View from garden | 02 Open movement zone | 03 Cloak room orange group | 04 Ground floor plan

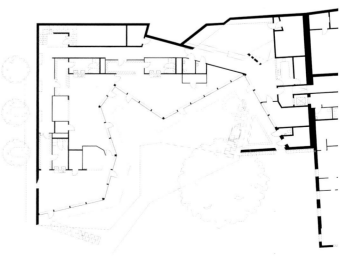

03

04

01

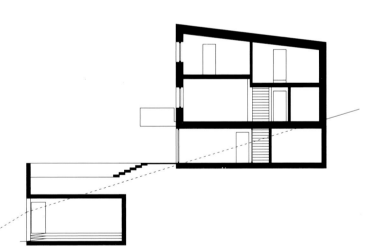

04

06

02

03

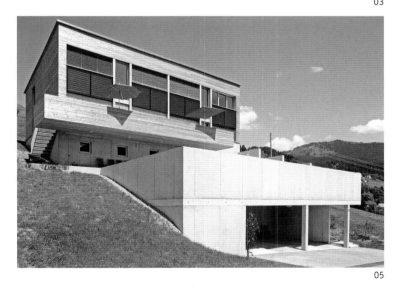

05

Schmid House

This terraced building blends harmoniously into the surrounding area. The solid reinforced concrete part rising out of the terrain provides the base for the wooden structure of the residential and office building and the front terrace. The tiered wall, with its cantilevered roofs, accentuates the stairs that lead up to the house entrance. The height difference between the gable and the ridge of the roof allows generous headroom in the spacious living area. This feature, together with the jutting out balcony and the large windows, which allow magnificent views across the mountain landscape, create a feeling of spaciousness.

01 Staircase | 02 View from northwest | 03 Living area | 04 Cross section | 05 Exterior with parking | 06 Kitchen and dining area

01

02

Eybesfeld Open Air Swimming Pool

In this project, the pool, sundeck, playgrounds and seating areas are defined as separate zones within a single outline; unified by a coating of polyester or polyurethane, they lie within the green lawn. At some points, this outline rises out of the lawn to create seating areas and space for changing cubicles and a shower room is created underneath the cantilevering concrete structure. The entrances to the pools and the seating areas are shaped like waves, which naturally makes molds for sitting and lying.

01 Pool with undulating ramp area | 02 Changing cubicles and shower room space | 03 Floor plan | 04 Sculpted pool area made of one single surface

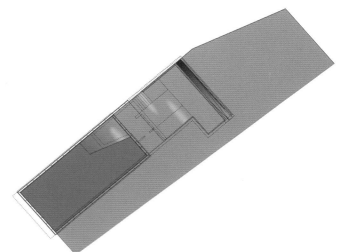

03

04

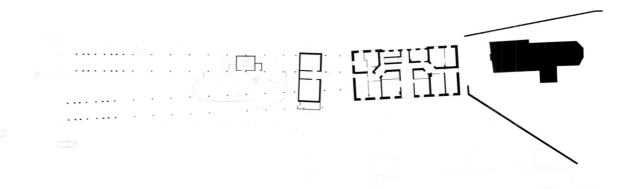

01

New Office Building Mayr-Melnhof

This new office building is built entirely from wood and consists of two elongated rectangular shapes, with a hall positioned between the two. To prevent exposing the new offices to the traffic, the entire building has been raised one story in height. The entrance foyer and conference room, with sound insulated glazing, are situated on the ground floor. A two-story, glazed hall creates a light-flooded intermediate zone, where offices are located that are clad in a warm-toned wood, creating a contrast to the brightness of the hall. Atria and galleries introduce transparency, drawing light and sun into the entire building. The office zone is based on the model of individual offices, these can be combined ensuring flexibility.

01 Ground floor plan | 02 Exterior view | 03 Middle zone with café | 04 Hall atrium | 05 Office detail

02

03

04

05

01

Sports Park Lissfeld

The Linz Sports Park occupies a 56,000-square meter site, in very close proximity to the A7 motorway. The volume of the L-shaped structure follows the slope of the site, resulting in the roof of the sports hall and the neighboring park being on the same level. The main areas, consisting of a central building with table tennis hall, a sports hall with connecting beach volleyball hall and multifunctional ball room or gymnastics hall are all joined together underground. The main building is made of wood and finished with an accessible, projecting timber roof, the lightweight nature of which is emphasized by its generous glazing. The sports hall is raised on three V-shaped supports of reinforced concrete.

01 Exterior view at night | 02 Trend sports hall | 03 Gymnastics hall | 04 Ground floor plan and trend sport hall section

02

03

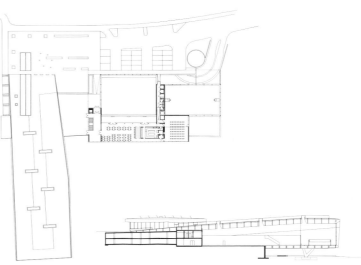

04

01

My Home is My Patio

A mix of stacked volumes structures this building. Commercial space lies above the underground parking, one-floor apartments are located above the commercial area, topped with two-story apartments on the upper level. Extended wooden poles help to integrate the banisters and specifically placed areas of color accentuate the centrally located inner courtyard as the core of the development. Two-story apartments, each with a surface area of 92 square meters, are located on the upper floor. The corner location on Feilstraße is accentuated by the materiality of the façade: along the west façade, the building has been covered with white stucco, on the east side, the roof of trapezoidal sheet metal is continued down the side of the building to the commercial area on the ground floor.

01 Variation in façades seen from street | 02 Cross section | 03 Central courtyard | 04 Strong colors accentuate the space

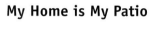

02

03

04

01

02

Living on a Hillside

This steeply sloping site lies at the foot of the Froschberg, west of the old town in the city of Linz. Terracing and roof areas are built parallel to the hill and integrate the building into the slope. The majority of the rooms in each apartment merge into the loggia area to create large spaces and a light and varied living area despite the tight financial margin in social housing. All flats were built towards the south and are provided with entrances via the outdoor corridor to ensure an equal quality of living for all. The building's façade has a multi-layered structure. Perforated, anthracite-grey façade elements emphasize the building's original form in the loggia area.

01 Exterior with balconies | 02 Façade detail | 03 Northeast elevation | 04 Exterior view

03

04

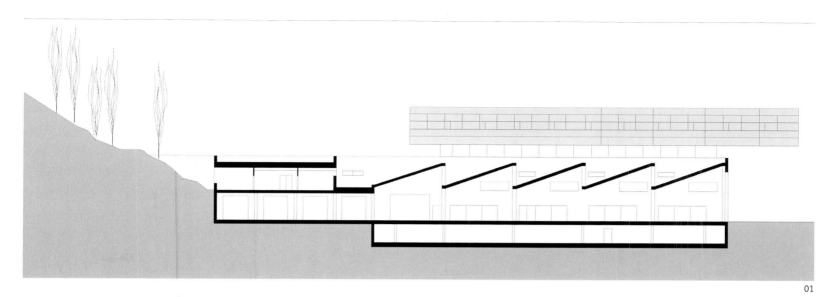

01

ÖAMTC OÖ State Headquarters

This project involved the construction and extension of the ÖAMTC OÖ state headquarters to include an underground garage, offices, call center, seminar rooms and testing areas. Of utmost importance was the large service area, which makes use of transparency and interior openness to bring to the fore the company's diverse expertise. Over this area is the prominent headquarters where open, free space increases communication opportunities. The service hall is visible from the reception area, allowing customers to oversee the work undertaken on their vehicles, making the core competences of the firm transparent. The roof of the hall functions not only to reflect the incoming light but also as a sound absorbing, acoustic device.

01 Section | 02 Waiting area | 03 Exterior view

02

03

01

02

03

04

Power Tower

This 74-meter office tower of the new headquarters of Energie AG marks the beginning of the regenerated train station quarter in Linz. The high-rise building is enclosed by a two-story base, which comprises public functions such as seminar and exhibition spaces. A landscaped inner courtyard serves as relaxation area for visitors and users. The building has passive house characteristics, as it is attached to the district heating network and uses no fossil fuels. Energy is provided by geothermal heating, ground water and a photovoltaic system. Two thirds of the façade shell is transparent, with solar control blinds positioned between the glass panels, which also reflects heat. A light installation "art on buildings" uses bands of LED lights, allowing the building to shine out at night.

01 Southeast view | 02 Atrium | 03 Foyer | 04 Northwest view | 05 Ground floor plan

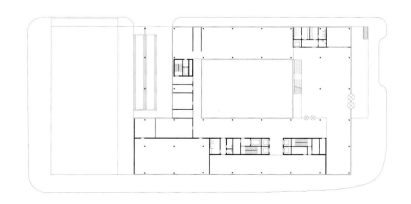

05

01

02

03

Austria Chapel

This chapel was conceived as a temporary, moveable structure. It measures two and a half by five meters, exactly the same size as a parking space and the height allows it to fit through underpasses, allowing easy transportation by road. The chapel is typical in shape, with a rectangular body and pointed roof. A small door at the front of the structure provides access. The interior is of horizontal wooden lattices, over one centimeter apart, which help to create the desired cozy interior. The exterior is covered with a white translucent membrane; the resulting structure is reminiscent of a tent, underlining the chapel's mobility. Natural light penetrates into the space through the fabric and wood, simultaneously illuminating both the interior and exterior.

01 Chapel opened on one side and illuminated | 02 Transportation of the chapel | 03 Open chapel at night | 04 Construction plans

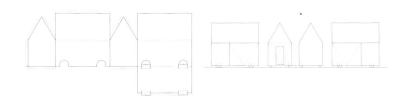

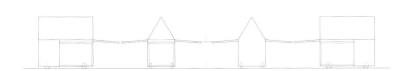

04

01

Kapitel 4

Kapitel 4 is moveable, expandable and suitable for lifelong use. It was developed as an innovative building system for future demands – especially concerning mobility, flexibility and sustainability. The system is based on the separation of a building into serving space and 'naked' space. The serving space is a completely prefabricated serving unit that provides all staircases, kitchens, baths, installations, electricity, heating and cooling systems for the entire building. All 'naked' elements are also prefabricated and are delivered directly from factory to building site, where everything can be assembled in a few days. The combination of units and elements in one system is a new approach in prefabrication.

01 West view | 02 North view | 03 Southeast view | 04 Interior view | 05 Ground floor and upper floor plan

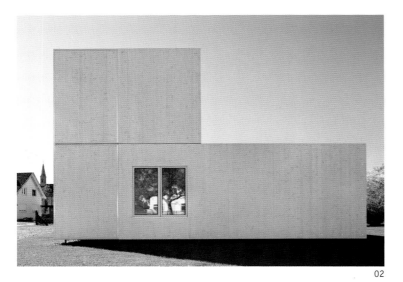

02

03

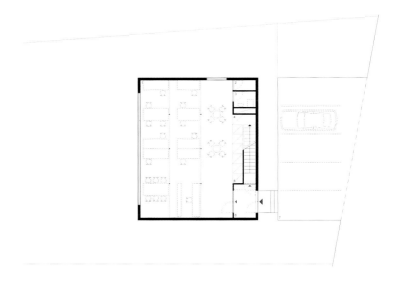

04

05

01

02

ICub – Incubator

The Incubator is a business, technology and research building where companies in the starting-up phase can be "incubated" and also looked after by means of a range of secondary functions. An architectural infrastructure supports this focus, with seminar rooms, a lounge and a café, as well as providing supporting facilities for management. Because the tendency is towards nurturing small innovative companies, the design of a community-focused social area is of particular importance. In the Incubator, it is the striking lounge area that serves this purpose: an outward-looking interior or an open terrace that can be closed depending on requirements.

01 Exterior view with entrance ramp | 02 Entrance | 03 Foyer | 04 Second floor plan

03

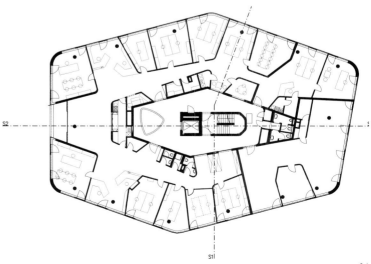

04

01

02

03

Sun Lifestyle Resort Mellau

Clear forms and authentic architecture dominate the appearance of this new hotel. Designed by the company Typico, the simple balustrades of the balconies and the plinth sections, consisting of textile façade elements, appear slight and unpretentious. A structure, wrapped completely in wood, floats above. Built on a passive house concept, the design is supported by the optimal adjustment and the compact form of the building. Together with the careful reconstruction of the interior and the new appearance of the building, the architects have created a symbiosis between old and new, a new lifestyle for the village of Mellau.

01 Exterior view | 02 Restaurant | 03 Northeast view | 04 Lobby | 05 Southwest elevation

04

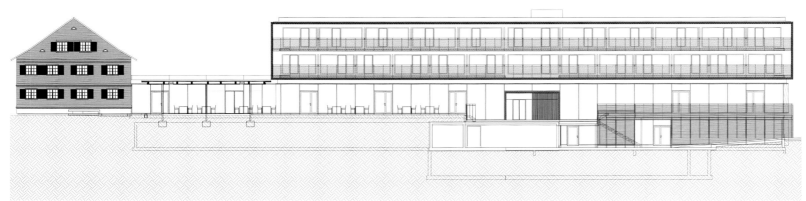

05

01

Berger House

This building is harmoniously positioned on a wooden platform, which also serves as a terrace and walkway on the south and east sides of the house. The subtle gray color and clear façade construction are the building's main exterior features. The gray, pitched roof functions as a ventilator, with two outlets on the north and south façades; these outlets offer a special aesthetic appeal. Inside, the west facing entrance allows light to flow through into the dining and living areas, two large glazed areas have also been installed in this area, allowing access to the terrace and the garden.

01 Southeast view | 02 Ground floor plan | 03 Corridor from bathroom | 04 Living room | 05 North view

02

03

04

05

01

03

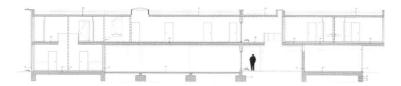

02

Self Check-In Hotel Caldor

A fallow site, just eight minutes from the city border of Vienna and very close to Austria's biggest shopping center, gave the landlord the idea to create a self check-in hotel. The site is next to a main road, the B16, and the structure of the hotel emerges along this road. The building has a bend at the center cross-point, which gives the hotel a high profile from the main road in both directions. Interesting spaces, both inside and outside, have an emphasis on communication between individual areas. The well thought-out combination of colors and the use of a glass wall to separate the individual bedrooms from their en-suite bathroom creates rooms which appear larger than they are.

01 Exterior view at night | 02 Section | 03 Exterior view with stairs | 04 Detail double room and bath | 05 Façade

04

05

01

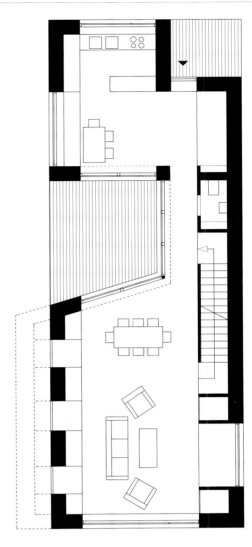

02

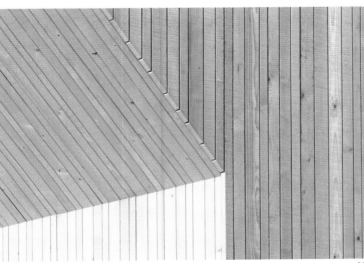

03

Sunlighthouse

The Sunlighthouse is the first CO_2-neutral family house in Austria, receiving an above average proportion of daylight. The three-story house is situated on a northeast sloping hillside, with a view to the Wienerwald Lake. A three-sided, enclosed atrium is cut into the main building on the west side. Because of its shape and orientation, the building receives the maximum amount of afternoon sun deep into the house and provides a private, protected outdoor area with access to the garden. Exclusively environmental and partially recycled materials were used in the construction and the design focused on maximizing the sustainable value. The pine wood paneling of the interior is oiled white, allowing daylight to be reflected deep inside the rooms.

01 Southeast view | 02 Ground floor plan | 03 Façade detail | 04 Staircase

04

01

Dr. Petra Freudenthaler-Karan Doctor's Office

This two-story doctor's office uses the topography of the area to allow both the ground level doctor's office as well as the overlying residential area and social areas to be accessed at ground level. The office is around 180 square meters and is open-plan and fully accessible by wheelchair. A central atrium compensates for the unfavorable alignment of the north slope. The climatically conditioned, in parts far projecting, flat roof defines the external appearance of the building.

01 West façade | 02 Ground floor plan | 03 Waiting area with atrium | 04 Reception

02

03

04

01

Logistics Center Tschabrun

Several planning teams, in collaboration with architects and structural engineers, created the competition-winning design for this logistics center. In addition to the fixed requirements, a naturally lit hall made of wood with supporting columns of between 27 and 18 meters high and a clear ceiling height of nine meters were the focus of considerations. The structure of the hall must, of course, compete with other designs in economic terms. Despite its inherent rationality and economical efficiency of the building, the exterior of the building shows a playful side. The simple rubber profile is punctuated with round windows, set flush into the outer façade and vaguely reminiscent of floating soap bubbles.

01 West view at night | 02 Cross sections | 03 Interior view | 04 Southwest view

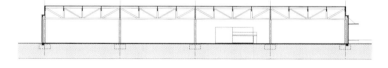

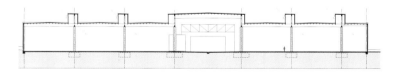

02

03

04

01

02

Passive House EF_Fah

Passive House EF_Fah features a large carport and storage room. The kitchen and living space are open-plan and accessed via an entrance on the ground floor. The room-width window opens out towards a chain of hills opposite the valley and an exit way onto the covered roof and a shaded balcony create a connection to nature and sunlight. The music and study room is oriented towards the east and is presented as a colorful box in the center of the space. The bedrooms and bathrooms, with access to terraces and garden, are located on the lower levels of the house. The cellar, with exit route, is situated underneath the carport. The photovoltaic system is integrated into the roof as an amorphous coating.

01 Southwest view | 02 Living room | 03 Outside stairs | 04 Section

03

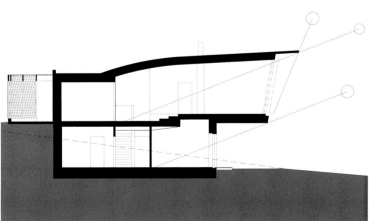

04

01

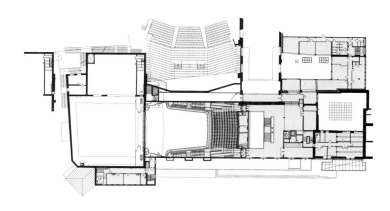

02

House for Mozart

The renovation of the existing theater included the large auditorium, stage area and the stage tower facilities, as well as the foyer area and stairwells. The auditorium of the small theater was made wider and the stage and the auditorium were lowered. Two new rows of seating were also added on both sides of the stage, giving the renovated "Haus für Mozart" a new audience capacity of 1,590. The foyer was also completely redesigned; this was necessary for technical as well as functional reasons. The main façade was restructured; the existing terraces were removed and replaced with terraces, which correspond to the scale of the building, reaching almost to the Faistauer foyer. The emerging new space takes on the function of a colonnade and allows access to the auditorium from three sides.

01 Exterior at night | 02 Upper floor plan | 03 Ground floor plan | 04 Large auditorium

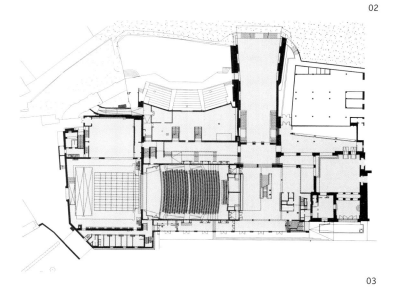

03

04

01

ARGEkultur Salzburg

02

The ARGEkultur in Salzburg produces and organizes with a cultural focus. Its displays and events question and confront social issues. The variety of the ARGEkultur is interpreted as the main theme of the design. The area is a platform, a forum for the presentation of art and culture. The platform winds upwards, the folds becoming ever smaller as they gain in height, eventually terminating in a formatted bar. This bar is the main feature of the building design, leading to the main building and connecting all the outlying sections. It establishes the communication between the individual levels of the building.

01 Exterior view | 02 Ground floor plan | 03 Bar detail | 04 Corner detail | 05 Entrance | 06 Interior view

03

04

05

06

01

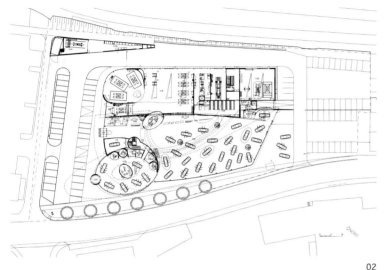

02

03

Toyota Lexus Salzburg

The site for the new Toyota and Lexus car dealership has been divided lengthways into two main areas: workshops and sales- and show-rooms. The glazed surfaces of the façade are sloped, strengthening the dynamic appearance of the building form. This has the advantage of reducing reflection while optimizing the view into the showroom. Two differing undulating roofs above the workshop area and the showroom share a formal tension and enclose a teardrop-shaped glass dome. Inside, the dynamic of the flowing lines can be seen in the intersections of the roof, which correspond with the elegant sweep of the interior lines and find a continuation in the sculpturally formed walls. The continuously changing patterns of light and shadow also contribute to this interesting effect.

01 Exterior side view | 02 Ground floor plan | 03 Showroom, view over ground floor | 04 Showroom with traversing footbridge | 05 Restroom | 06 Showroom, stairs

04

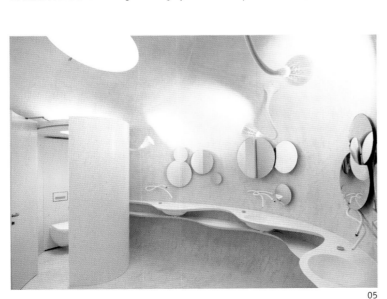

05

06

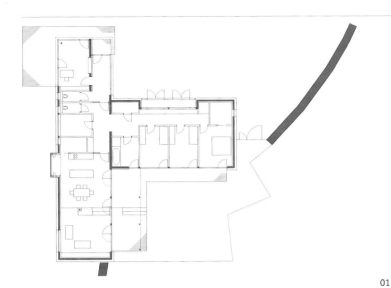

01

House at the Wall

This project was realized in a rambling wildlife park which is owned by the Esterházy family. The park is surrounded by a high limestone wall with the gamekeeper's house and the office located at one of the entrances. To remain consistent with the forestry operations of Esterházy the house was built of wood. The design is influenced by the theme wall and fence and plays with the ideas of camouflage, hiding and observation – inspired by the hunting environment. Nature, walls and the main structure are fused into one by the natural aging process of the wood panels. The project was presented with the Burgenland Wood Awards in 2008.

01 Ground floor plan | 02 Northeast view and wall | 03 Living room and southwest atrium | 04 Façade towards wildlife park

02

03

04

01

Gaislachkogl Mountain Gondola Neu Sölden Tirol

The characteristics of these three massive cable car stations give them an unusually light appearance. The transparency of the building gives a comfortable feeling of security, everything can be seen and there are no hidden corners. The transparent nature of the construction also affords a panoramic view into the light-filled space. From the beginning on, the user is a part of nature. The transparent shell, in connection with flowing light, makes the coming and going gondolas entirely visible. The middle station has a large floor area and the seven-meter-high entrance platform transforms it into a viewing platform. From the exit zone, visitors can enjoy the breathtaking view into the valley below.

01 Mountain station | 02 Section of the mountain station | 03 Interior view mountain station | 04 Middle station with garages | 05 Valley station

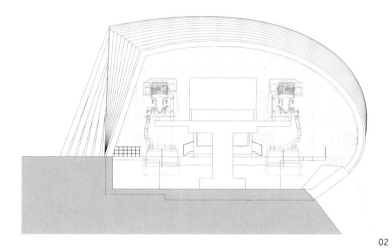

02

03

04

05

01

02

Gabriel Residential and Office Building

The profile of this building shows itself as a horizontal U-shape, which captures the landscape and at the same time releases the openness of the living area. The roof offers shelter from the hillside – the Ossiacher Tauern. The trapezoid shape of the building focuses on the view, framing it and setting the landscape in sequence. The office level forms the base – set into the hillside and blending into the site, the projection arranges the volume. From the mountainside, the building appears as a one-story bungalow while from the valley side it appears structured, varied and yet quiet body with a simple appearance. The basement is enveloped in the ground, raised in steps to match the surrounding area.

01 Office entrance ground floor | 02 Exterior view | 03 Detail upper floor | 04 Upper floor plan | 05 Dining room | 06 Living room | 07 Bathroom and bedroom

03

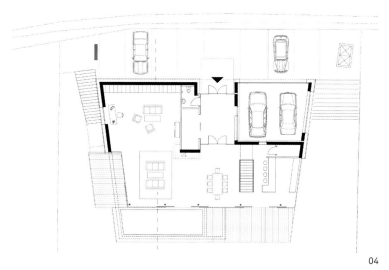

04

05

06

07

01

02

03

500 m² Living Room

Following the wishes of the client, the architects built this house on the outskirts of
Vienna on a site area of approximately 500 square meters. A total of 300 square meters
of living space was created, across three aboveground levels and one underground level.
To maintain the character of the undeveloped garden, the living and dining area on the
ground floor have been united with the garden by the large patio and pool. This design
creates an atmospheric living area that appears to be much larger than it is in reality.
The connection between exterior and interior is reinforced by the curved furniture installations, swimming pool and the curving line of the terrace. The façade is created from a
material with a distinctive, ephemeral quality, which appears to float above the glazed
lower floor.

01 Exterior view gardenside | 02 Roof garden | 03 Shadowing | 04 Living room |
05 Sections

04

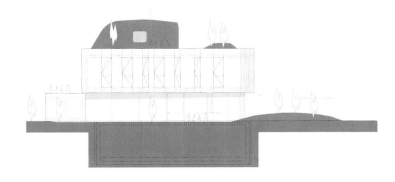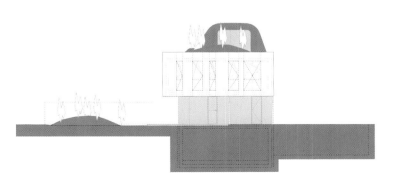

05

01

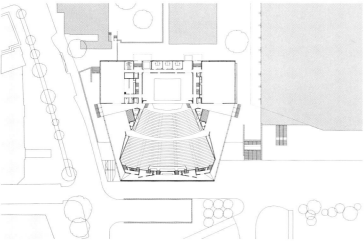

04

06

02

03

05

City Hall F

This project involved the extension of Vienna's city hall. The existing structure consisted of a large building, offering space for 15,000 people, as well as a smaller building for 500–1,000 visitors. The size of the new building is between these two, with a capacity of 1,800–2,200 people. The architects were chosen by means of an architectural competition in 2002. The design by Vorarlberger architectural office Dietrich | Untertrifaller was of a homogenous building, coated with silver aluminum elements. The existing building by Roland Rainer remains fully visible and the overall area is harmonized by the new building.

01 Evening atmosphere | 02 Main stage | 03 Old and new | 04 Floor plan with stage | 05 Main view | 06 Foyer

01

krautgarten

Living on the outskirts of town is similar, in terms of atmosphere, with living in the country; but, not everyone has to become a Do-It-Yourself builder. Caramel has stacked houses to create a residential building project that doesn't require any DIY builders and only needs someone to decorate the terraces. The individual residential units are constructed as separate multi-story houses with different views of the surroundings and then interconnected to create a complete building. Each apartment has an individual floor plan, recognizable from the outside by the different projections and balconies. Gardens, roof gardens, balconies and loggia provide each apartment with a green space – just like a family house in the country.

01 Exterior view | 02 Exterior view, individual gardens | 03 Detail terrace exits | 04 Ground floor and first floor plan

02

03

04

01

02

Spittelau Skyline

This project occupies one of Vienna's most unique locations, the northern end of the Vienna ring road. It stands near one of the city's main traffic arteries, marking the area's transition from one of Vienna's most coveted residential areas to administrative buildings and the train station facilities. The curving structure follows the movement of the former railway line, taking the form of a displaced circular arc. A light swing outwards, towards the ring road creates a dialogue between the old and new buildings. The four-story building stands out clearly from the huge arched structure. The arches open out towards the courtyard and ring road; point-clamped glazing allows maximum transparency in this area.

01 Skyline at night | 02 Inner courtyard with restaurants | 03 Site plan | 04 Aerial view

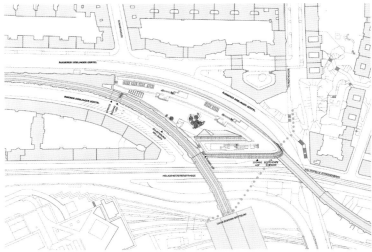

03

04

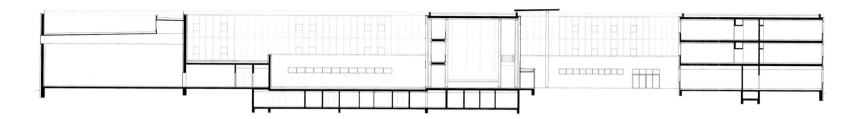

01

Hertha Firnberg School

The new Hertha Firnberg School, together with the Bernoulli Gymnasium, makes up this new campus for 2,000 students. The three-story entrance hall provides a central location for school events. The proportions and materiality of the hall is reminiscent more of a hotel lobby than a school hall, while the clear and unobtrusive nature of the architecture is deliberately free and timeless. High-quality materials, a dazzling light show, the alternation of lounge areas with space for movement, together with a strong visual relationship between terraces, balconies, bridges, courtyards and glass gangways create a continuous space of high-quality design.

01 Longitudinal section | 02 Entrance hall and lobby | 03 Main entrance

02

03

01

02

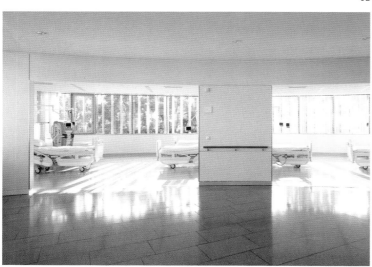

03

Dialysis Center

The new Dialysis Center presents itself as a clearly structured, welcoming building. The building is made of two circular elements, joined together. The entrance of the new building opens out towards the north. A separate conference area and administration rooms follow the brightly lit foyer. 72 treatment areas are located on the two upper levels, with views of the surrounding landscape. The design principle aimed to establish the greatest possible clarity with the shortest possible distances for staff and patients to negotiate. The wards are divided into four separate areas within the circular buildings, each of which has a central care base, with direct line-of-site care. Staff and examination rooms are located in the eastern compound of the structure.

01 Exterior view | 02 Reception desk with view to surgerys | 03 Surgery rooms | 04 First floor plan

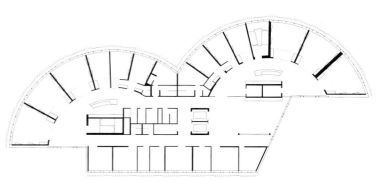

04

01

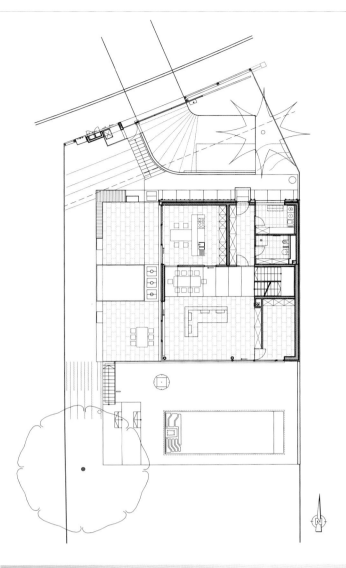

02

03

04

House D

This family house is situated on a south-sloping site on the outskirts of Vienna. The north face of the building, with its extended, barrel-like metal roof, appears closed and introverted. The building opens out to the south and west by using the topography of the site and the installation of a large glass façade that connects to the projecting terrace and the garden. Large sliding doors connect the exterior and interior spaces. The rounded roof continues dynamically over the roof terrace, which is shaded by a retractable sunshade. A skylight of transparent glass reaches across the roof, allowing sufficient natural daylight to penetrate deep into the rooms below.

01 Southwest view at night | 02 Ground floor plan | 03 North view at night | 04 Kitchen | 05 Living room

05

01

Secondary School - AHS Contiweg

This new school in Vienna-Hirschstetten was designed as a complex with two horizontally emphasized classroom wings and a distinctive entrance atrium. The school library sits like a tree house over the glazed, three-story foyer and gives the peripheral location a distinctive identity. The inner courtyard, with its stage and terrace elements, rises into the landscape with its free seating and stairway. In the interior, open seating niches in the corridors in front of the classrooms offer additional communication and retreat areas. Lens shapes form a decorative light motif on the façades, in open space and in the interior of the building, giving the building a special profile.

01 Exterior view at night | 02 Elevation | 03 Inner courtyard | 04 Façade main entrance | 05 Connecting bridge

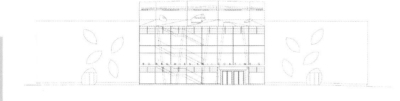

02

03

04

05

01

02

03

04

05

06

Thermal Baths Vienna Oberlaa

Embedded in the spa garden landscape of Vienna Oberlaa, the "Therme Wien", Austria's biggest thermal baths offers a diverse program of various thermal pools, quiet areas, dining options and beauty treatments, which all work together to create a special re-laxation experience. The design idea was inspired by nature: the basic motif is a creek, winding its way through stones, spilling over them and becoming, at times, wider and then narrower again. The starting point is one of the two thermal springs. The building follows the topography towards the south like the path of a wandering river, washing over several "stones", which rise out of the roof landscape like pebbles in a creek.

01 Water slide | 02 Water action in "Erlebnisstein" | 03 Green spring colors dominate thermal hall 2 | 04 Water cascade | 05 Relaxation zone | 06 Site plan

01

02

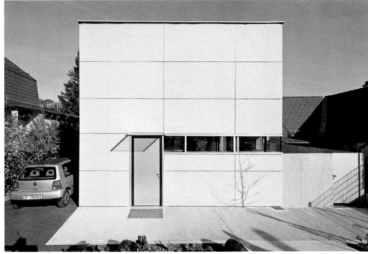

03

04

05

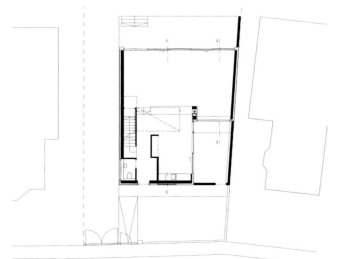

06

House H

House H is located on the outskirts of Vienna and offers a lot of privacy. Seen from the street, the house appears completely closed, just a narrow horizontal slit allows a view to the woods at the back of the house. The living rooms on the ground floor are oriented towards a courtyard, which lets light in from above and from the south. This compensates for the orientation and slope of the site towards the north and provides an intimate outdoor space. The different volumes of the building are ordered in varying cubes, so that the privacy of the enclosed space becomes apparent. With exception of the bathrooms and bedrooms, the house is a three-dimensional single space.

01 South façade | 02 View from garden | 03 Street facing façade | 04 Interior view | 05 Atrium | 06 Ground floor plan

01

02

03

Embedded House

The concept parameters for the design of this house are the existing structures in the surroundings, the topography, the far-reaching views of the landscape, building restrictions and the future growth of the family. Situated along the slope, it shares a dialogue with the scenery. Exterior terraces in each level are possible through the embedding of the building into the slope. The astonishing views from each room in the house over the valley and into the mountains allow the user to experience rural living in a modern transformation of traditional elements of this area. The side of the house facing the hill is closed, while the front opens out to the countryside, allowing natural light to flood the space.

01 Total view | 02 West façade with private terrace | 03 Southwest façade | 04 Ground floor plan | 05 Living space | 06 South façade

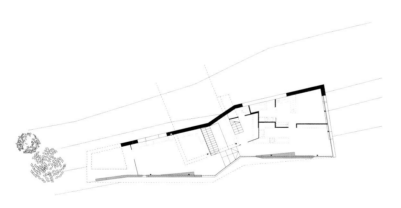

04

05

06

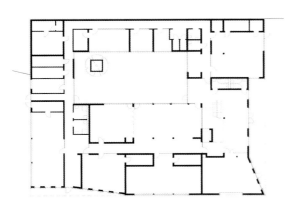

01

02

Lebenshilfe Sheltered Workshop

The new Lebenshilfe Sheltered Workshop in Weiz is located on a slightly sloping site on the eastern edge of the Weiz Becken. On the west side of the site is a large four-story residential building, built in the 1960s. The remaining area is surrounded by older family houses. The goal of the project was to mediate between these two opposing poles. This was achieved in that the new building, on the side of the residential block, presents a two-story façade to the street, resulting in the formulation of a representative urban situation. The building is dug into the side of the slope, allowing it to share a dialogue with the smaller neighboring houses through its one-story façade.

01 Ground floor plan | 02 Interior with view to patio | 03 Terrace | 04 Exterior view

03

04

01

02

Interspar Hypermarket Weiz

The cantilevered canopies of the new shopping center represent the architectural appearance. The dominating composition was chosen because the functional building was barely visible through the fore-lying buildings on the street side. These 'wings' are supported by forked columns, covering the parking area and leading to the entrances of the mall, as well as surrounding a centrally located restaurant. Artificial and natural light sources are integrated in order to emphasize the lightweight nature of the structure. The façade of the shopping areas are kept mostly transparent. Additional spaces such as storage rooms, social areas and utilities are located in a darker, two-story block.

01 Exterior view at night | 02 Interior view | 03 Detail exterior view | 04 Ground floor plan

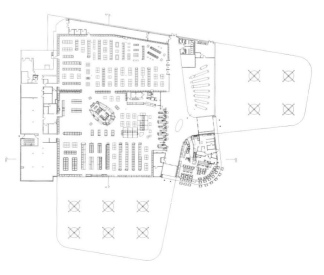

03

04

01

02

03

New Messe Center Wels

The main entrance to the New Messe Center Wels is situated between the existing Messe 18 building and the new foyer. This transparent foyer was conceived as a wind trap and connects Messezentrum West with the Bosch Halle and forms, in conjunction with the western foyer, the circulation and recreation zones of the new hall. The entrance foyer provides access to the restaurant and VIP lounge on the first floor and the seminar complex on the second floor. The foyer and office areas are connected by bridges and flooded with natural light, extending to form a bar-lounge and reception area. Inside, the generously sized space can be sub-divided by flexible partitions. A massive timber roof covers the new, flexible exhibition space.

01 Exterior view at night | 02 Timber roof | 03 Roof detail | 04 Ground floor plan | 05 Generously sized exhibition space | 06 New foyer with bridges

04

05

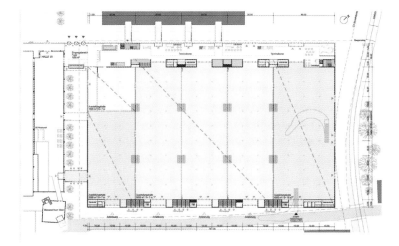

06

01

22 tops

This new residential building considers the existing building shape as well as the small structure of the neighboring family houses, maintaining suitable proportions and views of the landscape. It faces the challenge of providing for the different needs of users, while also respecting the surrounding scenery. The design spatially combines open public space including a children's play area with private terraces and stretches across the underlying, natural light supported parking deck. The construction offers different sizes of apartments, for single persons, couples and families with up to two children.

01 Northeast façade with outdoor corridor | 02 South façade with terraces | 03 Ground floor plan | 04 South view with open green space | 05 Southeast façade detail

02

03

04

05

01

02

Widra Areal

This new residential building has been built on the former site of Widra scales factory in Aachen. New buildings and the partial destruction of the old factory work to disguise the previous use of the site. Leasable gardens and a play area have been created on the once-sealed industrial site. The new developments and the renovated sections of the old factory now house 23 apartments and two group residences as well as space for two doctor's offices. On the ground floor, the former production hall today offers apartments for senior citizens, with direct access to the garden. The upper floors are shared by two residential care homes for senior citizens, each with eight residents.

01 Exterior view | 02 Courtyard with garden | 03 Courtyard | 04 Entrance brick building | 05 Ground floor plan | 06 Entrance area

03

04

05

06

01

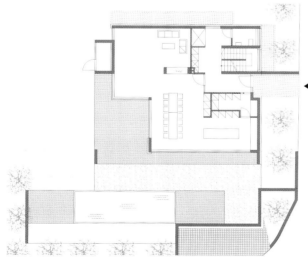

02

Residence S

This site is located in a suburban residential district on a south-facing slope with impressive views. With an adjacent park to the west, the building is designed to accommodate four people and has the necessary space and locations quality to suit this purpose. The clearly structured façade opens out to the southwest, while the expressive building frames project outwards, creating passive solar shading. The building is closed to the east mend the north. The reduced use of materials in the façade and the facilities result in a corresponding continuity, generosity and quality.

01 Exterior at dusk | 02 Ground floor plan | 03 Street view at dusk

03

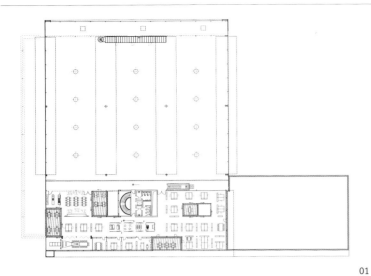

01

02

Sipos Aktorik GmbH

The structure of the Sipos Aktorik GmbH is divided into three parts: the assembly hall with automated warehouse, the two-story office and, attached to both of these areas, a loading and unloading area. The close proximity of the individual areas allows for easy internal communication. The usual separation between the assembly area and offices is reversed by use of a floor to ceiling glass wall, which promotes communication between these two different working environments. The naturally lit atriums in the office area connect exterior and interior, serving as an extension of the workspace. The black, reflecting glossiness of the façade is created by a transparent chromium oxide layer on the surface of the stainless steel panels.

01 Second floor plan | 02 Detail west façade | 03 Northeast view at night | 04 Northwest façade with atrium

03

04

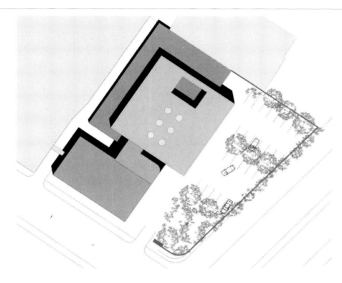

01

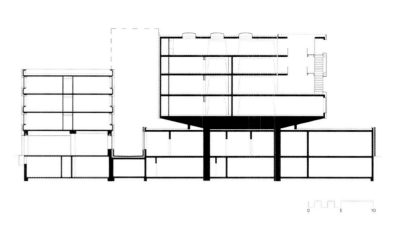

02

Training Center for Apprentice Butchers

This 1970s workshops and a boarding school area were converted and supplemented with a new building containing teaching rooms, offices and additional residential rooms. The central staircase connects the old building's four stories with the new cube, which seems to float above the single-story workshop area. As the old building was unable to support any additional load, four props support the new upper stories on a sculpturally designed table. The building's outer shell is a glass mosaic façade, its various shades of brown contrast with the white window elements, which extend the 'hygienic' white interior to the building's external appearance. The new cubic structure is distinctive enough to do justice to its exposed position and stands.

01 Situation | 02 Longitudinal section | 03 Entrance | 04 Meeting room | 05 Leisure area | 06 Hygienic surfaces

03

04

05

06

01

02

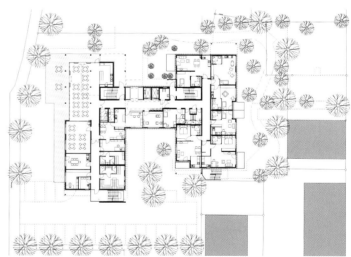

03

04

Nursing Home Aspacher Tor

Various interacting units form this senior center at Aspacher Tor; including 21 serviced apartments, a nursing home with 50 care places and 15 additionally integrated senior apartments. A shared social and meeting area is centrally located between the various buildings and a café offers space for relaxation and the opportunity to meet people. The bold, fresh tones of the color scheme underline the project's unique identity. The quality of both community and private experience is a focus of the design. The rooms of the nursing home are structured so that they offer, depending on individual mood, the choice of spending time in the public areas, in the café or the meeting area while also ensuring that retiring to one's personal room or care-group area, is also always possible.

01 Exterior view | 02 Living room | 03 Floor plan | 04 Sundial

01

Leonardo Glass Cube

This atmospheric building connects architecture, interior design, graphic design and landscape planning to create aesthetic homogeneity. The most significant design element is the impressive glass façade. The shapes of the graphically illustrated elements on the façade are taken from objects of the surrounding architecture and landscape; these generate a puzzling effect when seen in conjunction with the reflections of the real elements. The structure consists of a rectangular shell and an incorporated free-form wall. Sculptural, white structures – 'genetics' – link the zones of the building to each other. Inside, a void crossed by bridges connects the upper and lower level and the free-form wall forms niches or lounges and presentation zones.

01 Graphically printed glass façade | 02 Function room | 03 Ground floor plan | 04 Interior view

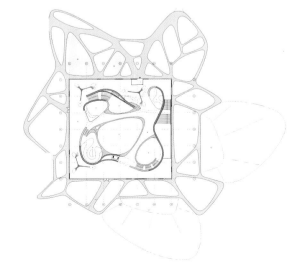

02

03

04

01

02

03

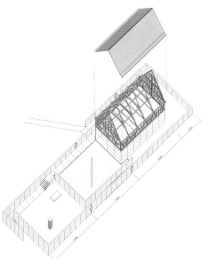

04

05

06

Stone Sculpture Museum

This is a small museum dedicated to displaying the work of sculptors Wolfgang Kubach and Anna Maria Kubach-Wilmsen. The face of the gable roof was replaced by a curtain wall of glass, fitted within the original timber framework. Natural light shines through the openings into the double-height space to give life to the sculptures. The lower portion of the building consists of a new concrete wall that contrasts the old woodwork of the shed. L-shaped walls around the perimeter of the building create a layered spatial division and a court for the display of sculptures. This wall, which at once opens and closes the realm of the museum to its surroundings, allows the architecture to be assimilated into the beautiful natural landscape.

01 Exterior terrace with pool | 02 Timber work modernized by glazing | 03 Concrete creates a contrast to timber frame of old building | 04 Axonometry | 05 Floor plan | 06 Interior under construction

01

02

03

Ostertor Gallery

The challenges of this project included embedding the volume within the cityscape and the integration of different functions in one building complex. To resolve these challenges, the building today has an area of 12,650 square meters and houses a convenience store, a four star hotel with 98 rooms, an underground car park, a conference center, a restaurant and the town library as well as diverse retail space and offices. The recognizable building is a landmark within the city, very close to the old town and is distinguished particularly by its stone façade.

01 North view | 02 Façade detail | 03 Exterior at night | 04 Ground floor plan

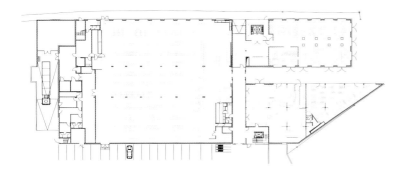

04

01

02

03

04

05

Sports Center Petkus

The basic design idea for this construction was to create a reduced events and sports box, formulating a one-story connection between the old and new buildings. This allows both spaces to open out, offers a grandstand for the sports field and separates the two buildings when necessary, so that they can fulfill individual functions. The concept envisioned a transparent space within the Brandenburg landscape, but with a closed south façade in wooden-frame construction. This façade has eight 'light points', reducing glare and offering protection from overheating. Another architectural feature of the building was the use of larch wood on both the interior and exterior, which connects the inside and outside, and also visually connects the acoustic ceilings and the impact-protection wall.

01 View along the façade | 02 Panoramic view | 03 Interior | 04 Sports hall at dusk | 05 Façade with 'light points' | 06 Situation

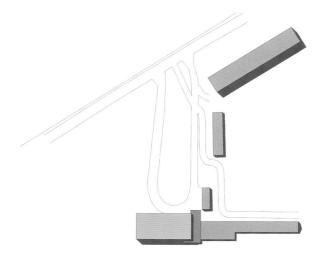

06

01

02

03

04

Synagogue Renovation

The 1922 building served as a transformer station, substation, and illumination laboratory for street lighting. With its classical façade, the building fits in well in the neighborhood of wealthy homes. Purchased by a Jewish foundation in 2004, the building was
placed at the disposal of the orthodox Jewish "Chabad Lubavitch" organization. The
exterior was retained to a great extent, except for the addition of a prestigious portal
opening onto the street. The orthodox synagogue was built in the former transformer
hall, with a traditional ritual bath (mikveh) located in the cellar. In addition there are
rooms for seminars and childrens' services, a library, café, and a ballroom, with a kosher
kitchen for the community members and visitors.

01 Prayer room | 02 Lobby | 03 Main façade | 04 Interior | 05 First floor plan

05

01

04

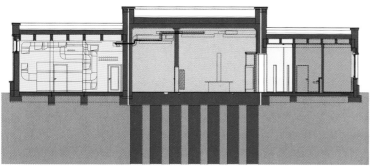

06

02

03

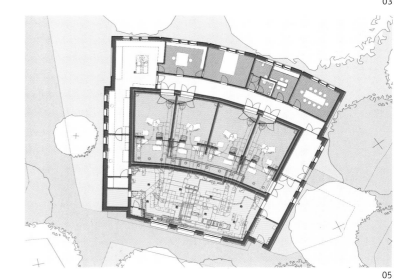

05

Transmission Electron Microscope Building TU Berlin

The TEM is an unusual building; inside, advanced transmission electron microscopes take incredibly accurate images of atoms for the research institute of the TU Berlin. To achieve this, the institution must provide very exact conditions: vibrations and temperature fluctuations from the surrounding environment must not be allowed to reach the microscope. All sections of the structure were built extremely stiffly and metal materials were avoided. The building's exterior corresponds to this stability and solidity through the use of a plaster and natural stone façade: high-tech research encased in low-tech architecture, which connects to the neighboring buildings in terms of its color and materials.

01 Façade detail | 02 Main entrance | 03 View from southwest | 04 View to the old building | 05 Situation | 06 Longitudinal section

01

02

Hotel Concorde

This five star hotel is located directly on the Kurfürstendamm, one of Berlin's main avenues. It offers 267 generously sized bedrooms, 44 suites, eight conference rooms, a banquet room, restaurant, bar and a wellness area. The design of Hotel Concorde presents the rare oppertunity for architect Jan Kleihues to design not just the building, but also the interior. Every detail of both the interior and exterior have been carefully selected, the corner buildings are piled on top of one another, and staggered along the street side. The strongly-profiled horizontal bands of the structure divide the building horizontally.

01 Exterior view | 02 Meander Suite | 03 Situation | 04 Bathroom | 05 Façade

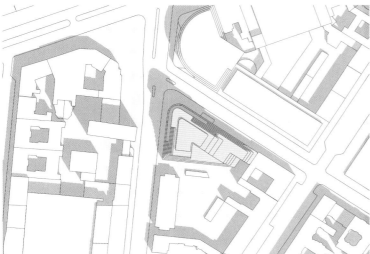

03

04

05

01

Music- and Lifestyle-Hotel 'nhow'

This four star hotel lies between the Spree in the south and Stralauer Allee in the north. It offers 304 rooms, two restaurants, conference rooms and ballrooms, a spa area and even a recording studio. The building layout and façade design contribute to the location within this former port area. The brick façade forges a deliberate connection to the adjacent warehouses and office buildings. The exterior is enhanced by the dynamic play of the different shades of brickwork. Dominating over the entire structure is a prominent, cantilevered three-story structure, reminiscent of El Lissitzky's "Cloud Hangers". This is made of highly reflective aluminum and juts approximately 21 meters out from the main structure.

01 View from bank | 02 Longitudinal section | 03 Detail façade | 04 Detail of material

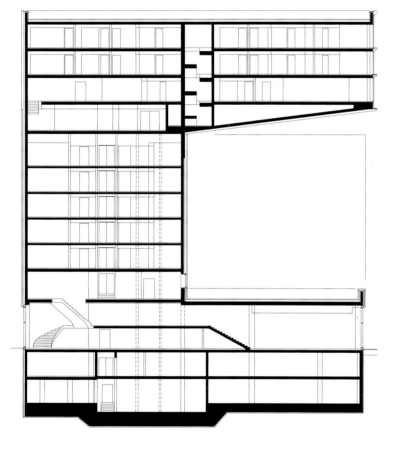

02

03

04

01

02

03

Hamburger Hof

This building ensemble constitutes a mature and constantly evolving combination of residential and commercial buildings, offering space for craftwork, Wilhelminian entertainment venues and dining areas from the last 200 years. In terms of the renovation and expansion concepts, the mix of functions, from craftwork to the arts trade, to the culture industry and provision of residential space, were all developed in close coordination with the conservation authorities. Only two barrack-style buildings from the 1960s were removed. Sloping roofs were added, along with a glass-enclosed upper floor and a fire safety wall. The new structure juts out above the older, brick architecture.

01 Front view | 02 Raised building | 03 Courtyard | 04 Longitudinal section

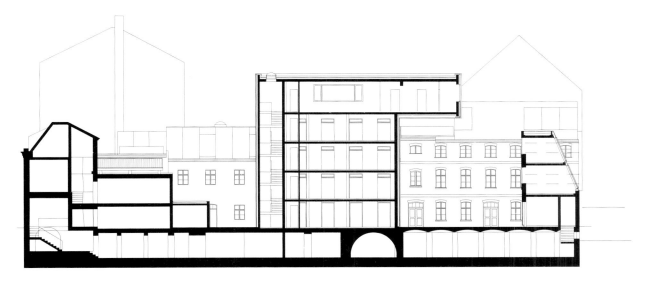

04

01

02

Residential and Office Building Jägerstraße 34–35

This new residential and office building emerged as the winner of an architecture and tendering procedure competition. The project is considered to be, together with the townhouses at Friedrichswerder, one of the most ambitious developments in the re-urbanization of downtown Berlin. Until 1945, the building site housed the main building of the german Reichsbank. The goal of the architects, Wiegand/Hoffmann, and the private investors was to enliven the historical area with an example of elegant, timeless architecture. A sand-colored limestone was used for the façade, architectural bronze and anodized aluminum for the window frames. The new coveted apartment buildings provide a view over Berlin's vibrant down-town area.

01 Main view | 02 Second to fourth floor plan of apartments | 03 Lobby | 04 Façade detail | 05 Entrance hall

03

04

05

01

Berlin Central Station

Berlin's new Central Station – Europe's largest train station for long-distance, regional, and local transport – was built on a historical site in the Tiergarten district. The platform hall is spanned with a large, lightweight glass roof. From an urban planning and architectural aspect, the arched buildings form a unity with the glazed halls of the train station. The station hall is also covered by a fine, vaulted glass roof structure. The hall offers an inviting gesture towards the Moabit district on one side as well as the government district on the other, consequently taking on an additional connecting function between government district and urban quarter. The glass roof of the entrance hall is connected to the lateral arch buildings.

01 Exterior view at night | 02 Design sketch by Meinhard von Gerkan | 03 Crossing of the two halls

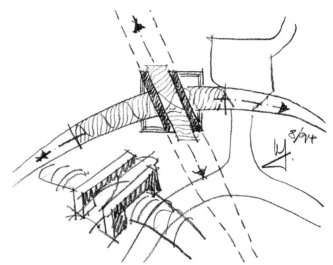

02

03

01

State Ballet School

This stage of construction of the State School of Ballet took 30 months to complete, and comprises a new hall with ten dance rooms plus the refurbishment of the existing school building dating from the 1960s. The overall architectural concept focuses on the special nature of the school, with its constant ebb and flow of pupils, between the creative world of dance and the classic functions of fulltime schooling. A curved hall runs through the new building, with the adjacent four-story school and ballet rooms facing each other. The various areas of the ensemble are related to each other above this linking space. Large display-window openings in the façade provide a view of the outside world and give passersby a glimpse of the ballet rooms and dance training.

01 Exterior view at night | 02 Curved hall | 03 Situation

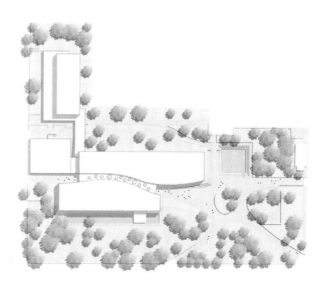

02

03

01

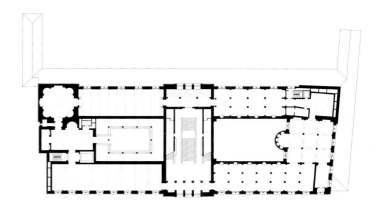

02

Neues Museum

The so-called New Museum on Berlin's Museum Island was constructed between 1841 and 1859, based on plans by the architect Friedrich August Stüler. The building was badly damaged by bombs in the Second World War. The restoration of the building followed a principle of conservation rather than reconstruction and involved the repair and restoration of the remaining sections, as well as the reinstatement of the original volume and spatial sequence through newly built sections. The new exhibition rooms are built out of large, prefabricated concrete elements made of white cement with marble aggregate. The main staircase is situated in a majestic hall preserved only as a brick volume. It is made from the same concrete elements and repeats the original volume without replicating it.

01 East façade | 02 Ground floor plan | 03 Roman room | 04 Egyptian courtyard, view towards platform | 05 Staircase hall

03

04

05

01

02

03

04

sc11

This building is one of the first building blocks in the development of the Mauerstreifen, where the Berlin Wall formerly stood. In the 1960s, due to the construction of the Berlin Wall, large areas of blocks of houses were demolished, which left a scar in the urban setting. The building is defined by a single element: an L-shaped band of reinforced concrete, which connects the building with the ground, defines the structure of all the stories and represents the completion of the building. At some points the façade can open into full room width and ceiling height, transforming the living space into room-sized loggias. At other points the façade runs inwards, leaving room for a terrace. The façade is a solid construction made out of cast-in-place concrete. The plastic surface structure was attained by inserting matrices into the formwork.

01 Exterior view | 02 Interior | 03 Façade detail | 04 Interior with outside view | 05 Ground floor plan

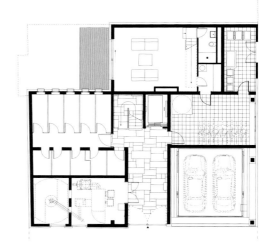

05

01

02

03

Moa-Bogen in the Stephankiez

A shopping center, a four star hotel, sport and leisure facilities as well as a parking lot and community area create this new, urban reference point on the site of the former Paechbrot bread factory. The new construction pushes into the urban space, with its modern, fully glazed façade, while the set-back alignment generates a small forecourt and entry space. The façade is designed with a glazed ceramic finish, changing in color from yellow to violet and then to blue.

01 Corner view | 02 Façade | 03 Community area | 04 Section | 05 Interior shopping center | 06 Hotel lobby

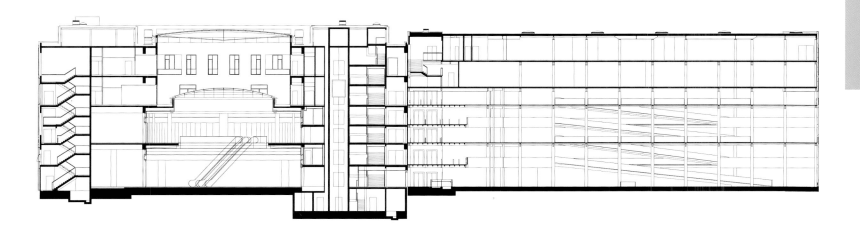

04

05

06

01

02

03

04

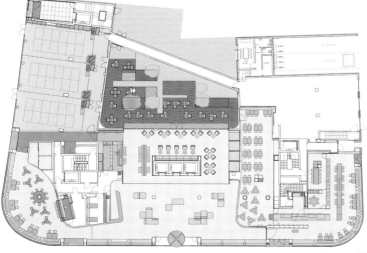

05

Sana Hotel

The Sana Hotel is situated in the center of the German capital. For this reason, black granite stone has been chosen for the façade. The design of the façade and the round corners maintain a clear dialogue with the inside of the building aiming for an integrating philosophy, the essence of the architect's studio in Barcelona. The layout of the granite pieces of the façade has its origin in the windows, which strategically rest against green-colored retro-illuminated modules, emphasizing the lines of the building. Both the lobby and the restaurants are located on the ground floor and have been delimited by transparent glass in order to offer visibility to the public areas of the hotel. Only the main entrance revolving door is made of green laminated glass.

01 Exterior with view to lobby | 02 Restaurant | 03 Hotel room | 04 Lobby | 05 Ground floor plan

01

02

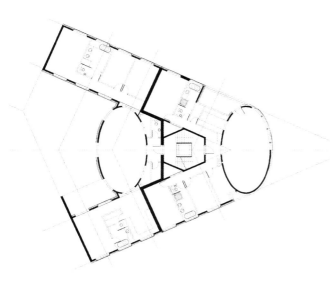

04

03

House 27°– Living and Working in Berlin

The corner location on two very different streets in a central district of Berlin strongly influenced this design concept of single units positioned around a central elliptical space. The double-layered façade is organized as a bris-soleil and can be folded and opened. The façade is oriented towards the existing buildings and newly interprets these. The variable spatial relationships stand in the foreground of the design of this very urban structure. Both sides of the building form a successive spatial sequence behind the elliptical reception and living space. The rooms can be closed off from each other and used as working and living space. The space is heated and cooled with geothermal energy and also incorporates solar thermal energy.

01 Double-layered façade | 02 Entrance area | 03 Elliptical living room | 04 First floor plan

1 Wood   2 Daylight   6 Cooling system   3 Photovoltaic

4 Rainwater   5 Geothermal energy

01

Rewe Green Building – Konzept Zukunft

This pilot project tests new ground and is a pioneer of sustainable retail-building design. The concept for the new Rewe supermarket in Berlin was inspired by historical market hall design. Modern architecture has been combined with energy-saving technology, insulation, sustainable material and the use of renewable energy sources, resulting in an environmentally friendly construction concept. Heating, ventilation and air conditioning systems don't pollute the air with carbon dioxide – the market is carbon neutral. The architecture uses daylight and wood to symbolize the building's sustainability. It is the first retail building in the world to be awarded the gold "Gütesiegel" for sustainable building.

01 Scheme | 02 Sketch | 03 Entrance area | 04 Main entrance | 05 Exterior view arcade

02

03

04

05

01

02

03

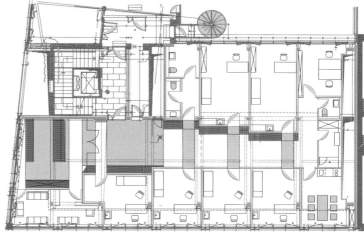

05

04

Cardiology Practice

The cardiology practice of Dr. Beckmann / Dr. Ehlers surprises with its generous size and the high-quality space of the semi-public areas. The reception area becomes a welcoming foyer, offering not only waiting rooms, but also space for lectures and reception rooms. Benches, wardrobes and shelves fuse into a graphic game and enclose the space. The open central spaces are located opposite to treatment rooms and functional areas. The intimacy of the treatment rooms is intensified by the quiet structure and high quality design. The patient feels like a guest inside the welcoming lobby and like an important interlocutor in the treatment room.

01 Treatment room | 02 Waiting area | 03 Seating in waiting area | 04 Floor plan | 05 Entrance area with way markers on the floor

01

The Wave

The Wave is a nine-story building complex located in close proximity to Alexanderplatz in Berlin: In addition to a four star hotel and a two star hotel, the complex also houses office and administration space. The different functional areas are made clear by the building's façade. The four-star area is emphasized by a gold band, which changes to silver as it runs over the two star area. The office complex combines the black and gold colors of the design in a narrow, horizontal layout. The horizontal emphasis of the façade share a a dialogue with the existing GDR architecture, signaling an interaction between the past and the present.

01 View to Alexanderplatz | 02 Northeast view | 03 Façade detail | 04 The Wave at night

02

03

04

01

02

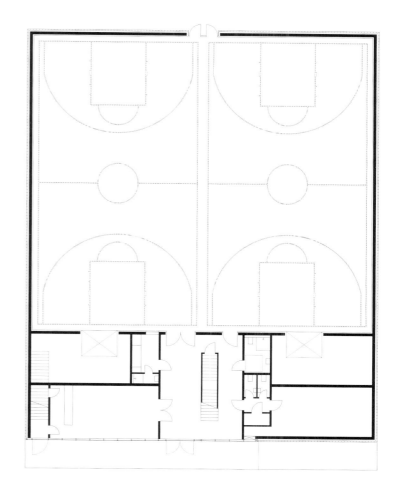

03

Double Sports Hall Bielefeld-Ubbedissen

This project involved the construction of a new sports hall for a primary school in the Bielefeld area of Ubbedissen. The old hall no longer met modern requirements and a new, more suitable space was called for. The new sports hall was required to serve the primary school as both sports hall and auditorium as well as to provide space for various sports clubs. The new hall presents itself as a simple, glass cube. The entrance is oriented towards the primary school and is emphasized by its projecting, canopy roof. Changing rooms, toilets and wash rooms are located on the second floor, keeping the floor area of the construction compact. The foyer on the ground floor is connected to the sports hall and the club space by double-winged doors. The sports hall was awarded the BDA prize Ostwestfalen-Lippe in 2010.

01 Front view | 02 Staircase | 03 Floor plan | 04 Sports hall | 05 Section

04

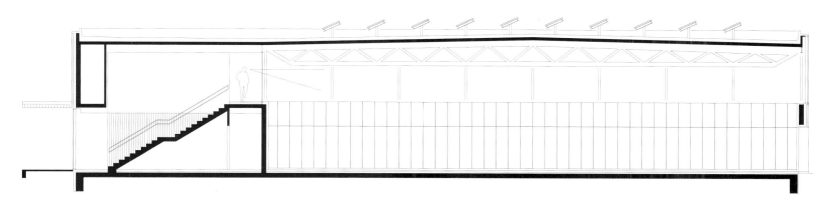

05

01

02

03

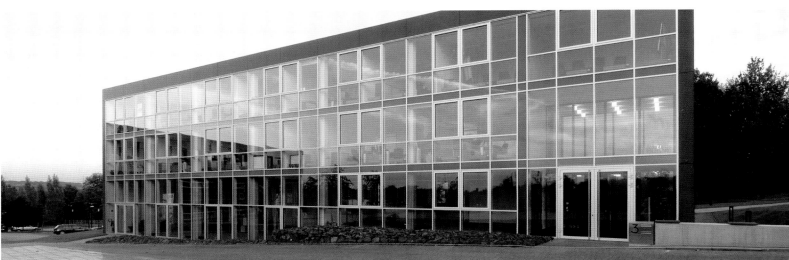

04

Immira

The Bochum Technologie-Quartier is located on the former site of the Mansfeld coal mine area. The scenic location in the Ruhr valley and the direct proximity to the universities of Bochum have made it an attractive location for technology ventures. The Immira building is the main urban feature of the Leonardo da Vinci Platz. Its façade, which is open to the north side, forms a window offering views of the quarter's central square. In addition to two office floors, the flexible and energy-optimized building offers space for exhibitions and catering on the ground floor.

01 West façade | 02 South view | 03 Exterior | 04 Northeast view | 05 Situation

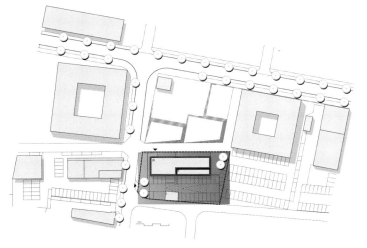

05

01

02

03

T-Home Campus Bonn

Positioned as the terminal point of Bonn's major thoroughfare, across from the Telekom headquarters, the alternating heights of these four U-shaped buildings present an attractive variation and create pleasant, urban transitions via open, green courtyards. The high quality style of the buildings – white concrete pilaster strips, Tyrolean natural stone, highly efficient double-glazed windows – create a comfortable sense of calm. The blocks are connected via five glass vestibules – the serpentines. The interior design is warm, bright and complies with the high demands of networked work processes. The team areas and the generous cafeteria further enhance the project's quality.

01 Casino | 02 Campus | 03 Courtyard | 04 Board room | 05 Ground floor plan with outdoor facility

04

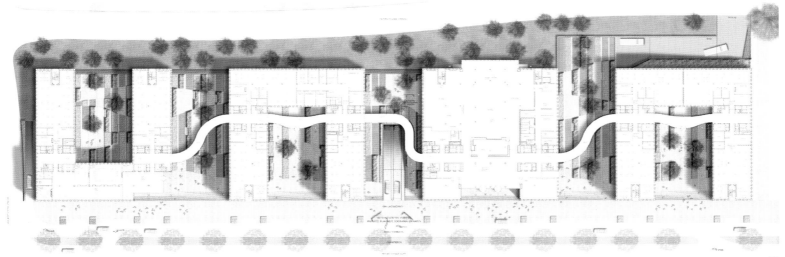

05

01

03

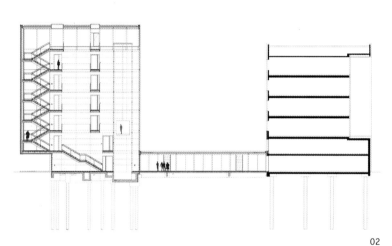

02

t.i.m.e.Port III

Through the gesture of the additional arch as a connecting circulation element, the restrained, yet clear architecture of this new building connects it to t.i.m.e.Port II without dominating over it. Access to the building is at ground level, via a glass walkway, this has the advantage of maintaining the visual relationship to the port. The ample stairwell offers views of the port and the town and corresponds to the entrance axis of t.i.m.e.Port II. The façade is designed as a double window façade. On the outside, simple glazing protects the inter-lying spaces from strong winds and salty air.

01 Exterior view at night | 02 Section t.i.m.e.Port III - t.i.m.e.Port II | 03 Staircase | 04 Staircase with offices | 05 Panorama view

04

05

01

02

Max Ernst Museum

Built in 1844, this classical, U-shaped building has undergone a transformation. The space has been restored to its original form, preserving the character of the original building. The new part of the development has been constructed, half hidden, under the earth so that the roof area appears as a slightly raised stone platform in the park. An open staircase leads visitors down to the temporary exhibition space; skylights fill the space with light. A concert hall is positioned next to the exhibition space and can be used independently, outside of the opening times. Artwork from Max Ernst is housed primarily in the old building, where the permanent collection is located.

01 Temporary exhibition space | 02 Pavilion | 03 Longitudinal section | 04 South view

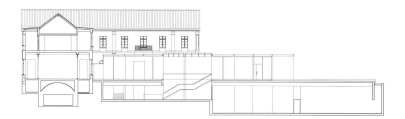

03

04

01

04

02

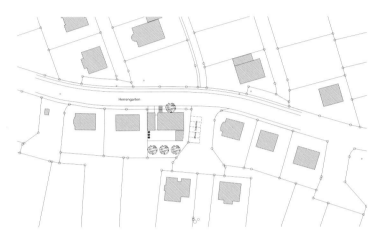

03

05

Single Family House PR05

The goal of this project was to design a house for a family with space for two or three children, an energy efficient design and a modern appearance. The garage, house and terrace are clear additions to the main buildings, separated from each other by a gap. The main building surrounds the garden, offering protection and privacy from the nearby street. The chosen materials used on the exterior were limited to those with a natural appearance. The house has a sculptural appearance and is lined with a casing made of rough sawn Siberian larch. The terrace and the garage are built from concrete and this material has been left visible. The different materials emphasize the principle of primary energy demand, 35 kilowatts per square meter.

01 Northwest view | 02 South view | 03 Situation | 04 Bathroom | 05 Northeast view

01

art'otel SEO

The challenge presented by this site was that an architectural answer must be found to suit the very different characters of the area – the traffic on the street and the quiet side facing the water, as well as the view towards Cologne Cathedral. Towards the street, colorful window openings are positioned in the façade. Towards the water, glass cubes project out of the façade and offer views of the harbor and other tourist attractions. The interior design of the building was not permitted a dominant role as a balance must be found. The work of the artist SEO, that this hotel is dedicated to, captivates through its powerful use of color and it is up to the architecture to respond to this.

01 Exterior view | 02 Foyer | 03 Façade detail | 04 Floor plans

02

03

04

01

02

03

RheinauArtOffice

The distinctive shape of Microsoft's office in North-Rhine Westphalia makes it a prominent landmark in Cologne's docks. Essentially, the building volume consists of two supporting, asymmetrical 'belts' which, shifted against each other, loop through the whole
edifice, thus connecting two individual rhomboid building units in a sculptural way. A
two-story bridge construction connects the volumes, which stand on a flood protection
platform, to ensure maximum spatial efficiency. The open space under the bridge presents a stage-like view of the docks. Generous glass surfaces constitute a transparent and
dynamic architecture, through which both city and river remain perceptible.

01 Under the bridge | 02 View from harbor | 03 Side view | 04 Office on bridge level |
05 Concept idea

04

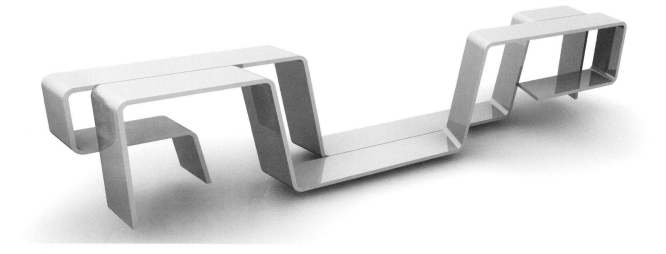

05

01

02

03

Residential and Office Building Volksgartenstraße

This pension fund office building in Volksgarten, a suburb in the south of the city, was built in the 1950s. Demolition of the premises was problematic as legally, the use of the property as office space was only secured by right of continuance law. The solution was a partial demolition. While the old building on the corner site of the pension fund building was left intact, the extension was conceived as an open-use space, functioning as both working and living space. The suspended ceramic façade unites the old and new building, forming a sedate cube. The perforated façade was maintained along the side-street, only broken at the corner to add emphasis.

01 Main façade | 02 Corner | 03 Exterior view with main façade | 04 Ground floor plan

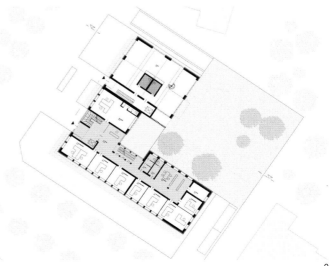

04

01

02

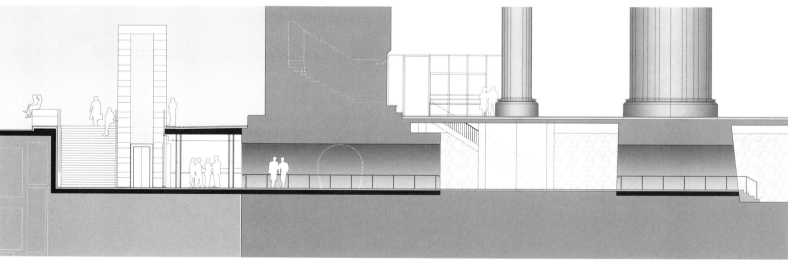

03

Entrance Building Cathedral Tower

The construction of the entrance building to the south tower of the Cologne Cathedral attempts to complement the cathedral with a significant but restrained architectural language. Its design needed to fit the dignity of the situation, the desired symbolism and show restraint appropriate to its location, situated at the foot of one of the most important and powerful structures in the west of Germany. The interior design of the kiosk consists of clear and well-structured furnishings, which answer commercial demands. The southern alignment of the building together with large glazed areas allow a generous amount of daylight into the foyer and kiosk areas.

01 View from southwest at night | 02 Sunken courtyard with view to the Roman cellar | 03 Longitudinal section | 04 Tunnel

04

01

02

Townhouse, Schwalbengasse 32

This townhouse has been built on a site only 4.6 meters wide. The entire area is 96 square meters and the house is built over 12 split-levels, this provides space for two separate units with different uses. The lower six levels provide space for work while the upper six contain the living areas. The open area in the center of the house allows for a light filled, continuous space, reaching from the cellar to the roof with views to many of the levels. Within the urban area, the house has a simple and unspectacular appearance, a clearly articulated house executed with simple and precise detail.

01 View from street | 02 View from courtyard | 03 Townhouse in its context | 04 Floor plans - working area | 05 Floor plans - living area

03

  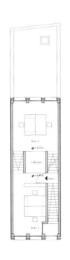

04

05

01

02

03

04

P & C Department Store

This new Peek & Cloppenburg flagship store is a savant blend of glass, steel, stone and wood: classic materials to dress a modern building. A wooden construction supports and shapes the glass jacket. On the fourth story, the supporting framework of the roof and façade construction rests vertically on the reinforced concrete skeleton. The curves meet to form a transparent dome overlooking the bell towers of the nearby Cologne Cathedral. The roof of the glass structure is lower at the center of the building to avoid rivaling the neighboring Brothers of St Anthony church. This curvature also carves out enough space to create a public square just in front of the church.

01 Interior | 02 Curved glass façade | 03 Top floor where wood ribbing forms a peak | 04 Aerial view of extended structure | 05 Floor plan of sales area

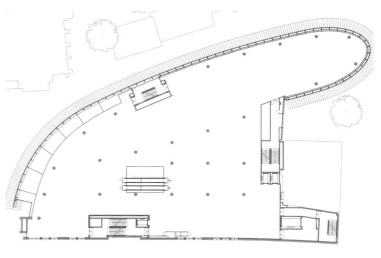

05

01

Kolumba

Kolumba is a museum for religious art of the archdiocese of Cologne, named after the former church St. Kolumba. The new building incorporates fragments of the late-gothic church, which was destroyed in World War II, and uses the original floor plan. It also incorporates the building of a 1950s chapel called "Madonna in the Ruins" by Gottfried Böhm, already situated on the site. The new building encompasses this entirely, making it simultaneously part of the new building and a part of the museum's exhibition. Typical for Zumthor is the concentration on one kind of material for the façades – in this case rectangular handmade bricks, used to deliberately evoke the architecture of the antiquity.

01 New building incorporating gothic fragments of former church | 02 Interior built on old foundations | 03 Exhibition piece

02   03

01

02

opusHouse

The original house on this site was built in the late 19th century. In contrast to the neighboring buildings, it had just two stories and was adjacent to an empty lot. The building, on Ploenniestraße 14–16, was increased two levels in height, although the original dimensions and architecture of the old building were maintained. In contrast, the empty building lot was filled with a modern three-story transparent extension, the façade proportions of this building are designed to respond to the surrounding architectural style. The raising of the house and the additional office space are designed in accordance with the passive house concept and solar panels have been added to the roof. This project successfully closed a gap in the urban landscape.

01 Roof terrace | 02 Situation | 03 Solar roof | 04 Street view

03

04

01

02

Schader Forum

The Schader Forum was conceived as a work and communication facility for the Schader foundation. The building consists of two intersecting cubes: The "Steinwinkel" houses the office and meeting rooms as well as secondary spaces. The glass cube is formed as a flexible open structure with a vertical development of contrasting elements, stairs and elevators. Reception area, office space, combi-offices and communal areas are located on the three upper levels. A flexible, divisible auditorium is located in the basement level and can accommodate up to 400 people for events and exhibitions. Important technical and service rooms are also situated here.

01 General view from street | 02 Foyer on upper floor | 03 Spiral stairs | 04 Section

03

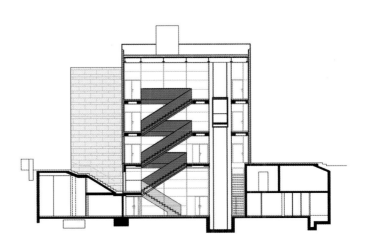

04

01

02

Residence Heinrich-Delp-Straße

This new house was built for a busy, professional couple and guarantees privacy in both the living and working areas. The exterior space with its old trees becomes part of the interior through the open floor plan. The building opens out towards the south by means of large glazed sections, but remains closed to the north, with just small window openings facing in this direction. The living area is located on the ground floor, while the sleeping or retreat areas are organized on the upper levels. The spatially separate workspaces include the ground and basement levels and also feature a meditation courtyard. This area is more introverted, obtaining its intimacy through its orientation towards the west and its interior organization.

01 West view | 02 South view | 03 East view | 04 Living room | 05 Working space | 06 Ground floor plan | 07 Upper floor plan

03

04

05

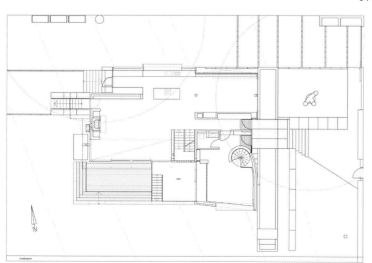

06

07

01

Winery in Dasing

This new winery building, belonging to Kunzmann, Germany's oldest mulled wine producers, has been built on a narrow site just a few meters behind the main building. The delivery and collection of the raw materials is carried out on the narrow side of the building facing the street. The production area is positioned at the end of the hall and has a large glass façade, which allows a beautiful view of the surrounding landscape. The glass façade also permits views into the production area from the nearby railway line; nothing is hidden. Head office and loading bridges are located in the roadside extension. The building has a controlled appearance and the green fiberglass façade allows the building to glow impressively at night time.

01 West façade | 02 East façade | 03 Sketch | 04 Exterior at night | 05 Bottle shelf | 06 Conference room and bottling plant

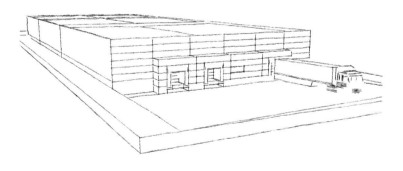

02

03

04

05

06

01

02

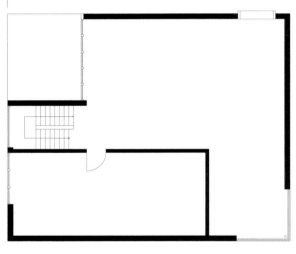

03

04

Office and Exhibition Building Holzbau Rössner

Since the founding of Bauhaus in Weimar 90 years ago, the dream of an architect, and sometimes even of a carpenter, is said to be the simple box. This modern office and exhibition building has been constructed on the foundations of an old storage barn. The building newly formulates the entrance to the Frankish village of Euerfeld and the design follows a sculptural approach. The corners have been cut out of the monolithic, rectangular main building. The timber frame construction was constructed by the Rössner firm, itself, thus documenting the firm's handwork traditions and its openness towards modern architecture.

01 Detail façade | 02 View to landscape | 03 Floor plan | 04 View from west | 05 Exterior view

05

01

02

Evangelical Parish Hall with Kindergarten

This parish hall is a listed property, dating from 1913. Over the years it has been extended to include a kindergarten and youth center. The project aimed to restore parts of the old building and unite the existing structure, giving it a more unified appearance. The new, one-story Alette Meyer kindergarten has been added to the garden side, extending the existing L-shaped structure to an rectangular unity. The main house has been restored and the white plaster façade is complemented by the wood clad exterior of the new building. The choice of natural, simple materials is a theme that unites both the old and new structures.

01 View from garden to kindergarten | 02 Main house | 03 Detail north view | 04 Basement plan kindergarten | 05 Main floor plan parish hall

04

03

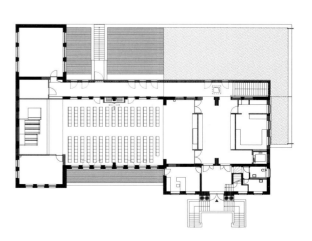

05

01

02

Kassenärztliche Vereinigung Westfalen-Lippe

The main building of the Association of Statutory Health Insurance Physicians in West-falen-Lippe was built in the 1970s and completely renovated in 2009. Large parts of the façades, the building services and the interior were modernized. The new heart of the building is the expressive new two-story forum containing reception, employee canteen, customer service, information and the modern media technology-equipped conference center and connects all the components together. Open plan offices provide a new work-ing area for staff. The energy efficiency of the entire complex, achieved by the intelli-gent use of technology, has resulted in significant savings in energy costs.

01 Forum | 02 Situation | 03 Plenary hall | 04 Interior forum

03

04

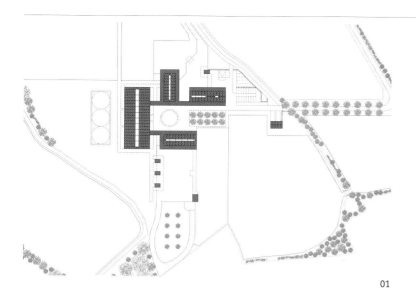

01

02

Riding Stables on the Estate Ashege

The idea behind the riding stables on the Ashege estate was to create a simple and realistic interpretation of a typical Westphalia farm. The new ensemble was developed slightly offset from the historical estate. Buildings of different sizes are grouped around the central yard and the riding arena is positioned, as is traditional, in a north to south orientation. Two parallel paths through the arcade create a visual connection between the buildings and ensure that both people and animals can remain dry when it rains.

01 Site plan | 02 South façade of riding arena | 03 Colonnade | 04 Interior riding arena

03

04

01

British Hotel

Situated among the reconstructed buildings of the Dresden Neumarkt and next to the Frauenkirche, the British Hotel occupies an extremely important position in Dresden's city center. 63 years after the destruction caused by World War II, the distinctive and rich Baroque façade design of the former palace enriches the urban space and gives the hotel an adequately historical appearance. Hapimag is a Swiss provider with 57 resorts in 16 countries; this Hapimag resort welcomes guests into a spacious entrance hall, with a historical context. The adjoining courtyard projects a modern clarity, while sections of the old building and historical finds have been incorporated into the courtyard, reinforcing the relation between the building and its historical past.

01 Exterior view | 02 Courtyard | 03 Longitudinal section | 04 Foyer | 05 Vaulted cellar

02

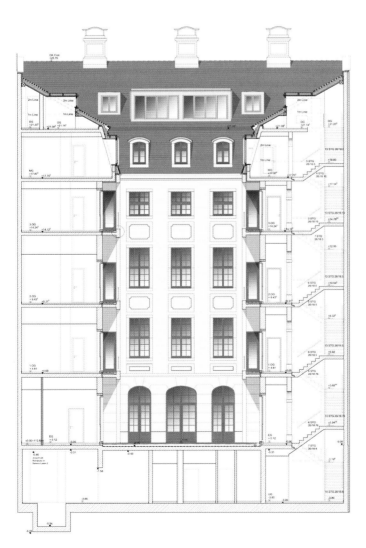

03

04

05

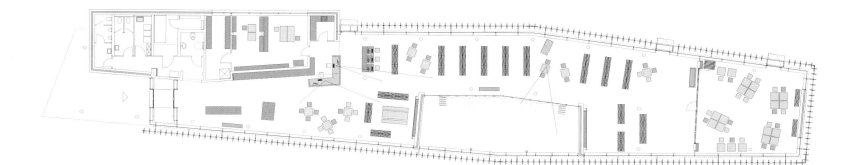

01

Library and Media Center

This elongated building, situated between street and railway line in the town center, stands out because of its façade of wide vertical lamella of anodized aluminum. The façade, with its steeped beige and brown tones, adopts the natural colors of the Swabian Alps. The lamellas adapt to the sunlight and awaken curiosity from passersby. They prevent a direct view from the outside to the interior but are transparent from the inside outwards. The building edge follows a curve of the street; at this point the library opens out into a large, glazed reading area. The school media library at the end of the building can also be used as a function room of the library.

01 Ground floor plan | 02 Street view | 03 Façade

02

03

01

02

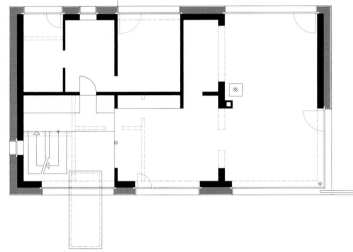

03

04

05

Family House Glück

The layout of this property was respected during the redevelopment, while new energetic aspects optimized the façade and the roof. At the same time, the local tradition of a simple and clearly formed pitched-roof shape was maintained. The elegant and significant effect of the renovations resulted in 90 percent less artificial heating and shows that ecology and aesthetics can work together. The respectable form serves the sustainability as well as technical content.

01 Street view | 02 Gable end | 03 Ground floor plan | 04 View from garden | 05 Staircase | 06 Façade detail

06

01

Day Care Center Rappelkiste

The existing kindergarten has been energetically renovated and expanded with a multi-purpose room. The large glazed sections of the façade allow generous amounts of natural light into the interior. The projecting roof provides a small covered area around the building and the brightly colored supports add character fitting to a kindergarten. The enclosed grounds of the kindergarten were completed with the construction of a two-group day nursery for children under the age of three. Common formal elements of the façade combine old and new to a harmonious ensemble.

01 Exterior | 02 Extension scope | 03 Façade | 04 Ground floor plan | 05 Playroom | 06 Washing room

02

03

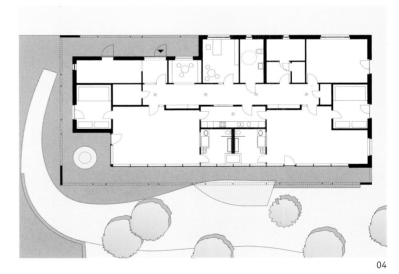

04

05

06

01

02

Sport and Leisure Swimming Pool Fildorado

Fildorado was built in the 1970s and was one of the first family and leisure oriented swimming pools. It has now been completely renovated and extended in size. A part of the old building was kept and integrated into the new structure. An entrance area with changing rooms hovers, like a bridge, over an open swimming area, which follows the natural slope of the topography. Space and color are used to fluidly combine old and new areas with entertainment attractions, sport and relaxation possibilities. In addition to this, there is an exclusive fitness club and a two-story spa area. The modeling of the surrounding landscaping divides the outer area into zones and offers privacy.

01 Exterior view with main entrance | 02 Redeveloped sport swimming pool | 03 Sections | 04 Water park and locker rooms above

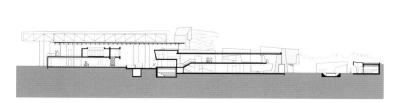

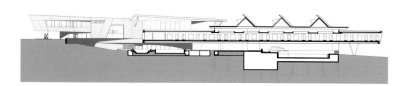

03

04

Campus Westend of Goethe-University

Based on the design concept for the upgrade of Campus Westend, all departments will be situated in a park-like campus. At its heart, the campus contains a span of extensions to the existing Hans Poelzig buildings, where the central services are located. The new departmental buildings are positioned along the edge, constituting a curb to the city. In addition to planning the entire masterplan of the premises, Ferdinand Heide designed the lecture hall building and the cafeteria. Both buildings present themselves as similarly shaped structures positioned across from each other near the new university square. Their architecture is based on a central theme: they conceptually respond to Poelzig's architecture with an individual contemporary interpretation.

01 Situation | 02 Axis Campus Westend | 03 Floor plan lecture hall | 04 Exterior view | 05 Lecture hall

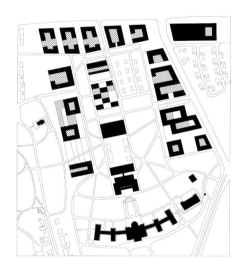

01

02

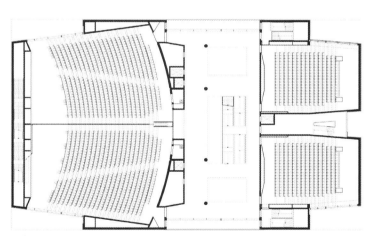

03

04

05

01

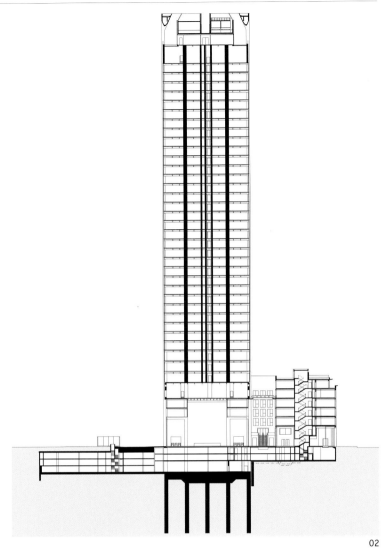

02

03

OpernTurm

This 170-meter tall OpernTurm, built as a block around an open, central area, completes the historically important ensemble on Opernplatz, linking it with a closed courtyard space. The façade is of natural stone and continues the stone cladding of the surrounding buildings and the old opera house. In classical form, the plinth of the tower houses the entrance hall, the middle section provides office space while the 'stadtloggia' is located at the top of the tower. The entrance hall is 18 meters high, making it a unique structure in Germany. The OpernTurm was one of the first office buildings in Europe, which was awarded the LEED-Gold certificate for green, sustainable building development.

01 Exterior view | 02 Section | 03 Lobby | 04 Main entrance

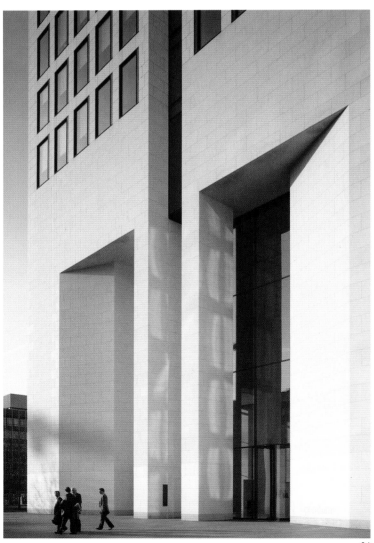

04

01

Cargo Center Messe Frankfurt

The new Cargo Center is located in the extension of the Frankfurt Trade fair and serves as the central, goods receiving and distribution area. It is comprised of a 5,600-square meter hall and an adjacent administration building for the dispatchers. In terms of urban planning, the dimensions of the construction fit into the existing part of the trade fair. The building should be recognizable as part of the trade fair, without being mistaken for an exhibition room. Conspicuous doors and a striking container façade make the building recognizable as a freight distribution building. The shell consists of a modular façade-system that plays with different profile widths and eight different colors.

01 North façade with large windows | 02 Logistics hall | 03 Ground floor plan | 04 Southwest view with Cargo gates | 05 Close-up of expanded gates

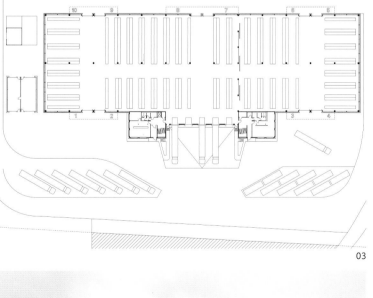

02

03

05

04

01

New Façade Zeilgalerie

The new façade of the Zeilgalerie, a project of IFM Immobilien AG, has a unique black and white design. The delicate ornamentation, together with the integrative combination of architecture, graphic design and lighting, gives the structure a distinctive appearance. The fragmented look of the previous façade has been transformed into a more homogenous surface. A significant design feature is the complex light installation: the softly pulsing light ornamentation produces a wide variety of aesthetic images. Geometric patterns transform fluidly into an organic-looking play of light and shadow. Fine, linear accents change with impressive, large-scale effects.

01 Façade | 02 Shopping street | 03 Façade detail | 04 Schematic of media façade

02

03

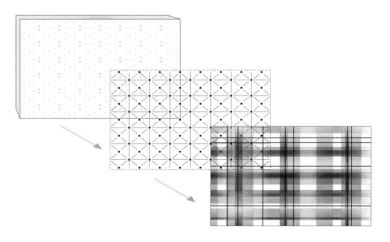

04

01

02

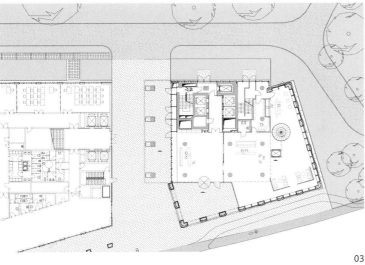

03

Parktower

This slender structure, opposite the old opera house, belongs to the group of pioneer buildings that formed the foundation of the "Mainhattan" skyline. The office tower was built in 1972 and has been enhanced by AS&P Albert Speer & Partner GmbH. The existing structure and the recent enhancements contrast each other in the cubing and façade development, responding differently to the urban conditions. The old structure is oriented towards the speer park and has a glass façade, whereas the new extension has a façade of light, natural stone and dominates over Opernplatz. The vertical window arrangement gives the slender building an elegant appearance. The new ensemble was completed at the end of 2007.

01 General view | 02 Façade detail | 03 Floor plan | 04 Parktower with the old opera house

04

01

02

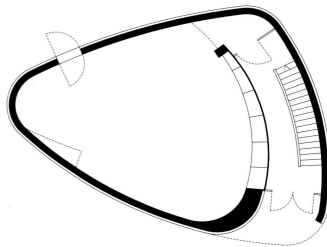

03

04

House of Silence

The House of Silence is a reflection, meditation and prayer area with an intercultural focus. Both the buildings and the interiors reflect the distinctiveness of the area and religious symbols and images have been deliberately avoided. The basic design of the building is based on interlocking parabolas, forming a protective, meditative interior, which also offers an urban contrast to the orthogonal and cubic neighboring buildings. The widespread walls of the gentrance area open out the introverted building in a welcoming gesture. The contemplative atmosphere in the interior is strengthened by the use of indirect lighting.

01 Entrance | 02 Gallery | 03 Ground floor plan | 04 Room of silence

01

04

06

02

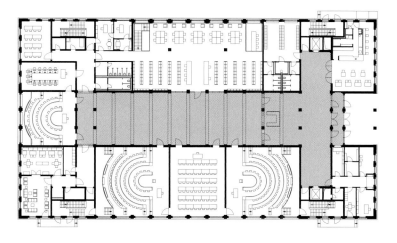

03

05

House of Finance, Campus Westend

With its accentuated façade projections, enclosed building corners and the three-dimensional development of the openings in the monolithic main building, the House of Finance continues the model of the nearby IG-Farben-Ensemble, built by Hans Poelzig. The opening out of the main building on the upper floors and the choice of material emphasizes this idea. A prominent base projects out towards the deeper-lying Gruneberg-park. The main useable area is 7,000 square meters and offers space for the institution's 300 employees and 900 students. The ground floor houses the executive teaching space with large lecture rooms and information center. Accessible teaching areas are located in the upper levels.

01 West façade | 02 East façade with main entrance | 03 Ground floor plan | 04 Situation | 05 Northeast façade | 06 Foyer

01

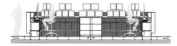 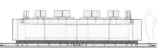

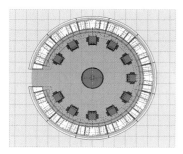 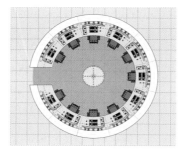

02

Börse Frankfurt

The trading floor in Frankfurt is the icon of the German Stock Exchange and the image of the Deutsche Börse worldwide. Through architecture, the trading floor portrays corporate identity. The high-quality, sleek design expresses the message of the Deutsche Börse brand. The space-defining elements of the hall are the ergonomic trading counters, the DAX-Board, and the world map light installation showing the Börse Frankfurt within the global context. Transparency and openness are reflected in the architecture and are evident through the use of contemporary mediums in the visitors' gallery. The light concept allows for a flexible and dynamic use of the trading floor.

01 Trading floor | 02 Trading counters | 03 Entrance between lobby and newsfeed | 04 Visitors' gallery

03

04

01

Messehalle 11 and Portalhaus West

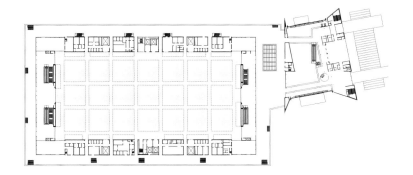

This building ensemble is comprised of Messehalle 11 and the Portalhaus with conference room and breathes new life into the trade fair area; forming the interface between
the large exhibition halls and the residential development. Despite its 30-meter height,
the different design of the building, with base, upper levels and flat roof, provides a
contrast. The new Portalhaus forms a concise structure, offering a new interpretation of
the form of a gateway and staging a highly visible gesture of welcome. Escalators, panoramic elevators, walkways and open galleries cut through the four-story space, leading
visitors into the trade fair area.

01 New main entrance and neighboring Messehalle 11 forming the western edge of the
complex | 02 First floor plan | 03 Open square leading to entrance and distribution

02

03

01

02

03

Energy Saving House

This 'multiple generation' house is located in the east of Frauenau, an historical town and important center for the glass industry. The volume has a reinforced-concrete core, covered by an insulating wooden construction and clad with translucent corrugated sheets. The façade is back-lit and at night shines out like a lantern. The south façade is oriented towards the garden and is fully glazed for the purpose of passive energy gain. It can be fully extended in the summer, while the other window openings within the building have been kept small. Inside, sliding doors and built-in cupboards optimize the functionality and flexibility of the space. The house is an excellent example of sustainable building; heating and warm water are provided by energy from a solar-collection system.

01 Exterior view | 02 Kitchen | 03 Exterior view at night | 04 Ground floor plan | 05 Panoramic window

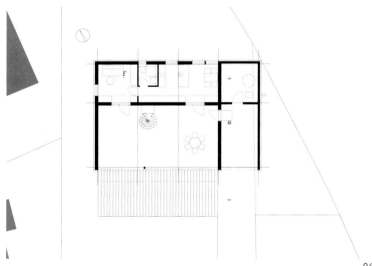

04

05

01

02

03

04

Center for Psychiatry

This new building is embedded in the campus of the clinical center, on a slight gradient with picturesque orchards, leading to Lake Constance. The building is integrated into the sloping surroundings and consequently designed as a stepped hillside house, enclosing a generously-sized interior courtyard. A bridge frames the view in the hilly landscape, allowing one to feel the natural incline of the terrain even in the courtyard. The psychiatry center is visible from the landscape and provides spectacular views. A combination of exposed concrete and wood define the surfaces of both the exterior and the interior. The vertically oriented cladding of untreated wood appears transparent and gives the building a light and open impression.

01 Detail of façade and projections | 02 View along south façade | 03 View of entrance hall | 04 Ground floor plan | 05 Northwest façade

05

01

02

Dornier Museum

The Dornier Museum is directly connected to the runway of Friedrichshafen Regional Airport. The museum presents the technology of aircraft design and construction as well as the history of Dornier factories, which were founded in 1922. The museum's exhibition includes examples of historic aircrafts, some of which are still in working order. The shape of the museum comes from the direct access of the aircraft to the runway. Accompanying the curved path, translucent shells denote the interior space. Transparent doors close the end façades, which are orientated towards the airport. The transparency of the modern façade allows natural light to flood into the spaces.

01 Exterior view at dusk | 02 Terrace | 03 Ground floor plan | 04 Exhibition room

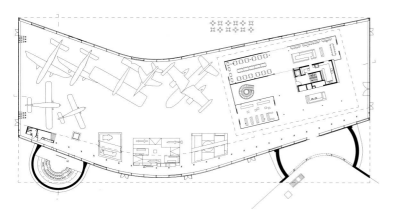

03

04

01

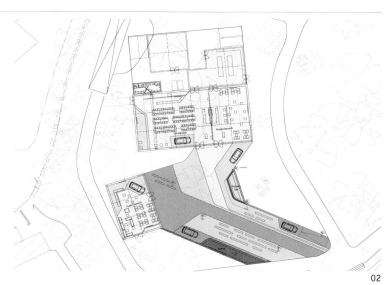

02

Audi – Ski WM 2011

As part of the World Ski Championships in 2011, event spaces for the main sponsor, Audi, were designed; situated in three locations in Garmisch-Partenkirchen – Kurpark, Kandahar und Gudiberg. In the Kurpark, two pavilions and an extensive outdoor area, built in the Audi Terminal style, present the Audi brand. The brand equity, dynamics, sportiness, innovation and quality have been translated into architecture. A continuous floor surface, platforms and benches develop to form the exterior bar area and stage backdrop, which are further enhanced with large, LED-lit areas. In the terminals, flowing transitions between public, VIP and press areas have been created and space is available for presentations and conferences.

01 LED wall with presentation stage | 02 Site plan | 03 Main view of the area | 04 Audi standing desk | 05 Floor detail with LED light strips | 06 View of the area from entrance

03

04

05

06

01

Renovation Double Sports Hall Silberberg School

This sports hall was built in the 1970s and had major deficiencies in terms of energy provision, technology and function. Because of this, it has been completely renovated and given a new façade cladding. The old façade projected out along the long side of the building, but the gables consisted only of unstructured exposed aggregate concrete. In order to unify the new façade and to integrate all of the projections and new installations, such as sun-protection elements, a continuous band of fiber cement has been wrapped around the building. The remaining façade has been clad with colored panels. The color, format and divisions of the panels give the cladding a dynamic appearance.

01 Gable end of the hall | 02 Long side of the hall | 03 Total view from southwest | 04 Design sketch

02

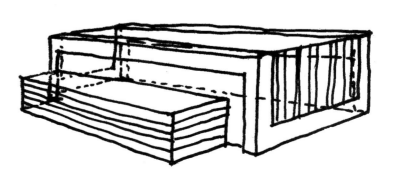

03

04

01

02

Arena Geisingen

The Uhrig family developed the idea of building a training circuit for inline skating. This developed into a business venture and became Arena Geisingen, the first circuit of its kind in Europe. With elaborate landscaping, the oval circuit, with its curved peaks, and the inner field fits perfectly into the existing Danube floodplains. Walls were also built to offer protection agains flooding. The arena lies like a recently-landed UFO, its translucent double-façade giving it a weightless appearance while the gently curving, wooden roof structure of the interior protects the entire space. The training conditions have been highly praised and the race circuit is considered by professionals to be one of the fastest in the world.

01 Northwest view | 02 Interior | 03 Situation | 04 Track at night

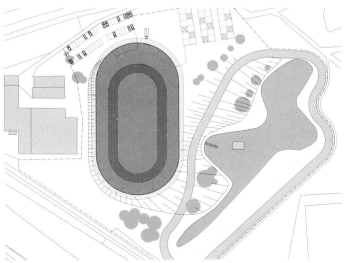

03

04

01

Shopping Center Staufers

The client wished for high quality architecture, in conjunction with an efficient energy concept. The result is a construction with 1,100 square meters of retail space that offers not only an open and welcoming architectural style, a stylish timber roof construction and a roof design that allows natural light to flood into the space, but also innovative and highly efficent technology. The energy for the entire building is supplied without any fossil fuel being used, halving operating costs. Through the use of geothermal energy, energy saving systems, heat recovery, concrete core activation and photovoltaics, the shopping center saves around 80 tons of CO_2 emmissions every year, setting new standards.

01 Exterior view at dusk | 02 Ground floor plan | 03 Entrance | 04 Interior space with timber girder | 05 Coffee bar and sun terrace | 06 Covered forecourt

02

04

03

05

06

01

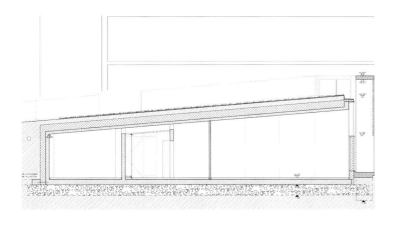

02

Dr. Urban and Mr. Hide – Childcare Center

Despang's second day care center is designed with the post-fossil age in mind and draws its inspiration from a range of different sources. It is situated on the 1970s university campus of Göttingen and interacts with both the concrete buildings and the flora and fauna. While the concept refers to Le Corbusier's "female" monol-house, the tectonic purity results from R.M. Schindler's Kings Road House. The material honesty also serves various pedagogical purposes and the new flooring from DLW Armstrong enhances the tactile quality of the linoleum with the use of aluminum particles, an exciting interior design that is not just attractive for children.

01 Glazed exterior façade at dusk | 02 Interior seating area | 03 Cross section | 04 Childcare center in front of university complex

03

04

01

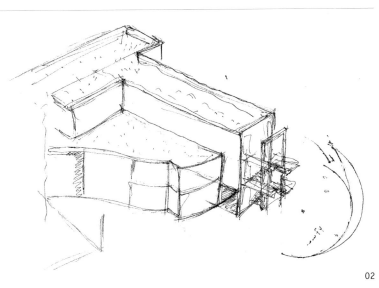

02

Hans-Sachs School

Two separate school locations on Hans Sachs Street have been merged together to create one large, full-day school, with several classes in each year group. The general classrooms are situated in the old building. The new building is structurally attached to the stairwell of the old building and offers, in addition to the two-story canteen, rooms for the full-day school program, teaching areas, specialist rooms and the staff room. The new forum space is located near the main entrance and can accommodate, including the gallery area, 190 people for special performances and occasions. This area is multifunctional; the lights can be fully dimmed for lectures using multi-media and it also functions as communication, lounge and recreation area, as well as providing the town with a space for hosting extracurricular events.

01 Façade forum | 02 Sketch of entrance | 03 Entrance area | 04 North view

03

04

01

02

03

04

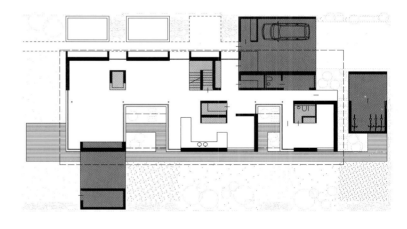

05

06

House AU29

This building is situated to the northwest of Munich. Two atriums structure the volume into the areas and allow the vertical and introverted exposure of the individual areas within the attic space. The ground floor is designed in the form of individual cubes that rise from the ground as homogenous, solid structures; these are assigned various functions. Entrance, garage and outdoor seating work to connect the building with its surroundings, while large, frameless glazing also works to create a fluid connection between the interior and exterior. The upper level appears to float above the cubic base, clad on every side in a light wood. The atmosphere of the house reflects the naturalness of the surrounding area.

01 Living atrium | 02 Entrance | 03 Garden corridor | 04 Fireplace between dining and living area | 05 Ground floor plan | 06 Second floor

01

Office Building le2

This project is situated on an exposed location in the entrance zone of a newly developed commercial area. The client, an insurance agency, demanded a building, which matches the company's philosophy, namely that maximum transparency and communication be optimized in all working areas. Glazed private offices combined with centralized communal areas throughout the different levels of the building resulted from an intensive dialogue between client and architect. The successful implementation of the design becomes particularly clear with coming darkness, when the building lights up from the inside, becoming transparent and opening up the internal functioning of the office to the public.

01 West view at dusk | 02 Ground floor plan | 03 West view | 04 Rooftop terrace

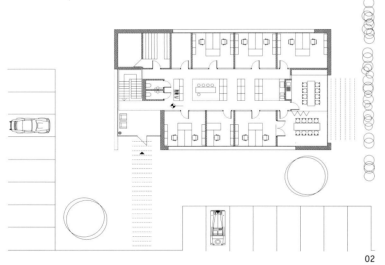

02

03

04

01

02

Residential Building and Doctor's Office

The immediate environment of this object is influenced by four townhouses, which beautifully reflect the architectural styles of the past 80 years. The site is marked by an old beech tree, which reaches far over the crown of the new building. In addition to the form and shape of the site, this tree was also one of the deciding influences in terms of the design. The plan follows the waving form of the site, the brick monolith has undergone a subtractive design principal and incisions have been cut into the entrance, creating a terrace on the upper level. The building has an area of 300 square meters and offers space for a doctor's office with a public area on the ground floor and a laboratory, staffroom and an office in the basement.

01 Beech tree on site | 02 Incisions cut into entrance of house | 03 Ground floor plan |
04 Interior | 05 Terrace

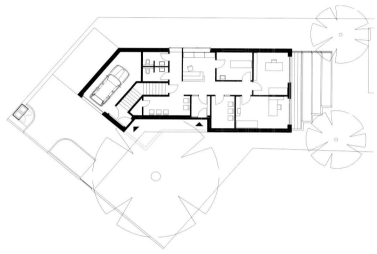

03

04

05

01

02

03

04

La Taille Vent

La Taille Vent "formed by the wind" is a detached building in HafenCity, Hamburg with 20 high quality apartments. A succinct design that plays with sculptural and dynamic elements, it references sand, the wind and yacht architecture without overemphasizing the metaphor. The main focus and central element of the design was to value the special location, on the banks of the river Elbe. Each apartment offers views of the Elbe, this is made possible by the core idea of tailoring the building to suit the location and gives it a special character.

01 View from Elbe | 02 View from east | 03 Dining area | 04 Living area | 05 Second floor plan

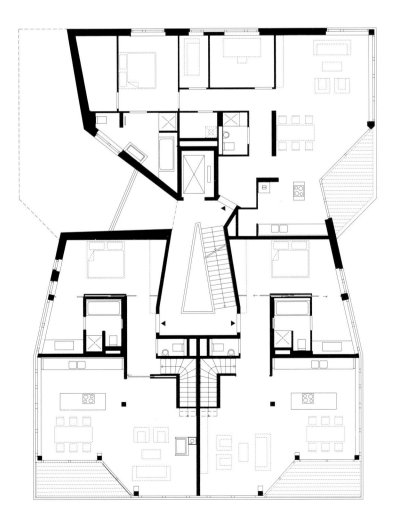

05

01

02

Freshfields House

The eight-story Freshfields House in Hamburg's city center is reminiscent, in terms of its cubature, of the 'stack houses' in Hansestadt. The ground floor offers 10,800 square meters of office and shop space. The building is staggered slightly from the fifth floor and fits harmoniously into the surrounding development. Terraces and balconies on the south side and a large roof terrace enrich the office space and give the building a welcoming impression. The tectonic layering of the façade, of glass, natural stone and supports creates a play of shadows that divides the building. The slim, tall supports give the house a vertical emphasis and support the hanseatic character of the building.

01 Exterior view at night | 02 Foyer | 03 Longitudinal section | 04 Roof terrace

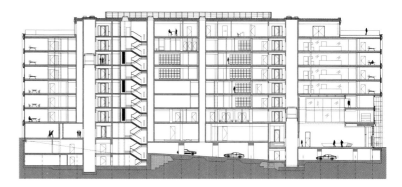

03

04

01

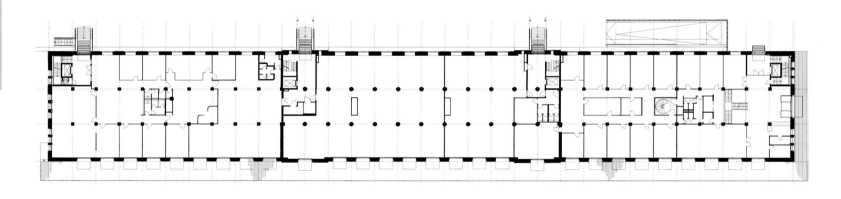

02

Altonaer Kaispeicher

This warehouse was built in 1924 and has been renovated and restored, enabling it to correspond with the overall upgrading process of the entire area. The warehouse has remained unchanged in its external appearance, allowing it to stand out from other warehouses in the area, as many of these have been extended or in some way altered. The internal structure has been used as a main defining element of the space. It was important that the interior space remained waterproof and well insulated. Because of this, the brick façade, with its historical traces, was permitted to remain. The modern window units interpret the nature of originals.

01 South façade | 02 Façade detail | 03 Floor plan | 04 Interior with view to the river | 05 Perspective view

03

04

05

01

02

03

ADA 1

The building site is situated at the intersection between Hamburg's lively downtown and its urban landscape, rich in water and mature trees. The horizontal, striped façade, with its floating 'eyes', celebrates the view onto this unique context. A public park in front of the building continues the design strategy of the façade into the landscape. The 'eyes' in the façade and the platforms in the park create places to meet and contemplate. Large spans provide for various office layout configurations in combination with balconies and climatically tempered outdoor spaces of the 'eyes'. The office building 'An der Alster 1', short ADA 1, links interior and exterior spaces to the public park in front of the building and to the city context of Hamburg.

01 Main façade at night | 02 Section | 03 Corner with 'eye' at night | 04 Main entrance |
05 Ground floor plan

04

05

01

02

03

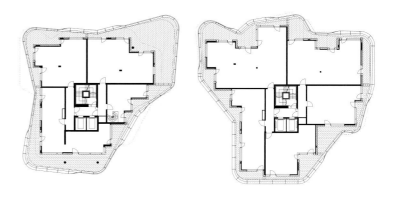

04

Marco Polo Tower

The Marco Polo Tower is situated directly on the river Elbe and commands a prominent position in Hafencity. It has been constructed next to the Unilever headquarters, also built by Behnisch Architekten. The 55-meter high tower is a sculptured, architectural addition to the area. The building has 17 floors and the slight rotation of each floor on its axis affords all 58 of the apartments superb views across the harbor area and the city. Overhanging terraces protect the recessed façades from strong sunlight, so that additional sunshades are not needed. Sound insulated louvers allow for natural ventilation without increasing the amount of noise pollution from outside.

01 Overhanging terraces | 02 Exterior view | 03 Interior space | 04 Floor plans fourth and eleventh floor

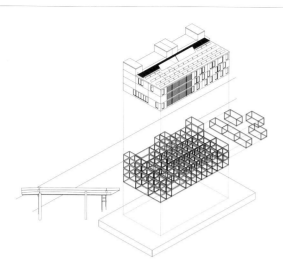

01

IBA DOCK

This is Germany's biggest floating building, situated in Zollhafen, Hamburg. The building moves with the tide, rising and falling three and a half meters and even floats with the water in a storm tide. The building rests on a concrete pontoon and the entrance is reached via a bridge. It offers a varied exhibition space spread over three levels. The three-story structures are made of steel and can be de- and re-constructed, this allows the building to be moved if necessary. The module frames are prefabricated and were assembled on the pontoon in just two weeks. The building requires no additional energy source. It functions entirely from the water of the river Elbe and from solar energy.

01 Axonometry | 02 Exhibition space | 03 Drawbridge | 04 Exterior

02

03

04

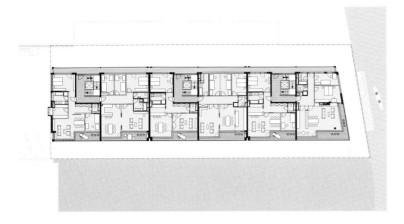

01

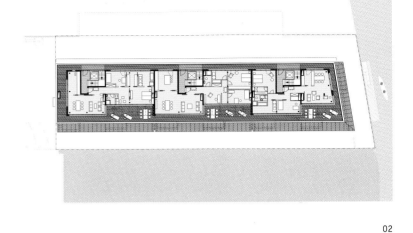

02

03

Apartment House Hamburg-Winterhude

This apartment building is located on Jarrestraße, on a backyard site with views over the Osterbekkanal. It includes 26 apartments of between 82 and 140 square meters in size, with private balconies and terraces protected from the views of curious neighbors and passersby. The apartments are designed for families. Bedrooms, playrooms and studies are located in the 'private zone', to the east. The communal areas, such as living room and dining area open out towards the west. A special feature is the 10.5-meter span. This allowes for an arbitrary choice of apartment layout; a flexibilty that is able to react to changing conditions and phases.

01 Regular story plan | 02 Stacked story plan | 03 Façade | 04 Exterior | 05 Perspective of entrance

04

05

01

02

The Hamburg Philharmonic Hall Pavilion

The pavilion on Magellan Terraces in Hamburg's HafenCity is in direct line of sight from the Hamburg Philharmonic Hall. The superstructure, known as a floating structure, bears its own weight and can easily be dismantled. The exhibition is open to the public and is located on the ground floor on both sides of a ten meter long passageway. The pavilion façade is encased by an installation of visual and acoustic elements. A model of the concert hall, located on the first floor, weighs three and a half tons and resembles the interior of the actual concert hall down to the very last detail. Light effects and illumination give the impression that the superstructure is floating above the Magellan Terraces.

01 Axonometry | 02 Façade with 'eye and ear trumpets' | 03 Exhibition on the passageway | 04 Exterior view at night

03

04

01

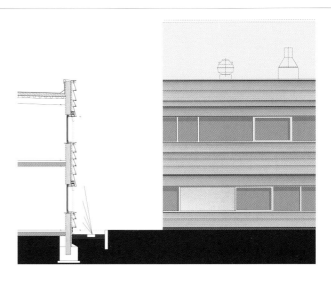

02

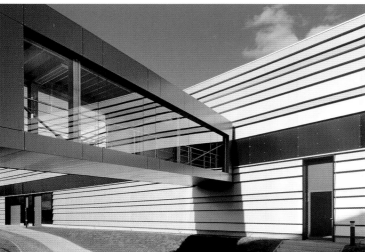

03

DESY Experimental Hall PETRA III

The façade of the 300-meter-long experimental hall Petra III, the world's largest cyclic accelerator, in the DESY research center reflects the dynamics of particle acceleration. The arc-shaped hall building is covered with horizontal, slightly tilted aluminum bands of different widths. The expressive slant and the continuous joints interpret the theme of acceleration and speed, becoming a metaphor for the physical process taking place in the hall. The dynamic impact is strengthened by the colorfully designed underside of the panels. The colors bring a playful element to the shimmering metal façade, which changes appearance depending on the daylight.

01 Front view | 02 Section and elevation of the façade | 03 Connection between the buildings | 04 Entrance | 05 West façade

04

05

01

Farmhouse Voges

The vernacular half-timbered housing type of northern Germany grants an innovation potential for the contemporary demand for open space. Natural lighting and energy efficiency requirements inspired a strategic concept for the reduced nature of this building. The living space on the ground floor 'shrinks' horizontally and contracts vertically into the inner core of the building. A new glazed spatial and thermal zone is set back from the structure, creating an inhabitable outdoor buffer zone. The intervention gives hierarchy and characteristic expression to the space: from below the space appears open and more public; from above, it is more private.

01 Exterior view with garden | 02 Façade | 03 Ground floor plan | 04 Living space

02

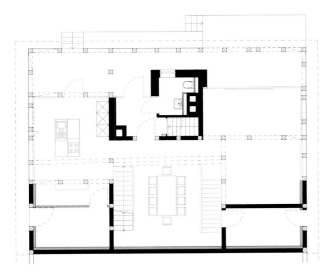

03

04

01

Jibi Bioclimatic Community Grocery

This local grocery store adds to the neighborhood, where concern for the environment has resulted in both typological and architectural changes. The client wanted the building to be a significant social, 'eco- and archi-friendly' place with prototype qualities. Inside, photovoltaics and cooling components with closable lids add to the building's efficiency. Two volumes form the center, the grocery box is covered with planted ivy as a thermal buffer and as graffiti-protection and a ceramic green façade. The transparent and translucent beverage volume, with bioclimatically performative mesh membrane screen, acts as an urban loggia and gives the volume presence and typological significance.

01 Exterior view | 02 Interior space | 03 Situation | 04 Ceramic green façade

02

03

04

01

02

03

04

Headquarters VHV Hanover

This new building for the VHV-Group is a dense urban ensemble, made out of three blocks. The addition of the three massive office blocks around a glazed atrium allows the development of a square as a spacious entrance. The atrium creates the central access area of the new building, extending fluidly into the stone 'streets' between the blocks. Stairways, elevators and bridges link the offices of the upper levels, where private, group and open plan areas are located. The central training, meeting and dining areas on the ground and first floor are opened up by a two-story foyer, which also offers space for larger events.

01 Main entrance | 02 Staircase system | 03 Entrance courtyard | 04 Atrium | 05 Ground floor plan

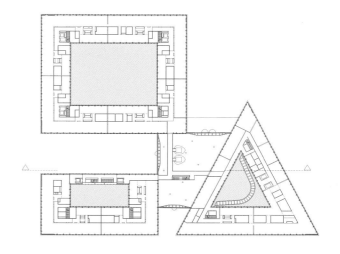

05

01

Rainbow Ribbon

This client enterprise specializes in digital transfer printing. The design for a new storage, production and office building alludes to the performance of the company in an abstract way: a colored façade emphasizes the unity of the building. On the southeast side the band is interrupted by a staircase – a glass façade with horizontal 'print plates' indicates the visitor's way to the entrance. A staircase with a gray cement facing provides access to three different levels. The corridors are decorated in simple white to emphasize the high quality seamless floor design and offer a contrast to the colorful exterior.

01 Front view | 02 Staircase | 03 Sections | 04 Colors matching natural surroundings

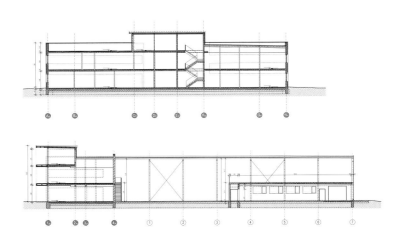

02

03

04

01

02

Bird Watching Tower

Located on the projecting peninsula of Graswarder, which belongs to the Baltic seaside resort of Heiligenhafen, is an extensive nature reserve that is a favored site not only for ornithologists but also for vacationers and other travelers. In order to observe birds in this unspoiled environment without disturbing them, the directors of the bird reserve wished to erect a suitable observation tower, which would also provide an exceptionally good view of the entire area and would allow visitors to study details with the aid of a telescope. As a sculpture made of beams and ledgers with diagonal bracing, it depicts a stylized figure of a sitting bird. A two-flight staircase provides access to tower, which is easily able to accommodate large groups of visitors.

01 Exterior view | 02 Interior space | 03 Section | 04 Bird watching platform

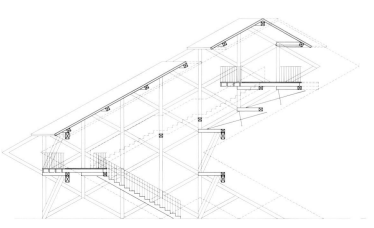

03

04

01

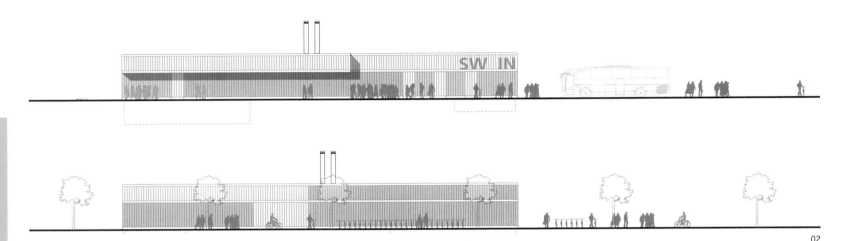

02

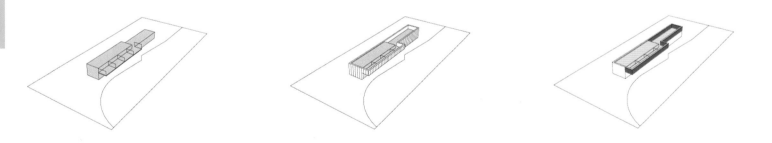

03

04

Energy Center at Audi Sportpark

This new energy center is located in close proximity to the new stadium building of FC Ingolstadt and provides the stadium with heating and cooling energy. A 76.5-square-meter roof space is situated on the north side, which also serves to cover the public transport stop, offering waiting passengers protection from the weather. A cladding of profile glass completes the character of this purely functional construction of reinforced concrete. The interaction of the massive concrete core and the transparent skin work together to create an interesting tension. A nine by three meter opening allows a view of the plant's internal energy systems.

01 Front view | 02 North and south elevation | 03 Conceptual design | 04 Exterior

01

02

Coffee Roastery Dinzler

In addition to office and seminar rooms, this complex consists of a large restaurant with a spacious exhibition area and a coffee roaster, where visitors can watch the coffee roasting processes. Two thirds of the complex are covered with a green roof, the separate sections of which are interconnected and allow the building to melt into the surrounding scenery. The green roof creates a hill that disperses the volume into the landscape and makes it possible for visitors to walk over the building. Above the green areas rises a structure with a saddle roof, which blends in with the typical architectural style of the area. By shaping the building according to the topography, interesting spatial situations and paths are created.

01 Green roof | 02 Northwest view | 03 Entry level plan | 04 Lounge

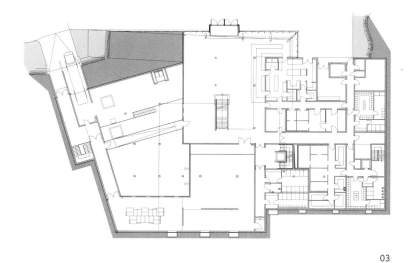

03

04

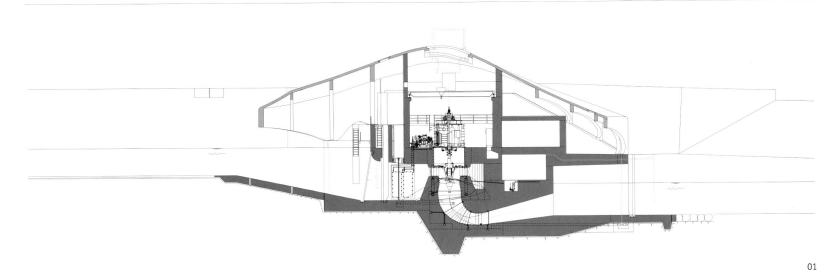

01

Iller – Overground Hydroelectric Powerplant

This hydroelectric power plant is situated among an ensemble of listed buildings including a former spinnery/weavery and the natural space along the river Iller. The design was realized in collaboration with structural engineers KBK - Konstruktionsgruppe Bauen Kempten and symbolizes the dynamics of the water, which change from a calm state at the water inlet to the churning and pitching of the water near to the turbines, before subsequently returning to a calm state after the electricity generation. Further associations include the river-washed rock formations in close proximity to the location of the power plant. As part of a public 'Hydro-power experience', the ecological energy source provides around 3,000 households with 10.5 million kilowatt-hours of environmentally friendly power per year.

01 Longitudinal section | 02 Exterior view | 03 View from river side | 04 Turbines | 05 Bird's-eye view

02

03

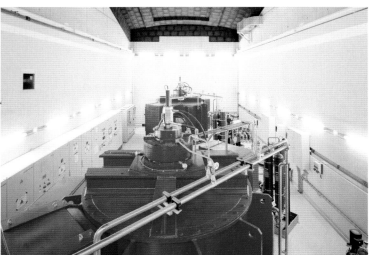

04

05

01

02

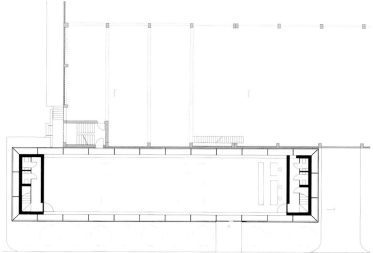

03

Interior – Competence Center GlasTrösch

The massive concrete vessels contrast with the representation of the diversity of the material glass, in both the interior and exterior of the building. This symbiosis emphasizes the ambivalence of glass: transparent and opaque, light and heavy, material and immaterial. During the day, the suspended, insulated glass curtain is in the foreground and receives the play of light and weather conditions at different times of day. By night, the building undergoes a metamorphosis the glass skin disappears through the use of artificial illumination and reveals the bold, static bridge construction in the interior, which now takes on a crystalline appearance.

01 Exterior at night | 02 Exterior by day | 03 Ground floor plan | 04 Contrast between glass façade and concrete vessels | 05 Skylight

04

05

01

Judges Tower Vogtland Arena

This design proposed a long compact, cylindrical volume, seemingly floating above the slope. The cylindrical tube corresponds in shape and material with the flying capsule of the 'Inrun'. Skeletal pillars lift the tube into the air expressing its lightness and providing the perfect position and distance to view the athletes. Due to large covered terraces integrated into the building, both the media and jury members view the event from the same vantage point. The jury tower is the connecting element between the viewing areas for spectators in the valley and the 'Inrun' on the top of the mountain.

01 Front view | 02 Exterior | 03 Axonometry | 04 Total view

02

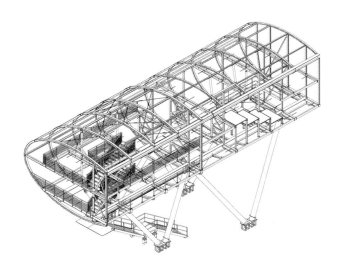

03

04

01

House W2

This house is divided into three parts. The access is defined by the curvature of two-story components. The entrance area opens to views of the living room and towards the nearby fortress. A padded pool separates the kitchen and dining area as a central recreation area in the living space. The dark wooden floor of the living room continues into the terrace, which houses the building with the integrated pool house on the west side. The large openings of the house reach down to the lower-lying city, forming a contrast to the street side, which is more closed. A continuous band of light gives the second floor a floating character, allowing soft light to flow inside.

01 East view at dusk | 02 Ground floor plan | 03 Northwest | 04 Kitchen and dining area

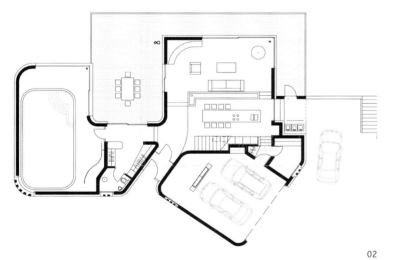

02

03

04

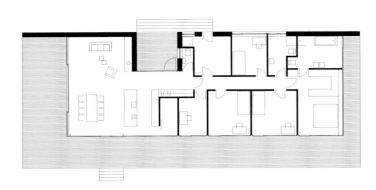

01

02

Family House Langenargen

This family house was planned and built during the creation of the surrounding agricultural farmstead. The new house is located a short distance from the farm complex, in the middle of an orchard. An elongated one-story building appears to float slightly above the flat lawn. The flat roof and the north façade, together with a slightly raised floor envelope, are all clad in copper and protectively encase the floor to ceiling glazing on the east, west and south façades. The large glazed areas and the flat roof make optimal use of solar energy. The large roof overhangs the main core, protecting it from overheating in the summer. The energy concept is supplemented with a photovoltaic system on the roof of the adjacent farm buildings.

01 Ground floor plan | 02 South façade | 03 Southeast façade | 04 Interior | 05 West façade | 06 Living room suite | 07 Northeast façade

03

04

05

06

07

01

Catholic Community Center St. Georg

This building reflects the urban texture in terms of scale, composition and volume. The church square was created to connect the community hall with the church. The new ensemble strengthens the qualities of the place; the church receives a direct counterpart and becomes an influential addition to the overall system. In contrast to the church, which is closed to the outside, the community center is opened invitingly to the church square. Positioned in the front of the building, the mediation room and the space-defining elements wood and staircase frame the churchyard and complement the church building.

01 Church square | 02 South view | 03 Foyer | 04 Ground floor plan

02

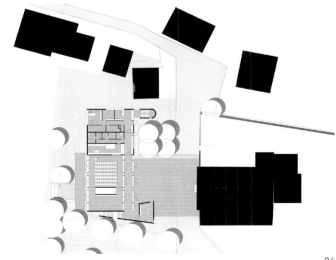

03

04

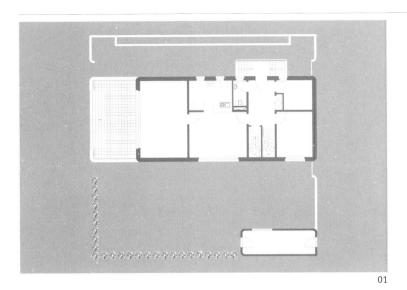

01

02

Private Residential House

The site of this residential house is located in the Leipzig district of Leutzsch, in an area mainly consisting of villas and family residences. The structure is rectangular and each floor steps back towards the garden. The living room, study and garden terrace are all located on the ground floor. The upper floor includes the bedrooms, children's rooms and a second terrace. The interior is uniformly decorated, reducing the type and quantity of the materials. The interior walls are plastered in the same way as the outside façade – the windows and doors are painted white. All rooms are fitted with colored linoleum. The building is designed and realized as a low energy house.

01 Ground floor plan | 02 Northeast view | 03 East façade | 04 Bathroom | 05 View from garden | 06 Dining room

03

04

05

06

01

02

03

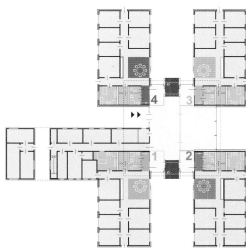

04

Care Home for Children and Adolescents with Disabilities

This care home accommodates 32 mentally and visually impaired children and adolescents and is divided into four residential groups. The residential grouping is oriented around a high central hall with a flexible floor plan for multi-purpose and therapeutic use. The organization of the residential areas forms separate and comprehensive units. The colors and surfaces of each section were chosen to suit the differential sensibility of the residents. To allow for easy orientation, specific color profiles are linked with each group and these colors reoccur throughout the separate spaces. The bedrooms have room-height glazing, creating a strong relationship between the interior and exterior.

01 Group entrance and cloakroom | 02 Wooden façade with window | 03 Group courtyard | 04 Ground floor plan | 05 Central hall, mixed-use area

05

01

02

03

Social Pediatric Center SPC Leipzig

Released from the strictly symmetrical and dominant main building, the imperfections of which have been reconstructed, this project extends parallel to the old building and has a trapezoidal layout based on existing alignments. The building responds to the topography and uses this to give the different spaces an individual character, as well as to build over as little ground surface as possible. The existing green space will remain largely intact and is fundamentally connected to the building concept. The individual functional areas are clearly separated according to the requirements.

01 Mixed-use hall | 02 Northeast view | 03 Main elevation | 04 North view | 05 Southwest view | 06 Ground floor plan

04

05

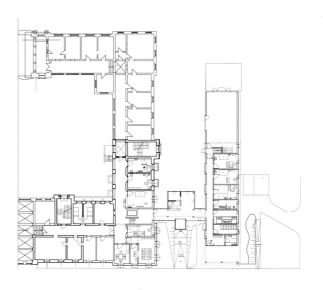

06

01

Mensa Leonberg

Instead of continuing the heterogeneous urban structure of the school complex, the new Leonberg cafeteria can be understood as a space positioned between the existing buildings, a part of the open area. The vertically oriented structure of the building defines exterior and interior space without separating these from each other. This creates a flowing, light-filled volume with differentiated zones, which allow a variety of functional uses. The preliminary design was developed by Hadi A. Tandawardaja and Tobias Bochmann from SOMAA. Architecture Office, on behalf of Dongus Architekten. Dongus Architekten carried out all services after the blueprint planning.

01 Exterior view at dusk | 02 Situation | 03 Mensa | 04 Interior view

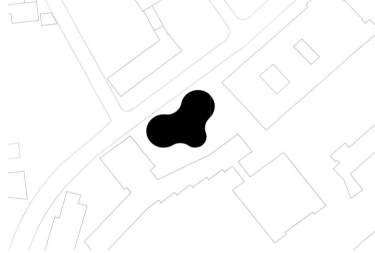

02

03

04

01

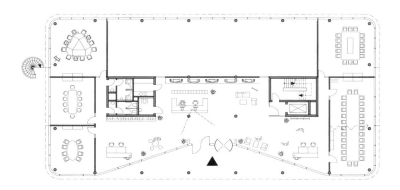

02

03

04

HBPO GmbH Lippstadt

In Lippstadt, the global headquarters of HBPO GmbH was built within a timeframe of just ten months. The building has an innovative, independent and unified appearance, reflecting the philosophy of its successful, future-oriented users and supporting modern workplace organization with a communicative, bright and flexible space. The 3,000-square meter space accommodates 120 employees who share the various work areas, which are divided into office, project work and development spaces. A workshop for prototype assembly is integrated into the ground floor and the central atrium connects the upper levels, facilitating internal communication.

01 Foyer | 02 Ground floor plan | 03 Exterior at night | 04 Corridor | 05 Meeting point atrium

05

01

Krogmann Headquarters

The woodworking company Krogmann, well known for its cooperation with architects, constructed the corporate headquarters itself, based upon a plan by an architect. Designed as an architectural résumé, the modern building not only demonstrates the characteristics of various woods – such as sound protection optimization, thermal storage capacity and humidity control, and their symbiotic interaction with concrete, glass, and fiber cement – but also symbolizes the generation change in the company management and the new status of the construction culture among medium-sized businesses. The distinctive trapezoid shape avoids the winter winds on the low northern side, while seeking daylight and passive solar optimization in its main façade.

01 Distinctive façade offers protection | 02 Ground floor plan | 03 Wood clad interior | 04 Trapezoidal-shaped building with wooden façade

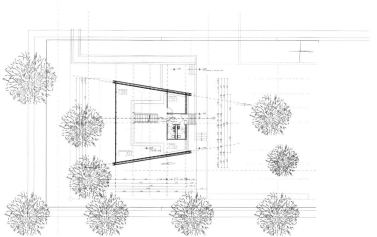

02

03

04

01

03

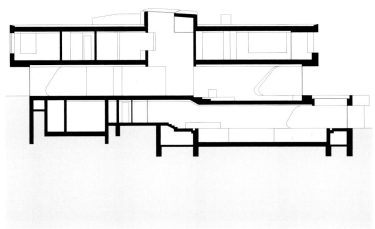

02

Dupli.Casa

The geometry of the building is based on the footprint of the house that was previously located on this site. Originally built in 1984 and with many extensions and modifications since then, the new building echoes the 'family archaeology' by duplication and rotation. Lifted up, it creates a semi-public space at ground level between two more discrete levels. The skin of the villa performs a sophisticated connection between inside and outside and offers spectacular views onto the old town of Marbach and the German national literature archive on the other side of the Neckar valley.

01 Terrace | 02 Section | 03 Serpentines | 04 Dining area | 05 Exterior view at night

04

05

01

02

03

Black Cube with Colani-UFO

This building complex is comprised of the Colani-UFO, the shaft hall and the Black Cube and is the result of a competition. Built in 1995, the UFO was reconstructed to create a unique conference room. With its white, fiberglass-reinforced plastic hull, it is the highly visible symbol of Lünen and offers a 360 degree panoramic view. The shaft hall, which was used previously as a storage hall, was reconstructed to provide a multifunctional conference room. The Black Cube completes the ensemble with a large area and energy-efficient office building. This was given the title of artwork of the year by the Art Association Lünen shortly after its completion.

01 Building complex | 02 Function room | 03 Entrance shaft hall | 04 Situation |
05 Business Lounge Colani-UFO

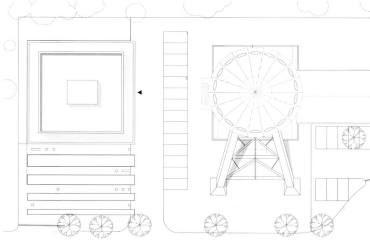

04

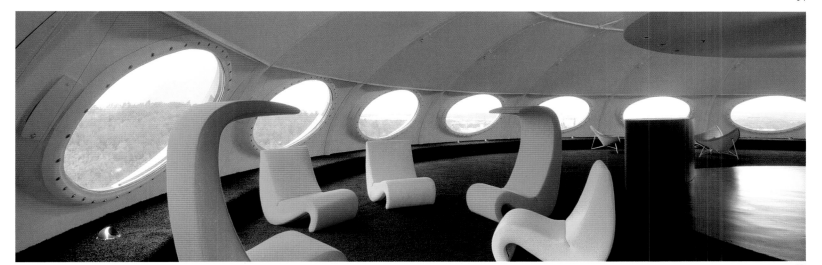

05

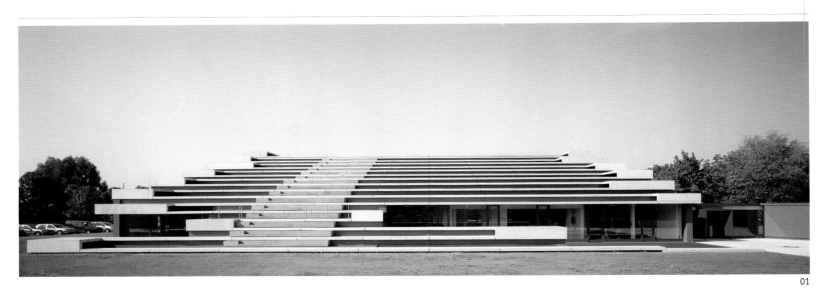

01

ZDF News Reports Studio

The new ZDF News Reports Studio is characterized by a set of large open stairs, at the top of which lies the ZDF logo. The building is constructed of 3,000 cubic meters of concrete and 670 tons of steel. It offers a useable area of 2,900 square meters and combines all the areas necessary for modern news transmission. At the heart of the building are two studios, with a surface area of 1,050 square meters. The functions block is located in front of the studios and includes the director's room and appliance, meeting and sanitary facilities. Additional day-lit offices and editorial rooms are located further along and slightly to the side.

01 Main view | 02 Cross section | 03 Bird's-eye view | 04 Steps detail | 05 TV studio | 06 Connecting walkway

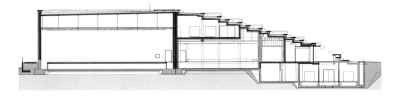

02

03

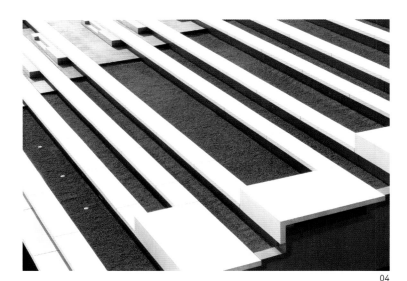

04

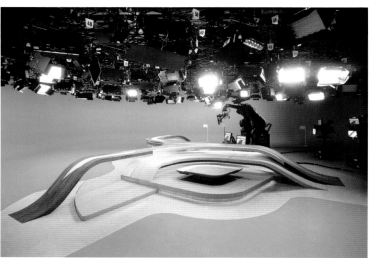

05

06

01

02

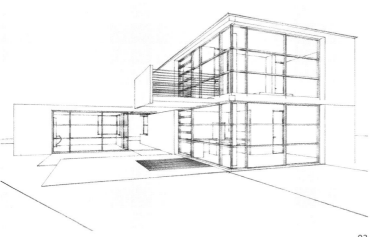

03

Hill Müller House - House with Orangery

Open living spaces, not closed in by four walls, are what gives the house its character. A flow is established, enhanced by the furniture and different views. The house is planned from inside to outside with a focus on simplicity and functionality, without forgetting the importance of atmosphere. Exterior and interior are oriented through openings towards the movement of daylight. Energy is supplied by geothermal energy, and solar energy provided by a photovoltaic system. House, orangery and carport connect to form a consistent line. The exterior of the house is a warm gray, while the interior is more colorful.

01 Flowing internal organization | 02 Glazing and neutral tones of façade | 03 Sketch of main view | 04 Glazed façade | 05 Large balcony at front

04

05

01

02

03

Kunsthalle Mainz

As a sign of its renovation and reuse, this listed, former energy center of the port has been upgraded with a 21-meter tower of reinforced concreted, tilted at an angle of seven degrees. The tower stands on the site where the chimney of the historic boiler house was originally located. As a new symbol for the port region, the building marks the main entrance to the Kunsthalle. The old building houses 800 square meters of exhibition space. The historical window openings in the exhibition area have been covered over with steel lamellar binds. The tower consists of an insulated concrete structure, which is superimposed with a façade of green translucent panels of security glass.

01 Perspective with students | 02 Exhibition room second floor | 03 Exhibition tower | 04 Panorama window third floor | 05 Longitudinal section

04

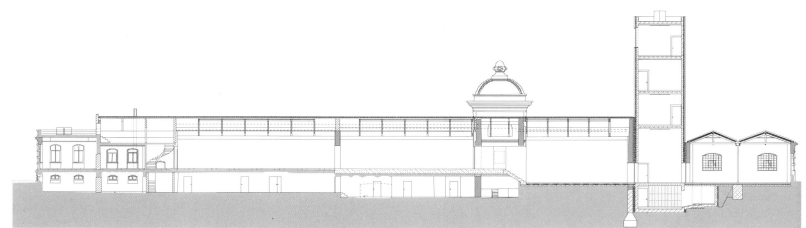

05

01

02

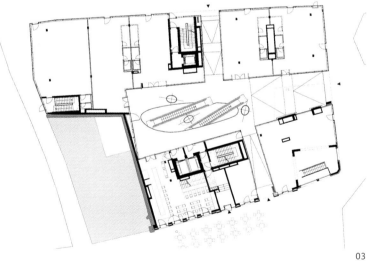

03

04

Houses on Markt 11–13

This building is located in the center of the city of Mainz. The façade looks towards a historical pedestrian square and towards Mainz Cathedral. Like many other European city centers, this important location has been compromised by thoughtless projects and post-war repair work. A downward-sloping roof design has been used to restore the façade and a striking external skin has been added. This white ceramic skin envelops almost the whole structure, with an irregular pattern of windows and openings, but leaves the old façade on the front section free and visible. As visitors enter the building, they walk through the full-height, five-story lobby, a small vertical square linking together the different functions.

01 Naturally lit interior | 02 Glazed roof | 03 Ground floor plan | 04 Central atrium allows natural light into building | 05 Façade with new external skin

05

01

02

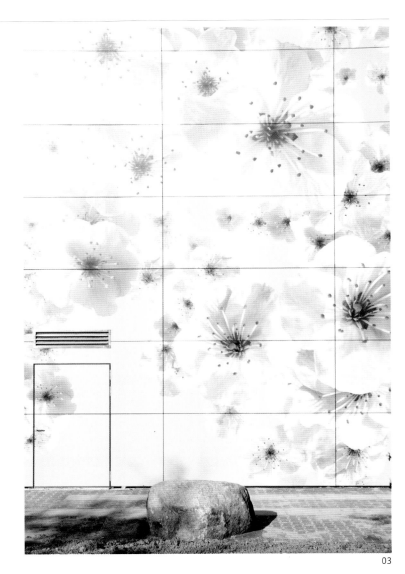

03

Käthe-Kollwitz-School

The Käthe-Kollwitz-School was the first of a total of five schools to integrate a day care center. The design concept of the building consists of two buildings, which are connected to a central access area. Class and group rooms are located in the west of the building, while all other functions are organized in the east. Enclosed staircases are located in the corners of the building and are clad with a distinctive façade. The façade print design, which was developed for each of the schools, makes each building unique.

01 South façade | 02 East façade | 03 Detail of the cherry blossom motif | 04 Staircase | 05 North, south and east elevation | 06 Ground floor plan

04

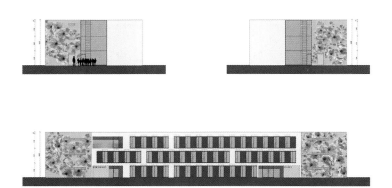

05

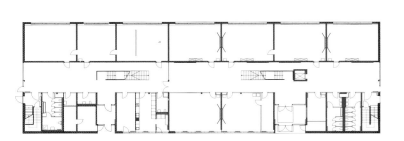

06

01

02

House Dr. L

The shape of this building results from the interior design and energy concept, as well as from the requirements of the development plan. The north side is closed to the street. A few openings in the street side and in the gable walls ensure minimal heat loss and also offer protection from the inquisitive gaze of passersby. The north façade was tilted by 18 degrees and counts, in terms of legal building requirements, as a roof area with an eave height of zero. The living area on the ground floor incorporates a 12-meter wide glass façade that can be opened or closed as required. The upper floor projects out over the ground floor, shading almost the entire glass façade during the summer. In winter, significant solar gains can be achieved with the glass façade.

01 View from street | 02 Exterior with terrace and garden | 03 Façade detail | 04 Site plan | 05 Staircase | 06 Exterior view

03

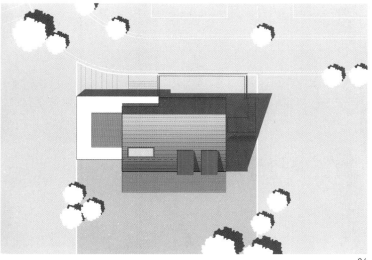

04

05

06

01

02

Holy Designer Outlets

This project is an urban design concept in the former Schwenkel area and includes the construction of six buildings and the renovation of one building to create designer outlets with 3,500 square meters of retail space. Blocher Blocher Partners have developed an ensemble consisting of architecturally original retail space in the style of flagship outlets. The revitalization of one of the last urban construction sites has enhanced the southwestern outskirts of Metzingen. Materials such as metal, glass, concrete and plaster mediate between the large-scale outlet architecture in the north and the small-scale, mixed residential development to the west and east. The rectangular structures arrange themselves harmoniously within the urban context.

01 Metal façade | 02 Façade | 03 Situation | 04 Exterior at night

03

04

01

City Villa EM35

Strict building regulations reduced the design margins for this project. From these requirements, the architects developed a three-dimensional structure that is characterized by its sculptural appearance. The original clear shape is a cube, the edges of which are defined in both height and length by the building. As with a sculptural work, the corners are cut out, creating differently proportioned indoor and outdoor spaces. The living area is placed on the top floor, a flowing space that narrows and widens, or opens across the corner. Built-in furniture divides the smooth transitions between the different residential areas. The deep-cut terraces offer either private or open space, rubbing shoulders with the city and the adjoining vineyard.

01 Front view | 02 Upper floor plan | 03 Exterior view | 04 Living area

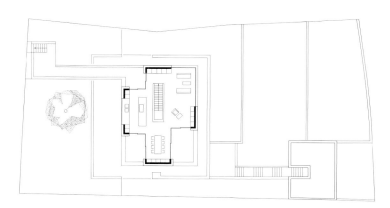

02

03

04

01

02

03

Training and Exhibition Center Altendorf

This new Training and Exhibition Center was inaugurated at the company's headquarters in Minden, on the 100th anniversary of this inventor and world market leader in panel saws. Clear lines dominate the façade, where large glazed areas combine with exposed concrete and zinc panels. The building consists of numerous offices, training classrooms and an exhibition room, spread across more than 2,000 square meters of floor space. The upper floor includes training classrooms and combi-offices around a bright patio. The purist interior follows the clarity of the façade, which is dominated by exposed concrete, natural stone, extensive wood paneling and white walls.

01 Exterior detail | 02 Corridor | 03 Section | 04 Exterior

04

01

Lift

The project 'Lift' was designed by *platzhalter architektur and includes the 23 square meter extension of an apartment with a terraced area. The conceptual idea of the design is that the building defines the space, functioning as a "platzhalter" (place holder). The slim white building is made of exposed concrete and reaches across the roof of a brick factory building. Living space and the existing building are connected with each other. Light colors and large windows define the building and create an open and friendly atmosphere, both in terms of the interior and exterior. The projections and form extend the living space and provide a contrast to the original building.

01 Projecting structure seen from street | 02 Exterior | 03 Interior | 04 Situation | 05 Sections

02

03

04

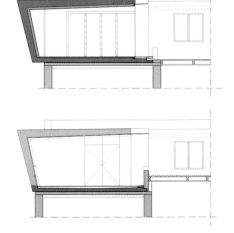

05

01

02

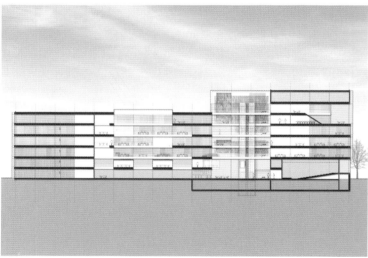

03

04

Office and Congress Center

This office and congress center of Engineering Dobersek GmbH is currently being developed in prominent proximity to the Borussia Park in Mönchengladbach. At the core of the new building is the meeting and conference center. On the ground floor, a representative lounge with café bar serves both guests and employees. Special highlights of the building include a welcoming atrium, a training area with flexible floor plan, a gallery on the first floor, which functions to join the separate areas together; a canteen, accessed via a bridge; a winter garden and lounge areas.

01 Main façade | 02 View at night | 03 Cross section | 04 Interior view with walkways

01

02

03

Vocational School

This Vocational School in Montabaur needed to be extended to accommodate 21 additional classes and renovated to meet modern fire safety standards. Even the original plans of the school allocated a particular area for an expansion to the building. The three-story extension, with 18 classrooms, occupies this allotted space and, in this respect, completes the main building. An additional one story construction, with three further classrooms and a large canopy, forms a second entrance and a covered rest area. In case of fire, external escape stairs and steel platforms lead the students over the roof of the building into the open. The many windows of the classroom buildings allow natural light to flood into the structure, and permit views of the surrounding area.

01 Façade | 02 Schoolyard | 03 Ground floor plan | 04 Classroom | 05 Exterior view | 06 Corridor

04

05

06

01

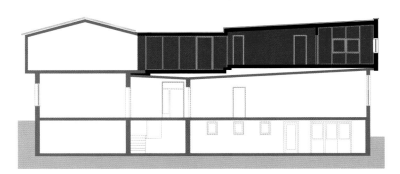

02

Extension Hannah-Arendt-School Iznang

The original building ensemble of this school is situated on a hill, with views over the Lake of Constance, and is a patchwork of different building phases (1956, 1996). Three wood-framed office rooms and a panorama room, offering views across the lake, have been attached to the roof of one of the rooms. These are accessed by a glazed groove, attached to the already existing administration building, and were constructed in a time frame of just eight weeks. The sloping roof was left intact and forms the basis of the new building form. The new roof of the building takes the same form, but is folded backwards at the same inclination. A panorama window offers unobstructed views of the lake. The lateral, set back, glass façade of the office space are shaded by wooden slats that follow the angle of the roof.

01 Façade detail | 02 Longitudinal section | 03 Interior space | 04 Exterior view at night

03

04

01

02

03

House S

This house is situated in a suburb on the edge of the town that offers imposing views across Mühlhausen and its important church. The design of the house takes this view into consideration, and the church has a presence in every room, from dining and living areas to the workspace on the gallery. The design subdivides the land into an ornamental garden to the south and a functional garden to the north. These areas, together with the sauna, create a building complex, joined together by the surrounding terraces. A central interior core divides the house, and the surrounding rooms are connected by peripheral enfilade. The house has two stories and successfully conveys a generous sense of space

01 Front view | 02 Kitchen | 03 Living room with gallery | 04 Exterior view | 05 West elevation

04

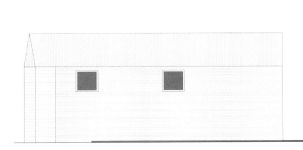

05

01

02

03

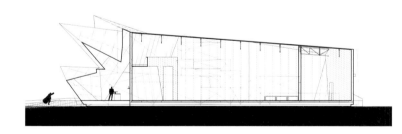

04

Pavilion 21 Mini Opera Space

This pavilion was built to create a space with 300 seats for experimental performances of the Bavarian State Opera. The Pavilion 21 was designed to be dismountable, transportable and remountable and to make the respective urban space distinctive through its shape. The architects aimed to introduce elements which involve both the spatial transformation of sound sequences and also develop sound reflecting and absorbing properties through their pyramid-like shape: 'Soundscaping'. The strategy to achieve soundscaping comprises three steps: Firstly, to realize the shielding effect between square and street, secondly, to shape the geometry of the pavilion in such a way that the surface deflects noise, and thirdly, to design the surface so that it reflects and absorbs sound.

01 Façade | 02 Bar | 03 Exterior view | 04 Section | 05 Bird's-eye view

05

01

02

03

BMW Welt

In 2000, the BMW Group decided to build a brand-experience and car-delivery center in close vicinity to the corporate headquarters and the BMW Museum. 275 architects participated in an open international competition for the project. In a multi-stage selection procedure, the design by Coop Himmelb(l)au was chosen as the winner in July 2001. One of the central design ideas was to expand the existing configuration of the BMW tower and the museum with an additional element so as to create a spatial, ideal, and identity-forming architectural ensemble. The design proposal consists of a large transparent hall with a sculptural roof and a double cone informed by its relation to the existing company headquarters building.

01 Stairway to the lounge | 02 Premiere | 03 Double cone | 04 Façade detail of the double cone | 05 Section

04

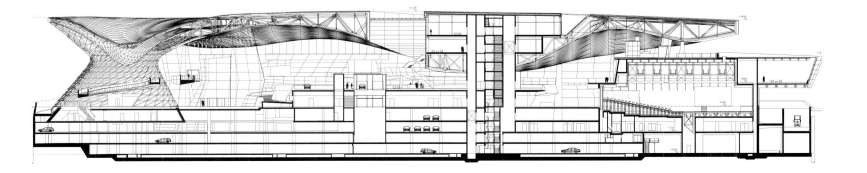

05

01

02

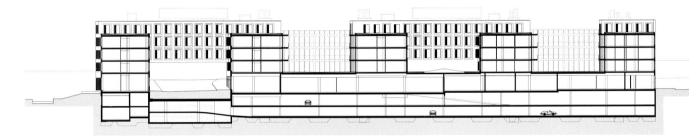

03

Pasinger Hofgärten

This was the first building to be constructed in the redesign of Pasing in Munich. An urban structure was required that would adequately complement the nearby ICE train station. This large scale, inner city building offers a strong urban edge to the north, facing the ICE railway line. Its design has also allowed it to be successfully integrated into Pasing's town center, which is defined by its small-scale buildings and open squares. Open courtyards have been cut out of the massive block-structure to the north and the south, creating a meandering building plan. The outer façade is plastered while the frontal sections of the façade facing the courtyard are clad with a ceramic finish.

01 View from south | 02 Exterior view | 03 Longitudinal section | 04 Courtyard |
05 Ground floor plan

04

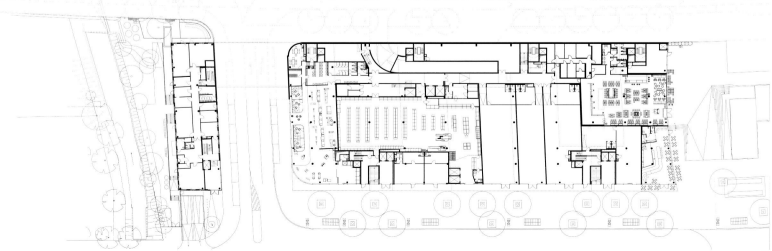

05

01

02

03

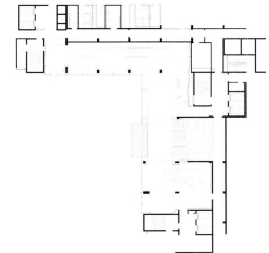

04

Kustermann Park

The complex is entered through an extension; the foyer. This is divided into three zones; the reception area, containing the Barista Bar, and the central circulation area. The consistent formulation of the design leads the visitor to the training area on the first floor. Light plays a decisive role in the design. Light slots and flat light strengthen the contours and the plasticity of the structure. The dining area presents itself as a complex spatial structure. The guest room, a VIP area and the interface to the kitchen space cover a total area of 800 square meters. The VIP area is separated from the guest room by mobile, colored structures and curtains. This area can be used as a meeting and event space.

01 Foyer and entrance area | 02 Employees restaurant | 03 VIP area | 04 Ground floor plan | 05 Outdoor terrace area

05

01

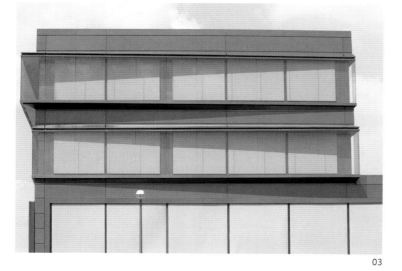

02

mk6 WerkRaumWest

This black building sits imposingly on the first corner location in Freiham, off of the main north-south axis. The upper levels are glazed; the glazing is accentuated by black aluminum. This gives the building surfaces a dynamic appearance, attracting the gaze of passersby, as it appears to move in the wavering sunlight. The mk6 WerkRaumWest itself is four stories high, with a staircase on the south side, providing access to the two upper-stories. The mk6 building can serve very different functions. In addition to retail space, offices, and administration areas, there is also space for cultural and social facilities such as an exhibition hall or a gallery.

01 View from west | 02 View from northwest | 03 Double façade | 04 Section | 05 Façade interspace

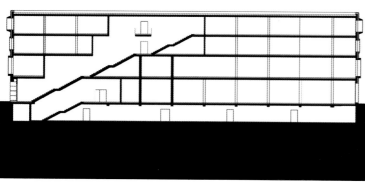

03

04

05

01

69 Apartments and an Underground Garage

This new building in Munich-Sendling, situated between Bruderhof and Schwaneck-straße, on the site of a former Lechner brother's timber merchants, consists of 69 apartments and an underground car park with 75 spaces. The dominating design elements of the façade are the ornamental balustrades, designed in collaboration with the artist Sabrina Hohmann. The projecting balconies give the façade a lightweight appearance. The large window units are made of wood and come from the former timber merchant, connecting the past with the present – a link that can be felt in every apartment.

01 Façade | 02 Section | 03 Staircase | 04 View from courtyard

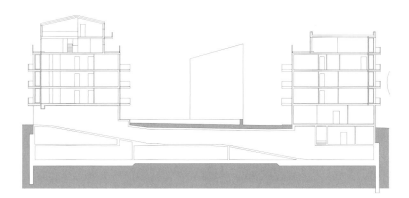

02

03

04

01

Technology Center MTZ

The Technology Center MTZ in Munich frames the western edge of the Technology Park M-Campus and lies within view of the Olympic Park. It offers a home to new entrepreneurs and existing companies in the technology industry. The building structure, with its eight different modules, creates a uniform structural grid for the office space – this systematic approach is flexible and allows endless options for expansion. The winter garden on the ground level takes over the circulation and organization and enables easy orientation within the building. The eastern and the western façades feature a curtain-like layer of mobile, vertically arranged sliding units of printed glass, which provide a very effective sun shield.

01 General view from west | 02 Winter garden, entrance | 03 Situation | 04 Winter garden | 05 East façade detail

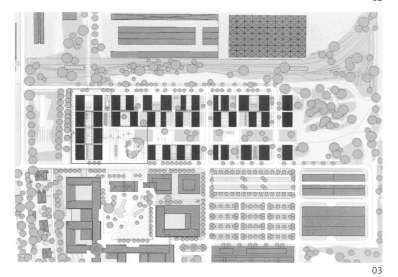

02

03

04

05

01

02

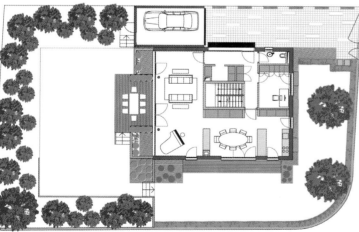

03

04

House Bogenhausen

Located in Munich-Bogenhausen, this family house is distinguished by a modern, clear architecture. Large, light-filled rooms create a feeling of spaciousness and allow various views of the landscaped garden. The basement is lit by a leafy, sunken court and offers additional space and optimal use of the property. The large, open ground floor is the meeting place for the whole family. The upper floor includes three children's rooms and two bathrooms. The master bedroom, with a private roof terrace, is located on the second floor and is an ideal retreat.

01 Bathroom | 02 Exterior view | 03 Ground floor plan | 04 Living room | 05 Upper floor plan

05

01

02

03

04

House Strathmann

The row of villas hangs like a string of pearls within the surrounding greenery. The new building slides discretely into these serene surroundings. The three-story corner house accentuates the cross roads between the connecting streets, while the stacked nature of the structure defines the transition to the neighboring houses. Large incisions cut into the façade play with the static nature of the building. An office is located on the ground floor, while the two family apartments are on the upper level. The house refers to its own history in that it is clad in a covering of salvaged bricks. Mortar, plaster and paint work together to create a new image, framed by black aluminum.

01 Southeast view | 02 Southwest view | 03 East façade | 04 Façade detail | 05 Ground floor plan

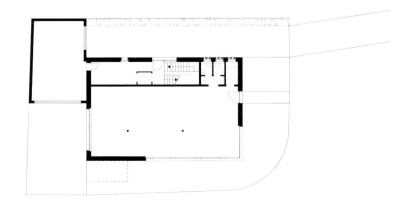

05

01

Reconstruction and Extension Waldhilsbach House

Built in 1970, this house is located on the outskirts of town and is adjacent to a nature reserve. The program for the reconstruction and extension resulted from the personal connection between the client and the old house. With its monolithic expression, the new extension looks more compact than the old house. This contrast was continued in the details of the façade. Large, glazed façade panels correspond to the small-scale, rough bonds of the brick. Ridge line, roof pitch and the north wall of the old building set tight boundaries for the extension. The extension is both an autonomous structure and a recognizable 'relative'.

01 Façade | 02 Backside view | 03 Existence and extension | 04 Ground floor plan

02

03

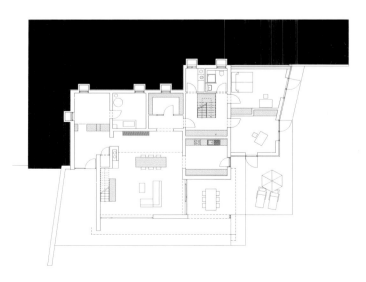

04

01

02

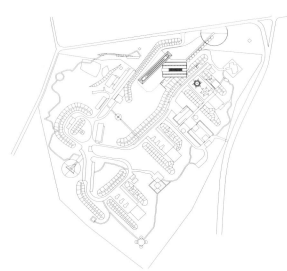

03

Langen Foundation / Hombroich

Near the Erft river in the suburbs of Dusseldorf, there is an art museum called Insel Hombroich. A new museum was planned about one kilometer northwest of Insel Hombroich. Tadao Ando Architect & Associates were commissioned to design one of the galleries. The museum contains a collection of oriental and modern art accumulated by Mr. and Mrs. Langen, who financed the building. The permanent exhibition wing is surrounded with a buffer area like the engawa (veranda) of Japanese architecture. In the temporary exhibition wing, the architect conceived the story of a volume entirely embedded underground, with dramatic light brought into this sealed box by means of skylights.

01 Exterior at dusk | 02 Interior | 03 Site plan | 04 Interior with view to outside | 05 Exterior by daylight

04

05

01

02

03

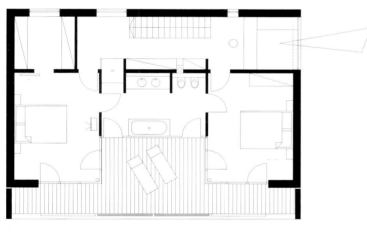

04

05

House on the Steinberg

This house is situated in the midst of cultivated land and features a balcony on the upper level, offering an outside retreat sheltered by the protective building envelope. The house receives its inhabitants in a two-story entrance area with a spacious room sequence, flowing from kitchen to dining to living. One impressive element of the building is the projecting balcony. On the upper level, bedrooms and bathrooms open out to the patio, which together with wood elements and the incision cut into the roof create an intimate outdoor space. The house has attained the energy-plus-house standard, through its use of insulation, triple glazing, large openings towards the south and west, and a geothermal heat pump.

01 Staircase | 02 Entrance | 03 View from southwest | 04 Upper floor plan | 05 Loggia | 06 Section

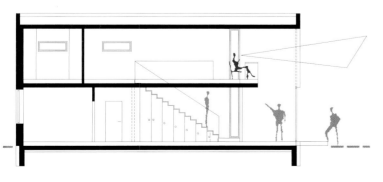

06

01

02

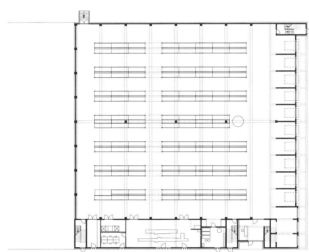

03

Logistic Center and Head Office Partyrent

Optimally functioning processes were the central concern of planning. The architects developed a spatial concept that is sufficient for the operating procedures. The analysis revealed five areas that needed to be combined: incoming and outgoing goods, processing, storage, sales and administration and a social area for staff. To link the stages efficiently, a reduced body was chosen as a connecting element. The geometric simplicity gives the complex production flow a regulative frame. The shiny smooth material of the building envelope highlights the compactness of the building. The volume opens with specific functions: the loading zone for trucks, the visitor portal and the staff areas for employees.

01 Overall view east façade | 02 Façade detail | 03 Ground floor plan | 04 Lounge area | 05 South façade

04

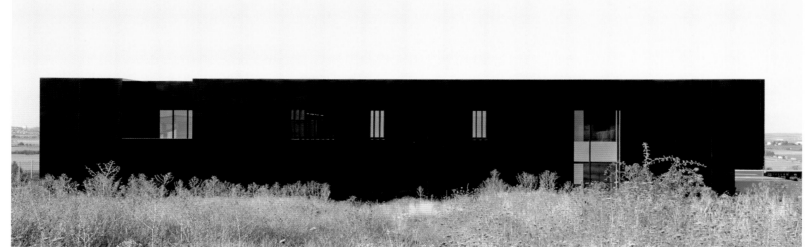

05

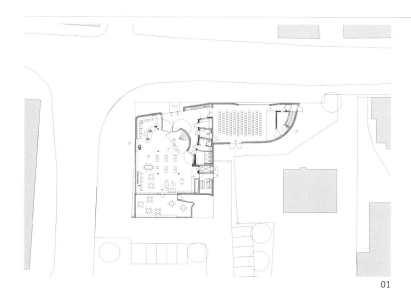

01

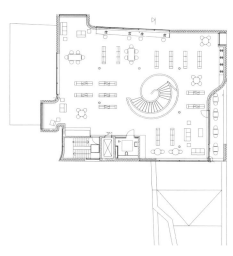

02

Mediathek Oberkirch

This three-story media center is connected by an organically formed stairwell. This centrally positioned opening serves not only as circulation space but also works in conjunction with the large glazed area above to serve as a lighting element, illuminating the interior areas. The sculptured façades act as display windows, allowing a wide view of the surrounding urban area. The outer, lighter spaces serve as a lounge, where undisturbed reading or computer work is possible. During the planning stages the focus was on designing a high quality interior and the inclusion of the outdoor space in the library concept.

01 Site plan with ground floor | 02 Second floor plan | 03 Exterior with garden of reading | 04 Staircase system | 05 Entrance | 06 Staircase first floor | 07 Exterior of meeting room

03

04

05

06

07

01

Façade Design for Galeria Kaufhof Department Store

Angelis & Partner have developed an exterior façade for the Kaufhof department store that respects the famous design of the previous façade by Egon Eiermann but also provides the building with a new, modern skin. It shares a clear dialogue with the more classical style of the town of Oldenburg. The new building envelope consists of large, horizontal, translucent glass elements on some surfaces and perforated metal elements, each with a height of 275 centimeters, on other sides of the building. The façade is an abstract, soft and shimmering skin, which constantly changes in appearance, sometimes disappearing against the gray of the sky, sometimes turning into a shining crystal within the town and sometimes reflecting the surroundings. At night, the façade transforms the building into a shining beacon.

01 Light play on perforated façade | 02 Glazed front façade | 03 Elevation with surroundings

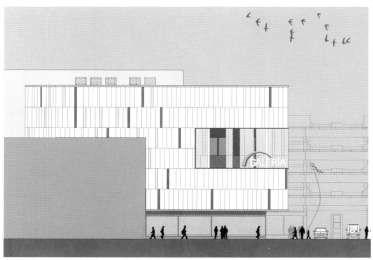

02

03

01

HHGO - Garden Residence

This detached residence is situated on an ample garden lot. The building shares a dialogue with an existing building also built on this site. The two independent retreats have separate entrances and both include master bedrooms, baths and studies. The houses are linked by the joint, fully glazed garden level to the dining and living areas. The two retreats are shaped like individual buildings, formally based on the same grammar but with different dialects, meeting the lifestyle of their inhabitants. The interior is tastefully thought out; natural daylight flows deep into the house and the large rooms with white walls and wooden floors have a very natural appearance.

01 Entrance yard and the two retreats | 02 Front door between retreats | 03 Ground floor plan

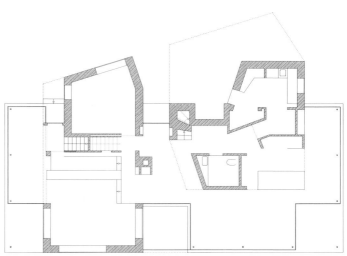

02

03

01

02

Executive Academy

This restored villa and its extension are used as an executive academy for the EWE AG. The design concept evolved out of the tension created between old and new and thus reflects the company's position between tradition and innovation. The old building was partly restored in a historical style but with a modern interpretation. The existing volume was extended with a modern annex, which serves various functions as well as providing more public space. The newly modeled building was given a minimalistic glass façade, creating an exciting dialogue between the old and new. The entire building is finished with a great depth of detail and presents a modern image, underlined by an elegant restraint.

01 Street view | 02 Lounge | 03 Ground floor plan | 04 Dining area

03   04

01

Pavilion Emilie F.

This pavilion building is used primarily as a staff canteen for 150 people and as a catering area for guests of the Frech Company; however, it can also be used for hosting
special events. The one-story building is influenced by the folded structure of the roof,
which is repeated in the interior of the building and the geometry of the floor plan. The
precise edges reflect the technical standards of the engineering company. The large,
raised terrace has a wooden deck, emphasizing its relationship to the surrounding environment. The landscape flows through the glass structure.

01 Edge | 02 Floor plan | 03 Pavilion with terrace at night | 04 Interior space

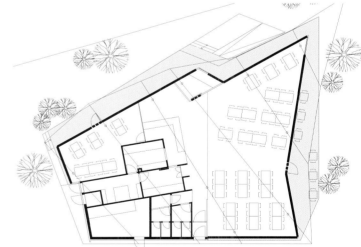

02

03

04

01

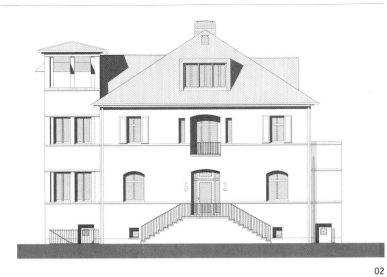

02

Apartment House in Potsdam

Potsdam's cultural landscape is famous for its villas, grouped around the historical parks, like Sanssouci Park and "Neuer Garten". In close proximity to this area, architects Wiegand/Hoffman were given the task of developing a masterplan for the art collector clients, which must relate to the historical houses and new adjoining buildings. The developed apartment building, flanking the site, plays a key role in this project. Based on an old building, the new façades and terraces were overhauled completely and extended with a lookout. This tower is a special motif of Potsdam and gives view to fascinating surroundings – the UNESCO World Heritage Site.

01 Front view | 02 Elevation | 03 Master bathroom | 04 Penthouse apartment with fireplace | 05 Exterior view | 06 Room on first floor | 07 Staircase detail

03

04

05

06

07

01

02

Information and Visitor Center

This annex, in close proximity to a 17th century moated castle and a zoo, is a significant architectural and cultural monument of Westphalia. Located close to the castle and in front of a forest, the information and visitor center opens up a dialogue between nature and culture. An exhibition offers space to impart knowledge of nature and the interplay between man and nature. The dialogues between volume and transparency, openness and enclosure, light and shadow define the building. The reflections of the surrounding forest allow boundaries between building and forest, inside and outside to melt together. The deliberately reduced architectural style and the choice of materials complement the natural diversity of the environment.

01 Front view | 02 Exterior | 03 Interior | 04 Exhibition space | 05 Ground floor plan

04

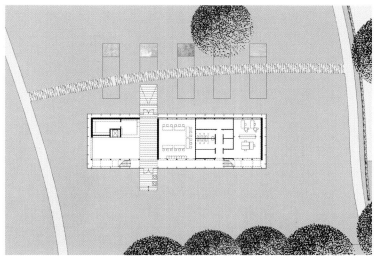

05

03

01

02

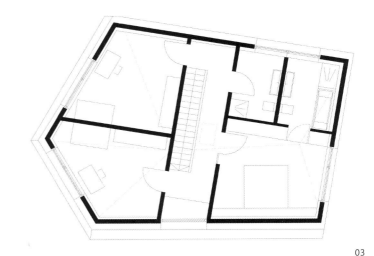

03

04

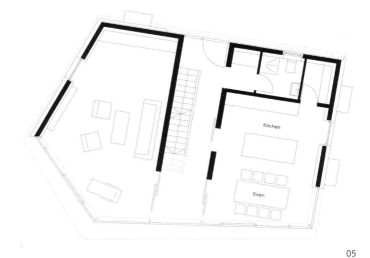

05

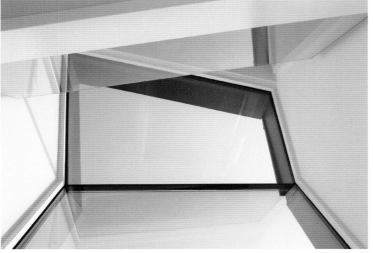

06

Haus der Zukunft – SolarAktivHaus

At the request of Sonnenkraft GmbH, fabi architekten developed the 'Home of the Future which aims to set the standard for the year 2020. Instead of the well known passive house type, a new, more developed building concept, the Solar-active-house, which is not only based on energy saving, but also on solar power generation, was created. The new building form, similar to a crystal, follows the sun and allows a maximum of active, useable solar energy even if plot is not perfect adjusted. The tilt angles of the wall and the roof are perfectly fitted to the actual orientation and using to solarthermics and photovoltaiks.

01 Terrace | 02 Entrance | 03 Second floor plan | 04 Exterior view | 05 Ground floor plan | 06 Skylight

01

02

03

Bosch Training Center

This industrial building, a test center for 200 millimeter silicon wafers and their end products, is situated, together with the new Wafer Fab building, in Reutlingen. It has four stories with a partial cellar underground; the building structure is flexible, made of reinforced concrete slabs and concrete columns. Core-steel composite columns support the two testing areas. This allows for a simple, cube-shaped building structure on the outside and differentiation and flexibility on the inside. The walls and ceilings in the foyer and the circulation areas are made of exposed concrete, while the first and second floors have been given a glass façade. The building has been given a unified appearance with the consistent use of a few main colors and materials.

01 Exterior | 02 Night view | 03 Staircase system | 04 Façade | 05 Ground floor plan | 06 Third floor plan

04

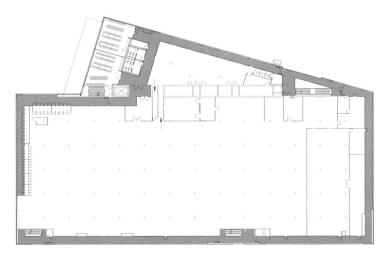

05

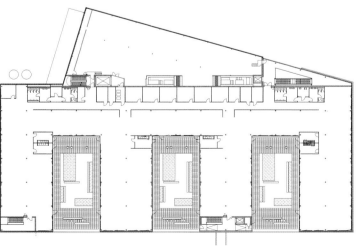

06

01

02

Lütkehellweg House

The typology and urban character of the project is based on the space defining contrast between a two-story brick building and the nearby exposed concrete garage, which is situated parallel to the street. The anthracite colored house appears large and solid. It is closed to the street side but opens to the south and west with a large glass façade, supported by several elegant concrete columns. The building forms a differentiated structural transition, dividing public, semi-public and private space while also complementing the immediate surroundings.

01 West façade | 02 Entrance | 03 Ground floor plan | 04 View from south

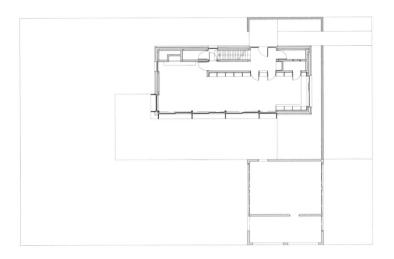

03

04

01

Wellness Area Beach Hotel Hübner Warnemünde

The Hübner beach hotel was built in the 1990s, on Warnemünde's beach promenade. The design of the wellness area was determined by the sensitive presentation of the upper levels in the silhouette of the Baltic Sea beach in Warnemünde. The areas containing the swimming pool and sun terrace are oriented towards the beach and the promenade. A magnificent view of the open sea can also be enjoyed from the sauna and quiet zones. The hotel's yellow and glazed façade tones down the angular lines of the building, making it an impressive and valuable addition to the beach landscape.

01 Sun terrace | 02 View from beach | 03 Floor plan | 04 Swimming pool

02

03

04

01

Office Building Ergosign

As visitors approach this building from the north entrance of the main train station, they are faced with an inviting, covered entrance ramp. A lounge is located on the first floor and serves as a reception area for business guests, as well as a meeting place for employees. A single staircase leads to the working areas. The split-level organization of the building, combined with the open staircases, promotes sufficient communication between the different levels. In addition to classic office space, there are also retreat areas and communication zones, these counter the restrained choice of materials in other parts of the building and have been finished with red material and leather. The exterior of the building consists of silver colored, shimmering alucobond plates.

01 Front view with covered entrance ramp | 02 Street view | 03 Interior with staircase and office space | 04 Ground floor plan in its situation

02

03

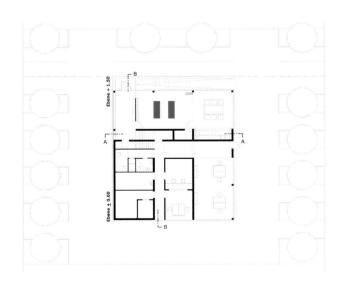

04

01

02

03

Renovation of the State Parliament of Saarland

This state parliament building in Saarland was built by Julius Carl Raschdorff in 1864 and has been a listed building since 1974. Until 1939, the building was used as a casino and wine store. It was then used for a short time by the Third Reich before being converted into a parliament building in 1947. The renovation and restoration work included the chamber, stairwells, the foyer, the entrance area and the cellar. A fundamental requirement was to unify architectural styles of the various construction periods, from the establishment of the original building to the styles of the 1950s and today.

01 Exterior view | 02 Chamber | 03 Bird's-eye view of the Chamber | 04 Ceiling detail | 05 Elevation

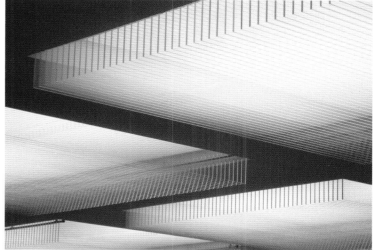

04

05

01

02

Extension DFKI

The extension of the existing DFKI building on the university campus in Saarbrücken was constructed during the third building phase and is at the end of a row of buildings. The building consists of two different structures: the base, which consists of a transparent unit together with the functional complex from the second building phase, and a horizontal bar, which is open to the north and east sides and projects out over the lower level. The three-story façade features large lamella, which offer protection against sunlight. On the north side these are stationary, whereas on the east side they are programmed by computer to follow the path of the sun.

01 Staircase | 02 Stairs | 03 Colonnade | 04 Exterior view | 05 Elevation

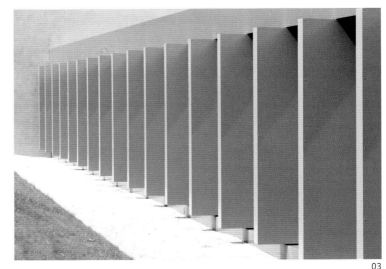

03

04

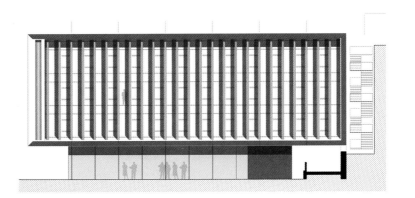

05

01

02

03

04

Beach House "Auf der Freiheit"

The "Auf der Freiheit" peninsula in Schleswig is situated between Holmer Noor and Schlei and was used as a naval base until several years ago. This attractive area, in close proximity to the sea, has been developed into a residential area of high recreational value. The beach house is located in the south part of the residential area, forming, as a multi-level point building, the transition between the residential development to the north and Schlei to the south. The beach house offers two apartments of different sizes on each level, arranged floor by floor in an alternating pattern; the upper level houses a large penthouse. Loggias form the transition to the exterior, giving the building shell a transparent appearance.

01 Southeast view | 02 East view | 03 Ground floor, first floor, attic floor plans | 04 Front view | 05 Rooftop terrace

05

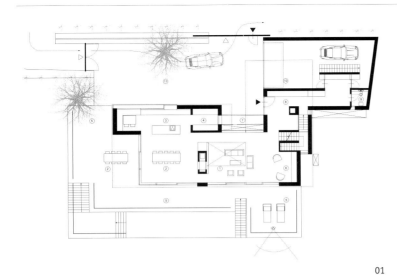

01

02

House TG, Ammersee

Three different levels form the structure of this building. The massive base draws its inspiration from the appearance of a cave. It is only on the side facing the lake that the stone volume can be seen – the basement level is embedded into the side of the hill. The site dictates the organization of windows and openings, with few windows facing the street but large windows facing the lake. The volume of the upper level appears to float over the glazed ground floor. The generous living areas, from ground to first floor, are connected by an open space. A pool of water flooded with light adorns the entrance area, forging connection between the outside and the wellness area in the basement.

01 Ground floor plan | 02 Street view with open gate | 03 South façade with garden | 04 Living room | 05 South façade at dusk | 06 Courtyard

03

05

04

06

01

02

House G

The main part of this building is deliberately turned away from the public road. In contrast to the closed façade at the front, the building opens out towards the garden at the back of the premises. The vertical slits in the façade serve as a central axis and entrance point; place, space and function interact with each other at this incision. This feature also divides the two main sections of the structure, providing a welcome contrast to the horizontally oriented glazing at the back of the building.

01 View from street | 02 View from garden | 03 Entrance and main circulation | 04 Central atrium | 05 Ground floor and first floor plans

03

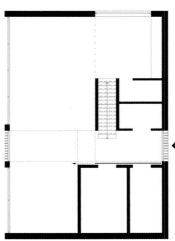

04

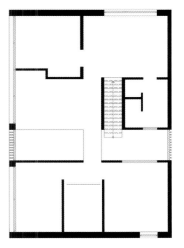

05

01

02

Event and Congress Center Forum Schönblick

The newly constructed Forum Schönblick is embedded in the surrounding park landscape at the edge of the Rems Valley. Seminar rooms and a chapel that serves as a place for quiet contemplation are grouped around the hall where church services and cultural events take place. The hall is positioned between the other buildings and is closed towards the north. Facing the south, the building opens out towards the landscape. Natural light, the acoustics of the room and the artistic design from sculptor Karl Imfeld permeate the atmosphere. The shape of the seminar room is adjusted to fit the overall plan of the building. As a light, transparent skeleton structure, this part of the building is set in front of the other sections.

01 Panoramic view | 02 Hall | 03 Site plan | 04 Interior | 05 Biblical wall

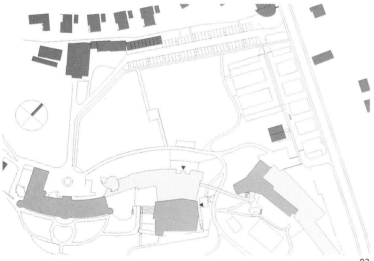

03

04

05

01

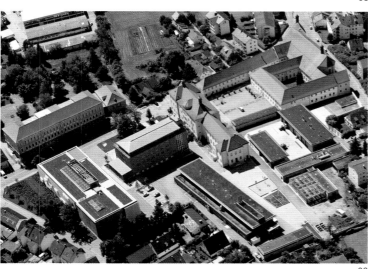

02

03

Competence Center for Renewable Resources

The Competence Center for Renewable Resources in Straubing brings together all components of the state government of Bavaria that are concerned with renewable resources. Three independent institutions; the Science Center, Technology and Support Center and the Central Agricultural Commodity Marketing and Development Network work together hand in hand; combining basic research, applied research and promotion of implementation together under one roof. The building offers 1,000 square meters of useable space. During the second building phase, a depot, research greenhouse, warehouse and surrounding grounds were developed. A third stage includes a interdisciplinary scientific laboratory. The core of this construction is going to be a wood-powered heating system with a maximum power output of 1.2 MW.

01 Entrance | 02 Aerial view of all three stages | 03 Circulation floor with laboratories |
04 Section of first building stage | 05 Central view of laboratories in first stage

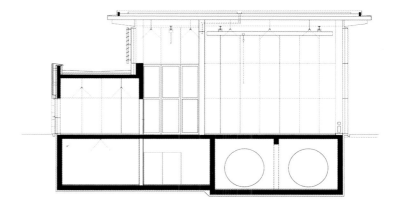

04

05

01

02

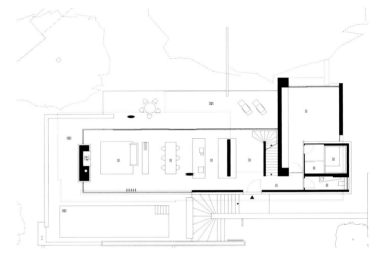

03

04

05

06

Heidehof House

The Heidehof House is screened from public view on the northeast side by a wood-paneled garage wall; protective walls, stacked in a line on top of each other; as well as by the closed façade of the white, cube-shaped main building, which is positioned over a 'zebra' striped, lower section. The entrance area on the ground floor is accessible by a small courtyard and set of stairs. This area has a view of the nearby pool, which is not visible from the street but still receives sunlight in the morning. Daylight can also stream into the living areas, through a floor-level window. The glazed entrance hall is two stories high and offers views over the garden and a huge sycamore tree. All living areas are on the ground floor, while bedrooms, bathrooms and the roof garden are situated on the upper level, aligned with the sycamore tree.

01 View from garden | 02 Exterior view at night | 03 Ground floor plan | 04 Swimming pool | 05 Entrance with a wood-paneled garage | 06 Living room

01

02

Children and Youth Center Helene P.

This youth center is a former villa, built in the 1870s, that has been fully renovated and fitted with a new extension. The extension seeks to re-establish the validity of the old building, helping to incorporate it into the surroundings. The new rooms have been developed according to orientation and view. The different functions of the premises, such as youth work and childcare, function independently of each other but are also connected through the open plan lower floor and cafe and the multi purpose space. The area is characterized by the busy access areas that lead into the city on one side, the youth center, which is sealed off from this, and the green hillside which overlooks the city on the other side. The building opens out in this direction.

01 Exterior view | 02 Roof terrace | 03 Joining basement with coffee bar | 04 Offices and workshops in the restructured villa

03

04

01

Königsbau-Passagen

The Königsbau-Passagen trade and service center forms, in conjunction with the new Kleiner Schlossplatz and the new art museum, a representative and vibrant building ensemble. Located directly behind the historic Königsbau, the new building respects the historic listed building. Passages lead through the Königsbau, connecting Königsstraße to the central atrium of the new building. The nine-story atrium offers a spectacular interior, which is based on different uses and creates attractive spaces for offices and retail businesses. The transparent, curved roof becomes the second façade and provides an attractive outer cover.

01 Shopping mall | 02 Atrium | 03 Sketch

02

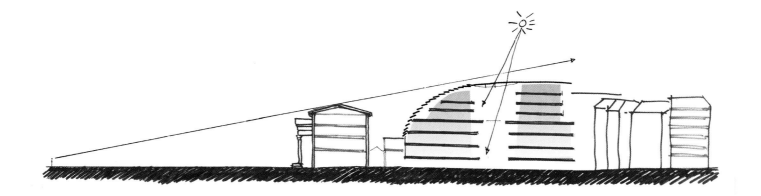

03

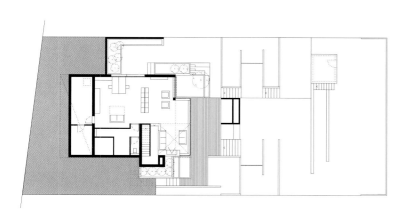

01

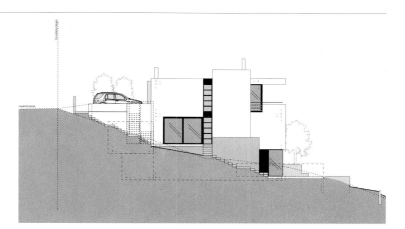

02

House RZ

This family house is located on a south-sloping site. The main building is consists of several different parts. The façade of white fair-faced plaster is interrupted by the room-height window elements. The base of the building is largely glazed and a sun deck is fitted to the slope of the hill. The entrance area and garage are located on the upper-most level. The intermediate level includes a living and a sleeping area and can be accessed from the other two levels by an open stairway in a large, central atrium. This forges a visual connection between the levels and brings the volume and the sloping situation to life.

01 Ground floor plan | 02 West elevation | 03 South façade | 04 Staircase system | 05 Southeast façade at night | 06 Interior ground floor | 07 Entrance area

03

04

05

06

07

01

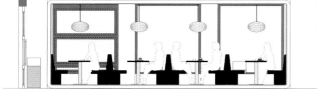

03

05

02

04

The Cupcake Boutique Stuttgart

After the opening of the first Cupcake Boutique in Weinstadt-Beutelsbach in December 2009, the new branch opened its doors in Stuttgart on June 2010. Upon entrance to the boutique, the main components of the boutique concept are immediately visible. A large glass display cabinet next to the checkout area contains the main offerings of the café: a wide assortment of cupcakes. The seating areas in the boutique are oriented towards the front display window. For customers who don't have much time, a bar is available in the center of the shop. The cupcake theme is reflected in small details throughout the store, such as in the wall graphics and the lights.

01 Bar | 02 Sitting area | 03 Sections | 04 Lounge | 05 Cash box area

01

02

03

04

Residence AM

This villa is positioned in an area of Stuttgart that offers the best views across the city. The house has a generous living space and the fantastic view can be enjoyed from all three floors. The villa was completely gutted and newly renovated and the façade facing the city was opened out. The open plan layout provides lots of room for flexibility and the use of coordinated materials permit flowing transitions between the individual living areas. A deliberately clear and formal language, both inside and outside, underlines the generous size and openness of the house. The façade and open plan areas with visual orientation create a modern property with a Mediterranean feel.

01 Fireplace | 02 Bathroom | 03 View from living room | 04 Living room with fireplace | 05 Kitchen

05

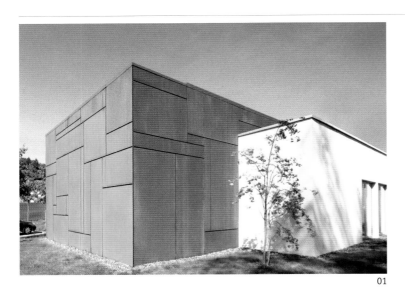

01

02

Chapel Bethesda

Designed by Herbert Hofer, this chapel in Bethesda House was conceived as a bright, meditative retreat for senior citizens. When completely opened, the timber swing doors connect the chapel to the entrance area of the residential home for senior citizens, creating a place of worship with a choir area. Due to the direction of the lighting, the view is guided into a small atrium. Glass pieces appear to float in space, forming a dynamic, lightweight cross, which casts dappled sunlight across the room depending on the light. The altar is a main feature of the space, formed from four solid oak blocks. The reduction of form and the use of color-matched materials, works to place the human being at the center of the space.

01 Exterior view | 02 Entrance area | 03 Floor plan | 04 Interior view | 05 Glass pieces floating above the cross | 06 Altar

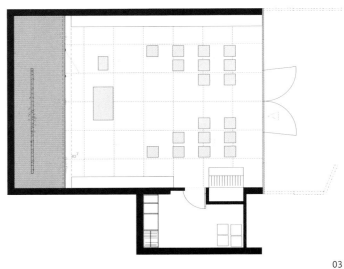

03

04

05

06

01

Joint Building Venture "Zukunft"

02

Mühlenviertel is a newly developed quarter within the town of Tübingen. The dynamic façade of this prominent building attracts attention through its colorful exterior, patterned with a combination of calm and cloudy surfaces. The lime plaster gives the building a Mediterranean feel and the design of the façade creates a contrast to the delicate pergolas and balustrades in front of the window openings. The apartments are individually tailored, many of them featuring a large hall area; three of the apartments are connected together, forming a duplex. The materials and components have been chosen for their ecological qualities and the house is also a low-energy building.

01 South façade | 02 Entrance hall | 03 Ground floor plan | 04 View from west

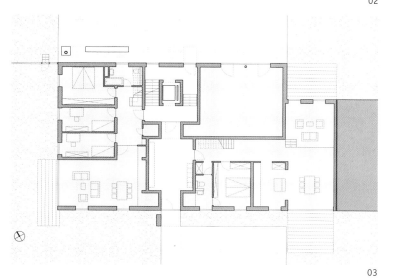

03

04

01

02

Sparkasse and Department Store Münstertor

Since the destruction caused in World War II, New Street in Ulm disrupts the flow of the city's old town. On one side lies Münster cathedral and the new town hall, while on the other side lies the medieval town hall and the new town library. The Sparkasse bank and Kaufhaus department store at Münstertor are centrally located and formulate new urban areas, filling in the gaps in the old town. The Sparkasse is divided into two sections, permeating at an acute angle, resulting in a light channel, through to Rathausplatz, which opens out the business and office premises. The wedge-shaped Kaufhaus department store offers panoramic views from its restaurant.

01 Head of the department store | 02 Flight of steps | 03 Situation | 04 Rathausplatz

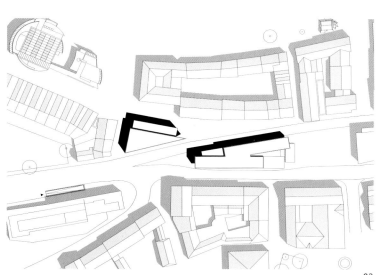

03

04

01

Max Müller I

"Wanderlust, tolerance, open to new things but still with roots in the old" – this is the motto of the Müllers, a family of winemakers. Thanks to this open approach, this listed 18th century building has been transformed into a new, light winery. An historical stairway of dark oak wood shows itself in the white modern building as a relic of the old wine bar. Oak wood is then used in a lighter tone throughout the room, marking the counter area and lining the exhibition wall opposite. The artists Marcel Neundörfer and Blagovesta Bakardjieva took a ceiling ornament from a guest bedroom on the upper floor and made it more abstract, sandblasted onto three, room height, glass panels in the wine bar.

01 Oak wood counter | 02 Seating and furnishings | 03 Entrance | 04 Floor plan

02

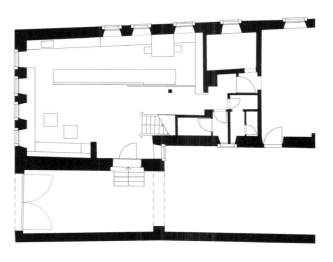

03

04

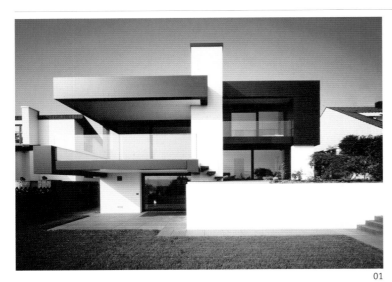

01

02

03

04

Family House R

Frank_Architekten carried out the restoration of this building. The restoration work allows the building to meet current housing standards and communicates a modern architectural language. The client wished for a dynamic renovation that portrayed a creative appreciation of a family house from the 1960s. Typical for this type of house was the split-level design; this makes optimal use of the building's sloping situation. The interplay of windows and large façade panels express the building's significance. The façade cladding forms an important formal and functional part of the renovation. The interior concept has a consistent high quality representation.

01 Front view | 02 Front view at night | 03 Interior | 04 South view | 05 Façade detail | 06 West elevation

05

06

01

Subsidized Housing Warendorf

This project is an example of subsidized, affordable housing. The concept of the semi-detached house was to interlace several cubes and to provide them with different materials, creating a unified whole. The structure does not only form the living rooms, it also consists of entrance canopies and storage rooms. The idea of the design is to experiment with materials. The façade of each cube is made of different materials: wood, plaster, brass, aluminum and synthetic turf. Irregularly arranged rows of windows complete the building.

01 Perspective of cubes with different surfaces | 02 Front view with synthetic turf |
03 Rear view with metal and wood panels | 04 Ground floor plan

02

03

04

01

Bissendorf Citizens' House

This historical government and domestic building is part of a group that forms this listed building ensemble. A characteristic feature of the structure is the large roof surface, interrupted by just a few dormer windows. The new citizens' hall is located behind these dormers, where the unusual length of the timber frame building can be experienced on the inside. A bistro, a bookstore and a gallery are located on the ground floor, while the foyer serves as a temporary event space. The individual areas are divided into zones that are clearly legible from both the inside and outside. In this project, an unusual approach has been taken to establishing the building detail, due to the special needs of the historical timber frame construction. For example, untreated oak wood lamella offer protection from the sun and privacy from the gaze of passersby.

01 Front view | 02 Exterior | 03 Interior new citizens' hall | 04 Ground and attic floor plan | 05 Stairs ground floor

02

03

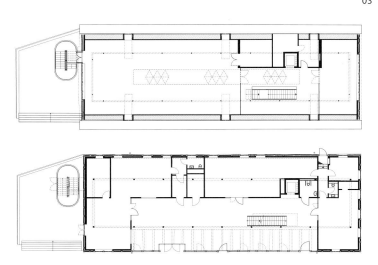

04

05

01

VitraHaus

The VitraHaus, built by Swiss architects Herzog & de Meuron, is home to the Vitra Home Collection. The concept of this five-story building connects two themes: the archetypal house and stacked volumes. The individual stacked houses, which are glazed at the gable ends, act as presentation rooms and have to be considered as abstract elements. Intersecting the underlying gables, the twelve houses have a nearly chaotic exterior appearance. To give priority to the presentation of the furniture, large spaces and white walls dominate the interior. The intention of the architects was to create a horizontal building, giving visitors an overview of the Vitra Home Collection and the beautiful surroundings.

01 Exterior view at night | 02 Interior | 03 Stacked houses

02

03

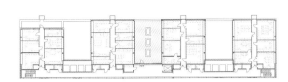

01

02

Center for Intelligent Building (CIB)

Weimar's current research institutions and the Materials Research and Testing Laboratory of the Bauhaus University are brought together under one roof in the Center for Intelligent Building in Weimar. The purpose of the new building is the advancement of materials, methods, products and processes in construction. The building provides 1,200 square meters of floor area for testing facilities, 850 square meters for laboratories and 1,500 square meters of office space. The two-story column-free hall on the ground floor extends over the whole building length and opens up an 87-meter long testing hall for multiple users. The upper stories have four cubic office and laboratory modules which are connected to one another by a glazed stairwell.

01 Second floor plan and section | 02 Patio on the roof of the testing hall | 03 Cubic modules | 04 Street view by night

03

04

01

02

Earth Observation Center

The old and the new are always the subject of provocative encounters. What doesn't go together needs a point of contact, connections, a common denominator. The concept of space forges ties between the old and new and vice versa. On different levels, research, teaching or events take place. The space is 14 meters high, 60 meters in length and offers an ideal climate, provided by an air exchange system in the ground, realized through 280 meters of pipes. At the top, glass domes 'bubble' and fill the spaces with daylight. Visitors and users experience the transformation from functional to sculptural.

01 Interior of atrium | 02 Atrium at night | 03 Second floor plan | 04 South façade

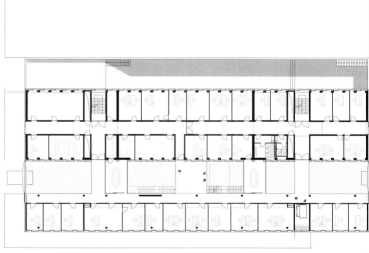

03

04

01

02

03

Renovation of a Single Family House

The renovation of this small, timber-framed house below Gleiberg Castle involved the creation of a spacious living area within a small area in a historic environment. Parts of the building have been carefully dismantled allowing for more space and an abundance of natural daylight. Particular attention was paid to the design of the building façade, which covers the former rough plaster façade with boards of larch wood. The restraint of the design is shown in the invisible transition from façade to roof and the windows, which are set flush into the façade. A rooftop terrace with a view of the castle creates the desired exterior space.

01 Exterior | 02 Living room | 03 View from glass base | 04 Section

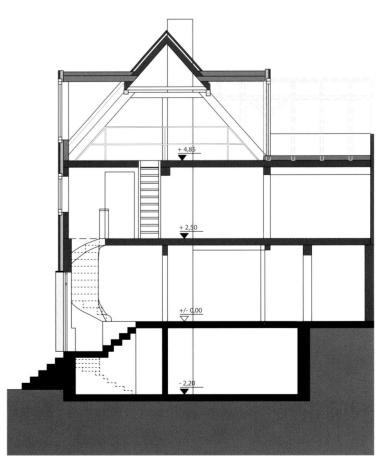

04

01

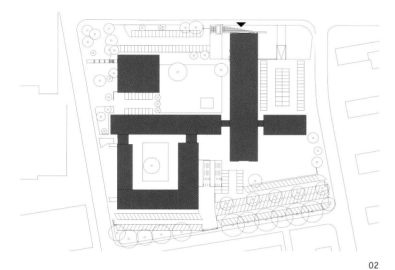

02

03

Renovation Census Bureau

The building of the German Census Bureau, which is landmarked as a typical high rise of the 1950s, had to be completely renovated due to faulty fire protection and contaminant-laden elements. The entrance hall and main hallways with functioning paternoster lifts remained unchanged. The improvement of the office quality and the hallways was the main focus of the project. Small, dark hallways were replaced by optimized zones with high comfort qualities. Room-high glazing created an almost daylight atmosphere. The building shell was updated with contemporary elements such as aluminum and glass. The proportions, patterns and colors of the 1950s were nevertheless integrated into the design.

01 Exterior view | 02 Situation | 03 Corridor | 04 Conference room | 05 Façade detail

04

05

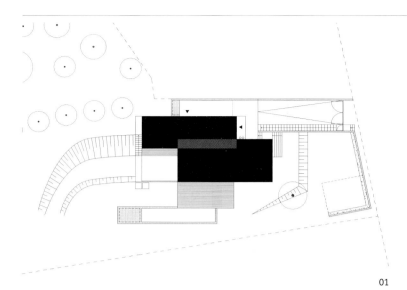

01

02

House B

This building concept consists of the intersection of two rectangular structures that are adapted to the topography of the site by their different heights. The white southwest oriented structure contains the living areas, while the gray northeast oriented structure includes the adjoining rooms and an annex. The format and placement of the windows in the gallery are effectively positioned to provide views of the surrounding hills. The swimming pool, which is situated on the downhill side of the house, is heated by the solar heating system on the roof of the building.

01 Situation | 02 Exterior at night | 03 Exterior with swimming pool and terrace

03

01

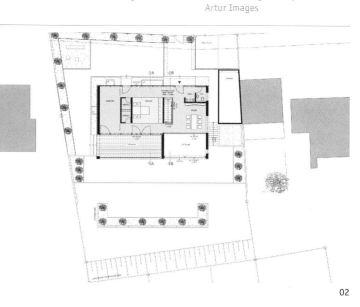

02

03

Family House F

The realization of this family house carefully introduces modern architecture into the rural townscape. The building is situated on an exposed slope, closing a gap in the existing street. The size of the construction has been tailored to suit a family of four. The full-surface glazing of the main side of the building ensures transparency and permeability. The shorter sides of the building are closed and form the walls adjoining the neighboring buildings. Through the full-height glazing the striking exterior is linked to the interior, creating an impressive spatial effect. The light is reflected by the solar control coating on the glass, creating reflections of the surrounding countryside, integrating the building into the area.

01 Front view | 02 Ground floor plan | 03 Southeast view | 04 Staircase | 05 Living area

04

05

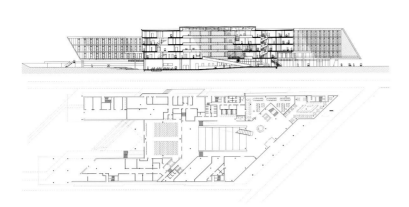

01

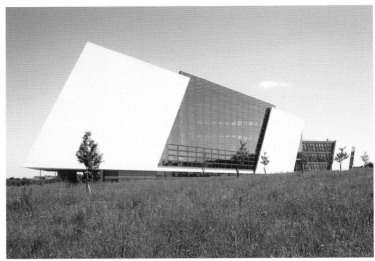

02

03

MobileLifeCampus

The central idea behind the design is an encircling, crossed over and apparently never-ending band. Cast in concrete, it picks out the tectonics of the buildings as a central theme. Overlays and intersections form the matrix, the translation of the idea of generating knowledge, transformed into concrete. The structural and organizational heart of the MobileLifeCampus is at the center. All paths lead to the campus' glazed atrium that rises over four floors. Conscious linking of the pathways underscore the openness of the campus. The seminar rooms are freely grouped around the atrium and extend upwards, to varying heights, into the center.

01 Longitudinal section and first floor plan | 02 Exterior | 03 Staircase system | 04 Detail glazed atrium | 05 Interior

04

05

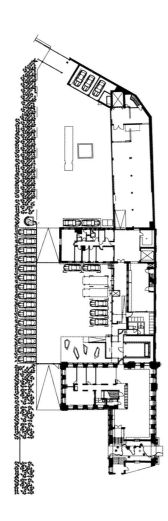

01

02

03

05

Stately Wine Cellar Würzburg

This wine shop with tasting and administration areas has been constructed in one of the finest wine cellars in the world, in the middle of the UNESCO protected Würzburg residence in Germany. Through the development of a clear corporate design – from website design to architecture – the public wine cellar is presented as a significant trademark. The choice of wines is originally and thoughtfully presented and a guidance system makes shopping easier. The deliberate contrast between Baroque and the 21st century positions the winery between the traditional and the modern.

01 Ground floor plan | 02 Access to winery | 03 Sales counter | 04 Exterior view | 05 Tasting area | 06 Street view

04

06

01

02

03

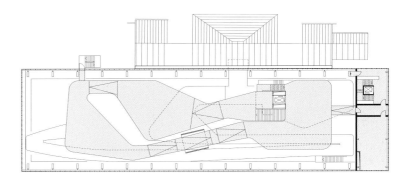

04

RömerMuseum in Xanten Archeological Park

This new museum building complements the older building that was built in the 1990s to protect the thermal baths and allows the entire Roman baths complex to be experienced as a building once more. The concept uses modern means to present the visitor with the huge dimensions of the old basilica. The large interior displays the historical room proportions and is based on the historical walls. The exhibition levels develop within the space continuum, free in the space. The development of the rising levels is experienced as accessible 'time bands' and supports the exhibition as an historical journey through the era of the Romans in Xanten.

01 Entrance | 02 Interior | 03 Museum within Xanten Archeological Park | 04 Third floor plan | 05 Interior with historic foundations

05

01

02

03

University Collection Historical Automobiles

The unusual feature of this university collection is the nature of the objects: historical automobiles. The new building is designed as a show window, situated in a central area of the university campus. The longitudinal sides are completely glazed, allowing unimpeded views of the cars within the surrounding environment. Sliding doors extend the interior space, which is lined like a display case. On the Scheffelberg Campus, the new building has been giving the name "Mobile Forum".

01 View to lecture room | 02 North façade | 03 View from campus | 04 Ground floor plan

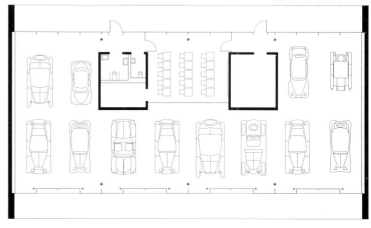

04

01

Vogt House

This house is located at the base of a hill in the middle of Balzers in Liechtenstein, near a castle, a church, and very high mountains. All these important elements are linked with the building through the openings in the strong concrete structure. The layout of the house centers around an open patio, to protect the inner living space from the street and the other buildings. The material is black concrete and the color is the same as the stone of the hill.

01 View from street | 02 Internal patio | 03 Living room with mezzanine | 04 Floor plan

02

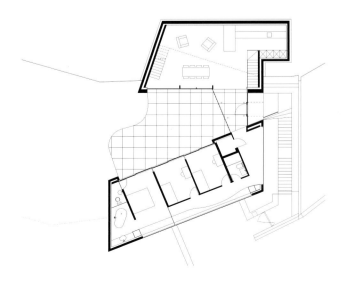

03

04

01

House on Rebberg

This hillside house is distinguished by three very distinctive stories. The basement is dictated by the topography. A wall, cut into the slope, extends along a forecourt and leads inside, turning into a roughly rendered spiral stairwell. The ground floor opens out into a generous living room with floor-to-ceiling sliding windows that provide views over the extensive terrace to the hilly landscape beyond. Minimalist architectural and structural elements strengthen the sense of continuity between inside and out. A narrow staircase leads to the upper floor, with its individual private rooms. The rambling room design is reflected in the façade, with its openings of various sizes set at different heights in the roughly rendered walls.

01 Exterior view | 02 Terrace | 03 Living room | 04 First floor plan

02

03

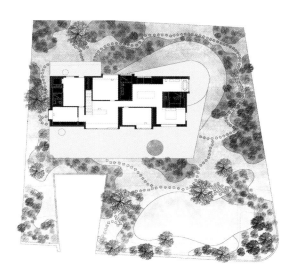

04

01

Spa Resort Tschuggen Bergoase

The "Bergoase" spa resort in Arosa, Graubünden, stands in a natural basin next to the pre-existing Tschuggen Hotel; the two are linked together by means of a glass walkway. The aim was to affirm the presence of the new structure only through the nine skylights, which become unmistakable signs of the big volume underground. The four levels of the hypogeal space correspond to the different functions required by the program. The modular design permits the distribution and interrelation of the different parts with the utmost flexibility: the fitness facilities are on the ground floor, the treatment areas on the first floor, the so-called 'sauna world' is on the second floor, while the swimming pools are situated on the third floor.

01 Snowy landscape | 02 Swimming pool | 03 Site plan | 04 Night view of the building

02

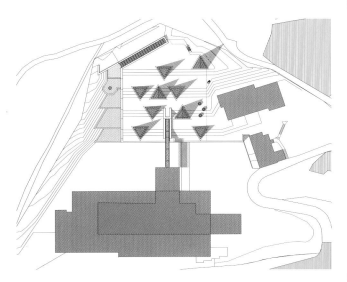

03

04

01

02

03

04

Tamina Thermal Bath

The project for the Tamina Thermal Bath is the result of a two-stage competition from 2003, won by Smolenicky & Partner Architektur. Instead of being freestanding, the form of the building volume emerges from the enclosing of exterior spaces. In the area of the open-air baths, the volume of the building is stepped back and opens out the sunbathing lawn and to the wooded slopes of the mountain ridge. The cultural and aesthetic identity of the project seeks an affinity to both Swiss tradition Iend the grand hotels of the Baltic coast. The thermal baths are intended to relativize the almost 'urban' stonework character of the spa spring hall. This explains the snow-white woodwork of the thermal baths, lending it the pavilion-like character of the architecture of a historical holiday resort.

01 Open entrance pavilion | 02 Seating area in pavilion | 03 Indoor pool | 04 Outside pool at night | 05 Cross section

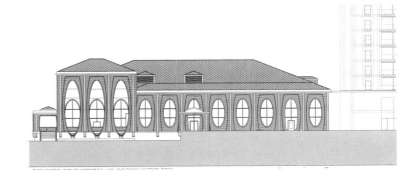

05

01

02

Laboratory Building

This research and production site in Basel for the pharmaceutical company Novartis is currently being transformed into a new campus, based on a masterplan by Vittorio Magnago Lampugnani. David Chipperfield Architects is responsible for the design of a five-story laboratory building. The first volume, completed in 2010, has a cubic form with a deep plan; creating an open square together with a second L-shaped building. The façade, made out of precast concrete elements, together with the two building cores and the concrete beams, provides the supporting structure and allows for a flexible column-free floor plan. An open garden courtyard on the fourth floor accommodates the permanent installation "Molecular (BASEL)" by the artist Serge Spitzer.

01 South view | 02 West view | 03 Isometry | 04 Art installation "Molecular (BASEL)" | 05 Restaurant | 06 West view, entrance level with colonnade

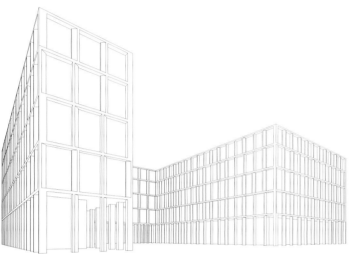

03

04

05

06

01

02

03

04

05

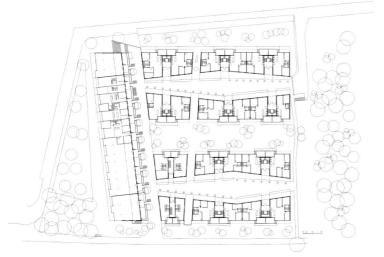

06

House Complex Weissenstein

On the border between Berne and Köniz lies an empty area of fallow land between the two city centers. New housing creates a separate living area with its own architectural language and its own range of exciting outdoor spaces. Private garden areas and shared courtyards, as well as a settlement site, structure the complex. The living space is continuous and links the courtyard with the garden. The kitchen can be used opened or closed and the flexible design permits different arrangements of the dining and living areas. A balcony or a patio offers private outdoor space, while a courtyard terrace or a floor-to-ceiling French window enables a direct connection with the courtyard.

01 Courtyard 1 with building project | 02 Access to courtyards 1 and 2 | 03 Balcony | 04 Façade with garden | 05 Interior with kitchen | 06 Site plan with ground floor plan

01

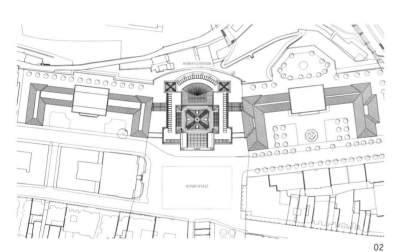

02

03

Modification and Improvement Houses of Parliament

This parliament building was built by architect Wilhelm Auer and is one part of a larger building complex. This renovation was the first comprehensive regeneration of the building since it was first opened in 1902. The beginning of the renovation project focused on exposing the hidden qualities of the building and allowing the historic exterior to shine with a new freshness. In addition to restoration and reconstruction, some areas were also completely rebuilt or newly constructed in order to meet modern building requirements. These procedures were designed in line with Auer's concepts for the building. Uniformity has been given to the old and the new, a unity that symbolizes the power of the building and the democratic understanding of the state.

01 North façade from Bundesplatz | 02 Site plan | 03 Staircase with the new elevator | 04 Multifunctional media room | 05 Cupola | 06 Visitor entrance

04

05

06

01

02

Renovation and Extension of Rossfeld Residential School

The aim of this project was to renovate and extend this boarding school for disabled children. The three main buildings were left relatively untouched, although the lighting was improved and the reduced architecture of the old building was returned to its former prestige. The main goal of this renovation focused on the need to create more space for classrooms and also on making them more attractive. The existing, elongated building was demolished and replaced with a new building. This is pavilion-like in form and also traces the streetscape and an architectonic relationship to the nearby church. The division between school and group rooms and the living and therapy areas were also clarified. Particular attention was paid to the basement levels, which were made fully functional by the introduction of new, large windows.

01 Exterior view | 02 Corridor | 03 Classroom | 04 Corridor with staircase | 05 Section

03

04

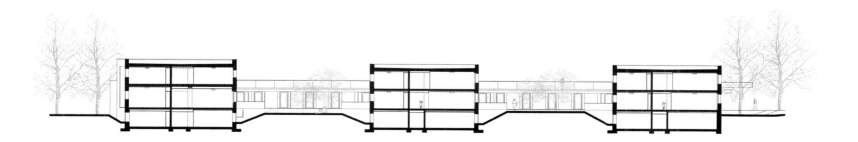

05

01

Family House on Altenberg

The slim form of this building has been pushed back close to the supporting wall. The building's footprint has also been minimized, to cause the minimum amount of discription to the attractive garden. The standard internal organization of a typical family house – lower, living; upper, sleeping – has been turned on its head, so that the inhabitants can make the most of the view of Berne's Old City. The reverse entrance on the ground floor opens out above in the main areas and connects both functional areas. A greened pitched roof keeps the rear roofline low and increases the effect of the glass front. The red lacquered metal grille creates a poetic element in the strong concrete structure.

01 Exterior view at night | 02 Living room with kitchen | 03 Bathroom | 04 Section

02

03

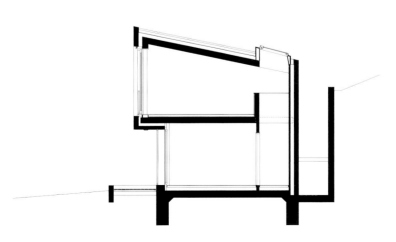

04

01

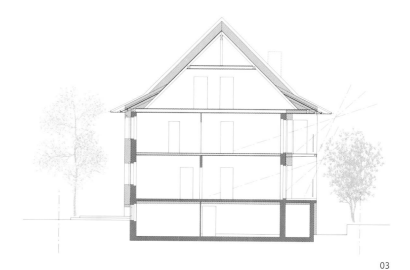

02

Renovation Sulgenheimweg House

A new façade has been developed for an existing, freestanding building with a high quality interior. The design pays more attention to the management of natural daylight, while also affording a better quality of living through an extremely well insulated building envelope. The new large window openings allow more daylight to stream in to the previously dark rooms and promote the passive use of solar energy. The kitchen and dining areas are joined by means of a new staircase, to the open-plan garden. The renovation concept, with its solar and ventilation system, reaches the passive house standard, Minergie-P, for old buildings.

01 Dining room | 02 Bedroom | 03 Section | 04 Exterior view

03

04

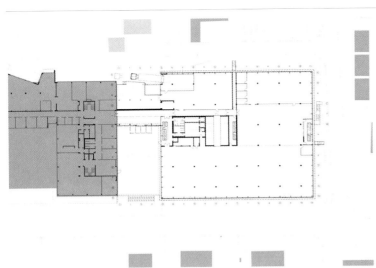

01

02

Hamilton Bonaduz AG

The main architectural idea of this design focused on extending the Hamilton Bonaduz AG complex and designing a building that, despite its size, still appears light, transparent, timeless and elegant. The full-height glazing and the sophisticated, horizontally structured façade are the primary elements that take the dominance from the cube shape and optimize integration into the building complex. The building's four floors are designed with a flexible internal structure, organized to match the various work processes. The high quality post and beam construction in steel and glass allows a maximum amount of daylight and meets the standard Minergie requirements.

01 Ground floor plan | 02 Exterior at dusk | 03 Connection element | 04 Office area |
05 Façade with windows opened | 06 Façade with windows closed | 07 Façade at night

03

04

05

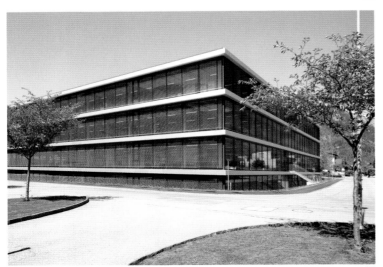

06

07

01

Family House Ruchenbergstrasse

The three different levels of this building are organized into the site plan and stacked one above the other, forming a unified concrete sculptural form. The lower level is built into the slope of the site and, together with the pool, builds a platform for the living area on the ground floor. This consists of a retaining space, which connects the interior to the exterior. The size of the upper floor is determined by the site boundaries – the interior geometry follows that of the ground floor, creating interesting spatial effects and structures. The use of in-situ concrete with two different types of formwork and the differing surface structure that this creates connects the different levels together to form a unified whole and supports the sculptural nature of the building.

01 West view | 02 Pool | 03 Dining room | 04 Ground floor plan

02

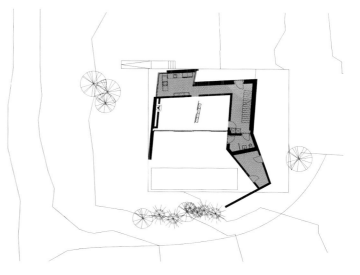

03

04

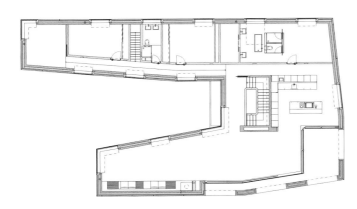

01

02

House in Canton Aargau

The starting point of the design concept was to model the building on the cubic nature of the site. One volume was developed, the center of which was then divided into two building sections of different sizes. The materiality of the façade underlines this characteristic. A latex matrix supplied the form of the black, precast concrete, generating an irregular surface structure. The structure of the heavy concrete elements is interrupted by the exterior window elements, which cut into the volume and make the strength of the walls visible.

01 First floor plan | 02 View of dining area and staircase | 03 Façade detail | 04 Exterior with patio

03

04

01

02

Cafeteria and Media Center

The extension of the 1933 Frank Wedekind House entwines itself with the existing building and accommodates the extended park area. The combination of old and new is portrayed in the interior space, the form of which extends across both building sections. The façade was also developed from this concept. The building base is made from colored and smoothed in-situ concrete, which continues the concrete base of the old building. On the upper levels, the limestone façade of the old building is continued on the new structure. Story-high, pre-made concrete elements are refined by the limestone and enclose the differing volume of the new building.

01 Northwest view | 02 Extension | 03 Interior media center | 04 First floor plan

03

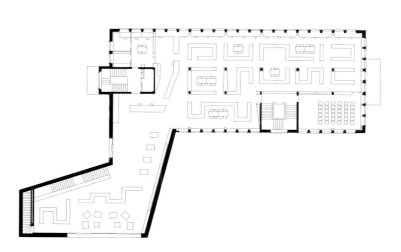

04

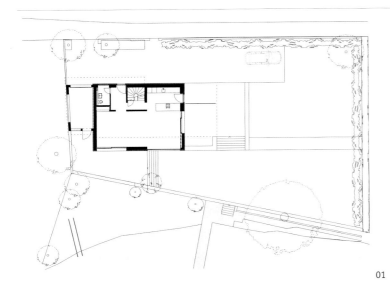

01

02

03

Lake House

The starting point for this project was a plot of land with an existing family house. This situation presented the challenge of accommodating the restrictive requirements of the authorities, while at the same time serving the wishes of the client. A partial demolition and reconstruction were granted, which in reality allowed the creation of a new building. The entire main building, except for the ground floor, has been completely renovated or restored. A wood-system construction provides the house with a projecting upper floor and a façade of wooden slats has been added. The ground floor is formulated as an open space, with a weather protected terrace. The house is Minergie certified and uses geothermal energy and comfort ventilation. The exterior space uses materials, cultivation and lighting that work in accordance with the building.

01 Floor plan garden level | 02 Exterior view | 03 Dining room | 04 View towards lake

04

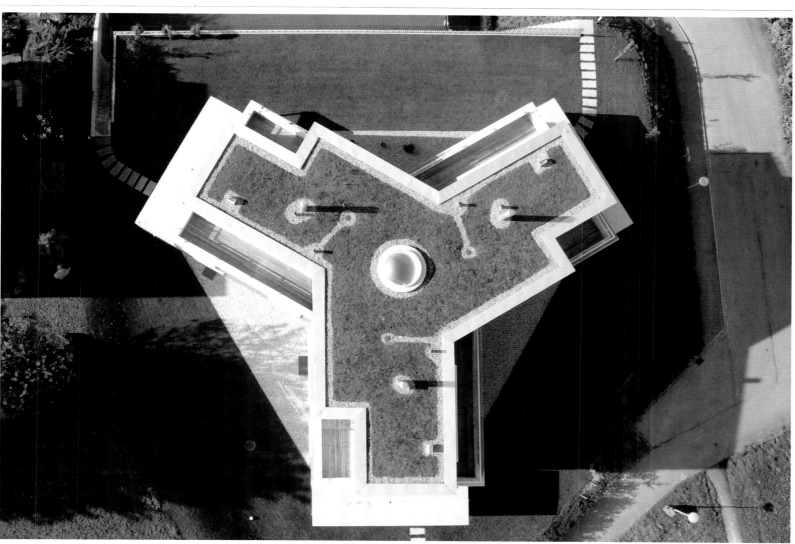

01

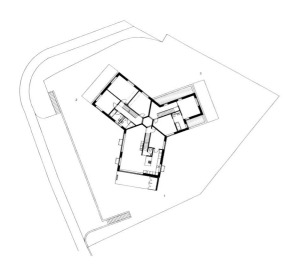

02

Trident – Three Family Houses

This plot of land is raised on an end moraine, where the highest point offers fantastic 360 degree views. The idea of combining the three existing family houses, each with a 120 degree view, into one multiple-family house proved, in terms of the relationship between site and residence and planning, to be ideal. The three houses benefit from being merged together but still obtain their own autonomy. The units are identical and are situated around a common courtyard. The entrance level offers communal access as well as direct access from the garages. The Minergie certified building has a compact exterior façade with flush metal windows in different formats. The building's exterior is built to a high standard and the color scheme is discrete.

01 Bird's-eye view | 02 Combination of ground floor plan, first floor plan and attic | 03 Exterior view | 04 Kitchen

03   04

01

Summer House

During the construction of this summer house in Kanton Thurgau, a light wooden structure was decided upon. This choice was taken because the previous house built on the site was too heavy and sank into the marshland. The structure of the new building allows for a smaller foundation pile, in addition to this, eight columns of larch wood have been used as supports. These supports carry the roof, which is covered with a hollow wooden box. The A-shaped wall sections help to support the roof and make the upper floor solid. The larch wood columns are visible, the less-prominent woodwork is stained a darker color and the weather-exposed façade of the upper level is covered with steel sheet.

01 Summer house on the moor | 02 Elevation | 03 Front view | 04 Living room | 05 Corridor

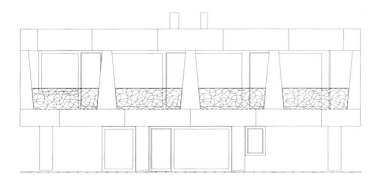

02

03

04

05

01

02

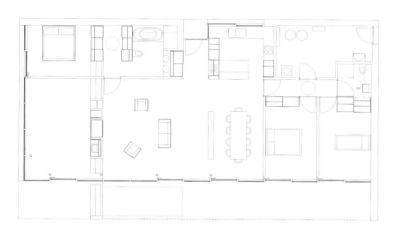

03

04

Les Grèves House

This site, with a population of mature trees, lies in a prime location between the street and the Neuchâtel Lake. The floor plan of the villa consists of two L-shapes – one L is made of concrete and functions to distinguish the premises from both the street and the neighboring property; the second L is glazed, allowing a view over the lake. A few shallow steps adapt the building to the gently sloping site. In terms of its typology, the building takes the lightweight appearance of a pavilion while reduction characterizes both its appearance and materiality. The structure is made of exposed concrete and the floors are of slate. The interior design is consistent with the exterior: the deliberate focus on what is essential continues inside, where light is permitted to play the main role.

01 Side view | 02 Workshop with fireplace | 03 Ground floor plan | 04 Main façade |
05 Living room | 06 Frontal view

05

06

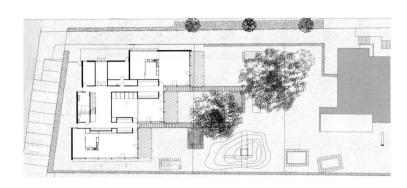

01

New Building, Double Kindergarten

This kindergarten is closed protectively towards the street side but opens out towards the garden, inviting the morning sun into the three group rooms. Inside, meandering walls create different spatial situations with niches and ceiling lights, through a series of different ceiling heights. The three volumes are staggered in height, each with a spatial relationship to its neighbor. They are situated towards the south, capturing light through their offset positioning. The group rooms in the middle can be combined to serve as a third kindergarten. All main buildings are separated from each other by corridors and additional rooms. The path from the building ensemble continues into the garden to the covered terrace, flowerbed, play-hills and large trees.

01 Ground floor plan in site plan | 02 Detail façade | 03 Foyer | 04 Street facing façade

02

03

04

01

Lankenberg

This house is a contemporary multipurpose building nestled against the hillside. It is notable for its use of sustainable design as well as for the stunning views of the lake. The site covers approximately 900 square meters; a third of which is devoted to the high-perched house. The structure is oriented northwards facing the lake, while following the contours of the land. The structure's northern orientation also reduces the solar impact on the glass. Its southern elevations are almost entirely enclosed by the hillside, while skylights allow daylight to penetrate deep into the building. The firm additionally specified a number of sustainable materials such as low-E glass and PU surfacing.

01 Exterior at night | 02 Interior staircase | 03 Kitchen | 04 Outdoor pool | 05 Site plan | 06 Section

02

03

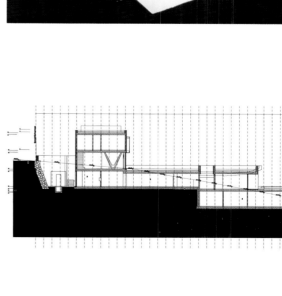

04

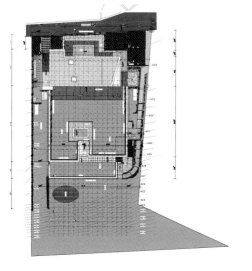

05

06

01

02

New Building Hotel, UBS Training Center Wolfsberg

This U-shaped building surrounds a large courtyard space and replaces a former inn. The three-story building connects seamlessly to the existing building, which houses a large, brick swimming pool and the central congress room. Horizontal bands of dark-gray concrete on the façade separate the stories from each other and emphasize the horizontal lines of the building. A gallery-like terrace on each floor gives the rooms an especially light, transparent quality. An open connection to outside space, the view of the lake and the green oasis of the interior courtyard, together with a simple, yet high-quality interior determine the visitor's sense of well-being.

01 North view | 02 View to courtyard | 03 Foyer and visitors' area | 04 Site plan

03

04

01

Waterflux Museum of Ice

This project involved the design of a building for an art museum/alpine ice research station. R&Sie(n) sought to combine organic forms and materials with a fantastical design. Cavities have been scooped out of the volume, as if it were an ice block. The construction of the building will use computer numerical control drilling, which will manufacture 180 pieces of wood; these will be assembled on site. The finished building will look like a chiseled piece of ice, responding harmoniously to the environment.

01 Exterior view | 02 Front view | 03 Rear view | 04 Site plan

02

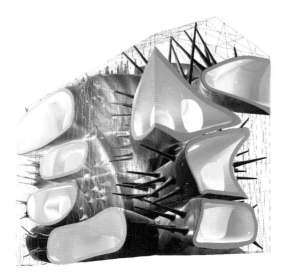

03

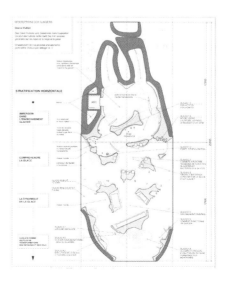

04

01

Chairlift Mutta Rodunda Weisse Arena Flims Laax Falera

"Reduce to the max" was the key phrase behind this design. The new construction involved replacing three ski lifts. The architecture of the lift station building is dominated by wood and concrete and takes a clear, angular form. The station at the bottom of the valley is clad in wood and reminiscent of the traditional building style of the region, the wooden cladding also relates to the building's function as storage space for the ski lifts. The building on the mountain-top gives the impression of strength, relating to its function as the control building for the ski lifts. The expressive form, as the only creative building in the landscape, creates an intense contrast to the raw mountain world.

01 Mountain station | 02 Sketch mountain station | 03 Section | 04 Detail valley station | 05 Floor plan mountain station | 06 Valley station

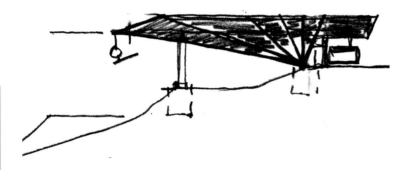

02

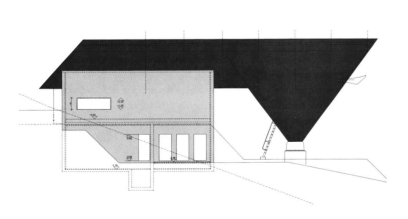

03

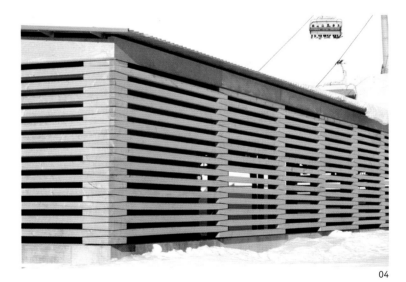

04

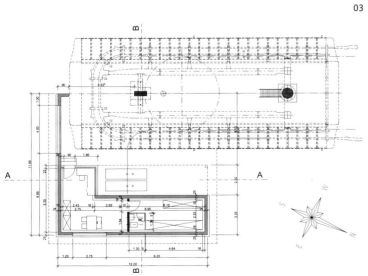

05

06

01

02

03

Extension Kunsthaus

A slightly meandering, single-story building; this structure has a façade of woven steel bands and is situated on the site of an old washhouse. The design defines the surrounding architecture of the Bahnhofstrasse and also shows a clear respect for the existing art gallery, lying to the northwest. The mobile walls of this new, ground level, column-free exhibition space, are extremely flexible, providing a range of display possibilities for temporary exhibitions. The garden door permits views over the sculpture garden and also allows for exhibitions combined with open space.

01 Exterior view | 02 Exhibition room | 03 Courtyard | 04 Entrance | 05 Longitudinal section

04

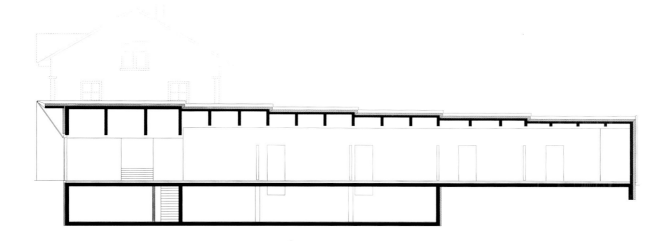

05

01

02

03

Single Family Home S·10

This house is located on a gently sloping site, with views of the Bernese Highlands in the Alps. The living area is accessed at ground level from the street while the garden-level provides space for bedrooms, offering a direct view of the swimming pool. Two L-shaped constructions of exposed concrete define the form of the façade, while the position, sequence and layering of the wall panels determine the interior design. The interior and exterior are connected by floor to ceiling glazing and the covered, elongated terraces. The large interior space emphasizes the contrast between the huge concrete walls and the lightweight quality of the glazing.

01 North façade | 02 Living room | 03 Exterior view with glass façade | 04 Longitudinal section

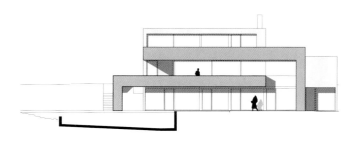

04

01

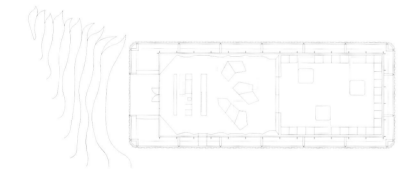

iHomeLab, Lucerne University Technique & Architecture

The iHomeLab is an independent Swiss think-tank and research laboratory for 'intelligent living'. An encounter with the iHomeLab should be an enduring experience. The façade serves as a metaphor for the inner workings of the iHomeLab. Proactively recorded and provoking a reaction from the visitors, the building shell is a signal of the function for the subject of intelligent living. A virtual assistant guides visitors through different areas, starting for example at a wall-length presentation. After this audiovisual introduction, the doors are opened to the 'treasure chamber' of the iHomeLab; the research lab is divided into three cubes, focusing on the core themes of security, energy and comfort.

01 Exterior view at night | 02 Ground floor plan | 03 Façade, vertical blinds open | 04 Interior view lounge and laboratory

02

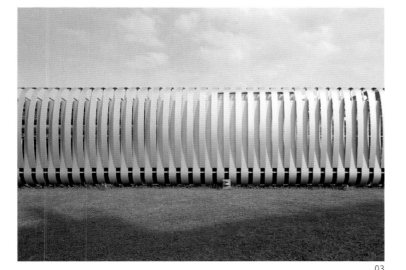

03

04

01

02

03

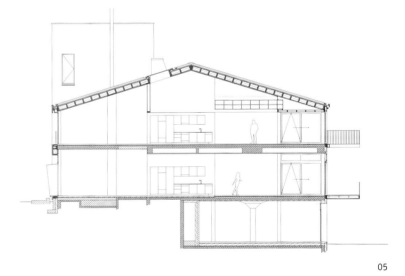

04

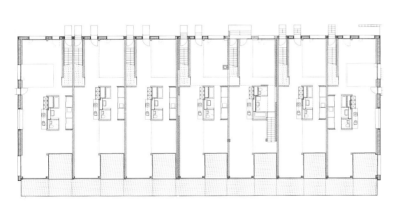

05

06

Loft Apartments Alte Sagi Innerberg

In Innerberg, this former sawmill has been converted into an apartment building. The height of the building and the room height of over three meters establish the identity and character of the residential units. The distinct floor plan concept offers unusual flexibility. The kitchen and bathroom together create the structural core. Anything is possible, from loft space to three-room apartments. A seasonal room increases the flexibility of the additional space. With controlled ventilation, solar powered heating, a compact volume and passive sun protection, the house uses very little additional energy and achieves the Swiss Minergie passiv standard.

01 Façade and balconies | 02 Loft units | 03 Three-story apartment | 04 Ground floor plan | 05 Cross section | 06 Side view

01

Double Kindergarten Itingen

The challenge in designing this building was to integrate a 600-square meter property into a residential area of family homes. This was achieved by structuring the new building into large and small volumes; the red cubes of the design are reminiscent of children's building blocks. The volumes are organized so that, when necessary, the building can be extended by an area of 200 square meters for a possible future kindergarten or school classes. A large entrance and cloakroom are situated between the individual buildings. The structure boasts an insulated building envelope and controlled ventilation with waste heat recovery; these measures resulted in it obtaining the Minergie certificate in 2009.

01 Exterior view | 02 Cloakroom | 03 Ground floor plan | 04 Center room | 05 Corridor

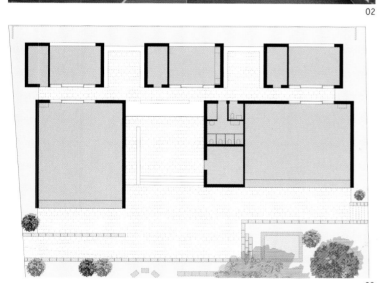

02

03

04

05

01

02

03

04

05

Le Monolithe et la Grange

Built in the Vaud countryside, on the edge of a forest, this home offers a sensitive solution to the client's desire to create a building that shares a dialogue with the surrounding landscape. The design should preserve the spirit of the place and meet the binding regulations of the building authority. The building must care for the environment as well as respect the proposed budget. The project was born from the idea of placing a box-type structure under a traditional barn roof. Larch wood was used for the house while the supporting posts are made of bamboo. Hot water is supplied to the house by energy from solar panels.

01 Entrance | 02 Southwest façade | 03 Northwest façade | 04 Mezzanine | 05 Northwest façade detail | 06 Ground floor and first floor plan

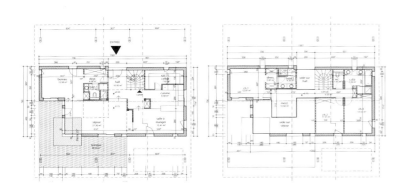

06

01

02

03

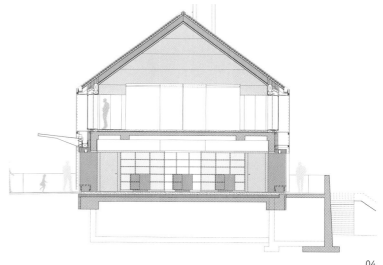

04

Rhine Falls Visitor Center

Located in Canton Zurich, the Rhine Falls Visitor Center defines the entry to Laufen castle and the pathway leading to Europe's largest waterfall. The program required the integration of a souvenir shop, bistro, public toilet facilities and a multipurpose hall into an existing staff house. The difficult task of transforming the nondescript house into a public building was achieved by extending the pitched roof and developing a new skin that wraps the entire structure. The new façade, made of weatherproof steel plates, forms a suit of armor which unifies the building into a primary form. On the ground level, folded canopies reveal a second layer with entries, vitrines and a ticket counter. The perforated steel elements on the upper level filter sunlight into the multipurpose hall.

01 Double façade | 02 Façade detail | 03 View from southwest | 04 Section hall and shop | 05 Multipurpose hall with felt-lined roof

05

01

02

03

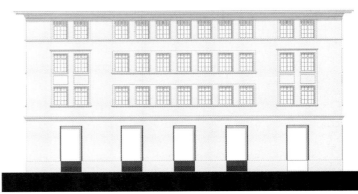

04

Port-Franc 9

This renovation project was carried out on an old building located in the district of Flon in Lausanne. A previous project on this site included the replacement of the original windows with insulating glass. This time, the new project involved rethinking the spaces on the ground floor in order to best meet the requirements for their new commercial use. This implied a reflection on the degree of openness required for such surfaces: maximum aperture guaranteeing full visibility of products, or selective openings respecting the character of the old warehouses? The strategy adopted includes openings that are generous, but that nevertheless respect the structural logic and method of construction of the building.

01 South view | 02 North view | 03 Detail of steel frame | 04 Rhythm of metallic boxes | 05 Elevation

05

01

02

Two Family House

This previously unused plot of land is situated directly at the edge of the wood, at the top of the garden city quarter of Köniz. The building code requirements, with regard to volume and design, were limiting. This led to a compact layout, which developed from the central access, resulting in a typologically 'garden-city' conceptual approach. Staggered levels complement the sloping terrain and allow for an exciting sequence of rooms and vistas. A finely-plastered façade with large, staggered window openings, coupled with the simple building volume and the flush pitched roof create a modern, urban building.

01 Exterior view | 02 Ground floor plan | 03 Living room | 04 Kitchen

03

04

01

02

03

04

05

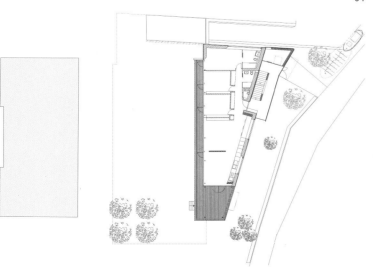

06

Multi-family House Gebhartstrasse

This wooden house nestles into the existing structure of the district, taking its form from the small, trapezoidal plot of land. The load-bearing façade design allows for a free, loft-like division of the interior space and demonstrates a unique, bright approach to individual adaptable spatial experience. The three levels are joined by an open stair-well which, together with the plumbing system, forms a static core in the otherwise 'fluid' space. The use of wood made a light, transparent façade design possible. To the south, the glass façade opens to the loggia completely. Wooden blinds act as filters on the west façade and depending on the wish of the residents the façade appears more or less closed.

01 Open stairwell | 02 Exterior view at night | 03 Façade, wooden blinds open | 04 Interior | 05 Façade, wooden blinds partly closed | 06 Ground floor plan

01

House in Graubünden

This house appears as an ensemble of several parts, stacked behind and over each other. The concept of layered units was inspired by the rising course of the surrounding terrain. The impressive building with its sloping roof references the mountain range in the background. Inside, the house is surprisingly open and coherent. Different room heights, sloping ceilings and hidden nooks allow for moments of surprise and an unexpectedly atmospheric space. The house offers an open, happy experience: a lot of art, cultures, family and friends. This is a cosmopolitan house, situated within the beauty and silence of the Swiss Alps.

01 Exterior with Alps | 02 Kitchen | 03 Dining room | 04 Ground floor plan

02

03

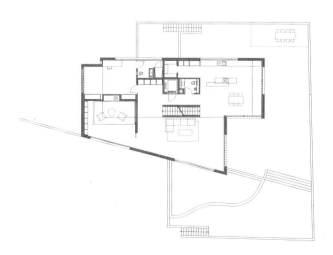

04

01

Reflection Room Boldern

The reflection room of Boldern Study Center is a mysterious-looking, concrete sculpture with a closed appearance, placed between different types of buildings. Two intertwined, hyperbolic concrete walls lie protectively around an amorphous interior; the room sculpture reveals itself out of the movement. A compact entrance leads from the busy outside world in a meditative inner world. Reduced to a minimum, the openings are not visible between the components. The contemplative atmosphere is determined by changing rays of light. A continuous bench leads visitors from the reflection room to a screened gravel area.

01 Interior view | 02 South view | 03 West view at night | 04 Floor plan

02

03

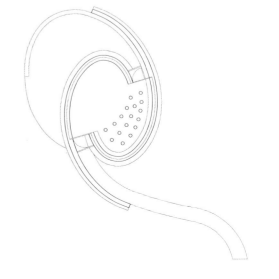

04

01

02

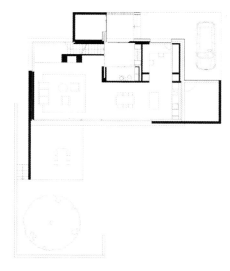

04

03

05

House in Haslital

This archaic stone house lies in the green fields and looks as if it has simply broken off the nearby rocky cliffs. The use of stone and wood shows a clear reference to the nearby boulder-strewn mountain forest. The house gives the impression of silence, strength and indestructability. The living and bedrooms are positioned to make the most of the view and have been given large windows, while the other rooms have just single windows. The magnificent landscape is captured and framed like a picture. An ensemble of wing and retaining walls connect the building to the stepped terrain, creating level spaces and offering protection from the wind.

01 Southwest façade | 02 Living room | 03 Northeast façade | 04 Ground floor plan | 05 Entrance

01

02

03

04

House on Lake Biel

This house is located on the south side of Lake Biel, in close proximity to a villa designed in the 1970s by the architect Fritz Haller. The views across the lake landscape, the Jura Mountains with their vineyards and the moorland conservation area are breathtaking. Nature and the adjacent villa were defining elements for the architects when drafting the design concept. On the ground floor, the theme of flowing space clearly relates to the spatial concept of the adjacent villa and also strengthens connections to exterior areas and the stunning views of the surrounding landscape.

01 Exterior with pool | 02 Entrance with bamboo garden | 03 Exterior with Zen garden | 04 Seating area | 05 Sections

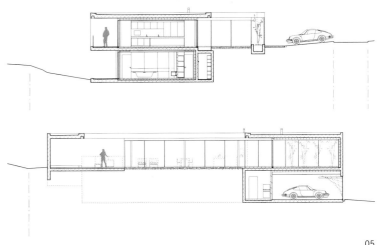

05

01

Campus Arc 1

This educational building is located in close proximity to the railway line and hosts two different institutions. The building consists of three main elements; a main wing; a kind of 'backbone' with four levels featuring two-story, transparent openings, which help to structure the main wing; and a two-story structure, with volumes that interlock into the wing. The rear side of the building is marked by a clear boundary to the railway building and structures the district's central square with its overhanging volume. The building has a high-quality thermal envelope. A controlled air replacement system functions in winter. These options reduce heat loss and cut heating needs. The controlled air replacement system guarantees a constant supply of fresh air without reliance on opening windows and thus efficiently manages external noise disturbance from the urban context.

01 Section | 02 North view | 03 Transparent openings | 04 Square in front of the building | 05 Aerial view of Ecoparc district

02

03

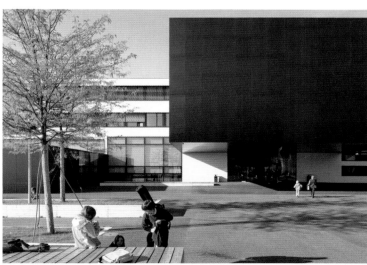

04

05

01

02

BKW Office Building Nidau

This mixed-use building from the 1970s has been converted into a highly flexible office building. Various firms within the BKW use the open and closed office levels. The central hall is located on the ground floor and is a central hub of the building. The urban character of the new façade responds to the future development of the city and marks the entrance to the entire complex. In accordance with the philosophy of the BKW energy company, the building envelope and utilities were all built to the highest standard. Transparency and unity of the design of the façade and interior work together to create a harmonious whole.

01 Exterior view with main entrance | 02 Site plan | 03 Exterior with floating roof | 04 Corridor

03

04

01

02

03

04

Giraffe House and Enclosure, Knies Children's Zoo

The curved, cantilevered roof of this giraffe house acts as a prominent symbol, positioned near the entrance of the zoo. The giraffe house continues the zoo's tradition of expressive architecture, which has always been considered as an important part of the zoo experience. Furthermore, the structure is reminiscent of both the tops of the acacia tree and the curved horns of Watussi cattles, who share the area with the giraffes, zebras and guinea fowl. Inside the enclosure, the air is fresh, dust free and lit with natural light, a minimum temperature of 15 degrees celsius is maintained for the health of the animals. The enclosure is heated and has little in common with a traditional stable.

01 Exterior view with enclosure | 02 Interior | 03 Exterior view | 04 Detail | 05 Section

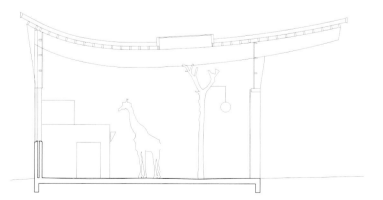

05

01

02

03

04

Convention Center

This project involved the new construction of a monolithic concrete building and renovation works in the basement, concerning the historic vaulted wine cellar of the ancient hotel, that was consumed by fire years ago. The ancient part was restored, changed to a wine and cigar lounge, as well as being extended and opened to the atrium. Featuring a waterpool, a cascade and covered with a glass dome, this area with its total height of 13 meters and multilevel in-and-outside views, is used multifunctional as lobby, bar and exhibition area. Behind the spacious kitchen area, the VIP-dining area offers direct views to the work space of the famous maitre de cuisine. The large and divisible ballroom is fully glazed both to the landscape and the atrium same for the conference rooms on the second floor, which can be reached from the atrium or a separate entrance.

01 Entrance area | 02 Glass buildings in the garden | 03 Main entrance from Landstrasse | 04 View from the show kitchen to the VIP lounge | 05 Section

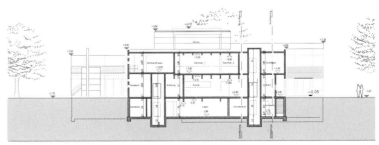

05

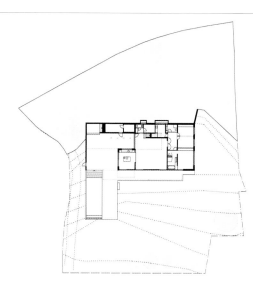

01

Family House in Savièse

This villa is built on gently sloping terrain, facing south and overlooking the Rhone Valley. The house is arranged on two levels. Outdoor spaces are treated as extensions of the interior and defined by white concrete walls, which emphasize unity and spatial continuity. The house is built back into the slope and has a large swimming pool surrounded by a wooden terrace. The spacious house is comprised of a generously sized kitchen, living room, dining room, three bedrooms, an office, utility rooms and a double garage.

01 Floor plan | 02 Interior view | 03 Glazed areas offer views of surroundings | 04 Exterior view | 05 Pool | 06 Rear view

02

03

04

05

06

01

Künzle-Heim Schaffhausen

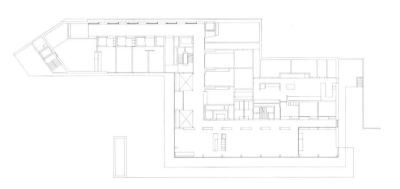

After the demolition of the existing building a new 60-room, Z-shaped volume has been developed in the middle of the park. The residential home for senior citizens is accessible from all sides, surrounded by various, multi-purpose outdoor spaces. Many of the individually designed rooms are fitted with bathrooms with disabled access. Two-room apartments have been furnished to suit couples, each equipped with a small kitchen. The well-insulated wooden façade is protected by a projecting overhang and its appearance changes depending on the light. The building has been fitted with both solar and photovoltaic systems.

01 Ground floor cafeteria | 02 Ground floor plan | 03 Terrace | 04 Rhythmic corridor

02

03

04

01

Natural Stone House in Sent

This freestanding, three-story family house is situated above the village of Sent in Lower Engadine, close to the edge of the forest. The house is a stone clad, cube shape, with a solid shell of two layers: interior of exposed concrete, exterior of stone. The metal roof is a typical architectural feature of this area and the decision to not allow a roof overhang strengthens the clear geometry of the cube. The windows are cut deeply into the façade and a large corner in the lower level has been cut out of the stone shape, allowing for a large glazed area, which draws light into the building.

01 Southwest view | 02 Ground floor plan | 03 Southeast view | 04 Entrée | 05 Stairs

02

03

04

05

01

02

03

Parking de l'Europe

This car park is located at the Place de l'Europe and completes the redevelopment of the site. It is a compact volume, comprising of three underground levels, organized with staggered levels of circulating vehicle ramps, ensuring a continuous flow of traffic. Each parking level is naturally illuminated by three skylights and the building offers views of the surrounding park and garden landscape. The structure clearly defines the west area of the square and redefines the existing boundaries and connections to surrounding streets.

01 South entrance | 02 Southern stairwell | 03 Parking lot | 04 Floor plan

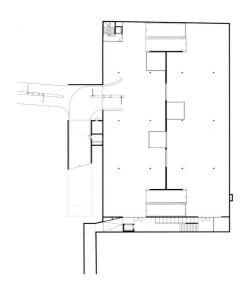

04

01

02

03

Kulturfabrik Kofmehl

The space and structure of this building are similar to the much bigger established concert halls such as Rem Koolhaas' Casa de Musica in Porto or the KKL, although the former functions rather differently: the core is a concert hall which is set as a cube within a bigger cube although structurally and acoustically separated from the latter. This configuration differs from the usual ones in as much as it prevents sound from travelling to the outside rather than the other way round. Technical appliances and air conditioning are located in the remaining space below the roof. All is housed in a cube, which is covered in steel sheets. Each side is individually designed with a few elements. The front wall is directed towards the street and is marked by eye-catching features such as the inscription and the sliding gate that seems to disconnect itself almost weightlessly from the wall.

01 North façade open | 02 Hall | 03 Fire escape | 04 Ground floor plan

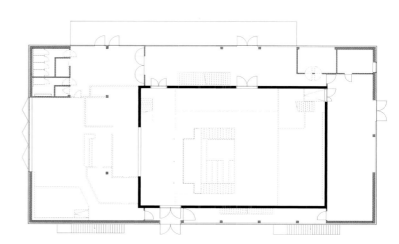

04

01

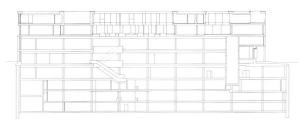

02

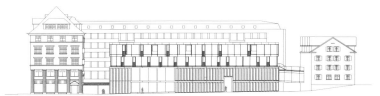

03

04

05

06

Residential and Commercial Building in Webersbleiche

The unique character of this project is achieved by the development of the block-courtyard typology, evolved from the urban fabric of medieval towns. Based on the new use, the design seeks to provide a modern response to the archetypal architecture of the town. Various courtyards arrange the urban spatial sequence from public to private exterior space. The position of the prismatic building also illustrates the irregular configuration of previous expansion work. As an 'overbuilt market hall' the specific architecture was required to work in harmony with the courtyard to the rear of the premises, developing a dialogue with its surroundings. The project has been realized in collaboration with Bollhalder und Eberle.

01 Bird's-eye view | 02 Longitudinal section and west façade | 03 West view | 04 Living room | 05 North view | 06 Shopping area

01

Viamala Road House

The façade and the structural layout of the windows allow this building to respond to the surrounding mountain silhouettes and certain attraction points in the landscape. The large-sized windows open the space to the landscape, which changes throughout the seasons. The folds of the roof structure the interior and create tensions within the space. The exterior of the building is made of folded metal, which offers a link between the building and the automobiles that it serves; the interior is lined with local timber. The deliberate contrast between inside and outside and the natural integration of the building form the great qualities of this building.

01 Exterior view at twilight | 02 Ground floor plan | 03 Gas station | 04 Rest stop dining room | 05 Bar

02

03

04

05

01

02

03

04

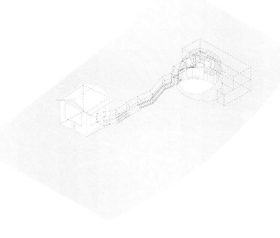

05

Villa Vals

The concept for this project was the question of how to conceal a house in an alpine slope, while still maintaining wonderful views. The introduction of a central patio into the steep incline creates a large façade with considerable potential for window openings. The viewing angle from the building is slightly inclined, providing a dramatic view of the mountains on the opposite side of the valley. The scheme was not perceived as a typical structure but rather an example of pragmatic unobtrusive development in a sensitive location. The placing of the entrance via an old Graubünder barn and an underground tunnel further convinced local planning authorities that the concept, while slightly absurd, could still be permitted.

01 Cardboard room designed by Jeroen van Mechelen, Studio JVM | 02 Exterior view in the snow | 03 Façade details, windows reflecting the mountains | 04 Exterior view | 05 Isometry

01

02

Punto Bregaglia Commercial Center

The ground plan of this design permitted the regulated arrangement of different office and retail spaces that can be altered depending on demand. To achieve maximum flexibility, the exterior supporting walls and the interior dividing walls between the functional space and the circulation areas have been reduced. The building envelope has been constructed with cross-shaped supports; this strengthens the structure and makes it more solid. Because of the diagonal crosses and the glazing on the façade, the building offers a strong contrast to the surrounding architecture. Despite this, the use of larch wood offers enough similarity to the area's architecture to allow for some unity.

01 Southeast view | 02 Detail | 03 Section

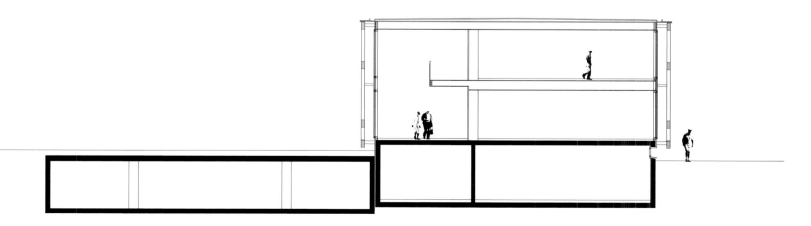

03

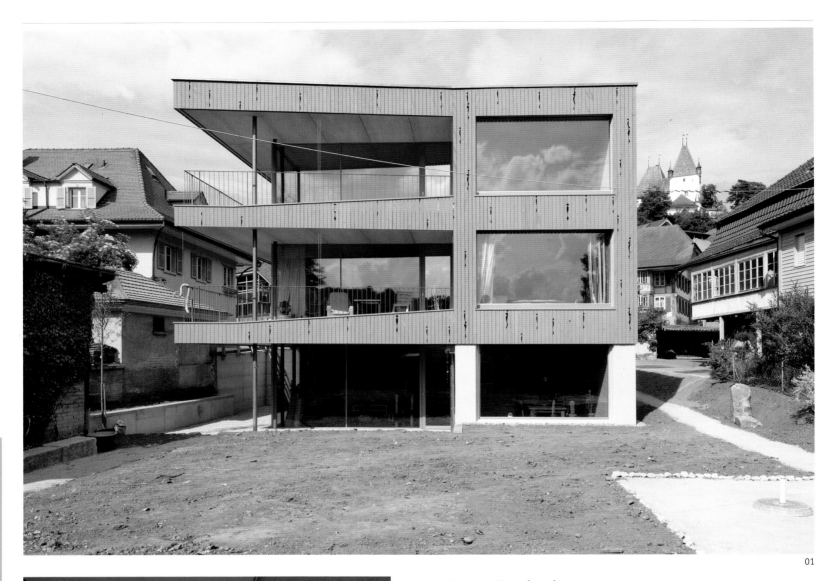

01

House Enggisteinstrasse

After a fire destroyed the original, the ensemble of historical buildings surrounding the nearby church had to be completed with a new building. It acts as an important space forming element and, being built of wood, adopts the traditional building style of the area. However, the cubic form of the structure functions to highlight its modernity. The three apartments have flexible, divisible floor plans, organized around a space-forming core. The building is characterized through the interpretation of site-specific elements, such as stairs and loggia. The perforated, painted wood façade relates to the traditional architecture of the area.

01 Exterior view | 02 Terrace | 03 Kitchen | 04 Section

02

03

04

01

02

03

04

Living and Business Building Seestrasse

The projecting building volume, with its dark façade of natural stone and large window openings, asserts itself as an elegant monolith in the heterogeneous environment. The entrance is at street level and the two upper floors offer space for offices, culminating in a 210-square meter attic apartment. On the lower level, the elegant entrance area flows smoothly into the residential and library areas, which offer views of the nearby lake. The living areas in the attic are accessed by a stairway, which leads to a large terrace with panoramic views of the landscape. The view stretches from the Glarus Alps in the south, across the lake to the Uetliberg mountain chain and towards Zurich.

01 Exterior view northwest corner | 02 Exterior view southwest corner | 03 Roof terrace |
04 Dining room and kitchen attic apartment | 05 Section

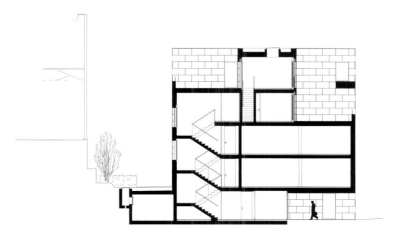

05

01

02

Schwarz Family House

This family house marks the corner location of two streets. The horizontal emphasis of the stories through prefabricated concrete elements fits the sloping site. The filler wall gives the impression of movement in the façade through the vertical folded brass panels. The stories have been twisted in their arrangement, giving the house its visual expression. An apartement was added on the garden floor to improve the view from the upper floors, raising them slightly and thus allowing a better view of the Zurich lake. The living room on the middle floor is the central place in the home. The house has been awarded with the Minergie certificate.

01 Façade detail with protective panels | 02 First floor plan | 03 Staggered levels with terraces, southwest façade | 04 Living room

03

04

01

V-ZUG Logistic Center

This project presented a challenge to the architects in that a 130-meter long logistics center with a height of 35 meters must be built within a large industrial area in the middle of the town. While the base, characterized by large delivery gates, and the over-lying level stretch across the complete building surface, the high-bay warehouse occupies just a part of the surface. The glazed high-bay warehouse assumes the color of the sky and molds optically into its surroundings. The pixelated nature of the façade creates an optical illusion; as the distance between viewer and building increase, the building appears a uniform blue, melting into the blue sky in the background.

01 Building in surroundings | 02 West façade | 03 Section | 04 View of high-bay warehouse | 05 Delivery gates below pixelated façade

02

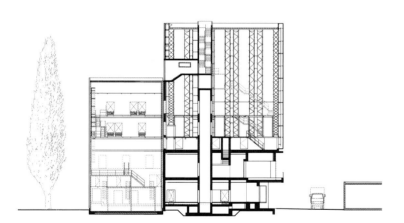

03

04

05

01

02

03

04

focusTerra

"focusTerra" is the Earth Science Research and Information Center at the Swiss Federal Institute of Technology in Zurich. The concept and design of the exhibition connect the existing historical mineralogical-geological collection with contemporary research done at the institute. The centerpiece of the exhibition is a tower located in the atrium. Analogous to the forces at work below the earth's surface, the tower spirals up three levels, reaching just below the skylight of the inner courtyard. A staircase and a continuous ribbon of showcases connect different levels of the exhibition in a seamless continuum, and guide visitors through the fascinating layers of the earth: from the dynamic processes inside the earth's core, the treasures hidden below its surface, to the intriguing archives preserved in its strata through the ages.

01 Exhibition tower in atrium | 02 Spiral staircase on level D, "Dynamics of the Earth" | 03 View into exhibition level E "Treasures of the Earth" | 04 Atrium | 05 Section

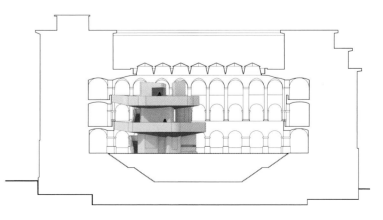

05

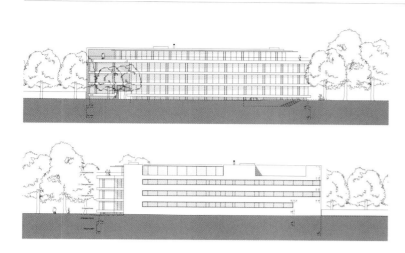

01

02

Office Building Bellerive

This area presented various challenges due to the presence of light rail and tram lines, which cut through Zurich. These surround the project's location, which at the same time offers a beautiful view of the nearby lake and mountains. The proximity of the city and the transition between the development of the block and the road design has resulted in a building with two different faces. The side facing towards the train lines appears elongated, dark and closed. The side facing the sea opens out with horizontal concrete layers and a glazed façade. The floor plan follows the line of the light-railway and the curve of the tramlines. At night, the building is illuminated and the middle story seems to float above the ground light a lantern at the entrance to the city.

01 Elevations | 02 Façade towards railway | 03 Glass façade detail | 04 Northwest view at night

03

04

01

Radisson Blu Hotel

The Radisson Blu Hotel opened on the first of August 2008 and was the first hotel situated the site of Zurich Airport, directly connected to the terminal. The building asserts itself through its strong, monolithic character and its simple façade, the dominance of which is relaxed by two multi-story loggias. Just two years after its opening – and not without thanks to the architectural presentation – the hotel, with 330 bedrooms and suites, two restaurants, numerous meeting rooms, two fitness and wellness areas and the unique 16-meter tall 'wine tower' in the atrium-lobby, has established itself as a leading business and conference hotel.

01 Frontal exterior view | 02 Interior atrium | 03 System of elevators, atrium | 04 Section

02

03

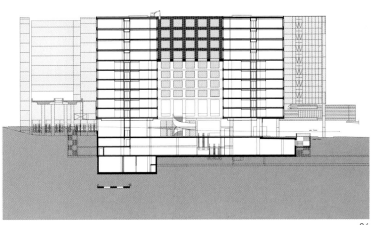

04

01

Stadion Letzigrund

The floating, far projecting steel roof of Letzigrund stadium is supported by pairs of columns and is visible from a distance. The specific inclusion of this large structure, complete with bistro and training grounds, was made possible by lowering the competition area by seven meters. The main entrance of the stadium is free of steps and opens out towards Herdernstrasse, while the rest of the area rises by 14 meters towards the west. Visitors can stroll around the stadium on a wide, gently rising gallery. From Herdernstrasse, the entire interior of the stadium can be seen. Instead of the typical arrangement of four down lights, 31 lights are used here, providing perfect lighting conditions.

01 Floating, far projecting steel roof | 02 Stadium at night with 31 lights | 03 Interior with seatings | 04 Ambulatory at night | 05 Exterior view

02

04

05

03

01

02

03

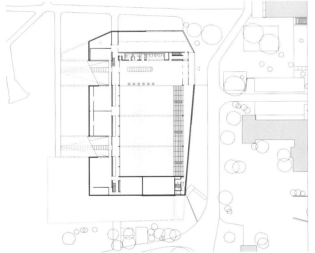

04

05

ETH Science City

Located on the Hönggerberg, on the east side of the vigorously developed campus, this new sports center formulates the transition between the campus and the surrounding landscape. A narrow, dark green glass crystal is turned towards the campus and forms the edge of the terrain. Behind this, a five-story building with a white interior is pushed back under the slope of the Käferberg, a layer of grass covering the roof. The strict horizontal character of the playing fields and their access ramps blur the boundary between building and landscape.

01 Entrance area | 02 Ramp | 03 Platform | 04 Ground floor plan | 05 Bird's-eye view | 06 Walkway

06

01

02

03

Trellis and Teahouse

Small trellis structures rearrange the rigid space situation at Zurichberg, creating a new spatial continuum with a sophisticated lighting atmosphere. Changing in structure, new recreational spaces were created. The light flowing through the trellis changes with the seasons, presenting the user with different functional alternatives. The teahouse is located on the steepest part of the site. The construction is geometric, organized in three equal arcs; this gives the room three equivalent directions: towards the city, the lake and the mountains. The interior consists of a polished walnut shell with leather Bordeaux-colored panels and a multilayered shell of folding glass and independent folding wicker frames.

01 Pergola of cedar wood | 02 Cedar wood pergola forming an arch | 03 Plan of pergola | 04 Teahouse | 05 Teahouse interior

04

05

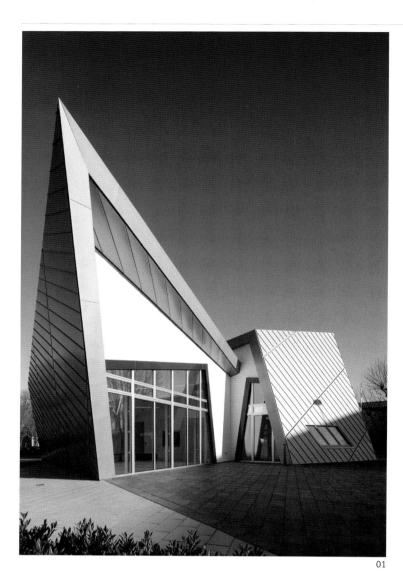

01

02

03

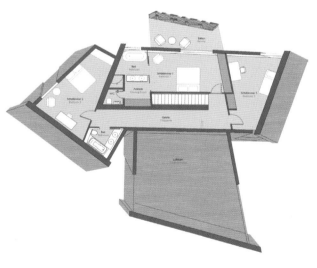

04

05

Libeskind Villa

The Libeskind Villa is a dynamic, 464-square meter signature series home that can be constructed anywhere in the world. Like a crystal growing from rock, the villa creates a new dialogue between contemporary living and a completely new experience of space. Built from premium wood and zinc, this German-made, sculptural living space meets the highest standards of design, craftsmanship and sustainability. In addition to the design standards, it complies with some of the toughest energy-saving standards worldwide. The villa awakens the senses: light floods through glass expanses, clean lines invite calm while elegant halls and staircases offer seamless transitions.

01 Exterior of prototype | 02 Front view | 03 Second floor study | 04 Second floor plan | 05 Exterior view | 06 Ground floor plan

06

01

02

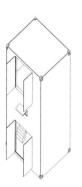  

03

HomeBox

This wooden construction has been built with the same dimensions as an internationally standardized freight container and can be transported and installed worldwide. Only the interior is different. Living within wooden walls is more comfortable and healthier than living in a building made from steel. Wood containers can be altered, adapted and converted easier and more cost-effectively than a steel container. The vertical positioning of the HomeBox allows for a small footprint and different zoning: entrance and supply units are well connected to public areas and a private lounge area, allows views out and sunlight in.

01 Front opened | 02 Front closed | 03 Opened, closed and transported box | 04 Second type - HomeBox 2

04

EASTERN EUROPE

01

02

03

04

The National Library of Belarus

The new building of the National Library of Belarus is located on the main avenue of
the capital. It has the shape of a diamond, placed in the center of the three-storied
surrounding stylobate. The main entrance is constructed in the shape of two open book
pages, which reflect the development of the world and Slavonic writing. The 20 reading rooms of the library are differentiated by materials in accordance with subject and
category. They offer 2,000 workstations, equipped with electronic circulation desks,
scanning, copying and printing devices. All reading rooms are light and comfortable, allowing a view to the riverside and the park area. The uniqueness of the library is its book
stack, which is located in the high-rise part of the building.

01 Main entrance | 02 Main atrium | 03 Illumination at night | 04 Main atrium | 05 Ground
floor plan

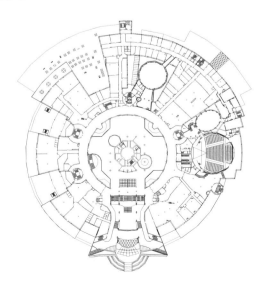

05

01

02

03

04

Conservatory House

The Conservatory House is a place for relaxation through enjoyment of natural serenity and arts. The brief called for a customized, green residence with disabled access and a large flower conservatory suitable for hosting music performances. Inspired by local trees, the new structure fills an old sand quarry pit, reinforces the terrain around it and branches out to accommodate its functions. The conservatory music room is placed on top of the residence for catching maximum sunlight and views, which become its most prominent feature. It welcomes family and guests and provides access to all levels. The utilization of an advanced geothermal system provides for all heating and cooling needs of the house and minimizes the carbon footprint.

01 Daylight flooding the interior | 02 Kitchen and dining area | 03 Exterior view | 04 Living area | 05 Axonometry

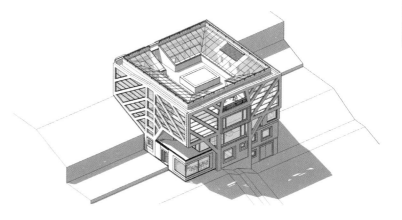

05

01

02

03

04

Church of the Brethren Church in Černošice

The House of Prayer in Černošice, Vráž is made of bricks and takes a gently waving shape. The concrete parts of the building have been left visible and the façade is continuously fluted to highlight its plasticity. The architects use the term plasticity to describe the adaptation of a building to the environment. It is a flexible reaction to the nature of the place where it is situated. Both buildings have the same program: to serve the religious and social life of the community, which is the investor. The buildings include the preacher's apartment on the second floor. Both houses were built for half of the original budget.

01 View from north | 02 View from east | 03 Internet coffee room | 04 Altar | 05 Ground floor plan

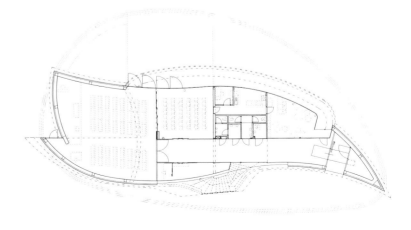

05

01

Bohemian Paradise Family House

This family house is situated in the central part of the Protected Landscape Area Bohemian Paradise. The location affected the main design concept. Influencing the integration of the house and its garden within the surrounding countryside, by using natural materials such as sandstone, merbau wood or Cembonit roofing. The concept of the house is based on the interconnection of classical forms and a modern approach. It was also necessary to follow the Protected Landscape Area regulatory requirements. The multi-generation house is designed to accomodate for large family gatherings. The interior is opened to the landscape and connects the inside and outside. Large glass windows, an outdoor kitchen, a spacious terrace with a fireplace and a pool communicate with the interior.

01 Terrace | 02 Exterior view | 03 Entrance hall | 04 Ground floor plan

02

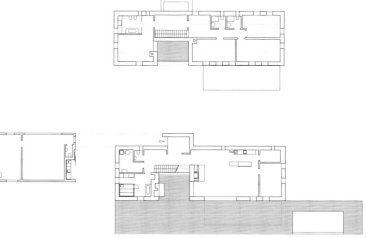

03

04

01

02

03

04

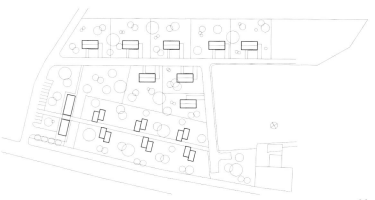

05

Bečva Villa Resort

This complex of wooden houses, available for rent, is located on a meadow in the municipality of Horní Bečva in the Beskydy protected natural area. The completed project, consisting of eight houses, 12 bungalows, an administration building, roads, green areas and other facilities presents a unified urban complex with a recreational function. The housing project makes use of traditional materials from the Beskydy region, such as wooden house constructions, wooden cladding on the façade and wooden windows as well as traditional forms such as rectangular floor plans, entrances on the longer side of the floor plans and slanting roofs with dormer windows.

01 Entrance to the complex | 02 Aerial view | 03 Single house | 04 Side view | 05 Interior view | 06 Site plan

06

01

02

03

Research Library

This five-story building consists of a concrete construction also visible in the monolithic fair-faced concrete façade. The building is shaped like an X. The main vertical component, illuminated by a circular roof light, is located in the center of the X. The distribution of visitors, librarians and books takes place from the central vertical point to the four wings of the X. The library space, with bookshelves and study rooms, is located in the two eastern wings and occupies three floors. In the other wings, there are offices, storage and a conference hall. The interior atmosphere is created by fair-faced concrete walls and ceilings, colored floors and wooden accents. An important part of the building design is the energy-saving concept.

01 Façade detail | 02 Staircase | 03 Study room | 04 Exterior view from the street | 05 Site plan

04

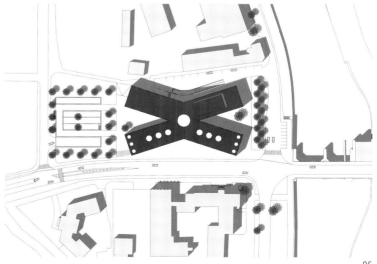

05

01

02

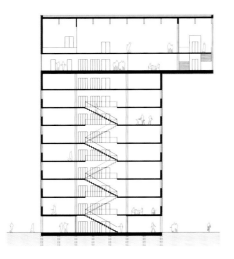

03

04

Townhouse

This project was designed for the town of Jesenik, situated in the Jesenik Mountains in the Czech Republic. The urban design is restricted by the existing situation: there is no proper place for a representative and important townhouse. The aim was to create a dominant building in this problematic town area. The building's façades are made from natural timber cladding, inspired by a traditional local material. Its windows are insulated from sunshine by the shutters, which complement local mountain architecture. The roof is a green color, matching the surrounding landscape. The construction has no basement because of unsatisfactory ground with underground water.

01 Day view | 02 Night view | 03 Section | 04 Hall interior | 05 Bird's-eye view

05

01

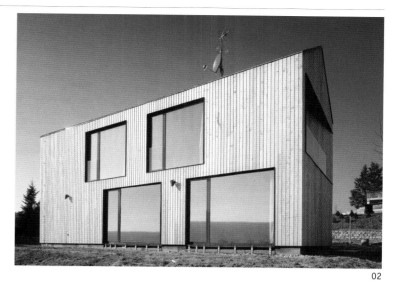

02

Family House in Lety

The goal of this design was to create a house that would, in terms of its size, comfort and architectonic conception, correspond to the modest needs of a young family. The house is made of wood, with the basic load-bearing structure supplemented and further developed by the integrated interior. This approach allowed for the optimal use of space even in relatively small rooms. The basis of the design is a transparent, logical layout, with a sufficiency of storage areas in its contemporary economical spatial concept. The resulting appearance of the house is minimalistic, grounded merely in the refinement of the chosen natural materials, the composition of windows, the mastery of proportional relations and purity of detail.

01 Side view | 02 Rear façade | 03 Street view | 04 Living area | 05 Ground floor plan | 06 View from kitchen

03

04

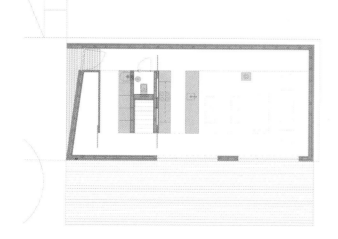

05

06

01

02

03

Church of the Brethren Church in Litomyšl

The roof of this structure acts as a continuation of the façade and carries all substantial information about the building. It has been abstracted to the maximum. The building exterior is of concrete, while the interior is of plywood. The vertical nature of the façades and their visual representation symbolize the dilemma of most sacral buildings. The connection between heaven and earth need not necessarily be a monologue; it can be an invitation for a journey, and for a gradual ascend upwards. The architect was contracted to build two prayer houses for the Church of Brethren. Both buildings have the same program: to serve the religious and social life of the community.

01 Street view | 02 Main entrance | 03 Corridor | 04 Main hall | 05 Ground floor plan | 06 Altar

04

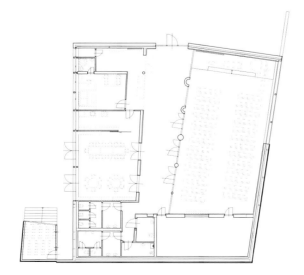

05

06

01

02

03

04

Apartment on Top of a Grain Silo in Olomouc

The concept of this project is based on the principle of vertical arrangement of fragments, an entrance patio, a garden, a double-story living area and asymmetrically positioned cuboid - "cube", and their integration through opening elevator doors. Each of the fragments is designed differently. The project represents a radical conversion, as well as an intervention into the city. The overblown dimensions and asymmetry of the "cube" embody an actual change. The radical nature of the gesture is probably the only reason why the project works despite the changes effected during execution. The cuboid is a further attempt to play with the modernist form, still repeatedly used in the Czech environment.

01 View from park | 02 View from southeast | 03 Entrance patio | 04 View from east | 05 Section

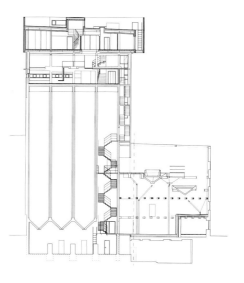

05

01

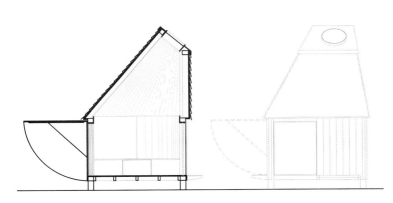

02

Hat Teahouse

"Hat" is the smallest of three already-designed teahouses. The name derives from its tall roof, which resembling a big hat left in the garden. Its inner space is meant for two guests and a host. A wide larch bench provides seating for guests. The almost square layout transforms upwards into the round shape of the skylight. Because available space is limited, the hearth is designed as a drawer hidden under the bench. The view is oriented to the uniquely picturesque garden and can be adjusted by sliding windows and outer shutters. Suitable and elegant material plays an important role when designing a teahouse.

01 Entrance from garden | 02 Sections | 03 Interior with skylight

03

01

Bextra

The fundamental concept of the design is the division of the structure into two clearly defined buildings – hall and administration. It is a dialogue between the static warehouse and the dynamic administration and sales areas. The hall design allows variable divisions of the interior, which appears as a clear cube within the circumferential casing. The administration section playfully hints that the projecting mass of the upper level is supported by the fragile structure of the receding ground floor, while clearly displaying energy, direction and impulse.

01 Staircase, seen from the top | 02 First floor plan | 03 View from east

02

03

01

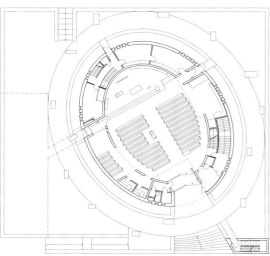

03

St. Spirit Church

This church is located in an area with a high crime rate, which is why it is designed like a citadel. When entering, visitors have to pass through different layers – a plateau, a moat, a wall and a ring of lateral rooms – before reaching the core. This passage reflects the transition from the material to the sacred world. The abstract-symbolic interior features liturgical pieces made of massive cubic limestone and colored glass. Its cellar contains the parish community center of Jean Paul II. With a capacity of 650 people, it is the biggest church built in the Czech Republic after the Velvet Revolution.

01 Main entrance with campanile | 02 Entrance and choir | 03 Floor plan | 04 Stairway to choir

02

04

01

Faculty Buildings, Pardubice University

The mass volume concept reflects the grid pattern of the surrounding area and corresponds to the construction plot. The ground floor areas of the new buildings do not fully lie on the ground surface. Instead, the ground surface flows horizontally underneath and the ground floor is freely passable for pedestrians. Corridors interconnect the buildings on the second floor. The complex consists of three buildings: the central axial building is the entrance point in the faculty, containing rooms that the whole building shares. The flanking buildings mainly contain large teaching laboratories, on the third to fifth floors, tutors' offices and their laboratories are also located here.

01 View from south | 02 Ramp | 03 First floor plan | 04 Entrance hall | 05 Exterior view from north | 06 Hallway

02

03

04

05

06

01

02

03

Mountain House

This house is located 820 meters above sea level near to the German border, in a valley characterized by a wild water stream. The house represents a hybrid typology of a small residential retreat and a guesthouse with facilities for skiing and nature hiking. The form and scale of the house are largely defined by its context, topography and the desired orientation towards views of landscape and towards sunlight. The external walls are made of 500-millimeter thick super-insulated clay blocks. The final cost was 100,000 euros, inclusive of the plot purchase, internal fittings and furniture.

01 Exterior view | 02 View from north | 03 Upstairs living space | 04 Floor plans

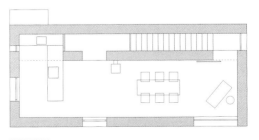

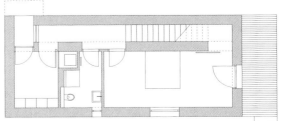

04

01

02

03

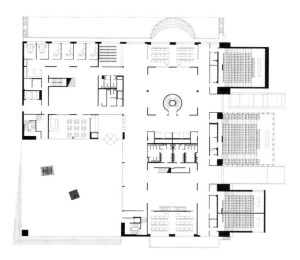

04

New CTU Building in Prague

The New CTU Building provides a home for the Faculty of Architecture. The floor plan is divided into four quadrants, three of these create the L-shaped form of the building and one quadrant is empty and serves as entrance courtyard. The building has eight floors above ground and three underground. The floors aboveground are vertically connected by three atriums. Workplaces for students and rooms for teachers are transparently connected through glass walls. The ground floor provides free, open space and includes small study rooms and four lecture halls of capacity 80, 100, 180 and 300 seats. Underground floors include garage and technical equipment.

01 Main view | 02 View from street | 03 Interior façade detail | 04 Ground floor plan | 05 Interior view

05

01

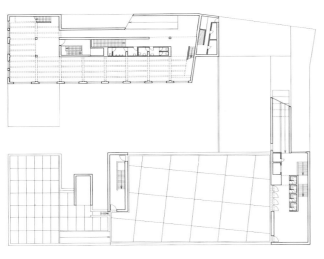

03

02

04

DOX – Centrum Soucasného Umeni

The architecture here is an integral part of this specific quarter, an industrial district from the turn of the 19th to the 20th century, that is currently undergoing intensive development. This project does not exploit the plot's maximum possible volume, but leaves empty space above the original buildings, in which the dense urban structure can rest. The project, which was carried out gradually between 2004 and 2008 as a private initiative, is about taking a sensitive approach to the place and its atmosphere. The process and time span of the construction were strongly controlled by the low budget. Today the complex houses 12 exhibition spaces, a café with a terrace, a bookshop and service facilities.

01 Tower building | 02 Main entrance ramp | 03 Third floor plan | 04 Interior view to tower | 05 Roof terrace

05

01

National Technical Library

This project is the architects' answer to the role of the library in today's society. The building should be environmentally friendly and important in the context of urban development. The ground floor houses public spaces like the café, exhibition hall, bookshop, cloakroom and night study room. The entrance to the library is right in the middle of the atrium. The actual library occupies the upper four floors. Part of the concept is the surrounding area – social spaces on the west and a green park on the east. The art and the graphic design follow the concept of 'the technological schoolbook', so that illustrations are deliberately shown to allow a better understanding of the building's design and functions.

01 Lobby | 02 Exterior view | 03 Reading room | 04 Second floor plan | 05 Main hall library

02

03

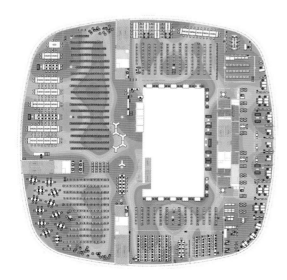

04

05

01

02

03

Hostivar Golf Club

This plot of land was ideal for a driving range with covered practice tees. The lightweight steel structure is covered by a textile membrane. As the course grew, a new clubhouse with restaurant, meeting rooms, relaxation areas and golf simulators for virtual practice was added. The main façade is open to the natural landscape with a pond. Besides the outdoor restaurant, protected from rain by suspended 'sails', the most impressive element of the clubhouse is the hall façade covered in expressively arranged wooden boards, creating a work of art at low cost.

01 Golf restaurant | 02 Indoor teeing | 03 Red lit hall | 04 General situation | 05 Green lit hall

04

05

01

Nova Brumlovka

This wellness center has two floors devoted to sports. A shed roof with a very slight pitch conceals a retreating relaxation terrace that extends from the aqua-zone one level below from the gaze of higher buildings. The ground floor has two restaurants, a post office, small shops and a bar. The building creates optical harmony between the center and neighboring office buildings. With the exception of expanses of glass, the exterior cladding is made of perforated trapezoidal sheet metal, whose color changes throughout the day.

01 Indoor swimming pool | 02 Section | 03 View from the pedestrian bridge | 04 East façade | 05 Façade detail

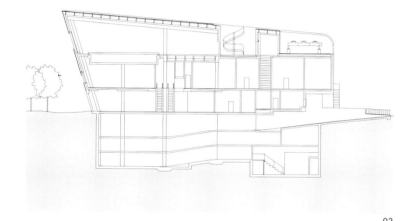

02

03

04

05

01

04

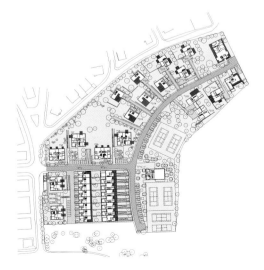

02

03

05

Na Krutci Residential Complex

This new residential complex design stems from its location at the boundary between a housing area and the countryside. The upper, only slightly sloping southern part of the area, containing residences, terraced family houses and the entrance building, connects to the street pattern of the neighboring suburb. The row of four residential houses situated at the edge of the northwards slope forms a dividing line in the character of the buildings. The 13 family houses in the northeastern part are connected, by their concept of free-standing houses, to the original building along Na Krutci Str.

01 Outside area in front of the apartment houses | 02 Courtyards | 03 Family houses | 04 Apartment house with wooden façade | 05 Terraced houses | 06 Site plan

06

02

01

Teahouse in the Garden

This teahouse adheres to the Japanese tradition of minimizing space and is intended as a place to receive guests for a cup of tea. It contains a world hidden inside, where time flows at its own pace, a vacant space which leaves an impression just by its spaciousness. When first considering the design for such a place, the architect thought of the places that had made an impression upon him, and came to the decision to build on a circular platform enclosed by a translucent dome, breathing the inner peace of small sacred buildings. Diffused rays of light illuminate the quarters within; the translucent dome resembles the sky and its spherical shape directs your attention to the hearth.

01 Dome | 02 Interior view | 03 View through window | 04 View from the ceiling | 05 Exterior view | 06 Section

03

04

05

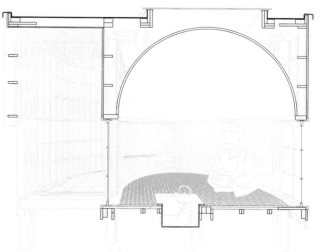

06

01

02

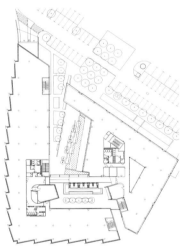

03

BB Centrum Objekt Gamma

The complex shape of the premises corresponds to the building's size, which includes ten aboveground and three underground floors. Its immediate location near the road means visibility for the tenants, but unwanted noise from the high-capacity road. Gamma consistently solved the noise reflection from the building to the opposite block of apartments with a sound-absorbing façade with a curved ground floor articulated to the individual scales. Apart from the extensive atria with an artificially ventilated inside environment, the building offers parking space in the courtyard which also has a water surface and complete noise screening.

01 Central atrium | 02 View of meeting room inside atrium | 03 Ground floor plan | 04 View from road | 05 East façade detail

04

05

01

02

03

04

Palladium

A unique shopping and service center was created in the heart of historical Prague with the opening of the Palladium. In addition to retail and gastronomic spaces and places for artistic events, the complex offers flexible-use office space and a three-story below-ground garage with a 900-car capacity. Two highly prized, historic buildings (an old barracks and a riding hall from 1859) have been integrated into the concept. Interconnected and accessible via two entrances are over 160 stores and more than 30 restaurants on five levels. The latter are found on the topmost floor, and form a unique constellation of Central European epicurean offerings.

01 Historic façade | 02 Atrium | 03 Exterior | 04 View to light tunnel | 05 Site plan

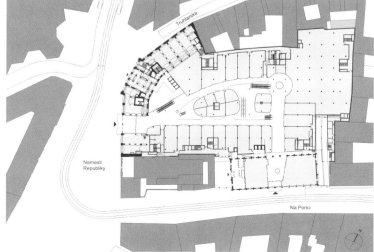

05

01

02

Villa Pod Devinem

This family villa has been built on one of the hills surrounding Prague, overlooking the Vltava river basin to the south. The site is a strip of former back garden at the center of established older villas. Adopting the trapezoid form and opening the southern façade with large format glazing (with external sun blinds) really helped to gain the most from the site, its aspect and view. The design features a simple slice of minimal building and clear lines with its funnel-shape orientated towards the view. The central, open plan staircase stitches the two functional halves of the villa's interior together. The house is organized with entry, bathrooms, kitchen and a plunge pool to the north while living, dining and bedroom areas are situated to the south.

01 View from valley | 02 Street view | 03 Section | 04 Living room | 05 Dining room / gallery | 06 View from valley | 07 Detail staircase

03

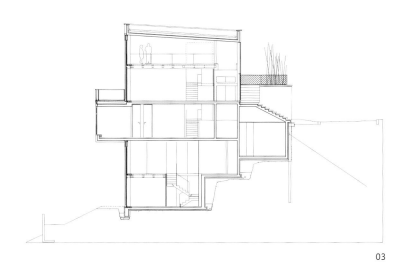

04

05

06

07

02

01

03

House in a Meadow

Built in a village at the foothills of the mountains, the dimensions and character of this house come from the environment of a sparsely developed country area. The living space is open, defined only by the cladding, and is connected to the landscape by large windows. A studio with a gallery in the attic forms the essential space of the building. The wooden shelter along the whole house fulfills the role of a sheltered parking, as well as a living platform with view of the hills. The house was structurally designed as timber framing with aluminum building panels. The construction is set on concrete foot blocks to interfere as little as possible with the landscape in terms of building operations.

01 Detail | 02 Rear view | 03 Exterior view | 04 Ground floor plan | 05 Dining area | 06 Entrance area and terrace

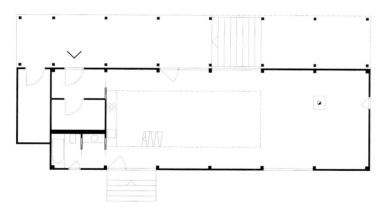

04

05

06

01

02

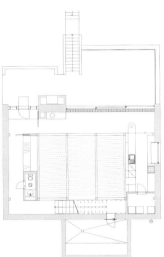

03

Family House in Talinska

The site of this family house is situated on sloping terrain. Right from the start, the overall concept was based on the orientation and shape of the south-facing terrain and incorporating the house into the surrounding landscape. The side views have been left almost without apertures, corresponding to the plot's narrow character. The house is accessed only by stairs and is designed in a combined construction system. The ground floor, the greater part of which is built into the slope, is solved by peripheral reinforced concrete walls and internal wooden posts. The second aboveground story is designed with brick peripheral walls, which are combined with wooden posts on the glazed southern façade.

01 Exterior view | 02 Terrace | 03 Ground floor plan | 04 Dining area

04

01

Bell Tower at Horečky

This bell tower is situated in the unique locality of Horečky on the border of the municipality of Trojanovice and the city of Frenštát pod Radhoštěm. The bell tower symbolizes the struggle against the potentates of the mining lobby, whose plans threaten the municipality's historical and future values. As a symbolic contribution to the struggle against the miner's plans, the bell will toll the passing of the Frenštát mine. The modern appearance and traditional craftsmanship used to build the bell tower symbolize the vision of a better future as well as a return to traditional values.

01 View towards mountains | 02 Inside the structure | 03 Elevations

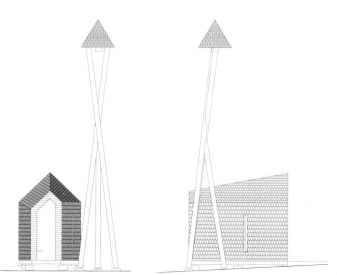

02

03

01

02

Multi-Purpose Building, Cauliflower

The surrounding neighborhood is the result of historical city development of various eras, mainly the 19th century. Across the street is an eclectic synagogue. The corrugated iron fencing became the inspiration for solving the problem of the irregular plot. The street façade was built as a harmonic curve, reflecting the ornamental decor of the synagogue. The curving of the northeast façade lets in the sun during the whole morning. The underground corner part of the building houses a coffee bar that extends to the ground floor. The main part of the ground floor contains a commercial area for rent

01 Corner view | 02 Southeast view | 03 Northwest view | 04 Floor plan | 05 Interior view

03

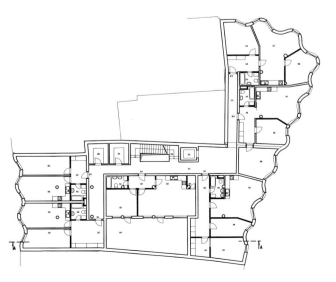

04

05

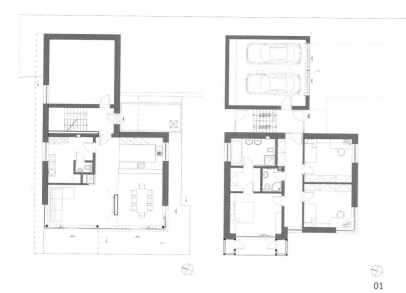

01

Family House Všechovice

This new two-story family house is located in the village of Všechovice near Tišnov. The house is positioned on a steeply sloping site and respects the surrounding area. Because of the steep land, the main access area is upstairs. Two blocks create the basic architectural design of this house, one block is plastered with white plaster and the second is lined with wood. The materials of this family house are traditional local materials; softwoods stained to a dark color and white lime-cast. The southwest side of the house features glass walls, these allow for passive accumulation of solar energy. Beside the house, there are several other buildings, including a wintering place for bonsai and a seating area with a fireplace and wine cellar.

01 Floor plans | 02 South façade | 03 Southwest view | 04 Southeast view | 05 Living room | 06 Kitchen and dining room

02

03

04

05

06

01

Kumu

This site with a 20-meter-high limestone slope is located at the southern end of the Kadriorg Park, three kilometers from Tallinn city center. In order to leave the park as intact as possible and to reduce the impact of this large building, the museum was integrated into the slope, partly underground. A curved wall unifies the plan, externally enclosing a courtyard and internally dividing the functions. The exhibition halls are simple and unassuming, directing the focus to the artwork. The ascetics of the interior continue in the exterior, which relies on the power of plain geometric forms. The main façade materials are limestone, green-aeruginous copper and glass.

01 Courtyard with terraced sculpture garden | 02 Main entrance | 03 Entrance from the rear | 04 Site plan | 05 Exhibition space

02

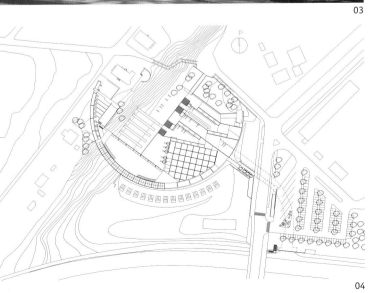

03

04

05

01

Synagogue

This synagogue is situated in central Tallinn in a quiet neighborhood near the main harbor. It is built as an extension to the existing Jewish High School and Cultural Center. The new building has a clear axial character. The main axis is north to south, as a synagogue in the Jewish Diaspora is always oriented in the direction of the original temple site in Jerusalem. The architecture of the building is based on two principal elements. The vault, as a form, is quite specific to sacral buildings. The vaulted form is entirely of the same natural stone as if carved from a single rock. Beneath that is a waving colonnade, which allows the building to deviate from the strictness of the vaulted form and gives it a floating quality.

01 Side view | 02 Front view | 03 Section

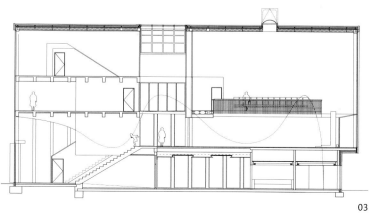

02

03

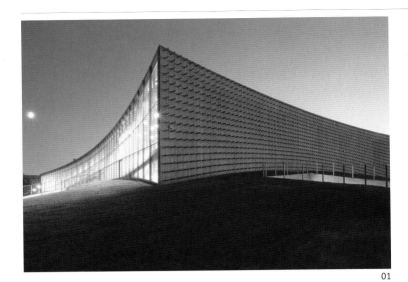

01

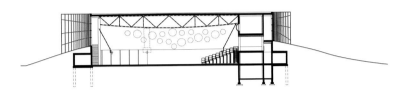

Sports Hall of the Estonian University of Life Sciences

This building and its landscaping integrates and organizes the scattered campus of the university. In addition, the roadside location on the very verge of the city makes the sports hall something of an entrance mark. Due to its location, one of the considerations was that one should be able to grasp the basic design idea at the first glimpse, upon driving by. As a solution, all corners of the cubic volume are slightly stretched, and the elevated ground forms a 'cushion' for the entrenched building. This integrates the building with landscape and lightens its overall appearance. The stretched-out corners create concave lines both in plan and elevation, creating unconventional spaces inside and varying optical effects outside.

01 Façade at night | 02 Wooden façade detail | 03 Sections | 04 Glazed façade

02

03

04

01

02

03

04

Casa CV

A disruption in the homogeneity of the surroundings, the form of this project is inspired by the traditional, drawn-out architecture of the panonian space and interprets the needs of time, place and the user's character. The house merges the boundaries between inside and outside, giving the inhabitant the feeling of living in the landscape. To enable an unhindered view and to preserve the tree population, the living deck has been situated above the existing terrain. Everything is dipped in off-white. The white increases the constantly changing colors of the lake, nature and the sky. The exterior is covered with a graphic design inspired by embroidery of Hungarian costumes.

01 Patio and sun bed | 02 Minimalist interior | 03 Exterior view | 04 Master bedroom | 05 Floor plan

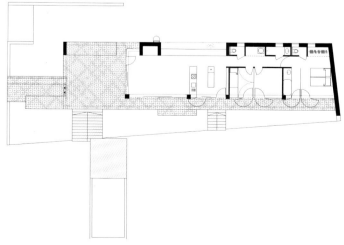

05

01

Bazaltbor Winery

The wines of the Laposa-cellar (designed by Péter Kis and Bea Molnár) became renowned under the name "Bazaltbor". The regions where the grapes grow are on the basalt hills and this gives the wine its characteristic mineral aroma, reflecting the mineral-rich region where they are cultivated. Two elements of the architecture – the symmetrical gable with its closed roof abstraction of the old press houses and the basalt bands that erupt to the surface – connect together into a new system. The basic elements flow freely, in any direction where there are no obstacles. A transformed pattern of grapevines, copied from own old house twining, is etched into the concrete facing panels. Perforated metal sheets allow light into the interior.

01 View from hill | 02 View at sunset | 03 Side view | 04 Section | 05 Façade

02

03

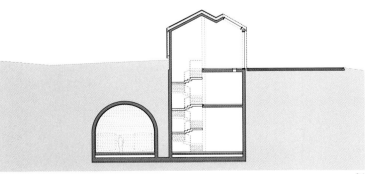

04

05

01

02

03

04

05

Füleky Winery

In the historical center of the small Tokaj village, on a plot directly adjacent to a 15th century church, this project entailed the design of a winery that is to produce quality Tokaj wines. The basic concept underlying the design was to build a new winery by making use of all valuable elements of the original stone building. During the procedure, the original stonewalls were uncovered, hidden under layers of plaster. The traditionally laid stonewalls were then integrated into the new building so as to result in a house that now displays these original elements.

01 New cellar | 02 Gallery | 03 View from street | 04 Aerial view | 05 Stone façade | 06 Ground floor plan

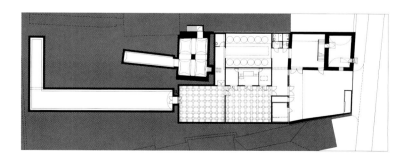

06

01

02

Karcsi's House

The key idea in this architectural concept is for the outer layer of the building to surround the inner space, like a clamshell. As an important element of the plan, an open atrium is placed in between the living room, kitchen and bedroom, thus forming a mini garden with an intimate atmosphere. The bulk of the building stretches out above the garage entrance, providing a rather imposing portal. The house itself is located on the east slope of Aranyhegy (Golden hill), and the building site has a panoramic view of Mocsárosdűlő.

01 Model view | 02 Atmospheric view | 03 Model | 04 Ground floor plan

03

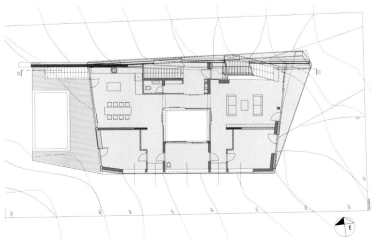

04

01

02

03

CET Budapest

CET is Central European Time and is also synonymous with a whale. The mixed-use development CET at the Közraktárak, between the Petofi and the Szabadság Bridge, symbolizes both. The CET concept refers to Budapest as an important metropolitan center in the heart of Central Europe, while the CET shape refers to the smooth and streamlined body of a whale. The smooth exterior slides unobtrusively over the edges of a neighboring building, allowing the structure to adapt to its allotted space. The alternating pattern of the outer shell gives the structure a dynamic appearance. The name and shape of the CET symbolizes its cultural potential and commercial pole position in one of the best-preserved cities in the world.

01 View from Danube | 02 View of warehouses | 03 View from main plaza | 04 Interior view of atrium | 05 Section

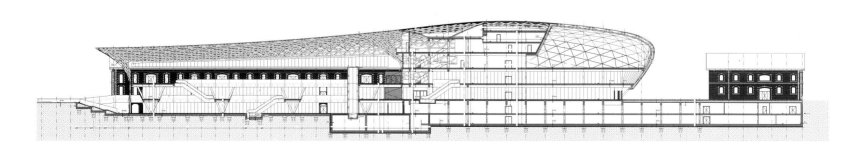

04

05

01

02

Institute for Physically Disabled Children

Two 100-year-old buildings used by physically handicapped children were the starting point of this project. The main challenge was to place the huge program, as unobtrusively as possible, between the two volumes. To achieve this, parts of the building were built under the earth, while a green roof covers other parts. The additions respect these not by imitating them, but by keeping their essence. The old brick body is balanced by new and massive concrete walls. Zsolnay ceramics, colors and rich details with ornamental patterns are interpreted as patterned, colored concrete surfaces in the annex. A new axis cuts its way through the rear garden, joining and merging old and new.

01 Exterior view | 02 New school building | 03 Main entrance | 04 Section | 05 Swimming pool | 06 Hall | 07 Canteen

03

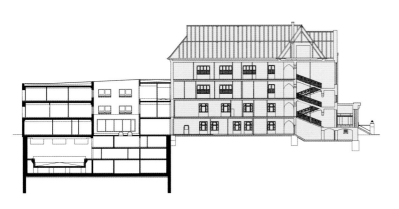
04

05

06

07

01

02

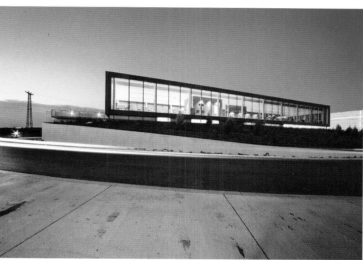

03

04

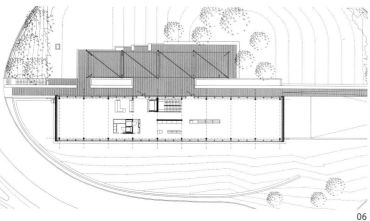

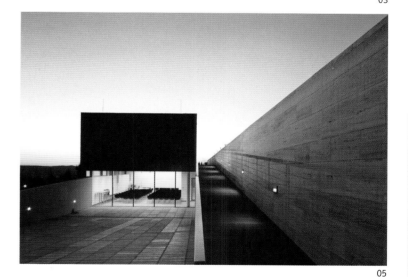

05

New Visitor Center of the Pannonhalma Arch-abbey

This building is located in the immediate vicinity of the World Heritage listed Archabbey. Designers paid close attention to the surrounding buildings to ensure that the new addition fitted into the architectural history of the environment. Since the 1970s the area had been used as a parking lot for tourists. The most important aspect of the concept was to restore the natural environment of the site. The restoration work of the Kosaras Hill conceals the parking area. The conference hall and the service areas are on the lower floor, enhancing the accessible and flexible utilization of the upper floor: the glass façade of the restaurant floats above the hill overlooking the valley.

01 Restaurant terrace | 02 Aerial view | 03 Restaurant exterior | 04 Restaurant interior | 05 Night view | 06 Floor plan

06

01

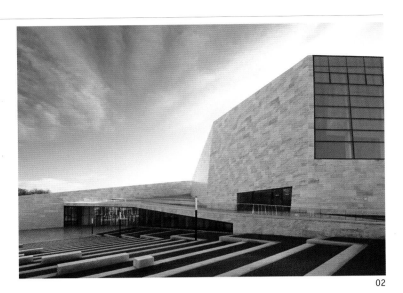

02

Kodály Center

This building has been designed so that visitors can walk around it unimpeded, both on the outside and the inside. The hall is at the center, surrounding visitors with music. The building is vivid and full of motion. The building works to bridge the gap between opposites, forging together inside and outside, object and space, community and internal silence. Large glazed areas open out the undulating exterior, while the interior widens out into the large central hall. The enduring impression is one of spaciousness and modernity.

01 Lobby | 02 Entrance | 03 Auditorium | 04 Corridor alongside auditorium | 05 Exterior at dusk | 06 Front view

03

04

05

06

01

02

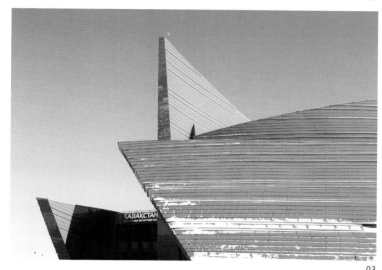

03

04

05

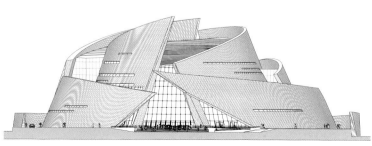

06

Central Concert Hall Kazakhstan

This auditorium was awarded to Studio Nicoletti as the result of an international re-stricted competition. The nucleus of the new capital, Astana, occupies a rectangular area whose organizational axis is based upon a system of three piazzas. In the largest of these, the Central Concert Hall faces the Senate House. The vastness of the location is reminiscent of the Kazakh Steppe. Amidst this monumental void, the structures of the auditorium rise like the petals of a flower. The music hall is one of the largest in the world with a vineyard conformation, designed for classical music but able to adapt itself to any kind of performance thanks to a special system of false ceilings mobile panels and acoustic tents.

01 Exterior view | 02 General view | 03 Façade detail | 04 Outside the auditorium | 05 Inside the auditorium | 06 Elevation

01

The Khan Shatyr Entertainment Center

The Khan Shatyr Entertainment Center represents a major new civic, cultural and social venue for the people of Astana, bringing together a wide range of activities within a sheltered, climatic envelope. The building encloses an area in excess of 100,000 square meters, with dramatic views over the city and the steppes beyond. Contained within it is an urban-scale park, along with a wide variety of entertainment and leisure facilities that can accommodate a varied program of events and exhibitions. In winter, a key challenge is to prevent the formation of ice on the inside of the envelope. This is achieved by a combination of temperature control and directing warm air currents up the inner surface of the fabric.

01 Interior view | 02 Dining area | 03 Exterior view

02

03

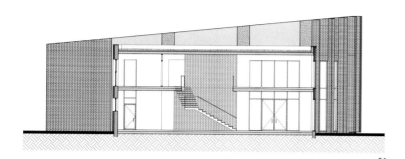

01

Flower Shop in Jelgava

This two-story combined flower shop and office building is located in the center of Jelgava, near the St. John church. Red brick has been used for the façade, allowing it to blend into its historical surroundings. Large brick buttresses are a response to the architecture of the nearby church. The building establishes a connection between the city's new and old architecture, while simultaneousy serving its functional purpose.

01 Section | 02 South façade | 03 View from Pasta Street | 04 Rounded red brick façade | 05 View from north

02

03

04

05

01

Villa Guna

This pine tree covered narrow lot, situated on Jurmala's Baltic coast, is adjacent to an apartment building, built in 2001 and also designed by Meinhard von Gerkan. The primary feature of the design is the spatial experience, characterized by a dialogue with nature and the view towards the Baltic Sea. The bedrooms, with bathrooms and dressing rooms for the lady of the house and her guests, are located on the upper floors. The whole villa is organized as a split-level house with staggered floors, which are linked by a multi-flight ramp. A narrow stairway connects the two living floors directly. In the northwest corner of the villa a tower rises up to a height of 15 meters. This completes the sculptural appearance of the white, cubic building volume.

01 Exterior view | 02 Living room | 03 Axonometry

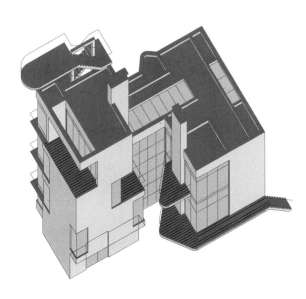

02

03

01

02

03

04

Commercial Center Sky & More

This shopping mall consists of two main volumes: one for commerce and its support areas and the other for parking. The commerce building has a large supermarket, together with its supporting and delivery spaces, on the ground floor. The second floor has a gallery with small shops and stands. The multicolored glass panels of the façades, contrast with the rigid, monochrome and massive concrete walls. The sweeping lines of the exterior, coupled with its gently curving shape give the impression of movement and add a modern feel to the structure. The white sections of the façade are part of the external lighting system, lighting the building up at night. The striped sections glow like a beacon, welcoming visitors.

01 Exterior view | 02 Escalators and panoramic elevator | 03 Main entrance | 04 Interior view | 05 Site plan

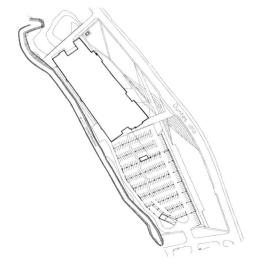

05

01

04

02

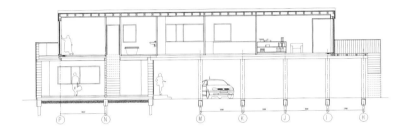

03

Two Sisters House

This project consists of two independent residential premises, based on reinforced concrete piles that form covered external spaces. The first floor is a connecting space, housing the entrance zone and common areas. The two volumes are connected in such away as to create individual living environments with maximum privacy and a view over Langstini Lake. Columns, creating a covered space in front of the buildings, support the upper levels of the red volumes. There is also a wooden deck area, providing a comfortable outside space for relaxation and enjoying the view.

01 Terrace | 02 Wooden deck and large windows | 03 Section | 04 Exterior view | 05 Front façade | 06 Rear view

05

06

01

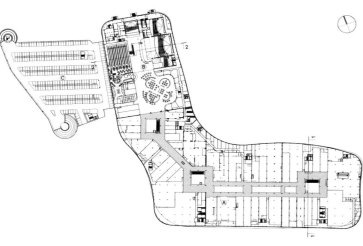

02

03

Riga Plaza

The idea of this commercial and entertainment center was to integrate the functional requirements of the two-story shopping mall with a dynamic, long and flexible façade that is reminiscent of a belt. The 'active' surface of the façade responds to the dynamic surroundings and can be easily identified from distant points of the city. The Daugava River, which runs along the entire country as a long ribbon, inspired the architects to create the sinuous form of the façades. The dynamic character of the building is accentuated by the use of multicolored metallic sheets in the façades. The selected colors – gray, white, light blue and black – come from native costume motifs.

01 South entrance at night | 02 First floor plan | 03 Façade detail | 04 East façade |
05 South entrance

04

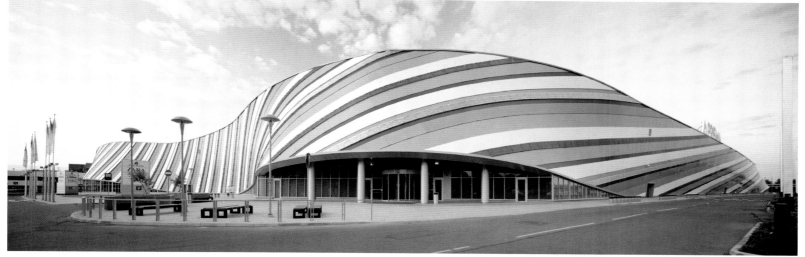

05

01

02

03

04

DnB Nord Office Building

The angular location of a newly developed multifunction block suggested the DnB Nord Office Building should be a clear boundary/corner formant of the block. But at the same time the building was created as an open and inviting space, actively involving both visitors and workers. The building consists of two separate ten-story volumes connected by a transparent vertical communication unit. A rectangular one-story roof slab covers the volumes and an open area under the roof slab creates a new type of space, which seeks to blur the boundaries between inside and outside.

01 Entrance | 02 Employee entrance hall | 03 North façade | 04 Worm's-eye view of roof | 05 Section

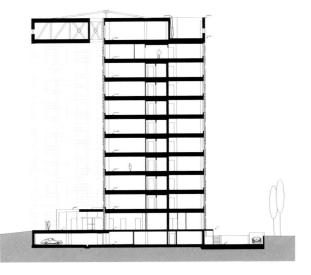

05

01

02

Residential House in Domeikava

The design of this residential house in Lithuania is based on an 'all in one' concept. The building is a solid box shape, mirroring the functional quality of the interior. The low volume is unobtursive and does not disrupt the undulating pattern of the lanscape. The roof projects over the walls, creating a sheltered space below. The generous glass façade allows views of the landscape and also allows ample light into the interior. The flat roof offeres a contrast to the pitched roof of the surrounding houses and contributes to the unobtrusive appearance of the house.

01 View from garden | 02 View from street | 03 North façade | 04 Site plan | 05 View from bridge | 06 Southeast façade | 07 Main entrance

03

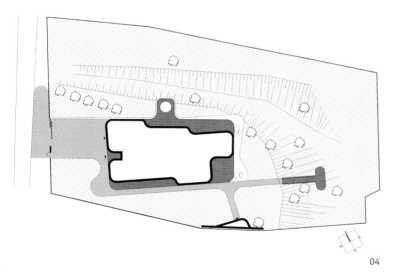

04

05

06

07

01

02

Medical Clinic

The mother and baby clinic is the first such clinic in Lithuania to specialize in independent assisted reproduction and home birth. Over the past few years, there has been a growth of clinical services, which indicated the needs to expand the existing premises. The clinic had limited ward and administrative premises, but the old building offered enough space to house the surgery premises. This situation indicated the solution for the expansion. The old building was renovated and the new one is designed according the land plot perimeter – the new building encloses the old in an inner courtyard, creating the idea of 'baby in mother's womb'.

01 View from street | 02 Courtyard | 03 Sections

03

01

02

03

04

Office Center '1000'

The design of this class A office and service center is based on a LTL 1,000 banknote dating from 1925; the period of Lithuania's independence between the two devastating world wars. The façade is covered from top to the bottom in a striking illustration consisting of 4,500 different pieces of glass. Produced in the Netherlands, all pieces were assembled like a puzzle. Complicated silk graphic technology was chosen so the required ornamentation could be painted on the glass. To depict the original banknote image, the building façade lights up with white, green and blue lights in the evening. During the day it reflects white and dark gray colors. Falling shadows indoors leave watermark reflections, giving the interior a dynamic feel.

01 Front view | 02 Façade | 03 Interior detail | 04 Façade at night | 05 Section

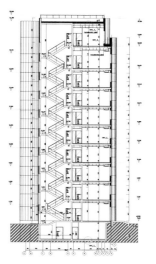

05

01

Swedbank Headquarters

A distinctive feature of this new office building is its openness and accessibility to the public. The site has been developed on the old Ukmerges street, which becomes the main axis of the buildings composition. The internal pedestrian street and the flowing spaces on the building's ground floor are planned as a public urban space. The building consists of two parts: high-rise part of two 15 and 16 story structures and the lower part. The highlight of the building is the over 4,500-square meter terrace, constructed on the stylobate part and offering excellent views of the river.

01 South façade | 02 South façade detail | 03 Interior view | 04 Ground floor plan

02

03

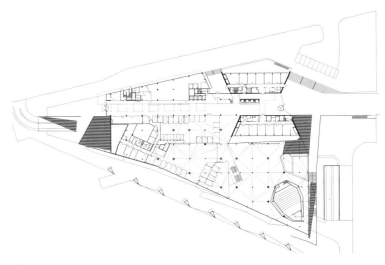

04

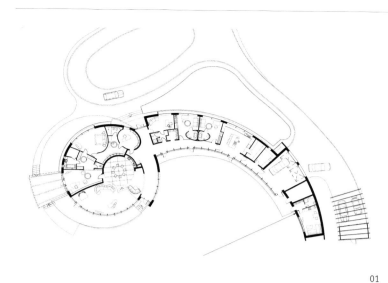

01

02

Villa N

This curved villa is situated in a breathtaking landscape on a slope above the river on the outskirts of Vilnius city. The landscape has had a visible impact on the architectural solution. The very first impression suggests that the building appears from the ground and vanishes somewhere in the surroundings. The slight curve of the building shapes both the inner courtyard with a magnificent view of the landscape and semi-closed outer façade that protects from the curiosity of neighbors. There are almost no boundaries between outside and inside, allowing the courtyard, fringed with woodland and the river, to remain visible from the armchair inside.

01 Ground floor plan | 02 Interior view | 03 Façade detail | 04 Backyard view

03

04

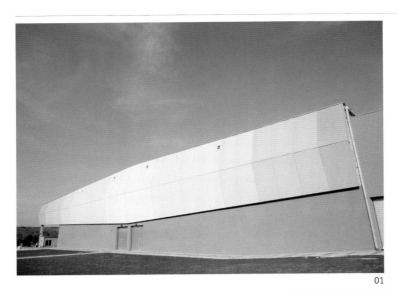

01

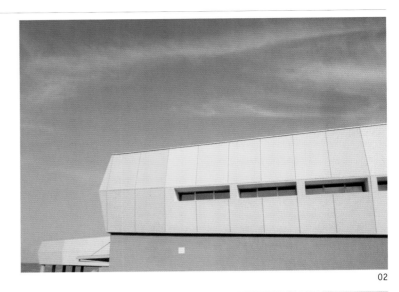

02

03

Stobi Winery

Stobi Winery is one of Macedonia's more recent wineries, situated near the archeological site Stobi. The winery's geometric module covers an area of 15,400 square meters, buildings and green areas. It consists of three continuously connected modules, which due to the natural topographical characteristics of the terrain and full use of the location are arranged perimetrally, forming a linear U-shape. The spatial and structural organization of the specific modules makes this building particularly compact in terms of functionality and shape. Linear configuration is employed for the purposes of retaining the openness of the complex, its integration with the surrounding nature, creating a spacious open green area in the central part and insulating each unit.

01 Inner yard | 02 Northeast module | 03 Entrance | 04 Connection between modules | 05 Wooden ceiling inside | 06 Façade detail

04

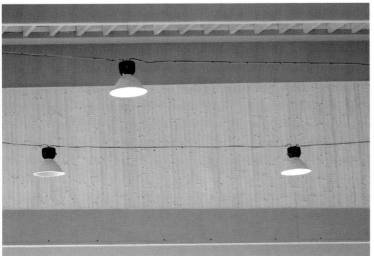

05

06

01

04

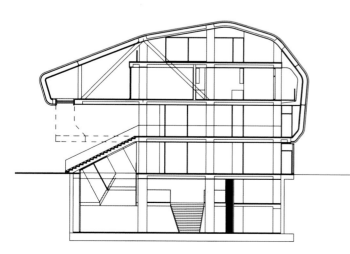

02

03

05

Commercial Center Skopje

At the foremost point towards the city square in Skopje, between the two lines that infuse in the square, this is an object that enfolds the external public area along with the closed usable area. The object is both a large sculptural structure in the public space, and a folded area that is filled with changing contents, brands and other products that reflect new dynamic economic trends. The generous glazing of the façade serves a dual purpose, allowing natural light to flood into the space while simultaneously acting as a large display window for the products.

01 Entrance area | 02 View from south | 03 View from the existing trade center | 04 View from north | 05 View from the pedestrian street | 06 Section

06

01

02

Macedonian - Italian Education Center

Located in close proximity to the monumental concrete structure of the University "Ss. Cyril and Methodius" is the House of the Macedonian-Italian Educational Center in which the contents of learning fold and differentiate the interior. This dynamic interior is separated into areas of different coor. The auditorium is green while the corridor, glallery and library areas are red. The metal sections of the façade continue into the interior to devlope a creative S-shape. The rest of the façade is glazed, allowing passersby a glimpse of the colorful interior and providing students with natural light and views of the surroundings.

01 View from south | 02 View from north | 03 Sections | 04 Corridor with gallery | 05 Entrance | 06 View from east

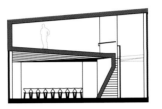

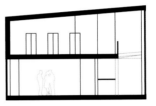

03

04

05

06

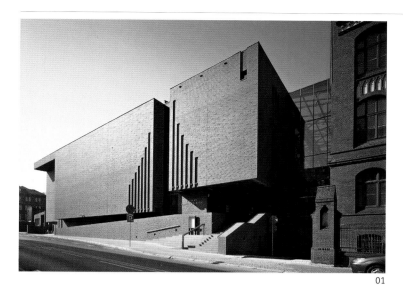

01

Symphony Science and Musical Education Center

Both the atmosphere of this place, generated by its musical function, and the neighbor-hood of neo-Gothic brick walls indicated the need for continuation. The wooden struc-ture of the concert hall was enclosed within a shell of reinforced concrete, the exterior of which was then clad with brick. This consistent, layered idea expresses the simplicity and clarity of the structure. The new structure clearly establishes a dialogue with the historical building of the academy. The consistent composition culminates in a spacious glazed atrium, where two important historic periods of the academy meet. Despite clear-ly different treatment in terms of texture and ornament, the carefully matched façade brick unifies the past with the present.

01 Exterior view from Damrota street | 02 Section | 03 Entrance at night | 04 Atrium | 05 Auditorium

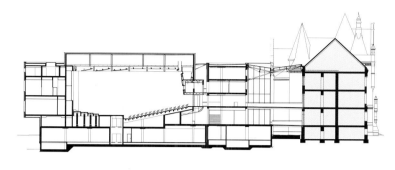

02

03

04

05

01

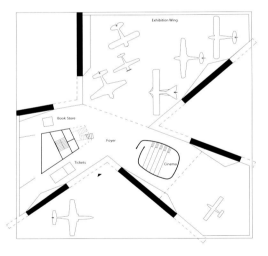

02

03

Museum of Polish Aviation

The idea of flying, the spirit of the place, the structure of the historical aerodrome –
this new museum building takes these ideas and compresses them into an expressive
building structure. The three-story building provides 4,500 square meters of space. The
old hangers provide the module size of the base, while the shape, cut and folded like
a windmill or a propeller, allows for an impressive, sculptural building. The exhibition
and the 3D cinema are situated on the ground floor. The restaurant and bar, library and
a lecture room with 150 seats are all located on the first floor. Offices and conference
rooms are all on the second floor. Justus Pysall, Peter Ruge and Bartlomiej Kisielewski
were the design authors of this building by Pysall Architekten.

01 East view | 02 Floor plan | 03 Main exhibition wing | 04 Cinema

04

01

02

03

04

CO$_2$ Saver House

This house, located on Lake Laka, blends in with its surrounding landscape. Colorful panels set into the timber façade reflect the tones of the country site. The outer countenance of the building is symmetrical, whereas the interior violates the symmetrical order following the functional requirements of the space. In addition to aesthetic considerations, the form was chosen in order to optimize solar energy absorbance. The ground floor was externally clad with untreated larch boarding, and a set-in glazed patio was integrated to gain solar energy. Additional solar collection panels were mounted on the roof, and a ventilation plant with a thermal recovery system ensures energy cost reduction for heating and lighting.

01 Detail of wood paneled façade | 02 "Black box" | 03 South view | 04 Untreated larch wood cladding | 05 Ground floor plan

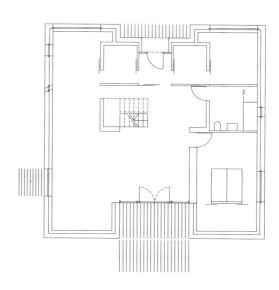

05

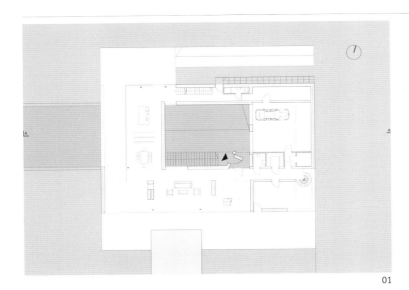

01

02

03

Aatrial House

This site has only one weak point, the southwestern access. A conflict develops between the driveway and the garden. The idea arose to lower the driveway in order to separate it from the garden. This prompted the design of a driveway leading inside to the ground floor level, from underneath the building. This was made possible thanks to the creation of an inner atrium with the driveway contained within it. As a result, the building opens up onto all sides with its terraces and the only way to get into the garden is through the atrium and the house. This in turn has made it possible to obtain a new spatial model of the house, which is the reverse of an atrial building.

01 Ground floor plan | 02 Atrium | 03 View from garden | 04 Driveway | 05 Driveway at night | 06 Interior view

04

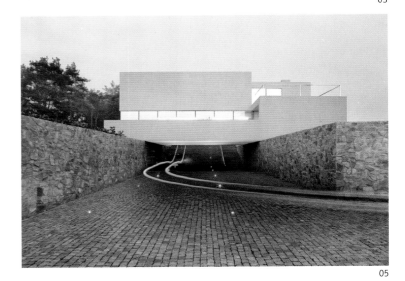

05

06

01

02

03

MAN Assembly Plant

Heavy-duty trucks destined for the Central and Eastern European markets undergo final assembly at this plant. The factory premises are divided in a modular fashion into supply, assembly, logistics, and accessory manufacture functional zones, all positioned in accordance with the production flow. This makes it possible for all functional elements to be expanded individually in the future. The central factory gate is constructed using dark gray brick and serves all deliveries, employees, and customers. Assembly takes place in a compact, equally expandable hall. The paint shop and auto finish areas are added to the side as independent units. Material choice and details project an image of precision and accuracy, as well as of genuineness and sturdiness.

01 Main gate | 02 Interior of integration center | 03 Stairway in integration center | 04 Ground floor plan | 05 Main entrance at night

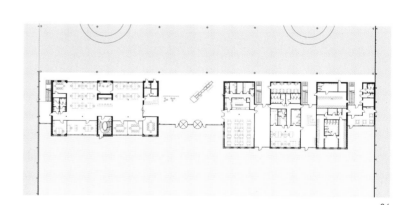

04

05

01

02

03

04

05

Maja's House

After the construction of the family house, there were some wooden elevation boards left over. As a result of this, the architects were asked to design a so-called tree house for a little girl named Maja. Unfortunately, none of the trees on the plot was suitable for this purpose. The only place good enough for the small house was the top of an earth mound in the garden. Maja drew her idea of the house, with a chimney and a gabled roof; these wishes were realized by the architects. The chimney providing ventilation and the gabled roof giving the house a large, open feel. The side walls of the house can be completely opened for when the weather is nice, or kept closed.

01 Interior view | 02 Slide | 03 Side view | 04 View trough opened façade | 05 Front view | 06 Exterior elevation and floor plan

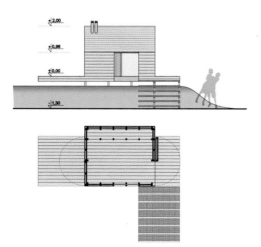

06

01

University of Poznan Library

The library is located in the heart of Poznan – in close proximity to historical buildings from the beginning of 20th century. The parcel is bordered on three sides by the Collegium Maius and by the building of the Regional Government Office. The building's structure is halved horizontally, with a massive sandstone bottom and a light glass top – merging historical content with a very contemporary form. The building's façades are dominated by glass and sandstone. The stone pattern is identical to the existing one at the façades of Collegium Maius facility. At the same time, some light rhythmic disturbances were introduced by the sandstone forms that appear throughout the entire building elevations, and which are also further reflected in the interior.

01 Exterior view | 02 Reading room | 03 Entrance hall | 04 Section

02

03

04

01

02

House near Poznan

This project is located on a picturesque plot that was originally a home to a seed drying installation, belonging to an agricultural university. The plot included a population of acacia trees and posed a challenge to the architects. The main task was to create a new structure that would accommodate a spacious single-story living space with a kitchen and dining area. The existing building was to be refurbished to accommodate a garage and storage space on the ground floor and bedrooms in the upper level. A staircase joins the new structure to the existing one. The entire building is clearly divided into two volumes – the old one with its historical charm and the addition with its clean, contemporary form.

01 Exterior view | 02 View from street | 03 Exterior at night | 04 Interior view | 05 Dining area | 06 Night view | 07 Ground floor plan

03

04

05

06

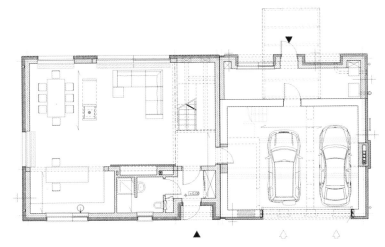

07

01

02

03

04

Siercza Petrol Station

This independent petrol station building is the architect's protest against the ugliness of typical gas station chain architecture across Europe, and indeed most of the world. This building is located in the center of the village, with a view to the mountains, and plays the role of local shop, cafeteria, and social space. Concrete, glass and layered board, which are commonly used in buildings of this kind, were deliberately applied to show another usage of the material. The filled slope is made of local stone debris and emphasizes the relation of the project to the area. Birchwood plywood was used as an inner wall covering to add a rural atmosphere.

01 Corner view | 02 Southwest view | 03 West view | 04 South terrace | 05 Floor plan

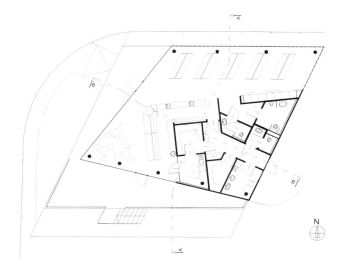

05

01

02

03

Industrie Maurizio Peruzzo Comfort Factory

The IMP Comfort Co Ltd. belongs to the Industry Maurizio Peruzzo Group, which deals with recycling plastic bottles into other products. The outstanding durability of plastic bottles is used positively here. The factory produces Geo-fibers, car carpets and furniture, amongst other things. Instead of being thrown away to contaminate the environment, the plastic is given a new use. The colors of the building give it a unique, sculptural appearance. The architecture is untypical of this type of industrial building. It is far more playful and eye-catching on the outside, as well as being modern and highly functional on the inside.

01 View from southeast | 02 View from northeast | 03 Front façade | 04 Ground floor plan | 05 Façade detail | 06 Interior view | 07 South façade

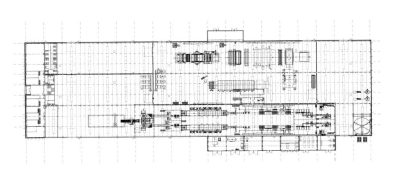

04

05

06

07

01

02

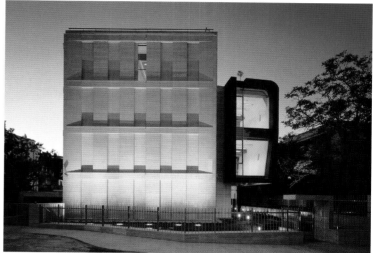

03

04

05

Wolf Nullo Office Building

The Wolf Nullo Office Building is situated in the prestigious part of Warsaw city center. The architecture of the building is determined by two elements. The main part is a classically shaped block finished in travertine. The movable elements of the façades, stone screens, and blinds, allow for individual regulation of the interior climate, signaling the state of activity within the building at the same time. The eastern façade is a surface of black basalt, easily twining around the block of the building. Its form is shaped freely, following its own rules, changing its shape and opening according to interior logic.

01 Façade detail | 02 Exterior view | 03 Exterior view at night | 04 West façade at night |
05 Exterior detail | 06 Floor plan

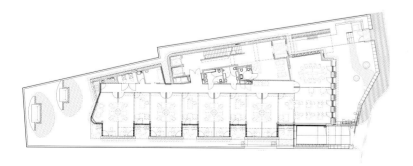

06

01

Golden Terraces

Surrounding the interior plaza, a three-level retail and entertainment center is organized in terraces, as suggested by the project's name. Towers rising above the three-level center will house office space. Designed to weave the urban fabric of central Warsaw back together, the center recreates the historic urban grid that was lost during World War II, and revitalizes public spaces nearby. Located near the Warszaw Central train station and the Palace of Culture, the mall is a landmark destination, and the center of a large urban system of the city's proposed new high-rise district. Designed as an extension of the city's 'necklace' of historic parks, the plaza is enclosed by an innovative glass roof with an undulating surface inspired by tree canopies.

01 Exterior | 02 Interior | 03 Food court | 04 Area master plan

02

03

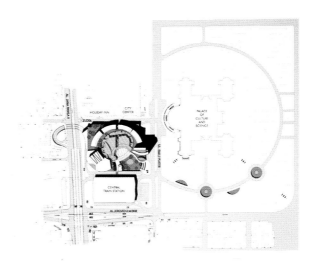

04

01

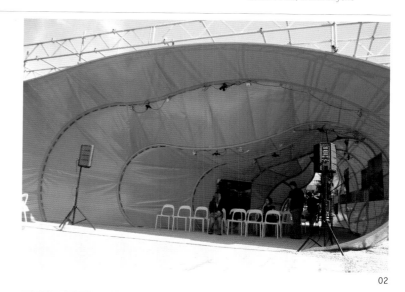

02

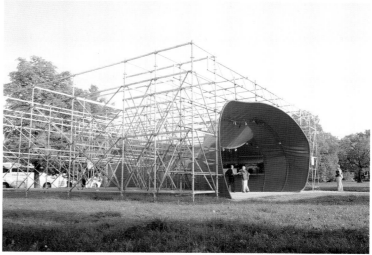

03

04

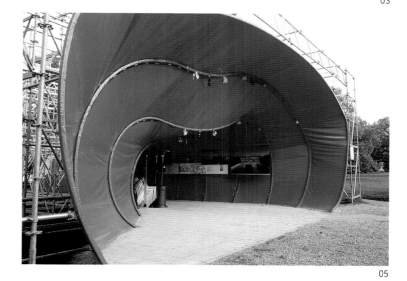

05

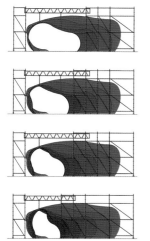
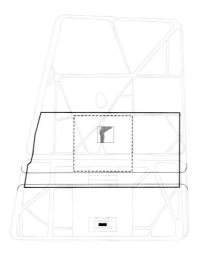

Ohel - Temporary Pavilion

The term "Ohel" carries a lot of connotations in the Jewish culture. It symbolizes bringing people together. The architect's tent gives the very first idea of the structure of the future Museum of the History of Polish Jews in Warsaw. The main aim of the pavilion was to inform about the building to be erected on the site. The "Ohel" pavilion was a temporary folding, textile structure, consisting of a blue PCV cover pitched over a steel structure made of scaffolding. Part of the idea for the pavilion was for it to be built on several of Warsaw's main squares. Krzysztof Banaszewski, Malgorzata Kuciewicz and Jakub Szczesny were working for Centrala on this project.

01 Rear view | 02 Entrance | 03 Front view | 04 Side view | 05 Entrance detail | 06 Plan

06

01

02

03

Corte Verona Apartment Building

The Corte Verona Apartment Building continues a Wroclaw tradition; the use of brick in large-scale constructions. The architecture complements the surrounding buildings and so called 'small architecture', as many local buildings, as well as benches, fences and walls are also built of brick. It was the last of those objects, an open-work brick wall in the neighborhood, that became inspirational in shaping the structure of this new building. The building was given the easily recognizable and well-functioning form of an urban block. The space was divided into: public (outside), private (flats) and semi-public (courtyard).

01 Façade detail | 02 Courtyard | 03 View from southwest | 04 View from northwest | 05 Floor plan

04

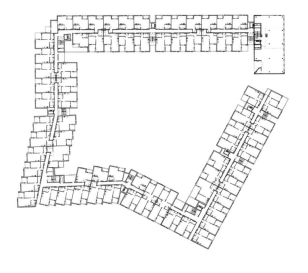

05

01

02

03

04

Black Cube House

This project involved the total makeover of a typical polish house from the 1970s. The clients wanted to increase the size of the house to almost double and change the elevation, whilst incorporating the old structure of the building. At the end of the facelift, the architects Rafal Specylak and Kuba Wozniczka turned the old white cube into a black cube. The existing house was extended in two directions, both towards the garden and the site's western boundary, creating extra living spaces. One of the most important aspects of this project was the creation of a smooth transition between house and landscaped area. On the garden side, a steel frame has been designed surrounding the terrace and supporting the projecting bedroom box.

01 Entrance | 02 Steel frame surrounding terrace zone | 03 Front façade | 04 View from garden | 05 Ground floor plan

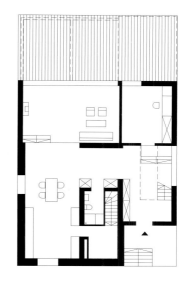

05

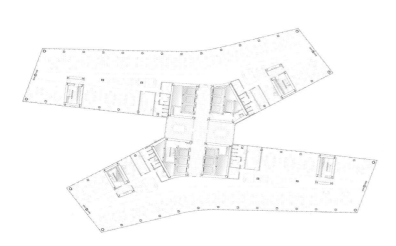

01

Orhideea Towers

The office building Orhideea Towers is a visible landmark on the banks of the Dâmbovita River. A soft cushioning of green shrubs creates a green buffer between the building and the nearby traffic network, providing a comfortable microclimate. The glazed monolithic appearance of the building consists of two black, convex wings, which are connected to each other in the middle via transparent bridges. Efficient logistics and reversible office space in differently sized units allow for a number of different combinations and uses. The communication center of the towers is the inviting, light-flooded lobby.

01 Standard office floor | 02 West view | 03 View from east

02

03

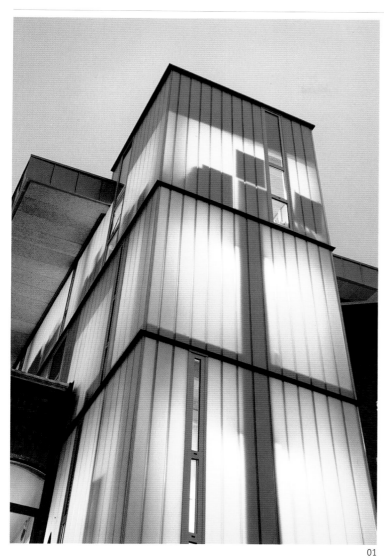

01

02

03

04

Renovation of Rahova Commodities Exchange

This building needed to be adapted to allow it to serve its new function. The architects therefore chose to restore the valuable part of the building and to rebuild the rest with a completely new concept, in stark contrast with the existing situation – exactly the kind of approach that is lacking in Bucharest. This former goods exchange building was the most prominent part of the Customs Goods Exchange Warehouses ensemble. The architects restored the long-vacant building to its nostalgic charm, framing it with a modern environment, using the candid and simple beauty of technology.

01 Façade detail | 02 Entrance | 03 Exterior view | 04 Office area | 05 Second floor plan

05

01

02

Litro Service Station

The Litro Service Station, designed by Eight Inc., brings a refreshing, contemporary environment to the traditional gas station concept. By using colored light, the architects aimed to embody the spirit of the new Rompetrol brand, Litro, conceived by Saffron Brand consultants. The design of the station reflects this fresh and playful identity through its use of light and incorporation of reflective and streamlined materials. The distinctive, ultra-thin canopy highlights the dynamic, indirect lighting and the signage, which is illuminated by color-changing LEDs. Fueling is designed on a bias, and was implemented to improve the efficiency and ease of entering and exiting.

01 Detail | 02 Cross sections | 03 Front view | 04 Main entrance

03

04

01

02

Petrom City

Petrom City merges together ten former offices from in and around Bucharest. The 100,000-square meter surface provides new work places for 2,500 employees. In addition to the building's main use as an office and administration space, complementary facilities such as medical facilities and a canteen, as well as a power plant and parking area have also been realized. The representative atria of the loop building are connected with each other via bridges; these optimize circulation in the building and are equipped with meeting points and conference rooms. The façade is a single, grid-like skin designed with integrated sun protection. The 11-story headquarters offers, in addition to conventional office space, sheltered green areas and roof gardens.

01 Petrom Plaza | 02 General view | 03 Façade detail | 04 Site plan | 05 Interior

03

04

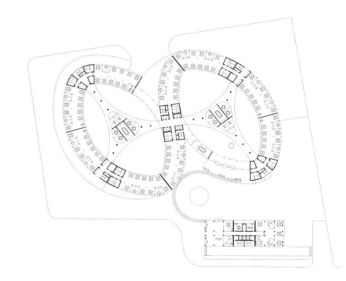

05

01

02

Green Gate

Green Gate is an A-class office building in the fifth district of Bucharest. The building will have a usable area of approximately 31,000 square meters, mostly comprising of offices, with some retail space on the ground floor, plus 16,000 square meters of underground parking. The intention is for the highest occupied floor to be below 45 meters, keeping the building within the limits of a 'high' building. The plan is to enable each floor to be split into four tenancies, each with independent access and metering. The office floors will be handed over to the tenants as a 'shell and core', with capped supply connection but without internal distribution or equipment. The architect's main objective is to create an economic but quality design.

01 Interior view | 02 Lobby | 03 Entrance | 04 Exterior view

03

04

01

02

03

04

05

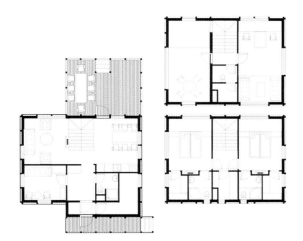

04

Russian Wood Patchwork House "Dacha"

The artistic design of this house is a combination of a simple layout with a clear function and a façade composed of wooden patchworks of various shapes and colors. The design envisaged a comfortable living space for two adult couples and their grown up children. The program also required ample space to accommodate guests. On the ground floor are the kitchen and adjoining dining room, a guest room, the boiler room, a summer veranda and a bathroom. The first floor consists of two bedrooms, two wardrobe rooms, a washing room, two toilets and shower rooms, while the work shop or studio, sauna, summer veranda, toilet and shower room are all located on the second floor.

01 Staircase | 02 Living area | 03 Bedroom | 04 Exterior view | 05 Living and dining area | 06 Ground, first and second floor plan

06

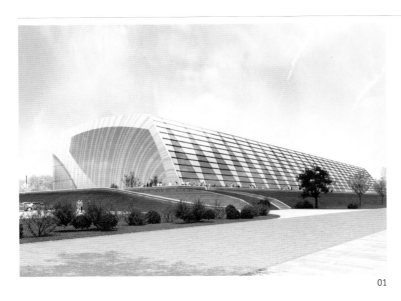

01

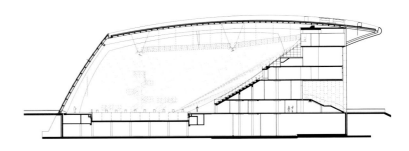

02

Water Stadium Kazan

This new water stadium, on the banks of the Kasanka, is integrated into an urban park area. It lies among other sporting facilities, built for a student sports competition, the Summer Universiade, which will take place here in 2013. The stadium is designed to cater for both professional swimming competitions and to serve as a public swimming pool. From a base embedded in the landscape, the construction develops into a wide, wave-like form. Between the V-shaped wooden constructions is a transparent roof. This takes a regular, alternating pattern, changing from rough to clear glass and creating a delicate pattern on the water. The entrance to the stadium lies in the raised base, together with the service facilities.

01 Street view | 02 Street view at night | 03 Cross section | 04 View of entrance at night | 05 View of entrance | 06 Interior with stands | 07 Swimming pool

03

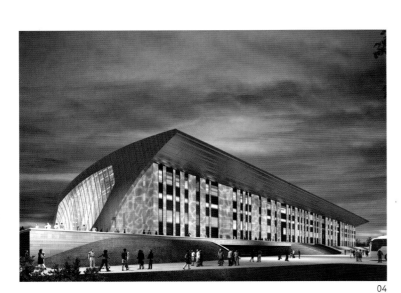

04

05

06

07

01

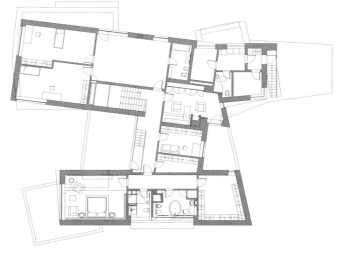

02

03

04

House of Mr. R.

This house has a solid-cast reinforced concrete frame with piers, bridging and walls made of brick. One wall is sloped. There are two apartment floors and a basement story; this has been dug in just over one meter below ground level. The rooftop is made of a single piece and has the maximum slope angle of 12 degrees. It is provided with clerestories to lighten a stairwell and a dormer. There is an accessible roof area for sunbathing or picnicing located between the house wings. There are two balconies and one recessed balcony on the second apartment floor. Outflows made of thin stainless pipes are being raised above the rooftop level and sloped against the house space to intensify the aesthetic impression.

01 Bar counter | 02 Ground and first floor plan | 03 Front façade | 04 Living room | 05 Master bedroom

05

01

02

03

04

Federal Arbitration Court of Moscow Region

The building is divided into two blocks – a seven-floor ancillary building located in the depth of the site, and a three-floor public building on Seleznevskaya Street. The buildings have separate entrances and are connected by two passages on the second and third floors. One of the passages houses a winter garden. The upper levels of the ancillary building are law offices and other departments. The sixth floor houses the office of the arbitration court chairman. The public building is designed for visitors. A round staircase and elevator lead to the court rooms on the second and third floors.

01 Interior view | 02 Exterior view | 03 View from street | 04 Projecting façade | 05 Second floor plan

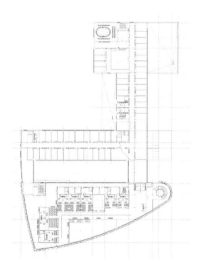

05

01

T-House

This private house, with a total area of 750 square meters, is located on a site of 0,9 hectares in a cottage settlement near Moscow. The house is a symmetrical rectangular volume with a protruding 'wings' – a balcony, which stretches more than six meters each side. Their beams equilibrate, together with a vertical concrete core, to form the framework of the building. The protruding balconies create dialogue between the house and the surrounding context, thereby creating the organic blend of rectangular volume within the existing landscape.

01 Exterior view | 02 Cantilevered balconies | 03 Staircase | 04 Floor plan | 05 Atrium

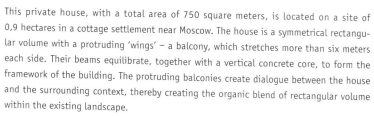

02

03

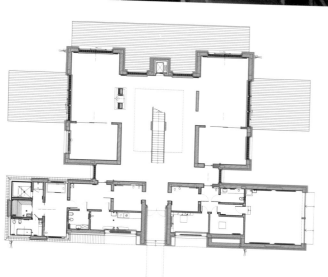

04

01

02

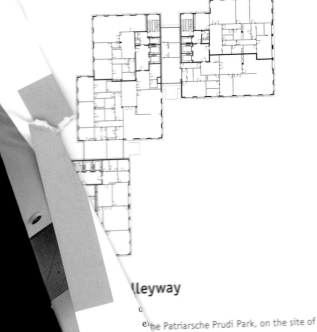

03

04

lleyway

e Patriarsche Prudi Park, on the site of a for-
fe favorite residence of the affluent members
tat homes from the 19th century and a few
Cen tiques and art galleries are established
shap of the complex, with its rich ornamen-
ate s re; in particular, by the neighboring

01 Ext by Andrej Burow. The three cube-
view at glass walkways. The volumes cre-

e fourth level | 04 Exterior

05

01

T-House

This private house, with a total area of 750 square meters, is located on a site of 0,9 hectares in a cottage settlement near Moscow. The house is a symmetrical rectangular volume with a protruding 'wings' – a balcony, which stretches more than six meters each side. Their beams equilibrate, together with a vertical concrete core, to form the framework of the building. The protruding balconies create dialogue between the house and the surrounding context, thereby creating the organic blend of rectangular volume within the existing landscape.

01 Exterior view | 02 Cantilevered balconies | 03 Staircase | 04 Floor plan | 05 Atrium

02

03

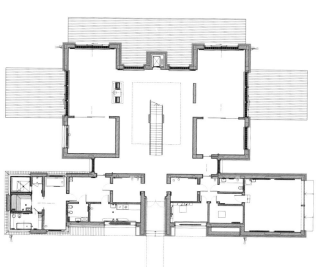

04

05

01

02

03

04

Apartments Granatny Alleyway

The Granatny Alleyway is situated near to the Patriarsche Prudi Park, on the site of a former gunpowder factory. The area has been a favorite residence of the affluent members of Russian society for several decades. Stately homes from the 19th century and a few exclusive businesses, housing restaurants, boutiques and art galleries are established features of this district. The exterior appearance of the complex, with its rich ornamentation, is influenced by the surrounding architecture; in particular, by the neighboring Central House of Architects, with its spectacular portal by Andrej Burow. The three cube-shaped volumes differ in height and are connected by glass walkways. The volumes create space for a central courtyard.

01 Exterior view | 02 Interior façade detail | 03 Plan of the fourth level | 04 Exterior view at night | 05 Window detail

05

01

02

03

Novatek Headquarters

This 12-story building is situated at the busy intersection between Leninsky Prospekt and Ulisa Udaltsova and was tailored to meet the needs of the Novatek gas company, right from the beginning stages of planning. A row of projecting bay windows take the shape of a curtain that has been pushed to one side, giving the main façades a fluent, dynamic and inviting character. The generous glazing on the façade has the added advantage of appearing to reduce the height of the building. Ridged, vertical limestone plates highlight the architectonic structure, while the light and shadow effect of the slopingindented façade elements enhances the structure's vitality.

01 General view | 02 Entrance | 03 Floor plan | 04 Corner view

04

01

02

House on Nikolina Gora

This architectural design complements the complexity of the landscape. The two-level lot allocated for the construction of the house has an elevation difference of three and a half meters. The main entrance is on the second floor and the first floor overlooks a beautiful meadow. The two sections of the house are mostly hidden inside the hill. In the small section there are guest and staff apartments, technical facilities and the boiler. Public areas such as the living room, kitchen and the dining room are in the large section. Private zones are on the bottom floor, which is hidden from the road and other houses located higher on the hill.

01 Bedroom | 02 Cabinet | 03 Front façade | 04 Service unit | 05 Ground floor plan

03

04

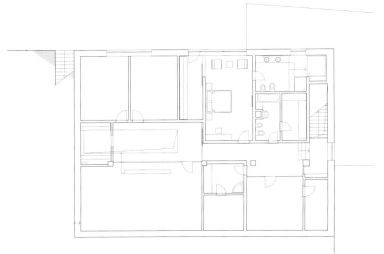

05

01

02

03

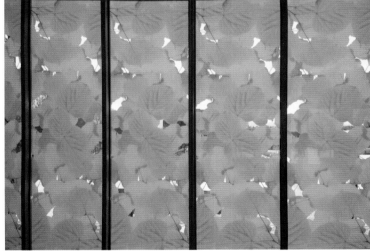

04

Administrative Building "Korpus 25" Renovation

"Korpus 25" is located in a Saint Petersburg park that formerly belonged to the tsars. Following the Russian revolution, this habitat was destroyed to a large extent by targeted relocation of industrial factories into the area. The building's frame remains a component of the post-revolutionary industrial architecture, with two additional stories stacked on top. The glass envelope is printed with summer leaves and flower motifs and is deliberately reminiscent of the park that was once here. The building, decorated along its almost entire surface, offers inhabitants on the upper floors views through the openings in the floral design, while along the ground floor, on the back façade, the building opens itself up through a fully glazed winter garden towards an old pond.

01 General view | 02 Flower curtain | 03 Opening in façade pattern | 04 View fixed glazing | 05 Ground floor plan

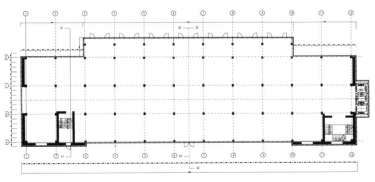

05

01

Benois House

A partially derelict industrial building stands at the former location of Russian artist Alexandre Benois's house at the border of the Kuschelev-Besborod-ko mansion gardens and today's Piskarevski Prospect. The building was redeveloped and converted into a multifunctional business center. The design is dedicated to Benois's theater work, which helped to bring Russian art and theater to world attention. The digital figurine prints on the glass of the front façade are based on Benois's theater costume sketches. The glass is set in an aluminum post-and-beam construction that supports the entire façade.

01 View from the street | 02 Site plan | 03 Rear façade | 04 Façade detail

02

03

04

01

02

03

04

05

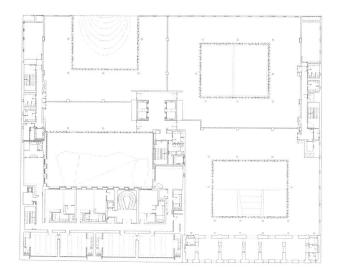

06

Quattro Corti Business Center

The Quattro Corti Business Center is located in the historic area of Saint Petersburg. The project called for the realization of a contemporary building, while still maintaining the historic façades of the two buildings that previously existed. Within the volume, four courts were created to illuminate the interior spaces. Their façades are composed of reflective glass panels of gold, green, blue and red, set at different angles and inspired by the chromatic richness of the city's historic architecture. The result is the fracturing of the overall reflection, which generates a kaleidoscopic light effect. The complex is mainly dedicated to offices, but also hosts a panoramic restaurant.

01 Courtyard | 02 Interior façade | 03 View of metal roof | 04 Green courtyard | 05 View from restaurant | 06 Floor plan

01

02

House at the Sea

North of Saint Petersburg city center, in the middle of a park area and in very close proximity to the sea, stands this apartment complex; an ensemble of 12 housing units, each joined to the next by a common base. The S-shaped arrangement of the building creates two different spaces, both different in character. One is the central Parade Esplanade, which extends the axis of the Grebny Canal, the other is a more private, quiet relaxation zone. The façade works to combine modern style with the historical appearance of Saint Petersburg. The architectural detail is inspired by French and Italian architecture; blinds and window shutters have been transformed into decorative stone elements, creating a surprise interpretation.

01 Detail façade | 02 General view | 03 House type "Korpus B" | 04 Historic villa and new buildings | 05 Detail façade "Korpus A" | 06 Site plan with typical floor plan

03

04

05

06

01

02

03

04

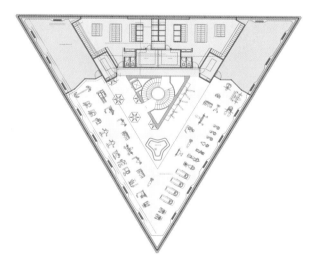

05

WellnessSky

The main volume of the building, triangular in plan, is elevated some fifteen meters above the river and the ground level with the pedestrian esplanade. It is supported solely by the central core, which contains two elevator shafts and a double spiral staircase. The concrete floor-slab and ceiling shell are not connected at the perimeter of the building, allowing for the continuity of the glass façade to the full extent. An uninterrupted glass strip, with a total length of 150 meters, is wrapped around the building. The ceiling design consists of a sequence of geometric transformations and subdivisions applied to the original grid. As a result, approximately 390 backlit panels with a finite variation in shape and size are suspended from the triangular steel construction.

01 Fitness room | 02 Exterior view | 03 Interior view | 04 Running machines with panoramic view | 05 Floor plan

01

02

03

Villa Klzawa

This rectangular-shaped plot is located on exposed, steeply sloping terrain with southerly orientation. The villa adapts to the terrain with retreating terraces, characteristic adaptations and original configuration. The longitudinal mass of the house is not composed of right angles, but is adapted to the shape of the site; the eastern façade in particular responds to the site boundary. The design of the house is focused around making optimal use of the city views; the large, glazed section of the façade facilitates this idea.

01 Front façade | 02 View from staircase | 03 Side view | 04 Interior | 05 Ground floor plan

04

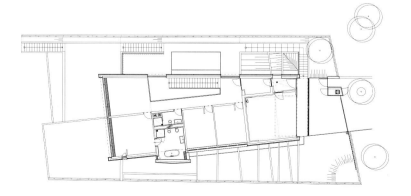

05

01

02

03

04

House Grunty

This family house is situated in a neighborhood of newly built houses in the locality of Stare Grunty. The position and building concept are based on the characteristics of the property and investor's requirements, with respect to the limits and regulations of the developed territory. The architect's aim was to find the optimal interior layout connecting to the outside environment, orienting the property around the ideal panoramic view. The design of the south-facing façade focuses on simplicity and functionality, thus fixed cantilever frames have been introduced to shield the interior. The frame line 'rewinds' through the east side to the west façades.

01 Wooden patio | 02 South view | 03 East view | 04 Wooden façade | 05 Ground floor plan

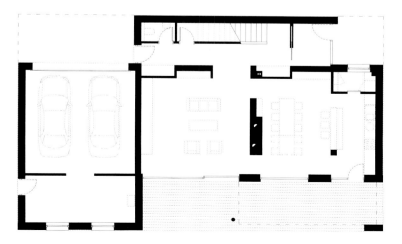

05

01

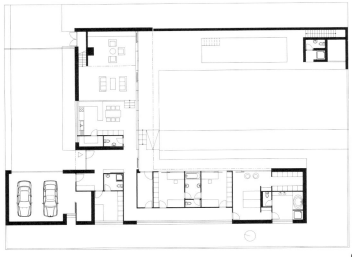

02

House B

House B is located in a new housing structure close to Bratislava. Close surroundings do not offer attractive views, while surrounding houses differ in architectural quality. The plan of the house is split into two separate wings. The 'day part' is represented by an open space on several levels, while the living room reaches a two-floor height, which includes a gallery and study-room. This space is lit by a skylight, which provides afternoon sunlight. The 'night part' is ordered linearly, where each room has access to the inner yard. The private space is separated from the street by a perforated concrete wall, allowing morning light to penetrate, creating an intimate and unique atmosphere.

01 View from garden | 02 Floor plan | 03 Night view from street | 04 View into kitchen and living area | 05 Rear façade and pool

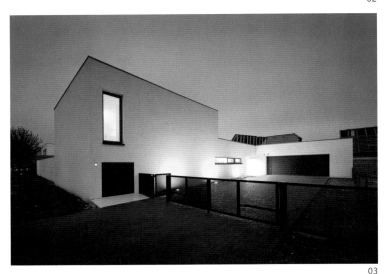

03

04

05

01

Apartment Building Smrek

This appartment building with kindergarten is located at Štrbské Pleso in the High Tatras. It has 35 standard, mainly two-room apartments, accesible via a naturally lit hallway with a light steel staircase. Light penetrates into the circulation space through tall rifts that split the building's volume. The proportion and form of the apartment building are articulated by tall shapes with oblique roofs that fit into the landscape. The metaphoric connection to the common spruce tree, found throughout the widespread mountain terrain, emphasizes the simplicity and uniqueness of the building's intervention in the wilderness of the High Tatra landscape.

01 General view | 02 Exterior view | 03 Interior view | 04 Regular floor plan

02

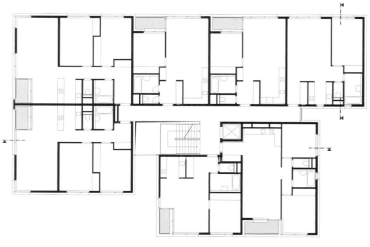

03

04

01

Villa A

Villa A is built near the forest, above the village of Kostoľany. The concept is based on a shell that protects the body from the outside. It is oriented to the east with a view towards the village and the church. The surface is made of tin and the interior is of wooden. The building itself is very simple, with an embedded basement and ground floor. The residential area containing the dining room and the kitchen is glazed and oriented to the east and west. The entrance is situated at the lowest level, covered areas near the stream serves also as a parking place. Walls consist of a sandwich construction surrounded by either wood or tin. The roof has ten-degree elevation and connects all rooms.

01 Rear façade | 02 Side view | 03 Front façade | 04 Floor plan

02

03

04

01

02

03

04

House U / Patio House

This house is located on the outskirts of Bratislava, in a new urban housing structure. The plan is based on a square. The main impression is of a circle, but really it is a spiral that is the leitmotif. A smooth spiral movement from the entrance hall to the open living space, continuing upstairs to roof terrace before flowing down to the patio, bedroom and study/window – a living landscape. Fixed furniture, like a bookcase, fireplace, kitchen box and wooden gallery, separates the various spaces. The relationship between the rooms and patio causes a palette of spatial experiences. The newly created patio space has all the advantages of an outer garden while remaining a safe, semi-internal zone within the house.

01 Patio | 02 Kitchen interior | 03 Exterior view | 04 Living room | 05 Elevations

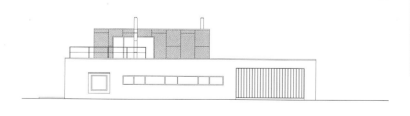

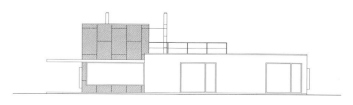

05

01

02

03

Schmitz Truck & Trailer Center

Located in an as yet undeveloped area with strong transport connections, the architects' intention was to announce the position of a building at this significant road junction. Having no desire to design the classic industrial boxed shed, they derived inspiration from the landscape. In folding and bending terrain facets, the architects enclosed an envelope around the required functions and also defined the external traffic flow. These include a showroom, administration, driver interface, five repair bays, and associated storage and parking lots.

01 Front façade | 02 Rear view | 03 Detail of triangular roof shape | 04 Site plan | 05 General view

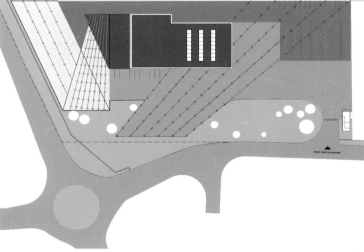

04

05

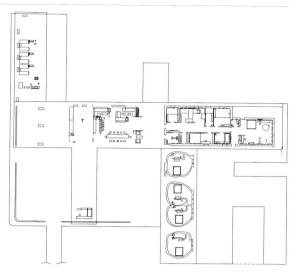

01

Friend House Hotel

The Friend House eco-hotel is located on the banks of the river Orel, 30 kilometers away from Dnepropetrovsk. It is a single-floor group of buildings with open yards, parking, terraces, gardens and park areas. In this project, the architects used exclusively ecological, harmless materials: clay, reed and wood. The building intentionally shares a dialogue with the surrounding environment, communicating with the forest and river. Another distinctive feature of this eco-hotel is an apple tree garden, emphasizing nature's bounty and highlighting the connection between the development and nature. The manufacturing company Ryntovt Design designs all furniture and lighting.

01 Floor plan | 02 General view | 03 Exterior view | 04 Hotel room | 05 Communal space | 06 Bathroom

02

03

04

05

06

01

02

03

04

Platinum Plaza

Kharkov is a city where every epoch spoke its own architectural language, 'the old' and 'the new' being interwoven in a dualistic unity. This building is located in the vicinity of the main square. A small atrium inside the building functions as an exhibition hall and is open to general public. A U-shaped layout was adopted, which solved a whole range of issues. Locating volumes along the perimeter of the plot ensured circulation between the old and the new buildings. The glazed, lower level of the building creates an interesting contrast to the heavier upper volume. The towers house conference halls and meeting rooms. In case of further development of the plot, open spaces are supposed to continue into the neighboring street.

01 View from street | 02 Courtyard | 03 Entrance area | 04 Passage | 05 Floor plan

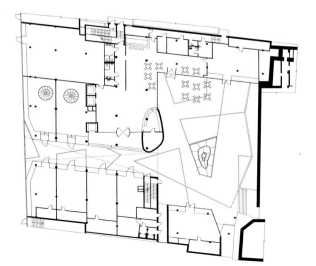

05

01

02

Pinchuk Art Center

Patron Victor Pinchuk, Chief Executive Officer of one of the main Ukrainian groups, wanted his foundation to close the gap between Eastern and Western European cultures. When Philippe Chiambaretta/PCA designed the Pinchuk Art Center, he wanted to embody this stance by designing a beacon for contemporary art in Eastern Europe. Located in the heart of Kiev, the Pinchuk Art Center distinguishes itself from the rest of the old neighborhood by its interior architecture, which develops a fictional journey through an architectural flux. On 2,600 square meters, the Pinchuk Art Center comprises two exhibition levels, a video lounge and a bar on the top floor.

01 Bar | 02 Interior view | 03 Dividing wall between exhibition spaces | 04 Exhibition room | 05 Seating in exhibition space | 06 Stairs | 07 Perspective of cross section

03

04

05

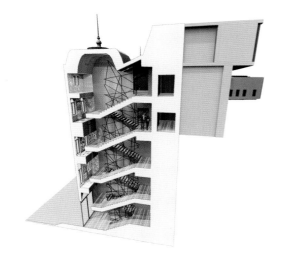

06

07

SOUTHERN EUROPE

02

01

Virtual Air Conditioners

In the process of this façade enhancement, the architects chose to authenticate the existing little white boxes with their round, off-center Cyclops-eye-vents. Sites for future acclimatizers were added, in the form of white rectangles, a strategy, which instantly legitimized the random placement of those already in service. The building itself is homogenized with red and orange stripes, faithfully scaled-up from the original watercolor sketch. The building is located between the Albanian Parliament and the former Dictator's Villa. An adjacent project for a Boutique Hotel proposed low-tech air conditioners: brise-soleil, freestanding in front of the reconstituted villa.

01 Exterior | 02 Façade detail | 03 Sketch of the façade

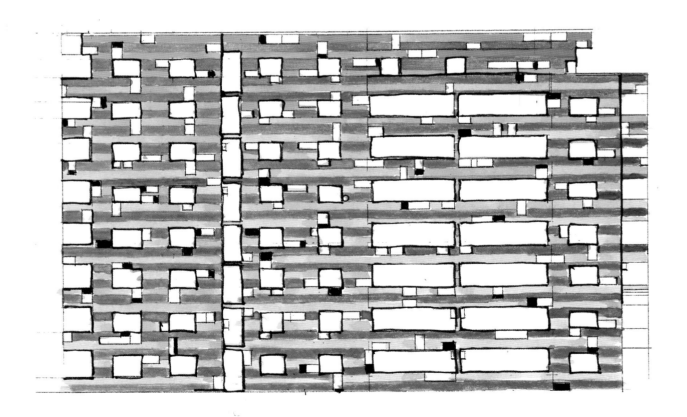
03

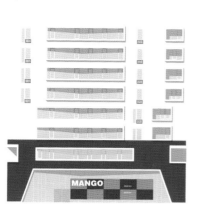

01

02

Rationalist Apartments

This eight-story building respects the formal language and compositional strategies of its travertine neighbors. Window slips bring a contemporary asymmetrical tension to façade compositions, balconies are internalized as loggias and materials are reduced to those fitting the historical context and the possibilities of construction in Albania. Broken and discarded roof-tile fragments were bought cheaply. Only two and a half centimeters high, they were laid edge to edge on a two centimeter wide mortar joint. Chinese bricklayers were imported (small-world networks), the precise horizontal striation having proved beyond the skills of local craftsmen. The rich tactility of this surface is the result, not of preconceived conceptual determinism, but of an open-ended and pragmatic approach to process.

01 Elevations | 02 Façade in context | 03 Floor plan | 04 Exterior view

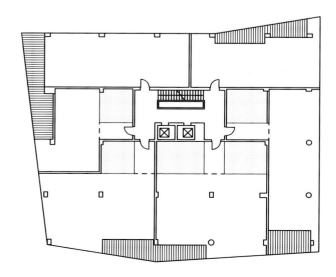

03   04

01

02

Bale Sports Hall

Bale is a small village in Croatia with a mostly agricultural population of 1,000. The Mediterranean's rich historical and cultural context was taken into consideration when building the new sports hall. The solution interprets the traditional ways of building with new technologies. Inspiration was found in the traditional stone hut – ka-un, a small multifunctional building used as a shepherds' shelter. The traditional local dry stone wall motif is used as a pattern for the surfacing of the sports hall. The concept was made to meet the design and construction time schedule by using RC prefabricated elements.

01 Front view | 02 Side view entrance | 03 Sports hall | 04 Ground floor plan | 05 Side view | 06 Rear view

03

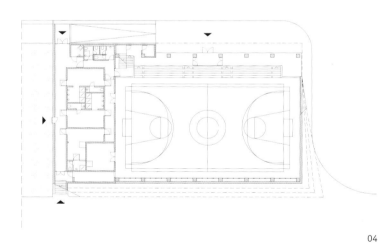

04

05

06

01

Gymnasium 46° 09′ N / 16° 50′ E

This high school building and sports hall are located at the end of a series of ambitious town projects, facing the American-style suburb. The complex is divided into two parts, contrasting black and green, full and empty, spiritual and physical, one facing the city and the other facing the residential area. The enigmatically compressed high school and sports complex constitutes a dynamic space experience contrasting with the surrounding flat landscape. It is centrally positioned as an entire whole without a frontal or back plan, free of any hierarchy or authority.

01 East façade with classrooms | 02 Multipurpose building at night | 03 Sports hall | 04 Cross section | 05 Multi-story 'internal street'

02

03

04

05

01

02

03

04

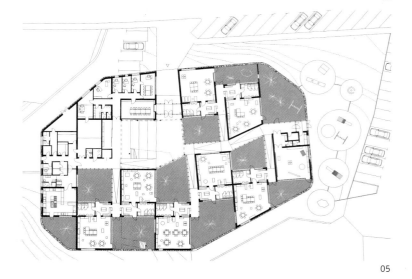

05

Katarina Frankopan Kindergarten

Shaped as an introverted insula and bordered by soaring stone walls, this kindergarten detaches itself from the unattractive surroundings of apartments and shopping malls. Inside, individual units are combined with open gardens and connected with pedestrian walkways. Due to the relatively small area of the site, the units for the smallest children, along with open roof terraces, are located on the first floor. The kindergarten is defined by a series of halls, or kale (local name for small streets), that are slanted upwards or downwards according to the topography of the site. A small piazza in the center of the kindergarten serves as a location for events and celebrations.

01 Stonewall façade | 02 Main entrance | 03 Aerial view | 04 Lobby | 05 Floor plan | 06 Playroom

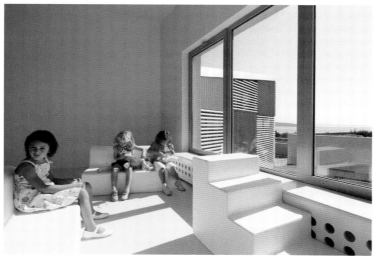

06

01

02

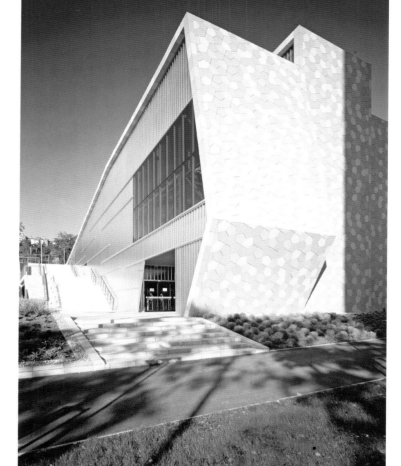

03

Zamet Center

Zamet Center is a hybrid building comprised of a sports hall, city library, local government committee rooms and commercial features, all of which create a new community center. The main architectural element of the center is the 'ribbons' stretching in a north to south direction. These function as an architectural design element and as a zoning element, which forms a public square and a link between the park on the north and B. Vidas street on the south. The ribbon-like stripes were inspired by "gromača", a type of rock specific to Rijeka, which the center artificially reinterprets in color and shape. The stripes are covered with ceramic tiles designed by 3LHD architects and manufactured specially for the center.

01 View from B. Vidas Street | 02 Exterior view | 03 Side view | 04 First floor plan | 05 Entrance

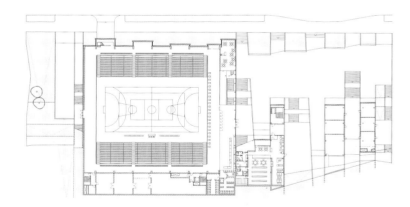

04

05

01

02

03

04

05

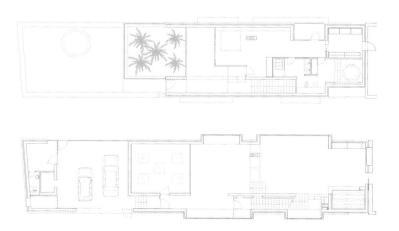

06

Varaždin Residence

The Varaždin residence consists of two parts, one older and one more recent. The living room comprises the entire ground floor of the house and everyday life takes place between two conservatories. One of these is located at the gable end of the new house and is dynamic and modern in its design. The other is inspired by the old house and is designed as an abstract aluminum cube with strict geometrical lines, emphasizing abstract character and providing a contrast to the old house. This house is an example of a modern building that respects its traditional location, forging together both the past and the present.

01 Interior view | 02 Street façade | 03 Side view | 04 Interior view | 05 View from garden | 06 Ground and first floor plan

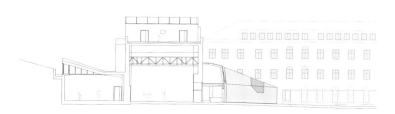

01

02

03

Dance Center

The opening of movieplex cinemas in Zagreb has led to the dying out of old cinemas in the city. The city of Zagreb decided to reuse those spaces for new cultural facilities. The old Lika cinema was converted into a dance center. It is located in a dilapidated block one hundred meters away from Zagreb's main square. The entire project was placed in the old cinema shell. The only new architectural element is the entrance lobby, a communication and meeting space. The volume and its broken form suggest dance movement, creating a connection between the courtyard and the roof terrace, which is an important part of the preservation and restoration of Zagreb's last open roof stage.

01 Section | 02 Entrance lobby | 03 Hallway | 04 Exterior from the courtyard | 05 Interior view

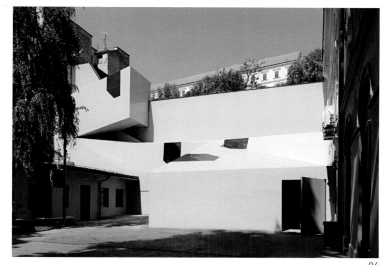

04

05

01

02

03

04

J2 House

This family house for a couple with children is located in the green residential part of the city of Zagreb. The 'L' layout with closed fronts protects the house from the street and the neighboring building, while the garden has been redesigned with all the main rooms in the house oriented towards it. The kitchen, living and dining rooms form a unique space, and together with a swimming pool are built underground. The house entrance is above, at street level, together with garage, storages, closet-space and studio. The living and dining spaces are separated by glass walls connecting the living space to the exterior, while the bedroom walls are paneled with wooden boards.

01 Terrace | 02 Stairs leading to bedrooms | 03 Exterior view at night | 04 Indoor swimming pool | 05 Cross section

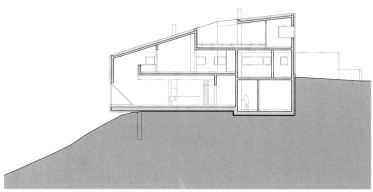

05

01

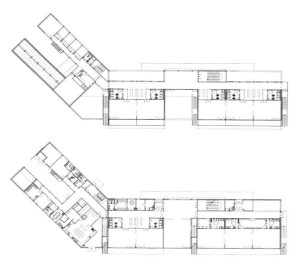

04

06

02

03

05

Jarun Kindergarten and Nursery

Space is provided for ten educational groups in this kindergarten and nursery, which combines optimal functionality, accessibility, transparency, and openness in its linear structure. Three interconnected units comprise the interior: the nursery on the ground floor, the kindergarten units on both the ground and first floors, and the service rooms organized around a housekeeping yard. The units can be completely opened onto sheltered terraces or deep canopied balconies on warm days, spaces which also serve to activate the linear volume and decode the function of the interior spaces. Materials such as aluminum, glass, linoleum, and colored Trespa plates further emphasize the main features.

01 Staircase leading to playground | 02 Façade with colored Trespa plates | 03 Playground | 04 Floor plans | 05 Detail of building volume | 06 Hallway

01

03

02

MB Kindergarten

MB Kindergarten was conceived as a single-story mat building - compact and introverted with clearly defined borders - as a response to the challenges of the site, which
is overshadowed by a nine-story block to the south and surrounded by heavy traffic.
A repetitive small-scale structure of units and patios echoes the local suburban matrix
and creates a variety of open-air spaces, including covered (winter) terraces and a rooftop garden. The interior is organized as a sequence of spaces linked with "The Children's
Street". Its meandering character and multitude of in-between spaces, supported by
transparency and color coding, create a scenery of true 'urban' experience for the child.

01 Classroom | 02 Interior with transparent glass walls | 03 Playground | 04 Floor plan |
05 Street view

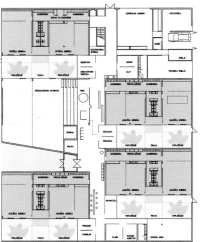

04

05

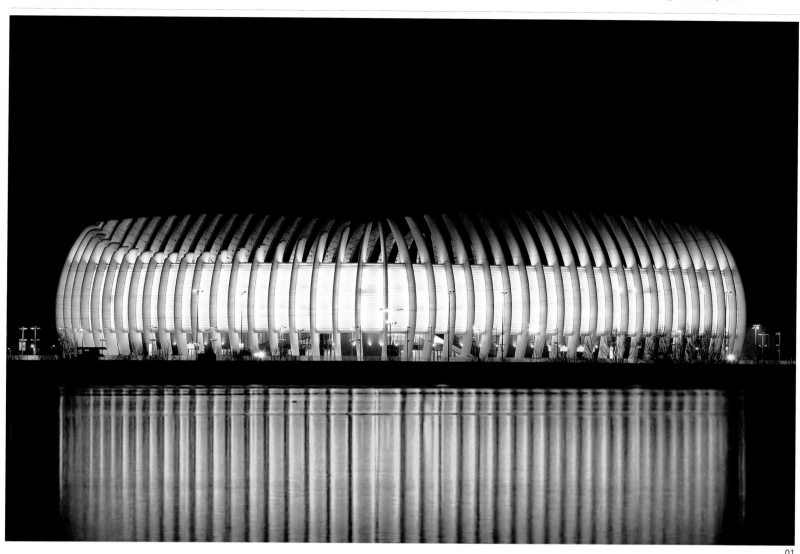

01

Arena Zagreb

Arena Zagreb is a multifunctional indoor arena built to host the 2009 World Men's Handball Championship. It is located in the southwestern part of Zagreb, Croatia. Thanks to its iconic design and position at one of the main city entrances, it has immediately become a landmark of the city. The unique shape of this building is strongly inspired by its significance in the city context, and also by its mega-structural characteristics that predefined main bearing elements. The arena was designed as a multifunctional hall with many special spatial and functional characteristics that enable maximal flexibility and allow for the realization of numerous events.

01 View from lake | 02 Exterior view | 03 Arena | 04 Explosion view

02

03

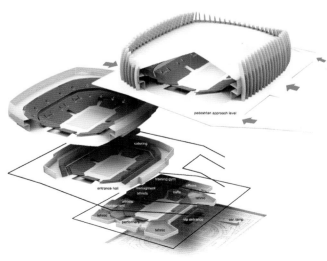

04

01

02

03

04

House K

House K is a family house situated on a large residential plot on a moderate eastern-facing slope at the edge of a forest near the base of Sljeme hill. By placing the object next to the street in the northwestern corner of the plot, preference was given to a beautiful forest view; the uneven terrain was used as a means of developing the object's volume. The concept of the house is inspired by the shape of a snail's shell, which involves a spiral twisting around its own axis, and as such all functional elements of the house follow each other and are built around a central atrium. The atrium was made in order to compensate for a lack of sunlight in the living room area and enabled two-way lighting of certain rooms.

01 Exterior view | 02 Staircase | 03 View from forest | 04 Living room | 05 Ground floor plan

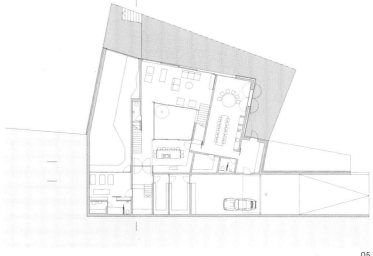

05

01

Acropolis Museum

Located at the foot of the Acropolis, this site includes sensitive archeological excavations, the contemporary street grid and the Parthenon itself. The base of the museum floats on pilotis over the existing archeological excavations, while a network of columns dominates the building. A glass ramp overlooking the archeological excavations leads to the galleries in the middle, in the form of a double-height room. The top, containing the rectangular Parthenon gallery, rotates to position the marbles of the Frieze exactly as they were at the Parthenon centuries ago.

01 Parthenon gallery | 02 East façade | 03 Sculptures between round pillars | 04 Parthenon gallery floor plan | 05 New building above excavations

02

03

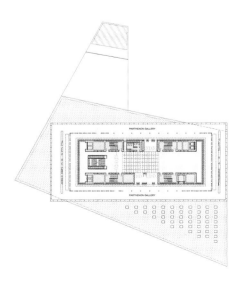

04

05

01

02

Athens International Airport

The concept of flow has driven this architectural design through geometric forms that reflect but also facilitate the flow of space. The functional section of an airplane engine, in the form of a funnel, is a symbolic reference within the design but is also a suitable form to maneuver the flow of passengers from the screening area to the enclosed walkway of the bridge. Connecting the two terminals with the aboveground, the enclosed walkway significantly upgrades the operational use of the Satellite Terminal Building (STB). The new buildings that compose this specific design are the footbridge, which unifies the Main Terminal Building (MTB) and the STB, and the building adjacent to the southwestern side of the MTB between the control tower and the main entrance of the MTB.

01 Bird's-eye view | 02 Exterior footbridge | 03 Sketch of footbridge | 04 Interior main terminal building

03

04

01

02

03

04

05

Placebo Pharmacy

The design process for this large pharmacy forced the architects to shift their viewpoint and come up with a virtual building – a placebo pharmacy. The octagonal shape of the existing structure was reformed into a cylinder and a spiral around it to converse with the rapid motion of its context. The Braille perforated façade alludes to the pharmaceutical packaging and allows light to find its way into the interior. Inside a ramp up to the upper level extends the dynamism of the exterior spiral into the interior space. Its arranged in a radial pattern to give a natural flow to the space and allow light enter inside throughout the day, with the cashiers desk as the focal point and distributed over two floors, the ground floor as the shop space with the mezzanine as office space.

01 Counter | 02 Exterior view | 03 Exterior at night | 04 Skin detail | 05 Ramp | 06 First floor plan

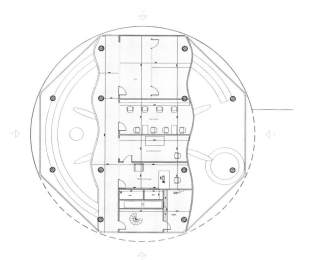

06

01

Two Houses in Anixi

This project concerns two private residences with a common yard. The construction process involved the use of a metal frame resting on concrete walls. The roof is clad with zinc and glazed windows form the façade. Basic synthetic principals of the design include the dissolution of limits between lived space and natural and organization between private and common spaces. This is achieved through the use of a concrete wall, connecting the two sides of the building. The structure also creates a unique geometry through the use of metal construction. Interior and exterior views are framed through adapted openings in the metal roof.

01 Main view, south façade | 02 View from courtyard | 03 View from north | 04 Interior view | 05 Conceptual diagrams

02

03

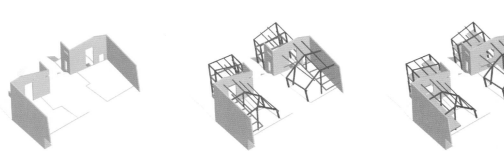

04

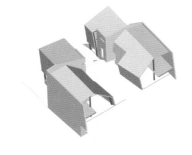

05

01

Aloni

The design of this house is a dual response to the topography of the site and to the rural domestication techniques that shaped the raw landscape of the Cycladic island in the past. In the north to south axis, the slope rises between two hills, while in the east to west axis the slope drops, opening to the sea views. The house nestles in the space while maintaining the continuity of the landscape which flows over it. This simple strategy blurs the edges of the house and makes its mass imperceptible within the broader context. The courtyards separate the living spaces into five interior areas. As a result, the house is protected from the elements yet is full of natural light, with a compact but rich relationship to its setting.

01 Aerial view | 02 Interior terrace | 03 West view with pool | 04 Section

02

03

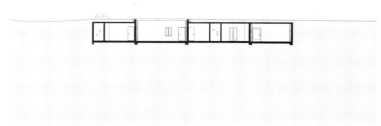

04

01

Split & Rotate

Responding to the spirit of the place, the general layout is austere, with clear geometric elements, industrial aesthetics and dynamic yet controllable tension. The general layout results from the split in two unequal parts: the main residence and the children's pavilion that are bridged with a transparent glass passage way. The composition results from the simultaneous rotation of the volumes on two axes according to the topography and the views, thus ensuring a dialectic composition of the entirety, with clear, relatively independently functioning yet connected parts.

01 Rear view | 02 General view | 03 Floor plan | 04 Exterior detail | 05 Hallway

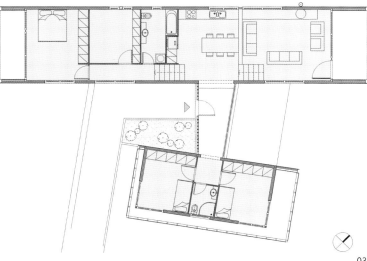

02

03

04

05

01

02

03

Patras Museum

This group of asymmetrical prismatic volumes was designed to accommodate the discoveries of a past culture. It is a modern composition which, through its irregular order, attempts to express the harmony of the volumes, the surfaces, the movements, and circulation through the spaces where the exhibits are displayed. At the same time, it consists of an organic and functionally structured deconstruction, exempted from a static symmetry that seeks to form a dialogue with the environment, the visitors and the users. The design of the building along the National road of Athens–Patras, an urban central highway, renders the museum a landmark for the area and provides easy and direct access to it.

01 Entrance | 02 Creased wall | 03 Elevated course | 04 Site plan

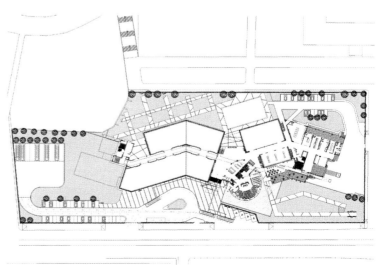

04

01

02

03

04

Hotel Arcadia

Hotel Arcadia is located on the first square encountered by visitors entering the city of Tripoli on the Peloponnese. Since pre-war times a hotel was situated here, originally three-stories high and later extended to five. In order to create the contemporary but comfortable appearance required, the hotel was entirely renovated both internally and externally. To emphasize the clarity of the design, white and black are the dominant colors of the materials applied. Decorative elements were avoided, apart from the graphic interventions by Vangelis Tzimopoulos. For the elevation, the glass boards of the balconies were engraved with graphics similar to the ones used in the rooms of the hotel.

01 Exterior view | 02 Hotel room detail | 03 Foyer with black and white decor | 04 Hotel room | 05 Ground floor plan

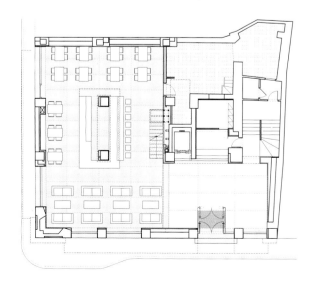

05

01

02

03

04

Museion – Museum of Modern and Contemporary Art

The effect of this museum building is derived from the contrast between the closed metal skin and the funnel-shaped, transparent entrance façades. These consist of an exterior, point-fixed glass layer and a glazing with insulating properties. Mobile, matt glass lamellas that act to regulate daylight and sun rays are located in the interstitial space between the inner and the outer glass layers. At night, they form a screen for projections; during the day, they accentuate the entrance by creating a slanting doorway in the full height of the building. The interstitial space of the façade is used as an active climate layer for the creation of an energy efficient buffer.

01 Glass façade | 02 Studios and museum | 03 General view at night | 04 Façade detail | 05 Longitudinal section

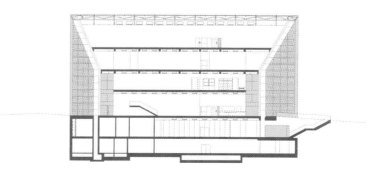

05

01

02

03

Blaas General Partnership

The company Blaas in Bolzano specializes in electro-mechanics. At its new headquarters, the company presents its new product range and offers repair services. On the ground floor of the building there is the sales division, with the showroom and the repair shop located on the first floor. All administration offices are situated on the second floor. The overall impression of the structure is a homogenous and closed building. Nevertheless, there is a clear and formal separation between the public and the private sector, which can be perceived from the outside. The glass façade on the northern side provides maximum visibility and transparency for the exhibition and sales area.

01 South view | 02 Main stairway with rooflight | 03 Roof garden with skylight | 04 Workplace | 05 Third floor office | 06 Third floor plan | 07 Main stairway

04

05

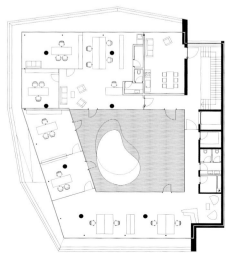

06

07

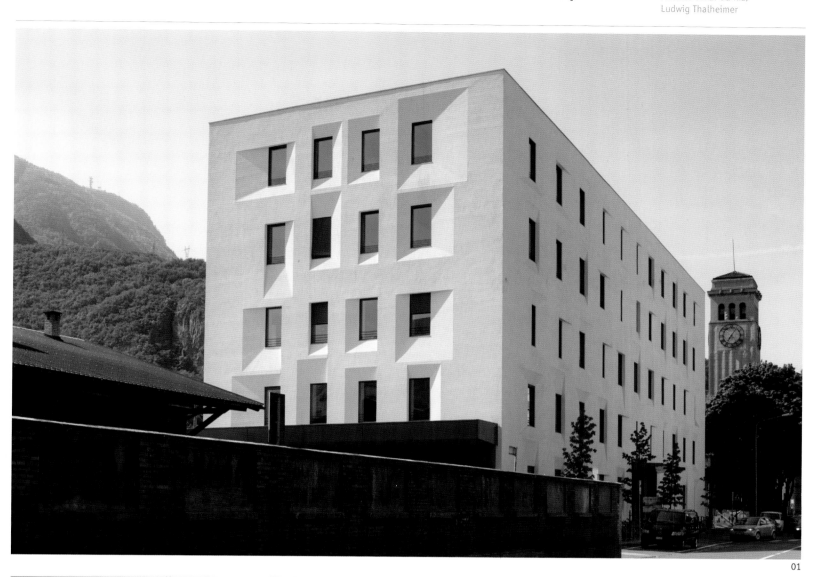

01

Ex-Post

The former post office from 1954 has been modified to create a modern office building for government agencies and constitutes the first public passive energy house in Italy, with a computed consumption of one liter of heating oil per square meter. Due to the high energy savings, all operating costs for the office building were reduced by approximately 90 percent. Insulated with a highly efficient building shell consisting of a polystyrene brick work and triple-pane glazing, it was possible to forgo a traditional heating system altogether. A ventilation unit with a heat recovery function is used for heating and cooling the offices, allowing individual thermal control for each room.

01 View from main street | 02 Back façade and photovoltaic plant | 03 Ventilation system | 04 Pipeline plan

02

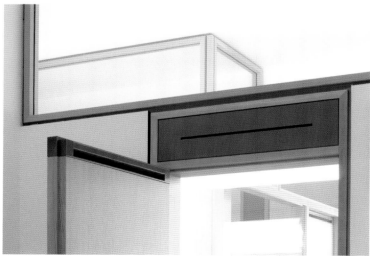

03

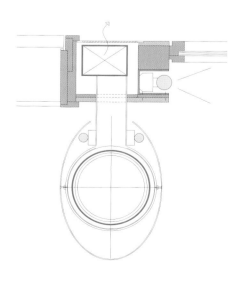

04

01

02

03

04

Fincube 1

'Natural high-tech' is the concept behind this modular, sustainable and transportable low-energy house. Entirely constructed using local wood, the building provides 47 square meters of living space with a minimal carbon footprint. Local suppliers and craftspeople using local, long-lasting, and recyclable materials were employed in the construction. The wooden space with 360-degree triple glazing is furnished with a second façade layer, providing shade and giving the building a unique mushroom-like shape. It is easy to dismantle and relocate, and requires only two meters of soil sealing, which is easily renatured once the Fincube has been moved to a new location.

01 General view | 02 View of bedroom from garden | 03 Wooden fins dominate the exterior | 04 Double façade detail | 05 Architectural models and axonometric projection

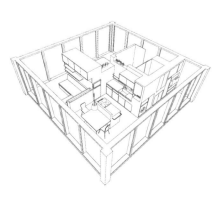

05

01

02

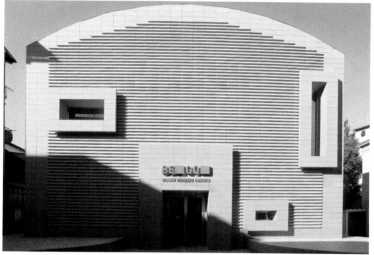

03

04

05

Benozzo Gozzoli Museum

The design of the Benozzo Gozzoli Museum, which has a total area of 400 square meters, closely follows the ground traces of an old building that has been demolished. The building is rooted to the ground through a functional island-shaped base, which solves the problem of urban furnishing: the base becomes a bench, a play area for children and a theater for small outdoor events. The ground floor is partly characterized by a low ceiling: a shaded area, which quickly runs to the full-height space where the "Tabernacolo della Visitazione" is placed. On the first floor, recessed into the corner-wall, is the "Tabernacolo della Madonna".

01 Exterior view at night | 02 Exterior view | 03 Front façade | 04 Interior view | 05 New meets old | 06 Ground, first and second floor plan

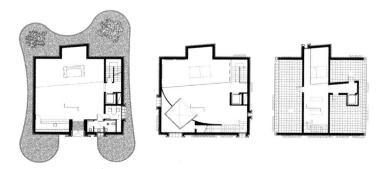

06

01

02

VC 1

This project includes the realization of a residential building on a site with no public access. The new access road now leads along two sides of the quadrangle lot. The form of the building is based on a box shape and contains a basement car park, eight apartments on the first two floors, and a garret apartment. The outer appearance of the building is compact and modern, with the variation of the façade cladding giving the structure a unique look. The structure refuses the homogeny of its surroundings, asserting itself with a dynamic presence into the surroundings.

01 View from public garden | 02 View from street | 03 Side view | 04 Parking lot | 05 Façade | 06 Ground floor plan

03

04

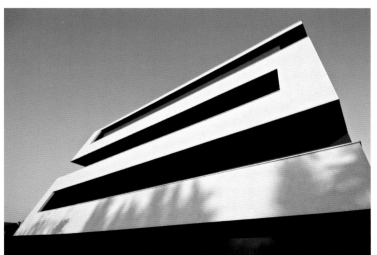

05

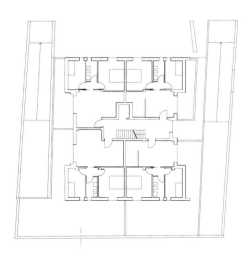

06

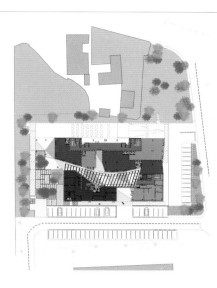

01

02

Ecoforum

The Ecoforum's general layout conceptually overcomes common practice in urban design, by designing the termination of the existing productive district. The Ecoforum is meant to be a flow connector; a system in place of a single building. The main building has a diversified depth, which makes possible the subdivision of each floor into five different independent units. Each building front is subject to different thermal loads and this naturally translates into the need to locally vary the performance of the façade system. The use of a 'double-skin' passive technology allowed the architects to design a fully-glazed, low energy-consumption environment with an optimized use of daylight. An electronically controlled dynamic system allows a controlled ventilation of the air layer.

01 Ground floor plan in situation | 02 Interior view | 03 Exterior view | 04 Façade | 05 Detail | 06 Rear view

03

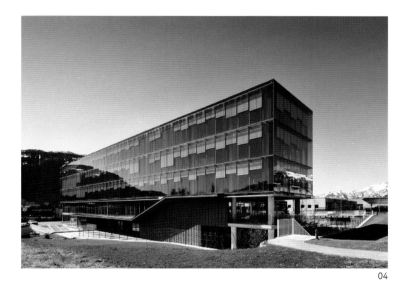

04

05

06

01

02

03

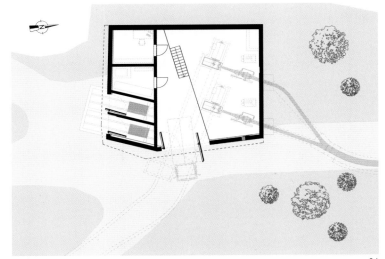

04

Hydroelectric Power Station Winnebach

This hydroelectric power station is partly built into the slope, significantly reducing the building area. The project consists of a simple polygonal volume, which is formally adapted to the landscape and the local conditions. The station is conceived as an artificial rock quarried out of the slope. The 'veins' that cross the building volume consist of light bands of layered glass and run around the building. The building has two stories, the basement shelters the generating set, the distributing unit and the control tank as well as a storage room. The ground floor offers space for the utility companies and the control room of the power station.

01 View from east | 02 View from south | 03 Exterior at nigt | 04 Site plan | 05 View from southeast | 06 Interior view | 07 Interior from walkway

05

06

07

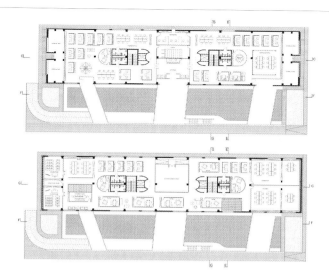

01

02

03

04

Cabel Industry

Cabel Industry covers an area of 4,500 square meters and it is incorporated into a small industrial estate. The building is composed of two extended floors. The visitor arrives on the ground level through three suspended bridges launched on a large excavation. At nighttime this empty space becomes a pool of light. Inside the building, the underground level holds a printing facility and other spaces; the ground floor features all different sorts of glazed spaces, ranging from open plan spaces to small isolated cells. The first floor accommodates the management space, with a small internal patio and terrace in-between them. The building is constructed out of prefabricated concrete elements.

01 Ground and first floor plan | 02 Interior view | 03 Suspended bridge | 04 Main entrance | 05 General view

05

01

02

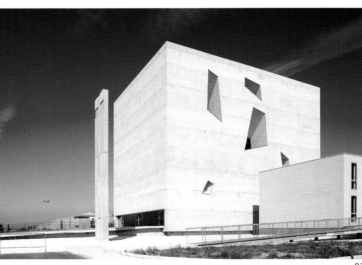

03

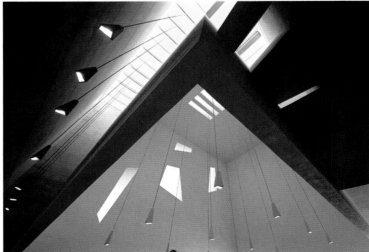

04

San Paolo Parish Complex

This project won a national competition, organized by the Italian Episcopal Conference to design new parish centers. The new parish complex is composed of two main elements, which also serve the purpose of providing a religious center. A thrust towards spirituality and quiet prayer blend together in an interplay of beams of natural light crossing the structure both transversely and vertically, projecting towards the main features: the altar, ambo and baptismal font. The striking structure is raised one a half meters above grade level. It can be reached by crossing a parvis, a long walkway leading to the entrance, a clean horizontal cut into the absolute compactness marking the entire front elevation.

01 External view | 02 Interior view | 03 Side view | 04 Ceiling detail | 05 Design sketch

05

01

02

03

House Cellina von Mannstein

This new villa, designed for renowned photographer Cellina von Mannstein, is located in the northern part of Italy, surrounded by the Alps. The housing part is distributed across two levels, which are slightly shifted over each other to create a canopied entrance on the northern part of the first level and a balcony on the south side of the second level. The first level contains the living area and connects onto the south oriented terrace and pool. An eye-catching feature is the tree in the atrium, which is accessible by large sliding glass windows. The photo studio is characterized by a large glass façade at the end. This 'screen' provides light or can alternatively be transformed into a vast projection wall.

01 Exterior view | 02 General view | 03 Interior view | 04 Section

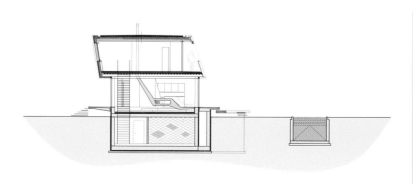

04

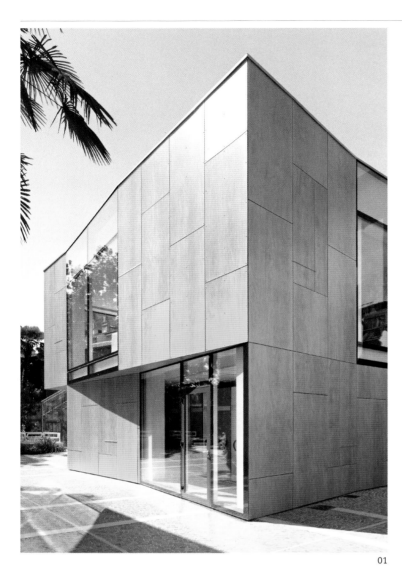

01

02

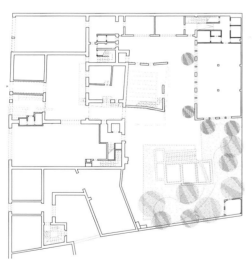

03

04

KBCenter and Qubik Bar

The KBCenter is a cultural space dedicated to the Slovenian community in the town. It consists of a renovated and a new library building. The choice of façade materials, wood and large glass surfaces, supports the insertion of a large piece of furniture, which slides on the courtyard floor. Windows are fixed and frameless, while natural ventilation passes through panels hidden in the façade. The skin is made of plain surfaces, to provoke ambiguity. From a distance, the glass surface is more distinct than the wood. Up close, it reflects the garden and the life around, almost disappearing.

01 New library building in the courtyard | 02 Courtyard | 03 Ground floor plan | 04 Passage through the existing building | 05 Street side bar

05

01

02

Seaside Single House

This house is located in the Monte Argentario National Park on top of a hill with an amazing view; facing the sea and the islands just in front of the Tuscany. The house regeneration uses recovered stones and the roof system is designed in the local tradition. New openings create windows, which allow a beautiful view of the landscape from all sides of the house. Passive solar systems make the house completely self-sufficient in terms of additional heating. The design of the building disturbs the surroundings as little as possible, while the large windows forge a connection between interior and exterior as well as allowing optimal warmth and daylight into the house.

01 Façade | 02 Exterior view | 03 Interior view | 04 Floor plan

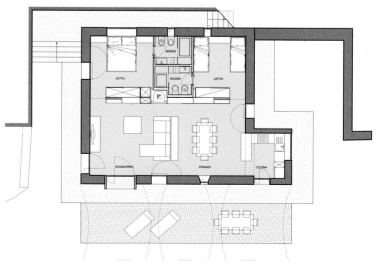

03

04

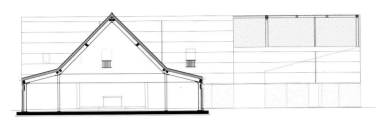

01

02

Church of San Bernardino and Celestinian Dining Hall

The competition guidelines called for the construction of a religious complex for liturgical functions and a small monastery, as well as the construction of a dining hall for charitable assistance. This proposal took a different approach with respect to the guidelines, organizing the footprint on the basis of the model of a Cistercian abbey and combining the functions in a single organism with an internal courtyard. The connection between the church and the volume of the monastery, and the creation of an internal void, though with the separation of the dining hall, permitted use of the area in a much more efficient way, generating a large set-back in front of the church, an area exclusively for pedestrians.

01 Section | 02 Main façade | 03 Exterior view | 04 Path to dining hall and lodgings | 05 Parvise and bell tower | 06 North view of church

03

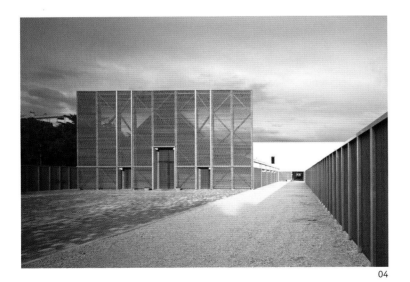

04

05

06

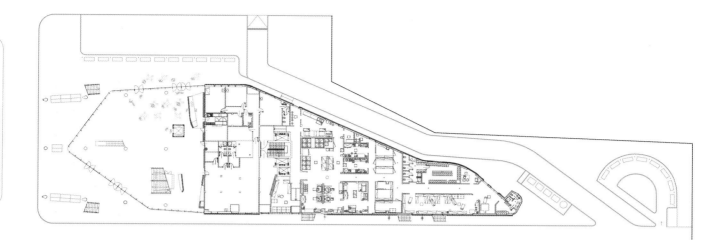

01

Ferrari Company Restaurant

The basics of the design consist of linking the juxtaposing two volumes to concepts of aerodynamics as represented by the great hanging wing-shaped pavilion, which is placed in a flight position, supported by another staggered axis wing positioned vertically on the ground. Besides the aerodynamic design of the external appearance, a main goal for the architects was to create a recreational space enabling the experience of the surrounding nature.

01 Floor plan restaurant | 02 General view | 03 Transparency as constituting design feature

02

03

01

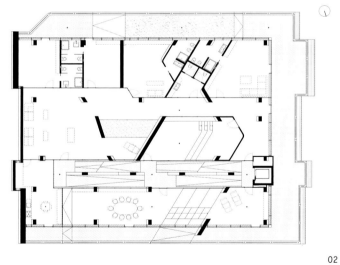

02

03

Lemon Factory

Simone Gatto is a citric essence manufacturer based in Messina. This project involves the expansion of the factory floor area to double its current size and provides much needed administrative space. The program was complex and demanded a new office, children's crèche and direct accommodations. The building folds the complex organizational diagram into a continuous wrapping and warping space where shortcuts and quick links are intended to connect the different areas effectively and efficiently. This also allows strategic open and closure of such thresholds to be configured. The unusual shape of the structure is eye-catching and dynamic; the angled walls create a bold impression, fitting to the successful company it houses.

01 South façade | 02 First floor plan | 03 Ramp | 04 Exterior view from southeast

04

→ Antonio Citterio Patricia Viel and Partners with
Studio di Architettura Beretta Associati
   → Office   → 2008   → Milan   → Italy   → Photos: Leo Torri

01

02

New Headquarters Ermenegildo Zegna

The structure overlooks the street from a glazed tunnel which opens on Via Savona through a narrow foyer. Zegna's headquarters have a showroom for each of its collections, the commercial and public relation offices and a presentation area on the ground floor. All the functional spaces are grouped around an inner court-terrace which overlooks the activities happening inside. The front façade is only partly glazed and treated with reflecting materials. It utilizes inclined plane shapes to reflect the surrounding industrial scenery.

01 Inner courtyard terrace | 02 Main entrance | 03 Longitudinal section | 04 Staircase | 05 Lobby | 06 Meeting room

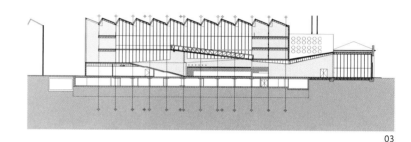

03

05

04

06

01

02

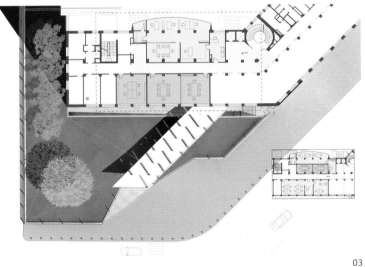

03

04

Tiziano 32 Headquarters

The renovation of the common areas of this 1950s building in Via Tiziano involved moving the building's entrance to the basement to redistribute previously unused spaces and to provide the whole complex with a new image. A canopy serves as the entrance to the new hall. It is covered in a skin of expanded metal panels that appear to be cut out of the surrounding lawn. The project also involves a general revision of the distribution of the spaces on all the floors, as well as the recuperation of the building's attic. Finally, the general refurbishment of the volume's front is now enhanced by a series of thin, continuous vertical wings of micro-perforated aluminum sheets.

01 Entrance area | 02 Entrance | 03 Ground floor plan | 04 Façade and canopy | 05 Entrance hall

05

01

02

03

04

Dolce & Gabbana Headquarters

The D&G headquarters in Milan is the result of a careful process of consolidation and re-modeling of two adjacent buildings, dating from the 1920s and the 1960s. The façade of the most recent building has been completely redone in glass, its rhythm marked out by a series of vertical blinds in opal glass. With five floors above ground and two below, the complex hosts the offices and the open-space showrooms. The ground floor opens onto an interior courtyard paved with white stones bordered by sinuously contoured garden areas. Facing the courtyard is the new structure that connects the two buildings, with the sheet metal staircases inside.

01 Metal staircase | 02 Inner courtyard | 03 General view at night | 04 Top floor restaurant | 05 Elevation

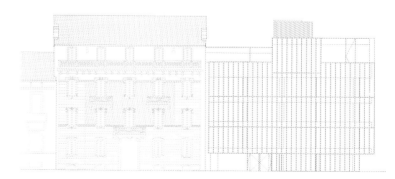

05

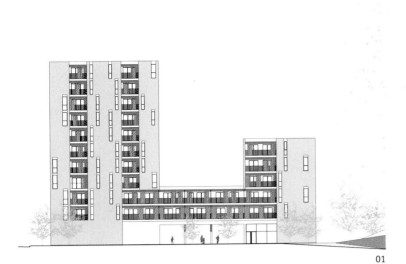

01

02

Social Housing, Public Space and Park in Via Gallarate

This project consists of 184 apartments of social housing, as well as services and public space. The main aim was to establish places of new 'urbanity' in marginal areas of the city. It is based on a concept of cohabitation between housing and public space, where the tenants can live in a pedestrian environment, supported by a strong infrastructure, commerce and public services. The buildings are conceived as four blocks along the park: their density allows more free space for utilities, green areas and playgrounds. The apartments are designed with a focus on solar exposure and crossed ventilation: all of them have buffer zones between interior and exterior in form of wide loggias, protected by aluminum shutters.

01 Block D west façade | 02 Block D north façade | 03 View of Block A from park promenade | 04 Block A west façade

03

04

01

02

03

04

Horizontal Tower

Horizontal tower is the new directional building of Fiera Milano. From dawn to dusk in open land, natural light turns into a material capable of transforming how a landscape is perceived, whether it be natural or man-made. In the peculiar setting of a trade fair, an environment where light flows in and is reflected in the whites, grays and patches of color, it can become a material shimmering from north to south, from east to west, emphasizing the deep color of dawn and dusk. The new building is characterized by the color gold, whose preciousness refers to the theme of sunlight and its reflections, the capacity to create an atmosphere of transparency and reflections with its surroundings, within the territorial perspectives crossing the area at different speeds and at all times of day.

01 Exterior view | 02 Staircase and 'bubble' lights | 03 Fifth floor terrace | 04 General view | 05 Site plan

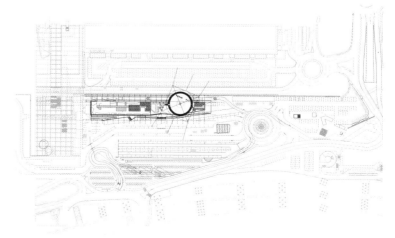

05

01

02

03

04

Tortona 37

Tortona 37 is a mixed-use complex, consisting of five separate buildings. These are constructed around a central courtyard with several trees growing in the center. The structures consist of single units, with a higher than average ceiling height of seven meters. This open area features integrated mezzanines which add versatility to the space. A prominent white grid dominates the outer façade, interrupted at intervals by wood-clad bay windows. The large glass windows work to unite the entire complex, connecting the different buildings. The panoramic roof gardens also offer true urban space, with views reaching to the horizon.

01 Courtyard | 02 Interior view | 03 Night view | 04 Entrance area | 05 Ground floor plan

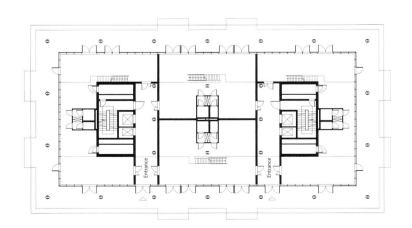

05

01

02

03

04

05

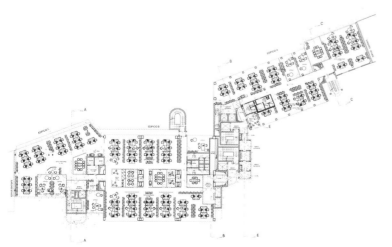

06

Data Center

An obsolete data center has been rejuvenated and refitted into high-tech offices. Construction was completed in less than 11 months. The refit was designed to accommodate the needs of a single tenant, Italease Bank, which needed to relocate its headquaters. The project included extensive demolitions, the addition of extra floors and new volumes, the complete redesign of internal circulation and workspace distribution, the implementation of up-to-date equipment, the creation of a two floor, underground parking with 120 spaces. The office complex now hosts 800 workstations, meeting rooms and support spaces, a cafeteria and terraces for outdoor use.

01 Side view | 02 Street view | 03 Street façade | 04 Interior view | 05 Exterior view | 06 Fourth floor plan

01

Barbapapa Kindergarten

Located on a hill on the city outskirts, this kindergarten accommodates 60 children in four classrooms. The project responds to the natural environment of the Emilia Romagna region by expressing through its architecture a consciousness of the importance of sustainability, which is then transmitted to the children. A green deck ensures excellent thermal insulation, while integrated green areas reduce the visual impact of the volume. Glass openings are strategically placed along the façade to control the infiltration of light and heat from the sun at different times of the day. The colors, materials and forms all express a sustainable system in a consistent contemporary architectural language.

01 View from garden | 02 Classroom | 03 Sleeping and play room | 04 Diagrams

02

03

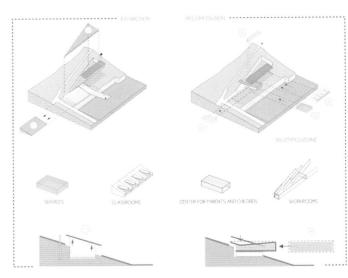

04

01

02

Dietro la Vigna

Meaning 'behind the vineyard', this nursery follows certain features of the existing site to amplify its peculiarity and unique qualities. The main hall, where most of the learning activities take place, faces the vineyard, offering a unique opportunity for the children to be in constant contact with the landscape, and receives a substantial amount of soft light from the north. All internal spaces follow the concepts of promoting learning and stimulating the sensorial experience of architecture, whether a broad or a narrow room, a high or low ceiling, a dynamic or fixed space. In each space, pedagogical concepts cohere with architectonic solutions to determine the children's behavior and awareness.

01 Theater | 02 North façade overlooking vineyards | 03 Play area | 04 Play and dining area | 05 View from second floor | 06 Floor plan

03

04

05

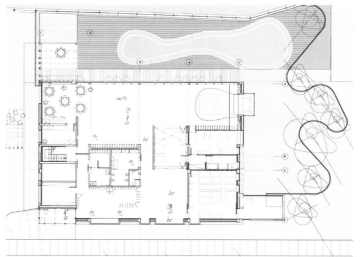

06

01

Library in Nembro

The city requested that the original building, erected in 1897, be renovated and turned into a library. The architectural character of the structure, closed on three sides, and the need for more space made it necessary to add a new wing. The new wing, detached from the old structure on all sides, is connected with the existing building through the basement. Its completely transparent body is characterized by a façade 40 x 40 centimeter earthenware tiles, glazed in carmine red. This construction makes it possible to screen and filter the daylight. While the use of earthenware evokes traditional building methods, the building also looks extremely contemporary.

01 Exterior view of new wing and original building | 02 Façade with ceramic tiles | 03 Interior view from the upper floor of the new wing | 04 Floor plan

02

03

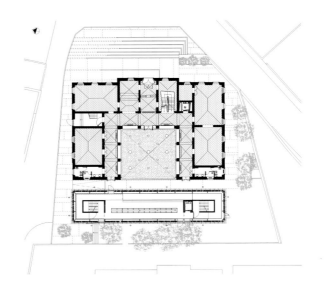

04

01

02

03

04

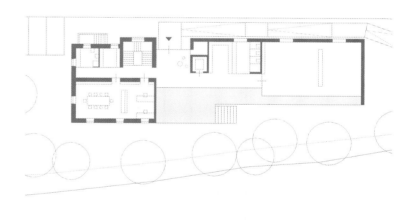

05

Kindergarten Niederdorf

This existing kindergarten in a Wilhelminian era villa dating from 1906 was renovated and augmented with a linear, two-story annex. At floor height the new structure is oriented towards the old building and the two are connected by a narrow glass caesura. The street side of the building is more closed, but opens up expansively on the south side to the sun, the river and its luxurious bank vegetation. The façade is a simple composition of triple glazings and wood panels alternatingly installed between the floor slabs. The whole kindergarten is usable without obstruction and in addition features an in-house kitchen, a multi-purpose and exercise room and a Kneipp facility.

01 Southern façade at night | 02 View from river | 03 Interior second floor | 04 Classroom | 05 Floor plan | 06 Washroom

06

01

02

Dex Showroom

Dex S.p.a., a company owned by the Tanini family, commissioned this building. As a contrast to most of the buildings in the area, which are solid and set with neon lights and giant advertising billboards, the Dex showroom concept focuses on silence and dematerialization. The project was influenced by the search for a dialogue with the landscape, obtained through the understated elegance of the façade. Made by 270 laser-cut metal frames, the skin of the building appears like a pixelated picture of the trees that are in front of it. The exhibition hall develops as a long alley, divided into three sections and elevated from the ground level of the entrance.

01 Exterior view | 02 Window detail and façade | 03 Interior view | 04 Floor plan

03

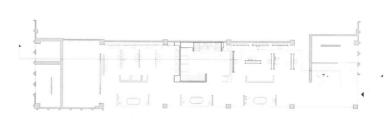

04

01

02

03

04

New Offices for Local Authorities

This project was built to provide new spaces for public facilities. These are divided into two buildings: the Center for Childhood and office space for local authorities. The new buildings are developed over three levels: archive and garages on the ground floor, public reception and offices on the two upper floors. The projecting sections of the structure, coupled with recesses and height differences give the building a modern, dynamic appearance. Some portions of the façade are glazed, while wooden strips complement others. These additions give the large structure and more lightweight appearance.

01 View from street | 02 East façade | 03 View from municipal park | 04 Interior view | 05 First floor plan

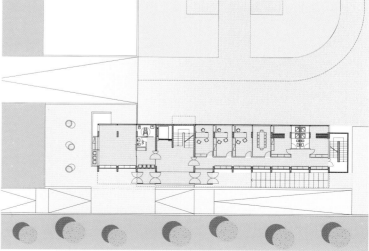

05

01

02

03

04

Family Chapel

For this chapel the architects proposed designing a small space within the city that would function as a personal and private space where the client could go to think, meditate, concentrate and, above all, gain a closer spiritual proximity to loved ones. The architects decided to develop a comfortable space where the client could sit and stay in contact with the atmospheric agent. The roof, with its passage of soft and changing light would allow the appreciation of passing time and, if it rains, the water can drain through holes inside the chapel. The floor, made of white gravel, drains the water leaving the floor dry.

01 Interior detail | 02 South façade | 03 View of the ceiling | 04 Interior walls | 05 Ground floor plan

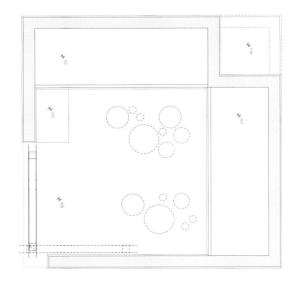

05

01

02

03

PPS. Ponzano Primary School

Ponzano Primary School is a sustainable building in terms of energy and cost. The building is open to the community after school hours. The school is designed to accommodate 375 children aged from six to ten. It has 15 classrooms and additional special classrooms for art, music, computer studies, languages and science. It also offers a gymnasium, a canteen and a library. The school becomes a society building, where collective spaces are very important as they underline the central role of relationships between people. This concept is reminiscent of the model of the famous industrial districts of the Veneto region, where people are incited to learn from each other by exchanging experiences.

01 Roof garden | 02 Inner courtyard | 03 View of arcade | 04 Sections | 05 Southeastern view

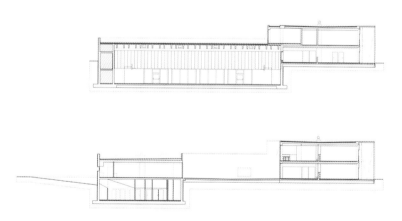

04

05

01

02

03

Kindergarten and Library

This new two-story building, which includes a kindergarten, a library and the elementary school cafeteria, was built 1,400 meter above sea level. The ground floor includes the library, kitchen, foyer and a mixed-use area, which can be used as the dining area. The second floor houses a kindergarten for up to 30 children. The monolithic structure is located in the center of the village and reacts to the growing village in terms of its building volume, the roof shape and the selection of materials. In addition to the cuts in the façade, the interior is lit by wooden box-type windows, which vary in size. The saddle roof covers all areas of the upper floor and provides space for smaller rooms, such as painting studio and picture book corner.

01 Main entrance | 02 Group room | 03 Interior view | 04 Elevations

04

02

01

03

04

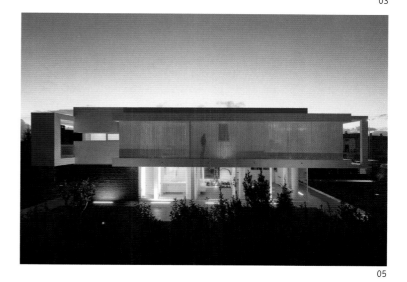

05

Villa PM

This building reveals its own identity through the combination of simple volumes. The structure has a lightweight appearance, aided by the contrast between large windows, dark surfaces and white walls. Cantilevered frames characterize the first floor with sliding panels that act as a vertical aluminum sunscreen. Large circular columns and a central glass patio define the interior space. Through its surfaces and contemporary design the villa stands out from the more traditional buildings surrounding it.

01 View from garden | 02 West façade | 03 Night view | 04 Interior view | 05 Combined simple volumes | 06 Site plan

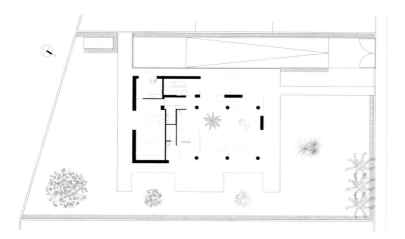

06

01

02

New Cultural Center

The new Cultural Center in Ranica contains a public library, an auditorium, a kinder-garten, and a school for dance and theater. The building represents a sort of threshold between the scale of the city and the scale of the surrounding territory. The aim of this project is to trigger a dialogue between the new building, the city center and the infra-structural system. The upper volume is cantilevered out from the lower floor and seems to float above ground. The distinction between the two volumes is emphasized by the choice of materials: the ground floor is enclosed by glazed and plastered walls, while the façades of the upper volume are made of colored, sometimes semi-opaque polycarbonate panels, allowing for silhouettes of people inside the building to be revealed outside.

01 Front view | 02 Façade detail | 03 Interior view | 04 Ground floor plan | 05 Courtyard

03

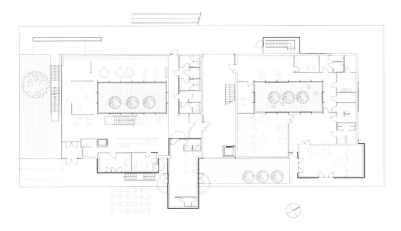

04

05

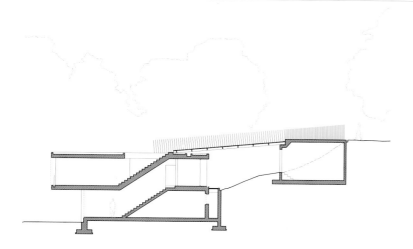

01

02

Green Vision

This rectangular-shaped plot is located on the side of a steeply sloping hill, facing south. The site is positioned high up, on the verge of a wooded area. The two-story semi-detached house is made up of two separate dwelling units with a total area of 300 square meters. The main aim was to establish a dialogue between the house building and the landscape that surrounds it. The load-bearing structure is made from steel and reinforced concrete, with partitions and pillars. The closing walls are made from brickwork and glass panes with printed adhesive films. The outer facing was created by using phenolic multilayer wood panels following the ventilated façade method. Synthetic grass covering has been glued onto the exposed surfaces.

01 Section of the two separate dwelling units | 02 Synthetic grass covering | 03 Roof | 04 Exterior at night

03

04

01

MAXXI – National Museum of the 21st Century Arts

This center, located in a former army barracks, has a public dimension within the city. The external as well as internal pathways follow the overall drift of the geometry. Vertical and oblique circulatory elements are located at areas of confluence, interference and turbulence; the notion of a 'drift' takes on an embodied form. The drifting emerges, therefore, as both an architectural motif, and as a way to navigate through the museum. The 'signature' aspect of an institution of this caliber is sublimated into a more pliable and porous organism that promotes several forms of identification at once.

01 Panoramic view | 02 Façade at night | 03 Ground floor | 04 Study painting by Zaha Hadid | 05 Staircase

02

03

04

05

01

02

03

04

CMB Headquarters Office

The design of this building, by one of Italy's most important construction firms, is based on the original design of the main structure, combining large windows with integrated Schüco photovoltaic cells and a ventilated façade in brick: a construction material rooted in the Italian tradition. The large structural windows with integrated photovoltaic cells open towards the central part, allowing the sun to permeate the interior, and emphasizing the volume towards the outside. CMB's new Rome office is therefore a communication structure on an urban scale, projecting the innovative language and sophisticated energy-saving technology used in its construction.

01 Building angle | 02 Entrance | 03 Front view | 04 Façade detail | 05 Site plan

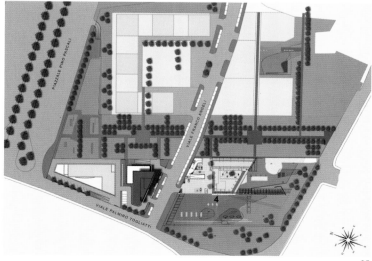

05

01

02

Dutch Embassy in Rome

Located in a Renaissance-style urban villa built in 1929, the Dutch embassy in Rome was drastically renovated. The main building had a lot of interesting details, whose splendor was restored and highlighted as much as possible by cepezed architects. The architects installed a secondary façade of weathering steel around the much less remarkable annex. On the inside, they stripped the buildings down to their concrete skeletons and provided them with a new, drastically revised and unifying arrangement, aimed at lightness, transparency, and good communication possibilities.

01 Exterior view | 02 Roof terrace | 03 Meeting room | 04 Hallway | 05 Elevation | 06 Stairwell

03

04

06

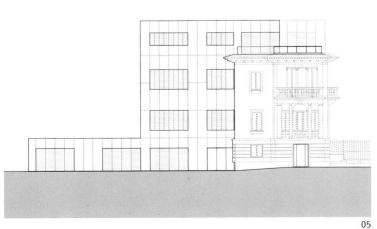

05

01

02

03

04

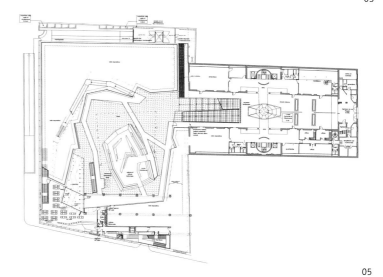

05

MACRO Museo d'Arte Contemporanea Roma

Inserted into the complexity of an old industrial estate, this new museum dynamically responds to the existing static condition of the site. The old and the new, the exhibition spaces and the other activities connected to it, are simultaneously articulate and distinctive. The roof surface is a landscape, a projection of the art trail below, creating an abstract continuity. This landscaped terrace is offered to the visitors of the museum and to the city. The terrace is a place of calm, freshness and sensual textures. In opposition to the dynamism of the surrounding space, the exhibition areas are perceived as more neutral.

01 Lobby | 02 Bird's-eye view | 03 Skylight in lobby | 04 Entrance | 05 Ground floor plan | 06 View from street

06

01

Laurentino Center

The Laurentino Center is part of an urban development program and is organized around a large civic square with shopping mall and public and private offices. This spacious square is designed to be a venue for cultural, recreational and commercial events. The specific plans for the shopping mall include a hypermarket, a 1,300-seat multiplex cinema, shops, a fitness center and restaurants. The extension, adjacency and modularity of the buildings' volume give the overall impression of a great horizontal whale. The façade links all the above functional programs together providing a clear volumetric whole. The part facing on to the square is open and connected to the square, almost making them an extension of each other.

01 View from street | 02 Plaza | 03 Interior view | 04 Section

02

03

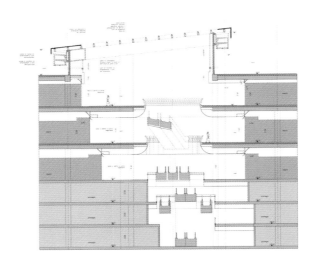

04

01

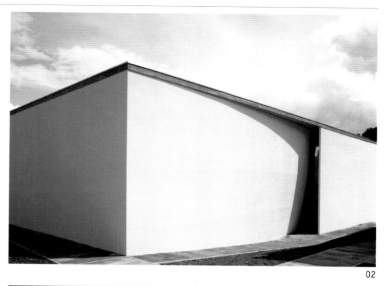

02

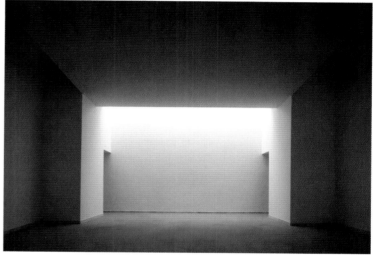

03

04

05

Stefanacci School Extension

The extension of this primary and secondary school in San Piero a Sieve is very close to the city of Florence. It is composed according to the character and the materials of the Tuscan countryside, projected in a contemporary horizon. The building consists of two rectangular volumes covered with white plaster, which are orientated differently. The main volume is defined by a big, solid wall containing a small auditorium, and the main corridor is illuminated from the ceiling. The smaller volume, naturally lit by windows with a variety of dimensions, is organized on two levels containing offices, laboratories and a small library.

01 Interior view | 02 Exterior view | 03 Auditorium | 04 Exterior at dusk | 05 Façade | 06 Elevation and floor plan

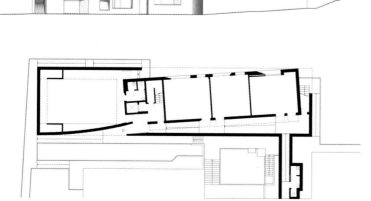

06

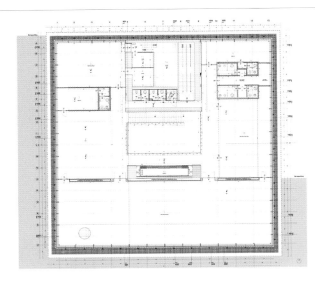

01

House of the Sea

The House of the Sea is a glass and basalt prism that cantilevers over the water. It is part of the recovery and restructuring project, aimed at creating a public and mixed-use complex surrounding the harbor of the ex-military Arsenale at La Maddalena. The new construction hosts a large event and conference hall, suspended six meters above water and looking out towards the extraordinary panorama of the Gallura. A dislocated geometry, underlined by the structural feat and the modular bee-hive like façade made of opaline glass, characterizes the new landmark that reinterprets the relation between the power of the surrounding natural elements and the rigorous forms of Italy's traditional military architecture.

01 Main floor plan | 02 External glass skin | 03 Ground floor view | 04 Aerial view | 05 View from harbor

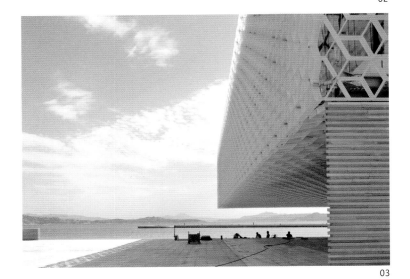

02

03

04

05

01

02

03

Indoor and Outdoor Swimming Pool Balneum

This swimming pool consists of two levels, open to visitors. The swimming pool area is on the ground floors and offers various pools and attractions. A large wellness area with sauna, beauty and relaxation areas is on the upper floor. A clear linear form, combined with room-height glazing, characterizes the building. Providing a transparent view of the surrounding mountains was a key point of the design. Through an incision in the roof on the upper floor, a spacious and sheltered outdoor terrace has been created. Locally sourced materials and a friendly color scheme characterize the building's interior.

01 Southwest view | 02 Outdoor pool | 03 Relax pool with flow passage | 04 Ground floor plan | 05 Stone sauna | 06 Section

04

05

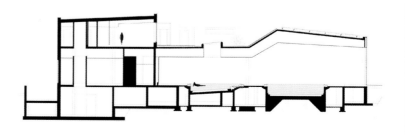

06

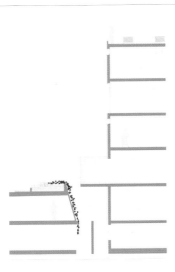

01

New Studio Altieri Headquarters

The internal environment of this new company headquarters guarantees a high quality employee experience, in line with the firm scale and work type. Productivity, working conditions, light and air quality all contribute to well being. The project is designed to achieve environmental comfort, save energy and lower energy costs. Use and control of natural light results in a shadow effect during the summer season. A high proportion of natural daylight is guaranteed during winter for all of the 150 workers. The used materials are natural and simple, wood, white stone and concrete, while the technology adopted is extremely modern. The building is four stories high with two underground levels dedicated to parking and the technological plant area.

01 Section | 02 Central staircase | 03 Exterior view | 04 Exterior view at night | 05 Meeting room

03

04

05

01

Nursery School in Covolo di Pederobba

Hidden among the vineyards and wheat fields, the Nursery School in Covolo comprises a collection of modest structures linked by a continuous series of stone walls. The new building forms an enclosure that both embraces and allows itself to be defined by the features of the landscape. A rough concrete wall is colored to match the surrounding landscape, reflecting light in various ways. The wall opens to the south, revealing the massive structure, before retracting and doubling, coloring itself to emphasize its passages. The overhang, the stabilized gravel paving, and the lighting transform the threshold into a space where classroom spaces and garden meet and form the imagination of a possible world.

01 View from garden | 02 Glass façade connecting interior and exterior | 03 Courtyard | 04 Main entrance | 05 Stone wall linking building structures

02

03

04

05

01

02

Daycare Center for Benetton

The square box housing this daycare center is composed of nine smaller squares, the central one emerging above the rest to allow in extra light. This space recalls a haman in the way sunlight is gathered through perforations in the ceiling and façades. Classrooms are arranged in the surrounding squares. A larger, circular enclosure made up of double-circular walls embraces the square structure. Four courtyards, tensed between the curved and straight walls and open to the air, evoke the four elements: air, earth, fire and water. The space between the perimeter walls serves as a 'secret place' for the children.

01 Paneled courtyard | 02 Courtyard with lawn | 03 Floor plan | 04 Vestibule | 05 Courtyard | 06 Exterior view

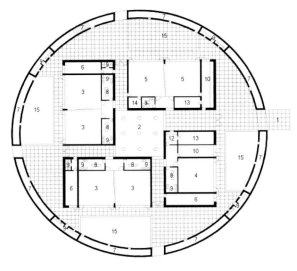

03

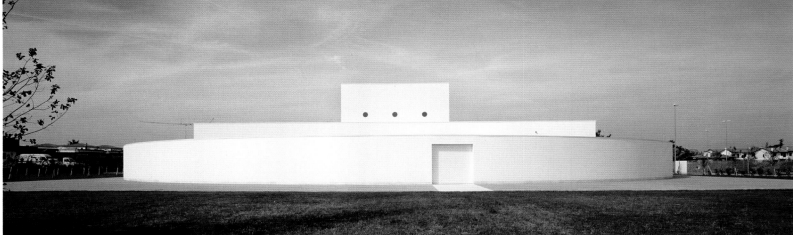

04

05

06

01

7Corti.Townhouse

This project involves redefinition of a suburban area. The site is characterized by two rivers and previously housed an office building. The client wished to change the function by creating six independent houses. The project involves the construction of six housing units along a central axis, which contains the internal courtyards that serve as private outdoor space. The apartment units each have two floors, plus an attic, and heating needs will be provided by geothermal energy. Chromatically emerge only the entrances to housing. The boxy and stacked appearance of the building conveys its modernity, while its discreet gray and white exterior gives it a suitably refined appearance.

01 Exterior view | 02 East façade | 03 South façade | 04 Site plan

02

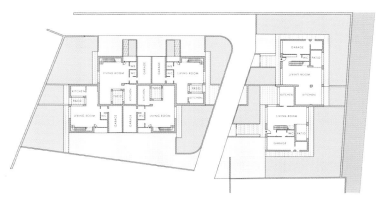

03

04

01

02

Casa sul Sile

This building is located near the Sile River just outside Treviso's historical town walls in the Veneto region. It shares some similarities to an historical villa although the white of the exterior contrasts the neighboring buildings and gardens. The townhouse has a large, long volume, predominantly white in color, but with projecting black sections and sunken gray sections. It houses nine apartments, spread across three different levels. The architecture is clearly rationalist and deliberately shares a dialogue with the surrounding 20th century Italian architecture. The riverside can be seen from every apartment and from the common areas.

01 Interior with terrace | 02 Hall | 03 Exterior view | 04 Section | 05 Projecting black sections

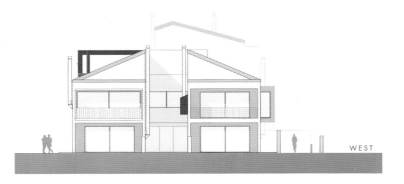

WEST

03

04

05

01

02

03

Casa X 5

Casa X 5 is a big apartment building on the outskirts of the city, near the railway. The principal floor is for everyday functions while the upper floor is for the body, for relaxing or playing. A central part is rounded by a black wall/furniture/wall. This black wall/furniture/wall is like a scenic curtain, a filter between day and night and viceversa. The big living and kitchen area is completely white: walls, furniture, ceiling and lamps. The flooring is like a water surface, reflecting the white color. The interior design concept gives every part an individual character. Every part contains space, light, color and is composed of elementary volumes. All the surfaces reflect natural and artificial light giving the space an overexposed look. The house has a night and a day zone. The difference between the two parts is the flooring: gray resin for day, cool gray wood for night.

01 Pool at dusk | 02 Interior view to living room | 03 Interior view to cloakroom | 04 Fifth floor plan

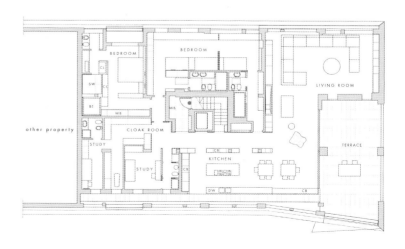

04

01

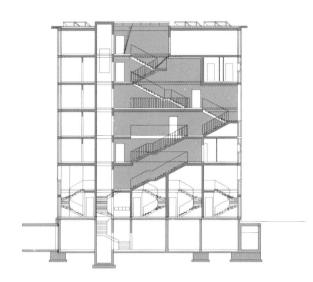

02

Turin Olympic Village

The Olympic Village for the 2006 Winter Olympic Games in Turin, a city developed on a grid, explored the continuation and extension of that structure. This permitted the development of multi-purpose squares and courtyards for the community based on an ordered structure. Form, façade, and color are the defining themes of this quarter. It was inspired by the idea of a colorful forest of international flags. From there, a friendly struggle developed between two color tones that competed for dominance. While this appears very emblematic at first glance, it has mostly met with amused approval. The office of Otto Steidle, who sadly died in 2004, established an international reputation for developing people-friendly residential buildings, a factor that also emerges from a glance at the floor plans for this project.

01 View towards "mercato generali" | 02 Unity and variety | 03 Section | 04 Density of space and color

03

04

01

02

Punta della Dogana Contemporary Art Center

This project involved remodeling the 15th century government-owned Âgcustom house in the sea into a modern art museum. The design was chosen by means of a competition. The volume forms a triangle that directly corresponds to the shape of the tip of Dorsoduro Island. Through exposing the brick walls and wooden roof trusses, the space retrieved its energy and the memories of the former sea customs were revived. In the center of the building, a square space spans over two rows as a result of an earlier renovation. This structure was retained and a concrete box was inserted that dramatically transformed the space. Through a dialogue between old and new elements, the building links its past history to the present and the future.

01 General view | 02 Interior view | 03 Exhibition hall | 04 Sections

03

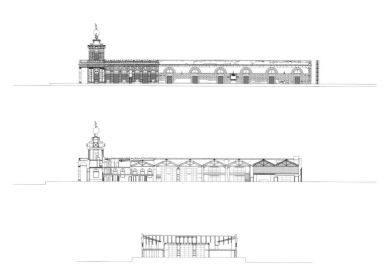

04

01

02

03

Shoe Manufacture Louis Vuitton

This manufacturing depot was designed to be perceived as an anonymous box from the outside, hiding its content and unveiling itself progressively. A lateral entrance leads to a hallway, which gives access to the core of the project, the element around which everything is organized. A uniform stainless steel mesh covers the walls of the building, giving the structure a uniform appearance. The mesh has three functions: it smooths the perception of the building's exterior, prevents passersby seeing into the building and stops direct sunlight from streaming in through the windows. Inside, all work spaces face the indoor garden, organized around the central element, the 'cloister'.

01 Front porch | 02 Lobby | 03 'Cloister' | 04 Design sketches

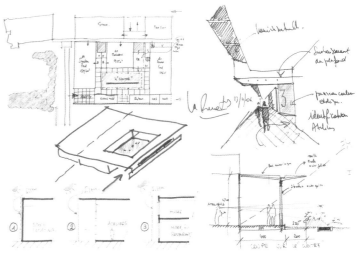

04

01

02

New Mestre Hospital

The main building is composed of two separate parts – the technological platform area and the inpatient room block. This block contains a three-floor platform area and seven floors above ground, five of which accommodate hospitalized patients. The platform area is a reinforced concrete construction; the single 'residential' block construction on top is a mix of steel and concrete. A large, sail-shaped glass structure the same height as the building links the two parts, stretching along the length of the building and covering a spacious, bright entrance hall linked to all facilities and contact areas.

01 Fully glazed façade | 02 Exterior view | 03 Entrance view | 04 Entrance hall | 05 Section | 06 Glazed ceiling

03

04

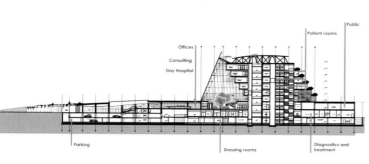

05

06

01

02

03

04

Joshua Tree

Joshua Tree is a mobile home conceived for a vacation at a high altitude; it imitates the profile of an Alpine refuge, with its sloping roof, the panoramic views of peaks and the use of combined stave wood on the interior. The external covering employs steel, zinc, and titanium to form large plates according to the method of traditional wooden shingles. Over time the materials oxidize, adding a more opaque tonality to the structure. Designed to be entirely built in the factory, Joshua Tree offers a reinterpreted version of the mountain dwelling: a continuous metal structure combined with a unique interior enhanced by the warmth of natural wood. It accommodates three to four people.

01 Bedroom with skylight | 02 Kitchen | 03 House on lake side | 04 View to main entrance | 05 Sections

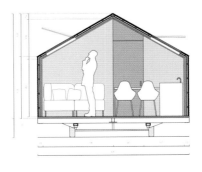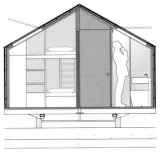

05

01

02

03

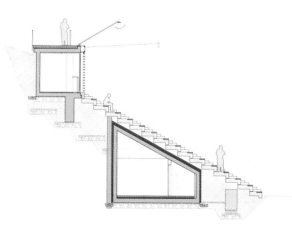

04

05

Rowing Center Bled – Spectator Stand

As part of a comprehensive new image for the Rowing Center Bled, which hosted the 2011 World Rowing Championships, the viewers will be able to watch the rowers from the new stands in the finish line area. These are distinguished by sustainable placement in a part of the area directly on the lakeshore. This area is characterized by the steep configuration of the terrain and the line placement of the stand facility further highlights the natural image of the area. The stand facility is defined by two sets: the lower open viewing platform with seats and a closed, uniform area, designated to house commentators and as VIP room. The cut in the shore emphasizes limited and carefully selected materials: concrete, wood, glass and metal.

01 Platform detail | 02 View from promenade | 03 View of lake from stand | 04 View across the lake | 05 Interior view | 06 Section

06

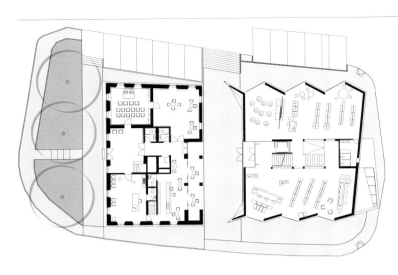

01

Grosuplje Public Library

The existing library operated in an old townhouse, the only preserved representative of quality architecture from 19th century in Grosuplje, which is protected as a listed building. Next to it, the new wing was added, which is twice as large. Inside it, a modern, open and fluid library space was designed with efficient use of light and energy in mind. The façade of the annex stretches like an accordion across the plot and with the repetitive exchange of glass and wall surfaces, opens the new library space towards the ambiance of the town's center. Neutrality and monumentality are repeated in a manner that allows the pavilion to become 'grown' into the town's fibre and its unimposing presence allows the old building to retain the dominant role.

01 Ground floor plan of old and new part | 02 Northeast view | 03 Reading area | 04 New building with passage to old building | 05 Reading area flooded with natural light

02

03

04

05

01

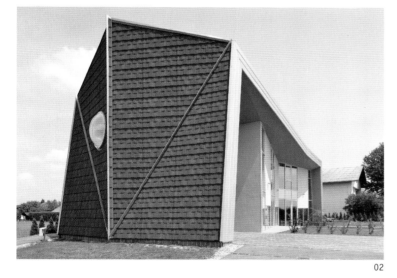

02

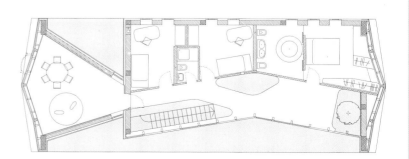

03

Stairway to Heaven

This whole house becomes a system of bridges and as such brings a sense of freshness. As one moves along this system, new spaces and environments open out. They connect the lower floor with the upper level, stretching through both levels by means of a connecting staircase and a two-story chandelier. The concept of the house is based on the idea of a conservatory. The living spaces on the ground floor and the bridge system form a conservatory that opens up to the south, this allows natural light to flood into the house, drawing light deep into the building. The glass surface is divided into a mosaic mesh-vitrage.

01 South façade and swimming pool | 02 Exterior view | 03 Stairs to upper floor | 04 First floor plan

04

01

02

Tetris Apartments

This apartment block is a social project and was sold to the Slovenian Housing Fund. Since the orientation of the building faces the busy highway the balconies are shifted, with windows angled at 30 degrees towards the quieter south side. Each apartment overlooks its own balcony. This way privacy is assured, with no direct view from other apartments in the opposite block. The apartments of different sizes are made of economic but quality materials such as wooden oak floors, granite tiled bathrooms and large windows with external metal blinds. Many people compared the design to the game of Tetris.

01 Corner view | 02 Sketch | 03 Site plan | 04 Exterior view | 05 Façade detail

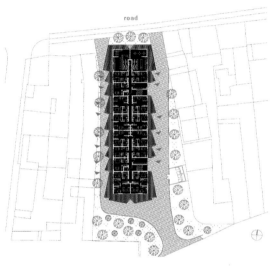
03

04

05

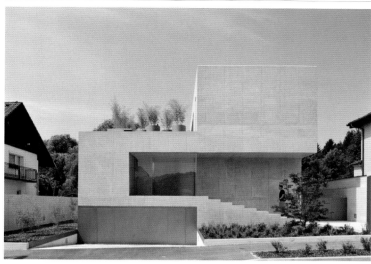

01

02

House D

House D is located in a prestigious neighborhood in the center of Ljubljana. The couple wanted a lot from the relatively small plot of land; therefore part of the house is hidden in the ground forming an introvert world secluded from the surroundings. The underground gymnasium, containing sauna, swimming pool, music room and three atriums, forms a vast base of the house, which covers almost the entire plot. The living room with reception area, open kitchen and dining area fills the first floor and continues over the external terraces, doubling the space. There is a smooth system of circulation within different fields of activity, which are also stressed by the different use of materials.

01 Front façade | 02 Garden with swimming pool | 03 Ground floor plan | 04 View into living space at night | 05 Kitchen and living room | 06 Workspace

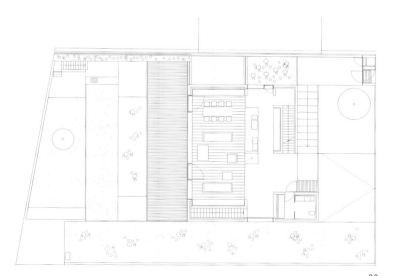

03

04

05

06

01

02

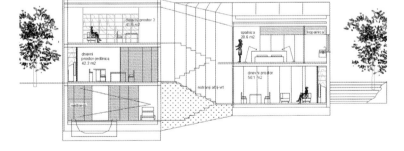

03

04

Villa Old Oaks

This residence, situated in a new neighborhood of six larger villas, has the unique feature of a splendid view of oak trees over 100 years old. To guarantee that most of the spaces have access to this view, the house is organized in stepped levels following the terrain. The heart of the house is an external covered courtyard, with the entrance lobby, staircase, children's playroom, dining, living, bedroom and work areas all overlooking this space. These rooms, plus the wellness area with its small pool, also have a view of the park. The staircase roof is glazed, while the courtyard roof is part glass, part wood, providing views of the sky and treetops, creating a link between inside and outside.

01 Exterior view | 02 Detail of angles | 03 Section | 04 Exterior in winter | 05 Vertical louvers

05

01

Multi-Purpose Sports Hall and Football Stadium Stožice

The Sports Park Stožice integrates a football stadium and a multi-purpose sports hall with a big shopping center, covered by the artificial landscape of the recreational park. The football stadium for 16,000 spectators is laid out below the niveau of the park. As a structure, it is 'sunk' into the park. Only the roof rises above the plane of the park like a monolithic crater. The sports hall for 12,000 spectators is located in the northwestern part of the park. The four levels of concourses and the lower, VIP, and upper stands are covered by a shell-shaped dome. As a result, the 182,000-square meter Sports Park Stožice becomes one of the major focal points of Ljubljana's urban life.

01 Multi-purpose sports hall | 02 Multi-purpose sports hall detail | 03 Interior of multi-purpose sports hall | 04 Aerial view sports park | 05 Football stadium, detail stands | 06 Football stadium

02

03

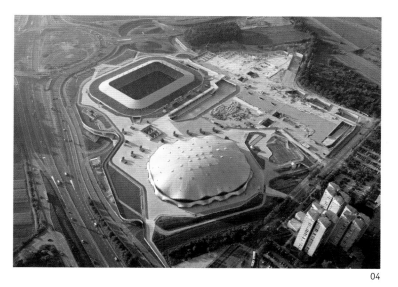

04

05

06

01

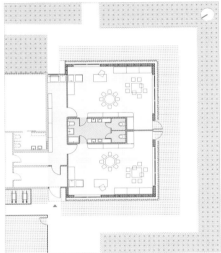
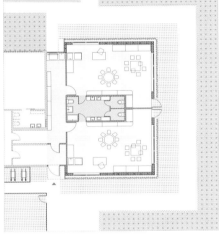

02

03

Kekec Kindergarten

The main design concept derives from the kindergarten's lack of play space. The new façade solves this weakness by offering a play element along all three exterior walls. It consists of dark brown timber slats, revolving around their vertical axis. The slats are the color of natural wood on one side but painted with nine different colors on the other side. Aside from serving as a shading element, the slats provide for children's play and learning: as the children manipulate the colorful wooden planks they get to know different colors, experience wood as a natural material and constantly change the appearance of their kindergarten, all at the same time.

01 Side view and entrance | 02 Floor plan | 03 Classroom interior | 04 Interactive façade | 05 Interactive façade

04

05

01

02

03

04

05

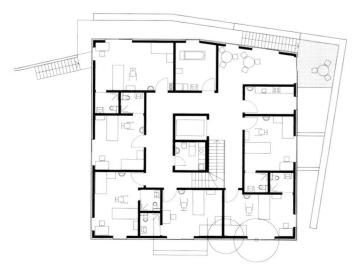

06

Hospic Building

The Hospic Building is a center for palliative care. It occupies a small plot between a steep slope and a busy road, leaning against the slope with terraced retaining wall and terraces. The ground floor is for management and training; while the first and second floors are occupied by patient's rooms, fitted to accommodate disabled users. A staircase, connecting common areas on all floors, spirals around the central core, opening different perspective with different daylight on each of landings. Rooms lie on the perimeter of the building, each offering a nice view through the full-length picture windows. The façade is made of brick tiles reminiscent of traditional fabric.

01 Rear façade detail | 02 Front façade and entrance | 03 Entrance canopy | 04 View from street | 05 Interior view | 06 Second floor plan

01

02

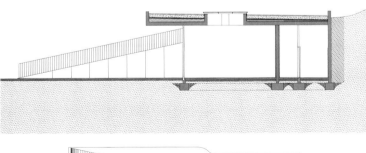

03

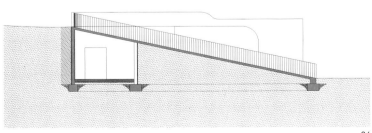

04

Farewell Chapel

This chapel cuts into the rising landscape and the building shape follows the natural contours of the land around the graveyard. The program comes together with the three embracing curved walls, which divide the space. The external curve divides the chapel plateau from the surrounding hill and also reinstates the main supporting wall. Service spaces are all placed along the back wall. The internal curve encompasses the main farewell space. It is partly glazed and opens towards the outside plateau for summer gatherings. The cross is positioned on the rooftop above the main farewell space as a source of daylight and night-time light.

01 Exterior view | 02 Entrance | 03 View from roof | 04 Sections | 05 Chapel interior

05

01

Ring – The Football Stadium Extension

The task was to convert the field into a football stadium by extending the existing build-ing with covered tribunes and additional public elements. The project proposed a ring of tribunes weaving above an enclosed base. The entrances to the tribunes are placed in the corners. The ring is pulled down to the level of the entry plateau, to rise gently and reach the highest point at about midfield, where the maximum number of the seats is placed, with the best view. The corridor provides rooms for VIP, press and refreshment sections. The sport halls and shops are in the basement.

01 General view at night | 02 Main stands | 03 Floor plan

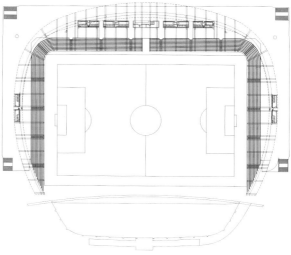

02

03

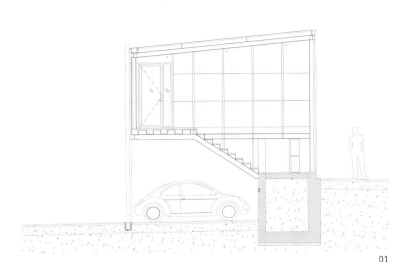

01

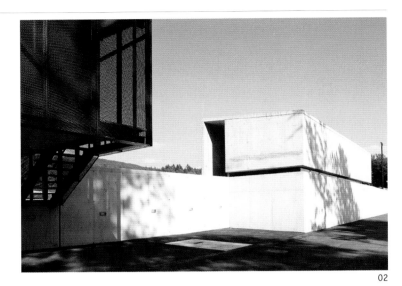

02

Metal Recycling Plant Odpad

What is long-lasting and what is recycle friendly was the key question considered by the architects in this project. The project consists of an immense production plateau and two small buildings on the edge of it. The small 100 percent metal office building works as a specific control deck, supervising the weighing of the in-coming waste and out-going metals. Since this specificity means non-adaptability the architects had to allow for easy on-site recycling when this building is not needed anymore. The two buildings are of the same volume, but materially very different: one is made entirely out of concrete, whereas the other is all steel – from structure to cladding.

01 Cross section | 02 Exterior view | 03 View from street | 04 Rear view with parking

03

04

01

02

03

04

Hotel Sotelia

Hotel Sotelia fills the gap between two existing hotels. During the design process, the
primary concern was to avoid creating an immense building mass which would have
blocked the last remaining view of the forest. The volume is broken up into small units
arranged in landscape-hugging tiers. As a result, the four-story building appears much
lower and smaller. The specific shape of the hotel was dictated by the folds in the
landscape and offers passersby a strong spatial experience. The front of the building is
perceived as a two-dimensional set composed of parallel planes placed one behind the
other. A walk around the hotel reveals entirely different views of the timber façade.

01 Terrace | 02 Façade detail | 03 Entrance | 04 Exterior | 05 Situation

05

01

Podčetrtek Sports Hall

This municipal sports hall is located on the main road that leads to the small town of Podčetrtek. Although primarily designed for sports activities, the hall also represents the single large community indoor venue for cultural and other events. It is this dual role that led to the specific design of the facility. Its primary design element is a 'red carpet' spatially designed path, bounded by the dyke on one side and incised into the building on the other. This works to shield the entrance from the direct influence of the road. Presented in vivid colors and attractive shapes it widens in front of the entrance to form a quality, almost square-like area.

01 Lit-up façade | 02 Main entrance | 03 Pathway | 04 Ground floor plan

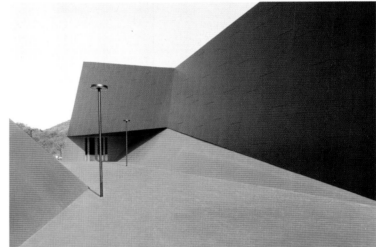

02

03

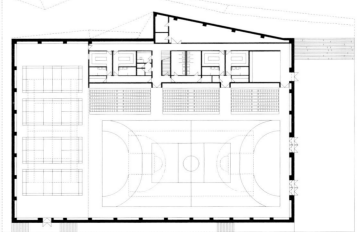

04

01

02

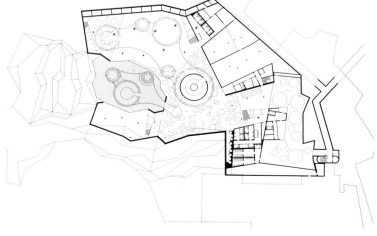

03

Wellness Orhidelia

The main focus of the design for the Wellness Orhidelia was to diminish its impact on the surroundings as much as possible. Since the program requirements of a wellness center are very extensive, erecting a classically conceived building on the central green section would have occupied the last remaining open area in the thermal complex and largely degraded the spatial quality. The new wellness center is thus designed more like a landscape arrangement than a building. Folded elevations appear like supporting walls, dividing different levels of landscape surfaces. A central walking path stretches over the roof and gives visitors a completely new sense of the site.

01 Exterior view | 02 Atrium at dusk | 03 Public square | 04 Ground floor plan

04

01

02

03

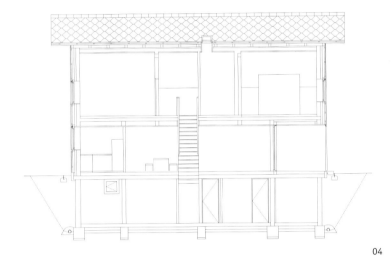

04

House R

This typical Alpine, yet contemporary vacation, home boasts a steeply-sloping roofline atop a simple cube base. The entire house was wrapped in wooden planks which, when shut, cover the entire structure, as well as windows and doors. This modern minimal exterior is complemented by an equally simple interior with large windows, a bright and spacious layout, and a white palette accented by naturally finished woods. A main staircase divides both the individual living areas in this open-concept layout, but also connects one floor to the next.

01 Exterior with open shutters | 02 Exterior with closed shutters | 03 Side view | 04 Section | 05 Dining room | 06 Open terrace | 07 Interior

05

06

07

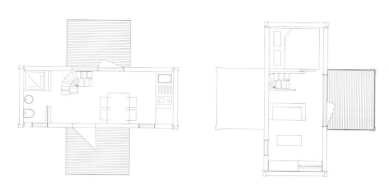

01

Conhouse 2+

The Conhouse 2+ weekend house is a two-level mini housing unit composed of two ISO containers placed perpendicular to each other. It shows that a minimal number of containers combined in an innovative fashion offer fresh yet functional architectural solutions. The upper container provides a projecting roof above the entrance and shelters the back terrace. The ceiling of the bottom container is also the terrace of the first floor. The pink-dotted façade illustrates the wide range of possibilities for tailor-made exteriors and the system's modular nature enables containers to be added or removed, so that the Conhouse 2+ can grow or contract depending on the spatial needs of the people using it.

01 Ground and first floor plans | 02 First floor interior view | 03 Side view | 04 Detail of building volumes

02

03

04

01

House D

This house features an abstract façade that sections off the east side, a Californian façade, as well as a pool, a terrace and plenty of green surroundings. The four different sections create 'micro-ambiences' which give the house its identity. These sections include the garage; the entrance to the house, which is located below the pool complex; the surrounding environment, which is reflected in the façade's reflective glazing; and the fluid living space, which is illuminated by gaps between the sections. The kitchen protrudes towards the exterior terraces, which connet the bathroom and the bedroom.

01 Front façade | 02 Section | 03 Rear façade with garden | 04 Side view

02

03

04

01

Bursa Wholesale Greengrocer and Fishmonger Market

02

Both the produce market and the fish market are modern facilities designed for whole-sale trade, providing the city with a centralized control point from which the quality and the price of Bursa's food supply can be monitored. The buildings are of reinforced concrete with a steel roof construction. Nowadays, when large market buildings are most often relegated to architecturally insignificant spaces, Bursa Wholesale revitalizes the idiom of the high, vaulted Central Asian bazaar. The naturally-ventilated and lit spaces result in a friendly atmosphere, avoiding the hermetic enclosure of a box-like facility. The elliptical floor plan is designed to facilitate easy orientation, efficient exchange and optimal routing.

01 Bird's-eye view | 02 Interior view | 03 Entrance gate | 04 Sections

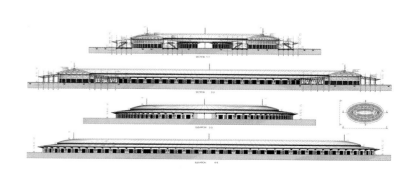

03

04

01

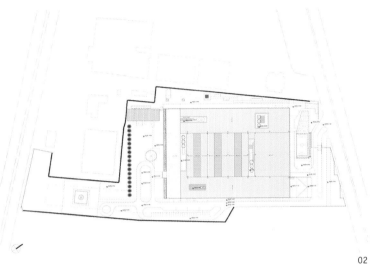

02

03

Ipekyol Textile Factory

The design of this building, located on the outskirts of Edirne, was based on the technical descriptions of the cyclic relations of the type of production, the limited size of the area, the constraints of service, and possibilities of connecting to the main road, and those of the local production techniques. The administrative section was more directly associated with production and thus, instead of different buildings, a large structure took shape. This building, which reaches the outer borders of the lot due to the spatial constraints, was implicitly loosened by linear gardens located between sections.

01 General view at night | 02 Site plan | 03 Exterior view of cafeteria at night | 04 Employees cafeteria | 05 Ramp

04

05

01

02

Prestige Mall

Prestige mall is a building in which structure correlates with form. Shiny materials and illuminated surfaces, exposed concrete and black plaster give the feeling of grace, purity, humility and infinity. The proportions of matte black plaster and shiny glass create a balanced aesthetic and allow the building to appear almost camouflaged. The curved horizontal lines of the building bring a sense of flow and dynamism. Reflective surfaces carry on inside to create never-ending illusionary perspectives.

01 General view | 02 Side view | 03 Entrance | 04 Floor plans | 05 Shop | 06 View from inside out | 07 Interior view

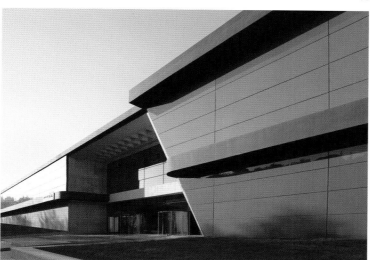

03

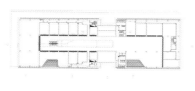
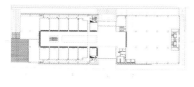
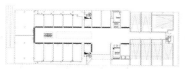

04

05

06

07

01

02

03

04

05

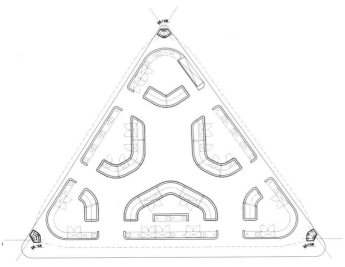

06

Besiktas Fish Market

Located in one of Istanbul's most populated and diverse neighborhoods, the Besiktas Fish Market, located on a triangular site, is an iconic venue for both locals and visitors who come to buy fresh fish. The old construction was in very poor shape and needed to be replaced. The design solution was to maintain its iconic neighborhood presence, while also reaffirming its welcoming feeling. GAD designed a triangular shaped concrete shell, covering the entire site with large openings to the street level and providing a column-free interior space, optimizing the project's programmatic needs. The new design injects a contemporary and pragmatic solution, but still preserves the fish market's history.

01 Bird's-eye view | 02 Exterior view | 03 Side view | 04 Interior view | 05 Displays | 06 Floor plan

01

Enviroloo

A system of public dry toilets for different locations, using the La Trobe evaporating and dehydrating cycle. Dry toilets work with a little bit of wind or a little bit of sun. No chemicals, no water, no sewerage. The architects proposed low-tech construction, with six posts, galva-steel bands and riveted wooden slats, on an earth-crete base. There are three very simple modules of uniformed size and shape and each with a wide, sliding door. The locations are natural environments where there are urban visitors: the architects chose to resort to an image recognisable by city people, the Parisian cabin, but a low-tech rural version.

01 General view | 02 Installed in a park in France | 03 Rear view | 04 Plans

02

03

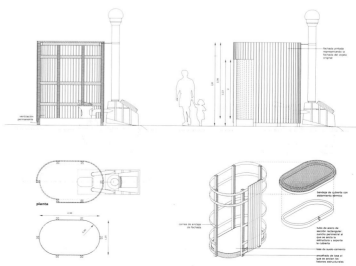

04

ARCHITECTS INDEX